The Body in History: Europe from the
Palaeolithic to the Future

This book is a long-term history of how the human body has been understood in
Europe from the Palaeolithic to the present day, focusing on specific moments
of change. Developing a multi-scalar approach to the past, and drawing on the
work of an interdisciplinary team of experts, the authors examine how the body
has been treated in life, art and death for the last 40,000 years. Key case-study
chapters examine Palaeolithic, Neolithic, Bronze Age, Classical, Medieval, Early
Modern and Modern bodies. What emerges is not merely a history of different
understandings of the body, but a history of the different human bodies that
have existed. Furthermore, the book argues, these bodies are not merely the
product of historical circumstance, but are themselves key elements in shaping
the changes that have swept across Europe since the arrival of modern humans.

John Robb is Reader in European Prehistory at Cambridge University. He has
worked extensively in Central Mediterranean prehistory, archaeological theory
and human skeletal studies, and is the author of *The Early Mediterranean Village*
(Cambridge University Press, 2007). He edits the *Cambridge Archaeological
Journal* and is currently researching prehistoric art in Europe.

Oliver J. T. Harris is Lecturer in Archaeology at the University of Leicester.
He is the co-director of the Ardnamurchan Transitions Project, which examines
the long-term occupation of the Ardnamurchan peninsula in western Scotland
and excavates sites from all periods including Neolithic, Bronze Age, Iron Age,
Viking and post-medieval. He has published on Neolithic Britain and archaeological theory in a range of journals including *Archaeological Dialogues*, *World
Archaeology* and the *European Journal of Archaeology*. He is currently writing a
book on the archaeology of communities.

The Body in History

Europe from the Palaeolithic to the Future

Edited by

John Robb
University of Cambridge

Oliver J. T. Harris
University of Leicester

CAMBRIDGE
UNIVERSITY PRESS

CAMBRIDGE
UNIVERSITY PRESS

32 Avenue of the Americas, New York, NY 10013-2473, USA

Cambridge University Press is part of the University of Cambridge.

It furthers the University's mission by disseminating knowledge in the pursuit of education, learning and research at the highest international levels of excellence.

www.cambridge.org
Information on this title: www.cambridge.org/9780521195287

© Cambridge University Press 2013

First published 2013

Printed in the United States of America

A catalogue record for this publication is available from the British Library.

Library of Congress Cataloguing in Publication data
Robb, John, 1962 March 18–
The body in history : Europe from the Palaeolithic to the future / John Robb, University of Cambridge, Oliver J. T. Harris, University of Leicester.
  pages cm
Includes bibliographical references and index.
ISBN 978-0-521-19528-7 (hardback)
1. Human body – Social aspects – Europe.   2. Human body – Europe – History.
3. Human remains (Archaeology) – Europe.   I. Title.
GT497.E85R635   2013
306.4–dc23   2013012807

ISBN 978-0-521-19528-7 Hardback

Contents

Figures

Plates

Tables

Contributors

Dušan Borić is Lecturer in Archaeology at the University of Cardiff. He specialises in the prehistory of Europe and the Near East, particularly the interactions between foragers and farmers, and archaeological theory, especially issues of the body and memory.

Jessica Hughes is Lecturer in Classical Studies at the Open University. Her research focuses on the role of material culture, including votive deposits, in the ancient world especially in Greece and Rome. She is also interested in the reception of this material in later periods.

Maryon McDonald is Fellow in Social Anthropology at Robinson College, University of Cambridge. Her research focuses on the anthropology of Europe especially medical anthropology. She has studied the ethics of transplantation, and the role of regulation, in detail.

Preston Miracle is Senior Lecturer in Archaeology at the University of Cambridge. His research focuses on, amongst other areas, the role of consumption and feasting in the past, particularly in the Mesolithic and the way humans dealt with environmental change at the end of the last ice age.

Robin Osborne is Professor of Ancient History at the University of Cambridge. He has published extensively on the ancient world. His research examines the representation of life in Greece, the development of art and the manner in which bodies were depicted on material culture.

Katharina Rebay-Salisbury is a Post-Doctoral Research Associate at the University of Leicester. She is a specialist in the Bronze and Iron Ages of Central Europe, and her research focuses on the movement of ideas through networks in this period, alongside changing understandings of the human body.

Marie Louise Stig Sørensen is Reader in Archaeology at the University of Cambridge. An expert in the Bronze Age, she has focused on the way in which gender played a crucial role in this period, as well as examining the importance of heritage in today's society.

Simon Stoddart is Senior Lecturer in Archaeology at the University of Cambridge. His research focuses on Iron Age Europe, and in particular on

Italy and the Etruscans. He has also conducted extensive excavations on Neolithic sites in Malta.

Marilyn Strathern is Emeritus Professor of Anthropology at the University of Cambridge. Her research has bridged anthropology in Melanesia and Europe, incorporating issues of personhood, gender, bioethics and intellectual property.

Sarah Tarlow is Professor of Archaeology at the University of Leicester. Her research focuses on post-medieval Europe, and in particular the changing ways of thinking about and relating to dead bodies. She is also a specialist in archaeological theory, and has led the way in considerations of emotion in past contexts.

Acknowledgments

Books, like bodies, are the product of many hands. First and foremost, we are very grateful to the Leverhulme Trust for supporting the Leverhulme Research Programme 'Changing Beliefs of the Human Body' (2005–2010), which underwrote the research upon which this book was based and the writing process itself.

Besides our colleagues in the research program who have helped to co-author parts of this volume, we are grateful for the collaboration of Annia Cherryson, Zoe Crossland, Ben Davenport, Anna Evans, Sara Harrop, Alex Hemming and Sheila Kohring. We are indebted to Marilyn Strathern for contributing the epilogue. We also thank John Davis, Lin Foxhall and Alasdair Whittle for their critical input to the research programme. We are especially grateful to Helen Foxhall-Forbes and Craig Cessford for guidance and discussion on medieval things, and to Lin Foxhall for comments on Chapter 5. At the Cambridge University Museum of Archaeology and Anthropology, Anite Herle, Amiria Salmond, Mark Elliott and Rebecca Empson put together a stunning exhibition related to this project, and it has been stimulating to collaborate with them. Many people have offered thoughtful discussions on the vast array of topics covered in this book, or gone beyond the call of duty in supplying images or unpublished materials. No doubt we have forgotten many, but we would still like to thank Pwyll ap Stifin, Karina Croucher, Andrea Dolfini, Chris Fowler and Dani Hofmann. Starr Farr, Johanna Farr, Nicholas Robb and Ellie Rowley-Conwy have also supported the writing of this book in innumerable ways.

For kind and generous help in illustrating the book, we would like to thank not only the institutions listed in the picture credits but also many individuals, including Craig Alexander, Biancamaria Aranguren, Douglass Bailey, Wendy Brown, Nick Card, Craig Cessford, Andrew Cochrane, Sylvia Codreanu-Windauer, John Coles, Sean Conlon, Bradley Cook, John Donaldson, Annette Faux, Francesco Fedele, David Fontijn, Chris Fowler, Alain Gallay, Clive Gamble, Martyn Gorman, Leore Grosman, Imogen Gunn, Veronika Holzer, Vedia Izzet, Lila Janik, Anne King, Ian Kuijt, Daria Lanzuolo, Maria Malina, Monica Miari, Irena Kolistrkoska Nasteva, Olga Novoseltseva, Ronan O'Flaherty, Nona Palincas, Hamish Park, Sandy Paul, Ben Roberts, Chris Roberts, Mary Robertson, Warwick Rodwell, Gary Rollefson, Ian Russell, Klaus Schmidt, Elizabeth Shee Twohig, Danielle Stordeur, Laurie Talalay and Matthew Van Doren. Vicki Herring did an excellent job of drawing many figures, sometimes on short notice, and we are very grateful to her for her help. We would like to acknowledge our debt of gratitude to Aaron Watson who drew the colour reconstructions for Plates I–V. Working with Aaron was a truly collaborative experience that allowed us to think differently about the vignettes we were writing, and the body worlds we were describing. His talent and hard work have undoubtedly enriched the book.

For important administrative support at Cambridge University, we would like to thank the Department of Archaeology and Anthropology, the Faculty of Classics, and the Museum of Archaeology and Anthropology. The McDonald Institute for Archaeological Research provided us with project space and much organizational support as well as subvention for figures, and our colleagues in the Department of Archaeology kindly put up with rotating staff as project members cycled in and out of research leave. We are also grateful to the School of Archaeology and Ancient History at the University of Leicester.

People, like books, are the products of many hands. We would like to dedicate this book to our colleagues, and to my parents Ernest and Sylvia Robb (JR), and to my inspirational great-aunt, Dr Madeline Jones (OJTH).

Preface

Every book has a story behind it. This book originated in a five-year (2005–2009) research project coordinated at Cambridge University by John Robb and involving all the contributors; Oliver J. T. Harris joined the project in 2007 to work with John on synthesizing and contextualizing the research, and to co-edit this monograph.[1] This project, a research programme funded by the Leverhulme Trust and titled 'Changing Beliefs of the Human Body', was intended to answer a deceptively simple question: Why and how did bodily understandings and practices change through history? As case studies we had five parallel projects, situated within the general trajectory of the European past. Each one examined change in how humans understood and experienced their body at a particular moment in European history: from the Late Upper Palaeolithic through the beginnings of farming, from the Copper Age through the Late Bronze Age, during the Classical period, between the seventeenth and nineteenth centuries AD, and in the contemporary world of medical practice. The idea was to coordinate substantial original research on each of these to come up with a genuine cross-cultural answer to the question of changing beliefs. We felt a very broad comparative study would allow us to see how the process of change reflects social conditions better than a study focusing upon a single time and place. The body forms an excellent ground for such a comparative study: on the one hand, it provides a certain set of existential challenges such as birth, growth, identity and death which all societies have to deal with; on the other hand, there is huge variation ethnographically, historically and archaeologically in how people in different groups have understood their bodies. It is also the subject of some of the most important theoretical work in the humanities and social sciences.

Although this book began as an answer to the question of why beliefs change, it took on a life of its own. Our five studies grew into six as we added a discussion of the Medieval period. Although we still insist we are not trying to write a universal history of the body in Europe – surely an impossible goal if ever there was one – we have tried to trace the historical connections between the moments upon which we focus. It probably goes without saying that we have had to be extremely selective in our coverage; one could fill a volume this size entirely with just the bibliography of works on the body alone! We should also emphasize that, although the body looks more and more alien the further back in time we go, our story should not be understood as a simple, unidirectional evolutionary sequence in which one starts from an elemental or universal humanity, a Palaeolithic Everyperson, and gradually layers on the civilised graces of Us. Every culture, every historical moment is different and has its own particularity. In some ways twenty-first-century bodies may be more like Palaeolithic ones than they are like Classical or medieval ones. Appreciating and understanding these particularities is our goal.

There is an old joke that defines a camel as a horse designed by a committee. Given the original structure of our research programme, we faced important choices in designing this book. Given how widely the individual research projects varied in what they studied and especially in their disciplinary traditions for studying it, an edited volume in which each project reported its own results separately would not have provided a coherent answer to questions of historical process and change. Yet simply writing the book on our own would neither acknowledge fairly how much we have learned from our colleagues nor provide specialist control over accuracy and a guarantee that we treat each period reasonably. Hence we have taken a middle route. The original specialist research carried out within the project forms part of each chapter, but we write freely around it to provide a larger framework and to cover other material. The text, with the exception of the epilogue, has been written almost entirely by the two authors, but we do so with guidance from our specialist colleagues, who hopefully have kept us within the limits of the thinkable for each of their own fields as well as providing valuable discussion of the overall opus. Yet, because we are asking questions which are often never posed within each discipline, we reach interpretations our colleagues might not have come to on their own (and, occasionally, with which they may disagree). The unusual form of authorship we have devised (and for which we apologize in advance to bibliographers) is intended to recognize this modus operandi. We hope the result is a horse rather than a camel.

John Robb and Oliver J. T. Harris, Cambridge and Leicester, July 2012

NOTE

1. All chapters were collaboratively written; the order of authors listed for each chapter is alphabetical.

1

O brave new world, that has such people in it

Oliver J. T. Harris and John Robb

Bodies in crisis – or everyday invisible strangeness?

In the Western world, hardly a day goes by without the announcement of a crisis in the body. New, wonderful, disconcerting, horrifying possibilities continually bombard us. During the time we have been writing this book, these are only some of the actual issues which have hit public attention:

- Is it right to create 'designer babies' to provide organic materials for an older sibling who may need a life-saving transplant? Is it ethical to screen unborn children for genetic diseases? For a preferred sex? For socially desirable characteristics or against socially stigmatized ones?
- Should stem cells from human embryos be used as a research or therapeutic material? Who owns the commercial rights to the genome of the population of Iceland? Should it be legal to trade commercially in human organs for transplant?
- Who controls dead bodies? For people dying in hospitals, is it doctors and hospital administrators or relatives of the deceased? For archaeological skeletons, is it scientists and museum curators, religious communities or descendent groups? Can waste heat from cremating the dead be used to heat a public swimming pool? Is it right to transform dead bodies into works of art for public, commercial display, as in Günther Von Hagens's controversial exhibitions of dissected bodies?
- Should animal organs be custom grown for transplant into humans? Should human genes be spliced into mice for testing human medicines?
- Why are athletes allowed to enhance their performance with caffeine and painkillers but not with ster-

oids? Should students be banned from taking drugs enhancing mental performance during exams?
- When do media images cross the line from promoting attractively thin bodies to pushing girls towards anorexia? Should public health funds pay for cosmetic dental work, plastic surgery or sex reassignments? When is a surgical procedure 'traditional female circumcision' and when is it 'genital mutilation'? What are the social implications of full-face transplants?
- Who is a child's mother – the woman donating an egg for in vitro fertilization, the woman who bears the baby from an implanted egg or the adoptive parent actually raising the baby? Do women older than 60 years of age have a 'natural' right to bear children through surrogate mothers? Who controls the frozen eggs or sperm of persons now dead?
- Do people have a right to end their own lives when and how they wish? Should relatives or doctors be prosecuted for assisting them?

These are items culled from the daily news, not futuristic science fiction. Yet these things broach matters which only a few years ago were considered the stuff of dreams or nightmares. Miracle cures and illness-free lives? Socially engineered designer babies and commodified organs? Human-animal hybrids and robot-like prosthetics? Mix-and-match body parts? Endlessly cloned organs? Free-form parenthood hatched from test tubes? It is as if each news item is the thin end of a wedge opening cracks in how we experience the body. Cumulatively, as wedge after wedge pries open our[1] comfortable, familiar reality, it is almost inevitable that we see ourselves in a state of bodily crisis, with the plastinated corpses of Von Hagens's exhibition serving as a garish fin-de-siècle flourish.[2]

But perhaps we should not despair quite yet. The phrase 'Brave New World' was made famous in 1932 as the title of Aldous Huxley's dystopic novel of a grim future in which humans were vat-cloned industrially, tailored eugenically for their predestined social roles and made devoid of individuality and freedom. But it is now eighty years and counting from Huxley's vision. Throughout this time, we have always coped with change. We replace parts of our body with titanium hip joints, battery-run hearts, and dental implants you could chew bricks with, and it has not made us robots. Our vaccine- and antibiotic-fortified super-bodies are invulnerable to a whole range of killers, gaining us, on average, two additional decades of life; rather than basking in godlike arrogance, we spend this time pursuing retirement hobbies. We have decoded the secret of life in the human genome, but totalitarian dictators do not use it to eliminate undesirable races eugenically; instead, amateur genealogists can buy DNA analyses on the Internet to see how genetically similar they are to people who share their surname. Reading about face transplants might make us worry about identity crises, but the first ones, used to rehabilitate victims of severe accidents, have proven psychologically beneficial rather than detrimental. The conceptual challenges posed by technologically assisted reproduction are nowhere near as complex as some of the traditional kinship-and-reproduction systems which anthropologists have documented in Australia, Melanesia and South America – systems based on old-fashioned pregnancy and amazing metaphorical logic, perhaps augmented by the ritual sharing of food, semen, milk or blood.

So is there really a crisis in the body? Humans are amazingly creative and responsive beings; there is no sign that the future is about to throw something at us which we really cannot handle conceptually and socially. What these news items do demonstrate is something else: *these things matter to us*. They matter because the body is central to how we conduct our lives on a daily basis. Beyond these extremes, how we use, live through, think and talk about our bodies is at the heart of the social and material world we inhabit. Thus, we project our hopes and fears about the future on the body. Not only has Huxley's vision not come to pass, it has been supplanted by newer, previously unimaginable nightmares and dreamscapes. Indeed, from at least the eighteenth century onwards,[3] whenever writers have envisioned alternative human worlds – utopian, dystopian or simply different – they have inevitably populated them with alternative human bodies, a fact which in itself tells us how deeply social life is rooted in the body. Every society understands the human body in its own way, and virtually every society believes that their body is *the* true body, the body which has evolved or been created to be the way bodies have to be. This is where the 'crisis of the body' comes from; it is part of our own historical narrative of the body.

Natural bodies? differences around the world today

'Nature', Katherine Hepburn tells Humphrey Bogart in *The African Queen*, 'is what we were put on earth to rise above'. Since at least the seventeenth century our own 'true' body has been the 'natural' body, understood as purely physical apart from a soul or mind. Many of our master narratives tell about our rise from body's 'state of nature' – how civilized people wash it, clothe it, heal it, restrain it and educate it. But since some point in the nineteenth century – perhaps *Frankenstein* marks the watershed – the flip side of this narrative has told how we

may go too far, how the 'natural' body is being replaced by a futuristic body, unrecognizable and out of control.

This narrative, of course, depends upon the existence of a pre-cultural, biologically necessary body. Yet, when we look at it, there is little natural about our 'natural' body, aside perhaps from our conviction that it is so. We ordinarily find out how dependent upon social convention our body is when travel forces us out of our comfort zone and we encounter people living perfectly happy lives though clothed, fed, worked, washed, doctored and sexually satisfied according to entirely different standards than ours. Conversely, we continually do bodily things previous generations would have considered equally unnatural or improper – everything from unisex public bathrooms to vegetarianism, restrictions on corporal punishment, and open premarital sex. Unless we happen, miraculously, to be the first generation to achieve a genuinely natural bodily life – on the very cusp of technology devouring the natural body – a certain social conventionality appears in our own practice. Indeed, anthropologists have shown how people in different cultures have radically different views of what the human body is and how it should behave. We want to offer three quick examples of this here, to give a taste of the florid variations around the world today, but we will return to the topic in more detail in the next chapter.

How do differences in the body manifest themselves in the world today? Amongst many groups in the Amazon, what a person's body looks like is not fixed by their biology – their 'nature', in our common usage – but by who it is that is looking at them.[4] Accordingly, all beings, whether human or animal, share a single culture, and all look like humans to one another. So jaguars look like humans to other jaguars, but humans look like tapirs – prey animals – to jaguars. Tapirs look like humans to one another but look like tapirs to humans. Because the body here is a matter of perspective rather than biology, it is changeable, and particularly powerful individuals can take on the perspective (and thus the body) of another creature. The body in Amazonia is very different from the body in the West, but to understand this we need to place it in the context of a very different way of engaging with the world – a different set of social, political and ontological conventions.

In Trinidad, in contrast to the feigned indifference of those who cite the old proverb 'clothes do not make the man', clothes tell you who a person really is.[5] Here the efforts put into looking good, achieving status and being fashionable are recognized as telling people far more about you than whether you happen to have been born into wealth, intelligence or good looks. Truth is not hidden on the inside, as theories of psychoanalysis in the

West might have it, but rather displayed in public, on the body where people can see it.[6]

For the shamans of Siberia, gender is not a fixed category given by biology but something that emerges under certain circumstances and that can change through time. Mandelstam Balzer has pointed out how 'at times, and in some Siberian cultures, the shamanic use of sexual power and symbolism meant that male shamans turned themselves into females, for particular shamanic séances, and, in some cases, more permanently'.[7] Amongst the Chukchi of north-eastern Siberia, female shamans occasionally did the reverse and took on male identities. Male shamans who took on female qualities were known as soft-men.[8] These soft-men then took husbands, dressed, ate and behaved as women, but despite the connotations of the name in English, soft-men were believed to be especially powerful shamans. The same is true of the attested cases of female shamans, who took up male identities and married wives. Jacobs and Cromwell trace up to ten gender categories amongst the Chukchi.[9] These range from the taking up of certain female traits by males (or vice versa) to the total adoption of the other sex's way of life.

In three different worlds, three ways of understanding the body emerge. In each case the body is central to how society happens: it lies at the heart of how Trinidadians conceive of truth and honesty, identity and being; it drives the ability of shamans in Siberia to change gender, or those in Amazonia to transform into jaguars. Each of these body worlds has coherence to it and builds upon this everyday strangeness to form a richly evocative subject, central to the societies themselves.

Huxley stole the phrase 'brave new world' from Shakespeare's *The Tempest* (Act V, Scene 1). Miranda, who has been raised alone with her father on a deserted island following a shipwreck, beholds people other than themselves for the very first time, and exclaims:

> "O, wonder!
> How many goodly creatures are there here!
> How beauteous mankind is! O brave new world,
> That has such people in't!"

We agree with Miranda. As we hope to convince you in this book, the really astonishing thing is not any science fiction vision of future bodies, but the complex and often unbelievable bodies all humans live with, in everyday reality.

From 'body worlds' to body worlds

To capture the social life of the body, we want to subvert Von Hagens's title and talk not about 'Body Worlds' but about *body worlds*; not the shocking, skinless, sensationalist bodies he displays, but rather the equally compelling bodies of everyday life. A body world, as we use the term here, encompasses the totality of bodily experiences, practices and representations in a specific place and time. These, we suggest, are at the heart of how we understand the world. The body world of Western daily life involves all manner of engagements: eating, sleeping, sex, painkillers, alcohol, walking, exercise, communication, driving and so forth. All of these are bodily acts, involving specific, usually trained, ways of moving, of carrying and shaping the body, particular forms of gender-appropriate behaviour (that are more or less adhered to) and so on. As our anthropological examples show, this is one example of many, but for all human beings body worlds are the worlds all of us inhabit all the time. Far from being boring, natural or universal, they are in fact fascinating, diverse and culturally specific.

Anthropologically, there is nothing normal about normality; it passes unnoticed not because it is inevitable, or the only way one can live, or even because it necessarily makes much sense, but simply because we are used to it. As we will see in Chapters 2, 7 and 8, our body world has a history and a cultural logic; it too could have been different, and will be different in the future. The strangeness and conventionality of our world is invisible, subsumed into a multitude of bite-sized pieces of experience, lacking the in-your-face shock value of flayed bodies, copyrighted genomes and face transplants. But if we examine daily life analytically, by taking it apart and looking at the rules, habits and bodily practices that comprise it, the 'obvious' nature of what we do and how we live disappears. It is these different body worlds, then, that we seek to explore in this book and to outline how and why they changed.

Bodies have history

But one can also encounter different bodies by travelling in time as well as in space – not to an alien future but to an equally alien past. Roaming away from the present, the historical tourist encounters strange bodies everywhere. Many seventeenth-century Britons – including highly educated scientists – believed that a hanged man's hand could cure some diseases. Medieval theologians found cannibalism peculiarly abhorrent not because of the violence involved but because of the difficulty it implied in sorting out whose body the flesh which was eaten belonged to when Resurrection came. Ancient Greeks placed statues of Hermes consisting of only a head and an erect phallus around the streets as a kind of civic spiritual protection. The most complex technology of Bronze Age Europe was employed predominantly not to solve life's practical problems but simply to give bodies a shining appearance. Neolithic people risked their lives performing delicate cranial surgery with stone tools for little apparent medical reason. Mesolithic people buried dogs like humans and carved sculptures of people turning into fish (or perhaps fish turning into humans). The list goes on.

These apparently bizarre practices made perfect sense to people involved at the time, just as comparing a body to a machine or to a computer may make sense to us, though it would be utterly alien to these other groups. To understand the body, then, it is essential to set it in its own cultural, social, political and material frame of reference. In turn, this frame of reference has to be understood as *historical*. The body worlds we study in this book are the products of particular histories. To give one example, which we discuss in more detail in Chapters 7 and 8, it is impossible to understand our 'modern' bodies without an appreciation of a range of historical processes including medieval theology that set the body in opposition to the soul; the growth of science in the eighteenth century; the development of discipline in schools, hospitals, factories, asylums, prisons and the military in the nineteenth century and so on.[10] Our bodies carry these histories with them, in the way we move, exercise, sleep, eat and act in general. The body is not a universally shared physical object whose historical continuity comes from its unchanging biological structure, but rather something emergent through history. The body is in history; indeed, the body *is* history.

Yet bodies are not merely victims of historical circumstance. Body worlds and bodies themselves are historical agents in their own right. They embody – the pun is anything but accidental – and produce understandings of the world and so make certain developments possible and forestall others. The manner in which they are understood practically through action and engagement, and materially rather than verbally, means they are often more important in generating action than we give them credit for. Like material things, bodies can be humble and in the background,[11] even as they disclose a particular set of possible actions in any particular circumstance. Part of the aim of this book, therefore, is not just to examine how historical circumstances create particular kinds of bodies, but how particular kinds of bodies generate certain forms of history.

Not just another history of the body...

Of course, to many people it will be no surprise that how humans understand their body is situated historically, and therefore it is possible – indeed, necessary – to write a history of the human body. There is a huge literature on body histories in many fields, including archaeology, history, Classics and anthropology, and the specialized histories of medicine, science, art, religion, gender and sexuality. Without this literature our work here would not be possible, and as will become clear, we draw on it extensively.

Why then this project? This book is an unusual, perhaps very strange, project, in two ways. The first is just the sheer scale of the story we want to tell. Even 'comprehensive' treatments of the body[12] only deal with Classical times onwards. By integrating prehistory as well as historical and modern periods, we cover much more than twice this span. In the process we need to cross disciplines. A history of the body in which each period is written up by specialists in that period inevitably traverses fields with quite different materials, questions and methods of scholarship. Hence what one writes about the body magically changes as one goes from prehistory to the Greeks, from Greek to medieval, from medieval to modern. In such a history, how much of the apparent change is really attributable to differences between disciplines which rarely talk to each other? What would one learn from a history which treats different periods in an equal way?

The second reason is our focus. We do not want to write an encyclopedic volume, presenting everything about the history of the body for each of the periods we deal with. Many histories of the body attempted to date provide beautiful snapshots of one particular body world. This might be historians describing how medieval people existed in a world in which the body formed a canvas for identities and moralities,[13] or archaeologists discussing how Mesolithic hunter-gatherers in Scandinavia understood dogs as being something that could become part of a person rather than a separate living being.[14] When discussions of change are attempted, they tend to focus on one particular kind of practice or discourse, or one particular aspect of change. An example might be the change from thinking about the body as microcosm in the sixteenth century to thinking about it as machine in the eighteenth, as in the case of Jonathan Sawday's exemplary analysis.[15] While certain moments of change, say in the Early Modern period, or in the shift from Archaic to Classical sculpture in Ancient Greece, have been analyzed a lot, other transformations have not yet been thought through. Although this book attempts to narrate a continuous history for the body in Europe from the Palaeolithic to the present, we have inevitably left many stories untold, many problems ignored and much variation suppressed. This is the price of long-term cultural history. The result is not *the* history of the human body in

Europe, merely *a* history. We make no claims to totality or finality.

Instead, consider paradoxes of scale. Scholars tend to work inside historical comfort zones of a few decades or centuries. Only fools and archaeologists venture into millennia. But if you try to tell the story of ten thousand years, you inevitably do it differently than if you tell the story of one year ten thousand times. Pulling back to the big picture not only allows but actually forces one to see different kinds of patterns and processes. In the mirror of deep history, dramatic punctuational changes, such as between the medieval and modern periods, show much more continuity than could ever be suspected from the close-up view. At the same time, taken for granted parameters of daily life such as concepts of honor or gender become historically arbitrary. The surprising fact that ideas about the body can both be entirely conventional and last for a millennium or more itself demands theorization. In this sense, one of the main concerns of this book is not merely the substance of history, the ten thousand years of facts, but the process of history. How does history unfold at different scales? And how does this process of history involve the body? It is this focus on scale, time depth and historical process that really differentiates this book from conventional body histories.

Thinking outside the (disciplinary) box: A challenge to the reader

One of us (JR) frequently has an experience which could pass for a recurrent nightmare, except that it happens when awake. Imagine you find a book in a bookshop, which promises a fascinating account of a Big Topic. It is written by a World Expert – a historian, a sociologist, a psychologist, a biologist, a physicist, an architect or even a cook. Chapter 2 of *The Universal History of Topic* is always the foundation charter, the sketch of The Topic in Human Antiquity. It traces the prehistoric roots of our modern foodstuffs, or the evolutionary basis of political relationships, or how the modern cities began in Neolithic Anatolia, or the ancient basis of worldwide genetic or linguistic patterns, or prehistoric evidence for the social process of dying. And in nine cases out of ten, it is deeply disappointing. The World Expert in some other field has only the haziest idea of my own field, prehistory. Amidst sophisticated exposition of cutting-edge research in his or her own field are naiveties about archaeology or anthropology which would not pass muster in an undergraduate essay. By now, blasé, the prehistorian usually skips the prehistory chapter, which, anyway, normally serves only as the historical garnish to what the author is cooking up. The real problem is the second-order doubts: If World Experts can write absurdities on topics about which we happen to know a lot, why should we take their writing as authoritative on topics about which we know nothing?

Now the tables are turned, and we are writing a book in which easily two-thirds of the material covered comes from other disciplines, far from our own. We imagine – indeed, we hope – that our readers are quite likely to be experts in fields in which we are not. What is to prevent us from making the same hash of other people's fields that they often make of ours?

At this point, we would like to propose an agreement with the reader. On our part, we will try to avoid the mistakes people make with other fields. There are three reasons such errors regularly occur. One is simply lack of genuine interest – using another field as wallpaper or legitimation rather than as something important in its own right. The second (closely related, in this age of easy access to information for those motivated to seek it out) is lack of real contact with the field, relying on a few sources and impressions heard in an undergraduate lecture several decades ago rather than actually finding out what people in the field are doing now. For both of these we may plead that, as noted earlier, we have been working closely with our specialist colleagues in the fields we discuss to keep us closely engaged and *au courant*.

The third reason, the real killer, is disciplinary differences. Common sense in one field rarely matches common sense in another. To take just one example, it is usual in evolutionary studies, economics and some forms of political theory to assume that individuals' behaviour can be judged against some relatively straightforward, universal form of self-interest; this is gross anathema in most of sociology, psychology and anthropology, and the question of general explanation itself is rarely even considered in most work in history and Classics. Time scale and models of social process are another example; in some fields, history is a micro-narrative about people and their actions, and twenty years is considered the long term; in other fields, twenty years is a barely measurable blink of the eye, and history is a slow secular fugue of traditions and institutions. Our solution here has been to use a reasonably broad theoretical framework drawing upon theorists who will be familiar across much of the humanities and social sciences, even if different fields employ alternative readings of their works. Our specialist colleagues have been of great help here. We have also tried to phrase our concepts, and writing, in a straightforward, ecumenical, lowest-common-denominator way rather than in ways tied to specific disciplinary frameworks.

On your part, we ask two things of the reader. First, we would never ask the reader to suspend his or her critical judgement – indeed, we are very curious to know what readers will make of this work – but we do ask you to suspend your disciplinary defense mechanisms. We may not always use the familiar phrases or cite the intellectual genealogies that serve as the handshake of recognition in each field, we skate over an immense amount of detail, and within the scope of this project we cannot possibly acknowledge all the controversies and debates which define every disciplinary landscape. We hope that this does not mean that the data which we do present and the interpretations we give them do not merit consideration.

Secondly, we hope readers will simply take the book on its own terms. Books which aspire to big-picture history with serious intellectual content (as opposed to popular surveys) are so rare that it is worth asking why this should be so. The answer is simply that scholars in most disciplines do not pose questions on this scale. On the rare occasions on which they do, there are real difficulties to contend with. The vast territory one needs to cover to answer these questions is carved up amongst quite disparate specializations that have to be reduced to some common comprehensibility; otherwise one winds up seeing not differences between the Dutch and English countryside but between how Van Eyck and Constable painted, so to speak. It follows that if this project is worth doing in the first place, it will have to be done in a way which does not fit any single disciplinary pattern; one can only judge it on its own terms, for how well the book answers the questions it poses.

Or so we think. Enjoy the ride!

NOTES

1. In this chapter, and indeed throughout the book, we use terms like 'we', 'our' and 'us' to refer to a set of perspectives commonly held by many people in Europe and North America. Of course, such a move may make it seem that we presume these people are a homogeneous group, or that we are alienating people from other places and backgrounds. This is not our intention. Rather, the point is simply that readers of this book have a deep well of ethnographic experience to draw on in understanding the body – 'our' knowledge of 'our' own bodies – and this gives us an invaluable resource in discussing these issues. And understanding the historicity of our own bodies is part of the point of the book. One could easily write another book exploring the limits of who the 'us' here actually is, but for the sake of clear writing, we (i.e., JR and OH) have chosen to use these terms as an intentionally general and somewhat vague shorthand simply to invoke an experience of embodiedness many readers may share.

2. Images of plastinated bodies-as-art from Von Hagens's exhibition may be viewed at http://www.bodyworlds.com/en.html. We had hoped to include an image here from the 'Body Worlds'. However, after reviewing this chapter, the 'Body Worlds' press office declined to grant permission to use an image – in itself a fascinating example of the sensitivity surrounding the use of dead bodies, here manifested in the organisers' feeling that they need to control the discourse their images provoke. In our text, we do not actually take a judgemental position on 'Body Worlds' – we merely note what others have said about the exhibit. But clearly it hit a nerve.

3. Guadalupe and Manguel (1987) provide a fascinating compendium with many examples of imagined alternative bodies from antiquity to the present.

4. See Vilaça 2005; Viveiros de Castro 1998; 2004.

5. Miller 1994; 2010.

6. Miller 2010, 18.

7. Mandelstam Balzer 1996, 165.

8. Ibid.

9. Jacobs and Cromwell 1992.

10. Foucault 1977; 1978.

11. cf. Miller 1987; 2010; Heidegger 1962.

12. E.g., Bynum and Kalof 2010.

13. Kay and Rubin 1994.

14. Fowler 2004a.

15. Sawday 1995.

2

Body worlds and their history:
Some working concepts

Oliver J. T. Harris and John Robb

Body worlds: Social reality as bodily process

Chapter 1 provided some of the background to the aims of our project. Before tackling the history of the body, however, we need to introduce the reader to some working concepts. Many will be familiar to readers who have studied fields such as anthropology or social history. This will not be true of all; and, in general, we have tried to use theoretical concepts quietly rather than belabouring the reader with them. Thus we need to set out our general approach here.

The first step towards enlightenment is perplexity. Of all things, we take the body the most for granted; we have to make bodies strange before we can understand them. And this means starting with our own bodies and (in the phrase we used in Chapter 1) their 'everyday invisible strangeness'. We begin with our own body world once again, before moving through a series of vignettes that outline just a fraction of the range of differences that exist around the world today. Doing so allows us to identify a series of key concepts to which we return throughout the book. Finally, we turn to the issue of variation in time, rather than space, and consider the tools we need to deal with the histories we seek to write, from multi-temporal scales of analysis to a rethink of causation. Once we have these concepts in hand, we turn to our narrative itself in Chapter 3.

The world we live (bodily) in

The strangeness and conventionality of our own body world is invisible, subsumed into a multitude of bite-sized pieces of experience; the shocking poster children for the body controversies which opened Chapter 1 are really just the tip of the iceberg. By looking critically at the rules, habits and bodily practices that make up daily life, the 'obvious' nature of what we do and how we live disappears, and we see instead how a historically configured bodily reality works.

Life in space

You are in a queue at a supermarket, bank or bus stop. Superficially, it is a completely banal, invisible moment, forgotten as soon as it occurs, the epitome of wasted time. But it is nevertheless a highly structured moment, in unseen ways. Consider the precise management of distance between bodies. Too close is invasive; too distant leads to ambiguity about who is next in line. Distancing is materially controlled and cued: bodies are quietly put into place by seats, doors, sidewalks, pathways, aisles, bathroom cubicles, privacy screens and many other devices, such as the plastic bars which separate your groceries at the supermarket checkout from those of the next customer. Social distance is maintained by behavioural walls too – conventions of glance, talk, position and gesture. Hearing someone a metre away in your group is listening, hearing someone a metre away in another group is eavesdropping, and discouraged.

Theoretically, the fascinating question here is why we should actually care as deeply as we obviously do about how bodies are distanced. The answer is that we experience not only physical space but also social or psychological space. Spatial closeness is fundamental to defining different kinds of public or private interaction amongst groups such as strangers, companions, a family or a couple. Conversely, identities can define spaces, as when people occupying an unstructured 'public' space define a 'private' group by standing and talking as one. These proximities do not merely symbolize social relations; they actually create them. They are experienced emotionally as intimacy, familiarity, invasiveness, presumption, chilly distance, privacy or security. And this emotionally coded space is centred upon the body. In our normal model of personhood, a person is rather like an onion; one penetrates successive thresholds to achieve increasing intimacy, solidarity and understanding. Our moment of queuing happens in a relatively outer layer of the onion, but it presumes and reproduces a continuum extending into more formally defined private groups (at a restaurant, for instance), into the official 'private' space of the home – itself graded into more 'outer' places for guests and more 'inner' places such as bedroom and bathroom.[1] Finally, via channels as varied as sexual contact, medical imaging, introspection or psychological therapy, poetry or portraiture, we get beneath the skin to penetrate the physical and psychological interiorities where we feel one encounters the true 'inner' self.

This is not a universal model of personhood; it is a model which is defined in our own culture,[2] which relies upon concepts such as the interior self, and which is elaborated on and experienced in many ways, including our unconscious spatial reflexes in moments such as queuing. (We discuss the historical roots of this model in Chapter 7.) Here, it is worth noting that it is a model in which most bodily functions (particularly 'bad' or dysfunctional ones) are understood as intimate and appropriate only for restricted or private spaces.[3] These include appetite (hence eating publicly is often hedged with convention), sweating, crying, defecation, sexual activity, illness and, of course, death. Thus, many critics of Von Hagens's exhibition of anatomised bodies felt that the displaying of the dead, particularly without their skins on, was an invasion of the privacy of death.[4]

You, your body and perfect bodies

To eat or not to eat? It is surprising how loaded this apparently simple, 'natural' moment of decision is. In a room alone, a young woman struggles against anorexia, fighting against the devastating linkage of her sense of self-worth with her body image: eating requires defeating part of herself. But morality also pervades less extreme situations. For most people, daily decisions about how to eat are laced with two particular discourses: body image and the medicalization of life. Images of how bodies should look are promoted ubiquitously through the media, through consumer culture and even through government and public agencies. These surround us with an omnipresent universe of ideal bodies, a pantheon in which celebrities serve much the same function as Greek gods, providing exemplary bodies. Central to this is advertising which employs young women, and increasingly young men,[5] to promote all manner of products in ways that allow the camera to consume the flesh of the model as much as advertise the product on display. Such visuals are internalized and form part of our self-image, for better or worse. Medical discourses, in contrast, lead us to internalize the idea that decisions should be made according to medical criteria: you should eat bananas not because you like how they taste but because they contain potassium and fibre. Claims about nutrition and healthy diet, reliable or not, are present in almost every eating situation. White bread or brown in your sandwich? The eater can, and is often forced to, make an informed decision on something about which he or she may never have previously considered a decision necessary at all.[6]

It would be silly to deny that what you eat has important health consequences, but the point here is that the moral discourse of eating goes far beyond this. Even as governments claim that super-thin fashion models promote a culture of female starvation, they also specify a narrow ideal weight range for everybody and stigmatize people above this as overweight or obese. Such evaluations obviously depend upon constant comparison of the body with implicit or explicit ideals. Such ideals are not only bureaucratically standardized but are also sold. Diets, exercise, 'healthy' foods and clothing associated with ideal bodies are huge commercial commodities, and consumer culture develops care of the self into a narcissistic care of the body. Increasingly, the body acts as a source of symbolic capital, of value 'less because of what the body is able to *do* than because of how it *looks*'.[7]

Hence eating – an apparently transparent decision which one might expect to be based upon things such as taste, hunger, need and pleasure – turns out to be mediated by imagery and discourse. Like all discourses of the body, this one is politically loaded. A famous 1970s manifesto argued that '[f]at is a feminist issue', that ideologies of body form imposed harmful sexist stigmas upon women.[8] Perhaps the most recent incarnation of this is the idea that the health costs of obesity are borne by society as a whole; being overweight is thus not merely personal but becomes an antisocial act. Increasingly clear moral boundaries police body size, fatness, unhealthiness and unattractiveness, all associated with a moral failure to control and discipline the body.[9] This often deftly converts a sexist stereotype into class-based demonization. To be thin is also to be attractive, successful and a good member of society.

Gendered doorways

A man entering a building holds open a door for a woman to pass through before him. Courtesy or condescension?

This apparently trivial gesture became politically loaded with the feminist movements of the 1970s. Traditionally, a male allowed a female precedence in entering a doorway. This was thought of as simple courtesy; it was a form of respect based upon difference. Yet, as feminists pointed out, it summed up distinctions that prevented women from having equal status with men: it cast women as the weaker sex and men as protectors, and it differentiated between those who orchestrate movement and those who are orchestrated. Such distinctions had a light touch when they opened a door with a smile; they had a heavy hand when they restricted women to 'women's work', excluding them from domestic decision-making and from education or professions.

Several decades later, great steps have been made towards gender equality, and many people would probably consider opening a door a simple courtesy one would extend to anybody regardless of their gender. Yet, we still live with gender classifications, which begin from the moment the midwife or doctor holds the newborn baby (or looks at the ultrasound image) and announces "it's a girl!" Gender distinctions seem natural, yet they are historically constructed. Even looking at a body and declaring it to be biologically male or female is itself a social categorization which prioritizes some criteria over others and irons out variations.[10] The doctrine that men and women have different natures because they have different biological bodies certainly has a specific historical trajectory and may date to developments in the seventeenth and eighteenth centuries.[11] Today, we still believe in gender and spend a lot of time discussing it in various forms. Why are there disproportionately fewer women in engineering and the physical sciences, and why do girls outperform boys at school? What kind of cars do men and women drive, and do they drive them in different ways? How can women (but not men, apparently) balance career and family? Why do we have separate male and female public bathrooms, given that separate cubicles within them already create privacy?

There are two important points to understand here. First, these tangential discussions of gender help constitute gender as a fundamental domain whose existential reality we do not question and which forms part of who we think we are and who other people understand us to be. We might (and in fact often do) argue about the surface choices of gender, such as dress or whether the kinds of cars men and women drive is changing; but we take for granted the underlying existence of categories such as 'male' and 'female' which are continually validated by such discussions. Secondly, these categories are not only created through discourse; they are enacted through bodily idioms of similarity and difference, through gendered spaces in which we move, through gendered things we make and use, and through gendered ways of dressing, looking, speaking, touching and moving. In bathrooms, shops, cars and life choices, we still have gendered doorways. If you remain to be convinced, try going through the wrong one.

Order, authority, class

In a tranquil concert hall, the orchestra plays a classical concerto. It is a highly ordered moment. Bodies of performers are synchronized, subordinated to a harmonious plan rather than allowing individualism or spontaneity. The violins' bows are coordinated to within a fraction of a second, and the finest distinctions are audible in the carefully modulated sounds that have been rehearsed a hundred times. Order encompasses not only the orchestra but the audience and other participants as well. Bodies are restrained, fixed in place, made to conform to standards of dress and decorum. The listeners sit in soberly dressed, silent rows, perhaps nodding or waving a finger gently in rhythm, awaiting their cue for their own performance, the mannered applause.

The interesting thing here is what this bodily coordination tells us about the meaning of Classical music as a field of activity. Admirers of Classical music will speak of beauty and pleasure, but there are many other, less rigidly ordered ways of experiencing beauty and pleasure. Classical music is music of finely textured order, of balance, repetition, formality, fine distinction; its values are intellectuality, restraint, and subtle distinction. Its venues are formal; even the more riotous or avant-garde twentieth-century composers, ostensibly composing tavern drinking songs or revolutionary manifestos, are normally heard in concert halls rather than in rowdy taverns or at street barricades. This genre is often associated with class (as part of high culture), with education (how can one become discerning without long training?) and with money (going to the symphony can be an expensive pastime, and only the prosperous can devote years of time and money to forming themselves as discerning performers or listeners). Mozart and Beethoven are often promoted prescriptively as what every educated person 'should know' (in implicit contrast to what they actually *do* know). In short, it is a musical form of high culture associated with class and authority. As discussed later, Bourdieu's concept of habitus[12] captures the manner in which different social orders produce and are produced by different kinds of bodily practices. These are conducted often without conscious thought, but nevertheless reveal much about the way in which bodies are understood and relate to one another in a particular society. And one bodily idiom for class and authority is a habitus of careful bodily control, reserve, restraint and conformity.

Habitus and authority in music is something we understand instinctively better than discursively. In another concert hall, this world is turned upside down; randomly and extravagantly dressed performers and audience contort themselves wildly, limbs flying in abandoned gestures. The disorder might be as scripted as the classical order, of course, but the deafening music with crude, pulsing rhythms expresses anarchic primal energy and individual defiance rather than finely coordinated, subtle distinction. In yet another gathering, we might find jazz, an intellectual, complex counterpoint of individualism and coordination, or a hymn service where the congregation sing in unison sturdy choruses with rousing, lowest-common-denominator melodies to get across the fundamental message of solidarity and salvation.

There are really two points here. First, not only within a genre of music but across different genres, and for listeners as well as performers, features such as synchrony versus asynchrony, uniformity versus difference, measured versus unrestrained gestures, and subtlety versus directness form bodily idioms which go straight to our nerves and help get the basic social meaning of the performance across. Secondly, and more importantly, these codes are not restricted by any means to music; they extend across many fields of life. The precise coordination of the violin section is matched by the impossibly synchronic, mechanical gestures of the military parade;[13] the two contexts ostentatiously display different sides of the subordination of individuals to the design of a group. The conservative uniformity of formal dress expected at 'establishment' occasions shows restraint, conformity to authority, and belonging; the restrained, controlled gestures and clipped, reasoned tones of upper class discourse express the same semantic in a different register. Without this underlying equation of bodily restraint with class, authority and conformity, how could long hair on men, disordered dress, wild gestures, upraised voices, or disordered music provide such a handy and recurrent way to express permissiveness, protest or antistructure?[14]

The standard medical body

Then there is medicine (something we explore in more detail in Chapter 8). Many modern states have universal health care systems, and even ones which do not (such as the United States) may have very complex governmental systems which set standards for health care and uphold basic rights to get care. Such health care systems depend upon the idea that all bodies have equal rights to health and upon the concept of a universal body, a body with a standardized functionality which can be assessed through objective measurement. For example, health care now depends upon an increasingly bureaucratized specification of what a standard body should be – its body mass index, its reflex times, its blood chemistry, its metabolization of nutrients, its visual and auditory acuity, its vaccinated resistance to disease and many more features. The purpose of medicine (increasingly via preventive care and restorative interventions such as hip transplants) is to maintain the body to this universal standard and, when it is faulty, to restore it to it as far as possible.[15] Medicine thus functions just like car care: the annual road test or check-up detects deviations from the governmental, democratic standard, and repairs get the body back on the road.

The medicalization and management of the material body are evident in many other ways. Consider regulation. In medieval times, for example, the material body was rarely regulated out of consideration for its health. To the extent that it was regulated, the point was either to keep it in its social place (e.g. via sumptuary laws on dress, specifications for military service and so on) or for its spiritual good (e.g. in fasting, scripted participation in religious services, the regulation of sexuality and similar rules). To the extent that the government intervenes in bodies today, the situation is reversed. Although some moral strictures remain (such as limitations on public nudity), many have gone (such as restrictions on many forms of sexuality). In their place, there has occurred a huge growth in regulation aimed purely at the physical health of the body – rules about smoking, drinking alcohol, taking drugs, eating pure foods, conforming to a vast array of health and safety rules, obligatory insurance and, increasingly, the protection of minors. It is symptomatic of the historical reversal of priorities that we allow our citizens to believe anything they want about God but not to ride in a car without seat belts.

Back to social reality: Body worlds

In one sense these are trivial moments, but in many ways they are culturally more far-reaching than any Frankenstein-like new technology. Discovering DNA, growing new body parts from stem cells or developing thought-controlled prosthetics may feel like a tsunami or earthquake with the power to transform the landscape in an instant. Yet millions of small daily acts have a power of their own more akin to the constant carving of eroding wind and water. They can accomplish things cataclysms cannot, levelling mountains, filling ocean basins, building up sandstone and limestone hundreds of metres thick. Sedimenting history, they create the cultural landscape that determines whether an earthquake transforms an entire vista or passes harmlessly without effect.

What gives a coherent texture to experience is not each such moment but the tacit connections between them. If we trace the links between these moments, we see how gender norms cross-cut the question of eating and body weight and the doorways and paths men and women pass through. Reflexes of personal autonomy and space underlie the routines of bodily distancing and privacy and the idea of bodily control as a balance of individual rights and collective authority. The idiom of refinement, bodily restraint and class underwrites not only our music example but also eating, via a high cuisine in which distinction, not satisfaction of gross appetite, is the goal; extending the same logic makes obesity a giving-in to gross appetite, a class-based moral weakness. Such extendible logics allow both conformity and resistance; when we equate bodily restraint and authority, we make possible both the goose-stepping army regiments and the carnival. One could continue in this analytical vein at much greater length. As many social theorists have argued, although culture can never be reduced to a single, rigidly logical code, understandings of the body are conventional, constructed discourses; a core of practices and beliefs about the body which underlies a lot of social action, which we understand intuitively and rely upon every day to act and to understand each other's actions, but which we rarely ever put into words. Thus, as we pass from one moment of living to another, we experience a coherency of meanings rooted in the body.

Social reality is a bodily process; we live in body worlds. A body world, in the terms we defined in Chapter 1, captures all the elements of bodily life, from unconscious practices through discursive knowledge via burial and representation. We have described some aspects of our own body world, but any individual's experience of the body world he or she lives in is always partial rather than a totality, and the term itself refers to something which may well be analytically hypothetical. Nevertheless, the concept of a body world is useful in a loose, descriptive sense to highlight two qualities. One is the feeling of coherence when many apparently disparate events or practices nevertheless acquire a feeling of connectedness or familiarity born from their grounding in the reflexes and understandings the body uses to generate behaviour. The other is worldness, the feeling of absolute reality which emerges from the immanent experience of the same presuppositions encountered everywhere one turns. Body worlds are not univocal. They allow contradictions, individual expression and dissent. Nevertheless, because acts of subversion normally work by inverting norms, even while transforming an underlying logic, they still reproduce it; dissonance and coherence are inseparable.

Another way to see the coherence of our body world is to look not at how disparate experiences hang together but at the blank places on the map, the no-go zones. Gunther Von Hagens's 'Body Worlds' exhibition of dissected and plastinated dead bodies has riveted public attention. Yet, fascinatingly, there are two questions which (as far as we can see) nobody has ever asked about the 'Body Worlds' exhibition. One question is: 'are these things really human bodies?' People in other cultures might well define these objects differently, as no longer human, as no longer a body, as some new kind of being with different rights and powers. We, in contrast, accept the implicit assertion that the body is the material apparatus of a human being, and, therefore, these plastinated objects remain human bodies. In fact, we have trouble conceiving that it could be otherwise; we accept them as bodies even when they display a defiance of logic reminiscent of Magritte's *ceci n'est pas une pipe*.[16] The other unasked question is 'why is it actually so shocking to display cut-up bodies in public?' Many cultures have done so throughout history, including European cultures up until about two centuries ago (and even now if you include the skeletons often displayed in archaeological museums). The power to shock us is not an automatic consequence of displaying dead bodies; it derives from this network of bodily understandings that lurk intimately below our threshold of awareness. The fact that nobody has actually asked these questions shows how much we take for granted our own attitudes. They are the sedimented landscape of accumulated reflex actions which directs the force of storms (such as the exhibition). The result, ultimately, is a sense of depth and reality to our cumulative bodily experience. It is part of a body world.

Cultural difference

If our own body world is strange, other peoples' are equally so. Earlier, we took five examples from our own world to explore and defamiliarize aspects of our own body world. Here we look briefly at three anthropological examples to highlight how body worlds can be different.

In doing so we will also set out some of the key concepts that are useful in understanding all body worlds. Rather than ploughing through a dense literature review here, we prefer to present our working concepts by example. Such concepts have been developed by key thinkers in the humanities and social sciences, from Foucault's understandings of discipline and discourse, via Butler's theories of performativity, to Deleuze and Guattari's body without organs.[17] These and other theorists provide us with some of our inspiration throughout our historical narrative. In drawing on an eclectic range of texts, we do not mean to suggest that all the thinkers we draw upon use compatible conceptual tools; it is simply that the body is complex and requires multiple approaches to open different arenas for analysis. Thus we do not adopt the 'spirit guide' view of social theory;[18] no single set of ideas takes us into all the areas we want to go.

The soul in Huronia and the body in the Americas

Two worlds collided in the 1620s: Huron Indians stood face to face with French Jesuits in what is now Ontario. The Huron had only met Europeans for the first time about two decades before. Now a handful of Jesuits, journeying far beyond the frontier of a small, still tentative colony based in Montreal, lived amongst them and tried to convert them to Christianity. We know about this encounter from the reports the erudite and bureaucratic Jesuits sent back to their headquarters.[19] Their reports mostly relate perplexity and frustration.

To convert the Huron, the Jesuits had to translate Christian theology into terms the Huron could understand. The Jesuits, like other Christians (see Chapters 6 and 7), believed that people were made up of two components, the soul and the flesh. The soul was divine and immortal. The flesh was worldly and mortal. The body was a place of theological struggle as the moral Christian fought against the fleshly appetites for eating, sex, sloth, display and anger.

With this agenda, the Jesuits ran into trouble right away. The Huron treated them amicably enough, but translating Christian theology was a real problem. Take the notion of 'soul'. The Huron, too, believed that persons had souls, but along somewhat different lines. For one thing, people had more than one soul. Besides the most widely acknowledged soul, the *oki*, which the Jesuits finally decided to use to translate the Christian 'soul', people had at least one other soul and possibly more, constituting other qualities of existence.[20] Moreover, the *oki* soul was not unique to humans. What the Jesuits wanted to translate as 'soul', in fact, was a general category of spiritual being which included not only human souls but also powerful supernatural beings such as the sky, the earth, waters, winds, rocks and animals. The world of *oki*s was densely populated by things both human and non-human, both good and malign.

What was life like in a world in which body and soul were not opposed? Huron body practices were difficult for the Jesuits to understand. They could ascribe premarital and extra-marital sex to the loose morals one would expect of untutored children of nature, but what about when a dream commanded that people should engage in intercourse while a sick person watched in order to help heal him? Similarly, to the Jesuits, when the Huron gave guests food without payment, this was seen as laudable if unsophisticated generosity; when guests were required to eat all the food served at a feast, even if it was so much that it made them sick, this was incomprehensible gluttony. Similar examples could be cited for things such as dress and finery, dance and ritual, and violence.[21]

As a generalization, to the Jesuit priests, and to Europeans more widely, bodily action could oppose spiritual action, or it might express it, as an outward sign of an inner spiritual meaning; both of these are possible if you assume a priori that body and spirit are separate and distinct, with the spirit having ontological priority. What is not a possibility is that bodily action *is* spiritual action because there is no ontological dividing line between body and spirit.

It is, however, exactly this idea that underlay Huron bodily practices. A ritual dance did not express a state of healing, it enacted or created it. If foods such as maize embodied spiritual value, then eating was a spiritual act; eating corn meant literally incorporating this value, and the more the better. Similarly, the French were unable to understand why the generally kind and gentle Huron should torture Iroquois war captives to death in protracted ritual cruelty, sometimes eating them as well. If it was spiritually beneficial to war on their enemies and inflict harm on them, then the more one did, the more spiritual benefit accrued.[22]

This drama of mutual misunderstanding took place centuries ago, but it is helpful here to broaden it to more recent encounters. Ethnographic descriptions of Northeastern Native Americans generally show them to have inhabited a spiritual world like that of the Huron. To the Ojibwa, there was no simple distinction between animate and inanimate beings; everything which existed had the possibility of being animate.[23] As for the Huron, dreams were real living processes, and humans, animals, and things such as stones and winds could transform into each other fluidly. A similar situation has been discussed by Viveiros de Castro and Descola for South American natives.[24]

As Ingold[25] notes, this is very difficult for us to understand from a Western perspective. When we read that an Ojibwa man donning a mask turned himself into a bear, or an Amazonian native could transform into a jaguar to roam the forest by night, this seems to us a patent impossibility. Non-anthropological observers might see this as evidence of non-Westerners' credulous superstition; more sympathetic analysts tend to see it is a metaphorical transformation, a pretending for the purposes of story or ritual. Yet it is simply based upon different assumptions about bodies and reality. As we saw in Chapter 1, to Westerners, 'nature' is a material state which is fixed: either you are a human or you are a bear, and that is it. In contrast, what you do, say and wear – 'culture' – can be varied. Hence, a human in a bear mask remains firmly a human, albeit one who is behaving differently for the moment. In Ojibwa or Huron or Amazonian ontologies, all things can potentially be animated and possess personhood; this is the broad and varied world of spirits in which humans participate along with many other beings. This is the idea of transformability: the same being might appear in the material guise of a human or a bear; it is the person who is constant, not their material nature. Donning a bear mask can thus effect a genuine transformation from human to bear, not in the underlying social being but in the material state they exist in. We are familiar in the world we live in with the idea of multiculturalism – there are many cultures – and mononaturalism – there is only one nature. For many groups in the Americas, the reverse is true – there is only one culture, but many different natures: multinaturalism.[26]

The Jesuits never had more than indifferent success in converting the Hurons, and when other Native Americans adopted Christianity, it often seems to have been not by the wholesale ontological shift which missionaries hoped for but by a kind of syncretistic compromise which allowed Christian ritual practices to carry on side by side with traditional beliefs in different contexts.[27] Be that as it may, it is an instructive example to see how deep ontological beliefs structure the way people live through their bodies.[28] We return later to this issue of ontology – what the body actually is.

Relationality and substances in Melanesia

Nowhere in the world have these issues been at the forefront of anthropological theory as in New Guinea. Exotica abound, from headhunting and cannibalism to gender antagonism at a level difficult for us to believe, the exuberant display of ornamented bodies, ritualized sexuality, elaborate life-cycle rites, and the practice of witchcraft and sorcery. It is fortunate that Melanesia is a region where anthropological theorists have risen to the challenge of such florid otherness.

As with the Huron discussed in the previous section, the obvious otherness of Melanesian bodily practices has to be seen within a symbolic order radically different from our own. The single most salient difference is that, throughout Melanesia, the body is thought to be constituted socially: the physical body is created through relations it participates in.[29] Often these are thought of in terms of shared or transmitted bodily substances such as blood, bone, semen and food. A comparison may be useful. In medieval Europe, a human body was considered to be constituted by four fluid 'humours' (blood, phlegm, bile and choler) which existed in balance (see Chapter 6). But now imagine that (unlike in medieval Europe) a person received the blood in their body from their mother, the phlegm from their father, the black bile from a priest officiating at their first communion, and the

choler from their food. Bringing a person to adulthood would require regular administrations of these substances, often in ritualized ways, and the grown person would be bound to other people through specific bodily relations. It is this kind of logic, for instance, not sexual pleasure per se or a lifelong sexual orientation, which underlies the Etoro's ritual homosexual insemination of young boys[30] (semen conveys male life-force and boys approaching initiation into manhood need regular infusions of it). Similarly, children are often considered to receive blood from their mother. By extension, they are linked to their mother's lineage, particularly to her brothers, by blood in a way which creates close lifelong obligations of support; but other substances link them to their father's relations.

This potency of bodily substances and actions generates often quite complex corollaries, particularly when combined with the strong gender polarity, even antagonism, which characterizes many New Guinea societies. For example, if semen is considered a form of male life-force, and if men possess only a limited quantity of it during their lifetime, then ritual insemination of novices is a praiseworthy self-sacrifice which depletes this precious limited substance for the good of society; in contrast, sexual intercourse for its own sake may be gratuitously dangerous.[31] Similarly, women's blood is both powerful and potentially dangerous to men and their masculinity. Similar logics underlie other practices, such as the often elaborate and traumatic initiation ceremonies for young men and women. Head-hunting and ritualized sexuality amongst South Coast New Guinea groups serve as means of appropriating and circulating life-force, maintaining the strength of the group, and ensuring spiritual regeneration.[32] Colourful body ornamentation, often including traded or gifted items such as arm shells, is a way of displaying the sum of relationships making up the body.[33]

In such a context, bodily objects such as ornaments can be more than just symbols of these relationships. Often they *are* the relationships. Just as bodies are formed through exchange of substances, so objects too are forged from their relations. Both bodies and objects then are the subject of the same rules, the same metaphors, and thus both objects and bodies can be persons, and both can be parts of a person.[34] Such a claim may seem nonsensical: surely only human beings can be persons, and surely the boundary of this personhood is limited to the (human) body. This is fundamentally not the case in Melanesia, however, because what makes something a person is not the set of physical properties derived from a single object, the biological organism, but a range of relationships.[35] Perhaps the best example of this is the Sabarl axe

(Figure 1) made by the Sabarl people who inhabit a coral atoll off Papua New Guinea. Different parts of the axe are given the same names as different parts of the human body, and like the body, axes possess *hinona*, a vital substance or life-force.[36] The axe, like a body, can take part in relationships, and on the death of a (human) person, people gather axes together with food to make a 'corpse' which is then broken up, just as human beings are understood as being broken up into their relationships on death.[37]

People and things (and indeed plants, animals, clans and so on) in Melanesia are formed from relationships. Thus personhood is fundamentally *relational*. Whereas people in the West have traditionally seen themselves as individuals (singular indivisible entities), people in Melanesia are dividual, or better yet, partible.[38] The movement of substances and things in exchange relations means that parts of people's personhood, parts of their bodies, can be separated off and exchanged. Personhood, therefore, is not bounded by the skin. This relational conception has important implications in particular for how gender is understood. Rather than being something prefixed by the body's internal biology (the individualized Western perspective), gender too is relational. Thus, gender emerges differently in different circumstances, depending on the position a person takes within a particular relationship. As Strathern puts it, 'the corporeal body is presented as exclusively male or female for specific ritual effect: persons are not automatically conceived . . . as single sex'.[39] People who are biologically male, can thus be understood as female within certain kinds of (usually exchange) relationships, and substances too can take on different gendered qualities, for they too are relational.[40]

Honour in Algeria

If you visited a traditional Kabyle peasant's home in Algeria in the 1950s, you would find yourself entering a one-room house with a lower stable area to the left, a hearth area to the right and an upright loom and a rifle along the back wall (Figure 2a). As a guest, you would be seated in front of the back wall, near the hearth, in front of the loom. Seating you near the wall by which you entered would be a grave insult: the 'wall of darkness' was also the place for invalid's beds, for things which are idle, ill or dead, and in a broader sense uncooked or 'natural' things, animals, and nocturnal or secret activities.[41] In fact, seating someone against the 'wall of darkness' was tantamount to receiving them scornfully; it called their honour into question.

Does a detail like this actually matter? This example is drawn from one of the most famous ethnographies of the twentieth century, Bourdieu's analysis of Kabyle culture, and it is famous precisely because of how Bourdieu makes clear the relation between space, bodily practice, time and meaning, through his concept of the habitus, those repeated, unthinking, bodily actions we have already briefly encountered.[42] The Kabyle world was structured by pervasive oppositions between male and female, between light and dark, between public and private, between hot and cold, between dry and wet, between east and west, and between times such as night and day, summer and winter. The house, for example, formed a microcosm of these distinctions, differentiated into areas associated with women, darkness, pre-cultural substances, fertility, illness and death, and areas associated with men, public interactions, light and heat (Figure 2b). These divisions, however, were not stated baldly and synoptically; they were taught obliquely, through sayings and gestures, through the patterns of movement appropriate for different kinds of bodies. Thus men and women favoured different foods: dryer, hotter foods eaten in the centre of the room more fitting for men to eat; wet, boiled meals were more fitting for women. The guest's place was in a valued area near the household's sources of productivity and esteem: the man's rifle, the woman's loom. Dead bodies were washed at the entrance to the stable on the left; making a guest sleep in the loft above the stable was an insult, comparing their sleep with death. Liminal and sometimes dangerous places such as doorways and thresholds were often where ritual prohibitions took place.

Bourdieu details the way in which space was highly structured, and this structure had a lot to do with the body.[43] The qualities and oppositions attributed to space were the same ones which defined male bodies and female bodies. Moreover, there were distinct forms of honour for men and women, which were defined spatially as well. A valued woman made the house productive and fertile, appearing little outside it. Men, in contrast, ploughed, traded and carried out politics and fighting outside the house – all bodily activities; a man who spent too much time inside the house was considered effeminate and suspect and was politically discounted. The same values were expressed through other forms of action. The man of honour lived on the 'point of honour', always ready to fight if insulted or in defence of his property, interests, friends or women. He would skilfully and far-sightedly manipulate political alliances and timings of such matters as when to reciprocate both insults and gifts to avoid being shamed. This readiness for action was shown in many ways besides words and work; the man of honour

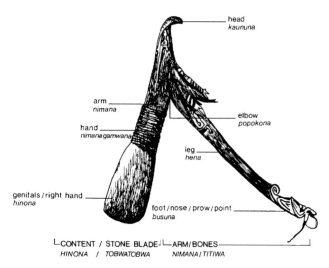

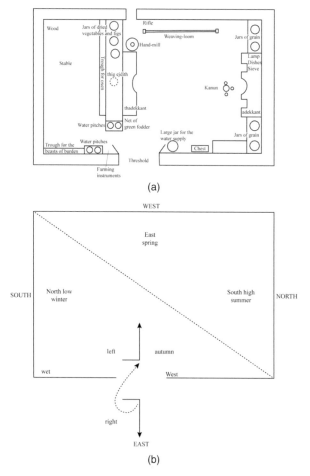

Figure 1. The Sabarl axe (Battaglia 1990: 9, reproduced with kind permission of Chicago University Press).

Figure 2. Space and the body: the Kabyle house. A. diagram of the house (after Bourdieu 1990, 272, redrawn by Vicki Herring). B. synoptic diagram of Berber house (after Bourdieu 1990, 280, redrawn by Vicki Herring).

was recognizable in public by his manner of walking – active, wary, tense and alert.

Bourdieu's analysis does not merely show how space and behaviour are structured by values such as gender, a point which many analyses have made. Instead, he shows how such practical logics work: how stable, generalized structures emerge from behaviour which is unscripted, which is simply people acting their way through daily situations. As people are raised within a culture, they learn a habitus, a set of 'generative dispositions'. The habitus consists of a set of generalized definitional principles: 'men are x, women are y'. This in turn provides the basic tools for how to 'wing it' in a way which makes sense culturally: how would a man act in this situation? What is appropriate ritual behaviour for a given time of year? What is important here is not only how people generate behaviour through such practical logic, but that such practical logics are embodied.[44] They are grounded in bodily identities such as gender and age and in bodily qualities such as masculinity and honour. They are performed and interpreted through bodily observances, not just dramatic performances such as fights and rituals, but the skilful execution of daily tasks such as farming, cooking, weaving, eating and the smallest gestures and habits. In each case, people find their way not through explicit thoughts of 'what do I do now?' but through non-discursive knowledge, habit and experience.

Practical ontology[45]

Experientially, the great thing about bodies is their immediacy. We experience bodies as real, but they are culture-bound. The great British pursuit of correct queuing

would probably be every bit as perplexing to a Huron, Melanesian or Kabyle anthropologist as feasting the spirits of the dead, the ritual insemination of novices or quarrelling to maintain one's honour are to our anthropologists. Yet in each case, simple everyday actions form dramas which build a unique body world. These different body worlds clearly show, in turn, the contingent nature of these practices and beliefs.

But the cultural variation and historical contingency of the body unexpectedly gets us into a philosophical hornet's nest. What is 'the body'?

What is the body anyway?

Our common-sense reaction is simple. We assume that people can understand the body differently, but the actual body itself, the physical stuff, stays pretty much the same. In other words, the real body is the 'natural' or 'physical' thing itself; what we have been talking about is simply various cultural interpretations of it. After all, Western scientific understandings of the body reveal a shared 'truth'; medicines work upon people who do not understand or believe in them. This position is widely held across the biological sciences, in many fields of the humanities and social sciences, and by ordinary people, politicians formulating public policy and so on. For instance, this position underwrites traditional gender studies, which began with a distinction between biological 'sex' and cultural 'gender'.

A recent critique of this 'standard view of the body', mounted in anthropology, sociology and cultural studies, starts with its dichotomy between naturalism and constructivism. The division between nature and culture has been central to how Western people have thought about the world since at least the seventeenth century (see Chapter 7). It is one of a series of so-called Cartesian dualisms, after the philosopher René Descartes. The nature-culture divide is not based on scientific investigation, but rather on assumed dualities about how the world works: mind is opposed to body, male to female, culture to nature. Given this duality, it is difficult to avoid privileging one of the two competing poles. If we assume that there exists a physical body which precedes culture and which is the 'real body', this position has been termed 'naturalism'. Such an argument says that as much as the Amazonian shaman might 'think' he can turn into a jaguar, he patently cannot, it is impossible. Equally, a Sabarl axe can never *really be* a person. In its more extreme forms, naturalism also sees human behaviour through the prism of biological determinism in which biology provides the bottom line explaining social relations, whether academically or in popular arguments such as why 'Men are from Mars and Women are from Venus'. It follows that the natives can think whatever they like about the body, but we (via scientific study of the biological body) know the real truth about it.

The reverse position is social constructivism, which argues that the body is largely socially constructed – that is, it varies through time and space to such an extent that there is little point in wondering about biological or physical connections. Instead, we need to concentrate on how differing social worlds make sense of and produce the body. There may be a natural or physical body somewhere beneath the socially constructed one, so say social constructivists, but this gives no help in capturing *cultural* difference. Most of the basic theoretical literature on the body has been written from a constructivist standpoint.[46] Constructivism helpfully forces us to pay attention to historical and social factors and is an entirely understandable response to an ahistorical emphasis on biology and nature. In its more extreme forms, however, it can write

the physical body totally out of existence,[47] and it fails to explain why similar systems of gender relations (for example) crop up in many, geographically unconnected, societies. Most problematically of all, it continues to buy into the nature-culture divide, even if it privileges the opposite end from naturalism.

Critics of the common-sense view of the body have targeted the nature-culture distinction. Judith Butler,[48] for example, argues that bodies do not have a given sex, they are ascribed one. For instance, when doctors classify newborns as either male or female, they ignore chromosomal variations or phenotypical variations in genitalia, or write them off as 'rare abnormalities'; sex is thus not an absolute biological reality which precedes socially constructed gender, it is socially constructed itself. A more general argument deals not with how the body is classified and defined but how it is actually produced.[49] Simply put, the body is produced within social relations; hence, no part of the body is ever solely 'natural' or 'biological'. A child is conceived through sexual intercourse, its specific genetic inheritance reflecting the social relations structuring mating within its society. Within the womb, the mother's diet and living conditions intimately shape the baby. From birth onwards, eating, working, and health are all carried out within social relations that affect its growth, disease burden, stress, violence, medicalization and bodily modifications. Human biology is plastic and responds in many ways, from the greater stature seen in upper classes of many societies, to the asymmetrical arm bones of a tennis player, whose racket arm will be up to 30 per cent thicker than the other.[50] In medicine, Lock has argued that people have a 'local biology' rather than a universal biology. Differences between American and Japanese women in the symptoms of menopause, for example, are not merely because of different cultural interpretations of the same biological symptoms; the two groups of women actually experience different physical conditions.[51] In other words, there is no opposition between an underlying 'biological' body and a veneer of a 'social' body. If you took away the social history of a body's actions in the world, you wouldn't have a 'natural' body – you simply would not have a body at all.[52] It follows that, historically, there is not one human body which is understood differently at different points in time. There are many different bodies which are inextricably different both socially and biologically.

Does this leave us any basis for comparing bodies? A social constructivist could argue that bodies are so specific to their cultural milieu that we cannot compare them; what is understood as the human body differs too much from one setting to another. We would take a somewhat different position. Such arguments write out the body's biological materiality from the picture; the body becomes infinitely malleable and plastic in the hands of society.[53] In contrast, we would suggest that the body poses similar existential challenges in all societies. Bodies require nutrition; genomes, however acquired, express themselves; at death, metabolic processes inevitably cease. It is not determinism to say that all societies have to make sense of such things. There is a shared *history* to the human body which underwrites its historical differentiation. Gender relations are creative and differentiated, but not entirely unstructured. The history of death is a history of the different ways in which humans have created, channelled and understood metabolic changes. Our evolutionary history is both of how DNA has changed biochemically and of how humans have migrated socially and formed groups across the globe. It is this shared history that allows us to make comparisons between different groups without simply imposing our conception of the body on others. We need to attend to both difference and similarity if we are to understand the complex ways in which multiple kinds of human bodies have existed through the histories we trace in Chapters 3 through 8. The body, as we will see, is the outcome of these complex shared histories and everyday practical engagements.

Terms of analysis

With this broad introduction, we now need to outline the axes of analysis we will use to study the body worlds we cover in Chapters 3 through 8. The ethnographic vignettes discussed earlier suggest both variation and similarity amongst body worlds. It is not that the worlds we uncover in the European past will be the same as those that exist for the Huron, in Melanesia or for the Kabyle – far from it – but these cases and our own body world supply some vocabulary of analysis.

Practical ontologies, embodiment and personhood. An ontology is a theory of being: the kinds of things which could potentially exist or happen within a particular reality. For example, in our own ontology (cf. Chapters 6, 7 and 8), we distinguish between bodies and minds; in other ontologies, such as the Huron example, such a distinction makes no sense. Similarly, in our ontology, people are understood to be bounded individuals whose identity and ability to make moral choices remains invariable as they pass from one situation to another. In contrast, in some Melanesian ontologies, people's identity is understood to change as they pass from one set of social relations to another. Such ontological principles are rarely expressed explicitly in so many words; instead they are enacted in practical and ritual actions, as in the examples discussed earlier.

In this book, we do not approach bodies as possessing internal minds, assessing sensory data fed to them by organs such as the eyes. Such a position separates mind from body and mind from world and drags us back to the Cartesian dualisms of which we have already been critical. Instead, we approach bodies as active, sensing beings already thrown into particular worlds. 'Embodiment' describes the manner in which people experience the world through their bodies, a world of which they are always a part, and points us in the direction of the sensory qualities of places and things. This is a claim not to a universal phenomenology but a specifically historicized one in which the nature of experience is disclosed against different historical, material and social backgrounds.[54] Concentrating on embodiment emphasizes a key tenet of this book: that in producing the world, people produce their bodies at the same time, it is through learning to move, talk and act in specific ways that those ways themselves are sustained and taught to others. Thus, the term 'body world' in this regard captures precisely the co-constitutive nature of body and world; the two emerge through each other ontologically through practice.

Fundamentally, therefore, body worlds are practical ontologies. This somewhat cumbersome term is designed to capture the sense that people think abstractly by doing things in historically concrete ways. It suggests internal logical connections without rigid systematicity. It also indicates that how people and their bodies relate to the world is not a matter of different ways of understanding the same thing, but rather the ways in which different bodies and different worlds emerge through practices which have genuine ontological impact. Throughout this book, we look for evidence of how these bodily ontologies changed and developed through time, particularly in the specific moments of transition we examine. How did the bodies of people and animals change in relation to one another as people began to farm in the Neolithic, for example? How did the currently dominant ontology of body-as-machine emerge in the Early Modern period?

Practical ontologies involve ideas about what a person is. As the Melanesian example reveals, what is understood as a person may differ radically amongst groups. Under what circumstances might things take on the characteristics of people? How might different kinds of personhood, relational or otherwise, coexist with one another? How do new modes of personhood emerge? In our case studies we examine how specific kinds of personhood grow, change or stay the same across specific transitions. Does the new use of metalwork in Copper Age Europe, for example, relate to a new form of personhood, as has often been argued; or is it instead bound up in older understandings of what people and bodies are?

Habitus, space and material things. Both the Kabyle example and our vignette of people listening to music in the Western world reveal how body worlds are centrally shaped through the use of space and the knowledge of how to move or sit still, speak or remain silent in appropriate circumstances. Habitus[55] – the idea that cultural worlds and human bodies are produced together through structured but not necessarily discursively rule-bound practices – has proved a central concept across the social sciences. The concept has not been without criticism, and Bourdieu's formulation tends to portray a group's habitus as a somewhat timeless abstraction, making it difficult to integrate with explanations of historical change. But it provides a useful way to relate the minutiae of daily life with the underlying meanings which people use to generate them through unscripted, spontaneous action. Such meanings often remain latent, expressed through words, gestures or proverbial senses, rather than synoptically. Space and material culture are central here. Different kinds of material culture and architecture play a crucial role in guiding these movements and engagements, just as we saw with the distancing technologies of our own society. When examining different past societies, it will be essential to examine how particular things, say classical statuary, helped to define a habitus that privileged certain forms of embodied experience, skill and movement over others. Thinking about habitus and embodiment together requires us to examine how people engaged with architecture and material culture from the perspectives of their bodies, how different spaces offered up different kinds of possibilities. For example, what new kinds of habitus or embodiment became possible as rooms became increasingly divided and specialized in the eighteenth century? How did this lead to a new emphasis on privacy in some quarters (especially the wealthy and middle class)?

In thinking about space, a useful notion is Tim Ingold's conception of the 'taskscape'.[56] The taskscape defines the way in which all elements of human action do not take place against a backdrop of undifferentiated space, but rather are part and parcel of the way in which landscape forms and the manner through which people understand and move through that landscape and experience time. In our own lives, the taskscape might be made up of the office, the home, the streets we move through, other places such as coffee shops, train stations, supermarkets, relatives' houses, the gym or pub. Each of these locations involves different kinds of tasks, and different tasks are appropriate: one would be happy to wash up at home, but less so in the pub. They also involve different forms of dress and sociality, and are associated with different times of the day and night. If you normally go to the cinema in the evening, a daytime trip can provide quite a shock when you walk out into the light (time here is defined by activity rather than chronological clocks). Landscape is not a background against which these tasks play out, but is instead formed through these tasks, and the forms of embodiment and habitus to which each of them refers. In the most obvious sense, we can think of builders erecting a building or a farmer ploughing a field as a means by which taskscape produces landscape. Taskscapes, however, are not just about what things look like but also about how they sound and feel, and therefore involve everything from ringing church bells to blaring mobile phones as well. The landscape is thus the congealed form of the taskscape, made up of all the tasks people undertake. These tasks may be repetitive long-term activities or single transformative events, but each has its place in the taskscape and each is formed by and in turn forms particular kinds of embodiment. Through the taskscape, bodies become constituted through landscape, and landscape through bodies.[57]

Gender and power. Gender is a form of identity central to all body worlds. It is important to stress from the outset that we do not necessarily mean male and female genders alone, as we saw with the Siberian shaman in Chapter 1. It is undoubtedly the case that many different societies focus around two particular gendered groups, which equate well in terms of bodily characteristics to our notions of male and female. This is unsurprising: bodily difference in this regard plays a crucial role in reproduction amongst other things. Nevertheless, there is extensive evidence for third gender and third sex groups around the world, including in our own society. What it means to be 'male' or 'female' is historically specific; not only do the roles men and women play in our own society emerge from specific histories of capitalism and feudalism, so even our understandings of what it means to be a man or a woman are historically contingent. One important thinker on gender in recent years has been Butler,[58] already mentioned, who draws on a range of eclectic writers[59] to problematize our basic understandings of sex, gender and identity. Butler argues that concepts such as male and female or man and woman are not absolute; rather they are regulatory ideals[60] 'whose materialisation is compelled, and this materialisation takes place (or fails to take place) through certain highly regulated practices'.[61] These practices are *performative*, Butler argues,[62] in that they produce and sustain the regulatory ideals they appear to follow, thus making the latter appear natural. This might sound complicated, but it is actually a very straightforward and powerful idea. Through dressing, walking and acting like a man people sustain the regulatory ideal of what a man is at the same time as making themselves into a man. These performances of gender are never entirely within a person's control.[63] This is demonstrated in Butler's classic example of the performative nature of sexing infants. As we saw earlier, when midwives lift up a baby, examine its genitalia, and pronounce 'it's a girl', they do not merely report a fact but instead performatively begin the process of binding sex and gender on to the baby.[64] Other societies may have very different regulatory ideals of gender.[65]

Power is equally central to the body worlds we uncover. Foucault's work has exposed the way power works through bodies. In *Discipline and Punish*,[66] for example, Foucault examined the shift in how the body was punished. In the Medieval and Early Modern periods, European societies punished criminals through exemplary public assaults on the body – public torture and execution, for example – which located and demonstrated political power in the ability to act upon the bodies of its subjects and produce pain and death. From the nineteenth century onwards, punishment shifted increasingly to private, controlled acts of imprisonment, understood not only as retribution but also as correction or reformation. In so doing, bodies were controlled in new ways, power worked through bodies in new ways and new forms of body were produced. In fact, the genius of Foucault is that he traces this move not just in prisons, but in many other contexts as well, such as schools, hospitals, asylums, factories and the military. New ways of punishing criminals made sense because they fitted into a new understanding of the body as a component which had to be treated mechanistically to fit it to its role in a social machine – the goal of the prison. All of this becomes part of a form of control exercised through the body that Foucault calls *biopower*.[67]

Foucault was writing about a time of nation states and the emergence of modern capitalism, and we return to this in Chapter 7. How does power relate to the body in other contexts, however? When we consider the prehistoric world, for example, we lack the large centralized power structures we have in later times. This does not mean power was not important. In Chapter 4, for example, we trace how power played out through the body and material culture in the worlds of Neolithic and Bronze Age Europe.

The structure of body worlds

If these different lines of enquiry help us to understand different aspects of the body world, we still need to say something more about how these worlds are structured. Habitus, personhood, embodiment, power and gender are all deeply intertwined. Body worlds are not experienced through clinical analyses but through the muddled and confused nature of getting on in the world. Each of these elements depends deeply on the others, and all come together in the way people have lived through the body worlds of history. It is not particularly useful, however, to regard body worlds as undifferentiated, quivering masses of embodied meaning, like giant jellyfishes. Here we outline just a few basic points.

Body worlds are internally structured. Generalized, abstract, often implicit beliefs underwrite a multitude of more concrete propositions and practices which are invoked or performed in specific settings. To take an obvious thumbnail example, wearing black for mourning presupposes a system of colour categories and terminology, beliefs about death, and semantic and embodied associations between colours and sentiments. To take a somewhat more subtle example inspired by Butler, in our society one may enact a gendered identity through more masculine and more feminine ways of dressing, of walking, of eating and drinking, of choosing consumer goods and so on. These prescribe, or at least suggest, different ways of performing gender in different settings. But, as we saw with our 'gendered doorways' earlier, these presuppose a more general belief in a distinction between males and females which comes into play across contexts and forms part of one's personal identity and social operating concepts. And this in turn supposes another concept – people come in two mutually exclusive, opposed, exhaustive categories which are rooted in biological difference and which are stable through a person's life. This is an idea about the fundamental nature of the body of which most natives who are not also anthropologists usually remain unaware. Thus body worlds not only contain multiple perspectives on the body but are organized at different scales, so that certain perspectives rest upon others.

Although reaction to totalizing, reductionist, top-down views of symbolism has led anthropologists in recent decades to focus upon the fluid and contextual aspects of culture, the hierarchical organization of bodily, practical ontologies has been acknowledged in some form by almost all anthropologists and sociologists of belief. This is generally presented in terms of a generative dialectic, as in Giddens' concept of the duality of structure or Bourdieu's concept of habitus as a set of learned, ingrained dispositions which generate a free flow of improvised behaviour. To the extent that culture is neither reinvented entirely afresh in every action nor simply the blind repetition of imprinted facts, some such conceptualization remains inescapable; there is little to be gained by objecting that any abstraction above the level of individual action is a reification, as this superficial objection presumes that individual behaviour provides the single, a priori immanently and objectively real scale of analysis.[68] In this book, we make use of the hierarchical organization of belief in a very general way. As a basic, minimal model, we posit a historically inherited world of abstract beliefs and tendencies, more or less in line with Bourdieu's concept of habitus (see Figure 3).[69] These in turn provide the materials called in to formulate specific fields of action (e.g. defined, rule-bound and meaningful ways of doing particular things). Fields of action, in turn, enable people to act in concrete, effective and creative ways. For example, for an individual to practice medicine, create art, cook dinner or conduct a business transaction, these activities must be defined as a kind of thing to do, each with its own conventions and meanings. Similarly, each field of action will be based upon explicit or implicit assumptions. To take an example, medical science generally presumes a functionalist, mechanistic view of the body; this bounds the practice of medicine as a field of action, such that (for instance) a consultation with a doctor conventionally deals with factors which can be related to illness within a mechanistic paradigm; it does not involve discussion of the position of the stars and planets or of the condition of the patient's soul.

Multiple examples from our brief vignettes bring this to mind. Going to a concert, for example, rests upon a whole set of context specific rules for behaviour that are not merely generated each time anew, but rest on the tradition of classical music reaching back a century or more. The behaviour of the body here rests upon implicit assumptions of class, wealth and sophistication that can be demonstrated through knowing how to act and when to clap (not at the end of a movement for example). To understand this, it makes no sense to analyse a single concert alone; we have to be aware of the way in which going to a concert relates precisely to a broader field of action. These are themselves not fixed and timeless but historical; so the attitude from an audience towards the actors in a theatre would have been very different in Shakespeare's time from the solemn silence we now expect.

Relations between fields of action and their underlying structures of meaning are not narrowly prescribed or fixed (Figure 4). Instead, a given practice can have a 'sheaf of meanings', in the anthropologist Barth's terms[70] – a ceremonial feast may be used to create solidarity and equality or to underline indebtedness and inequality between hosts and guests. Conversely, a highly abstract meaning may be expressed and recreated through many different fields of action, and if it is an important meaning it often will be. Social class in modern Britain, for instance, is expressed through fields of action as diverse as the accent with which you speak, where you go to school,

how you eat and even what kind of hunting or fishing you do. One surprising implication of this becomes clear when we move from anthropology (in which the relationship between meanings and fields of action is often presented as simple and static) to history. Over historical time, the relationship is remarkably fluid. Practices are continually reinterpreted within possible meaning structures; how meaning structures are expressed in action is continually redefined as the world of practical action changes. Thus, over centuries or millennia, practical actions and ontological interpretations are continually remapped onto each other in new ways. This turns out to be central to understanding change in beliefs about the body (Chapter 9).

It is essential to stress here that body worlds are the sedimented histories of practice, but that they do not simply unfold through bodies themselves. As Bourdieu showed, body worlds are found in architecture, in material culture, in the fields and in the monuments, in artwork and in burial. Houses, for example, shape the way people interact with each other, the way in which notions of privacy are understood, how certain bodily performances (sex, sleeping, going to the toilet) should be undertaken in public or in private. Body worlds are thus not limited simply to the bodies themselves, but are constituted through the material worlds that surround them even as these material worlds are themselves produced through people's understandings of what the body requires and entails. This sedimented character, the way much of a body world consists of what goes without saying, means that they are often resistant to sudden change and upheaval. Certain aspects of a body world may come up for intense transformation at certain times, whilst others sustain themselves unnoticed in the rhythms of daily life and the humility of things for thousands of years.[71]

The other concept we wish to introduce here is multimodality. We commonly speak of ontological systems or structures, but body worlds are never rigidly systematic; nor however are they entirely incoherent. Instead, one remarkable finding of this book is that all societies hold several contradictory ways of looking at the body at the same time. Ethnographies have often acknowledged this fact in passing (normally somewhat apologetically), but social theorists have never really realized its full scope. For example, in Chapter 7 we examine how Early Modern Western Europeans, when confronted with a dead body, alternated between seeing it theologically as a worthless material shell to a flown spirit, socially as a site for splendid display or stigmatising degradation, mechanistically as a functional structure to be dissected anatomically, or magically as a source of inherently potent substance to be used in witchcraft or healing. Each of these perspectives was enacted systematically and logically through its own

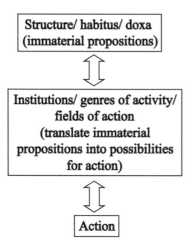

Figure 3. Habitus, fields of action and ongoing actions.

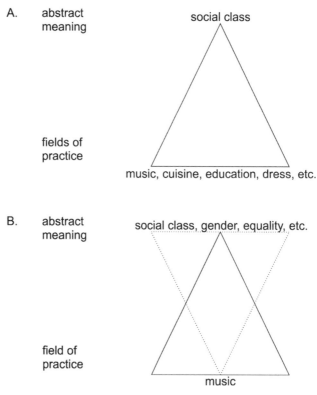

Figure 4. Relations between fields of action and doxic meanings. A. A single abstract meaning is enacted through many fields of practice. B. A single field of practice potentially reproduces various fields of meaning. Over time, these relations allow slippage where relations between practices and their meanings are remapped.

particular fields of action – theological discourse, sumptuous burial or judicial punishment, scientific investigation and magical rites. Not only were such different perspectives practiced simultaneously within society as a whole; individual people alternated between them as they passed from one context to another.

One effect of multimodality can be seen readily in the galleries of colour body images we include in this volume. Here we have grouped a variety of body representations over time. At any given point there is no single way of seeing the body – Palaeolithic Western Europeans saw human bodies as continuous with animal bodies in some contexts, but they defined distinctly human female figures in others. The split between body and soul was a paradigmatic anchor for understanding the medieval body in many ways, but what does it have to do with attempts to correlate zodiacal signs and body parts medically or with the bizarre torso-less figure of the 'gryllus' carved under a contemporary church seat ? Such multimodality is most visible in societies in which there is a concerted attempt to impose a unimodality – a single dominant meta-theory (as in the medieval and contemporary periods) – in which ontological tensions can be detected between the different modalities. But it is an omnipresent feature of human practical ontologies. Again, we underline it here because it turns out to be fundamental to how the long-term history of the body unfolds (Chapter 9).

The body as a historical problem

If we have demonstrated some of the potential difference in body worlds, we are still left with the fundamental historical problem that we posed in Chapter 1, and the topic of this book: where do body worlds come from?

We patently do not think the same things about our bodies we did a hundred years ago, let alone a thousand or ten thousand years ago. And if, as we argue earlier, we cannot separate a purely physical body from how people understand and live in the body, it is not just cultural understandings which have changed but the body itself. The human body has a history.

But what kind of history is this? How do body worlds come into being, change and disappear? These are the central questions of this book. Before we tackle it, we need to think about some relevant concepts of historical analysis.

For example ... modernist histories of the modern body

Let's take an example – indeed, *the* example par excellence – of the history of the body: our modern body.

The 'crisis' narrative

We began the previous chapter by discussing a sense of crisis in the body sometimes expressed in public discourse. Such a sense of crisis derives from a tacit, assumed, common-sense history of the body. The story might go something like this:

> Once upon a time, the body was natural, simple and obvious. You were born into your body, which was a human body, distinct both from animals (you might wear fur but you did not become an animal) and from mechanical things (obvious, easily detachable things such as eyeglasses and wooden legs did not make you a semi-robot). It came in two simple, permanent, easily distinguishable models (male and female) and passed through a self-evident, biological lifespan from birth to death. Both you and other people knew that your body defined who you were – your sex, age, height, strength, attractiveness and physical abilities. You passed on some of your own genetic material and characteristics to your children and raised them; they grew into who their own bodies made them. Eventually, like a machine deteriorating, your body wore out under the stresses of life. After medicine had done what it could, you died, leaving nothing of yourself behind besides the memories and feelings which remain to people who knew you and the lasting effects of your works and actions.

> Now new technologies are sweeping away all of the body's fixed points and we no longer know who we are…

This narrative, however, involves a deception. It goes without saying that the future is strange, uncharted territory. That is the nature of futures. But the sleight of hand here is the idea that we start out from a body which is biological, natural or inevitable. We tend to believe that our understanding of the body is simply a statement of empirical fact, grounded in biological reality. We feel that other peoples can believe in supernatural transformations, shamanic cures, body humours, astrology and alternative medicine; our biology simply reveals nature truly and our medical science actually works. As argued earlier in this chapter and in Chapters 7 and 8, however, our ideas about nature, culture and biology are historically situated. Our own narrative of the body – our story just told – has traceable historical roots; its story is not only that of the progressive accumulation of scientific knowledge but also of cultural change. For example, the concept of the body as a functional, soulless machine – an idea which arose between the seventeenth and twentieth centuries – is not a necessary concomitant of increased insight into its physiology; many outstanding anatomists and doctors have been, and are, devoutly religious. Instead, it grounds physiological knowledge in an abstract cosmology influenced by many other social factors, such

as industrial design and discipline (cf. Chapter 7). Similarly, concepts such as the boundedness and uniqueness of the human body, the stability of social identities rooted in the body, the link between individual identity and the innate characteristics of the body, how bodies relate through descent and kinship, the incommensurability of male and female bodies, and even the concept of 'nature' itself all have traceable historical pedigrees.[72]

Similarly, while this master narrative relies upon concepts of 'culture' and 'nature', it uses them simultaneously in contradictory ways. From one point of view, the master narrative sees history as the replacement of a biological body, which just happened naturally without human intervention, by an artificial, cultural and technological body. From another point of view, it is a story of how cultural understandings of the body (astrology, folk medicine, spiritualism) come to be superseded by purely natural understandings based upon empirical observation of the actual body.

Although the story serves as our society's flagship narrative, we also believe other, sometimes contradictory things about the body. In the terms discussed previously, we think multimodally. For example, as mentioned earlier and discussed at length in Chapters 7 and 8, one of our dominant metaphors of the body for the last few centuries has been that it is a purely material machine which functions or breaks down mechanically; but we also hold complicated beliefs about the body and personhood (so that bodies require personal space in a way which machines do not, for example; and disposing of a dead body is very different from disposing of a broken machine). We move seamlessly amongst alternative beliefs as we move from one context to another. Moreover, there are alternative modernities of the body. Modern science and medicine are practiced worldwide in cultures which have traditions of understanding the human body in very different ways. Rather than regarding such beliefs as ethnographic curiosities incompatible with modern technology and medicine, we find that scientific and medical techniques can fit within a wide latitude of beliefs.[73]

These considerations suggest that, in spite of how we may experience it, we are not in a transition from a world of 'natural' bodies to a world of 'artificial' bodies. Instead, the body forms part of a social and material order that encompasses and goes far beyond scientific knowledge and technological capacity. Are we experiencing a transition of the body? If we are (and we return to this question in Chapter 9), it is neither the takeover of the natural body by culture, nor the emergence of a scientific body grounded in a pure knowledge of nature. Instead, it is a shift from one body world to another.

Histories of the modern body

But we are not the first to point out these things. In fact, historicising the modern, Western body has been the focus, more or less explicitly, of most body scholars. This requires, of course, defining what is fundamentally different about the 'modern' body. In many ways, we are talking here about the historical roots of the body world we have described in our vignettes earlier – for instance, in concepts of privacy and civility and the notion of the individual.

It is really amazing how many distinct historical genealogies scholars in various fields have traced for the modern body (Table 1). We cannot review all of these in detail here, but the Table 1 summarizes some key arguments about when our body became what it is. We would stress that *their presence here in no way equals an endorsement by us* (our position on what is happening in each period is made clear in Chapters 3 through 8). One obvious point here – caveat lector – is how readily the body lends itself to legitimating political claims. This usually happens by arguing that the body is a universal object with 'natural' properties (as in most prescriptive arguments about gender that we touched on earlier) or by situating the body in a metanarrative about progress towards a more perfect age or a decline from one. We have not included here the more obvious of these origins stories (such as Gimbutas' tracing of the origins of Western male domination to supposed 'Indo-European' invasions at the end of the Neolithic),[74] but one must always consider the political context of narratives purporting to explain the present. For example, Classical statuary is often celebrated as signalling the growth of democracy and philosophical thought, in a manner that tells us more about our own origin myths than it does about the actual Greek context from which it emerges (cf. Chapter 5).

Looking at Table 1, we can only conclude that this is a staggering load of history for the poor body to bear! The body clearly supplies a windmill for every theorist to tilt at. The huge, often inspiring literature on the history of the body is spread across fields as diverse as gender and feminist studies, Classics, history, cultural studies, art history, the history of science and of medicine, historical anthropology, post-colonial studies and theology. We deal with many of these interpretations in the later chapters of this book, particularly in Chapters 5, 6 and 7. At present, these interpretations make one great point: the body *has* a history, and the interpretations listed in Table 1 give us potential fragments of this broader picture. At 1000 AD, the body was a theological battleground between the opposed forces of spirit and flesh, cared for through spiritual practice. At 2000 AD, it is a material mechanism defined by health and cared for through medical artifice. How did this change happen? Were there points of change where one body world gave way to another, like a photo album leaping from one snapshot to the next? Did people feel they were in 'crises' at every jump? Or was it a continuous and gradual development, with change perhaps even unnoticed at the time? In either case, what drove it? Did change in how people understood the body result from scientific causes such as the development of medical knowledge? Was it theologically or philosophically driven by the Reformation, by the Enlightenment, by materialist theorists such as Darwin and Marx? Can we blame economics, say the Industrial Revolution or twentieth century's consumer culture? Politics? Technology? Or did it just happen, a change in culture not determined by any external force?

And, keep in mind, this is only the last millennium of the many more discussed here...

Lessons from historiography: Designing this project

There is a huge literature on the body from all the different disciplines we draw on in this book: archaeology, history, art history, classics, anthropology, sociology and so on. In each of our case-study chapters, we draw our reader's attention to the sources that are of particular relevance to the narratives under discussion in a brief bibliographic essay. It would be impossible to cover all of the material that discusses the body (that would be a task more suited to a multivolume encyclopaedia!), but it is worth noting here a few points about the literature. First, certain thinkers occur with surprising regularity (most notably Foucault[75]), but often how their work is read and interpreted is dependent on quite different disciplinary traditions. Second, although the different literatures have specific strengths, few offer overarching understandings of the body across contexts, and they tend to focus on particular kinds of sources or lines of evidence. Larger theoretical treatments of the body have tended to be the domain of people working in the Early Modern period like Laqueur[76] or Elias.[77] Whilst historical change is important in these works, other studies have often focused on particular times and places, both in archaeology[78] (such as in studies of certain kinds of personhood) and in anthropology.[79] There are a number of interesting comparative studies in both fields,[80] but comparative study is more unusual in classics and history. Where anthropologists have delved into changing body worlds, it has normally been at moments of colonial encounter.[81] It goes without saying, of course, that there are always exceptions to these trends.[82]

Table 1. *Historical theorizations of the 'origins' of the 'modern body' in Western Europe*

Date	Supposed defining characteristics of the 'modern' body
Palaeolithic	'Behavioural modernity', including self-consciousness and use of symbols, originated after 200,000 years ago in Africa, Asia and Europe; representations of gendered bodies, ornaments and self-presentation, and burial become common in Europe after 40,000 years ago, coincidentally with the appearance of 'anatomically modern' humans. Language may begin earlier, but is assumed to be present in modern form by this point at the latest. Evolution stops, culture begins.
Neolithic	The start of farming. For some, the body, and society itself, now comes under the auspices of culture, opposed and contrasted to wild nature.[83] The emergence of large numbers of human representations, particularly in the Near East, is seen as playing a key role in this. Others see the sedentism of this period and the concomitant explosion of material culture as another central aspect of how the body and the world are understood in new ways.
Copper-Bronze Age	Some fourth and third millennium BC burials, particularly in Corded Ware and Bell Beaker traditions, show single burials with a standard kit of prestige goods, thus connoting the 'rise of the individual'.[84]
Copper-Bronze Age	Basic traditions of gender symbolism (weaponry, ornaments) appear in art and burial; these persist at least to the Classical world and arguably up to the present.
sixth – fifth centuries BC	A 'naturalistic' vision of the human body appears in Archaic and particularly Classical sculpture; this vision, which has been influential down to the present, has been traditionally associated with philosophical humanism, celebration of the individual, and political self-government.
fifth – fourth centuries BC	The Platonic tradition of mind-matter dualism sees the material world as a dark cave compared with the illumination of spirit.
Early Christianity	Early Christianity establishes a theological tradition of seeing humans as a contradictory bipartite union of eternal, divine spirit vs. base worldly matter prone to sin and corruption; this is expressed in doctrines such as the Incarnation and the Resurrection.
Late medieval – Early Modern	From the high Middle Ages through the Early Modern period, there was an increasing emphasis upon civility, privacy, control of violence as a social mannerism and control of bodily functions; this 'civilizing process' was associated with the politics of courtly manners.[85]
Late medieval – Early Modern	Development of modern attitudes towards death, childhood, etc. (for instance, childhood as a particular stage of life rather than children as miniature adults, and the increasing association of death and privacy).[86]
Renaissance	Return to a 'naturalistic' vision of body in Renaissance painting and sculpture, once again associated with humanism (for instance, the association of the body with rational geometric proportions in Leonardo's 'Vitruvian Man').
fifteenth – nineteenth centuries	Scientific and anatomical knowledge of the body expanded through experimentation and dissection, culminating in the nineteenth-century definition of the body as purely material structures defined by function.[87]
seventeenth century	Philosophical discussion (usually attributed to Descartes) of humans as consisting of sharply divided rational mind and material body; philosophical discourse privileges the individual reasoning mind as the dominant element of consciousness and discounts the body as merely material and mechanical.
seventeenth – eighteenth centuries	Political thinkers such as Hobbes and Adam Smith assume that the rational, presocial individual is an elemental political actor which uses rational means to fulfil universal, predefined will or goals; this forms the basis of modern legal codes and political systems.
seventeenth – eighteenth centuries	The 'body as machine' replaces the 'body as microcosm' as a basic metaphor for understanding the body.[88]
seventeenth – twenty-first centuries	The insistence on the separation of nature and culture ironically provides the potential for countless new hybrids that are always ready to spring into being, rising in number through the twenty-first century.[89] This affects the body most notably with the rise in concern over technological infringement on its basic structure.
eighteenth – nineteenth centuries	'Race' is developed as a key concept for classifying human variation; colonial contact with other kinds of people, inside relations of domination, is an important impetus.
eighteenth century	Male and female genders are defined as based upon fundamental biological difference for the first time in Western thought.[90]
eighteenth – nineteenth centuries	The disciplined body becomes the dominant discourse of cultural biopower, influencing widely diverse institutions such as punishment for crime, education and military and industrial organization.[91]

Date	Supposed defining characteristics of the 'modern' body
nineteenth – twentieth centuries	Major nineteenth-century thinkers build upon scientific thought to propose materialist views of bodies; their influence grows in the twentieth century. In Darwinian thought, the social characteristics of human bodies emerge from material-based biological and sociobiological processes. In Marxist thought, human consciousness has a material basis rooted in bodily needs and practices.
twentieth century	Freud and other twentieth-century psychologists, in contrast, establish the idea of the psychological body, which could not be divided neatly into physical and mental components (for instance, in sexuality as a basis of individual psychology, in bodily health as a manifestation of psychological state). Instead, they contrast the superficial feelings and experiences of a human being with the 'inner' or 'deep' processes reachable through therapy.
twentieth century	With the molecular characterization of human DNA, bodies are understood as the expression of genetic formulae, not only scientifically but also in popular conceptions of social relatedness.
twentieth century	The dieted, exercised, clothed and cared for body becomes a locus of self-definition in consumer culture, visible both in habits of self-fashioning and consumption and in ubiquitous discourse in popular culture about the body.

Why is this literature so complex? The first impression one gets is of fragmentation. Scholars in each discipline focus upon aspects they have been trained to study. Hence, for example, literary historians write the Early Modern body in terms of the metaphors which intellectuals used to discuss it in texts, while historians of popular culture look to unwritten practices of magic, superstition and belief amongst the unwashed, illiterate masses. Historians of medicine trace how knowledge of the body changed as a result of medical discoveries; political economists trace histories of population, need and industrial labour; gender historians examine sexual practices. And each of these choices implies not only different topical focuses but different methods and standards of demonstration as well. As in the cliché of the blind men studying the elephant, it is hard to recognize that they are all really talking about the same object. Beyond this banal point, however, this richness also reflects the inherent complexity of the body as an object of study. There are simply many different possible perspectives of study. This in itself warns us off any quixotic attempt to write a universal, exhaustive account of bodies in history.

Instead, one needs to start by defining a specific research question and building an appropriate methodology around it. In this book, we do not attempt to say everything there is to say about the body in each historical moment we study. Instead, the theme of this book is not only bodies but change – how (and why) one historically situated body world turns into another.

This problem, in turn, requires a specific set of approaches and methods. The most obvious one is that we have to work across rather than within disciplines. This is in part because the large sweep of history has been carved up into segments studied by prehistorians, Classicists and historians in different ways. It is

also because – as demonstrated in our ethnographic vignettes – understanding the richness and complexity of a body world means bringing together insights from a broad range of sources, from artistic representations and daily practices to scientific, medical and theological accounts. Working across disciplines inevitably means giving up some of the depth and sophistication of analysis within each field in exchange for a broader, multidimensional picture of the past.

Additionally, we are interested in body worlds as broad cultural phenomena rather than in individual intellectual histories. Hence, although it is impossible to deny the importance of particular philosophers, scientists, artists or theologians – Praxiteles, Augustine, Descartes, Vesalius or Darwin – intellectual life is only one strand of the story. The body emerges as much from daily life as it does from grand thinkers in salons, and such thinkers need to be seen as historical agents developing inherited means of thought and (indeed) living with their own bodies. Related to this, we choose to work at multiple scales, and particularly at the scale of grand historical narrative. In recent years amongst historians, this has been the road less taken, and it requires some particular conceptual apparatus (see following discussion).

Finally, as Table 1 suggests, one feature of body history has been a tendency towards narratives which divide history into two simple moments: Pre-Modern and Modern. This mirrors a tendency in anthropological literature – explicitly disavowed by all major theorists but nonetheless exerting a visible, irresistible suction on interpretation – towards understanding the body, personhood and ontology in terms of dualistic ideal types representing Us and The Other. The teleological narrative quest transforms history into a search for the quintessential moment when we became Us. Modernity is thus starkly opposed to everything that came before. Yet as Latour[92] points out, distinguishing 'the modern' from its predecessors is elusive, and no single moment of dramatic transformation could ever be identified. Even without the political dangers of grand origins narratives, such approaches impoverish history. We explicitly disavow any such intention in this book. Our history is not to be read as the historical laying-down of layers of similarity to ourselves. Instead, each period is unique, quietly adding, losing and reconfiguring elements from its past and future in its own way. Historical narrative does not mean moving along an inexorable, unidimensional rise to ourselves; it is like moving through a spectrum of colours, in which each band is related to its neighbours but resolutely and irreducibly itself.

Scale and causality: Intellectual tools for large-scale history

If this discussion makes clear just how widespread discussion of the body is, then there remains another set of issues to tackle in our project: issues of scale.

How long is the history of Britain? Problems of scale

In a famous essay,[93] the mathematician Benoit Mandelbrot pointed out that it is impossible to measure length of the coastline of Britain absolutely; the answer you get depends upon the scale at which you measure it.[94] Mandelbrot's point works equally well for time. Looking at the length of history is like measuring the coastline of England – we might intuitively expect big pictures to be more complex than small pictures, but, paradoxically, the closer you look at history, the more involuted and complex it gets.

Traditionally, historians have dealt with scale by two opposed strategies for engaging with the past: particularism and synthesis. Particularism is focusing upon a single aspect of the body, often in a narrow range of material ('The Three-Pronged Fork in European Table Manners: an Art Historical Study of 17th century Flemish painters'). Synthesis involves bringing many such aspects into relation ('Etiquette, Distance, and Social Class in Medieval and Modern Europe'). Each strategy has payoffs and dangers. Particularism usually means staying within a safe academic comfort zone of known data, but it often ignores the wider structures that condition particular possibilities for the body. Synthesis, in contrast, involves seeing the connections across topics and intellectual fields. The arch-systematiser is Foucault, whose analyses range

across history, literature, iconography, economics and even architecture and social planning; other Grand Synthesisers include Laqueur, Elias, Gombrich and many others. The advantages of synthesis are clear: big questions, big answers. The danger is analytical reductionism: reducing history to simple abstract system, the disciplining gaze of an intellectual panopticon. As historian Inga Clendinnen has noted, 'large theories may generate good questions, but they produce poor answers'.[95]

Within historical analysis, the assumption has generally been that particularism is the ultimate bottom line. If a proposition is not true 'on the ground', it cannot be true at any scale. The intellectual landscape thus tends to evolve as theoretical landmarks extrude violently like new volcanic cones – we like the image of the Saussurean, Levi-Straussian or Bourdieuean eruption! – only to lose their bold outlines as they erode under the weathering onslaught of deconstructing, particularistic studies. But this approach, however intuitively appealing, is intellectually weak. It assumes that the basic unit of narrative is the individual human agent. Yet, as in the 'coastline of Britain' example, rather than there being one exclusive scale of truth, what you say about history depends in part on the scale at which you look at it. We recognize this in many intellectual problems: we give a different account of an animal's social behaviour than we do of the metabolism of its individual cells or of how its species forms part of an ecosystem. Shifting analytical scales is like zooming the focus on a microscope, which makes some features of a tissue become visible and others vanish. For example, it is common to see a transition which is stark and clear when viewed over a century or a generation, over a whole page of history, but which, viewed in a time-slice of a few years, appears a ragged and undirected mixture of pixels;[96] Figure 5 expresses this relationship pictorially.

Analytical scales are thus not absolute visions at which truth resides; they are constructed as relevant to a particular question, and useful to the degree that they allow us to answer it. As Knauft points out in his cross-cultural survey of New Guinea societies, all scales involve analytical constructs.[97] One can contrast Melanesian societies with Polynesian or Australian groups, but only by overlooking huge variations within each grouping. Moving down a scale, the same is true for contrasts within New Guinea, for instance between people inhabiting the Central Highlands and the South Coast. And even amongst South Coast groups, it is difficult to make generalizations that are not contradicted by one or another group. Yet if we refuse to make general characterizations, we lose any vision bigger than an individual datum; we are trapped in the ant's-eye view. The solution is to identify the scale of analysis which is relevant to a particular intellectual

(a)   (b)

Figure 5. 'Reflexive representations' photomosaics – different patterns emerge according to the scale at which it is viewed. A. Parthenon frieze metope. B. zoomed-in version of the same image reveals it is constructed from a mosaic of images. These are returned from Google searches for key terms related to the picture theme, see Cochrane and Russell 2007 for full details on this (reproduced with kind permission of Andrew Cochrane and Ian Russell).

problem, and its strengths and shortcomings. In fact, this is evident in the 'origins of the modern body' discussed earlier. Although scholars agree that the contemporary European/American body differs fundamentally from its predecessors, there is no real consensus on what the defining features of this modernity are and when they emerged. Somewhat circularly, the dates of the origins of the 'modern body' depend upon what you take the modern body to be, and this is defined by the intellectual problem at hand.

In this book, we work at multiple scales, from fine-grained analysis to millennia-long generalization. This reflects the needs of the question of long-term change in the body. Particularism is a familiar intellectual tactic and needs little defence. But it presumes and requires a larger-scale synthesis for several reasons. Methodologically, particularism fragments the world of the body, which exists in the connections between experiences and phenomena. As we have argued previously, one feature of body worlds is that some smaller number of more general facts condition a larger number of more specific analyses by furnishing their basic presuppositions: things like the principles of a habitus, the ontological assumptions upon which fields of social action are based, and the networks of relationships through which people are constituted. One element called for, thus, is a kind of historical 'thick

description'[98] (in Geertz's famous phrase) revealing the texture and comprehensibility of bodily life in a given setting. Moreover, getting beyond thick description, as a practical ontology, a body world may exhibit patterns which are only evident in large-scale synthesis across disciplines. Theological ideas about the body changed radically between 0 and 500 AD; patterns of daily life tended to show continuity. A history based on only one or the other would miss something important. And as we have noted, rather than uniformity, body worlds have multiformity; yet even incoherences can be defined by their common terms of argument or by what they jointly are not. Some of us kill animals in hunting and butchery; others refrain from killing and practice vegetarian diets; but neither half of this contradiction forms part of a universe in which gaining and eating meat is not a meaningful social or political act.

In many ways, our call for multi-scalar analysis can be compared to that of the Annales historians, who looked at how surface events, medium-scale currents and the ebb and flow of the longue durée built up to form history. In a more recent formulation, time perspectivism, history is seen as a palimpsest of processes which unfold at different temporalities.[99] The key is not to privilege a single scale of analysis, but to look at relations between them. In the big picture, we see long-term continuities and grand changes. Specific institutions and practices figure the middle ground. In the picture of life 'on the ground' we see not only variations, alternations and contradictions of the larger scales, but also some intimation, in the processes to be observed closely, of why and how change should have occurred at all. To take an example, the development of medications in psychiatric treatment – generally from the 1950s on – in some ways represented a great change from preceding understandings of mental illness: it linked emotion and consciousness directly to biological events in the brain rather than to the patient's life history, social circumstances or moral practices in a way that many psychotherapists still find controversial. We might well see the moment when the first antidepressant medication was prescribed as an important watershed in practical understandings of the body. But in many ways, this simply extended to the nuts and bolts of the brain the materialist approach to the body largely developed by medical scientists in the nineteenth century: in this view, the body was viewed as a purely mechanical system that functioned without reference to any spiritual entity or state. Whereas this increasingly atheistic approach represented a disjuncture from a more pious past, the body-as-machine, in turn, may be traced to several prior and potentially more encompassing developments: the rise of industry and mechanical metaphors from the mid-eighteenth century and Enlightenment philosophers such as Descartes and natural philosophers such as Harvey. The point is that we can read this historical moment in terms of events and processes working at quite different scales. A new form of medication may certainly betoken important social changes, but these will probably be more closely tied to a specific social context or institution, and more circumscribed in time and general impact, than the change represented by the rise of medical science as a whole, which they presuppose both logically and historically. Similarly, the rise of medical science in turn presupposed the rise of the ontological categories of body and mind, which also predate and underwrite many other fields of endeavour. Hence we have nested processes of change: change or continuity at broad scales forms the context within which change at more localised scales can happen.

Body worlds and causation

History is not only about what happened, it is also about why it happened. Simply describing body worlds at multiple scales and in all their richness is not itself an explanation of change, that is to say an explanation of how one body world comes to be replaced with another. In other words, we need to understand causation.

The most basic model of causation is simple and straightforward: x causes y. For example (Table 1), one might argue that a new kind of body in the Neolithic was caused by sedentism and farming, new philosophical outlooks led to the 'naturalistic' body of Classical sculpture, or new medical discoveries in the seventeenth century led to a new understanding of the body as a physical mechanism. Such explanations usefully point out important factors in change, but they tend to unravel quickly. In caricature, it is like saying World War II happened because of Adolf Hitler. True, at one level, but Hitler's capacity to cause the war itself resulted from many other circumstances – how he had come to power, the rise of fascism across Europe, the Versailles treaty and hence World War I, nineteenth-century political coalitions, the growth of industrial capitalism that made this sort of war possible, the emergence of nation states (and so on). In the broadest sense, everything we could plausibly propose as a cause is also a result of many other things. The best we can say, therefore, is that historical events occur through the conjunction of many circumstances at all scales.

Thus, rather than simple causation ('x causes y'), we have to speak in terms of contingent causation ('x causes y given all the other processes creating the context in which x *can* cause y') (Figure 6). This rather commonsensical conclusion has implications for the language of causation. Causation, in this view, becomes not a deterministic relation but an analytical tool, a spotlight for focusing heuristically upon particular connections within a web of reciprocal, many-scaled relationships. What we are doing when we say things like 'science caused the modern body' is black-boxing. Taking this term from Bruno Latour,[100] a black box is something that has sufficient stability for us to hold it static so we can examine its external relationships. We take a single thing like 'agriculture', or 'scientific experimentation', or 'Hitler', and place all the complex historical relationships that form them into a black box. Rather than opening the black box and decomposing the term into its causes, we take it as a closed, fixed phenomenon for purposes of the analysis. Only then can we really talk about any kind of simple causation. Black-boxing is a necessary tactic for building an understanding of the world; to understand everything would be to unpack an infinite number of these boxes, ranging from 'who was Hitler?' to 'what kinds of things are human beings?' and proceeding all the way back to the geological and biological processes by which the world works.

Black-boxing is intimately linked to scale of analysis (Figure 7). For example, particularistic accounts normally unpack some black boxes (for instance, asking 'how did gender relations vary across social classes in ancient Greece?' rather than taking 'Classical gender' as a self-evident unit) while accepting others at face value ('social class in ancient Athens'). In fact, the often unconscious choice of what to black-box and what to investigate forms a strong part of an academic discipline; do you take gender as a known quantity and problematize religion or take religion as read and problematize gender? Different scales of analysis take different processes and place them inside black boxes. In all the levels of analysis we examine in this book, certain things will always be black-boxed: the chemical processes going on in individual cells that make up human organs, for example, or the digestive processes that allow food to become part of our bodies. At certain times things at another level might be black-boxed. We may talk about 'capitalism' or 'the Church' or 'science' at one moment, treating these things as fixed entities, but at other moments open up these black boxes to take apart what it is we mean by these terms and the histories of the relationships they encapsulate. This means that the history we write can never be exhaustive or total; instead, it always depends upon the analytical possibilities we choose, and indeed those our evidence offers up for us. Black-boxing, like writing at the large-scale as we discussed earlier, always comes at a cost. We repress the complex histories of these concepts and institutions but gain the ability to see a bigger sweep of history. Similarly, opening up black boxes means paying another price – that of privileging some topics over others and over the big picture. Telling history means making choices.

Where is causation in all this? If we unpacked all our black boxes, would change simply disappear to be replaced with gradual shifting of relationships? Perhaps, but this ignores the manner in which power works. 'The

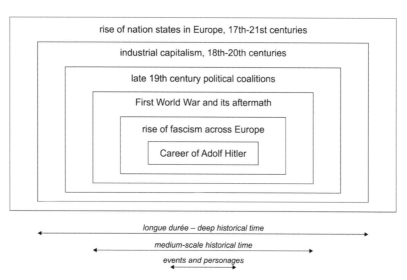

Figure 6. Contingent causality: a multi-scalar model.

Church in medieval Europe' might be a black box in one sense, combining into a single entity heterogeneous people, times, places, beliefs, embodied practices, agendas and perspectives, but it is difficult to deny that the Church's existence had a real effect on how body worlds were lived through and understood (see Chapter 6). Similarly, science did not cause the idea of the body as machine to emerge alone, but it did, for all its complex history, have a role to play. Studying causation, therefore, requires multiple scales of analysis, and the larger scales, for all their black-boxing, are not necessarily more false than the smaller ones. They are different and equally important. Thus histories that reduce change simply to the slow ebb and flow of daily life and dismiss big changes as modern inventions miss important historical trajectories. Equally, attempts to explain big moments of change at the largest scale miss the importance of these acts of daily acceptance and rejection, the on-the-ground way in which bodies themselves play a key role in reworking their own body worlds.

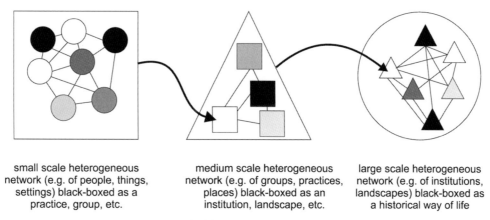

Figure 7. Black-boxing across scales of analysis.

A serious effort to cover history at these multiple scales is not often attempted. Cultural historians often try to deal with change at small local levels, with bigger accounts of change normally focusing on intellectual history. Where the large-scale and culture history do come together, it is often in unusual moments of abrupt profound alteration, such as colonial contact.[101] We are thus required here to do something quite unusual. We must seek out multiple scales of analysis and select particular black boxes and peer into them, moving from histories of grand subjects like science, down to how people ate and moved and buried their dead. Through thickly descriptive accounts, the case studies provide accounts of these body worlds and the changes within them at these multiple scales, and in Chapter 9 we return to issues of body world, belief, causation, scale and change to see what this journey through 40,000 years of history tells us about these topics and, indeed, about our future.

NOTES

1. Giddens 1984; Goffman 1974.
2. See for example Miller 2010; Strathern 1988; Strathern 1992a.
3. Elias 1978.
4. Burns 2007.
5. Gill, Henwood, and McLean 2005, 38.
6. Shilling 2003; 2005; Turner 1996.
7. Gill, Henwood, and McLean 2005, 40, original emphasis.
8. Orbach 1978.
9. Bordo 1993; Gill, Henwood, and McLean 2005, 55.
10. Butler 1990; 1993.
11. Laqueur 1991.
12. Bourdieu 1977; 1990.
13. Foucault 1977.
14. Douglas 1973; Turner 1969.
15. cf. Graham and Thrift 2007.
16. In Magritte's famous Surrealist painting, a detailed and accurate painting of a pipe is titled "This is not a pipe." And it isn't; despite what we think we see, it is, in strict accuracy, not a pipe but a picture of a pipe. Both fans and critics of the "Body Worlds" exhibition implicitly interpret an object which has been dead for a number of years yet is nevertheless incorrupt, which is missing skin, muscles, and other tissues and nevertheless stands in a jaunty attitude of sport, dance or thought, as a 'real' human body rather than, say, a representation, transformation or intimate model which flaunts rather than attempts to conceal its blatant impossibility.
17. From a *much* longer list: Butler 1990; 1993; Csordas 1994; Deleuze and Guattari 2004; Foucault 1977; 1978; Lambek and Strathern 1998; Merleau-Ponty 1962; Shilling 2003; 2005; Turner 1996.
18. sensu Thrift 2008, 18.

19. Thwaites 1898; Tooker 1964; Trigger 1976; 1978.
20. Pomedli 1991.
21. Robb 2008a.
22. Robb 2008a.
23. Hallowell 1955; 1960.
24. Descola 1992; Viveiros de Castro 1998.
25. Ingold 2000, 95.
26. Viveiros de Castro 1998.
27. Merritt 1997.
28. Harris and Robb 2012.
29. Knauft 1993, 201–203; Knauft 1989.
30. Kelly 1993; Knauft 1989.
31. Knauft 1993, 221.
32. Knauft 1993.
33. Strathern and Strathern 1971.
34. Strathern 1988.
35. Battaglia 1990; Fowler 2004a; Strathern 1988.
36. Battaglia 1990, 40.
37. Battaglia 1990, 177–178.
38. The term 'dividual' originates in ethnographies of India (Marriott 1976) and is only used by Strathern on a couple of occasions. The term 'partibility' more accurately captures the specific mode of personhood she traces in Melanesia. That this mode is specific is important, for there are multiple forms of relational personhood in both the present and the past (Fowler 2004a), including permeable persons (where people are viewed as permeable vessels for example in India (Busby 1997). Relational personhood also has a complex relationship with more individualising conceptions. It is not the case that some people are individuals and some are dividuals, but rather that different kinds of personhood are more or less common in different societies and emerge more or less often in different types of context (cf. Brittain and Harris 2010). For more exploration, see Fowler 2004a.
39. Strathern 1988, 122.
40. Strathern 1988.
41. Bourdieu 1990, 272–273.
42. We should note here that Bourdieu's ideas are not without their critics (e.g. Smith 2001).
43. Bourdieu 1990.
44. cf. Foucault 1977.
45. For a more detailed engagement with these theoretical themes see Harris and Robb 2012.
46. See, for example, Bourdieu 1977; 1990; Foucault 1977.
47. Kirby 1997. We are obviously glossing over a great deal of literature here and have no wish to suggest that all versions of constructivism write the physical body out completely (cf. Ahmed 2008); but even where biology is taken into account, it is still often taken to be the opposite of culture, and thus the two poles of nature and culture remain unhelpfully opposed (Davis 2009).
48. Butler 1990; 1993.
49. Interestingly, this argument has been best developed by scholars in the two branches of social thought who actually find themselves forced to deal with the nuts and bolts of physical bodies – archaeologists studying human remains

(e.g. Sofaer 2006) and medical anthropologists (e.g. Lock and Nguyen 2010).

50. Sofaer 2006, 72.
51. Lock and Kaufert 2001.
52. Our argument here is in part inspired by both our agreement and disagreement with a group of anthropologists who have set out to reinvigorate arguments about ontology (how the world really is) rather than epistemology (how people think the world is). Scholars such as Holbraad (2007) make a powerful case for examining the worlds other people live in not merely as mistaken representations of the 'real' world, but as places where different rules apply, and real ontological difference – alterity – can be glimpsed. On one level, we agree with this – we certainly accept the reality of differences between different cultural settings; bodies really are different and can do different things. On the other hand, we cannot accept that there is nothing shared between these worlds, that people in different settings have nothing in common. If that were the case, no act of comparison or translation would ever be possible. Moreover, such a standpoint leaves no room for the material world to intervene in any more than a trivial sense (Harris and Robb 2012).
53. See Ahmed 2008 for an important counterpoint to this argument.
54. Heidegger 1962.
55. Bourdieu 1977; 1990.
56. Ingold 2000, chapter 11.
57. Ingold 2000, 200.
58. Butler 1990; 1993; 2004.
59. These include Derrida, Hegel, Foucault, Irigaray, Lacan and Wittig.
60. Butler 1990, 43.
61. Butler 1993, 1.
62. Interestingly, Butler here echoes the understanding that the Huron held of how healing dances worked. They did not symbolize the healing, they actually brought the healing about – they were performative.
63. Butler 2004, 16.
64. Butler 1993, 232.
65. Herdt 1996; Jacobs and Cromwell 1992; Mandelstam Balzer 1996; Nanda 1999.
66. Foucault 1977.
67. Foucault 1978, 140.
68. DeLanda 2006.
69. Robb 2010.
70. Barth 1987; 2002.
71. Miller 1987; 2005a; 2010.
72. See Collingwood 1945; Olwig 1993; Thomas 1983; Thomas 2004.
73. e.g. Lock 2000.
74. Gimbutas 1991.
75. Foucault 1973; 1977; 1978; 1985; 1988.
76. Laqueur 1991.
77. Elias 1978; 1982.
78. e.g. Fowler 2001.
79. e.g. Strathern 1988.
80. e.g. Lambek and Strathern 1998; Meskell and Joyce 2003.
81. e.g. Sahlins 1985.
82. For example, see one study of very long-term change that deals extensively with the body and personhood (Gamble 2007).
83. Hodder 1990.
84. Shennan 1982.
85. Elias 1978.
86. Ariès 1962.
87. Sawday 1995.
88. Sawday 1995.
89. Latour 1993.
90. Laqueur 1991.
91. Foucault 1977; 1978.
92. Latour 1993.
93. Mandelbrot 1967.
94. He later went on to develop fractals as a way of describing shapes independently of their dimensions, see also Strathern 2004.
95. Clendinnen 1999, 17.
96. Cf. Robb and Pauketat 2012b; Strathern 2004.
97. Knauft 1993.
98. Geertz 1973.
99. Bailey 2007.
100. Latour 1987; 1999.
101. e.g. Sahlins 1985.

3

The limits of the body

Dušan Borić, Oliver J. T. Harris, Preston Miracle and John Robb

Death and the landscape in Mesolithic Denmark[1]

About 7,000 years ago on the coast of Denmark, a group of people gathered to bury two of their dead (Plate I). By an inlet running in from the sea, this was a place where the land became sea and sea became sky. Here they dug a grave as they had done many times before, and prepared it for use. First a swan's wing was laid in the grave. Then a small wooden structure was placed next to it, covered with a folded cloth decorated at one end; in the cloth's middle, they deposited pendants made from snail shells, red deer and wild boar teeth, and attached beads made of seal and elk parts. They spread red ochre pigment around the swan's wing; the red colour reflected the sun, which was beginning to set over the land to the west.

As the grave was prepared, more people, including several children and a couple of older adults, walked up from the small huts standing closer to the sea. One of the elders, a woman, pointed to each of the items entering the grave, telling the children about them. She emphasized the importance of the swan, a bird that could walk, swim and fly, a bird that could transcend the three realms. She pointed to the parts of boar, deer and elk, the three animal tribes that lived in land and shared those spaces with their people. The children had heard these stories many times. They knew that swans in the sky, the seals in the sea and deer in the woods were people like them, people who they might become one day, perhaps when they died, or when they donned their skins as the old people did at certain times of the year. As these stories and others began to draw to an end, their attention turned to the inlet, where a boat was approaching. Two people paddled it with intricately carved paddles, each wearing a highly decorated cloak made of different animal skins patched together. As the boat neared, the people on shore began to move rhythmically, to dance and to feel the growing

wave of heat spread through their bodies. The boat pulled ashore and the cloth that covered its middle was removed to reveal the body of the young woman and the child who had died, as one tried to give life to the other, just a few days before. They had been at sea in the boat for three days and nights, as was customary.

As the bodies were carried to the grave, the dancing intensified; the rhythmic sound contrasting with the silence elsewhere. Finally the bodies were lowered into the ground, the young woman's head resting on one set of beads, her pelvis on the other, separated from the ground by both the cloth and the wooden panels. The child was laid on the swan's wing. The two paddlers scattered ochre over the infant and the woman's head and waist. Others stepped forward to connect themselves with the deceased. One person placed a flat stone under each of the woman's ankles, and more ochre was placed beside her calves, now slightly raised. Another placed a hammer stone by the woman's head, a token both of their shared connection (they were sisters) and of the way that a hammer stone transforms flint from one form to another. Hopefully the hammer stone would help ease the transformation of the body in the grave. Finally, the old woman who had told the stories stepped up and selected one of the six flint blades she carried around her waist. Placing it on the body of the infant she stepped back, signalling the end of the ceremony. The grave was quickly filled in and the mourners began to disperse. Now it was time for the bodies of the dead to transform themselves into stones, animals and birds, to spread themselves around the landscape. At the same time burying them here, where others had been buried before, marked something else: this was their land.

Although aspects of this narrative have been embellished, the basic archaeological facts are supported by evidence from the Danish Mesolithic cemetery of Vedbaek-Bogebakken.[2] The Mesolithic burials discovered here reveal a concern with the boundaries of the body, with its capabilities, its limits and its relations with the world around it. The bodies of these Mesolithic people were not firmly bounded but were instead relationally linked, tied to other people, places, animals and things through histories of occupation, feeding, sharing, hunting and exchange. In the first half of this chapter, we examine how Palaeolithic and Mesolithic bodies came to be constituted through these different relations.

To do so, we work in the broadest framework, covering 30,000 years or more. In this chapter, we discuss both the Upper Palaeolithic – from 40,000 years ago onwards,[3] and the Mesolithic, which marks the period between the end of the Ice Age (around 10,000 BC) and the start of the Neolithic in Europe (cf. Figure 8).[4] Although both

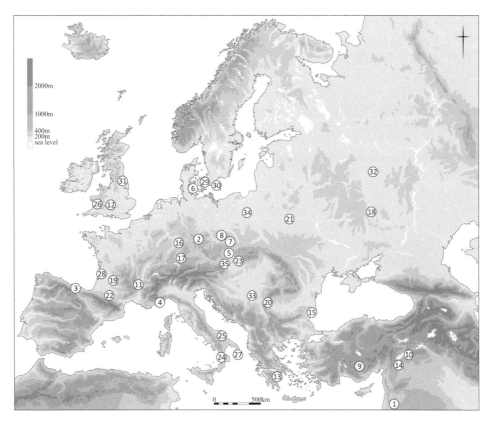

1. Ain Ghazal, 2. Aiterhofen, 3. Altamira, 4. Arene Candide, 5. Asparn-Schletz, 6. Bolkilde, 7. Brno, Dolni Věstonice, Pavlov, Předmosti, 8. Bylany, Milovice, 9. Çatalhöyük, 10. Cayönü, 11. Chauvet, 12. Crickley Hill, 13. Franchthi, 14. Gobekli, 15. Hamangia, 16. Herxheim, Talheim, Vaihingen, 17. Hohle Fels, Hohlenstein Stadel, 18. Kostenki, 19. Lascaux, 20. Lepenski Vir, Vlasac, 21. Mezhirich, 22. Montespan, Trois Frères, 23. Nitra, 24. Papasidero, 25. Passo di Corvo, Scaloria, 26. Paviland, 27. Porto Badisco, 28. S. Germain La Riviere, 29. Sigersdal, Vedbaek, 30. Skateholm, 31. Star Carr, 32. Sungir, 33. Vinča, 34. Wilczvce. 35. Willendorf

Figure 8. Sites mentioned in Chapter 3.

of the former periods display cultural variation and we do not want to treat all hunters and gatherers as homogeneous, timeless beings,[5] at the scale of this synthesis, there are features that broadly characterize the entire span.[6]

Such a sense of scale does not invalidate an approach that centres on the body but instead makes it more valuable, allowing us to link together apparently diverse histories and sequences to gain an understanding of big changes. Humans were caught up in two of the great transitions of history. Between the Middle and the Upper Palaeolithic, Europe was occupied by anatomically modern humans producing the first European art and symbolism and the first widespread use of burial. This is usually described as a 'cognitive revolution', but it is really the rise of a new form of embodied human existence. What was the body world of the earliest modern humans like? Our second key transition is between the Mesolithic and the Neolithic, or from hunting and gathering to farming. This too reveals differing forms of embodiment. What was the body world of Europe's first farmers?

The Upper Palaeolithic: New forms of embodiment

The 'origins of cognition' and modern humans

In the global story of humanity, the first cognitively modern humans evolved in Africa around 200,000 years ago. After an extended period colonizing Africa and then other continents, *Homo sapiens sapiens* appeared in Europe around 40,000 years ago, at the beginning of the period known archaeologically as the Upper Palaeolithic. Here they replaced or hybridized with indigenous Neanderthal populations. At about the same time or relatively shortly afterwards, a suite of new things appear for the first time in Europe:

- New stone tool industries, which not only produce new forms of tools using new techniques but which also show clear regional and chronological style (such as the Aurignacian, Gravettian, Solutrean and Magdalenian) for the first time.
- The first common use of bone tools.

- New hunting techniques.
- The extension of humanity's territorial range to new environments, principally northwards to a vast swathe of northern Eurasia.
- The first widespread burials; although Neanderthals sometimes buried their dead,[7] burial is more common, less ambiguous and more elaborated in the Upper Palaeolithic.
- The first personal ornaments, known principally from burials in the form of shell and stone beads.
- The first 'art', principally in small handheld forms such as incised designs on bone, ivory and stone artefacts, but also including three-dimensional carvings such as the famous 'Venus figurines' and paintings such as the famous examples from Lascaux, Chauvet, Altamira and other caves in France and Spain.

For many years, archaeologists have read these changes as a 'cognitive revolution', as evidence for new capacities for thinking symbolically, whether developed indigenously or introduced by new 'anatomically modern' peoples expanding from the Near East. The Upper Palaeolithic 'revolution' happened in the mind, not in the body.[8] Art in particular has played a special role in these arguments. Early Upper Palaeolithic Venus figurines such as the 'Venus of Willendorf' (Figure 12) have long stood as the symbol of humanity's new engagement with the world. Representational and abstract art such as the famous horse images from Lascaux or Chauvet Cave cannot (it has been argued) have been produced without the full trappings of the human mind, an ability to reach beyond the immediate physical setting and talk about abstract concepts, things and places. Unlike other animals, our species could now talk to each other of things beyond the day-to-day, of gods and monsters, of hopes and dreams, of future and past. The human body might only be subtly different from previous incarnations but the mind it housed was of a different order, a new world could be created.

Embodied foragers

This widely held point of view is problematic. The idea that cognition exists free of the body is based upon philosophical assumptions originating in Plato and other Classical philosophers and codified in the Enlightenment. Descartes' famous maxim, 'I think therefore I am', posits a disembodied intellect; the 'cognitive revolution' view transplants this view of intelligence into our Upper Palaeolithic ancestors. They are defined by a new ability to think, a consciousness floating free from the world. Critiques from philosophers,[9] anthropologists[10] and cog-

nitive scientists[11] have shown that such a perspective fails to capture the embodied nature of people's engagement with the world. We think through the body, not outside of it (see Chapter 1 and Chapter 2). In fact, a purely cognitive view separates the body from history; in reality the body is formed by social/material relations,[12] and if we were to raise a modern newborn infant in Palaeolithic society, she would not only differ from us cognitively and culturally but also in her very body.[13]

Thus, we suggest that the Upper Palaeolithic 'revolution' was not fundamentally about a form of cognition separated from the body, but it was instead about new forms of embodied thinking, new ways of engaging with the world through new social and material relations. To impose at least some boundaries on the scope of the book, we refrain from commenting upon Neanderthal body worlds, not least because of the different and hotly contested nature of the evidence in this regard.[14] What is certain is that the Upper Palaeolithic and Mesolithic are the first periods in which we can get a clear idea of the body worlds ancient Europeans inhabited.[15] We now turn to several key forms of action through which this body world was created.

Bodies and places

Archaeologists have traditionally understood Palaeolithic peoples through two master discourses: the closely intertwined topics of subsistence and mobility and stone tools. Both involve embodiment. We begin here with subsistence and mobility.

All Palaeolithic and Mesolithic people were hunter-gatherers; they lived in small groups spread thinly over the landscape, moving in sophisticated seasonal rounds to hunt, gather and fish as different resources became available. Rightly or wrongly, we normally understand this landscape mobility as motivated by ecological needs, and it was such an effective way of making a living that it lasted many times longer than the entire history of our farming world up to now. But hunter-gatherer landscapes are not equivalent to highly dispersed supermarkets; they are symbolic landscapes as well, rich in animal and ancestral spirits, memories, and myths and legends.[16]

This way of life, so different from ours, was nevertheless as embodied as that of the modern city-dweller growing plump and near-sighted at his computer terminal, merging seamlessly with her car amongst traffic or crammed in on the subway, and flowing between the tastes of coffee and concentration at work, beer and conviviality at the pub, and champagne and celebration at New Year's. The most direct evidence of this is the bodies of Palaeolithic and Mesolithic Europeans themselves. Bodies do not precede social relations but develop within them[17] (cf. Chapter 2). Upper Palaeolithic and Mesolithic Europeans may have been 'anatomically modern' in comparison with Neanderthals, but their bodies were developed through their experience of landscape. Compared with their Neolithic successors, they were tall with an average height comparable to historic Europeans, an adaptation costly in calories but useful for both traveling and hunting. They suffered from fractures fairly commonly, probably from both conflict and accidents such as falls. Yet they were relatively free from infections, typically a malady of sedentism and population aggregation, their teeth were longer-lasting than farmers thanks to relatively low carbohydrate consumption, there is little sign of malnutrition or childhood stress amongst them, and overall they seem to have lived longer than their farming descendants.[18]

The landscape produced embodied experiences as well as physical bodies. Upper Palaeolithic people lived in cultural places, not in abstract, ecologically functional space. Whereas Neanderthals (and indeed earlier hominids and non-human primates) had habitually frequented spaces, perhaps with a stable sense of 'home', something new is going on spatially in the Upper Palaeolithic. For example, Neanderthals do not seem to have cached tools with the intention of returning to the same place: 'the temporality of action changes as places for future action are created'.[19] It is only after about 40,000 BC that people in Europe began to create architecturally elaborate home bases, burial sites and places of ritual. It is certain that this newly emerged cultural landscape had embodied dimensions. Fundamental to any cultural taskscape are connections between places, times, work and food; and the landscape of early Europeans, like that of many ethnographically known hunter-gatherers, would have been strongly structured by seasonal changes. This seasonal regime would also have been a sensory, culinary and work regime.

It is difficult to say more without ethnographic pastiche – the summer dispersal of small family groups to gather forest products, the long dark evenings of storytelling during winter aggregation in group hunting camps perhaps – and without over-generalisation across such broad territories, long spans of time and varied environments. But we can make two further observations about Upper Palaeolithic and Mesolithic landscapes which hold true for all except a few late developments at the very end of the latter period. First, in contrast with the landscapes constructed by later Europeans, they seem very loosely structured. Within sites, architecture tends to be relatively informal and generalized, with little attempt to create repetitively formalized space.[20] There is little investment in large structures, in creating fixed places or

in created bounded settlements. Burial does not seem to have been used to create obvious, visible and lasting links between particular groups and territories. Ritual was certainly a part of life, but there are virtually no labour-intensive ritual sites (the possible exceptions are French and Spanish painted caves, and even these were probably used sporadically by small groups rather than continually and intensively). To the extent that space corresponds to social reflexes, the traditional anthropological picture of people living in fluid, open social networks is probably accurate. We get the impression of a society with little concern for rigid boundaries, formalized structures and fixed places, in which most important things happen outdoors in locales which are found rather than constructed, with the landscape as a participant in human action rather than a backdrop to it.

Secondly, when people did place iconography in the landscape, the major focus was not humans per se but animals. The French and Spanish painted caves, with their amazing art of animals, are the most obvious example, but other forms such as small carvings and engravings of animals – found over a broader area than painted caves, and often found on habitation sites – would have loomed much larger in everyday experience. In fact, animals were referenced in many other ways. For example, at Milovice in the Czech Republic,[21] Kostenki in Russia,[22] and Mezhirich in the Ukraine,[23] people actually lived in huts built of mammoth bones, sometimes decorated with red paint – a way of underlining the symbolic importance of the mammoth and its relation to humans and their landscape.

Embodied knowledge and identity

The other master discourse of Palaeolithic and Mesolithic archaeology is stone tools, mostly because these comprise the vast majority of archaeological finds from this period rather than because of any dominant role they had in social life. As archaeologists have traditionally recognized, the Upper Palaeolithic saw the emergence of regional and chronological styles of stone-working.[24] Although it is now clear that there are variations and changes within Middle Palaeolithic 'Mousterian' stone-working, these remain small in scale for 250,000 years. In comparison, the Upper Palaeolithic is a mosaic of different traditions, particularly after 33,000 years ago.[25] This suggests a new, community-based relationship between people and learned technological traditions.

Although archaeologists have regularly thought about stone tools in terms of abstract cognition, they often forget that every stone tool was produced by eyes seeing, by people learning from others and by the subtle and decisive movement of human hands.[26] In fact, at several

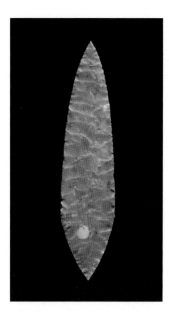

Figure 9. Ostentatious skill and size: Solutrean laurel leaf point from France (length 28.2cm) (© Trustees of the British Museum).

sites in Magdalenian period France, careful excavation has revealed how children learned knapping techniques from their elders, gradually acquiring embodied skills.[27] The historically varying styles of stone tools mentioned previously probably were not conscious badges of social identity, but resulted from varying local traditions of how to carry out the habitual gestures involved in flint-knapping – traditions determined by inculcated practice rather than by the nature of flint or the necessities of knapping. People learning to make the long flint blades found in some Gravettian burials in Italy,[28] or new kinds of bone and antler tools, shaped their bodies in particular ways, learning to work with the material in a manner that was culturally specific. Similar kinds of bodily practices could also be applied through different materials, particularly in the Aurignacian, so repeated habitual bodily movements could be applied to both stone and ivory, for example, in the production of various kinds of beads.[29] Indeed, making exquisite-flaked Solutrean spear points (Figure 9), which took skill, strength, patience and intricate planning, may have been a performative way of enacting the valued qualities of maleness.[30]

These new technologies hint at the ways in which people learned to shape their bodies in culturally constituted manners. Stone-working technology had always been an embodied act; the earlier Achuelean and Levallois technologies required dexterity, strength, appreciation of symmetry and aesthetics, and forward planning. But they did not involve the kinds of identity production through embodied difference that emerged in the technologies of the Upper Palaeolithic. The same is true for bone tools.[31]

New technologies, therefore, were not simply about new cognitive abilities; they were about new traditions of shaping the body and of learning to use it in new specific ways that allowed new kinds of difference to emerge.

Ornamenting the self
Beyond food and tools, the body turns up in many Upper Palaeolithic innovations. Jewellery dates to the earliest period of the Upper Palaeolithic, the Aurignacian. Typically people made beads from mammoth ivory, but ornaments were also carved from animal teeth and shells.[32] After 33,000 years ago, beads begin appearing regularly in graves as well as at living sites, and henceforth burials are the commonest find-spot for ornaments.[33] For example, a young woman who lived about 19,000 years ago at Saint-Germain-la-Rivière near Bordeaux in France was buried in a rock shelter. Her burial, recently reanalysed by Vanhaeren and d'Errico,[34] was accompanied by at least eighty-six objects, seventy-five of which were ornaments probably sewn onto now-vanished clothing. Of these, seventy-one were red deer canine teeth with holes drilled through them; the others included three perforated shells and a single steatite bead. Fascinatingly, the deer almost certainly came from more than 300 kilometres to the south across the Pyrenees in Spain.[35] Ornaments are similarly known in almost all regions where many Upper Palaeolithic burials are known, for instance amongst Gravettian burials in Liguria. In another burial-rich region, Moravia, one burial found at Brno was accompanied by more than 600 *Dentalium* shells.[36] In the same region, at Dolní Věstonice, a triple burial included two adolescent males on either side of a person of indeterminate sex, though probably female (Figure 10).[37] The bodies on the outside were accompanied by ivory and canine pendants. Shell ornaments were also included, most likely sewn onto caps and tunics.[38]

What do acts of decoration tell us? Whilst the evidence for Neanderthal behaviour in this regard is growing,[39] it remains small in scale compared to what happens after the arrival of *Homo sapiens sapiens*. Were 'modern' humans simply vainer than their Neanderthal predecessors? In one sense, yes. The body was now more regularly a scene for display, a place where statements were made about identity through what you wore and how you wore it. Ornaments created bodily difference; they were worn in varying ways, and these decorative items are rare enough that they certainly suggest that not everyone was wearing them. Whether or not this implies distinctions of power and status,[40] people now – as we have done in all subsequent periods – sought to employ the body as a means of social distinction and communication.

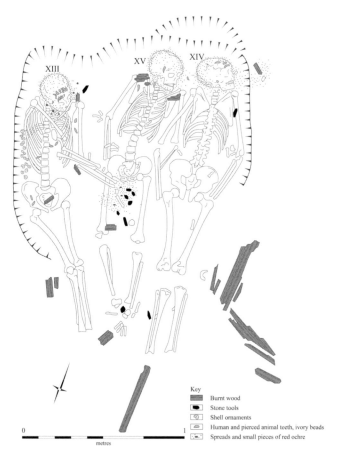

Figure 10. The famous triple burial from the Gravettian site of Dolní Věstonice, Czech Republic (after Gamble 1999, fig. 7.19; redrawn by Vicki Herring).

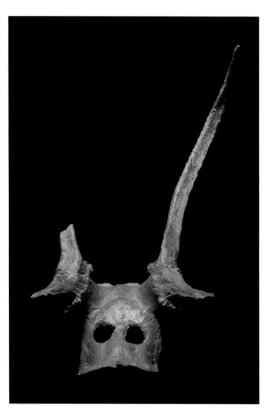

Figure 11. Red deer skull carved into a mask, Star Carr, Yorkshire, England (© Cambridge Museum of Archaeology and Anthropology).

Beyond this, the ornament evidence suggests how the body was divided in parts and bounded. The location of beads on headgear at Dolní Věstonice, or the ivory arm and leg rings in Ligurian burials, suggest that people were not decorating the body at random; they were signalling attention towards particular parts of it. Moreover, ornaments and clothing create a 'second skin', blurring the boundaries between the body and the world; they give the body a surface linking it to the world around it, by giving it qualities such as colour and texture, and references to materials, qualities and places.[41] Upper Palaeolithic people paid attention to the qualities and properties of the materials they worked with, drawing out the shine in ivory, steatite and bone through polishing.[42] Marine shells such as dentalium, imported far inland, would have carried connotations of far-away places, travels or exchanges with distant neighbours.

Ornaments and clothing made from animal materials such as deer canine teeth would have held significance in terms of memories of hunts, places and human relations with animals. The deer teeth at Saint-Germain-la-Rivière which had come from Spain connect the young woman to places far away from where she was buried. When we do not assume that people were alienated from their material worlds, such objects may not be clearly separated from the animals they come from, the places they were acquired and the person who now wears them.[43] Thus, through ornamentation, the young woman's body was not limited to the skin, but extended across time and space and linked with a particular animal. In fact, the use of dress and ornament to blur categories is even clearer with antler frontlets, found in north-western Europe thousands of years later in the earlier Mesolithic.[44] These are portions of deer skulls shaped so that humans could wear them as masks. The most famous examples are from Star Carr, England (Figure 11), but others are known from Germany. They may have served to ritually transform the body into something which was neither deer nor human, drawing on ideas of multinaturalism discussed in Chapter 2.[45] The use of ornaments in the Upper Palaeolithic and Mesolithic hints at a world in which the project of the body was now actively worked upon, adjusted, decorated and displayed, and in which the body was not clearly associated with a single place or a single species, nor necessarily bounded at the skin.

Burying the body

The new project of the body involved new attention to burying the dead. Our evidence for Upper Palaeolithic burial (as for almost everything else in this period) is patchy and spread over huge areas of space and time. Nevertheless, a change from Neanderthal burial is clear. Neanderthals seem to have buried their dead only occasionally, when they did simply caching the body in caves without recognizable grave goods.[46] Upper Palaeolithic people buried their dead more consistently and in more elaborate ways, though it is important to note that this is not something that begins with the arrival of modern humans onto the continent, but rather several thousand years after their arrival from around 29,000 years ago.[47] The classic examples are the Gravettian burials at Dolní Věstonice, Pavlov and Brno in Moravia, and elsewhere in Europe, for instance, at Paviland Cave in Wales.[48] There is also a substantial group of late Upper Palaeolithic burials at sites such as Arene Candide in Liguria and Papasidero Cave in Calabria, and the general tradition of burial continues unbroken right to the few Mesolithic cemeteries known such as Vedbaek (see earlier discussion). These burial sites generally involve small groups of single burials, mostly commonly laid out prone on their back, sometimes with ornaments (and no doubt clothing), red ochre, tools and ritual paraphernalia. Occasional burials were extremely elaborate, for instance at Sungir in Russia where two children were buried head to head in a very unusual burial, accompanied by thousands of ivory beads, probably sewn on to clothing, spears of straightened mammoth tusk, animal carvings and pins made from ivory, bracelets and pierced antler rods.[49]

There is much more to Upper Palaeolithic and Mesolithic dealings with the dead than simple inhumations; in fact, the relatively small total number of burials known suggests that most of the dead were disposed of in other, archaeologically invisible ways. To take the Moravian open-air sites as an example, parts of more than thirty bodies have been recovered from Dolní Věstonice, with another three from the nearby site of Pavlov. At these sites, people were buried within huts, close to hearths, placing the dead close to the living. At the nearby site of Předmostí, up to twenty people were discovered in double burials and a mass grave.[50] Moreover, only six of the 'burials' from Pavlov and Dolní Věstonice are complete inhumations; all are adults. These were quite unusual, therefore. All three of the Dolní Věstonice single burials appear to have been quite particular persons, each with healed cranial trauma. Similarly the middle body of the triple burial had a deformed right femur and a notable curvature of the spine.[51] Each skull in the triple burial, and the groin of the central person, was covered in ochre. The choice of persons with particular life histories, the use of beads and ochre, hints that these burials were important or perhaps special.[52] All the rest of the 'burials' at these sites are scattered remains which may come from burials which were allowed to become disturbed. In fact, the vast majority of the dead in the Upper Palaeolithic and the Mesolithic were not buried in a single place.[53] Instead, their bones are found scattered in caves, in the fills of pits, and as part of other graves. The dead were fragmented, mixed and scattered; some bones were retained amongst the living.

Similar patterns occur elsewhere, though most burials are known from caves rather than open air sites. To take a famous example, Arene Candide cave in Italy contains burials spanning most of the Upper Palaeolithic,[54] including a cemetery at the very end of the Upper Palaeolithic where twenty individuals were buried.[55] One burial dating to 24,000 years ago is of a young man laid on a bed of ochre wearing a cap with hundreds of perforated red deer teeth and shells attached, mammoth ivory pendants, perforated and decorated batons made of elk antler and a 23-centimetre long flint blade.[56] But such treatment certainly does not reflect the wealth of a 'prince' (as this individual has anachronistically and misleadingly been named). Instead, it shows us rather an unusually elaborate ritual moment, one in which the body is framed and related to the world around it through additions and citations. We have already discussed how the decorated cap in other burials begins the process of dividing the body into parts, how the red deer teeth connect it with other animals and places, and how, as we suggested speculatively in the vignette, ochre may have recalled life, death and blood. Here too the elk antler suggests further connections with other animals, as do the pendants of mammoth ivory. Such materials and things had histories and were technologies of memory, they stimulated people to recall particular past events.[57] But why decorate the dead just as well as the living? Clearly the project of working on the body did not come to an end with 'biological' death; they continued into the future. By placing the dead in significant locales, like the caves at Arene Candide and Saint-Germain-la-Rivière or the huts at Dolní Věstonice – places which hunter-gatherers returned to repeatedly in the course of their seasonal peregrinations – people began to bind the fluid social relations that created bodies into particular kinds of places.

The point is that Upper Palaeolithic 'burial' has little to do with burial as we often understand it,[58] as a way of recognizing individual status or preserving the memory of individual dead. Most people were probably disposed of through exposure or other rites which dissolved the dead into the broad landscape of the annual foraging round and which left little archaeological trace.[59] Body parts were sometimes kept as distributed relics accompanying groups as they moved, and were used on occasion for personal ornamentation.[60] This pattern continues in the Mesolithic with the exception of a few notable cases.[61] When whole burials are discovered in the Mesolithic, such as the 'shaman' burial at Bad Dürrenberg Germany, it is clear these are particular people marked out in particular ways.[62] Maintaining the body's unity in death required special measures, and went against the norm of dispersing the body out into the landscape. The memory of particular individuals was probably relatively short-lived, as opposed to a more diffuse association between generalized group ancestry and a broad landscape. The comparatively few complete burials we have excavated reflect a rare event, for unusual individuals or in special circumstances. Even so, the treatment of the body we find in this shows how it was composed through citations to their qualities, places and especially animals.

Art and bodies – human, animal and in between

'Art' is often cited as the ultimate trump card proving that Upper Palaeolithic Europeans had the same ability to think symbolically as we do today, unlike their Neanderthal predecessors. But what does this tell us about human bodies? Whether or not art indicates new cognitive capabilities (and both sides have been argued[63]), it suggests a new concern with the body. Neanderthals made no surviving representations of their own or other bodies; after 40,000 BC, humans in Europe left us numerous depictions.

The one genre of Palaeolithic art which foregrounds the human body clearly and emphatically is 'Venus' figurines, which are found across Europe from France to Russia (Figure 12). Venus figurines (the name is anachronistic and wildly inappropriate, but we seem to be stuck with it) are small stone or ivory figures of women, dating particularly from the Gravettian period. The meaning of the Venuses is controversial. Although they have been claimed to represent fertility, women at various stages of their lives[64] and self-portraits of pregnant women,[65] none of these is fully convincing, particularly for the Russian and Ukrainian figurines. There is no reason why they must have a single interpretation. What is more relevant here is *how* the body is depicted, rather than why it is depicted. The Venuses fall into distinct stylistic canons, as Leroi-Gourhan[66] showed long ago. Western and Central European examples emphasize a round, full body with prominent breasts and buttocks. Russian and Ukrainian examples are often much more schematic, at their most abstract consisting of a rod-like body

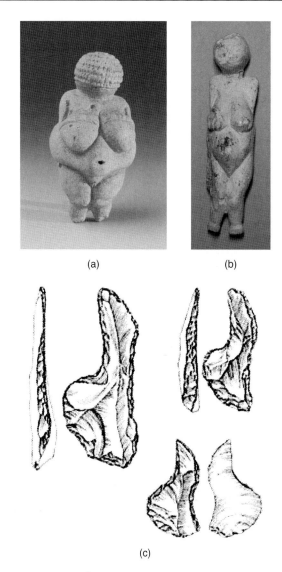

(a) (b)

(c)

Figure 12. 'Venus' figurines. A. Willendorf, Austria (© Naturhistorisches Museum Wien, photo: Alice Schumacher). B. Kostenki, Russia (photo courtesy of Lila Janik). C. Late Magdalenian female plaquettes from Wilczyce, Poland (Fiedorczuk et al. 2007, fig. 3; © Institute of Archaeology and Ethnology, Polish Academy of Sciences, drawing by Ewa Gumińska). See Plate VIb for another example.

with breasts. A third canon, found across the northern European plain from Belgium to Poland, shows a human figure with breasts and prominent buttocks in side view; these were made in ivory, bone, and remarkably, chipped flint.[67] In all canons, any attempt to depict individuality (for instance, via detailed facial features or dress) is extremely rare, and entire regions of the body – hands, feet, even arms and legs – are minimal or absent.

Humans turn up in other forms of Palaeolithic portable – or "mobiliary" – art in different ways. In the extensive groups of small bone and stone carvings from France, Spain and Italy, about 200 images have been identified as

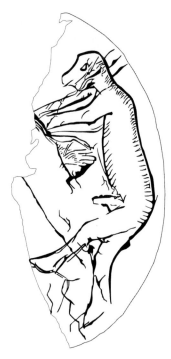

Figure 13. Engraved shoulder blade (fragment) showing hybrid human/animal male figure, from Mas d'Azil cave, France (Musée d'Archéologie Nationale, Paris, drawn by Vicki Herring).

humans. These are typically sketchy line drawings, normally depicting heads or whole bodies from the side, a mode of vision which may derive from the much more numerous animal representations. Stone plaques from Germany and Moravia likewise portray animals and geometrical designs, with a few line drawings of humans in profile included. Some are hard to classify, mixing human and animal features and postures (Figure 13). Similarly, small ivory carvings from Western Europe depict animals almost exclusively, though a few mix human and animal characteristics, such as the so-called Lion Man from Hohlenstein Stadel, Germany (Plate VIa). An ivory figurine from Dolní Věstonice with dysplasic facial features may have been intended to portray one of the individuals buried there. Then there are the amazing exploding figurines: thousands of fragments of clay figurines have been found at Dolní Věstonice I and Pavlov I.[68] Extraordinarily, experimental work has shown that these figurines were not accidentally broken but were intentionally exploded when heated.[69] Like the bodies of the dead then, that were often fragmented through disarticulation, the body of figurines could be separated, parted and divided.

Other than the Venuses, one of the stereotypes of Palaeolithic art is that it is all about animals, with few humans in it. The most famous Palaeolithic art is found in the painted caves of southern France and northern Spain, with a few other painted caves found in Italy. Much cave

art dates to between 18,000 and 10,000 years ago, at the height of the Ice Ages, but there are outstanding examples from both earlier (e.g. Chauvet Cave[70]) and later (e.g. the late examples from around Palermo, Sicily). Palaeolithic cave art certainly was made for quite varying reasons, but it is dominated by animal images, particularly naturalistic depictions of animals including bears, deer, bison, aurochs, rhinos and mammoths.

Yet the human body is present in painted caves in two ways. One is through human interactions with the art. These were not galleries of images for aesthetic contemplation in the modern sense of 'art'; they were flickering presences in special, dark, remote places frequented ritually, people interacted with images, sometimes adding to them or even stabbing them (such as the Montespan horse[71]), and like animals in Australian or African rock art they may have been considered living or spirit beings. One interpretation of animal art is that it taught young hunters how to observe and track game effectively projecting them into an imaginary scene of an embodied activity for which their eyes and hand needed to be trained.[72] Another is the shamanic theory, that animals formed part of a spirit world which humans could enter through shamanic transformations during altered states of consciousness.[73] If so, humans may be present *in* the animals on cave walls. The most direct reminder of human presence is handprints at Chauvet and other caves. These were produced either by covering the hand in paint and imprinting it onto the wall, or more usually by stencilling around the outside of the hand, perhaps by blowing.[74] Tubular finger marks in clay are also found. Handprints make the body present by abstracting a single gesture as a fixed sign of the whole body's presence.

Humans may also be represented directly but ambiguously. As mentioned earlier, a number of images seem to show human-animal hybrids. The most famous image, the 'sorcerer' from Trois Frères cave, has been criticized as heavily reconstructed by archaeologists, but another image from the same cave shows a hybrid being with what may be a musical instrument, and a scene from Lascaux may show a bird-headed man (Figure 14). In portable art, line drawings, figurines such as the 'Lion Man' and statuettes from cave sites on the Italian Riviera[75] combine human and animal characteristics. The tendency in recent archaeological thought has been to understand such hybrid images as resulting from shamanic practices.[76] Whether or not they derive specifically from shamanic rites of altered consciousness – a view which has proved controversial – they seem more generally to evidence a theory of being (an ontology) unlike our own, where the boundaries between human and animal may have been understood as permeable rather

Figure 14. Cave art hybrids from Les Trois Frères (first and third) and Lascaux (middle), France (redrawn by Vicki Herring).

than rigid.[77] Similarly, some millennia later, in the Mesolithic, hunter-gatherers at Lepenski Vir on the banks of the Danube in Serbia[78] carved boulders to represent hybrid human-fish beings (see Figure 17). The boulders at Lepenski Vir, connected in part to funerary rituals, appear to capture another form of bodily metamorphosis, one in which humans become fish, perhaps in the act of dying.[79]

We would draw several conclusions from this rapid review of Palaeolithic and Mesolithic art.

- Contrary to stereotypes, human bodies do not infrequently appear in Palaeolithic art, and not only in Venus figurines. They are directly represented in several ways, signified by handprints, implied in scenes involving animals and as hybrid human-animals.
- However, whereas animals tend to be represented obviously and often quite naturalistically, humans are represented contingently to a particular situation, as participants but not necessarily the sole or rigidly defined protagonists in the stories narrated by art; they hunt animals and they transform into animals, and even the predominant visual style for line drawings (representation in profile rather than frontally) is essentially geared to representing animals.
- Although the human body is present in art, it is handled in highly varied ways according to the situation. Even with Venus figurines, there are several ways of dividing the body and of schematizing or emphasizing particular parts. Sometimes the body is clearly present, but in other situations it is implied by its actions or signified by a single part as in handprints; sometimes it merges with the animal world, at other times it is clearly distinct from it. Abstracting different, sometimes contradictory dimensions of the body in different situations is typical of human embodiment, of body worlds (Chapter 1).

Embodying humanity

So, what changed between the Middle and Upper Palaeolithic in Europe? Whether or not humans had new capacities to think symbolically, they certainly related to their bodies differently, in ways typical of humans since. For the first time, there is clear and widespread evidence of people customizing their bodies to particular social roles and identities through dress and ornaments; teaching them group-specific, historically contextualized skills; manipulating the bodies of the dead to dissolve people into their landscapes and to commemorate unusual people; and abstracting varied qualities from them as relevant to different situations.

We would not speak of a 'revolution' in embodiment; human history tends to show continuity and change inseparably (Chapter 9). With emerging evidence for Neanderthal burials[80] and ornaments,[81] it may be an overstatement to claim there was a historical rupture 40,000 years ago. But it is clear that the changes that did take place were not only in how people thought; they were in how they thought through, or with, their bodies.

The body world of early human foragers

A body world is a set of assumptions about what kind of thing the body is, combined with discourses and practices which make the body a generator of social meanings and relations (Chapter 2). We are looking not at a stable, defined and essentialized object but at a set of 'cultural repertoires' or reflexes on which people could draw.[82] Can we talk about an Upper Palaeolithic-Mesolithic body world? Although the evidence is inevitably more fragmentary than one would like, we can perhaps outline some general features which appear mostly by contrast with later periods.

To start with everyday practices and routines, little energy seems to have been spent constructing formalized spaces – substantial houses and ritual sites, bounded or fortified settlements, internally differentiated architecture. This probably does not simply reflect the needs of a mobile lifestyle but a sense of social space as well. Stereotypically, hunter-gatherers have loose, flexible group structures with open territories; the spatial correlate would be a landscape characterized by shifting settlements, a lack of boundaries and rigidly fixed points. The symbolic attention which more sedentary peoples often lavish upon constructed sites – histories, myths, legends – is instead invested in the landscape itself. Identity tends to be relationally defined as groups reconfigure themselves; and identity is produced through 'sharing of food, residence, company, and memory'.[83] Experientially, a sense of pathways and movement may have been more important than ideas of bounded territories.[84] It is a converse of the situation typical of modern states in which the bounded territory and fixed, bounded personhood coincide.[85]

Death is an existential challenge; every society needs to make sense of the changes that accompany it. In comparison with most later European people, Palaeolithic and Mesolithic people show little concern with trying to halt or channel the flow of change by maintaining the integrity of the body or perpetuating its memory in visible memorials. Aside from a few large cemeteries at the very end of the Mesolithic, the relatively few burials we have to represent this 35,000-year swath of prehistory were not normal ways of displaying status or preserving memory, as our own burials often are, but rather unusual, often local, traditions or responses to clearly anomalous circumstances. The dead were seen within an essentially fluid ontology in which people became transformed into scattered residues and, perhaps, other beings. Their bodies were allowed to break up, ending up being deposited in multiple places, creating and enhancing connections with a broader landscape rather than singular defined cemeteries.

Within this landscape, the human body itself may have been seen as contingent and relational, more than fixed and bounded. One line of evidence here concerns animals. Animals are central to how landscapes are understood by people whose lives are so demonstrably interwoven with them. Human hunting is not simply ecological predation, but involves 'a moment in the unfolding of continuing – even lifelong – relationship between the hunter and the animal kind'.[86] In the cosmology of many forest dwellers the world cannot be divided into clear categories of 'nature' and 'culture', or 'human' and 'animal'.[87] Instead, relationships cross such boundaries. When hunting, relations of trust, in Ingold's term,[88] existed between humans and animals such as deer, so that animals '*present themselves*'[89] to hunters to be killed, in other words they continue to move predictably, return to the same locales, and act in ways that indicate their continued willingness to be killed and eaten by human beings. Respect would be accorded in killing the animal, and people in turn would be rewarded with the food the animal could offer, and the power in its associated material remains. We may, in this context, choose to think not of animals and people but of animal people and human people as co-occupants of the world, and sometimes as the same.

Such a view gives us a context for understanding relations between human and animal bodies. Ornaments such as deer canines composed the living and dead body in terms of citations to places and the powers of the animals found in them. The animals carved in portable and cave art were not neutral photographs of the scenery but active co-occupants of an interesting and dangerous world. Practices such as cave art may have been important in convincing animals to continue relations of reciprocity. Human-animal hybrid images provide 'clear indications of the existence of beliefs which included the possibility, for selected beings, of changing from one state to the next, from a fully human character to a non-human one'.[90] These capture moments of human and animal linkages, of transformation, and of mixtures of genders, bodies and species.[91]

In sum, to the extent we can reconstruct a forager body world archaeologically, the evidence suggests that the human body was not clearly bounded but a contextual amalgamation of relations and materials (or rather material relations) temporarily joined together. Relations between humans, animals and landscape could be bridged in life, death, art and hunting. The Lepenski Vir sculptures, for example, like the Star Carr masks and the much older Palaeolithic images blurring the boundaries of human and animal, reveal an underlying concept that the human body need not be seen as a stable given (as it is in our body world) but instead as something capable of transformation or metamorphosis.[92]

By way of conclusion, we can return briefly to the site with which we started the chapter, the Mesolithic cemetery at Vedbaek, Denmark, and two similar Swedish sites, Skateholm I and II.[93] These Ertebølle culture sites date to between 5600 BC and 4000 BC, and represent the final and most elaborate developments of the Palaeolithic and Mesolithic logic of the body. These cemeteries contained accumulations of graves – seventeen at Vedbaek, twenty-two at Skateholm I and sixty-four at Skateholm II.[94] Grave goods are included in many of the burials, particularly at Skateholm II and Vedbaek.

In the vignette beginning this chapter, we imaginatively reconstructed a moment of burial at Vedbaek. Underlying this reconstruction are several points we have been discussing. For instance, whereas later cemeteries almost always position the body in a single normative way, at these cemeteries bodies were carefully positioned in a great variety of ways – on their backs, on their sides and in sitting positions,[95] In positioning the body, the dead could be made to play different parts in the funerary ritual, to actively watch the proceedings or to turn away from it; the variety suggests that each burial was contingent upon its own circumstances. Similarly, social relations did not end at death; graves were sometimes opened to remove and reuse bones.[96] Like other forager barriers, it seems death may have been one that was more permeable than secure.

At these sites, the dead, animals and landscapes were brought together. People were buried wearing specific parts of different creatures – red deer teeth, pine marten heads, the bills and feet of water birds.[97] Some graves included deer antlers; in fact, one grave at Skateholm II held three deer antlers but no human body at all.

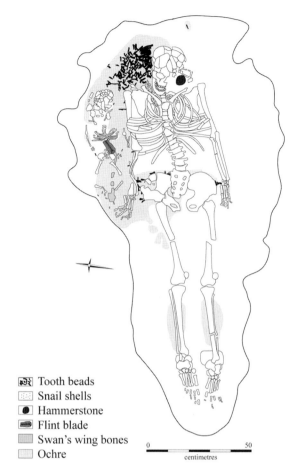

Tooth beads
Snail shells
Hammerstone
Flint blade
Swan's wing bones
Ochre

Figure 15. Grave 8 at Vedbaek, Denmark (Albrethsen and Brinch Petersen 1976, fig. 10; redrawn by Vicki Herring).

This is particularly evident with dogs. Dogs were sometimes included in people's graves (on occasions as sacrificial offerings); on other occasions, they were buried by themselves, sometimes with grave goods. Strikingly, the 'richest' burial at Skateholm II is of a dog, who was accompanied by a red deer antler laid along its spine, three flint blades in the hip region and a decorated antler hammer on its chest.[98] Clearly these dogs were not human, but they may have been persons, constituted from relations expressed through material connections.[99]

The burial at Vedbaek depicted in Plate I and drawn in Figure 15 is a famous burial of a woman with a newborn child. These coastal people had lived on land and sea, in close interaction with people and animals from both. The dead were buried by the shore, a liminal place where different landscapes and animals met. Here these two people were buried with deer tooth pendants and beads made from other materials, with the infant laid upon a swan's wing.[100] The choice of the swan is not arbitrary, nor is the position of the grave close to the sea. Swans are birds that can swim on water, fly and also walk on land; like humans they disappeared and reappeared annually, and

Figure 16. Trapezoidal hut from Lepenski Vir, Serbia (after Borić 2011, fig. 14; drawn by John Swogger).

they transcended the multiple categories against which the graves were situated. These assemblages of humans and animals connected and created relations together, and it was these relations that produced human bodies. Bodies were thus in part produced at these sites through relations with animals. They produced the food people ate, the clothes they wore and the jewellery that decorated them. Relational personhood was produced through these intersections, the way they bound up the biographies of people and animals together.[101]

Coda: The Mesolithic body in the time of farmers

At the end of the Mesolithic, not all European societies embraced farming; but foragers who turned their back on farming did not stand outside history as timeless holdovers. Some of the most florid exemplifications of the forager body world come from the very end of the Mesolithic, from an ever more circumscribed way of life. It is worth briefly visiting one of the most famous late Mesolithic groups – foragers of the Danube Gorges or Iron Gates.

On the border of Serbia and Romania, the Danube flows through dramatic canyon-like gorges, the Iron Gates. Foragers inhabited its banks throughout the Mesolithic,[102] subsisting largely upon regularly migrating large fish such as sturgeon,[103] a rich and stable food source, which might have permitted an unusual degree of year-round sedentism. Around 6200 BC at Lepenski Vir, Vlasac and Padina, these foragers built the most substantial settlements known for Mesolithic Europe. The largest settlement was at Lepenski Vir, with more than fifty trapezoidal huts with stone foundations and hearths and prepared lime-plaster floors (Figure 16). The Danube Gorges sites reveal an elaborate ritual life. At Lepenski Vir, as we have seen, statues carved from boulders and placed between houses or with burials depict beings that have both human-like and fish-like features (Figure 17). Burial of the dead was common and highly varied. Most burials are single, supine inhumations, but individual human bones or groups of scrambled bones were deposited on occasions; bones were sometimes burnt at Vlasac,[104] and skulls were sometimes removed from burials and singled out for special treatment and deposition.

The body world of the foragers who occupied the Danube Gorges was closely tied to the landscape in which they lived. The river played a crucial role in bringing life, and the burial of the deceased close to its banks, often with the head oriented downstream, cannot be coincidental.[105] In both life and death some individuals wore cloaks decorated with carp teeth.[106] As with the Neolithic groups we will meet later in this chapter, sedentism was accompanied by an increased symbolic commitment to places, a commitment signalled by placement of the dead. Associations with landscape and its animal inhabitants were also signalled through the burial of aurochs skulls and red deer antlers with the corpse.

The landscape provided the setting and symbolic resources for transformation, a key theme of the body at Lepenski Vir. One form of transformation was through treatment of the dead. Burial was partly structured by age and gender; for instance, the numerous infant burials were located within buildings and never buried with boulders,[107] and age certainly played a key role in the type of boulders associated with different burials, especially in relation to the depiction of eyes and other details.[108] Burial practices not only maintained the integrity of some burials but also fragmented other bodies and distributed them both around living sites and perhaps around the larger landscape. Such selective treatment channelled people of different kinds and dying in different circumstances into different forms of new beings and collective memories.[109] The other form of transformation was between humans and animals. As mentioned earlier, Lepenski Vir offers unusual evidence of boulder statuary apparently showing human-fish hybrids, suggesting fluidity between the categories of people and animals, particularly those who sustained them. Relations between the two forms of transformation are particularly interesting. Although many boulders were not sculpted iconographically, enough were shaped in this manner to suggest that all the boulders represent human-animal beings. Although not all boulders commemorated individual dead, enough did so to suggest that the dead may have been understood as transforming into animals. For example, adult male Burial 7/I was interred in House 21 behind the hearth. He was accompanied by an aurochs skull and a redeposited human skull, and a painted boulder was placed on his

forehead.[110] Boulders placed around sites but not associated with the dead may have been spirits present for other reasons. Thus, one interpretation linking the two forms of transformation is that of bodily metamorphosis between humans and fish through death.[111] In many ways, this is a logical extension of the forager body world outlined previously.

The Danube Gorges situation is particularly fascinating because of what it suggests about historical process. From at least 8000 BC onwards, at Vlasac and Lepenski Vir, foragers became increasingly settled down by the banks of the river, with experiments in increasingly elaborate burial. By about 6300 BC, Neolithic settlements began to appear in regions surrounding the rocky and – for farmers – inhospitable Danube Gorges; in the ensuing centuries, these villages were probably populated both by incoming farmers and by local foragers who had decided to adopt farming. In fact, to judge from the presence of pottery at Lepenski Vir throughout this period, foragers were in contact with nearby farmers.[112] It is precisely during this period that new practices emerged. Almost certainly, all of the burials associated with the phase of trapezoidal buildings (Phase I-II) at Lepenski Vir date to between 6200 BC and 5900 BC. It is difficult to escape the conclusion that Lepenski Vir represents foragers increasingly encapsulated amongst farmers and yet not succumbing to the Neolithic, using ever more floridly developed ritual and burial to emphasize their difference while at the same time adapting some elements of the Neolithic body decoration.[113] Much of this way of understanding the world revolved around bodies.

In this light, perhaps the most striking fact is how much developments at Lepenski Vir parallel Neolithic innovations at the same time as they resist them. Like many Neolithic groups, the Danube Gorges foragers developed the formalization of space through architecture, the intensified village ritual and the use of burial to establish lasting historical associations between people and particular places (as opposed to dispersing people into landscapes generally). They developed these practices independently. Unlike farmers elsewhere, the local Starčevo farmers had neither such substantial villages nor such elaborated burials. In many ways, the Danube Gorges may give us a glimpse into an alternative universe in which the organizational changes related to sedentism are decoupled from core beliefs about relations between humans and other beings – a society organizationally Neolithic but based upon a belief in the volatility of human bodies, the temporary moment in which the human form was enmeshed as part of a lifelong change from fish to human and back again.

Figure 17. Human-fish carved boulder from Lepenski Vir, Serbia (Borić 2005a: fig. 8, photo courtesy of Dušan Borić).

This leaves us with the question of reinserting Lepenski Vir into long-term history. In the latest phase at the site (Phase LVIII), a clear, full Neolithic enters with new material things, house forms and burial rites, as well as an economy based upon terrestrial animals and domesticated plants. The traditional way of life was clearly historically tenable – it had served people well for several centuries already, and there are many historic examples of animistic, sedentary farmers or fishers in native cultures of the Americas. Yet the body is fundamental to historic ways of life, and it may be that a key moment in giving up the fluid, animal-transformation view of the body was the adoption of domesticated animals, a step which implied or required redrawing categorizations of humans and animals (see following section).

Settling bodies down? The Neolithic body

The Neolithic is the period during which Europeans began to farm. From about 6500 BC onwards, people in Europe obtained domesticated plants and animals from early Near Eastern farmers and began to settle down and lead a farming lifestyle (see Tables 3 and 4 in Chapter 4 for a broader chronology in relation to social changes). The Neolithic and the transition from hunting and gathering to agriculture proved a major watershed in human history. Archaeologically, Neolithic groups differ from their foraging predecessors in a number of key institutions and material culture, particularly the so-called 'Neolithic package' of sedentary villages, cemeteries and often colourful burial rites; a reliance on domesticated animals and

plants, pottery, polished stone axes and tools for grinding grains; and rituals involving figurines (in some areas) and megaliths (in others).

Definitions like these are the simple bit. In fact, every term in this description has been challenged by archaeologists of different persuasions. There is a huge and often deeply divided literature on questions of how to define 'the Neolithic', many – perhaps most – Neolithic societies furnish exceptions to a tidy 'Neolithic package', and the very process by which farming spread from the Near East across Europe and into places like Britain remains controversial.[114] Here, although we hope to give a sense of the great variety of European Neolithic societies, we sidestep these traditional issues. Instead, we focus simply upon the question of what kind of world Neolithic villagers inhabited and how their understandings of the human body differed from that of their hunter-gatherer ancestors.

We do however have to confront the question of how economy, society and culture relate. In most of Europe, the Neolithic was an economic transition from a mobile foraging lifestyle to sedentary farming. The transition to farming has often been considered the second great human 'revolution', following the advent of anatomically and cognitively modern humans in the Palaeolithic.[115] Since Childe's work,[116] a series of prominent theorists have regarded the Neolithic as a radical economic disjuncture which changed not only how humans made their living but also how they organized landscapes, related to each other and conceptualized the world symbolically.[117]

We are only in partial agreement with this view. Contrary to the 'revolutions' view, becoming Neolithic was often gradual and varied rather than sudden and uniform, an elastically bounded envelope of possibilities rather than a single pathway, and there is much evidence for continuities between farmers and their foraging predecessors. But such a sweeping, if gradual, transformation of human life could not be confined to the economy alone. As Ingold notes,

> the domain in which human persons are involved as social beings with one another cannot be rigidly set apart from the domain of their involvement with non-human components of the environment. Hence, any qualitative transformation in environmental relations is likely to be manifested similarly both in the relationships that humans extend towards animals and in those that obtain among themselves in society.[118]

Social change in prehistory usually did not involve abrupt revolutions, but rather the slow revelation of new forms of identity produced through material metaphors – that is, how people come to understand the world around

Table 2. *The body in the agricultural transition in the Near East*

Period	Food	Space	The Dead	Representations
Natufian (12800–10000 BC)	Hunting (particularly) gazelles, intensive use of wild grains	Variable, but some substantial sedentary villages of round houses	Cemeteries of mostly single burials with ornaments and ritual goods	Animal qualities important in 'grave goods'; figurines of animals made, but only a few hybrid images[119]
Pre-Pottery Neolithic A (10000–8500 BC)	Hunting, intensive use and incipient domestication of wild grains	Growth of some very large villages with 'public' architecture (Jericho)	Single burials in and around houses; retrieval of skulls for skull cult	Shift to mostly human, often female figurines; wild animals still important (Göbekli Tepe)
Pre-Pottery Neolithic B (8500–6750 BC)	Domesticated plants and animals	Villages of square houses with increasingly formalised interiors	Single burials in and around houses; retrieval of skulls for skull cult	Figurines common, particularly females; males represented in other forms of art, animal representations focus upon wild animals; a few hybrids

them through the things they make and use, the places they live and so on.[120] With the Neolithic, as people began to settle down, to build permanent villages and to farm, and to bury their dead in new ways, new relationships and new understandings of the body emerged. We have discussed how Palaeolithic and Mesolithic hunter-gatherers constructed their understandings of their bodies in part through how they related to animals, landscapes, places and histories. New relationships to these things developed hand in hand with new understandings of the body.

The Near Eastern backdrop to European agriculture

Before plunging into the European Neolithic, it is important to have a quick glance at the Near Eastern roots of the Neolithic (Table 2). Not only does the Near East provide the essential backdrop for what happens in Europe; the detailed and well-studied Near Eastern sequence provides a fascinating insight into how ideas of the body can change through the transition to a settled farming life.

The transition to agriculture in the Near East was clearly under way by around 10,000 BC, and by about 6700 BC all the stereotypical technologies and institutions of early farming societies were present. But in human terms, we can scarcely call something several millennia long a 'transition', and still less a 'revolution'. Although farming, herding, towns and material culture such as pottery form a stable complex, which has supported most humans since the Neolithic, such a gradual onset surely explodes any determinist idea that these form a tight functional package in which all elements require each other to be viable.

At the beginning of the sequence, Natufian people were not farmers at all, but semi-sedentary hunter-gatherers who sometimes relied extensively on collecting and storing wild grains in the Levant.[121] Particularly in the Early Natufian, they sometimes lived in large villages of semi-subterranean round or oval huts and used non-portable technologies such as large grinding stones. Like late, semi-sedentary foragers in Scandinavia, Portugal and the Balkans, the Natufians buried their dead in cemeteries close to their settlements, perhaps grouped by kinship. They also built structures in areas that were already associated with funerary activities.[122] Single burials were most common, but (as at Vedbaek) there were lots of variations such as burial in small groups and redeposited burials.[123] The dead were adorned with beads, wristbands and other ornaments, mostly of imported marine shells but also of bone and carnivore teeth. An extraordinary burial from Hilazon Tachtit gives a sense of Natufian concerns at death (Figure 18). Here, an older woman with physical impairments in walking was buried with a staggering array of goods, including a human foot, more than fifty complete tortoise shells, two stone marten heads, a golden eagle wing-tip, an aurochs tail, a boar forearm, a leopard pelvis, a gazelle horn core, a basalt bowl fragment, three shells, a painted bone tool and a stone-working pebble.[124] This has been interpreted as the burial of a ritual specialist, perhaps a shaman, who was evidently feared as well as respected (to judge from the ten large stones holding her body down). What is interesting is how her outstanding attributes were evidently understood through reference to animals and their qualities, something not unusual in Natufian burials.[125]

The succeeding Pre-Pottery Neolithic A period sees both continuities and changes. The way people made

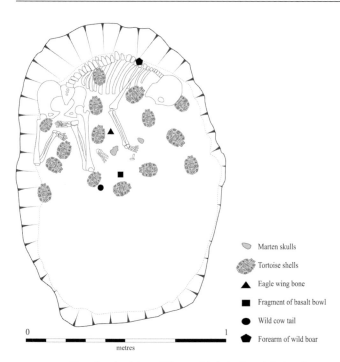

Marten skulls

Tortoise shells

▲ Eagle wing bone

■ Fragment of basalt bowl

● Wild cow tail

⬠ Forearm of wild boar

0   1

metres

Figure 18. Natufian burial at Hilazon Tachtit, Israel (after Grosman, Munro and Belfer-Cohen 2008, fig. 4; redrawn by Vicki Herring).

Figure 19. Neolithic plastered skull from Tell Aswad, Syria (photo courtesy of Danielle Stordeur).

a living continued more or less unchanged, although at some point grains and legumes were domesticated, probably a gradual and unconscious mutualistic response to selection pressures exerted in harvesting wild versions. People continued to live in villages of round huts, but some, such as Jericho, grew much larger, bringing together more people than ever before.[126] As far as the body goes, the real changes occur in burial and art. From the Late Natufian onwards, single burials around houses and sites become the norm; the dead were ornamented less in ways underlining their individuality, but it became increasingly common to retrieve the skull and reuse it in rites, sometimes adding a generic plastered face onto it (Figure 19).[127] In effect, the dead body becomes constructed less through its relations to settings and beings (such as animals) and more through its generic relation to the ancestral history of the human group. This shift in symbolic focus towards the human group becomes evident in figurines as well; although some animal figures continue to be made, human figures become dominant (Figure 20). Many of these are clearly female, although some are ambiguously gendered and may represent generic or fluid humans. Animals continue to play an important symbolic role in other ways; for instance, wild bull skulls were built into walls

and benches in houses.[128] The most spectacular evidence, however, comes from the recently excavated late Pre-Pottery Neolithic A (PPNA) to Pre-Pottery Neolithic B (PPNB) ritual site of Göbekli Tepe in Turkey,[129] where large stone circles contained massive anthropomorphic pillars carved with male snakes, turtles, lions, vultures and boars (Figure 21). Even as figurines and burials increasingly represented the bounded distinctly human body, wild animals continued to be a source of symbolic potency, and the combination of animal images emerging from schematised human forms may continue the belief in the potential metamorphosis of the human body.[130]

The PPNB is the first true 'Neolithic' period, with domesticated plants, sheep and goats, and (from late in

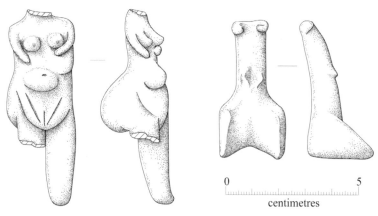

0   5

centimetres

Figure 20. PPNA figurines considered to be female, from Mureybet, Northern Levant (left) and Netiv Hagdud, Southern Levant (right) (after Bar-Yosef 1998, fig. 13; redrawn by Vicki Herring).

Figure 21. T-shaped statues from Göbekli Tepe, Turkey, with animal reliefs (photos courtesy of Klaus Schmidt and Deutsches Archäologisches Institut).

the PPNB) cattle.[131] The period is best known from excavations at Çatalhöyük in Turkey.[132] What is architecturally notable about Çatalhöyük is the formal, almost standardized layout of houses with repeated, well-defined features such as storage rooms, hearths, entrances, burials and ritual platforms; there was a highly structured, shared experience of space. As in the PPNA, the dead were mostly buried in and around houses, and it was common to return to bodies and remove their skulls for ritual use, occasionally replastering them with idealized faces;[133] one building at the PPNB site of Çayönü contained parts from 450 bodies, a remarkable attempt to reconstitute the living community amongst the dead.[134] As in the PPNA, clay female figurines continue to be commonly made, though in certain contexts (such as in art) reference to hunting male figures dominate.[135] The lime plaster figures from 'Ain Ghazal (Figure 22) are really statues rather than figurines, and, like the dead themselves, were buried beneath the floor of an abandoned house.[136] Animals are often represented and increasingly include domesticated beasts. Although hybrid human-animal representations are relatively rare,[137] some splayed figures at Çatalhöyük may represent bear-human hybrids.[138] Art generally portrays close linkages between humans and animals, with vultures accompanying headless humans in wall paintings, people wearing leopard skins and bull heads and vulture beaks protruding from the walls in the rooms in which people lived.

The Near Eastern sequence shows how gradual change was, with continuity rather than rupture clear at all points; every phase was a stable, inhabitable human world rather than an unstable moment of transition. Yet if we compare the beginning with the end, we see the

emergence of a new kind of body world with distinct characteristics. Movement (both within landscapes and within houses) became increasingly fixed and channelled by villages, walls, plazas, rooms and constructed spaces with particular uses. As spaces define relationships, rights and comportment, we may infer an increasing formalization of bodily movement and behaviour. For example, kinship relations probably became more fixed and represented architecturally and through burial in large villages. The body in death became a vehicle for enacting the community's ancestry and identity. It is particularly interesting how human-animal relations shifted. In media such as figurines, it was increasingly common to define the human body, particularly women's bodies, as an object of interest on its own, independent of links with animals or the world around it. Yet the interest in wild animals and their qualities always persisted, and relations between humans and wild animals became realigned; in some places wild animality was associated with maleness and with locales distant from living spaces (as at Göbekli Tepe), in other places it may have been associated with death as well (as at Çatalhöyük).[139]

The body in Neolithic Europe

The earliest farming villages in Europe appear around 6500 BC in Greece and spread west and north from there. Moving in fits and starts, the Neolithic moved from Greece and the Balkans westward along the Mediterranean and northwards across Hungary; crossing the Carpathians about 5500 BC, in the Linearbandkeramik (LBK) period, and by 5000 BC it had spread very rapidly westwards to Belgium. By 4000 BC, the Neolithic had reached Britain, Ireland and Scandinavia, transforming life across the continent. In Europe, unlike the Near East, plants and animals were not domesticated locally; wheat, barley, pulses, cattle, sheep, goats and pigs in Europe came from Near Eastern ancestors. Archaeologists discussing the 'origins of farming' in Europe have been split in an increasingly sterile division between those who see migrating farmers radiating out from the Near East and those who see local foragers adopting farming indigenously. Neither position captures the truth of a complex situation,[140] and to some extent the argument is beside the point here.

Regardless of how it came about, Neolithic life took a great variety of forms. The broadest division is between much of lowland Europe, where Neolithic groups clearly had a farming-based village economy, and the Atlantic and Scandinavian worlds, which entered the Neolithic later and where evidence for both sedentary villages and reliance upon agriculture is less clear. Instead, Atlantic

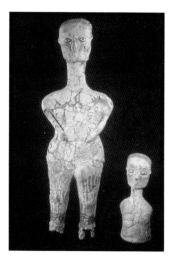

Figure 22. The figures from 'Ain Ghazal, Jordan (photo courtesy of Gary Rollefson and the Department of Antiquities, Jordan).

and Scandinavia Neolithic groups departed from their Mesolithic traditions in other ways, particularly in creating landscapes of monuments (such as megalithic tombs). We return to questions of historical process and variation later in this chapter and in Chapter 4; this discussion focuses principally upon periods before about 4000 BC (see Table 4, Chapter 4). Here we briefly review evidence for ideas of the human body, as the Neolithic involved reconceptualising the human body in many ways, both in practical activity and in ritual and art.

People, work, food and animals

Although archaeologists often equate the Neolithic with agriculture, how much Neolithic people actually relied upon farming and herding has been controversial; all Neolithic groups gathered wild fruits and plants, and some continued to hunt quite a bit. As a broad generalization, however, except for the Baltic and Atlantic fringes, there was a clear economic shift. Analysis of plant and animal remains shows that, throughout most of Europe, Neolithic groups relied substantially upon cultivated grains, and very rapidly shifted from eating hunted game to eating sheep, goats, pigs and cattle. In the northern and western maritime worlds and in highland zones such as the Alps, the economic consequences of the Neolithic were more varied, and farming economies gradually consolidated over centuries or even millennia.

Economic change affected the body directly through changed work regimes, nutrition and tastes, and indirectly through ideas of space and through redefinition of categories such as 'animals'. How did changes in daily routine and work affect the body? The best evidence for this comes from skeletal analysis. Throughout Europe,

adult stature dropped by 5–10 cm with the advent of farming.[141] This may reflect a seasonally poorer diet and lessened mechanical demands upon the skeleton with sedentism. Infectious disease begins to appear, perhaps because permanent sedentary living sites became contaminated with parasites, and perhaps because increased contact with domestic animals facilitated zoonotic diseases such as tuberculosis (the earliest evidence for which comes from Neolithic Israel and Italy).[142] With a diet based upon sticky, carbohydrate-rich grains, dental disease affected more people earlier in their lives. The data tentatively suggest a demographic shift as well. Neolithic people had more children per person than their foraging predecessors, but also died younger; we have to imagine more than half of Neolithic people being children.[143]

Conceptually, new economic practices were enmeshed in categorizations of animals. Although dairy products were used in some areas from the early Neolithic onwards, Neolithic people probably kept relatively small numbers of animals and the focus was upon eating them; specialized herding to exploit milk and wool seems to be a later development. Isotopic evidence suggests that Neolithic people ate varying amounts of meat and milk, with some groups consistent carnivores and others almost vegetarian.[144] However, domestic animals may have been used particularly for feasting. Conceptually, there is not much celebration of domestic animals in art, and little evidence for human-animal hybrids. Although the use of bucrania in Balkan architecture and occasionally in grave goods suggests the prestige associated with cattle consumption, they were not co-species in a world of multi-naturalism (as we saw in the Palaeolithic and Mesolithic).[145] Instead, they were property that required care and attention and which could be dominated and used for gain and perhaps as a source of wealth and prestige. To the extent that taste in Neolithic cuisine reflects social interaction, grains were probably the taste of household solidarity, meat the taste of inter-household sociality.[146]

At the same time, the role of hunting changed. Except in a few mountain ecologies, hunting became a small component of the economy, contributing supplementary foods such as small mammals, raw materials such as antler, fur, feathers, and shell, and probably drama and excitement as well. Economic changes redrew the boundaries between different kinds of animals (see discussion later in this chapter). This does not imply that domestic animals were simply eaten whilst wild animals were symbolically important; instead, domestic animals were regarded as social capital to be accumulated, used in important transactions and feasted upon.[147]

Bodies and (and as) objects

The Neolithic saw an explosion of things; people made, used, kept and deposited as archaeology far more material objects than their mobile ancestors had done. Whereas theoretical archaeologists have considered the general social effects of this fact,[148] we consider its implications for the body. These consequences are diffuse and inferential, but as significant as the more obvious changes in imagery and burial.

New forms of technology allow us to understand our bodies in new ways. It is remarkable that in both Palaeolithic Europe and the Near East clay was used for figurines before it was used for pottery. In Neolithic Europe, clay was used for both. There are more direct links as well. Sporadic anthropomorphic vessels are known from many Neolithic contexts, human figures are sometimes sketched on pots in both Central Europe and the Mediterranean, and human faces are occasionally modelled on the rims of Mediterranean Neolithic vessels. The placement of such faces suggests a latent isomorphism between pots and human bodies; decoration on some Balkan figurines suggests that bodies may have been decorated (through painting, tattooing or clothing) similarly to pots. Such an isomorphism received its most dramatic expression in anthropomorphic pots from Macedonia which add houses into the equation as symbolically equivalent to clay vessels and bodies (Plate VId).[149] Much as the machine in the eighteenth century, clay technology gave people a new metaphor for understanding the body, one which emphasized its substance, its plasticity and ability to take different forms, and its links to houses and places.[150]

The body was also a medium of action, and this brings us to the paradox of Neolithic skill. The abundance of Neolithic things is not functionally necessary; axes and pots were useful, but one could be a sedentary farmer without them, and there is greater variety and elaboration of both than warranted by a purely functional view. Many Neolithic things were made with consummate skill. Pots were decorated elaborately and burnished meticulously; flint blades were struck precisely from an expertly prepared core; axes were polished to a gloss far beyond what their physical uses required. In fact, some forms of pottery may have been attempted because of their ostentatious difficulty. Yet anthropologists have rarely contemplated skill per se.[151] It has been seen as a response to economic specialization, political hierarchy or functional need. None of these is the case for the Neolithic. We are thus left with the paradox of skill exercised for its own sake, simply to enhance the sense of the maker as skilful or as possessing specific qualities such as patience, judgment or strength. Skill was

embodied and materialized. As anybody who has tried to make Neolithic things knows, such skills are not cerebral; they reside in the body, in the practiced hands that know how to thin a vessel wall regularly or strike a flint strongly yet precisely. The logical conclusion is that there was a close relation between Neolithic material things and the body, and that one of the raisons d'etre for the explosion of Neolithic things was to provide arenas for the externalization of bodily skills tied to identity.

Finally, the body was completed through things. Whether they represent real or imagined painting, tattoos or clothing, many Balkan figurines show the body decorated with a wild range of swirls, spirals and geometric designs. A few, such as the famous Vinča figures, appear to be masked as if for rituals (Figure 23 and Plate VIc). Interestingly, to the extent that we can extrapolate an aesthetic reflex from these, it involves figuring the surface with ornate, fine detail, much as Neolithic pottery decoration does. This proliferation of difference creates a surface that allows multiple, heterarchical evaluations rather than a single, simple evaluation.[152] Headdresses and costumes are also shown in Levantine rock art. Elsewhere in Europe, dress is manifested archaeologically principally in durable ornaments, which are found in some quantity everywhere. Metals – experimented with from around 6000 BC in the Balkans and becoming widespread through the fifth millennium in the Balkan and Central Mediterranean Neolithic (the Early and Middle Neolithic)[153] – were probably of interest principally for their colour and shining appearance. Carnivore teeth cite the qualities of foxes, dogs and wolves. Pierced miniature axes in Italy and Malta and ornaments from variscite mines in Catalonia may cite the cosmological qualities of greenstone or specific trade histories. *Spondylus* shell ornaments found in Central Europe may have publicly attested renown in trade much as shell valuables from distant sources did in ethnohistoric Melanesia. Moreover, as objects such as polished stone rings passed from person to person, they may have been intentionally broken to distribute their powers amongst different people or to end their social biographies.[154] Some arm rings were often too small to have been taken on and off and probably formed a continuously worn extension of the body[155] – becoming truly inalienable property. Throughout Neolithic Europe, ornaments were not wealth in our conventional sense; for instance, there does not seem to have been any attempt to restrict production, and they seem to have been circulated rather than accumulated. Bodies were differentiated not to make them outstanding in terms of wealth but rather simply to create social difference of various kinds.

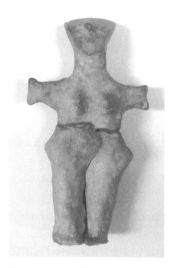

Figure 23. Vinča figurine, Vinča, Serbia (photo: Robb).

Finally, this is probably the context to understand the intentional modification of the body. Removing highly visible front teeth in Neolithic Italian women may have been part of creating adult females.[156] There may have been other experiments in body modification. The first instance of dental surgery known is in a Danish Neolithic skull whose tooth was drilled with a flint blade during life;[157] there is no suggestion of dental caries, which is common in Neolithic skulls, and this was not a normal therapy for it in any case. The most widespread modification was trepanation, the practice of cutting a hole in the skull during life. Neolithic trepanations are known from many areas of Europe, particularly Italy, France and Denmark. More than half were healed, indicating that the trepanee survived the operation,[158] but it would have been a dangerous and infrequent intervention. Trepanations probably were neither 'medical' nor 'magical' (an oft-invoked dichotomy which reveals more about our categories than about the Neolithic). Although they may have been prompted in some cases by medical symptoms (for instance, following severe cranial trauma which may have had effects upon the brain), in most cases there is no indication of this, and trepanations would have been carried out publicly within a native understanding of person and mental state – perhaps something like a ceremony of donning a potent yet risky mask to heal a dangerously spiritual or physical malady.

Space

Neolithic people settled down; rather than pursuing a seasonal foraging round over a broad landscape, they lived most or all of the year in a particular, much more limited place. Experientially, this meant that the body would not spend the year moving amongst widely separated places with which it was loosely associated; it would spend a lifetime in a much narrower world whose people and places it knew intimately.

Exactly how people settled down took many forms; there are several great traditions of Neolithic settlement. In much of the lowland Balkans and northern Greece, villagers lived in dense clusters of wattle and daub huts. In some places, over the generations, the accumulated debris from such houses built up settlement mounds, or 'tells'.[159] As landscape made through human occupation, tells anchored the world in terms of fixed human histories. Whether a tell site or flat site, architecture provided a structure for routinized, permanent interactions; houses were often rebuilt directly upon earlier ones. Cooking and many other activities were done in open-air areas between houses where people from different households interacted. Houses provided zones of private interaction and were identified with their occupants to the extent that they were often intentionally burnt at the end of the household's social lifespan.[160] This concern with boundedness and rights of access probably extended to other elements of the landscape; ethnographically, societies similar to European Neolithic groups tend not to have absolute property ownership but to consider that individuals and families 'own' places such as gardens to the extent that they are actively investing labour upon improving them.

The situation in the Central and Western Mediterranean is similar. Well-defined, often ditched Neolithic villages are known from much of Italy and parts of Iberia; in other places, people apparently lived in small hamlets of a few houses. Yet throughout, people were probably identified principally by their resident groups, and there was often considerable investment in defining the borders of the community through ditches or palisades around villages. Nested within the community, the life of the house was probably identified with the lives of the people living within it, to judge from the intentional, probably ritual destruction of many houses.[161]

Village life remains the theme in Central Europe, though tells are not found north of the Hungarian plain. Instead, people often lived in clusters of longhouses, massive structures up to 60 meters long[162] which probably housed multiple families living under one roof. Again, longhouse settlements represent a formalization of space, with many people coming together to erect an overbuilt, indeed monumental, structure which followed a widely shared formal layout that divided internal space into regularized sections probably associated with different family groups, animals, and special social functions. LBK longhouses were often abandoned long before the end of their useful use-lives, suggesting again a close tie between the social lives of living spaces and those of the groups living within them.[163] Central and Western European Neolithic villages were also often ditched or palisaded, particularly in the Middle Neolithic. Whether or not this is a response to warfare (and this is debated), it shows a concern with bounding areas of space and movement and defining categories of people within them. Moreover, as with monuments (see following discussion), such collectively built projects were themselves tangible reminders of a community whose membership was largely defined by living together and participating in such projects.

Space and identity created warfare. There has been a long tradition of regarding the Neolithic as a pacific time, in part because of the absence of obvious weapon symbolism (see Chapter 4). But in any Neolithic skeletal collection there are a fair number of injuries (such as cranial fractures) which probably resulted from violence. When archaeologists have tried to quantify the rate of injury, it is as high as any time in prehistory, and there are clearly documented Neolithic assaults at Crickley Hill (England)[164] and massacres at Talheim (Germany)[165] and Asparn-Schletz (Austria).[166] Neolithic violence affected men, women and children generally.[167] It includes many sub-lethal injuries such as healed traumas probably inflicted with clubs, suggesting that attacks were common but the goal was not necessarily systematic killing. One gets the picture of endemic low-level raiding and conflict between groups, occasionally culminating in a dramatic mass attack such as at Asparn-Schletz where sixty-seven people were massacred with clubs in their village.[168] Anthropologically, it suggests that a more rigidly divided social landscape created the potential for increased conflict, with much more closed, territorial and frequently hostile social groups than was the case in earlier periods.

The dead

Neolithic people related to the dead in new ways. For one thing, the dead were present amongst them to a much greater degree. The large-scale burial of dead bodies takes off in this period, on a level far greater and more widespread than had been seen previously. Particularly in the earlier Neolithic of mainland Europe (Neolithic burials after 4000 BC, particularly megalithic traditions, are mainly discussed in Chapter 4, though we do touch on them in this chapter), the dead were usually buried in and around settlements – within houses, in open spaces between houses or in pits and ditches around villages. In some areas, particularly Central Europe and the Central Mediterranean, such burials evolved into formal cemeter-

Figure 24. Scaloria Cave, Italy: cut marks on a child's collarbone made with a stone tool attest rites of defleshing bodies (photo: Robb).

ies near settlements; for the LBK, cemeteries such as Nitra,[169] Bylany and Aiterhofen[170] can include more than a hundred burials. Moreover, even when people buried their dead, funerary treatment was far more varied. In Southern Italy, for instance, burials were common, but we also see other processes, including disturbed burials around sites, possible ritual killings, ritual deposition of skulls, removal of skulls from earlier burials and skull caches within villages. At one site, Scaloria Cave, people stripped remaining flesh from the faces, skulls and bodies of the dead to clean the bones before depositing them (Figure 24). Similarly, in LBK villages such as Vaihingen (Germany), in addition to burials in cemeteries, it is common to find burials (particularly of children), partial bodies and stray bones in pits and ditches around villages. This suggests that many, perhaps most, people were actually buried around and amongst the houses. Disturbing the dead was part of life, with body parts perhaps being kept and manipulated afterwards. Unusual ritual processing of dead bodies is seen at Herxheim, Germany, where large numbers of the dead were brought from distant places to a ditched enclosure, intentionally broken (often to reduce the skull to a specific form of skull-cap) and deposited.[171]

At this point, it is worth asking what it meant to deposit grave goods with the dead. For some parts of Neolithic Europe, grave goods are very uncommon; however, they do occur repeatedly in areas such as in southeast Europe and amongst the LBK.[172] In the latter case, burials included grave goods such as red ochre, pottery, flint and bone tools, axes, and ornaments such as bracelets and pendants made from imported *spondylus* shell (Figure 25). Axes were deposited preferentially with adult males. To look a little forward in time, to the period after 4000 BC amongst Scandinavian Neolithic groups, people were buried with axes, pots and ornaments in flat graves, long barrows and in some closed dolmen megaliths.[173] Archaeologists have traditionally understood grave goods in terms of personal wealth and status, along the lines of 'whoever dies with the most things wins'. Neolithic

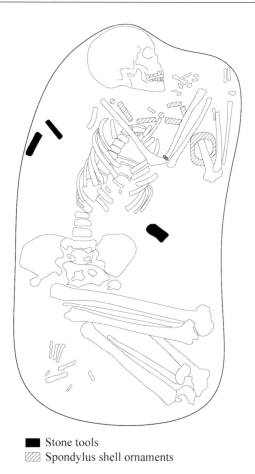

■ Stone tools
▨ Spondylus shell ornaments

Figure 25. Aiterhofen, Germany: LBK burial (original image courtesy of Sylvia Codreanu-Windauer, Bayerisches Landesamt für Denkmalpflege, redrawn by Vicki Herring).

grave goods, however, rarely fit such a model. They sometimes define social categories – especially gender and age – or refer to idiosyncratic ritual statuses or circumstances. Moreover, they often give a sense of being placed with the dead to redefine the body and its relations with people, to recreate a relational personhood via the social networks constituting the body.[174] Thus, in Scandinavian tombs, pots may relate to the ways in which the body was sustained through feeding, the axes to exchanges made with others and amber beads to the ways in which people could assemble decorative items that tied them into other places and times. On a more abstract level, like ritually depositing artefacts in bogs, placing grave goods within monuments was one part of the broader acts of assembly that gathered together dead bodies, living bodies, stones, wood and earth in the acts of building, provoking memories and emotions.[175] As we will see in more detail in the next chapter, the kinds of megalithic tombs that came to dominate in Europe in the late fifth and especially in the fourth millennia BC provided a focus for sociality, a place where people could come together and work to construct

a sense of community that was written on and through their bodies, and tied in the bodies of the dead alongside ideas of ancestry.[176] Markedly, a significant proportion of bodies buried in such Neolithic monuments in Britain may have been selected because of the fact they died violently.[177] It may have been people who died in particular ways who were selected to represent the community in these constructions, their bodies potentially both the source of anxiety and power.[178]

There are two points here about the body. First, Neolithic burial was not a final, one-way disposal programme intended to distance the living from the dead. Instead, varied burial programmes created ongoing contact with the dead, who were present in daily life and who therefore may have had powers for good or ill.[179] For example, keeping skulls and occasionally depositing them under houses may indicate a belief in their inherent power; similarly, in areas where villages were ringed by ditches, the dead were often buried in the ditches, implying perhaps a desire to interpose the dead between the village and the potentially hostile outside world. Secondly, burial was not usually about representing individual status or hierarchy. Instead, it was a way for people to reformulate the community of the living after death and to identify the history of the group with its specific landscape and territory of the village. It marked a new linkage between the history of the body, the history of the group, and places.[180] This gives us a context for interpreting a kind of burial found consistently in small numbers throughout Neolithic Europe – deviant burials, the victims of violence. Whereas in Neolithic Britain the violently killed were often selected for burial in monuments, elsewhere violent deaths seem to have led to quite different treatments of the deceased. For example, several individuals have been found strangled and deposited in Danish bogs at Sigersdal on Zealand and at Bolkilde on Als.[181] Similarly, at Passo di Corvo in Italy, a young woman was deposited – perhaps not buried – face down in a well. If burial rites provided the plan of action merging collective identity with the memory of places, such flagrantly different burials were a means of excising the people involved – presumably for political or ritual reasons – from history, a form of social forgetting.[182]

Representations

As in the Near East, Neolithic people in Europe made clay figurines. Figurines are common in Greece and the Balkans; moderate numbers are known in adjacent areas of Central Europe such as Hungary and Austria, and in Italy and Malta. Figurines are usually found discarded and broken amid 'domestic' refuse. This suggests that

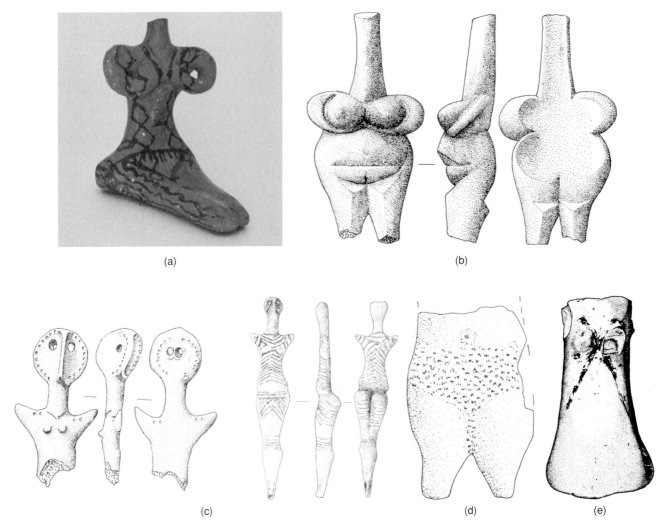

(a)

(b)

(c)   (d)   (e)

Figure 26. Balkan and Mediterranean Neolithic figurines. A. Franchthi Cave, Greece (Indiana University Archives, P0031514). B. Hamangia, Romania (Bailey 2005, fig. 3.2, reproduced with kind permission of Douglass Bailey, figure drawn by Howard Mason). C. Cucuteni/Tripolye, Romania (Bailey 2005, fig. 5.11, reproduced with kind permission of Douglass Bailey, drawn by Howard Mason). D. Rendina, Southern Italy (Robb 2007, fig. 5). E. Catignano, Italy (Robb 2007, fig. 6).

they were important for particular purposes but not of particularly high value. They may have been used as toys, as tokens of relationships or agreements, or in rituals.[183]

Most figurines depict humans, and the great majority of these are intended to show females, to judge from anatomical references such as breasts and pubic areas. In some areas, animals and males are also depicted.[184] It has never been satisfactorily answered why primarily women should be shown. Some archaeologists and popular writers have seen figurines as evidence of a Neolithic 'Mother Goddess' associated with the fertility of the earth. This is extremely doubtful; there is no inherent reason why Neolithic people should have associated crop fertility particularly with females and there is no other evidence for such a cult. Moreover, this is based upon a universalizing, essentialist concept of what it means to be a woman entirely at odds with what anthropolo-

gists know about the varied construction of gender.[185] Such a view is also based upon a doctrinal, monolithic view of religion much more reminiscent of Christianity than of anything known ethnographically in the tribal world. Balkan figurines make two important points for understanding Neolithic bodies (Figure 26a–c). First, they provide an excellent illustration of a theme which we will encounter repeatedly – the interplay of technology and the body (see especially Chapter 4 on metals and Chapter 8). As new technologies arise, they provide new ways of understanding the body. Here, as we mentioned earlier, we see a homology between pots, bodies, and houses that is underlain by a shared clay technology and made evident in things such as pots with anthropomorphic details such as faces added to the rim, houses whose lifespan parallels that of the social units inhabiting them, and even pottery sculptures merging

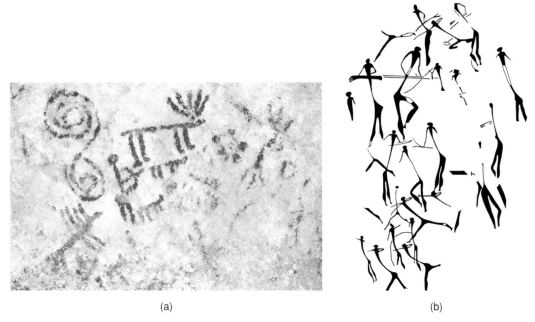

(a)   (b)

Figure 27. Neolithic cave art: (a) Porto Badisco, Italy, males in hunting scene (Graziosi 1974, fig. 157); (b) Levantine art, Spain, hunting scene (drawn by Vicki Herring).

houses and bodies (Plate VId). Secondly, figurines vary immensely. From Greece to Hungary, there is no single template for representing the body. At some sites, the lower torso is emphasized, the upper body shrunken to a simple rod; at others the torso is detailed and the limbs and head mere nubs; there are three-dimensional, 'naturalistic' bodies and flattened plaque-like bodies, there are stiffly rigid bodies and freely gesturing bodies, there are hollow vessel-like bodies and bodies constructed in segments specifically designed to be broken neatly apart. The act of abstraction and schematism[186] needed to go from the body as people saw and experienced it to the body as represented was governed by local tradition and by the needs of the particular context; the result was utter heterogeneity. Obvious as this sounds, it needs saying, because it stands in strong contrast to the uniform way in which the body was represented a few millennia later and it reveals a particular Neolithic understanding of the body.

In the Central and Western Mediterranean, the body appears in two forms of prehistoric art.[187] First, figurines are again known throughout Italy, Sicily, Sardinia and Malta. Although they are found in far fewer numbers than in the Balkans (altogether about 100 are known in the Central Mediterranean), they resemble the figurines discussed earlier: small, clay, female, found around domestic sites, and extremely heterogeneous in form (Figure 26d and e).[188] Like the Balkan figurines, they probably reflect both a particular context, practice or usage and how an extremely local community of practice read the body.[189]

The Neolithic also sees the rise of rock art, something which will increase in subsequent periods. Although dating is a major headache for most bodies of prehistoric rock art (and we discuss megalithic art in Chapter 4 as it dates principally to later in the Neolithic), it is worth mentioning several art traditions here. At Porto Badisco in south-easternmost Italy (Figure 27a),[190] males are shown hunting deer, whereas women identified by a dot between their legs are depicted in a characteristic pose, perhaps dancing. 'Praying' figures with upraised arms are known in Neolithic tombs on Sardinia, as are ox-heads. In Iberia, 'macro-schematic' cave art also includes anthropomorphic 'praying' figures. The most remarkable and justly famous Neolithic art is Levantine cave art from Eastern Spain (Figure 27b).[191] Images of men hunting deer with bows are prominent; as at Porto Badisco, in a society whose subsistence was based mostly upon farming and herding, hunting is shown as an important male pursuit. Groups of probable women are shown dancing together. Levantine art also includes scenes of warfare between groups armed with bows and of herding and other varied activities; some figures wear elaborate costumes such as feathered headdresses, and in one scene, a probable woman is shown collecting honey while bees buzz around her. The body world shown in Levantine cave art is one in which gender is clearly enacted through specific activities, particularly hunting for males and probably ritual dancing for women, but in which people participate in a wide range of pursuits which cannot simply be reduced to gender or prestige; value has a performative aspect and derives from differentiated activities.

The Neolithic body world: Humans and difference

Body worlds are ways of understanding the body through diverse practices (see Chapter 2). As we noted previously, although these body worlds create coherent textures of experience, they are probably best thought of as repertoires upon which people could draw, rather than a systematic and homogeneous way of understanding the world.[192] The evidence for Neolithic bodies – reviewed summarily in an earlier section – lacks resolution, and there is much regional and chronological variation; the Neolithic picture looks clearest when contrasted broadly with Palaeolithic and later prehistoric (Chapter 4) ways of doing things. Nevertheless, we can rudimentarily outline some very broad elements of Neolithic European body worlds.

Bodies in space. The Neolithic introduced new relationships between bodies and places. If we were to plot Palaeolithic and Neolithic bodies moving through space, the latter would move along dramatically more limited and more formalized grooves. On the scale of landscapes, people were situated experientially within much narrower vistas, with more fixed places, routes and uses. Within these, there may well have been divergent male and female, senior and junior taskscapes based around potentially gender specific tasks like cattle herding, ritual, and the gathering of different raw materials. Aggregation into sometimes substantial and sometimes bounded villages[193] suggests the development of firm, stable insider-outsider distinctions based upon co-residence. Intergroup raiding suggests that hostility between such groups was not infrequent. Within communities, participation in collective projects such as village ditches and monuments defined identity through bodily work; yet constructed spaces such as houses, zones within houses, hearths and work areas also created a nested set of distinctions within village groups based upon access, movement and knowledge: working together, sharing shelter, sharing food and sharing rituals. Finally, burial added a time dimension to this fixity. Whereas foragers tended to dispose of the dead in ways that dissolved them into landscapes, Neolithic people increasingly used burial to create relations with specific places. Even when (as in Greece and Britain) most Neolithic dead were disposed of offsite in ways archaeologically invisible to us, such rites presumably took place within a much more circumscribed home territory than previously and a representative fraction of the dead's remains were retained for ritual use or to create highly visible monuments. Moreover, the point of

Neolithic burial was not preserving the memory of individuals; through varied practices – collective burial, casual disturbance of graves in villages, recovery and reuse of body parts – the dead were dissolved in the living area to give substance to history, and presenced in the form of generic, collective ancestral bodies.

Humans and animals. Neolithic representations emphasize the humanness of the human body. With a few exceptional examples,[194] there are very few human-animal hybrids in Neolithic art. Instead, there are far more human representations, proportionally speaking, than in Palaeolithic art, and animal images themselves are far less important. Presenting humans as a fixed category conceptually distanced from animals was not entirely new (as the Palaeolithic Venus figurines show), but it becomes by far the dominant imagery in the Neolithic. Burial evidence of potential human-animal fluidity (as in the Danish Mesolithic examples discussed earlier) is also generally absent. This shift probably relates to new economic practices which carried new 'rules of engagement'.[195] Among hunter-gatherers, wild animals are often thought of as independent beings, potentially peers, sentient beings or spirits, as co-species occupying a landscape together with humans. Among herders, domesticated animals may be cherished and cared for, but they are normally regarded as property. In the Neolithic, the animals with which people engaged most became objects of intimate care, control and exchange – a form of property which mediated relations between people and which created new, less egalitarian and less bridgeable divisions between people and animals.

Wild animals remained important in the Neolithic – providing an alternative mode for understanding animality and humanity – but generally for non-nutritional reasons: they were a resource for raw materials such as antler, fur and feathers, and for citation of colours and qualities such as wildness or danger. Hence hunting is represented in art as a prestigious male activity even in societies which rarely ate game and, in a Palaeolithic survival, wolf, fox and dog canine teeth continue to be used widely as ornaments.

People and things. During the Neolithic, people created and used an unprecedented amount of material things. The sea of material extensions and environments through which the body swam grew larger, richer and more structured. New technologies, particularly clay, provided new metaphors for understanding and representing the body. New genres of things provided new arenas for cultivating and displaying bodily skill and defining people in terms of skilled bodies – an opportunity clearly exploited in the plethora of ostentatiously skilful Neolithic things. Moreover, the social body was created and transformed through assembling things such as ornaments, clothing, and bodily decorations.[196] In cases such as habitually worn shell rings and permanent modifications to the body, much as for our wedding rings, haircuts and dental implants today, it is impossible to draw a clear boundary between 'the body' and its 'things'.[197] Instead, we have bodies created through the assembly of disparate elements, each originating in different social relations, bearing its own qualities and stories and making its own contribution to the whole person. As an ensemble, Neolithic material culture illustrates well the interdependence of things and the bodies using and created by them; the social creation of the body was invested in things to a greater degree than ever before.

The body's potential for difference. The symbolic context for the human body shifted decisively in the Neolithic, from landscape and animals to the bounded body, bounded spaces and social networks, and material things. This is a huge transition in human embodiment; in these qualities, the Neolithic set the tone for all later periods. It is important, however, to consider how the Neolithic was unique too. The overriding impression one gets of the Neolithic body is that what was crucial was its potential for difference. We see many ways in which bodies were differentiated, but (in contrast to later periods, see Chapter 4) these were not subordinated to an overriding social plan.

For example, gender is a baseline principle, clearly signified by a range of varied references: physiological references in figurines, gendered activities in rock art, and burial positions, and no doubt many gendered practices now inaccessible to us too. Gender, however, appears not to have been particularly highly politicized. For example, although weaponry and warfare were probably male things everywhere, we see no attempt in art, burial goods or material culture to suggest that to be a successful member of society in other contexts, a male had to excel as a warrior. Similarly, there are isolated but parallel examples of women dancing in rock art in southern Italy, the Alps and Spain, but this was not developed into a widespread regional symbolism, and there is no evident attempt to indicate the gender of isolated 'praying' figures. So gender was present and salient in all groups, but it was not viewed as relevant to many contexts. Gender is occasionally represented ambiguously. The most striking examples of these are figurines from both the Balkans and Italy, which (seen one way) depict an erect phallus atop two testicles and (seen another way) depict an extremely schematic female torso with large buttocks and a shaft-like torso.[198] Such occasional but undeniable examples of gender ambiguity do not imply that Neolithic people did not have stable, widely acknowledged gender definitions,

as has occasionally been suggested; but they do suggest that, in very particular contexts, such definitions became fluid, permeable or objects of play.

Likewise, many distinctions were marked on the body – appearances, qualities, abilities, ritual statuses, relations – but these distinctions do not seem to have been organized around specific, recurrent dimensions of social difference – there was no single costume of power, for example. Material culture is rife with demonstrations of remarkable skill, yet this effort was not harnessed to some rational economy of investment, some calculus of political advantage; these products were prized, but they were also created, used and disposed of by ordinary people in ordinary moments, not accumulated as social capital, or displayed as trophies. The point seems to have been simply to create the qualities they display and the kinds of person with the skills needed to create them. Likewise, although food had an important social role (food linked people and animals were social valuables), people could have produced far more than they actually did; there is little evidence for centralized storage, accumulation, intensification or redistribution, or for the harnessing of subsistence resources to any greater ambition. This suggests that the food producing economy was not strongly linked to a political economy which might have encouraged overproduction. There was warfare, often lethally, but there was no systematic politicization of warfare (for instance, through explicit depictions of violence or dominance, celebration of martiality in grave goods, the development of specialized weaponry distinct from tools or hunting gear, or a strategic choice of victims as opposed to indiscriminate raiding). Burial, likewise, shows little attention to individual status through grave goods or tomb architecture, which instead draw attention to ritual circumstances, communities and places.

What we get out of this discussion is mostly a texture of practice, a set of social reflexes. Juxtaposing all of these various realms of bodily discourse does not reveal a simplifying set of recurrent themes, an attempt to organize social value around a few central roles such as hierarchies. Instead, they were context-specific, leading to an overall impression of heterogeneity and fluidity. We see many different activities carried out with great skill and attention, but they occur in separate spheres; none are generalized to provide a central, dominant political identity.[199] It is heterarchical, in that it defies reduction to a single simple axis of comparison.[200] The Neolithic body, as it is presented to us through these activities, does not convey a single dominant plan or model; instead we see a context-specific body, an assemblage of citations suited for the purpose at hand. It is the body's potential for difference which is socially productive.

Multimodality in Neolithic body worlds: Constant, unremarkable difference

In Chapter 2, we introduced the concept of multimodality, an important theme in how body worlds are lived through and understood. This term captures the way in which there is never a single, unified concept of the body in play; instead, all societies have multiple modes of being, multiple kinds of bodies if you will, that emerge in different kinds of context. We have not discussed this much in our Palaeolithic examples. For this period, the data is limited by the patchiness of the evidence which is spread over thousands of years and kilometres; it is hard to tell whether apparent differences really existed within groups or are because of historical difference between groups. However, there are occasional hints of multimodal contrast. The most obvious example is the polarity between the unambiguously human figures of the Venus figurines that emphasize a stylized, normally faceless corporeality, the two-dimensional humans sketched upon bones and stones that emphasize the head and face in profile, and the fluid permeability between humans and animals suggested in other images and practices.

Different modes of understanding the human body are more clearly detectable during the Neolithic; here the evidence becomes more concentrated. Neolithic body worlds abound in contradictions. We have already mentioned the dual forms which human-animal relations took; whereas domestic animals were social valuables to be controlled, circulated and consumed, wild animals were principally sources of raw materials and symbolic resources. At the same time, domestic animals could also be understood as the corollaries of their human counterparts, their bodies mixed together in burials,[201] or used as metaphors for human kinship.[202] Human bodies belonged to bounded local communities within which their social identity was defined, but they were ornamented with traded objects crossing boundaries and incorporating the lure of the exotic. People killed each other in warfare, raiding and probably violence within groups, but fighting per se was not glorified in material culture, burial or art – a fact which gives rise to mistaken archaeological stereotypes about the 'peaceful Neolithic'. In other words, there were contexts in which the body's capacity to hurt and be hurt mattered, and others in which it did not. Art at Porto Badisco and the Spanish Levant suggests that hunting was a source of male power, but it was peripheral to villages where figurines suggest female-oriented forms of ritual value.

But the texture of multimodality is different than that seen in later periods; the contrast with the Bronze Age and particularly with the medieval period is great. Without a bodily logic centred around a few central values, multimodal contradictions do not seem to take the form of towering clashes of symbolism or moral wars. Rather than a hierarchy of perspectives as we see in the medieval period, for example, we are better off thinking of these differing perspectives as being in themselves heterarchical: locked into parallel ways of understanding the body.[203] Thus these different bodily logics are a constant, omnipresent low-level feature of life – a feature of a body world centred around the body's potential for difference. In Chapter 9, we return to the important issue of why the nature of multimodality itself changes in the different time periods we encounter.

Conclusion: The body in historical process

In this chapter, we have considered two of the classic 'revolutions' of human prehistory: the Upper Palaeolithic (sometimes heralded as the 'origins of cognition') and the Neolithic beginning of sedentary farming life. Both have rightly been critiqued as origin myths,[204] but they both capture important social transitions. Amongst both foragers and farmers, the limits of the body were not given but were defined and sustained through practice and ritual. We argue that both involve the rise of new forms of embodiment. It is not at all clear that Upper Palaeolithic foragers were the first hominids able to use language or think symbolically; what the archaeological record really shows us is humans thinking and acting systemically in an embodied way – ornamenting bodies, burying bodies, categorizing and representing bodies, relating bodies to animals and landscapes – for the first time. This was a world of fluid and mobile bodies that related to animals as co-species and had the potential at times to transform into them, a potential found not only in Palaeolithic art but in the fish/human boulders of Lepenski Vir, the statues of Göbekli Tepe, and the baby on a swan's wing at Vedbaek. An even broader range of embodied behaviours is evident in the Neolithic, which reveals a different approach to understanding the body. Neolithic people understood their bodies in less fluid ways, through the social relations they had with their communities. It was more often a relationship with place or with other people that was seen as constituting a body's edges.

Having split history into two structurally distinct ideal types – a classic way of rendering it impossible to explain – we must now briefly stitch them back together in some sort of historical process. We return to this theme in Chapter 9, but it is important to flag up a couple of points here – if only because we will encounter similar patterns at every point in this book.

First, although we have emphasized the disjuncture between the Palaeolithic and Mesolithic and the Neolithic, historically, most European farmers were descended directly from local foragers, and there are many cultural continuities – Palaeolithic antecedents for Neolithic practices and Neolithic persistences of Palaeolithic traditions. For examples, ochre and ornaments are used similarly throughout both periods, there were probably continuities in gender and, in cases such as Scandinavia, the transition between them was long and gradual, without any clear point of inflection. In fact, the multimodality of culture means that wild animals remained symbolically important in many Neolithic groups long after hunting lost its economic centrality and most human-animal relations were redefined in completely different ways.

Secondly, this chapter provides a classic example of scale effects (see Chapter 2) – a picture of change which looks clear and distinct when seen at the largest scale looks blurry and patchy when we look close up at individual pixels. For example, there are always discrepancies between a homogenized picture drawn across Europe and a particular case: foragers may be sedentary or use pottery, or farmers may remain largely mobile or persist in creating human/animal hybrids. Is this a problem? If we view history as a Newtonian clockwork mechanism with a functional or deterministic logic, such slippages between scales mean we have either drawn our generalizations wrong or collected our data incorrectly. But history is not a clockwork mechanism turning out rigid stereotypes. To a more thoughtful reading, the play between large-scale patterns and such 'discrepancies' are actually informative about how historical processes unfold. They tell us, for instance, that although we can define general historical tendencies, what happens in a given situation reflects local contingencies rather non-deterministically. Moreover, the relationships underlying these general tendencies are not tight functional determinisms but elective affinities. For example, in both Neolithic groups and foragers such as Natufians and in the Danube Gorges, sedentism often seems to launch a decisive change in how the body in death is used to relate people to places. Yet this is not a universal either/or relationship – not all sedentary farmers used burial in this way, and mobile peoples sometimes used burial to establish similar meanings. Similarly, in Europe, the adoption of domesticated animals coincides neatly with the replacement of human-animal hybrid images by human images, yet this shift in imagery happens in the Near East several millennia before the first domesticated sheep or goat. It is history not running in narrow grooves but unfolding in elastic, fuzzy envelopes of possibility.

Finally, the temptation in narratives like this is see 'hard' factors such as technology and economy driving cultural change. This is all the more so for change between periods that have been defined basically by their economies; disciplinary narrative traditions urge us irresistibly to make up stories in which 'farming caused the Neolithic body'. We should resist this tendency. Theoretically, this reifies 'technology' and 'economy' as standing outside social life and prior to it. But technology and economy are social, and because the body is the medium of social life, technology and economy cannot be logically prior to the body. Instead, technology is embodied (see also Chapters 2 and 8). The transition to the Neolithic affords a concrete example of this. If we ascribe changes in beliefs about the body to sedentism or farming, we then have to answer the question: why did foragers decide to become sedentary farmers? It is hard, however, to answer this question without involving embodied logics and landscapes of action.

We can demonstrate this using both modes of looking at causality proposed in the preceding chapter. In a 'contingent causation' view, the world is seen as a network of relations, each of which contributes to structuring the others at each point in time. Hence the future results from the ensemble of relations in the present – an array of relations to which the body is fundamental. For example, in asking how economic changes related to understandings of the human body, we have black-boxed 'economy' and 'the body' as bounded, distinct known quantities; we assume that 'the body' is constant in all ways except those which are proposed as potential effects of change and we assume that these potential effects of change do not simultaneously feed back reciprocally into the proposed causes of change. But this assumption is probably false. Many aspects of economic practice would have changed the body and how it was understood. The 'Neolithic demographic transition' is an obvious example; though archaeologists and demographers tend to regard such things as abstract population models, we are talking about women's and men's reproductive biographies, life risks, and potential breadth and depth of social relations through children and marriage partners.[205] New forms of gendered labour (such as herding or making pottery) and new gendered spaces would have been another, redefining how often and in what roles people encountered others. Redefining group identity based upon a shared commitment to living in the same place, and symbolising it through manipulation of the dead would have been another, with more fixed and salient insider-outsider distinctions and with deeper, more relevant group histories. And once such changes were in motion, they became part of the landscape of action structuring future pathways.[206]

For instance, some groups may have adopted sedentism and domesticates for social reasons, triggering a demographic shift which then made use of such new resources obligatory. Similarly, a sense of crowding in the landscape would not have been based upon gardening, for which plentiful land was available, but upon probably male-oriented forms of action such as pastoralism and hunting; hence economic models of Neolithic expansion which are based upon a sense of space would have had a gender dimension as well. Likewise, redefining the body in such a way as to tie it to local landscapes and groups formed the precondition for many important Neolithic institutions such as long-distance trade networks. As such 'unintended consequences of the body' show, it is difficult to distinguish external causes affecting the body, as the forms of action through which such causes act are themselves embodied. It is never safe to black-box the body!

The other way to approach causality is to devise traditional explanatory narratives which ascribe causation to particular factors rather than diffusing it generally throughout a network of circumstances – but to do so free from preconceptions about how social life must be structured. For example, in the European Neolithic, human-animal hybrids in representation tend to be replaced by images firmly foregrounding a bounded human body at about the same time as people start herding domesticated animals. It is straightforward to regard this as a functional compatibility: when animals became property of humans, they ceased being potential peers and transformations. But in the history of the Neolithic transition as a whole, such functional compatibilities tend to be assembled gradually and elastically, and the fact that they exist at one point does not necessarily tell us how they arose in earlier periods. Thus we begin to see a symbolic focus upon the bounded human body in Natufian figurines and burials, long before the first sheep or goat was domesticated in the Near East. If there is any causal lesson to be learned, it has to be that redefining the symbolic boundaries between human and animal bodies formed a precondition for the domestication of animals, not the reverse. So did shifts in body symbolism trigger the Neolithic? Perhaps. The elasticity of this narrative, however, is clear: whilst the human body became an increasing *matter of concern*[207] through the Natufian, the PPNA and the PPNB, so the relations between human and animal bodies came under scrutiny on the pillars of Göbekli Tepe and the walls of Çatalhöyük. Perhaps Lepenski Vir illustrates a complementary scenario, that of foragers who (like the Natufians) became sedentary, but (unlike the Natufians) held firmly to a forager view of a fluidly transformable living world, and in consequence resisted the encroachment of the farming world even as they were increasingly circumscribed and undergoing parallel changes to it. Whereas at Lepenski Vir humans and fish could transform into one another, the stelae at Göbekli and the murals at Çatalhöyük contrast the relationship between humans and animals, which may have embodied similar qualities but were now demonstrably different things. In both cases, even as other causal forces are at play, understandings of the body form an essential condition of how change unfolds. The body is a generator of historical process.

NOTES

1. At the start of each of our case-study chapters, we include a short bibliographic footnote to give the reader a sense of the key literature on the field. The material covered in this chapter falls between several literatures, which reflect the conceptual partitioning of the field. The study of the body in archaeology has become increasingly popular in the last two decades, emerging out of a combination of interests in post-structuralism (Fowler 2000; Nordbladh and Yates 1990; Thomas 2002) with the influence of Foucault particularly notable, gender and feminism (Gilchrist 1999) and phenomenology (Tilley 1994; Tilley 2008; Thomas 2002). These studies have explored the body both as a symbolic medium for social display and expression and via more experiential accounts of embodiment (Borić and Robb 2008; Hamilakis, Pluciennik, and Tarlow 2002; Houston, Stuart, and Taube 2006; Meskell and Joyce 2003; Perry and Joyce 2001). They range across case studies from the old world and the new, bridging topics such as the Classic Maya and Ancient Egypt, Neolithic Europe and Bronze Age rock art. Joyce (2005) provides a relatively recent and useful summary. Most of these accounts tend to deal with the description and interpretation of a particular aspect of a body world, as we would term it, and rarely engaged in how that body world came to be.

   For the debate on 'cognitive evolution' and the Middle to Upper Palaeolithic transition in Europe, see Mellars and Stringer (1989), and the more recent Mellars et al. (2007), Mithen (1996) and Zilhão (2007). For French and Spanish Palaeolithic art, the best general handbook remains Ucko and Rosenfeld (1967), although this predates the spectacular discovery at Chauvet; see Chauvet, Brunel Deschamps and Hillaire (1996). And see Lewis-Williams (2002) for a popular, if disputed, interpretation. The evidence for Palaeolithic burial has recently been synthesised by Pettitt (2011). For the general archaeology of the Palaeolithic, see Gamble (1999); and for the Mesolithic, see Bailey and Spikens (2008) and two recent collections of papers (Larsson et al. 2003; McCartan et al. 2009). There is a huge literature on the Mesolithic-Neolithic transition in Europe. For general models, see the arguments by Rowley-Conwy (2011) and Robb (in press

b) for differing positions. Bailey, Whittle and Cummings (2005), Finlayson and Warren (2010); Price (2000); and Whittle and Cummings (2007), offer edited volumes with more detailed studies. For the Near East, see Hodder (2006), Simmons (2007) and other papers in Finlayson and Warren (2010). The archaeology of the body in the Neolithic Near East has recently been reanalysed by Croucher (2012). For the Iron Gates, see Borić (2002; 2005a; 2005b; 2011). The best single authored overview of the European Neolithic is undoubtedly Whittle (1996); but see also Whittle (2003). Finally, the most theoretically provocative work on the body in all the periods covered by this chapter is Gamble (2007).

2. Albrethsen and Brinch Petersen 1976; Nilsson Stutz 2003.

3. For a more detailed take on the chronology of this period see Roebroeks et al. (2000).

4. Bailey 2008; Bailey and Spikins 2008.

5. cf. Gamble 2007.

6. Of course, there are real differences between the Mesolithic and the Palaeolithic (not least in the environments they explored and exploited), and authors such as Zvelebil (2009) have argued powerfully for a consideration of the Mesolithic on its own terms. At the scale at which we are working, however, there are clear continuities between the two periods, including commonalities of forager lifeways and understandings of human bodies.

7. Pettitt 2011.

8. e.g. Mellars and Stringer 1989; Mithen 1996.

9. e.g. Heidegger 1962; Merleau-Ponty 1962.

10. e.g. Ingold 2000, chapter 21.

11. e.g. Clark 1997.

12. Sofaer 2006.

13. Ingold 2000.

14. It is important as well to note that even where evidence is lacking for the kinds of body world we see in the Upper Palaeolithic and Mesolithic, this does not necessarily imply the absence of these kinds of engagement (cf. McBrearty 2007).

15. As Clive Gamble (2007) has so clearly demonstrated, this transition can be seen not as a revolution but as part of a long-term directional change in how humans understood their world and their bodies. His account takes an even deeper temporal perspective than ours, and where we differ in interpretation in places we have been inspired by his challenging and stimulating account.

16. Brody 1997; Ingold 2000; Myers 1986.

17. Sofaer 2006.

18. Cohen and Armelagos 1984. In discussing the shape of the body in this chapter and the next, but not in later ones, we do not mean to imply a categorical difference between our bodies and their bodies, nor between the bodies of historical periods and those of prehistoric ones. Instead, the different kinds of evidence from prehistory mean we need to draw on all the strands of evidence available to us when considering the body.

19. Gamble 1999, 356.

20. Gamble 1999.

21. Svoboda, Lozek, and Vleck 1996, 218.

22. Delson et al. 2000.

23. Soffer et al. 1997.

24. Gamble 1999, 370.

25. Gamble 1999, 288.

26. Leroi-Gourhan 1993.

27. Grimm 2000; Roux, Bril, and Dietrich 1995.

28. Mussi 2000, 361.

29. Gamble 1999, 334. In an excellent account of materials and their properties in the Upper Palaeolithic, Chantal Conneller (2011, 45) points out that Aurignacian beads made from stone and ivory were produced in the same manner even when this meant that the materials became much harder to work. It would have been simpler to make the beads differently out of ivory but people actively chose not to do so: there were set bodily movements when it came to the making of particular kinds of beads.

30. Sinclair 1995.

31. Dobres 2000.

32. White 1993.

33. It is worth noting that there are no known burials that date to the earliest part of the Upper Palaeolithic prior to this point (Pettitt 2011).

34. Vanhaeren and d'Errico 2005; see also Gamble 2007, 144–150.

35. Gamble 2007, 146.

36. Gamble 1999, 405; Oliva 2000.

37. Gamble 1999; Klíma 1988; Svoboda, Lozek, and Vleck 1996.

38. Gamble 2007, 197.

39. e.g. Peresani et al. 2011.

40. e.g. Vanhaeren and d'Errico 2005.

41. We will see how metals too became incorporated in surfacing the body in Chapter 4.

42. Conneller 2011; Ingold 2007; White 1997, 95.

43. Fowler 2004a.

44. Without wishing to suppress the differences between Palaeolithic and Mesolithic, as discussed in an earlier endnote, we do argue there is enough similarity to draw on shared concepts around the human body, as revealed in this example.

45. Conneller (2004) draws inspiration from understandings of perspectivism common in North and South America that we touched on in the last chapter (see Ingold 2000; Viveiros de Castro 1998). Rather than hold that the physical body is fixed whilst culture is malleable, Mesolithic people might have understood culture as fixed whilst nature itself was changeable. This in turn allows the body to transform itself, to reveal its inner deer-ness, by wearing particular kinds of masks.

46. Pettitt 2011.

47. Pettitt 2011, 38.

48. Aldhouse-Green and Pettitt 1998; Oliva 2000; Pettitt 2011; Svoboda, Lozek, and Vleck 1996.

49. Formicola and Buzhilova 2004.

50. Svoboda, Lozek, and Vleck 1996; Svoboda et al. 2000.

51. Gamble 1999, 409; Klíma 1988, 834. Such disabilities in persons who were buried as whole bodies may not be unusual – it also applied to the burial at Brno II in Moravia (Oliva 2000) and some of the Italian sites.

52. Pettitt 2011, 211–214.

53. Gamble 1999; Spikins 2008.

54. Mussi 2000.

55. Rowley-Conwy 2001, 51.

56. Pettitt et al. 2003.

57. Harris 2009; Jones 2007.

58. Pettitt 2011, 14.

59. Gamble 2007.

60. Pettitt 2011.

61. See Conneller (2005) for discussion of the British evidence for example.

62. This burial is made up of the fragmentary skeleton of a child and a complete adult female. This latter individual suffered from various pathologies, including ones that would have potentially affected her behaviour in life (Porr and Alt 2006). The grave goods are quite extraordinary and include fifty pendants made from animal teeth, a polished stone axe and the long bone of a crane used as a case for thirty-one well-made microliths (Porr and Alt 2006, 396).

63. Mellars and Stringer 1989; Zilhão 2007.

64. Rice 1981.

65. McDermott 1996.

66. Leroi-Gourhan 1968.

67. Fiedorczuk et al. 2007.

68. Soffer et al. 1993; Vandiver et al. 1989.

69. Soffer et al. 1993.

70. Clottes 2000; but see also Pettitt and Bahn 2003.

71. Sieveking 1979.

72. Mithen 1990.

73. Lewis-Williams 2002 and see the following discussion.

74. Morley 2007.

75. Mussi, Cinq-Mars, and Bolduc 2000.

76. Lewis-Williams and Clottes 1998.

77. Borić 2007. Like the example of Conneller's (2004) study of the Star Carr deer frontlets we touched on earlier, these studies too have been influenced by perspectivism.

78. Srejović 1972; Borić 2005a.

79. Borić 2005a.

80. Pettitt 2011.

81. Zilhão et al. 2010.

82. Thomas 1996.

83. Ingold 1999, 406.

84. cf. Barrett 1994.

85. Not surprisingly, when the two systems collided as Europeans began to colonize the globe, colonial governments typically tried to control mobile foragers by making them settle down and adopt a single, fixed identity.

86. Ingold 2000, 71.

87. Ingold 2000, 423; Vilaça 2005; Viveiros de Castro 1998.

88. Ingold 2000, Chapter 4.

89. Ingold 2000, 71, original emphasis.

90. Ingold 2000, 112.

91. Mussi, Cinq-Mars, and Bolduc 2000, 110–112.

92. cf. Conneller 2004; Borić 2005a; 2007.

93. Albrethsen and Brinch Petersen 1976; Brinch Petersen and Meikeljohn 2003; Larsson 1989.

94. Nilsson Stutz 2003.

95. Nilsson Stutz 2003, 173.

96. Nilsson Stutz 2003, 310.

97. Fowler 2004a.

98. Fowler 2004a; Larsson 1993.

99. Fowler 2004a.

100. Albrethsen and Brinch Petersen 1976, 8–9.

101. Fowler 2004a, 144.

102. Bonsall 2008, 238.

103. Borić 2005a.

104. Borić, Raičević, and Stefanović 2009.

105. Radovanović 1997.

106. Cristiani and Borić 2012.

107. Borić and Stefanović 2004.

108. Borić 2005a.

109. Borić 2010.

110. Borić 2005a, 59.

111. Borić 2005a.

112. Borić 2002; 2005b; Tringham 2000; cf. Bonsall 2008.

113. Borić 2011.

114. Cummings and Harris 2011; Robb and Miracle 2007; Rowley-Conwy 2004; 2011.

115. Gamble 2007.

116. e.g. Childe 1942.

117. Cauvin 2000; Hodder 1990; 2006; Renfrew 2007.

118. Ingold 2000, 61.

119. Boyd 2002.

120. Gamble 2007, 267; Tilley 1999.

121. Boyd 2005; 2006; Rowley-Conwy 2001.

122. Boyd 2006, 173.

123. Byrd and Monahan 1995.

124. Grosman, Munro, and Belfer-Cohen 2008.

125. Boyd 2002; Boyd 2006, 174.

126. Bar-Yosef 1998.

127. Kuijt 1996.

128. Cauvin 2000.

129. cf. Croucher 2011; Hodder and Meskell 2011; Schmidt 2003; 2004; 2006.

130. Miracle and Borić 2008.

131. Goring-Morris and Horwitz 2007.

132. Cessford 2005; Hodder 2006; Hodder and Cessford 2004; Hodder and Meskell 2011.

133. Kuijt 2008.

134. Croucher 2010; 2011; Verhoeven 2002.

135. Hodder and Meskell 2011.

136. Rollefson 1983; 1986; 1998.

137. Though see Verhoeven 2002, 338 for two examples from Nevali Cori.

138. Hodder 2006; cf. Borić 2007.

139. cf. Hodder and Meskell 2011.
140. Cummings and Harris 2011; Robb and Miracle 2007; Thomas 2007; Whittle and Cummings 2007.
141. Angel 1984; Meiklejohn et al. 1984; Mummert et al. 2011; Robb 1994.
142. Canci, Minozzi, and Tarli 1996; Hershkovitz et al. 2008; Mummert et al. 2011.
143. Bocquet-Appel 2002; 2009; Bocquet-Appel and Bar-Yosef 2008; Bocquet-Appel and Dubouloz 2004.
144. e.g. Hedges, Saville, and O'Connell 2008; Jackes, Lubell, and Meiklejohn 1997; Lightfoot et al. 2011; Richards 2000.
145. Different Neolithic groups may also have modelled their understandings of kinship on those that existed between their cattle herds (e.g. Ray and Thomas 2003), and on occasions created contexts in which cattle and humans became equivalent (see Harris 2011 for a discussion of one such moment).
146. Robb 2007.
147. Marciniak 2005; Robb 2007; Russell 1998.
148. Gamble 2007; Hodder 2006; Renfrew 2007.
149. Borić 2008, 121.
150. It is an interesting aside (although one we do not have the space to explore here), whether those areas where clay was used solely for pottery and not for figurines (e.g. Mesolithic Ertebølle groups in Scandinavia and Neolithic groups in Britain) had different conceptions of the body as a result.
151. With obvious exceptions, e.g. Ingold 2000.
152. Robb 2007, chapter 5.
153. Borić 2009.
154. Chapman 2000; Chapman and Gaydarska 2006.
155. Hofmann and Whittle 2008.
156. Robb 1997.
157. Bennike 1985.
158. Mallegni and Fornaciari 1980.
159. Borić 2008; Halstead 1999; Souvatzi 2008.
160. Stevanovic 1997.
161. Robb 2007.
162. This represents the upper limit of the size of these houses. Even an average longhouse would still have been a substantial 20 meters in length, however.
163. Bickle 2009; Bradley 2002; Whittle 2003.
164. Dixon 1988.
165. Whittle 2003.
166. Sommer 2001.
167. Schulting and Fibiger 2011.
168. Sommer 2001.
169. Pavuk 1972.
170. Hofmann and Whittle 2008.
171. Orschiedt and Haidle 2006. A recent alternative interpretation views Herxheim as an episode of mass cannibalism (Boulestin et al. 2009).
172. Borić in press; Hofmann and Whittle 2008.
173. Midgley 2008.
174. Fowler 2004a.
175. Harris 2009; McFadyen 2007.
176. Fowler 2004c; 2010; Whittle, Healy, and Bayliss 2011.
177. Fowler 2010; Schulting and Wysocki 2005.
178. Fowler 2010.
179. Whittle 2003.
180. Borić, in press.
181. Whittle 1996, 243.
182. Borić 2010; Forty and Küchler 1999; Harris in press; Rowlands 1999.
183. Bailey 2005; Beihl 2006; Chapman and Gaydarska 2006; Talalay 1993.
184. Male figurines dominate at some exceptional sites, as in the recent excavations at Pavlovac-Cukar in Serbia by one of us (DB).
185. Meskell 1995; Tringham and Conkey 1998.
186. Bailey 2005.
187. Robb in press a.
188. Fugazzola Delpino and Tinè 2003; Holmes and Whitehouse 1998; Robb 2007.
189. Wenger 1998.
190. Graziosi 1974; 1980.
191. Fairén-Jiménez, in press.
192. Bourdieu 1977; Thomas 1996.
193. Or, in other parts of Europe, the construction of enclosures where such gatherings could happen at particular times.
194. Hofmann and Whittle 2008; and further recent discoveries by one of us (DB) at the Serbian site of Pavlovac-Cukar.
195. Ingold 2000, 75.
196. This in itself was not entirely new, of course, but was built on and expanded a range of existing practices that had existed in the Palaeolithic and Mesolithic as we emphasize later in the chapter.
197. cf. Webmoor and Witmore 2008.
198. Bailey 2005; Holmes and Whitehouse 1998.
199. In this respect, it was probably similar to the "Great Man" societies described ethnographically in some areas of Melanesia (Godelier 1986). In such societies, people can gain prestige from a wide range of activities – gardening, hunting, warfare, oratory, ritual, exchange – but such forms of prestige are structurally separate and not convertible into each other or into some generalised sense of leadership; being a prominent orator or trader does not imply or require outstanding leadership in war ritual, and so on.
200. Crumley, Ehrenreich, and Levy 1995.
201. For examples in post LBK groups in Central Europe see Hofmann and Whittle (2008); for the Neolithic Balkans see Borić (in press); for interesting human and animal combinations at one site in Britain see Harris (2011).
202. Ray and Thomas 2003.
203. Harris and Robb 2012.
204. Gamble 2007.
205. Collard et al. 2010; Bocquet-Appel and Bar-Yosef 2008.
206. Robb in press b.
207. sensu Latour 2005.

4

The body in its social context

*Oliver J. T. Harris, Katharina Rebay-Salisbury,
John Robb and Marie Louise Stig Sørensen*

Reassembling the ashes[1]

A wooded clearing by a stream on the edge of the endless plain, two days journey from the still snowy Alps (Plate II). The woman had died of an illness which struck in the treacherous first cold days of spring. Her body had been laid alone in her small house for two days while preparations were made for the burial and neighbours gathered; the family, afraid of death, had moved into a neighbour's hut. Now it was time for the burning. All seven families from the hamlet were there – about fifty people, many of them children, all related in some way. There had been considerable discussion about whether to burn her body or to simply bury it. Burning it was a lot more work, but was considered fitting for somebody well-loved, somebody you would miss, one of the adults everybody turned to for help or care. Nowadays, almost all adults were burned when they died. She had come to the group from another village to the west where fewer people were burnt at death. Some people felt she should be buried like her own people, but she had lived here amongst them so long that it was decided to burn her.

First her closest family dressed her, with clothes and pins on her, bracelets on her arm. They placed the shining things they had given her over the years on her body, repeating the acts of respect and affection; nobody could doubt that she was an important woman and one of them. Meanwhile, others collected a large heap of wood. Then they laid her atop the pyre and lit it.

The burning had been done at night, the body crackling and hissing atop a pyre as tall as a man, the flames and sparks shooting high into the darkness. Then people ate, drank, and slept. Now it was time to lay her out in the way she would be remembered. Two or three elders gave directions, partly unheeded; the visitors from her birth village sang a mournful song on the side-lines. A

few adults picked her bones up amongst the cold ashes, picking out the longer shafts, bits of the spine, and the flat fragments of the skull and pelvis and laying them out in the outline of a body. Then at last they covered over the burnt ashes with a low mound, just as one would fill in a grave.

This vignette, this single moment from Bronze Age Austria around the middle of the second millennium BC, goes straight to the heart of major issues in prehistoric body worlds. Burying the dead individually with sets of things adorning the body and defining its gender and status was infrequent before the late Neolithic, except in unusual cases such as the LBK;[2] it became a common Bronze Age pattern. As we discuss in this chapter, this new way of treating the body in death was organically related to concepts about the body in life. It grew out of new ways in which the body grounded social relations. Later European prehistory is extraordinarily full of bodies – lived, buried, represented – and the same shift is visible in other media. For example, as a rough generalization, Neolithic body representations vary immensely between and within local traditions. They can be clearly gendered, as in the figurines shown in the previous chapter, or they can be ambiguous. They exaggerate or make invisible different parts of the body. They do not commonly link the body with other symbols; when they do, it may be in one-off, difficult to interpret ways. Britain gives an extreme example of the body's potential for difference. Aside from Late Neolithic chalk and flint phalli and the unique Folkton 'drums', only six Neolithic human representations are known. Small as this group is, no two items are the same. The group includes one potentially female figurine made of sandstone, one clay figurine whose gender is not clearly indicated, one stone figurine again without clear attribution of gender, one possible male figurine again made of clay, one wooden statue which is thought to have been enhanced by a detachable penis, and one hermaphroditic wooden sculpture (Figure 28).[3] The latter has been discussed as a ceremonial object, an incidental sculpture or a toy, but it clearly left the archaeologist who published it deeply puzzled, commenting:

if a toy, it was for a rather strange child by our standards[4]

In contrast, from about the mid-third millennium onwards, depictions of the body in Europe become increasingly standardized (see Figure 33). They coalesce around two repetitive clusters of symbols which are readily interpretable. What the body was about snaps into focus much more clearly, through a logic of symbols which has remained familiar to us from the Bronze Age onwards. These images, clearly gendered and indicating status like modern dolls and action figures, are the kind one might give to a 'normal' child!

The first part of this chapter outlines the major shift in body worlds between the earlier Neolithic and the Bronze Age – a shift which happened haltingly, raggedly, yet decisively across Europe between about 3500 BC and about 2000 BC. This grand shift in prehistoric culture is particularly fascinating because it happened without major economic reorganization and long before most of the factors usually proposed as causes for changing beliefs existed: not only literacy, science, and organized religion, but also any real large-scale or centralized social organization such as states or empires to which we might plausibly ascribe large-scale change. Thus the spotlight is really focused narrowly upon the most fundamental locus of change: the body in its social context.

Our Bronze Age cremation stands not only as a general example of life after this transition, but it also has important lessons to teach us about how the process of change unfolds. Archaeologists normally contrast cremation and inhumation as opposed practices. These villagers, living in the foothills of Austria in the Middle Bronze Age, did not know it, but they stood on the cusp of a huge transition. Behind them lay many millennia of burying people in graves; after them, for at least half a millennium, most of Europe cremated their dead. Seen from afar, the Bronze Age transition from inhumation to cremation is a stark change. Yet seen close up, the transition is anything but sudden: the people gathered in this clearing combined both rites for three or four generations as part of a normal way of life. Moreover, they did not make the shift to cremation as part of a grand ideological renewal, religious conversion or political evolution; it seems to have happened purely through local tinkering with ritual. The same tinkering sometimes resulted in baroque involutions such as putting the body back together for burial after it has been cremated. Such paradoxical rites are logical, but only within an understanding of the body far more complex than archaeologists usually allow prehistoric people to have had.

Thus our second theme, which we turn to at the end of the chapter, is scale and the process of change. How does the larger context give people the tools for thinking their way through on-the-ground situations such as burying a dead relative? Conversely, how does action on the small scale result in change on the large scale? We explore this through the transition from inhumation to cremation.

Figure 28. The Neolithic body's potential for difference is well-illustrated by British Neolithic bodies: there are only six representations known, five of which are illustrated here, but they nevertheless manage to illustrate heterogeneous gender symbolisms. Compare these with the far more homogenous examples from Europe in the third millennium BC in Figure 33. A and B Figurines from Links of Noltland, Orkney (© Historic Scotland). C. Figurine from Ness of Brodgar, Orkney (© ORCA, photograph courtesy of Nick Card). D. The Dagenham 'idol', Essex (© Colchester and Ipswich Museum Service). E. The Sweet Track 'god-dolly', Somerset (© Cambridge University Museum of Archaeology and Anthropology).

The big change in middle prehistory: Europe between 3500 BC and 1500 BC

At the end of Chapter 3, we left our story around 5000 BC, with the establishment of Neolithic farming villages throughout much of Europe, a development not so much narrowly economic as broadly social and cultural. It was accompanied by wide-ranging changes in how the body was understood. In most abstract terms, the shift was from more fluid bodies to more fixed ones. The line between humans and animals came to be drawn more rigidly; practices of nourishment, spatial intimacy and work became more routinized through institutions (such as the village); and the village dead were used to fix the relations between particular landscapes and communities.

By and large, these features will characterize European societies through the rest of prehistory. Yet many other things changed. At different times and different places between about 3500 BC and 1500 BC, European society changed dramatically: across the continent, one kind of prehistoric world gave way to another. We will explore many of these changes in this chapter (and see Table 4 and Table 5), but in brief:

- In many places, landscapes dominated by villages or hamlets evolved into ones dominated by burial sites ('landscapes of the dead' as they have sometimes been termed).
- Burial traditions began to include formal burial places set apart from settlements, often with collective tombs; considerably later, burials begin to have more elaborate, gendered grave goods which present status kits for particular identities.
- Settlement is extended to new areas such as high mountains and small offshore islands, which may indicate more extensive herding as a way of using ecologically different places.
- In economic production, horses, wheeled vehicles (such as carts) and ploughs become widespread features of life, and economic systems may include more extensive herding for wool and milk production.
- Metals – first copper, then bronze – become a widespread technology, first supplementing and eventually largely supplanting flint tools. New trade systems arise to circulate metals and metal objects. In many areas, there is an increasing emphasis upon visually gleaming pottery surfaces.

Archaeologists have long noted these changes in the character of society. For much of the twentieth century, the standard explanation was that invading peoples (often 'Indo-Europeans' from the Russian steppes) overturned a Neolithic social order.[5] The invading-hordes scenario, however, does not fit the evidence well. In most places, there is much more evidence of cultural continuity than of replacement, and change occurs in several moments of overlapping, partial shift, not as an instant wholesale substitution. Nor does the invasion model make much sense theoretically; it relies upon static, essentialized views of fixed ethnic identities, and once we give up nineteenth century romantic ideas of prehistoric ethnic groups filled with insatiable wanderlust, it lacks any real reason why large-scale migrations might have taken place.[6]

In the 1970s and 1980s, archaeologists tried determinedly to map these changes on to a steady increase in inequality or 'social complexity', but this does not fit any better. For much of Europe, there is little evidence for systematic, entrenched social inequality until almost the dawn of the historic period; rather than a 'rise of inequality', we are witnessing shifts amongst different ways of organizing more or less egalitarian societies.[7]

The last generation has seen a sturdy crop of alternative views, particularly within Anglophone archaeology where general models are favoured. This change has been seen as a shift from restricted horticultural economies to expanded pastoral economies,[8] from 'group-oriented' to 'individualizing' chiefdoms,[9] from a society regulated by ritual to one regulated by prestige competition,[10] from a 'corporate' to a 'network' political leadership strategy, and from a social world organized around generic ancestors to one anchored in specific genealogies.[11] Most recently, it has been seen as a period where ambitious individuals traversed wide distances across Europe to generate new sources of power and legitimation.[12] The last two decades of research have focused upon filling in or critiquing these general models. All of these capture elements of the change in some places and at some moments, but none really apply to the full panorama of change.

The body lies at the heart of these transformations. Without claiming to explain all social shifts in Europe between 3500 BC and 1500 BC, we argue that a central feature of this change was formulating new linkages between the body, social identity and politics.

A brief orientation in prehistory

As we summarize change across several thousand years and an entire continent, a chronological framework is useful. The archaeological terminology is confusing enough in itself, as it often changes with national borders and archaeological traditions. Table 3 gives an approximate outline; our focus is particularly the period between the Late Neolithic and the Middle Bronze Age.

Beyond questions of terminology, the structure of social history in this period itself is anything but orderly. People living in small, decentralized groups across the forests, mountains and plains of Europe reformulated novel ways of life generation after generation, and the transition we address did not happen in any centralized or systematic way. In fact, this makes it all the more remarkable that broad changes should emerge from the ferment of local innovation across Europe. We summarize the most salient changes and events in Table 4 (see also Figure 29).

This serves, however, mostly to underline the complexity of the process of change. Anywhere in Europe, life at 1500 BC was radically different than it had been 2,000 years earlier. Europeans held many things in common at 3500 BC, as part of a recognizably European Neolithic

Table 3. *Chronological framework for later European prehistory*

	Balkans and Central Mediterranean	Eastern, Central, Western Europe	Britain, Scandinavia
6500–6000 BC	Mesolithic/Early Neolithic	Mesolithic	Mesolithic
6000–5500 BC	Neolithic	Mesolithic	Mesolithic
5500–4500 BC	Middle Neolithic	Mesolithic/Neolithic	Mesolithic
4500–4000 BC	Middle-Late Neolithic	Middle Neolithic	Mesolithic
4000–3500 BC	Late Neolithic	Middle Neolithic	Earlier Neolithic
3500–3000 BC	Copper Age or Early Bronze Age	Middle-Late Neolithic	Middle Neolithic
3000–2500 BC	Copper Age or Early Bronze Age	Late Neolithic	Later Neolithic
2500–2000 BC	Early Bronze Age	Early Bronze Age	Later Neolithic/Early Bronze Age
2000–1500 BC	Middle Bronze Age	Early-Middle Bronze Age	Early-Middle Bronze Age
1500–1000 BC	Late Bronze Age	Middle-Late Bronze Age	Middle-Late Bronze Age
1000–500 BC	Iron Age/Classical	Late Bronze Age/Iron Age	Late Bronze Age/Iron Age
500–0 BC	Classical	Iron Age/Classical	Iron Age

Table 4. *Chronology and social developments in later prehistoric Europe*

6500–4000 BC	Transition to farming begins ca. 6500 BC in south-eastern Europe, moves slowly west and northwards, and reaches Britain and Scandinavia by about 4000 BC (Chapter 3).
4500–2400 BC	People begin to build megalithic structures containing collective burials – the earliest appear in western France and Iberia after 4500 BC, in Britain and Ireland after 4000 BC, and in northern Europe, Scandinavia, the Alps and the Central Mediterranean by 3500 BC. Pockets of megalith-building flourish in many areas until around 2000 BC.
Early-mid-fourth millennium BC	First experiments with metals (principally copper) in most areas of Balkans and Mediterranean; common uses are pins, pendants and axes.
3300–2000 BC	A series of new groups arises in which people are buried individually in single graves with kits of personal goods and drinking vessels: the Globular Amphora groups in East-Central Europe (3300–2800 BC), the Corded Ware and Single Grave groups in Eastern and Central Europe and Scandinavia (3000–2400 BC), and the Bell Beakers in Central and Western Europe (2400–2000 BC).
Ca. 3300–3000 BC	The 'Ice Man' lives and dies in Alpine valleys along the Italian-Austrian border.
Late fourth millennium – early third millennium BC	First widespread use of metals (principally copper) in most areas north of Alps; common items are pins, pendants, daggers and axes.
Ca. 3000–2000 BC	Rise of stone statue-stelae (life-sized human statues) which are found in about a dozen local traditions across Europe from Spain to the Ukraine; most traditions go out of use by 2000 BC.
Ca. 2000–1800 BC	Transition to expanded metallurgy based on bronze in most areas, with expanded range of objects including short swords and occasionally armour.
2000–1200 BC	Palace societies (Minoan and Mycenaean) arise in the Aegean and in Near Eastern urban groups.
From 2000 BC	Widespread tradition of large Bronze Age cemeteries of status-coded individual burials, often with barrows (mounds) over graves; occasional lavish burials such as Leubingen (Germany) and Bush Barrow (England) show political use of display.
1600 BC	Cremation increasingly replaces inhumation as a burial rite, particularly in Central Europe.
1300–800 BC	'Urnfields' – cemeteries of individual cremations buried in pottery urns – become the standard burial rite throughout Central Europe, with cremation widely practised in other regions too.
800 BC	Formation of Greek city-states in Aegean area (Chapter 5).
800 BC	Increasing interaction between Europe and Mediterranean urban, literate societies, first via Greek traders and colonists in Italy, France and the Black Sea, then via Roman trade and conquest (Chapter 5).

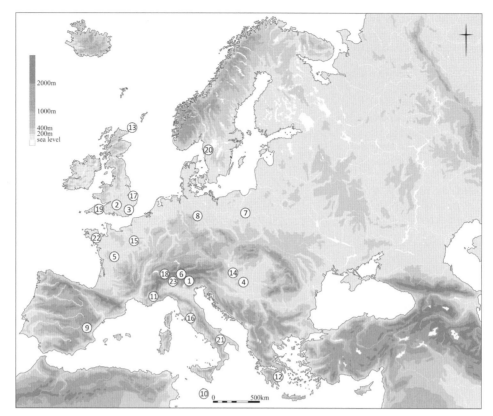

1. Alto Adige, 2. Bush Barrow, Hazleton, 3. Dagenham, 4. Encrusted Ware, Füzesabony, Vatya groups, 5. Grand-Pressigny, 6. Hauslobjoch (Ice Man), 7. Łeki Małe, 8. Leubingen, Nebra, 9. Levantine art, 10. Malta, 11. Mount Bego, 12. Mycenae, 13. Orkney, 14. Pitten, 15. Raget, 16. Rinaldone, 17. Seahenge, 18. Sion, 19. Sweet Track, 20. Tanum, 21. Toppo Daguzzo, 22. Tressé, 23. Valcamonica

Figure 29. Map of sites mentioned in Chapter 4.

world, just as they held many things in common at 1500 BC as part of a recognizably European Bronze Age counterpart. But it does *not* follow that European culture was homogeneous at either moment, or for that matter at any other point. In fact, the changes in Table 4 happened in different times and different combinations in different places. Nor does it follow that there was only one path by which people got from the Neolithic to the Bronze Age; without going into the complexities of prehistoric social history, this is demonstrably false. Comparing Europe at 3500 BC with Europe at 1500 BC is much like comparing Europe between 600 AD and 1400 AD, or between 1700 AD and 1900 AD. In each interval, groups of people moved about, innovations in political order were made, economic practices changed, and new beliefs were propagated. But all of these things happened in continuous, gradual sequences of change, and none of them suffices to describe, much less explain, the cultural differences between post-Roman Europe and high medieval Europe, or between Enlightenment Europe and industrialized Europe. Similarly, what we see in middle

prehistory is a qualitative change from one kind of prehistoric world to a very different one.

Living and dying, 3500 BC to 1500 BC

So how did conceptions of the body itself change through these transformations? In this section, we look at four aspects of embodiment and how they changed between 3500 BC and 1500 BC – the treatment of the body in death, the invention of weapons as gendered prosthetics and symbols, the use of metals to complete and ornament the body, and the way the body was represented in art.

Deathways

Megaliths, memory and place: The monumentalization of the landscape

Burial and landscape are good places to start. As we saw in Chapter 3, for most of Neolithic Europe until around 4000 BC, most people lived in a landscape defined by settlements – tells, ditched villages and clusters of longhouses. It is more difficult to generalize about burial. Earlier Neolithic burial practices are sometimes represented as consisting mostly of simple individual burials – a picture derived principally from the LBK cemeteries. Yet, as discussed in Chapter 3, the picture across Europe is far more varied. Even within the LBK there were many other ways of treating the dead,[13] and there are well-investigated areas such as Greece where we remain unable to say how most people were disposed of at death. It is easier to generalize about what deathways were not about. They were not monumental; there is almost no attempt before 4500 BC to presence the dead visibly in the landscape, and it does not even begin to become commonplace until after 4000 BC. Nor were burials about celebrating individual status, about commemorating prominent individuals and perpetuating their memory.[14] Instead, the intention seems generally to have been to let the remains of the dead return to the landscape and village in which they lived, to weave the biographical time and memory of the individual life back into the longer history of the group.

After about 4000 BC, burial changes in many places. The most visible feature is the rise of cemeteries standing apart from settlements. In many landscapes throughout Europe, villages become archaeologically much less visible, and the human landscape was defined in terms of the dead – so much so that many archaeological groups in this period are defined by burial sites. Many such cemeteries throughout the Mediterranean involve collective burials in rock-cut tombs or caves.

For most of Western Europe, this shift involves megaliths (Figure 30) – chambered tombs built of massive stone slabs and usually covered by a stone or earth mound (in some areas, timber or earthen tomb chambers were built and covered by a mound; the effect was much the same). Megaliths are found earliest in western France from about 4500 BC;[15] they spread much more widely after about 4000 BC, and reach their maximum extent between about 3500 BC and 2500 BC.[16] Megalithic tomb-building spans both areas which had already been Neolithic for a long time, such as Germany, Iberia and most of France, and areas which were just experiencing the Neolithic transition, such as Denmark, Sweden, Britain, Ireland, and western France. Archaeologists have often equated megalithic and collective tombs with new ways of

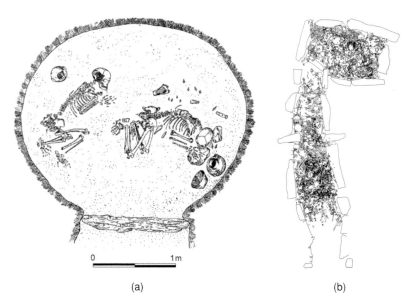

(a)   (b)

Figure 30. Fourth millennium BC burials. A. Collective rock-cut tomb, Rinaldone group, Central Italy (Miari 1995; reproduced with kind permission of Monica Miari). B. Megalithic chambered tomb, Hazleton North, England, south chamber (after Saville, Hall and Hoyle 1990, fig. 105, © English Heritage).

merging the bodily substance and identities of the dead. Many traditional accounts have seen them as places where bodies, already exposed to the elements and broken up, were taken to be deposited. From this perspective, the tomb represents solely the mixing of anonymous ancestors, in contrast to a perceived emphasis on single burial previously and later in Europe. Yet this misreads the nature of the change. Collective tombs do not necessarily involve the intentional mixture of individual bodies after prior excarnation, secondary deposition of bodies previously buried elsewhere or other practices. Where there has been careful analysis of burial practices inside collective tombs,[17] it is often clear that most or all people buried in tombs were deposited as complete bodies one by one as they died; their bones were subsequently disturbed and mixed when later bodies were deposited,[18] though on many occasions this may have been done in a deliberate and purposeful manner and involved some organization of the now disarticulated human remains. This is not radically different from previous burial practices in many areas. Moreover, there is accumulating evidence for alternative practices such as secondary burials and keeping and circulating selected bones of the dead in the kinds of groups we focused on in the second part of Chapter 3; groups that were Neolithic, in other words, but did not build megaliths.[19] Both before and after the construction of megaliths, it is clear that the human body in death, and most likely in life, was not clearly bounded, but rather something that incorporated multiple substances throughout life, and gave up many of these substances to be manipulated upon death.

The real change marked by megaliths has to do not with the body of the dead but with landscapes. In many areas of Europe, settlement becomes much more elusive after this point. This was probably associated with changes in how the landscape was used economically. New areas such as uplands were exploited, probably for more intensive pastoralism; spindle whorls (stone or clay weights used in spinning wool or linen fibres into thread) become common finds, suggesting that textiles became more common and culturally important. This extension of the economy in turn may have meant that people identified themselves with a broader landscape and social network rather than with a particular village or house. Hence, usually for the first time, cemeteries become prominent. The real point of the shift to megalithic tombs and free-standing cemeteries was to provide a new kind of highly visible, well-remembered anchor for the social landscape.[20]

A new emphasis upon visible burial places distinct from settlements is only part of the monumentalization of the landscape seen throughout Europe from the end of the fifth millennium BC onwards.[21] This is the period in which we begin to see labour committed to investing the landscape with historical significance through other means, particularly non-funerary ritual monuments such as the megalithic 'temples' of Malta,[22] rock art[23] and statue-stelae,[24] monumental human sculptures in stone which themselves often stood at burial-related sites (see the following discussion). To the extent that such monumentalization involved ideas about the human body, it may have revolved around isomorphisms equating stone, as a material, with the enduring ancestral substance of humans. Such a metaphorical equation would make stone particularly appropriate for death-related constructions.[25]

The third millennium BC: Single burials with a status kit
A second wave of change – one far more significant for the history of the body – happened 500 to 1,000 years later. It happened patchily, not consistently throughout Europe, but by about 2000 BC the general nature of burial had shifted. This change is detectable in the rise of burials with kits of grave goods expressing the personal identity of the deceased. In much of Europe, this development establishes what burial is about in a way which endures through the Iron Age and up to the end of prehistory.

The *locus classicus* to observe this shift archaeologically is in a series of groups living across northern Europe. These begin in the last few centuries of the fourth millennium BC in Poland and adjacent areas with the so-called Globular Amphora group. These groups

are known from cemeteries of single burials which are accompanied by repetitive combinations of grave goods including jugs and drinking vessels, weapons and ornaments. A few centuries later, in the early third millennium BC, with the 'Corded Ware' group, very similar burials extend westwards as far as Switzerland and France,[26] and the 'Single Grave' or 'Battle Axe' groups represent a Baltic version. The last such group, the 'Bell Beaker' culture, occurs from around 2400 BC and is found through Central and Western Europe, from Hungary to Spain and from Scandinavia to Sicily. The Bell Beakers usually straddle the threshold between the Neolithic or Copper Age and the Early Bronze Age. Bell Beakers largely occur within pre-existing communities and pottery traditions, and all three archaeological phenomena represent local adoption of widely shared things and practices rather than representing immigrant groups as was once thought.[27]

The transition represented by these groups is basically a change in burial treatment; it is no coincidence that archaeologists have named all of these groups after their most typical grave goods. But the transition was not a shift to single burial per se. As we have seen, single burial was already commonly practiced in megalithic collective tombs before the Corded Ware or Beakers showed up.[28] Moreover, across Europe, it was very common for Corded Ware and Beaker people to bury their dead by inserting them into earlier collective tombs.[29] And throughout Mediterranean Europe, from Cyprus to Spain, the kind of identity-signalling grave goods which typify Corded Ware or Beaker burials were found from about the mid-fourth millennium BC accompanying burials within traditional Copper Age collective tombs.[30]

The real point of these developments is that, for the first time, burial was used to emphasize the personal identity of the deceased rather than some other aspect of his or her death. Moreover, this identity was constructed or signalled through a consistent assemblage of material things which made the point that the dead had been, and perhaps continued to be, a particular kind of person. Finally, although we do not mean to imply that treatment of death necessarily summed up all aspects of someone's identity, it remains inescapable that only a restricted and stereotyped range of personas are represented in death.

Between about 3500 BC and 1500 BC, people were buried with three principal kinds of items. The first is pottery vessels. These are not a random selection of the vessels people used in everyday life, instead they usually included flasks, bowls and drinking vessels such as the Beakers themselves, which typically held 0.5–1 litre and were highly decorated.[31] These coherent sets of particular

Figure 31. Assemblage of material culture associated with 'Battle Axe' group grave, Denmark (© National Museum of Denmark).

kinds of pots refer to specific contexts, above all to conviviality or commensality, eating and drinking together as a way of forming social bonds amongst a group of equals. Secondly, both men and women were buried with ornaments, including pins, bracelets, beads (probably strung on necklaces) and buttons. These could be made of metal, stone such as jet, or bone; in many places obtaining them would have required participation in long-distance exchange networks. Such items suggest a newly heightened concern with appearance and with displaying objects which enhance or distinguish a particular body. Finally, people were buried with weaponry. Although one could argue that, in some cases, axes and small copper, bronze or stone knives were general-purpose tools rather than weapons, the same cannot be argued for the specialized battle-axes found in Baltic Europe (Figure 31), the elaborately flaked flint daggers found in Iberia, Italy, France and Scandinavia, and the arrow points and archers' wristguards found with many Beaker burials.

What kind of social persona do these items help create? Grave goods have little reference to most activities of daily life such as making things, farming, cooking or taking care of animals. These activities were important but not part of the specific persona referred to in burial. (We discuss weapons and gender later in this chapter.) Archaeologists have discussed single burials with grave goods in terms of the 'rise of the individual'[32] – ironically so, given how stereotyped and un-individual the identities involved seem to have been.[33] Even though such display often involved exotic materials and had an inherent potential for competition, it was not about wealth or political exclusion per se; the grave goods rarely include anything which probably would have been out of the economic reach of most adults within the group, and

the range of variation in grave goods is usually small. If they were competing, they were (in Shennan's happy phrase) 'competing for parity'.[34] But this kind of political display established a basis for the display of inequality later in the Bronze Age. The display of political status in Bronze Age burial treatment ranged from relatively modest local leadership[35] to the burial of lavish wealth beneath a massive tumulus[36] (as at Leubingen, Germany, Łęki Małe in Poland, the Bush Barrow in Wessex, England, and Toppo Daguzzo in Italy; in Greece the Shaft Graves representing the earliest phase at Mycenae are clearly part of this pattern). But such burial ostentation was often surprisingly unaccompanied by a similar level of inequality in life, and it is clear that hierarchical political structures tended to be fragile and short-lived.[37] The more general message about politics and the body to be read from these burials is the emergence of a sense of political personhood so enduring across contexts that it was important to endow the dead with it, and this personhood was created or expressed through bodily display and bodily practices such as drinking. The body in death displayed the relations from which it was constituted, the connections its material extensions embodied and its links to other people, places and worlds.[38]

Representations: The emergence of a standard body

In this new order of things, what happens to the human body conceptually? Fortunately, we have a great deal of Late Neolithic, Copper and Bronze Age prehistoric art to help answer this question.

The most obvious change is a wholesale shift in genres. The small clay figurines which typified the Balkan and Central Mediterranean Neolithic generally vanish along with the tradition of village life they formed part of. Interestingly, all the exceptions occur along the southern fringe of Europe: Cyprus, the Aegean islands, Malta, Sardinia and southern Iberia. In parallel independent developments, most of these exceptions combine a survival of the Neolithic-figurine emphasis on the female form with third millennium BC developments in material and style, notably a move towards larger sculpture, often in stone rather than clay, and increased schematism. But elsewhere in Europe, it is at least two millennia until small human figurines re-emerge, and when they do, they are typically in a completely different medium and with different themes – often small bronze male figures, perhaps warriors as in the Sardinian *bronzetti*,[39] or males, females, animals and chariots as in the Danish late Bronze Age site of Fårdal.[40]

Instead, in the fourth millennium BC, there are two new genres of landscape-oriented art: rock art (Table 5)

Table 5. *Sets of representations including anthropomorphic images in prehistoric European rock art and megalithic art. (Note that dates are approximate as rock art is often difficult to date; table omits art in northern Scandinavia and Russia primarily made by hunter-gatherers)*[41]

	Region	Dominant themes
5000–4000 BC	Porto Badisco, Italy	Hunting (males), female figures, handprints
	Levantine cave art, Spain	Hunting, dancing, fighting, varied human activities, animals
	Breton megalithic tombs	Geometrical motifs, axes, cattle horns, possibly female anthropomorphic beings
4000–3000 BC	Macro-schematic cave art, Spain	Human figures (sometimes elongated or distorted), animals
	Paris Basin, France	Female figures
	Sardinian Neolithic tombs	Cattle horns
3000–2000 BC	Valcamonica, Italy	Daggers, deer, human figures, spirals
2000–1000 BC	Mount Bego, France	Male figures, oxen, ploughing, weapons
	Southern Scandinavia	Cosmological scenes, boats, males, weapons, animals
1000–0 BC	Valcamonica, Italy	Geometric motifs, warrior figures, hunting scenes

and statue-stelae. Rock art occurs in open-air sites and caves, and in megalithic tombs (Figure 32). Most rock art in all contexts consists of simple geometric or abstract motifs such as circles, crosses or spirals, but a fair amount of it, outside of places like Britain and Ireland, is representational. Unlike Palaeolithic rock art, the human figure is more prominent and is almost always clearly recognizable as human, even when very schematic. Although rock art is notoriously hard to accurately date, we can outline a very general evolution. Before about 3000 BC, when males are depicted, they are generally hunting; the bow is the weapon of choice. When females are depicted, they may be dancing. Simple insect-like anthropomorphic figures (sometimes erroneously called 'oranti' or 'praying' figures) without a clear gender reference are also known. In Breton tombs, a highly schematic anthropomorphic image, perhaps female, is sometimes placed in the back wall of a tomb's main chamber, and third millennium BC tombs in the Paris Basin and Brittany are occasionally adorned with pairs of breasts combined with what appear to be necklaces.[42]

During the third millennium BC, weapons enter the repertory – for example daggers and halberds[43] – in Alpine rock art. Axes are known at Breton tombs such as Gavrinis, and recent laser-scanning of Stonehenge shows that some of the standing stones there were also decorated with daggers and axes. These are often shown as free-standing images, but when they are associated with a gendered human figure, it is usually male. Slightly later, at Mount Bego, France, weaponry and oxen are major themes of masculinity. Again, throughout southern Scandinavia, masculinity is a major theme in Bronze Age rock art, associated with boats, weapons and animals. Scandinavian rock art shows armed warriors on foot, on horseback, in boats and in combat with each other. Designs on Scandinavian metalwork portray warriors.[44]

New forms of small bronze statues on Sardinia similarly show armed males. Although identifiable female figures are not entirely absent, they are much less common than earlier in prehistory.

The other new genre is the statue-stela (Figure 33). Statue-stelae are roughly life-sized statues of people; made of flattish, often squared slabs, they sometimes look rather like large stone playing cards.[45] They mostly date to between 3000 BC and 2000 BC, with a few corpora continuing after this. Statue-stelae appear across Europe from the Ukraine to Iberia; there are about a dozen major concentrations of them in Spain, southern France, Switzerland, Italy and the Ukraine, with isolated examples in Germany, Hungary and other countries.[46] There are hints that similar representations may have been made of wood elsewhere. They typically depict both males and females, with schematic indications of faces, a few body features, and occasionally dress. Statue-stelae are often found in groups or alignments, either in open country or at burial sites; they are not found on habitation sites. They were generally found at sites associated with death. In some places, such as the Ukraine and Switzerland,[47] they marked graves; in other places, such as at Osimo-Anvòia in Valcamonica,[48] they created places where rites of ancestral veneration took place.[49] They thus form part of the general pattern of presencing the ancestral dead in the landscape particularly through stone installations.

In terms of gender imagery, statue-stelae echo the symbols seen in rock art of the same period. Aside from occasional depictions of clothing, they normally show little detail aside from basic gender markers. Stelae consistently portray two distinct categories, figures with weapons and figures with breasts and often necklaces; these presumably indicate males and females. This dualism confirms that this opposition furnished a major gender diacritic across Europe in this period. They

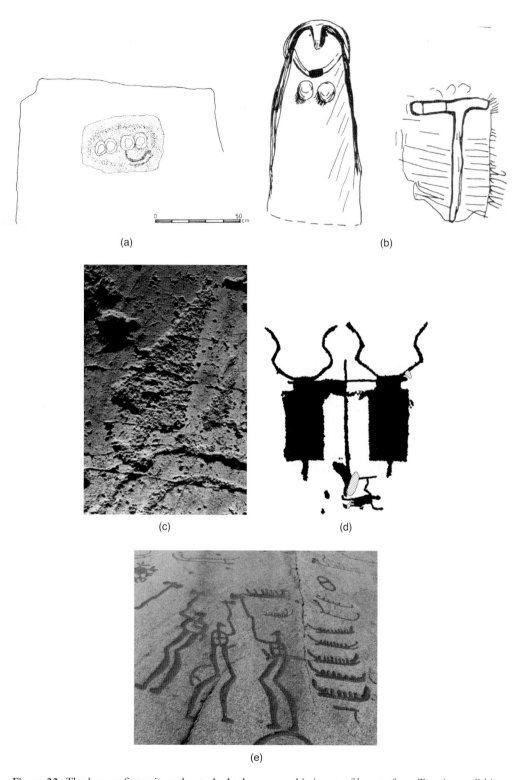

Figure 32. The human figure in rock art. A. Anthropomorphic image of breasts from Tressé megalithic tomb, Brittany (Shee Twohig 1981, fig. 149; reproduced with kind permission of Elizabeth Shee Twohig and Oxford University Press). B. Female imagery from Razet 28, megalithic tomb in the Paris Basin, France (Shee Twohig 1981, fig. 195, reproduced with kind permission of Elizabeth Shee Twohig and Oxford University Press). C. Weaponry from Valcamonica, Italy (photo courtesy of Hamish Park). D. Ploughing at Mount Bego, France (After De Lumley 1976: fig. 72; redrawn by Vicki Herring). E. Males, weapons and boats at Tanum, Sweden (photo: Harris).

represent personhood distilled to simpler, more widespread and standardized categories than before.

Statue-stelae are important to our story here not only for *what* they represent but also for *how* it is represented: their style and medium encode central concepts of the body. Aesthetically, statue-stelae treat the body differently from earlier figurines in two key ways. First, unlike the irregular three-dimensionality of figurines, the only departures from rigidly flat surfaces are the bas-relief details needed to convey formulaic identities. By flattening the body and reducing it to a tabular slab, they emphasize its surface over its interior substance or corporeality, which is no longer of interest. In effect, they reduce the three-dimensional, dynamic living body to a two-dimensional static surface for display. In this, they are entirely consonant with the new emphasis upon the performance of identity through display of key social icons, as we saw with the burials from this period. Secondly, in earlier body representations such as figurines, there is no consistent formula or template for representing the body. In the choice of body parts represented or omitted, in how divisions of the body are made, in the degree of stylization, each site or group is different. In contrast, statue-stelae across Europe share a formulaic layout.[50] The body is positioned rigidly standing straight with the arms at the sides, divided into either two zones (head and body) or three (head, torso and lower body distinguished by a horizontally drawn beltline). The face consists of a 'T' shaped brow and nose, rarely with any other detail. The upper body is the site of gender and social distinction, the lower body is an unornamented null zone (Plate VIe). Importantly, whereas Neolithic figurines tend to be an assemblage of parts deemed relevant to the purpose at hand, statue-stelae are designed according to a unifying template which subordinates the parts to a whole. Again, this suggests the emergence of a widely-shared standard body.[51]

Inventing weapons: Gender, violence, things and the body

Gender was surely important in the Neolithic, but the archaeological evidence is surprisingly mute or ambiguous about how it was experienced or symbolized – in other words, how a body that had the capability to display gender was made into a gendered body. This changed dramatically in the third millennium BC, in large part because of the new practice of placing grave goods relating to personal identity and new developments in artistic representations, both discussed previously. But earlier people could have placed grave goods and represented gendered bodies too; the fact that this new evidence exists tells us about a new social salience of gender.

From about 3000 BC onwards, the male object par excellence was the weapon. We need to resist the temptation to see this as obvious, natural or universal in any way. Weapons have a surprisingly intricate prehistory. The starting point is the observation that violence is a constant: Europeans have been killing and hurting each other throughout prehistory and history. However, this does not require the development of specialized tools whose exclusive purpose is violence. As noted earlier, Neolithic violence was relatively common, but it seems to have been carried out with general-purpose implements such as axes, also used for wood-working, and bows and arrows, also used for hunting.[52] Until about 3000 BC, there is nothing in the archaeology of Europe that we can identify as a specialized weapon for use on people.

The situation changes after 3000 BC. Three specialized tools of violence appear: battle-axes, daggers and halberds (Figure 34). It is likely that the late Neolithic and Copper Age stone axes with shaft-holes found across Europe were often intended specifically to be weapons, as the perforation for the shaft might weaken the axe too much for repeated high force work such as wood-cutting. This is generally acknowledged for the finely carved 'battle-axes' well known from the Baltic in the third millennium BC, which were often deposited in male graves and which often show no visible signs of use-wear. Daggers are another third-millennium BC invention. For northern Italy and Alpine areas, the so-called Remedello dagger featured a triangular copper blade with a rib down the middle. Copper daggers are known from other areas of Europe as well. Flint daggers are particularly common in Northern Europe, where they largely replace axes in later third millennium burials. The most famous of these are from southern Scandinavia, where they represent the apogee of skilled Holocene flintworking. Flint daggers, however, are also known widely from Central Europe to Spain and Italy; in some cases they are clearly intended to imitate metal daggers, but in other cases they are simply exceptionally long, thin flint blades, possibly with a preference for yellowish flint such as that from the Grand-Pressigny mines in France. When they can be associated with genders (as in burial) they are almost always associated with males. Their exquisite craftsmanship, particularly in later phases, probably made them traded status objects, and they were certainly preserved and curated on many occasions.[53] The final weapon was the halberd. Halberds – found mostly in the Alps and Southern Scandinavia and the United Kingdom and Ireland – consisted of metal or stone blades affixed crosswise to the end of a long pole. The pole does not survive archaeologically, but images of halberds in French Early Bronze Age rock art suggest how they were used. In addition to these clear-cut weapons, we also have the elaboration of hunting

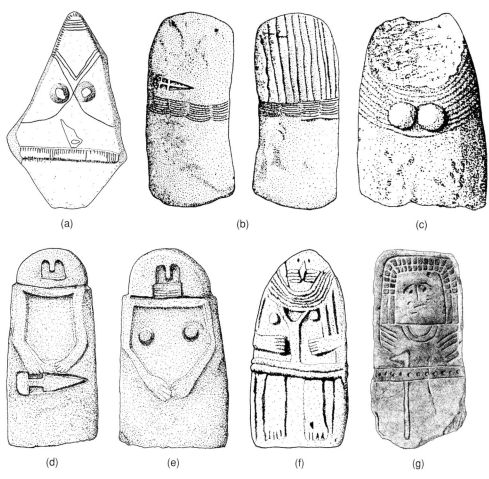

(a)   (b)   (c)

(d)   (e)   (f)   (g)

Figure 33. Statue-stelae. A. Southern Italy (female). B. Alto Adige (male). C. Alto Adige (female). D. Lunigiana (male). E. Lunigiana (female) F. Southern France (female). G. Spain (male). All images from Robb 2009a.

technology, in the form of bows and arrows. Bows had been used throughout the Neolithic for hunting and fighting, but in the fourth and third millennia BC their technology undergoes elaboration and specialization, not only in groups new to farming but also in long established agricultural communities.[54] For the first time, arrowheads – specialized flint objects rather than generic flakes or blade segments – are found. These appear from 4000 BC in Britain, in the form of leaf-shaped arrowheads, but reach their apogee in the oblique and barbed and tanged examples from the third millennium BC. These arrowheads were flaked with the same highly skilled bifacial pressure-flaking technique as daggers, a demanding way of shaping flint which had not been used since the Ice Age Solutrean style more than ten millennia earlier and which seems to have been used only for daggers, knives, arrowheads, and sickles in some Scandinavian areas.[55]

The fascinating thing about this new technology of violence is that it was not necessarily about hurting people effectively and efficiently. It was about the person the weapons were attached to. Several lines of evidence underline this. We have already mentioned how

weapons provided a diacritic marker of male gender in art. We have also seen how weapons are common male grave goods wherever single burials allow us to see associations between grave goods and gender. The most curious flourish on this story concerns the Bell Beaker version of the metal knife. Archers' wristguards and arrowheads are commonly found as grave goods in Bell Beaker graves, and they are almost always associated with male skeletons – the bow is clearly the 'male' artefact of violence here.[56] In some Beaker groups, however, bronze 'daggers' are surprisingly small and non-descript items, often less than 10 cm long. They are found with both male and female burials. In subsequent periods of the Early Bronze Age, when bronze knives speciated into several distinct forms, including knives, daggers and short swords, swords and halberds become found only with males.[57] The implication is not that weapons were buried with females as well as males, but that these bronze items were considered general-purpose knives used by both genders; when they developed into specialized weaponry, they also became restricted to men. Weapons thus evolved by several routes; in the third millennium BC, daggers

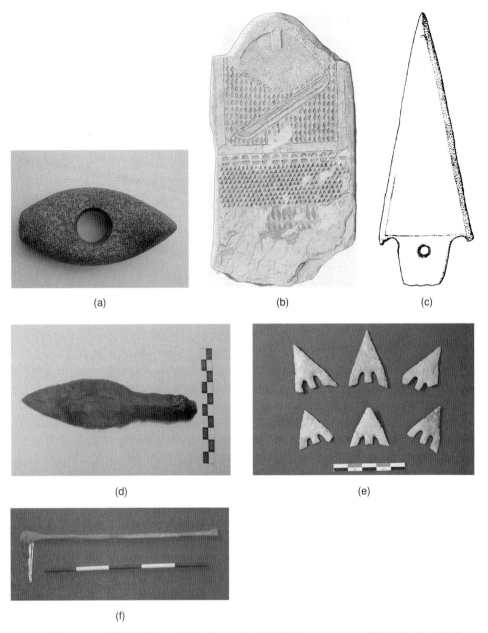

Figure 34. Weapons, 3000–2000 BC. A. Battle-axe, Scotland (photo courtesy of Chris Fowler). B. Statue-stela with bow, Sion, Switzerland (Gallay 1995, fig. 11; reproduced with kind permission of Alain Gallay). C. Copper Remedello dagger, Italy (Aranguran 2006; reproduced with kind permission of Biancamaria Aranguren). D. Flint dagger, Denmark (© Trustees of the British Museum). E. Barbed and tanged flint arrowheads (© Trustees of the British Museum). F. A reconstruction of an Irish Type Cotton Halberd (photo courtesy of Ronan O'Flaherty).

were prominent in some areas, and bows and axes in others, and metals began as small knives before branching out into specialized forms such as swords in the Early Bronze Age. By the Early Bronze Age, however, specialized, male-oriented tools of violence were common over most of Europe (Plate VIg).

Technologically, it was the *idea* of the dagger which was important, more than its *use*. The elaborately knapped flint daggers, found from Scandinavia[58] to the Mediterranean, show no sign that they were regarded as an inferior substitute to their bronze counterparts.[59]

Moreover, it is not clear how functional early metal blades were, particularly before harder tin bronzes came into use.[60] Thin copper blades may have bent easily with any determined thrust, and their riveted mounting upon a handle would have been a weak point. All weapons were potentially used, and some daggers in various areas of Europe do show evidence for re-sharpening,[61] but this use may not have been frequent or intense. Although it is not uncommon to find arrow points lodged in human skeletons[62] (one is lodged in Ötzi, the Alpine Ice Man), many battle-axes and flint daggers found in burials show

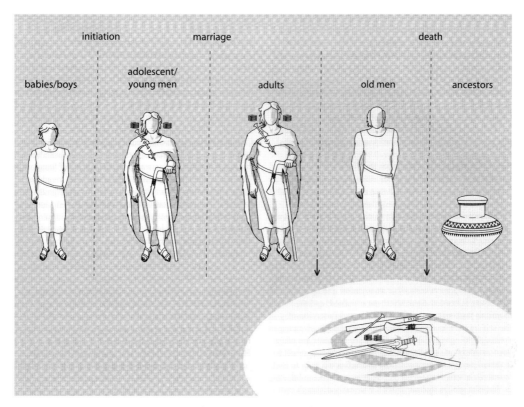

Figure 35. Weapons in the life cycle of males (Fontijn 2002, fig. 11.3, reproduced with kind permission of David Fontijn and the Faculty of Archaeology, University of Leiden).

no damage from use. Whilst there is variation in this pattern, a recent study of use-wear in Italian Copper Age objects concluded that copper axes were used for practical tasks as well as being potential instruments of violence, but that there was little use-wear on daggers; copper halberds were probably used only in ceremonial duelling between pairs of fighters.[63] The capacity for violence expressed by weapons may have been largely dramatic and metaphorical; actual levels of violence or warfare were not necessarily higher than in earlier periods.

Another expression of the capacity for violence may have been hunting, which experiences a resurgence in places in the fourth and third millennia BC (both as a prestigious male activity and in some areas as a food source), and is clearly linked to the emergence of the highly specialized arrowheads mentioned earlier.[64] Hunting was sufficiently prestigious that at the mid-third millennium BC henge monument of Durrington Walls in southern England, domestic pigs were killed by being shot with arrows.[65] Hardly efficient, such actions would have been part of a display of skill associated with the feast, emphasizing the regard hunting was held in.

Given the heavy symbolic emphasis upon displaying weapons, it is perhaps more accurate to regard weapons – particularly daggers, battle-axes and halberds – essentially as male jewellery. In much of Europe, weapons spent far more time being worked, exchanged, carried, and worn

in important social settings than in actually being used to harm other people. Violence is part of hexis, habituated gestures which express the social person.[66] As a symbolism, weaponry highlighted the readiness for violence, probably with connotations of defending the social group and one's rights. As such, the dagger was not a static icon but part of a habitus, a set of social reflexes which must be continually performed to be maintained and recognized. The dagger was thus a commitment to the responsibility to act with a certain aggression in appropriate circumstances. New weapons would also require the body to be trained and conditioned in different ways. The new weaponry changed the style of fighting. Rather than killing either close-up with clubs or axes, presumably in hit-and-run raids, or long-distance with arrows, fighting with short swords became close-up and face-to-face. As Harding argues, it seems clear that a new model of close-range fighting with swords became increasingly highly thought of through the Bronze Age, caught up in questions of status and prestige.[67] The short length of swords helped keep combat close; and the result was a contrived, dramatic situation of personal danger and courage, an opportunity to construct martial values in practice.[68]

Once weapons existed, they took on aesthetic, political and economic roles in the persona of the warlike male. Weaponry helped construct male appearances (Figure 35). At least some weaponry and armour, particularly thin sheet bronze items, may have been too fragile or too valuable to actually defend the body;[69] their role may have been to display wealth, the ability to command craftwork, and exotic connections in a visually striking way.[70] Some celebrated Bronze Age items underline this graphically; the famous Mycenaean boars' tusk helmets basically clothe the warrior in headgear made up entirely from painstakingly accumulated hunting trophies. Small personal cosmetic items such as razors, tweezers and ear-scoops were sometimes particularly associated with men, suggesting at times a concern for cultivating and celebrating the 'warrior's beauty'.[71] Weapons as artefacts had their own life-cycles. Whereas many metal weapons, including many swords,[72] were working weapons, some, particularly fine ones, were probably also inalienable possessions,[73] regarded almost as persons; some may have even been named. Such weapons probably had histories which would have been remembered and recounted, and making them, using them, obtaining them via patronage, trade, gift or inheritance, and depositing them would have been notable events.[74] Such events interlaced with the life-cycles of their owners, marking the passage of a male through boyhood, manhood, old age and death.[75]

Finally, weapons existed in an economic context. When social inequality developed, one way it was expressed was through weaponry. Some archaeologists have seen warrior aristocracies as a key feature of the very late Bronze Age and Iron Age.[76] In this model, metalwork functioned as a form of capital, to be controlled by leaders and monopolized and redistributed amongst clients as a motivational system. It is uncertain, however, how widely such a model applies to prehistoric Europe, which lacks clear evidence of systematic social inequality. Nonetheless it is clear that as weaponry developed into more elaborate forms through the Bronze Age, it allowed expression of social distinctions. Where males had 'competed for parity' through the presence of a simple dagger or bow, by the end of the Bronze Age in many areas, they could compete for distinction through a panoply of sword, spears, archery gear, helmet, corselet, greaves, shield and toilet articles.

The emergence of the warrior as a celebrated person is a widely discussed feature of the later Bronze Age, as much a hallmark of this period as the emergence of clergy in the early Christian period or the emergence of scientists in the Early Modern period.[77] Metalwork was thus fundamental to what Hanks terms 'the materiality of the warrior'[78] (Figure 36). All this leads to a somewhat counter-intuitive conclusion. The suite of weapons developed in the third millennium BC – which, with spears (another Bronze Age invention) were the ancestors of all European weaponry up to the development of fire-

arms – were not invented to provide functional ways of killing people efficiently. Prehistoric Europeans already did that perfectly well using whatever general-purpose instruments came to hand. Instead, weapons were a new social technology invented in response to the needs of identity – a need to constitute masculine values within a new body world. Making, wearing and using weapons created a new kind of embodiment through new relations and capacities for action. A new kind of body was constituted through its relations to these weapons in life, death and art.

Metals as a body technology

One of the major features of later prehistory is the development of metals as a major technology. The first, sporadic, often idiosyncratic forays into metals occurred during the Neolithic, in the Balkans and Central Mediterranean in the fifth millennium BC. By about 3000 BC, copper was in use consistently south of the Alps and patchily north of them; by about 2000 BC, almost all European groups were metal-users. As archaeologists have recognized for decades, the introduction of metals was not just a technological shift; it was also, or above all, a social change.

Any discussion of early metal use must start by dispelling one myth which is commonly held outside the field but rarely endorsed by archaeologists: the idea that metals were invented as part of technological advance because they were functionally better than stone tools at cutting things. The modern myth of technology sees technology purely as a technical way of accomplishing a task.[79] But well into the Bronze Age – at least a millennium after their introduction – metals were usually made and circulated in small quantities. They were fashioned into a narrow range of items, including ornaments such as pendants, pins and armbands, and weapons, mostly small triangular daggers or knives of uncertain functionality (see earlier discussion). The most functional tools made of metal were the axe, which was used for wood-cutting (as attested by chopping marks on Early Bronze Age timbers such as at Seahenge, England),[80] and in some areas, the sickle. In most areas, flint continued to provide the basic cutting edge right through the Early Bronze Age. All of this hardly suggests a revolution at the cutting edge of technology.

So what was the point of early metals? The place to start is by looking at what metals were used for and how. Women's use of metals provides a well-studied starting point. Women used metals principally as ornaments. (Men commonly wore ornaments as well, of course, but

Figure 36. Reconstruction of Bronze Age warrior (Harding 1999b, fig. 5, original drawing by John Coles, redrawn by Vicki Herring).

discussion of male self-presentation has tended to focus upon weaponry instead – see earlier discussion).

In the third millennium BC, statue-stelae with breasts and necklaces refer to women. In comparison, when single burials with grave goods become common, there is no simple set of grave goods which recurs across different regions to typify female burials. Other than pottery, however, the most common item in third and early second millennia BC female graves is some form of ornament which suggests a consistent emphasis upon decorating and presenting the body (see following discussion).[81] This use of metals expanded dramatically in many areas of Europe in the Middle and Late Bronze Age, a time in which dress became increasingly important. Physical appearance mediates social categories and identities in all situations, and dress provides an important medium through which social identities are constructed and communicated: it provides the materiality of a sense of self which is also an essential component of relations with others.[82] Our knowledge of prehistoric dress improves greatly from the Middle Bronze Age onwards, and this is not coincidence: it reflects a greatly heightened cultural attention to the presentation of self in material culture, particularly metalwork.

For women, this took the form of elaborate body adornment (Figure 37). Pottery figurines from Romania and Serbia (a rare form of representation in this period) show women wearing elaborate belts, sashes, and hair ornaments (Plate VIf).[83] In other contexts, two sets of

female ornaments defined distinct categories of women.[84] The best-known case, however, is that of Southern Germany (Figure 38).[85] Throughout the region, there were two distinct female costumes, one focusing attention upon the chest and the other on the waist. Cross-cutting this, there were five regional assemblages of ornaments which reflected identifiable ways of dressing amongst women living in different areas. Within each category, the number and quality of objects may have differentiated women between different contexts.

Whether it involves a Bronze Age woman fastening her tunic with a pin or a twenty-first-century businessman girding himself in suit, tie, watch, smart phone, briefcase and haircut, ornamenting the body involves making it conform to a look or aesthetic sense which is constructed socially and materially and is meaning-laden. Several elements converged in the Bronze Age look. On a superficial, economic level, metal was subject to scarcity; even if it was obtained through reciprocal gift-giving relationships rather than through barter or a market economy, maintaining such relations still would have had a cost. When the standard of adornment fell within a narrowly limited range of a few items, it set an ideal to which most women could presumably aspire; when the range expanded to comprise a large assortment of clothing, small objects and major bronzework, it set an ideal which allowed much more social distinction.

Economic considerations, though important, do not explain the real significance of metalwork by themselves. Metal's material characteristics were central. Aesthetically, few natural substances gleam. Metals provided new qualities such as shining brightness, which may have had metaphorical associations with the sun (this is suggested by some Copper Age rock art imagery in Valcamonica, Italy) as well as representing social prominence. Major symbols of power at this time, beyond weapons,

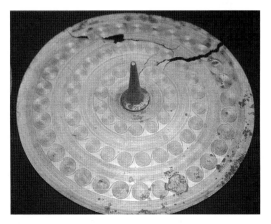

Figure 37. Large, shining metal ornament, hung from a woman's belt (Denmark, Middle Bronze Age). (National Museum, Copenhagen; photo: Robb).

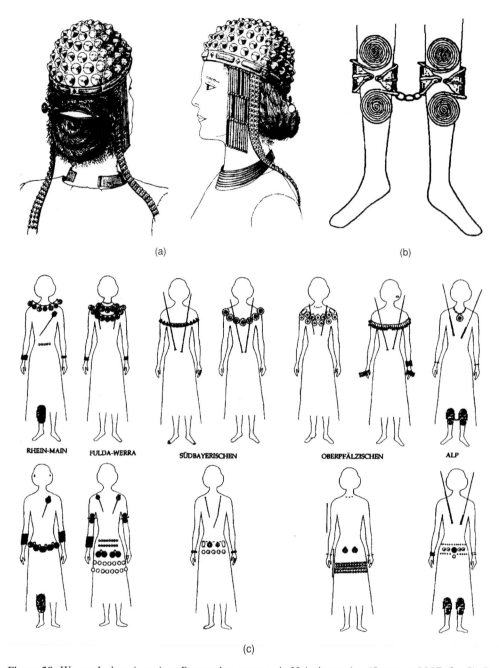

Figure 38. Women's dress in various Bronze Age groups. A. Hair decoration (Sørensen 1997, fig. 5). B. Leg ornaments that restrict movement (Sørensen 1997, fig. 6). C. Group differences in South Germany in display of ornaments on women's bodies (Sørensen 1997, fig. 3). All reproduced with kind permission of Marie Louise Stig Sørensen.

included large and lucid greenstone axes, and, in Britain and Ireland, sheet gold body ornaments. Interestingly, this aesthetic shift is sometimes observable in pottery as well, which in many places features highly burnished vessels which emphasize the lucid gleam of the surface. These do not imitate metal vessels, as is sometimes asserted; instead, pots, metals and axes in different regions all participate in the same general aesthetic. Significantly, whereas metal surfaces were sometimes elaborately engraved, the Copper and Bronze Age aesthetic of

gleaming similarity also presents something which can be readily assessed regardless of social distance, a feature highly relevant to the importance of inter-group trade and connectivity in this period. Bronze Age ornamentation involved making as much of the body as possible gleam with the shining yellow of bronze, placed strategically in areas of high salience, particularly the head, chest and arms.

Bodies clothed in metal may have sounded and moved differently as well. For some costumes, we can imagine

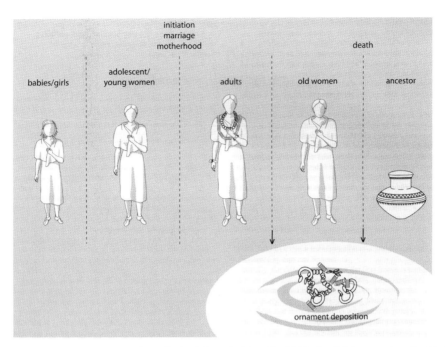

Figure 39. Women's ornaments through the life cycle (Fontijn 2002, fig. 12.3, reproduced with kind permission of David Fontijn and the Faculty of Archaeology, University of Leiden).

auditory effects – a gentle jingling and tinkling accompanying some movements.[86] Clothing the body in bronze, with sometimes quite substantial weight and momentum, may also have had kinetic effects of modulating sudden or jerky movements; a body garbed in metal may have moved with a certain decorousness. Heavy and elaborate head-dresses may have had a similar effect. In an extreme example, some women in Middle Bronze Age North-Central Europe wore leg-rings which consisted of bands around each leg connected by a short chain; these would have restricted the legs' motion, for instance preventing the woman from running (Figure 38b).[87] Such devices may have been tied into notions of habitus and how women were supposed to move.

As with weapons, metal ornaments would have had their own biographies. There are several ways we can see this. One is to see how items were brought together and used to form a costume (Figure 39). Some items were attached to the body so closely that they were difficult to remove, for instance some types of arm-rings and ankle-rings which were probably put on at a young age and grown into, so that they became permanent elements of the body.[88] These may have symbolized permanent and ubiquitous dimensions of identity, put on at specific life-transitions such as coming of age or marrying. Other objects could be assumed or taken off as occasion dictated, and would have been used to nuance the sense of self contextually. Alternatively, the same process of composition can be seen from the point of view of the arte-

facts. As Fontijn[89] points out, bronze objects had cultural biographies which were linked to a person's biography.[90] Many would have come from parents, friends, relatives or spouses; others would have come from exotic sources, perhaps via trade or gift partners. Such stories would have been intrinsic to their meaning to the woman or man wearing them. Ornamentation displayed the kind of relational self we described in Chapter 2.[91] To the extent that ornaments were given and received, mediating social relations, the ensemble would thus represent an assemblage of relations, virtually a social biography. A panoply of ornaments would have been a construction of self in terms of the relationships through which the ornaments had been gathered, the histories of exchange and gift giving they revealed; depositing them (in ritual hoards, for example) would have been a deconstruction of the social persona.

In summary, one of the primary uses of early metals was to ornament the self, but ornaments were no more about simply looking attractive than weapons were simply about being able to wound someone. Metals were a kind of 'social glue'[92] – a transformative material which linked the places where they were extracted and made, the life cycles of people and the cultural biographies of the artefacts themselves. This applies equally to both weapons and ornaments. Both men and women, thus, were 'competing for parity', although in different spheres of exchange.[93] Their aesthetic qualities of colour and sound embodied important cultural sensations. Metal objects were strongly gendered[94] and were central to creating and displaying gendered identities. More than any functional or technological necessity, ornaments and weapons developed as body enhancements – things which extended the body, made its surface hard and gleaming, or made it dangerous. Conversely, the result was a body and sense of personhood which was defined by its relation to new kinds of objects, and through them to people and places. The relationship between the body and technology, in which each defines and produces the other, recurs throughout history.[95] Its particular Bronze Age form was the prosthetic metallization of the body. The gilded faces of Bronze Age leaders at Mycenae perhaps supply its ne plus ultra, and show us a vision of a godlike Bronze Age robot (Plate VIh).

From many bodies to one body: The Bronze Age body world

As noted previously, one of the most striking things about the third millennium BC is how the archaeological picture suddenly snaps into focus. Before this period (as anybody who has tried to explain an everyday Neolithic site to an intelligent, sceptical school group can attest), it is surprisingly difficult to draw a clear picture about what gender, prestige and political life were about. It is not that evidence is particularly lacking; in places, it is extremely abundant. But the evidence gives us many incommensurate fragments of a picture. We can say a great deal about what people did, but, except in a few areas in which the evidence is mostly of hypertrophied ritual, it is difficult to add it up into a picture of an overall social order. There are no obvious terms through which to summarize the identities of people in this period, because of their contextually bound nature. There is no single sense of personhood to be defined, no central sense of an overarching political order that transcends different categories. This is why archaeologists trying to understand the experience of living in the Neolithic almost always end up discussing the power of places, cultural landscapes and the routines of daily life.[96]

In contrast, from some time in the third millennium BC, we suddenly have the luxury of a coherent cluster of symbols of personal identity. Because this is what we naively expect to find when looking for social agents in any context, and because many of these symbolisms (such as gendered weaponry and ornaments) remain familiar to us from later periods, it is easy for us to miss how great a change from the preceding period this is. This cluster of 'key symbols'[97] linked gendered objects such as weapons and ornaments, aesthetic qualities such as shininess and sound, and actual or potential social relations such as giv-

ing, exchanging, inheriting, or fighting. As discussed later in this chapter, these were not formulae applied rigidly throughout Europe; they were abstract possibilities which people could call into play in following local traditions or formulating new ways of acting.

This transition, as we saw with burial earlier, has sometimes been called 'the rise of the individual',[98] but this is misnomeric and anachronistic; these are not autonomous, self-interested individuals in the modern sociological sense.[99] This was not a shift simply from a form of relational personhood to a more individualistic one;[100] instead, it was a moment when new kinds of relational personhood emerged.[101] It is, therefore, more useful to see this as a shift from societies which were regulated by ritual authority to ones which were regulated by competition for prestige,[102] which was accessible through the careful management of relations with the wider community, rather than any sense of individualized power.[103] In particular, what emerges abruptly is a complex of material things which are associated with the singular body and its social relations rather than action on behalf of a larger collectivity. Rather than large, ritualistic monuments and collective village constructions, we find personal drinking vessels, tools to fit a person's hand, ornaments to distinguish a particular body in both life and death. The result was the emergence of a largely homogeneous set of actors, both male and female, who are competing not usually for pre-eminence but for parity of a rather limited, stereotyped, highly gendered kind.

The link between this class of actors and the body is via prestige and motivation. A key insight from recent ethnography is that societies vary greatly in how they organize prestige as a motivational system. In some groups,[104] different activities result in incommensurate forms of value; being prominent in one kind of endeavour does not necessarily result in prominence in other fields. In other groups, many different activities can contribute to a generalized form of the person's value or prestige. In the Neolithic body world, there is much more of a sense of context-specific value; there were many Neolithic bodies, each particular to a given context. With the transition discussed in this chapter, perhaps the most important aspect of this shift is that these new symbolisms are found *across* contexts. Weapons as signs of male gender, for example, turn up in burials fixing the gender of the dead, in rock art as isolated affirmations of this value in a specific context, in statuary as the minimal information needed to identify a being as male, in material culture as products of highly skilled flint-knappers and metalworkers, in exchange as the objects of long-distance movement of goods, in hunting as the tools of a valued activity, and in actual violence and warfare. Effectively, we are witnessing the invention of some concept of prestige such as honour; a range of contexts became linked through a generalized sense of male or female worth which is relevant in many previously independent spheres. And via the body, these symbolisms were internalized, experienced, lived. Like the sense of honour which Bourdieu[105] describes (see Chapter 2), these values formed part of habitus, part of the embodied constitution of the actors themselves. This may be the significance of the aesthetics of statue-stelae, which vividly show the change from an understanding of the body as an assemblage of often disparate parts, citations and qualities relevant to a particular context, to one of a body subordinated to a uniform template and set of qualities which are relevant across the settings of life. It is a shift from many bodies, which exploit the body's potential for difference, to a single, universal relevant body, which is defined in terms of similarity.

The process of change

As we have tried to show, the body in Bronze Age Europe was understood very differently than the Neolithic body had been. The body formed a central part of the large-scale change in prehistoric worlds which happened across the continent between about 3500 BC and about 1500 BC. However, change is rarely a simple story of one thing after another, it is always more complex than that. So far, we have been operating generally at a large-scale of analysis. As we argued in Chapter 2, however, to understand change we have to examine how it takes place at multiple scales. In what follows then, we take a more detailed look at some of the evidence for how this change happened. Whilst this examination still supports the 'big picture' we have outlined so far, it also allows us to see other things going on. Specifically, we first examine the complexities inherent in the transition to the Bronze Age body world that we have been discussing, in the context of the Alps in the third millennium BC. Then we turn to a second and different transition that took place within this body world a millennium later: the rise of cremation in Middle Bronze Age Central Europe.

Mediating multiple bodies in the Copper Age Alps: The mysterious case of Ötzi's Tattoos

Ötzi, or the Ice Man (as he has been nicknamed in the media), lived in the Italian Alps sometime between 3300 BC and 3000 BC – at the threshold between the Neolithic and the Copper Age, very early in the transition discussed in this chapter (Table 3, Table 4).[106] After he died at an age of 40–50 years in an isolated, high-

Figure 40. Ötzi, the reconstruction (© South Tyrol Museum).

altitude pass, he was naturally mummified under a glacier. This remarkable preservation makes the Ice Man the most famous prehistoric European body. The Ice Man's body gives us a unique opportunity to see how prehistoric bodies were defined through their relation to material things.

Ötzi's body fits the picture of bodies for this period surprisingly well. Most obviously, he was male not only in terms of physical characteristics such as genitalia; he was culturally gendered through the same objects seen in burials, rock art and stelae – principally weapons. In fact, he carried an entire Copper Age armoury of copper axe, bow, stone arrows and stone knife (Figure 40). The knife was fixed in position via a woven grass scabbard at the belt (the same position as on many statue-stele), in a way which implies that it was carried and drawn through habitual gestures. Moreover, these body-defining items were procured not only through metalworking (chemical traces of which were found in his hair) but through long-distance exchange; his metals, marble bead and flint tools show connections within areas up to 200 km away. As on the stele, the body is demarcated into the upper body, the locus of social marking, and an unmarked lower body; this is done through the foundation garment, a belt from which a loincloth hung. Intriguingly, the upper body was figured through an animal skin tunic with a striking pattern of vertical dark and light stripes, much like the vertical striping seen on the torsos of Trentino-Alto-Adige statue-stelae found nearby a few centuries later: such striping may have been a local tradition of clothing.[107] Items such as his bearskin cap and white marble bead recall the animal cosmological citations found in the nearby Valcamonica statue-stelae, not far away to the west. Ötzi's body is invaluable in confirming that the body world we have outlined in this chapter was not merely an image created in burial or art, but was actually lived in contexts of everyday life. Ötzi died through violence; a flint arrow point was found embedded in his left shoulder, in a way which suggests that the habitus of weaponry was not just for show but carried actual life risks; he lived and died in a drama of Copper Age masculinity. In this manner, he is a classic example of the new bodies produced through the relational practices that came to dominate Europe in the earliest metal ages.

However, there is one detail which does not fit. The Ice Man provides the earliest known example of tattooing, in a series of small, rather inconspicuous blue-black lines and crosses on the small of his back, his knee and his ankle (Figure 41). It was immediately realized that the tattoos seem not to have been intended for visual impact; they are small and rather inconspicuous, and located in areas which would usually have been covered by clothing.[108] (If they formed part of the display of important political symbols common in this time, we would perhaps expect something like a large rock-art style dagger tattooed somewhere highly visible such as his chest, biceps or face!). Hence, most researchers have proposed a medical interpretation: the tattoos were intended to ameliorate the osteoarthritis evident in Ötzi's back and legs.[109] Such an interpretation, however, is questionable: osteoarthritis such as the Ice Man's is often not accompanied by symptoms such as pain, and would have been completely normal at his age rather than requiring a special medical intervention.[110] Moreover, the medical interpretation is based upon vague analogies with acupuncture,[111] without any concrete specification of exactly how the tattoos would have been therapeutic, or even have been understood to have been so. Ice Man researchers seem to have felt that, because the tattoos do not fit our criteria for self-decoration, they must have been 'functional' in some way, but there is no real agreement upon how they actually would have been so.[112]

Tattoos are a permanent marking of the body; whatever else they do, they fix the body as a particular kind of social product. Visible or not, they often commemorate social relationships or identities, and in societies without commercial tattooists, the act of creating tattoos is often done publicly to attest these things.[113] The Ice Man's body is clearly a product of many hands: workmanship of several distinct people is evidence in the sewing of his garments, his accoutrements attest exchange relationships; even the tools he made and used show skills learned from others. As a permanent modification of the body for social purposes, and one which must have been made by others (especially as it is impossible to tattoo your own lower back!), his tattoos are probably the most eloquent witness of the relationality of his body. Why then should they not be visible? The obvious answer – if one can draw any lessons at all from modern tattooing – is that nuances of visibility and invisibility, concealment and revelation, are highly relevant to marking the body: different contexts, different eyes, different relationships, different markings.

Visibility was important. As we have seen, Copper and Bronze Age people marked and displayed their bodies prominently in many contexts. Hence, markings of the body which were either actively concealed or simply not important to display may have referred to other components of identity. Perhaps these were 'background' aspects of identity which required less ongoing, active public maintenance and instead were fixed permanently as an enduring element of social being – a ritual status or sponsorship perhaps, a clan identity or a record of parenthood. Whatever the case may have been, working from this premise, we thus have two quite distinct systems for marking the body, relevant to different aspects of personhood in different contexts. This makes two important points for our broader argument. First, the understanding of the body, even as new dominant approaches emerged, was never singular, there are always other ways of conceptualizing the boundaries and edges of the body. Second, to understand the changes that take place we cannot subdue difference to produce a single story. We need to appreciate how different concepts of the body took up space within particular contexts, and how they waxed and waned in relation to one another.

Much as Ötzi combines two different ways of understanding the body's social relationships in a single body, sites from the Alps in the third millennium BC show how tensions were resolved in art and burials. Valcamonica, in northern Italy, conforms well to many of the third-millennium BC generalizations we have made, particularly the rise in long-distance trade in metals and other items and the appearance of new symbolisms such as daggers (attested in rock art there). As elsewhere in the Alps, people adopted the idea of placing statue-stelae in the landscape, in groups or alignments associated with rituals commemorating the dead. For example, at Osimo-Anvòia, an alignment of statue-stele was placed in an area which may have been considered a *mana* ground with live ancestral presences.[114] But when the residents of Valcamonica fashioned large stone people, they did not adopt the carefully shaped stone slab and formal layout common to all other corpuses of stelae in Europe. Instead, they used barely formed boulders and continued the Neolithic tradition of composing the body as a mass of citations (Figure 42a and b). The resulting statue-menhirs differ radically from statue-stelae found anywhere else and are at times only debatably anthropomorphic. Why did they do this? Valcamonica is the only stela-making area with a pre-existing rock art tradition, and when they began to make stelae, they assimilated the form to an existing practice. Perhaps they were following the third-millennium BC meta-pattern of creating local identity through enclaves of ritual difference.[115] Perhaps there were other reasons we cannot know now. The point here, however, is the texture of geographical difference. The symbolic innovations of this period were not an unstoppable and indivisible ideological juggernaut rolling across Europe. They were a coherent but loosely linked set of concepts and values which afforded small-scale communities an opportunity for the local tinkering that anthropologists have termed bricolage. Like Ötzi's tattoos, they show us that there is always more than one thing going on, and even widespread changes continue to play out differently in local contexts.

One of the finest examples of how analysis has to unfold at multiple scales is that of the Petit-Chasseur site in Sion, Switzerland. This site was used for burials for almost a millennium, between about 2700 BC and 2000 BC (Figure 42c and d).[116] Sion belongs to its era. It includes megalithic tombs with statue-stelae erected before them, with burials deposited with valuable traded items in metal, flint and shell; it would look dramatically out of place a millennium earlier or later. It clearly reflects a widely shared zeitgeist. But Sion's long history shows clearly how people continually played with the possibilities this afforded rather than reproducing a pattern blindly. The site began with the construction of two megalithic tombs, each containing a burial chamber under a long mound. Stelae were then set up beside their entrances. Some centuries later, in the early Bell Beaker period, new stelae were set up, in a different style; they show elaborate woven garments and bows rather than daggers as the weapons of choice. Beakers are clearly integrated with a local tradition rather than challenging it. Then, still in

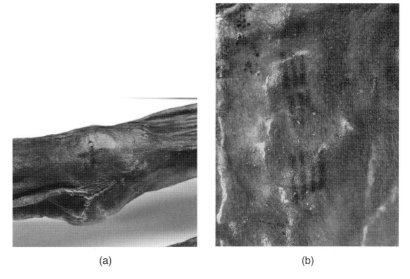

(a)   (b)

Figure 41. Close-up of Ötzi's tattoos. A. Tattoo on right knee. B. Tattoos on back. (Both images © South Tyrol Museum).

the Bell Beaker period, there is a significant rupture; the stelae are all broken in a major episode of iconoclasm, and the skulls and bones are taken out of the tombs and piled along their side. The megalithic tombs are no longer used. Following this, in the Early Bronze Age, people continued to be buried at the site, in what is probably a gesture of respect towards the antiquity of the place, but they are buried in small stone boxes which are often actually made of broken-up stelae. Finally, later in the Early Bronze Age, the dead are buried around the site as simple single burials.

When exactly does the broader transition we have highlighted in this chapter occur within this sequence at Sion? There is no single moment; at every point, change was combined with continuity and tradition. The creation of the original tomb combines older concerns with the monumental landscape with new ones about grave goods; then, the Beaker stelae and burials tie the monument into the changing world in which it was found – one of new regional styles of pottery and the display of weapons. Unlike other parts of the Beaker world, this was not initially associated with single burial; this then came later with the disuse of the megalithic tomb and the destruction of the stelae. Even here, however, a moment in the sequence where the change must have seemed radical at the time, involving the iconoclastic destruction of the stelae, as many elements were perpetuated as changed – in this case, the location of the burials, the use of stone boxes and the use of the stelae to make those boxes. The result of the history of a site like Sion is a historic shift similar to that in many other places across Europe, but this happens by small steps, by indirection and experimentation. Just as with Ötzi's tattoos or the stelae in Valcamonica, local sequences of incremental change add up to the dramatic shift we see across Europe in this period, but at no stage do they follow a simple linear sequence or an abrupt break.

Multiple bodies and change in the Bronze Age

Other Bronze Age bodies

These examples bring us back to a constant theme which was raised theoretically in Chapter 2. In all periods, there is never only one way of understanding the body, a monolithic totality. Even when there exist clearly articulated, coherent public symbolisms of the body – and these are the ones we are most likely to detect in normal archaeological circumstances – they never completely exclude alternative modalities of experiencing it. Here we discuss two modes of practice in which other modalities of the body emerged.

First, there are the forms in which both the practices of daily life, and elements of the treatment of dead bodies, helped to constitute alternative understandings. As in the example of the Ice Man's tattoos, presenting oneself in terms of the third-millennium BC model of generalized prestige does not preclude alternative forms of relatedness. In fact, paradoxically, a sense of individuality must itself be maintained relationally within social networks which treat the person in such a singular and bounded manner. In the third millennium BC there is abundant evidence for social interaction which was not subordinated closely to a unified sense of prestige. Crafts such as making pottery, working metal and weaving, show the cultivation of personal skill.[117] The treatment of material things like weapons, pottery and even houses in ways that are analogous to the human body (e.g. fragmentation and burning) indicates, as Brück argues, that these too may have been understood as being a kind of body.[118]

The human landscape was constructed at different scales: the household had a duration of about a generation; local burial groups of 50 or 100 people represented the historical continuity of the community; cult places and field systems had other histories revolving around other kinds of cross-cutting social relations.[119] Local relationships of solidarity were important and were probably reinforced in foodways such as feasting. In the Netherlands and Belgium, burial emphasized equality, cooperation and solidarity amongst a local community, at the same time as deposition of metalwork in rivers was a way of expressing wealth, status and supra-regional connections.[120] Gender, prestige and inequality formed part of a mosaic of many principles of social life.

Another example comes from ritual, which provided an important sphere of action which took metalwork, gender and prestige for granted but went beyond them. Throughout Europe, ritual knowledge and practice may have afforded social authority of a different kind than that derived from wealth, warfare or exchange. For example, metal figurines in Sardinia show ritual or tribal leaders distinct from warriors; in the Mycenaean world, terracotta figurines of women commonly interpreted as priestesses or goddesses counterbalance the overwhelmingly martial and masculine iconography of metalwork. Throughout later Bronze Age Central Europe, from Poland to the Alps, an iconography of the sun, birds, boats, horses and carts is found which has been generally interpreted as cosmological. The Nebra sky-disk, a remarkable bronze disc from Germany with the stars and moon picked out on it in gold,[121] suggests a preoccupation with celestial bodies.[122] In later Bronze Age Scandinavia, imagery in rock art and on metalwork suggests a cosmological narrative about the sun crossing the sky in a boat or pulled by a horse and returning beneath the earth in a boat.[123] In the relevant rock art in Denmark, Norway and Sweden,[124] the human body is referenced by life-sized footprints, which are at a completely different scale than the other imagery, suggesting that people were involved as observers or celebrants but not as protagonists. It is not that bodies produced through extended relations with metal work did not play their role in this context, rather that it was not these aspects of the body that were important within these broader cosmological spheres. Other elements of the body were at play here.

One of the most obvious tensions concerns what to do with the body at death. At one level, the Early Bronze Age tradition of single burial with grave goods served ritually to fix the social body of the deceased, surrounded by the material things which identified, extended, and enabled the body, in the collective memory at the moment of burial.[125] There is abundant evidence, however, that inhumation was by no means always a straightforward process, but rather involved all sorts of choices that potentially allowed the corpse to be manipulated in many different ways.[126] Despite this potential for variation, however, a more significant contrast emerges with the funerary treatment captured in our opening vignette: cremation. If our first transition in this chapter covered the change from a Neolithic body world to a Bronze Age body world, our second transition covers a change *within* the latter, and it is to this we now turn. Whilst differing practices were always part of the inhumation process, cremation, in contrast, apparently transformed the body radically, destroying it creatively and rendering

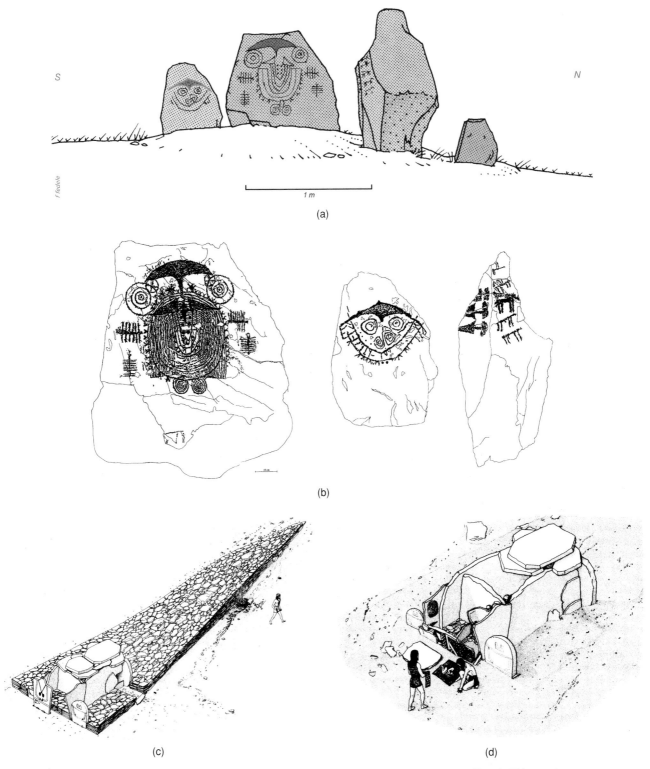

Figure 42. Mediating different approaches to the body in the third-millennium BC Alps. A. Valcamonica stelae in context (Ossimo, Borno) (Fedele 2007; fig. 4a). B. Valcamonica stelae detail (Fedele 2007; fig. 1) (both images reproduced with kind permission of Francesco Fedele). C. Sion reconstruction drawings showing the first phase of use of the monument (Gallay 1995, fig. 4). D. Sion reconstruction drawing of the second phase of use of the monument (Gallay 1995, fig. 5) (both images reproduced with kind permission of Alain Gallay).

its former being unrecognizable. How did such a practice begin? How was the attitude to the body this implies reconciled or accommodated within existing, dominant, understandings? As we will see a detailed study of this can tell us more about the ways in which body worlds change.

Cremation in Bronze Age Europe[127]

Cremation begins to be commonly practiced in Europe from about 1700 BC; and, by about 1400 BC across Europe from Poland to the North Sea and from Scandinavia to northern Italy, the dead body was treated radically differently from how it would have been a century or two before. This culminates in the 'Urnfield culture', found across most of Europe, which lasted from about 1300 BC to about 800 BC; the term refers to the very large cemeteries of cremations interred within urns.[128] Why did a rite so apparently different from preceding ones spread so widely, rapidly and uniformly? One traditional explanation was the migration of new peoples entering the region.[129] However, there is no convincing, widespread evidence of significant migration in the archaeological record at this point. In the other major interpretation, cremation has been viewed as a religious conversion, a new way of freeing the soul from the body. It was a 'spiritual revolution'.[130] As Harding comments, archaeologists have often considered that cremation 'indicates that the body itself is valueless, prone to decay, and but a feeble and intransient vehicle for higher things – emotions, reflective thought, spiritual conceptions'.[131] The implication is that the idea of a soul distinct from the body was invented at the same time.[132] In this view, based largely upon analogy with cremation practices in modern Hindu societies, the Urnfield period represents a period of profound religious change. A third, recent view, sees Urnfields as representing the solidarity of an egalitarian, local village community in resistance to a chiefly elite which attempted to dominate based upon control of long-distance trade in metalwork.[133]

All of these assume a single, regional cause for Urnfields, and all rest upon a simple, straightforward discontinuity: the profound divide is whether one buries the dead or cremates them, and these lead down radically divergent conceptual and interpretive pathways. Burial versus cremation thus provides a black and white opposition which supplies the touchstone for an entire structure of belief. This in turn poses the question of how such a change happened. How did one structure of belief about the body come to be replaced by another? One of the great blessings of Bronze Age burial archaeology, however, is large datasets with fine-grained chronology. These afford a unique opportunity to dissect change both geographically and temporally.

Death amongst neighbours: Middle Bronze Age Hungary

Our first view of Bronze Age burial under the microscope takes us to the Hungarian basin between about 1950 BC and 1650 BC.[134] This Middle Bronze Age social landscape shows how cremation interacted with other rites several centuries before the Urnfield period. The northwestern half of the Hungarian basin was occupied by three related groups, known archaeologically as the Encrusted Ware, the Vatya and the Füzesabony. These groups are roughly contemporary and in close proximity, and their people demonstrably interacted with their neighbours in other groups. To a certain extent, we can treat them as representing a real ethnographic landscape.

These three cultural groups share much of the taken-for-granted aspects of a way of life; at the broad level of generalization we have employed in the rest of this chapter, we would have little hesitation in lumping them together with many other groups under a common rubric. They largely used the same economic resources, technologies and productive techniques such as casting metals, potting and probably weaving. Things such as the basic iconography of gender and the use of bronze ornaments to dress the body were largely the same throughout. In death, too, there were recognizable commonalities.[135] All three groups buried the dead in cemeteries of individual pits not far from their settlements; all were familiar with both inhumation and cremation, and all deposited similar kinds of things with the dead, principally pottery and metalwork in combinations appropriate for the deceased's social persona. These commonalities betoken a firmly shared idea of the fundamental purpose of the burial rite.

But there were also marked differences in burial practice. Cremation and inhumation both occurred in each group, but the balance differed; Encrusted Ware burials were mostly cremations deposited in pits, Vatya burials were almost entirely cremations deposited within urns, and Füzesabony burials were mostly inhumations. The presence of alternative rites within each group makes clear that this was not simply blind adherence to an inherited tradition but a real local choice. The dead body was prepared for burial differently. Encrusted Ware cremations include few metal items, which were probably included simply because they were attached to the clothing the deceased was dressed in. In the Vatya group, cremations also include small ornaments and fittings, but items such as pins, bracelets, pendants and torcs were also deposited separately outside the urn when it was buried in the pit following the cremation. Füzesabony group inhumations include more bronze ornaments, particularly later in the period, and they sometimes include elaborate gender-specific kits such as weapons and whetstones for males and elaborate pins, necklaces, pendants, and hair ornaments for females.

Even when cremation was practiced, there were local variations in how it was done. Encrusted Ware cremations, for instance, were not particularly intended to destroy or efface the body; the body was probably placed on the pyre in the same crouched position it was given in inhumations, and burning left the body in relatively large fragments which were sometimes then placed in the grave in anatomical order. In the Vatya group, in contrast, bodies were more fragmented following cremation because of the repeated relocation of the bones both in and out of the urns. How pottery was used in burial provides another point of nuance. Encrusted Ware graves typically include a dozen or more vessels, including large storage jars and relatively esoteric types such as rattles, serving platters and miniature vessels. Pottery is used to outline the space of the grave; it probably represented the household or mourning community as well as marking the body's position. Some pots were deliberately smashed during the funeral. Vatya graves use pottery principally to contain the cremated body, in the form of large urns and their covers. There are examples of urns with anthropomorphic details which underline the analogy between the vessels and the bodies they contain. In Füzesabony inhumation graves, pottery is found mostly in standard sets of three vessels: a cup, a jug and a bowl. This eating or drinking set was sometimes placed in graves in a way implying that the idea was to feed the dead.

The point of such a fine reading of local difference is to see how such details add up to expressing different purposes and attitudes towards the dead. The Füzesabony group is perhaps the most faithful in adhering to the general tradition inherited from the Early Bronze Age. The inhumation graves of this group do not alter or dispute the body's corporeal existence; instead, they focus upon presenting the deceased person's social persona and maintaining it. Burial here fixes the dead in memory much as they were in life. The other two traditions, in contrast, transform the body by cremating it. But they also deal with the existential questions raised by cremation, such as the absence or reduction of the body – existential questions which were posed by existing orthodoxy in which the identity of the deceased was marked by the

Figure 43. Gendered pots from Bronze Age Hungary (Sørensen and Rebay-Salisbury 2008b, fig. 6; reproduced with kind permission of Katharina Rebay-Salisbury and Marie Louise Stig Sørensen).

presence of the body. Thus, for instance, Encrusted Ware burials place the body on the pyre in the same position it would have been buried in, and following the cremation they reconstitute the body spatially by constructing the grave around the scattered remains of the bones and marking its position with a frame of domestic vessels. As a technique of remembrance and acknowledgement of transformation, this would have been particularly effective if the whole community participated in placing vessels, as their sometimes large number suggests. In contrast, Vatya burials effectively use the urn to construct new, strongly marked bodily boundaries; the emphasis is upon closing the urn securely with lids and covers, and it is deposited within a small pit of a form familiar from Vatya settlements (and not found in the other two groups), hinting that actions involving familiar techniques and structures were used to incorporate the transformed remains in an unthreatening, routinized context. In several cases, gendered pots matching the gender of the deceased also preserved some of the social identity of the now-destroyed body (Figure 43).

These three closely linked communities shared a common vocabulary of death ritual. But rather than cremation and inhumation dictating monolithic, opposed traditions, we see a kind of geographical bricolage or tinkering. Each community selected elements and combined them to define a coherent ritual which met their particular concerns. As cremation emerges we see an undoubted set of changes, but rather than being simply transformative of the older concerns around bodily identity, we can trace how people paid attention to maintaining aspects of the singular, bounded Bronze Age body, even as they disposed of it in a new way. Thus, rather than a substantial transformation of the broader body world, as there was in the third millennium BC, we see instead how different practices can draw on the same overall understandings of the body.[136]

Cremation by degrees: Middle Bronze Age Austria

The previous discussion suggests that we need to understand how change happens by looking at it on a fine scale and by looking at concrete practices as well as abstract ideas. We now turn to a case in which it is possible to track such changes in detail over time.

About fifty kilometres south of Vienna in Lower Austria, the cemetery of Pitten was used by a small community of thirty to thirty-five people for about ten generations between about 1600 BC and 1350 BC.[137] This is the site on which we drew for the reconstruction drawing and vignette that opened this chapter. At Pitten, the burials can be divided into four phases within this span. Excavations at the cemetery revealed 235 burials in 195 structures of various kinds.[138] Burials took the form of either cremations or inhumations. They were made within and around a great variety of structures, including shaft pits, cylindrical graves, stone enclosures built on the ground and covered by low mounds, and they were also placed within urns covered by mounds. There were also platforms used to display things or perform activities upon. Grave goods were strongly gendered. Males, even as young as four years old, were buried with weapons. Women were buried with ornaments for their head, chest and legs, and had significantly more grave goods than males. Both males and females showed changes in grave goods around adolescence, suggesting a life transition to adulthood. Cremation, inhumation and other ritual practices showed no particular patterning of age and sex; nor did they correlate with the amount of grave goods.

The Pitten data allow a very fine-grained look at how change happened. In the first phase, the real conceptual division was between people buried *in* the ground, in shaft-graves, and those buried *on* the ground surface and covered with mounds. Mound burials could include either inhumations or cremations, and the distinction between them does not seem to have been important at this stage. Only two of nine excavated burials were cremations, but one of these (Burial 163) was an older male who was cremated, deposited in an urn, and buried in one of the largest mounds at the site. This permanently visible installation may have resulted from a rift with the then-dominant practice of inhumation in shaft-graves. In subsequent generations, the barrow may have formed an important precedent for the practice of cremation.

In the next phase, the cemetery grows larger and more populous. Earlier mounds are reused and new mounds constructed; people begin depositing more than one burial in a mound. Mounds begin to predominate over shaft-graves. Inasmuch as cremations at this site are deposited only in mounds, this is an important precondition for making the rise of cremations thinkable, but the actual proportion of cremations remains roughly constant. The biggest shift occurs in the third phase, the end of the Middle Bronze Age. In this phase, inhumation in shaft-graves goes completely out of use; all new burials are made within mounds built upon the ground surface. Moreover, cremations increase and become the majority rite, with thirty-five out of fifty burials including cremation. Whereas most burials are cremated in situ, this phase also sees the construction of several specific places where cremation pyres were made. In the final phase, cremation alone is practiced. What began two centuries earlier as an infrequent option whose meaning probably lay in opposition to the established way of doing things itself became a hegemonic rite. This does not mean, however, that burial became uniform; variation in this phase was expressed in how stone architecture was constructed to enclose the grave, of which there is a great variety including several completely new types.

Pitten thus allows us to immediately refute the two most common theories of cremation origins. If cremations were to be ascribed to an incoming group, we would expect an abrupt shift rather than a gradual transition; there is strong evidence for continuity of burial traditions here. The same argument tends to exclude the idea of a sudden mass conversion event to a new religious system. By the early Urnfield period, cremation is the normal rite, but they arrived at this state of things gradually, not suddenly.

The most important point, however, is not only how much cremation was done, but *how* it was done. As we saw in our opening vignette, cremating the body itself offers numerous choices and opportunities for action.[139] In most cases, a pyre was built on the surface of the ground, and the body was laid atop it, apparently as it would have been dressed for burial and in the same position. The pyre was then burnt down. The amount of bone destruction was variable, but, in most cases, major recognizable fragments would have remained in their bodily position. Following this, a grave enclosure or mound was constructed around the cremation, defining the space occupied by the original body, much as would have happened with an inhumation. This suggests that cremation was not thought of as a radically different alternative to inhumation burial. It did not destroy the body, or lead to its absence; as long as it was not moved away and separated from the rest of the pyre, the cremated body continued to be perceived and treated as a corporeal entity. Moreover, cremation was not a final good-bye, as we might expect if it were intended to definitively destroy the body. As in many contemporary cemeteries, disturbance to the grave customarily interpreted as 'grave robbing' probably happened during repeated ritual visits to the grave, perhaps to recover valuables which had been given to the dead for a delimited time. This pattern continues when cremation becomes the dominant rite at Pitten, and it is noteworthy that many of the Phase 3 and 4 architectural innovations on this site include door openings or other entrances to allow ongoing access to the dead. Instead, cremation seems to have merely involved inserting another step in the sequence of ritual operations. Effectively, people cremated a body and then buried it like an inhumation. Again this is suggestive of a change within aspects of a body world, rather than the body world itself transforming.

Cremation, however, posed new challenges to belief. By attenuating the recognizable bodiness of the body, it may have threatened the sense of identity attached to a particular dead person. In several cases, cremated remains were moved around within the grave to give them bodily features once again, for instance by gathering them together to make a bounded mass or by placing them in alignments representing the body. It is this that we see in our vignette that opened the chapter (and see Plate II). Here people picked out parts of the body from the cremation pyre, effectively ensuring the body was reconstituted into something alike in structure to the living body although demonstrably transformed. Similarly, this anxiety may account for some of the architectural elaboration of the stone features enclosing the burials in the cemetery's last two phases. These normally follow the size and outline of the body rather than that of the underlying pyre, which was substantially larger; the result is a range of kinds of body-sized and body-shaped containers built over part of a pyre. In contrast, selecting bones from the cremation and moving them to another site or placing them within a container may have been a much more significant action than the cremation itself, one which meant reconstituting the body in a completely transformed form. A number of burials show experimentation with defining new forms of container for the dead body such as pits in the pyre place: urns are the end point of this experimentation.

Thus, in most cases, the cremated body was still perceived as a whole corpse, but new understandings were emerging. The persistence of the idea of the whole body suggests that people began cremating as a practice which held a specific meaning as part of a suite of accepted alternatives in a specific context, rather than as a programmatic application of a new grand idea. In this early moment of transition, they surrounded cremation with ad hoc practices aimed at conserving the bodiness of the individual body even when it had been burnt. Here, they buried the burned body just as one would bury a whole body. In the Hungarian example, they used a range of options: they built a traditional grave around the cremated body, moved the identifying gender information to the pottery vessel, or even laid out burned bones in the outline of the burial. Again we see multimodality at play here; different conceptions of the body were in tension with one another. People both wanted to cremate the dead and to maintain another understanding of the body as something which retained connections to its previous form. Changes in practice, however, shifted the ground for future action; they made new possibilities comprehensible for the first time. These changes thus had historical momentum: once cremation had been common for a few generations, the need for such elaborations had passed and the destruction of the body was accepted as an alternative mode of dealing with the dead. Nevertheless, bones were still placed in urns which were buried individually, often with grave goods, preserving the emphasis upon the bounded integrity of the social person.

Scale and the process of change

Prehistory is messier than prehistorians would like. Rather than a tidy, easily explained transition in which institutions, values and practices all change from A to B simultaneously everywhere, the two millennia or so examined in this chapter show directed, continent-scale change emerging out of a disorderly heap of local experimentations. But this very messiness tells us important things about the texture of social life. We can sum up some of the lessons briefly.

- What is transitional depends upon our analytical perspective (which defines the beginning and end points between which distance is measured), and equally upon our scale of analysis. From the point of view of large-scale history, the period discussed in this chapter presents a clear transition between two distinct ways of living. On the scale of the human lives making it up, however, so-called transitions consisted of stable human worlds enduring many generations which were conceptually coherent enough to be inhabitable.
- When we look closely at them, in each case it is clear that apparently large transitions happen in small steps. Each step, incrementally, forms the preconditions which make the next ones possible or, sometimes, necessary.

- People share an entrenched, taken-for-granted value system which generates and authorizes practices (see Chapter 2). Given this, the incremental steps of change represent a process of historical bricolage, tinkering or problem-solving, which is not entirely free-form but is given structure by a regionally shared habitus that prescribes new forms of creativity and limits to the thinkable.

- Body worlds are coherent, but not homogeneous. In the situations discussed, there are several ways of understanding the body which came into play in different contexts and relationships. The body may be treated differently in death than in life, or in situations emphasizing individual distinctions than in contexts of lifelong solidarity and group unity. What people actually do in practice may represent a situational alternation between modes of understanding, as when Scandinavian Bronze Age cosmological rituals involved a different set of symbolisms than those coming into play in political self-presentation. Or it may represent an accommodation between contradictory ways of dealing with things, as in the example of the various ways Middle Bronze Age Central Europeans found to experiment with cremation while maintaining the integrity of the body in death.

- This multimodality provided the necessary materials for change. Change in how people understood the body rarely involved the invention of new basic concepts. Instead, it usually arises from modifications or inventions of concrete practices, often of quite limited extent, which are authorized by one or another existing understanding. In the shift from the Neolithic to post-Neolithic understandings, most or all elements were already present in some form; what changed was how they were related to each other via concepts of gender and prestige. Similarly, Bronze Age cremation began as a minor, situational variant of burial practice which probably did not mark any major conceptual significance.

We return to these observations in Chapter 9.

Using this model, widespread horizons of change in prehistory usually represent neither single, centralized causes such as the immigration of new peoples – which is probably much more often a symptom of change than a cause of it – nor the spread of a new religious idea or ideology whose unity and fidelity to a source is similar to what we might expect in the textual, hieratic world of history. In the absence of these traditional answers, the question remains: why did almost everyone, rather than just a few groups end up adopting cremation in this period? People throughout Europe in the Bronze Age faced similar life challenges using a generally similar repertoire of possible actions, thinkable ideas and ordering principles. It is no surprise, then, that their creativity often runs in similar directions, especially as each group is in contact with its neighbours and can use their innovations as potential models. The growth in population in this period in Central Europe in particular may have meant not only more contacts, but simply a greater number of funerals and a greater possibility for innovations to take hold. Over time and on a regional scale, both the cultural repertoire and the needs of creative action change, resulting in distinct moments of transformation.

Conclusions: The body in (and as) social context

European societies were very different at 5000 BC, 3000 BC and 1000 BC. It is clear that this change cannot be summed up by any simple formula such as a steady increase in inequality: instead, it was movement between qualitatively distinct social worlds, each of which contained the basis for egalitarian and inegalitarian politics. How people thought about the world and related to others changed. And it is clear – even from simply comparing how people composed the human body in Neolithic figurines (Figure 28), Copper Age stelae (Figure 33) and later Bronze Age ornamentation (Figures 37 and 38) – that the body changed in step with these changes.

The Neolithic world presents us with valued activities, places and social relations – making pots, trading axes, carrying out rituals, being a mother, building houses and many other things. But these do not interlock to form an obvious system of social statuses; inasmuch as clear themes emerge from the archaeology, these tend to underline the importance of places such as the village[140] and institutions such as ritual systems rather than particular social persons. The inference is not that Neolithic people did not consider themselves as persons, but rather that their way of understanding personhood differed from what we might expect. Personhood was contextually understood rather than absolute, and the composite of social relations that produced this personhood varied across different fields of action.[141] As in some ethnographically known tribes,[142] different pursuits probably generated different kinds of value which were qualitatively incommensurate. When inequality developed, it took the form of ritual authority in a world of hypertrophied ritual practices such as in Atlantic Europe or Malta after 4000 BC. We see this understanding of persons in the body in a number of ways. The division between human and animal bodies was much more strongly drawn than it was during the Mesolithic – probably as a result of the changing relations with animals following the introduction of domesticated beasts. Burial was not about asserting individual status; it was a way of fixing relations between people and places, of creating generic ancestors. Ornaments were used to differentiate bodies finely very much as surface decoration created layers of difference in pots. Human representations (such as figurines) showed highly heterogeneous approaches to the body, abstracting an enormous range of parts to emphasize and styles to show them with. In a world where people were defined by multiple, incommensurate forms of value, the body was understood in terms of its potential for difference.

Between about 3500 BC and 2500 BC – the dates vary regionally and change was gradual rather than abrupt – another ethnographic landscape replaced the Neolithic world. In the landscape, cemeteries and mounds become highly visible, villages often disappear, and many ritual sites go out of use. In communities, new forms of social value are organized not around places or practices but around persons. This is highly visible archaeologically in a cluster of gendered key symbols which are referenced across contexts rather than being confined to specific settings. For males, weapons become an element of habitus which is involved in fields of practice including warfare, craft, hunting, exchange and burial. For both genders, the presentation of self in dress was important.

As we have seen, some archaeologists have termed this shift the 'emergence' of the individual, of the warrior, and of politics based upon prestige competition. Although all of these encapsulate elements of it, none really go to the heart of the change. The underlying change is to a form of personhood in which the values and relations composing the person reference an identity held constant across different settings. It more closely resembles ethnographically known tribes in which people are understood in terms of a single form of prestige garnered in many situations. The body's potential for similarity rather than difference is central. The embodied aspects of this new form of personhood are obvious in terms of how important and standardized the display of gendered icons such as weaponry and ornaments becomes. As inequality developed, it often took the form of rich, ostentatious burials. These do not necessarily connote centralized political or economic control; it is display of the persona as a social principle taken

to extremes for its own sake. Representations of the body in stelae reflect the new model of personhood, showing the body not as a contextually defined collection of parts and citations but as a standard template which is found across contexts and communities, in which parts are subordinated to an integrated and constant whole, and which treats the body essentially as a surface for display.

This change, as we have seen, did not take place in a uniform way in all areas, but built on local understandings and always incorporated multiple ways of engaging with the body, from Ötzi's tattoos to the histories of burial at Sion. When cremation began to be incorporated into this body world, it built on the dominant understanding of the body we have developed, yet altered aspects of it. In the end cremation transformed the way the body was treated in death, without altering the fundamental understandings of people's need to situate their identities across context in relation to material things. This change too was not simply a switch from one way of treating the body to another, but rather played out through complex negotiations in the way the body was treated that drew on the modalities of understanding that lay behind *both* inhumation and cremation.

Of all the periods we discuss in this book, this period provides probably the clearest demonstration of a fundamental theoretical point. How do ideas about the body relate to social context? In other periods, we have to consider a range of things we might think of as 'external' structuring factors – for instance, specialized scientific knowledge, centrally-controlled religious doctrines, developed medical technologies, or the top-down diffusion of high culture. In this period, all of these are absent. We can look at connections between the body and its social context unencumbered by these apparently external factors. Here the body develops through the rhythms of social process alone. When we do look, we see that ideas about the body are isomorphic with social process; how people related to each other in the Neolithic or the Bronze Age, how they related to the dead, how they worked and clothed themselves and expressed their values in art, all originate in how they understood their own bodies.

More than this, because they generated millennia of history through living their lives every day, the shape of history is conditioned by understandings of the body. Neolithic concepts of bodily value generated a world of many narrowly differentiated social statuses and roles. The result was a structurally complex society with a low ceiling for social and economic intensification; when inequality developed, it tended to take the form of ritual knowledge. The Early Bronze Age model generated a world with fewer, more generalized statuses whose relationships were expressed through display in life, art, and burial. Metals were called into being as a technology to enhance the body and make its social value material and apparent. Once they existed as a material medium, however, they generated technological knowledge and an economic system geared to circulating them, and they afforded potential for developing new practices and new understandings – for instance, the concept of accumulation rather than display as a basis for hierarchy that would become important in later periods. Given this, we cannot see ideas about the body as a dependent consequence of social context. In Chapter 3, we saw how changes in the body world were not just a product of a large-scale transition, but also part and parcel of it. Here we see no such transition and yet the body continues to play a vital role in historical process. Thus, we see not just the body in society, but society in the body; not just the body in history but history in the body.

NOTES

1. This chapter draws on material from a range of sources. Because many archaeological accounts tend to study things by period, much of what we have written here draws on certain sources that focus on the Neolithic and other sources that specialize in the Bronze Age. For the Neolithic in Europe the best source remains Whittle (1996), but good regional accounts of the development of megaliths can be found in works by Scarre (2011) on Brittany, Midgley (2008) on northern Europe and Smith and Brickley (2009) on southern Britain. For an excellent recent site specific study see Benson and Whittle (2007). Bronze Age key texts include Coles and Harding (1979), Harding (2000), Kristiansen (1998) and Kristiansen and Larsson (2005). Excellent illustrations of Bronze Age grave goods from Britain can be found in Clarke, Cowie and Foxon's (1985) volume.

   The main references for prehistoric art in this period are also spread across different literatures. For rock art, the best sources for the rich evidence across Europe are Beltran Martinez (1982), Coles (2005), Graziosi (1974), Sanchidrián (2005), Sandars (1985), Scarre (2008), and Shee Twohig (1981). For insightful and highly stimulating discussions of British and Irish rock art, which is non-representational (and so is not discussed in this chapter) see the work of Andrew Jones (e.g. Jones 2006; 2007, chapters 8 and 9). For statue-stelae, see Casini, De Marinis and Pedrotti (1995), Casini and Fosatti (2004), and Robb (2009a). For Neolithic figurines, see Bailey (2005), Fugazzola Delpino and Tinè (2003), Giannitrapani (2002), Holmes and Whitehouse (1998), Nanoglou (2005), Scarre (2007) and Talalay (1993). Two of

the main topics in the chapter are gender and personhood. The key texts on gender in later prehistoric Europe are Whitehouse (2006) and the work of Sørensen (1997, inter alia). For personhood in the Bronze Age, there is the research of Chapman (2000), and especially Brück's papers (2004; 2006a; 2006b; 2009). The best general text on personhood remains Fowler 2004a, and he has recently offered several important texts on regional studies of personhood in the Early Bronze Age (e.g. Fowler 2004b). The literature we refer to here obviously has an Anglophone bias, but for a book published in English, we believe these will be of most use to our readers.

2. e.g. Nieszery 1995.

3. The first four come from Orkney – three from the Early Neolithic site of Links of Noltland and one from the later site of the Ness of Brodgar. The other two come from Dagenham and the Somerset levels in southern England. The third figurine from the Links of Noltland (not depicted here) was discovered only after the book had gone to press. This list does not include the possible figurine found at the Neolithic site of Grimes Graves, which is generally, though not universally, now accepted as a fake. For further discussion of Neolithic representations (and the lack of them) see Thomas 2005.

4. Coles 1968, 277.

5. Gimbutas 1965; 1974; Mallory 1989.

6. This does not mean that movements, by both families and individuals, sometimes over considerable distances did not take place, but that mass invasions and the movement of whole communities seems unlikely.

7. Gilman et al. 1981.

8. Sherratt 1981.

9. Renfrew 1974.

10. Braithwaite 1984; Shennan 1982; Sherratt 1984; Rowlands 1984; Thorpe and Richards 1984.

11. Barrett 1994; Thomas 1999.

12. Kristiansen and Larsson 2005.

13. Hofmann and Whittle 2008.

14. Similarly, the Palaeolithic and Mesolithic burials we saw in Chapter 3 were not about individual status, but about exploring the relations between people, things, animals and places.

15. Scarre 2011.

16. The acts of building are by no means consistent throughout this very long period, however. In Britain, for example, megalith building really gets going after 3800 BC and, although they stretch into the last quarter of that millennium, none are built after 3000 BC (Whittle, Healy, and Bayliss 2011). These dates are broadly matched by the megaliths of the TRB (or Funnel Beaker culture) in northern Europe (Midgley 2008). In other places (e.g. Brittany, see Scarre 2011), they start earlier, and continue in others (e.g. Malta, see Skeates 2011) after this date.

17. In the case of Britain, see, for example, Smith and Brickley (2009) and Fowler (2010).

18. Benson and Whittle 2007; Saville, Hall, and Hoyle 1990; Scarre 2011; Whittle, Healy, and Bayliss 2011. This is *not* to deny that secondary burial took place on occasion in Britain, for example, at Fussell's Lodge long barrow (Wysocki, Bayliss, and Whittle 2007), or more commonly at some Scandinavian dolmens and passage graves (Midgley 2008).

19. Hofmann and Whittle 2008; Robb 2007.

20. Cummings and Whittle 2004; Robb 2007; Scarre 2011; Tilley 1994. This transition is captured in moments in the archaeological sequence, such as in northern Europe where long barrows were built directly above older sites of occupation (Midgley 2008, 13).

21. Whittle 1996.

22. Evans 1971; Malone et al. 2009; Skeates 2011.

23. Chippindale and Taçon 1998; Shee Twohig 1981.

24. Robb 2009a.

25. Parker Pearson and Ramilisonina 1998; Tilley 2004; 2009.

26. Shennan 1993.

27. Kohring 2011; Shennan 1982; 1993; Vander Linden 2006; 2007a; 2007b; Whittle 1996.

28. Moreover, the treatment of the body in these graves is also often more complex than the term single burial often implies, with multiple burials, manipulation of the corpse, access after burial to remove bones and so on, far from unusual (Brück 2006a; 2009; Gibson 2004).

29. Barrett, Bradley, and Green 1991; Bradley 2000; 2007; Green 2000; Henshall 1972; Midgley 2008.

30. Lanting and Van der Waals 1976; Needham 2005; Vander Linden 2006; 2007a; 2007b.

31. On some occasions in Britain, these were made specifically for inclusion in the grave (Boast 1995).

32. Renfrew 1973; 1974; Shennan 1982.

33. For a thorough critique of the 'rise of the individual narrative', see the work of Joanna Brück (2004; 2006a; 2006b; 2009).

34. Shennan 1982.

35. For example, see O'Shea's (1996) study of Early Bronze Age Hungary.

36. Kienlin 2008; Renfrew 1973; Sherratt 1994.

37. Brück 2006b.

38. Brück 2004; 2009.

39. Vella Gregory 2007.

40. Brøndsted 1940, 310.

41. The references discussing this art can be found in various locations including: for Italy, Graziosi (1974); for Mount Bego, de Lumley (1976); Coles (2005) on southern Scandinavia; Scarre (2008) on France; Vella Gregory (2007) on Sardinia; and Shee Twohig (1981) and Sanchidrián (2005) for an overview of megalithic art.

42. Shee Twohig 1981.

43. Axes have a longer history of appearance in rock art, being present on Breton tombs going back to the fifth millennium, for example. However, these are less clearly weapons as we would understand the term today; instead, they were tools that could be used as weapons, but also stood as evidence for complex histories and relations of exchange, skill and status.

44. cf. Harding et al. 2008.

45. The terms and language around statue-stelae can be confusing. In the most common usage, statue-stelae differ from statue-menhirs in that the former are shaped stone statues whilst the latter are carved on to a pre-existing boulder.

46. Casini and Fossati 2004; Casini, De Marinis, and Pedrotti 1995; Robb 2008b; 2009a.

47. Gallay 1995; Mallory and Telehin 1995.

48. Anati 1994; Casini, De Marinis, and Pedrotti 1995; Casini and Fossati 2004; La Guardia 2001; Robb 2008b, 2009a.

49. Fedele 2008.

50. In this they share much with many Bronze Age burials, which also have a repetitive layout, drawing attention to certain parts of the body (Brück 2004; Lucas 1996).

51. Robb 2008b; 2009a; cf. Sørensen 2010.

52. Even clubs, for which we have some evidence in Neolithic Britain at least (Schulting and Wysocki 2005), do not seem to have been valorised as weapons in the manner in which Bronze Age examples were.

53. Frieman 2010a.

54. And in fact, in the unusual example of a society that returned to hunting and gathering in this period, the Pitted Ware group that dwelt in parts of southern Scandinavia.

55. Pressure flaking is a highly skilled technique, and elements of it require significant strength (for example, in the removal of flakes to make the barb and the tang on certain kinds of arrowheads (Lawrence Billington, personal communication)). It is likely that this form of technology itself was caught up in prestige and power relations (cf. Sinclair 1995).

56. Fitzpatrick 2011.

57. As were razors.

58. Lomborg 1973.

59. Frieman 2010a.

60. Even when tin bronze was used, on occasions the high amount of tin included (for example in Scandinavian metal hilted daggers) would also have made them brittle (Frieman 2010b, 159).

61. Frieman 2010a; 2010b.

62. Guilaine and Zammit 2005; Schulting and Fibiger 2011.

63. Dolfini 2011.

64. Boyle 2006; Orton 2008; Robb 2007.

65. Albarella and Serjeantson 2002.

66. Bourdieu 1977; Riches 1986.

67. Harding 2000, 281–284.

68. Fontijn 2002.

69. Coles 1962; Harding 1999a.

70. Kristiansen 2002, 326.

71. Treherne 1995.

72. Kristiansen 2002.

73. Inalienable possessions are those that cannot be separated from the context of their use, production and exchange. They are always caught up in their own histories. The simplest contrast to explain this is between a precious family heirloom wrapped in stories, emotions and memories, and a bottle of mineral water purchased in a shop, the same as all the others left behind. These latter possessions are entirely *alienated* in opposition to the former (Weiner 1992). See Brück (2004) for discussion of Bronze Age objects as inalienable.
74. Kristiansen 2002, 329ff.
75. Fontijn 2002.
76. García Sanjuán et al. 2006; Harding et al. 2008; Kristiansen 1999.
77. Guilaine and Zammit 2005; Hanks 2008; Harding 1999b; Harding 2007; Kristiansen 1999.
78. Hanks 2008, 269.
79. Pfaffenberger 1992 and see Chapter 2 and Chapter 8.
80. Brennand and Taylor 2003; Pryor 2001
81. O'Shea 1996.
82. Sørensen 1991; 1997; 2000; 2006; 2010. And see Chapter 2 of this volume.
83. Harding 2000, figure 11.3.1, 373; Palincaş 2010.
84. Sørensen 1997.
85. Wels-Weyrauch 1988; 1991; 2008.
86. Sørensen 1997.
87. Sørensen 1997.
88. Sørensen 1997.
89. Fontijn 2002.
90. See also Brück 2006a; 2006b.
91. Fowler 2004a; Strathern 1988; Sofaer Derevenski 2000; Sørensen 1997; Brück 2004.
92. Stevens 2008; cf. Fontijn 2002.
93. This is an important point to emphasize. As Brück (2004, 2) notes, there has been a tendency for the acquisition of weapons by men to be treated as an active agent-driven process, whilst the collection of ornaments by women has been seen as a passive system in which they are, in effect, decorated by someone else. The point is that both these constructions of self are parallel, both equally requiring active participation and both equally relational.
94. Sørensen 1987.
95. Brück 2006b, 307.
96. e.g. Harris 2009; 2010; Hodder 2007; Hodder 2006; Robb 2007; Souvatzi 2008; Tilley 1996; Whittle 1996; 2003.
97. Ortner 1972.
98. Bradley 1984; Renfrew 1974; Shennan 1982.
99. Brück 2004; 2006a; 2006b; 2009.
100. A switch that takes place much later in our history, and was never totalizing or complete.
101. For a discussion of the multiple kinds of relational and individual personhoods see Brittain and Harris 2010 and Fowler 2004a; specifically in relation to this context, see Fowler 2004b.

102. Shennan 1982; Thorpe and Richards 1984.
103. Whilst we concur entirely with Brück's critique of the rise of the individual narrative in the Bronze Age, we differ from her here in our interpretation. Brück (e.g. 2006a, 73; 2009, 9) is critical of attempts to read competitive individualism into the past, and where this draws on capitalist and neoliberal ideologies, she is certainly right to do so. However, competition itself is not solely a product of capitalism. Ethnographic examples demonstrate the potential for competition to exist alongside, and indeed to be productive of, particular kinds of relational personhood (Godelier and Strathern 1991).
104. Godelier 1986; Godelier and Strathern 1991.
105. Bourdieu 1977.
106. Barfield 1994; De Marinis and Brillante 1998; Höpfel, Platzer, and Spindler 1992; Spindler 1994; 1995.
107. Robb 2009b.
108. Spindler 1994.
109. Murphy et al. 2003; Spindler 1994; Sjøvold et al. 1995; zur Nedden and Wicke 1992.
110. Rogers and Waldron 1995.
111. Dorfer et al. 1998.
112. Robb 2009b.
113. Gell 1993.
114. Fedele 2008.
115. Robb 2001.
116. Gallay 1995; Harrison and Heyd 2007.
117. Michelaki 2008.
118. Brück 2006a; 2006b.
119. Gerritsen 2003.
120. Fontijn 2002.
121. Maraszek 2009; Meller 2002.
122. Kristiansen and Larsson 2005, 267.
123. Bradley 2006; Kaul 1998.
124. e.g. Coles 2005.
125. Brück 2004, 309.
126. Brück 2004; 2009.
127. This section of the chapter draws extensively on the research conducted by Marie Louise Stig Sørensen and Katharina Rebay-Salisbury as part of the wider project. The detail of their research can be found in Sørensen and Rebay-Salisbury 2008a; 2008b; 2008c; 2008d.
128. Harding 2000.
129. Childe 1950; Kimmig 1964.
130. Harding 1994, 318ff.
131. Harding 1994, 320–321.
132. Gräslund 1994; Oestigaard 2004.
133. Kristiansen 1998, 113ff.
134. This section draws heavily upon Sørensen and Rebay-Salisbury 2008d.
135. Sørensen and Rebay-Salisbury 2008d.
136. In some ways, this is similar to the transition to cremation in twentieth century Britain. Whilst there are clearly broader changes in beliefs behind this, it has not, by itself, radically transformed British body worlds.

137. This section draws heavily on Sørensen and Rebay-Salisbury 2008c.
138. Hampel, Kerchler, and Benkovsky-Pivovarová 1981; Sørensen and Rebay-Salisbury 2008a; 2008c.
139. See also Brück 2009, 7.
140. Robb 2007; Souvatzi 2008; Whittle 1996.
141. Brück 2004; Fowler 2004a.
142. Godelier 1986.

5

The body and politics

Oliver J. T. Harris, Jessica Hughes, Robin Osborne,
John Robb and Simon Stoddart

Perfect in death[1]

On a warm spring day in 430 BC, a group of people have assembled in the Kerameikos cemetery at Athens for a funeral (Plate III; Figure 44). It is a family group, but a large one – several dozen in all, counting the adults and the children who trail solemnly behind. A handful of slaves attend but remain apart. They have walked from their house inside the city out through the fortress-like Dipylon gate to the area beyond which forms the principal cemetery of the city. Here, their family grave plot stands amongst many others of the well-off Athenian citizenry. The varied forest of private commemorations spreads out before a backdrop of civic memory, the city's monuments to its war dead, and the massive wall built by Themistocles about fifty years ago. That was the heroic time of grandparents who still remember the great victories of Marathon and Salamis over the Persians which cemented Athens' freedom and leadership in the Greek world. Since then, Athens has come a long way. The city dominates a 'league' of subjugated allies which is in fact its empire, and it is the naval, commercial and military centre of Greece. It is a boom town, full of foreigners, and its poets, orators, sculptors, potters and craftsmen set the standard for the Mediterranean world. This is the long summer of Athens; the grim, grinding Peloponnesian War with its ultimate defeat has just begun, and the disasters of the coming century – the plague which will kill half of those present in the next year or two and the conquest by the Macedonians – are not even clouds on the horizon.

The funeral group gather around a freshly filled-in grave, its earth raw and moist. Nine days ago, they buried a young man, one of the heirs of the family, victim of a sudden illness. Now they are completing the first of the remembrance ceremonies which continue at intervals over the coming year. As the parents and family look

on, dressed in their finest tunics and cloaks, workmen are erecting a marble stela at the grave. The family have purchased it in haste from the sculptor's workshop. It shows a solidly built young man, beardless but mature in body, grave but attractive, his athletic body clothed in cloak and tunic. The scene chosen suits the death of a young man approaching his prime. He holds a strigil, a curving bronze accessory used by athletes in the gymnasium to scrape sweat and oil from their bodies. It marks him as a member of a wealthy cultural elite which frequented the gymnasia and the symposia. The young man's name has been added to the grave marker in the last few days.

The grave marker raised, the young man takes his place amongst the dead of Athens. The gravestone represents the individual buried there, but not in a quasi-photographic form. It is a remarkable transformation. Who outside his immediate circle will remember that his arms were stringier than portrayed or that his face was more often twisted in anger or laughter than gravely composed? Who will remember that he was always last in competitions of any kind or that he had recently been reproved by his parents for mistreating a household slave? Who will remember that his first military service a few months ago had been to help guard a goat track in an unmemorable bit of saber-rattling near Megara (no enemies appeared, only goats, for which he was profoundly grateful)? And who will remember that his unexpected death wrecks his parents' plans for his marriage and changed his brothers' prospects of inheriting land in the countryside outside Athens? It does not matter now; whatever else he was or wanted to be, Eupheros is now a grave, strong, young athlete for eternity.

Classical sculpture is famous amongst art historians for exactly this kind of transformation. Bodies such as Eupheros' are shown with 'realistic' detail rather than with the schematism typical of earlier and non-Greek sculpture, in 'natural' poses, with weight, posture and anatomical detail suggesting the genuine depiction of living human bodies. Yet at the same time, they are purified of individuating detail. They are reduced to idealized bodies projecting a narrow range of stories based around individual and civic virtues. We will discuss what this style means in this chapter. Here, it is worth noting that this 'technology of enchantment'[2] has cast a similar spell on modern viewers. We are used to seeing bodies such as Eupheros' on a pedestal, in a museum, or as pictures in a book, without living bodies around them. Isolated from the life around them, they can exemplify an abstract spirit of 'art' and 'civilization'.

Yet Classical 'art' occurred in the midst of life. The Kerameikos is no quiet place of contemplation like the vast cemeteries outside modern cities, the suburbs of

Figure 44. Grave stela of Eupheros, Kerameikos cemetery, Athens, ca. 430 BC (photo Robb; photo courtesy of 3rd Ephorate of Prehistoric and Classical Antiquities, Kerameikos Museum, Athens. © Hellenic Ministry of Education and Religions, Culture and Athletics).

the dead. It sits astride the most important road out of Athens, bustling with continual traffic: rich, poor, citizens, foreigners, slaves, soldiers, philosophers, prostitutes, beggars. All people and purposes are present. The chaotic mixture along the road contrasts with the resolutely staid, homogeneous membership of the gymnasium-going, monument-purchasing class. On the grave markers, women remain modestly in the home and men are athletic, martial or statesmanlike. On the road, women of all strata go about the city on errands, conducting friendship, and, often, their jobs or professions; men may also be lumpy, bald, weak, quarrelsome, physically or morally grubby, or simply tired. And the funeral ceremony which Eupheros' grieving family is conducting is not insulated from this personal and political richness. Death in Athens is not a private family affair; civic funerals, for instance, are always the occasion for major political speeches. At private funerals, by law, only relatives are allowed to be present, underlining ritually an often downplayed but sometimes highly important legal distinction between citizens and foreigners. The scale and

ostentation of the funeral is an important statement about a family, so much so that funerals both in Athens and elsewhere were restricted by sumptuary laws: in Athens stone grave monuments seem to have been effectively banned between 480 BC and 430 BC. Children are present in part because being present at the funeral is important to one's claim to inherit property.

What is the 'Classical body'? In this chapter, we focus principally upon the 'revolution' in how bodies were represented. Why did Greek artists show bodies such as Eupheros' naturalistically? This is a question which has provoked a vast amount of debate. It is not merely a question of art history; it turns out to have important implications for how the body relates to politics.

But to answer this question, we need to escape from art history and put the body in its social context. Most discussions have started from the stone bodies and grudgingly supplemented them with some reference to the living bodies around them – an approach as detached from flesh and blood as the marble itself, in a scholarly world in which even the modest claim that statues were sometimes painted gaudily is surprisingly controversial. We take the opposite tack. The 'Classical body' must be seen first and foremost as the bodies of Classical people, as they understood them and lived them; the various worlds of sculpture, vase painting, poetry, philosophy and medicine are all partial and interested systems of representation touching upon this matter but not defining it. The real question addressed by this chapter is how the gaze of Classical sculpture worked: how the stone bodies formed or changed, Gorgon-like, the living bodies which made them, saw them, worshipped them, bustled by them, and sometimes defaced or destroyed them. An important aspect of this is that these statues, with only a few exceptions such as herms, were usually encountered in very specific contexts: in the cemetery, the sanctuary and the temple. These were not contexts at random, but instead places which had both political and cosmological implications.[3]

The act of abstracting the body to an image or system of representation must always be a political act. Although the body is always central to politics, the Classical period is particularly appropriate for exploring this theme. Ever since art historians began to systematize and study Greek sculpture, there has been an almost irresistible tendency to associate the formal style of Classical art with Athenian democracy as a political system. In a traditional narrative, the dynamic naturalism of Classical sculpture entails a rejection of rigid, formalistic Oriental models. Its emphasis upon the idealized individual reflects an air of freedom and confidence blowing through the streets of Athens after the heroic, against-the-odds victory defeating the massed armies of the Persian invasions. At the same time, by making an idealized, 'naturalistic' humanity the aesthetic measure of all things (including the gods themselves), Classical Greeks placed humans at the centre of the cosmos, much as democracy placed the individual citizen capable of self-government at the centre of civic life.[4]

As an interpretation of the past, this has all the hall-marks of a legitimating origin myth. It derives modern European high culture and political systems from a heroic past, and links them through politically loaded modern terms such as 'individualism' and 'freedom'; it provides a historic basis for European Orientalism[5] by contrasting a vaguely defined Greek or Western 'spirit' or zeitgeist of individual freedom and expression with an equally vague Oriental despotism. Thus even recent and insightful scholarly treatments such as Fullerton's contrast the 'rational humanism of Greek culture' with 'the more spiritual and obeisant mentality implicit in Middle Eastern art'.[6]

We argue that there *is* a fundamental link between politics and the body in Classical art, but it is of quite a different nature. We first discuss the lived Classical body in a range of venues. Then, with this as a baseline, we ask two questions. First, how is the stereotypical 'Classical body', known above all in statuary, a political representation within the Greek world? Secondly, we tackle the same question on the margins of the Greek world. What happened to this representation of the human body, a key element of Greek 'civilization', when it encountered people outside the Greek world – Etruscans, Romans, Gauls and others? What does this tell us about the politics of colonization and empire?

The Classical world

Greece in the first millennium BC

The historic period in Greece begins around 800 BC and is subdivided into various periods such as the Archaic, the Classical and the Hellenistic (Table 6).[7] Although these subdivisions sound dry and academic, they exist because of an important fact: as a time of dramatic social change, 'Classical Greece' stands for histories rather than static objects. From the Archaic through the Hellenistic period, every century is different. In effect, it is as if we tried to characterize under a single epithet such as 'early historic Europe' the history of Western Europe from the rustic towns of the Viking or Anglo-Saxon period to the colonial empires of the eighteenth century.

Here we can only summarize a few key elements of the Classical world as background for discussing how people

understood the body in this period. The *polis* (city-state) is a good place to start. As a physical settlement, *poleis* varied greatly. A few were non-urban polities and the smallest were towns of a few hundred people, but the largest (such as Athens, Corinth and Sparta) were cities with more than a hundred thousand residents each. What they had in common was self-rule. 'Greece' never existed as a political entity in ancient times; although cities often acted in alliances or leagues, these were built out of fiercely independent building blocks. Even when one city-state subjected and exploited its nominal partners (the most outstanding example is Athens' domination of the Delian League of smaller Aegean city-states), such infringements were strongly resented and the subjected cities were always ready to rebel at any sign of weakening control.

City-states are often described as democracies, oligarchies or tyrannies, but such terms refer rather narrowly to their formal form of government rather than to the social relations making up the *polis*. All city-states included similar fundamental elements in their populations. There were three basic civil statuses: free citizens, foreigners and slaves. Each city rang its own changes upon these, of course; Athens, for instance, defined citizen status more rigidly and explicitly than many others, forbidding resident foreigners to own property, and Sparta reputedly used a particularly repressive form of control over its slaves. Cross-cutting these civil statuses were distinctions of gender and age. Very different basic natures, activities, and social and economic roles were prescribed for males and females (see discussion later in this chapter). It is difficult to estimate how the population would be broken down amongst these groups, as demographic records are both hazy and unrepresentative. The best known city, Athens, was also by far the largest and probably also had many more resident foreigners than most. As a general estimate, the Athenian state at its height in the Classical period probably held 300,000 to 400,000 people. Of these, about 10 per cent were adult male citizens; with their families, they made up about half of the population. Most would have been small landowners, but many were urban craftsmen or engaged in trade and this included an elite stratum of wealthy families. Slavery was universal, unquestioned and economically fundamental in the ancient world. In Athens, probably one-quarter to one-third of the population were slaves.

Governing a city-state such as this could be done in several ways. There was virtually always a stratum of old, wealthy families who provided most civic leaders regardless of the form of government. In the Archaic period, these civic elites alternated between different political idioms and lifestyles for promoting their interests,

Table 6. *Classical Greece: the chronological framework (dates relevant to art, literature, and human body representations are shown in italics)*

eighth century BC (700s) through 510 BC	Archaic period in Greece. Some institutions which span Archaic Greece include the independent *polis* (city-state) as a political unit; a generally aristocratic city government which oscillated in individual cities between a single ruler (tyranny, without negative connotations), an elite oligarchy, and a more or less popular assembly; and civic and pan-Hellenic religious festivals often associated with athletic games.
eighth century BC (700s)	*First surviving Greek poetry (Homer's and Hesiod's works); Geometric art includes human figures in metalwork and on vases.*
eighth century BC (700s) onwards	Beginning of Greek colonization of the Aegean, Black Sea, Adriatic and Central Mediterranean; more than 100 independent cities are founded between 800 BC and 550 BC.
seventh-sixth centuries BC (600s–500s)	*Archaic Greek poetry: short lyric poems by aristocratic poets such as Sappho, Archilochos and Alkman for performance at symposia or on formal public occasions.*
seventh-sixth centuries BC (600s–500s)	*Range of Archaic human body representations, including miniatures in stone, wood, ivory and metals, and monumental, naturalistic but formal and rigid statues of young men (kouroi) and women (korai).*
510 BC	Overthrow of 'tyrants' in Athens (single rulers chosen from aristocracy) and formation of democratic government (government by assembly of enfranchised citizens).
492 BC–490 BC, 481 BC–479 BC	First and second Persian invasions of Greece. Although Athens was sacked in 480 BC, primarily Athenian victories at Marathon (490 BC) and Salamis (480 BC) and Greek coalition victories at Plataea (479) and Mykale (479) ended the war.
480 BC–323 BC	Classical period in Greece.
fifth century BC (400s)	*Flowering of Classical literature, including tragedies by Aeschylus, Sophocles, and Euripides, comedies by Aristophanes and histories by Herodotus and Thucydides. Three generations of Classical philosophy represented by Socrates, Plato and Aristotle span the later fifth and fourth centuries BC.*
fifth century BC	*Classical medicine, represented by Hippocrates (460–370 BC), emphasizes external observation, diet and drugs.*
fifth – fourth centuries BC (400s–300s)	*Classical style in statuary depicts human body in 'naturalistic' manner and in wider range of positions and contexts.*
fifth – fourth centuries BC (400s–300s)	*Statuary used commonly in public monuments and religious architecture; Parthenon (Temple of Athena) at Athens built and decorated 447–431 BC. Particularly notable classical sculptures include Praxiteles' Aphrodite of Knidos (mid-fourth century BC; rare in portraying female nudity) and huge gilt statues of Zeus at Olympia and Athena at the Parthenon (mid-fifth century BC).*
431 BC–404 BC	Peloponnesian War between Athens (and allies) and Sparta (and allies), ultimately won by Sparta with punitive consequences for Athens, though the city regains prosperity after further fighting amongst Greek city-states reduces Sparta's dominance.
338 BC	Philip of Macedon's campaigns to conquer Greece culminate at the Battle of Chaeronea (338 BC), which ends Athens' independence and places mainland Greece under Macedonian domination.
336 BC–323 BC	After death of Philip, Alexander the Great conquers much of the Near East, Levant and Egypt, bringing it under Macedonian rule.
323 BC–146 BC	Hellenistic period, from death of Alexander to Roman conquest of Greece. After the death of Alexander, his empire fragments into major kingdoms based in Macedon, Iraq and Persia, and Egypt.
3rd–2nd centuries BC (300–100 BC)	*Hellenistic art develops new genres of depicting human body (in grotesques, in female nudes, in private sculpture) but also makes great use of Classical style in both new works and copies of earlier works – a trend which continues into the Roman era.*
third century BC – first century AD	Expansion of Rome, which conquers Italy (third century BC); Greece, Spain and North Africa (second century BC); Egypt and Gaul (first century BC); and Germany, Britain and Judea (first century AD).
second century AD	*Galen (129–200 AD) theorizes circulation of fluids in body, the basis of Roman and medieval physiology and medicine.*

a fact which impinges directly upon art and body representations.[8] One style of elite politics emphasizes their aristocratic roots, international connections and wealth. This was expressed in institutions such as the symposium, a closed, exclusive dining party formalizing relations amongst a group of 'companions'; it also resulted in avid adoption of Oriental art and imagery, aristocratic sports such as chariot racing, and ostentatious public dedication of expensive statues. The *kouroi* (Archaic male nude statues) fit directly into this lifestyle. Conversely, elites also practiced a democratizing style of politics which downplayed their wealth and exotic connections and appealed to a broader 'middling' base amongst the citizenry, rather like American politicians from old wealthy families and Ivy League educations wearing blue jeans and eating hot dogs at baseball games. Again, this was associated with specific forms of body representation, particularly herms (see discussion that follows). In the Archaic period, *poleis* tended to alternate between oligarchic government by small assemblies of leading citizens and tyrannies in which one such citizen seized control, usually through a populist appeal to the masses.

In the Classical period, democracy supplemented these models. In Athenian democracy, a citizen assembly governed the city. Any adult male citizen could participate, and about 6,000 citizens regularly attended the meetings about forty times a year. This assembly was guided by a council of 500 citizens chosen to represent the local communities making up the city. Although Classical Greece is often cited as the 'cradle of democracy', we should probably not take this too literally. For one thing, democracy was far from common in the Greek world. In fact, Athens is the only notable example; most other city-states were governed by oligarchic assemblies or by kings advised by such assemblies. It is also questionable to what extent Athens owed its success in cultural, economic and military affairs to its peculiar form of government rather than to other factors such as its wealth and trade; democracy may have been a result of these factors (for instance, a way of governing a hyper-large city with an active, prosperous mercantile and manufacturing class) rather than a cause of them. Moreover, although modern viewpoints tend to highlight the difference between democracy and other forms of government, democracy, monarchy and oligarchy were not qualitatively discrete options but formed part of a continuum, and arguably had more common elements than differences. For example, citizen assemblies were found in almost all governments, and they almost always included some status-related distinction excluding much of the population on grounds of gender, property, citizenship or family. Athens was highly unusual in having no property-ownership criterion for attendance at the Assembly, but only adult male citizens – perhaps 10–15 per cent of the total population at most as we noted earlier – were enfranchised. Athenian democracy was thus both similar and dissimilar to modern democracies; it involved the mass of citizens in civic discussion and decisions, but it was much more exclusionary and often acted to protect the rights of the enfranchised against the disenfranchised.

Outside Greece, there was a world of other people; indeed much of the 'Greek' world could be found beyond the boundaries of the modern nation state of Greece.

From early in the eighth century BC, Greek cities established settlements abroad around all the seas they knew. These existed from the Crimea, Armenia and Turkey around the Black Sea to Anatolia and Cyprus in the Eastern Mediterranean, Egypt and Libya, Sicily and Southern Italy, and Southern France and Iberia. With Greece itself, Southern Italy and Sicily formed part of *Magna Graecia*, an area of Greek language and civilization; important Greek poets such as Ibycus, philosophers such as Pythagoras, politicians such as the tyrants of Syracuse and scientists such as Archimedes came from these western regions. Greek colonization was very different from Roman or modern European colonialism. These 'colonies' were mostly opportunistic private ventures rather than planned government initiatives. Relations between colonies and their parent city were not particularly strong; Greek colonies functioned essentially as independent cities from their birth, and acted autonomously or even against their parent city.

The Greek world also differed from Roman and post-medieval imperialism in how it dealt with other peoples. Many of these were known to the Greeks: Scythians, Thracians, Persians, Anatolians, Phoenicians, Egyptians, Italics, Sicels, Etruscans, Gauls and more. In general, although Greeks recognized distinctive traits of people such as Scythians, Thracians and Persians, they seem to have been less concerned about stigmatizing and controlling people different from themselves than, say, the Romans in Gaul or the English, French and Spanish in the New World. There are a number of reasons why this may have been so. There was no real technological gap between Greeks and non-Greeks; indeed, with respect to Anatolia, Persia, the Levant and Egypt, Greeks were a newer, less populous culture which learned much from their powerful neighbours, and there was probably some level of shared general culture, at least in the Eastern and Central Mediterranean. Moreover, the Greek encounter with the other was less dictated by a one-sided, strategic calculation which would benefit from essentializing and dehumanizing the Other, and more attuned to needs of coexistence and trade which required some level of mutual understanding. The category of 'barbarian' was not really used until the fifth century BC and never employed as systematically and reductively as similar concepts (e.g. 'savage', 'Indian') were in later colonial worlds.

The kiss of the prince: The Classical body and the 'Greek Revolution'

Classical art has been appreciated since antiquity – Hellenistic and Roman patrons were avid collectors and imitators of it – and the rediscovery of Classical sculpture was fundamental to the Renaissance. Sculptors such as

(a)   (b)

Figure 45. Archaic sculpture. A. *Kouros* from Tenea, ca. 550 BC (© Staatliche Antikensammlungen und Glyptothek München). B. The 'Peplos *kore*', Acropolis, Athens, late sixth century BC, as found (right) and as originally painted (left) (© Museum of Classical Archaeology, Cambridge).

Michelangelo and painters such as Botticelli were directly inspired by Classical models (or at least by the more common Hellenistic and Roman copies of them). Classical paintings have almost entirely vanished with time, and bronze sculptures, thought to have been more highly valued than marble ones, were probably mostly melted down for reuse of the metal and are generally preserved only in exceptional circumstances such as shipwrecks. Appreciation of Classical art, hence, has been based principally upon sculpture in stone, and secondarily upon painted pottery. And it was recognized from the beginning that one of the most characteristic features of Classical art was how it placed the human body front and centre. The human body provides the dominant theme of Classical sculpture and vase painting.

Winckelmann and subsequent nineteenth and twentieth century art historians defined the periods known later as the Archaic, Classical and Hellenistic based upon sculpture. *Kouroi* were considered typical of the Archaic period. A *kouros* (plural *kouroi*) was a life-size or larger statue of a standing male youth, usually marble, usually nude but with elaborate hair styles, in a rigid, formal posture with arms at the sides and one foot advanced. *Kouroi* were used throughout the eastern Greek world as dedications at temples, and within Athenian territory were also used as grave markers. Their female counterpart, the *kore* (pl. *korai*) was always clothed. Both males and females bear a distant, somewhat enigmatic smile.

The big change came in the Classical period, from about 500 BC. It is what the art historian and theorist Gombrich called 'the Greek Revolution'. Compare the bodies in Figure 45 with the bodies in Figure 46.

(a)   (b)   (c)

Figure 46. Classical sculpture. A. Later copy of the Doryphoros of Polykleitos, ca. 440 BC (© Museum of Classical Archaeology, Cambridge). B. Grave marker, Athens, early fourth century BC (©bpk/Antikensammlung, SMB/Ingrid Geske). C. Dexileos stela, Kerameikos, Athens (© Museum of Classical Archaeology, Cambridge).

In summing up the canonical art-historical view of the change, it is hard to do better than quote Gombrich's wonderfully vivid description:

> There are few more exciting spectacles in the whole history of art than the great awakening of Greek sculpture and painting between the sixth century and the time of Plato's youth towards the end of the fifth century BC. Its dramatic phases have often been told in terms of an episode from 'The Sleeping Princess' when the kiss of the prince breaks the thousand-year-old spell and the whole court begins to stir from the rigors of unnatural sleep. We are shown how the stiff and frozen figures we call Apollines, or *kouroi*, first move one foot forward, then bend their arms, how their masklike smile softens, and how, at the time of the Persian wars, the symmetry of their tense posture is finally broken when their bodies receive a slight twist, so that life seems to enter the marble.[9]

Classical sculptures were used for a wide range of functions: as grave markers, as decoration on public monuments (such as temples), as venerated images within temples and as religious dedications and commemorations, though never for private art. A particularly common form was the herm, a square pillar with a male head (often representing Hermes) and an erect phallus (see Figure 56). Herms were erected by roadsides, in public places such as temples and markets and at the doorways to private houses.

The human body was also frequently depicted in painted pottery (Figure 47). Archaic vases featured black pictures on a red background; Classical vases bore red pictures on a black background. Like sculptures, decorated pots were made not as purely expressive 'art' but as things to be used upon specific occasions, such as formal male drinking parties (symposia), presentations to athletic victors, and in burial rites. Black- and red-figured vases show a wide range of scenes from mythology, story, history and daily life. White-painted cylindrical cosmetic jars were used mostly in burial rituals, a feature evident in their decoration. How the human body was painted on pottery parallels how it was depicted in sculpture. Before the sixth century BC, the body was shown very schematically; the presence of a body might be required for the narrative motivating a pot, but detail and realism were unimportant (Figure 47a). Black-figure painting (Figure 47b) introduced a new level of realism in both subject and style; yet figures still have a conventionalized appearance, as if they are formed out of geometric solids with smooth surfaces. Red-figure painting (Figure 47c) involved much more detailed depiction of surfaces and textures. Such detail proved a breakthrough in terms of ability to depict

things such as the texture of musculature which convey a sense of fleshy embodiment ('enfleshment' in Osborne's term[10]). Red-figure pottery, thus, has been written into the narrative of the classical body; like Classical sculpture, it has been seen as the apex of ancient art, when the medium really comes alive.

The history of scholarship on the human body thus sets up a grand narrative of a change in beliefs about the body and their causes:

a) Art (sculpture and pottery) reveals the fundamental essence of Classical civilization.

b) The defining moment was the transition to Classical sculpture around the beginning of the fifth century BC, with its focus upon the human body, portrayed in a style which is both 'naturalistic' and idealized and which continues to provide a standard of beauty in art down to the present day.

The big question, thus, is: What was the kiss that awoke the sleeping beauty and freed the human body from shackles of rigid marble? As we noted at the start of the chapter, for several centuries now, scholars have located the answer to this question in the relationship between politics – specifically Athenian democracy – and a general Classical Greek zeitgeist of freedom, individualism and humanism.[11]

> If the overall development of Greek art is from [Archaic] abstraction to [Classical] naturalism, it is clear that a major step in this direction occurred around 480 BC; given that date, explanation is inevitably found in the Persian Wars.

> The experience of having defeated the Persians is believed to have imbued the Greeks with an enhanced sense of liberty and personal responsibility, both of which are thought to be reflected in the 'humanism of Early Classical style. . . . Another view is that the individualistic qualities implicit in the Early Classical style evolved as a result of the establishment in democracy in Athens and were disseminated from that centre during and after the Persian Wars as Athenian power was waxing.[12]

Thus, victory over the Persians gave early Classical artists the self-confidence to undertake a 'new analysis of consciousness underpinned by the confident belief in the value of human thought and action'.[13]

Although politics, art and the body were anything but separable, there are serious reasons to question this facile, alluring, traditional narrative of the 'Greek Revolution'.[14] We will return to the question of the Classical body in sculpture later in this chapter, but first we must meet the Classical body in life.

(a)   (b)   (c)   (d)

Figure 47. Archaic and Classical pottery. A. Geometric amphora, c. 700 BC; note schematic human figures on neck (photo Robb; photo courtesy of 3rd Ephorate of Prehistoric and Classical Antiquities, Kerameikos Museum, Athens. © Hellenic Ministry of Education and Religions, Culture and Athletics). B. Archaic black-figure vase (© Trustees of the British Museum). C. Classical red-figure vase (© Trustees of the British Museum). D. Athenian cylindrical cosmetics jar (*lekythos*) with painted figures on white background (© Trustees of the British Museum).

The body world of Classical Greece: The view on the streets

There is a huge, argumentative literature on the human body in the Greco-Roman world, fragmented among, and within, the surprisingly distinct disciplines of Classical literature, philology, art, ancient history, archaeology and the history of medicine. Only two general floods have washed across these traditionally bounded disciplines and cross-fertilized them. The great cultural theorist Michel Foucault used Classical Greek masculinity and homosexuality as a centrepiece of his *History of Sexuality* (Volume 2),[15] provoking a storm of criticism and counter-criticism. More generally, as throughout all the humanities, the feminist movements of the 1970s and 1980s gave rise to extensive criticism of traditional, almost entirely male-centred scholarship. For the Classical world, this bias in scholarship is exacerbated by the fact that almost all of our literary and artistic sources are male-authored; men wrote the histories, tragedies and comedies, medical texts and most of the poetry, and they made the sculptures and vases. Hence gender study requires criticism of sources and their contexts. Notwithstanding this challenge, in every discipline mentioned here, there are now extensive bodies of work on gender, women and masculinity. Classical gender has been extensively studied.[16] Even so (and perhaps all the more so), controversies remain, and there are many obvious sides of the life of ancient bodies for which we simply have no real evidence.

What was it like to have a body, or to be a body, in this period? We have addressed this question in previous chapters through ideas of a 'body world' which relates structures of meanings, practices, and bodily experiences. Here, since Athens around the fifth century BC is both the context for the problem of art discussed earlier and the place from which the bulk of the evidence comes, with occasional digressions afield or into other centuries, we will imagine ourselves in the streets of that city.

Women, men and the household

Any account of the classical body has to begin with gender, both because most of the scholarship has focused upon gender and because gender was genuinely central to people's lives.[17] Ancient Greeks understood their world through conceptual dichotomies, and the opposition between male and female was one of the most sweeping. Men and women were understood as having fundamentally different natures. This was reflected not only in visible differences between male and female bodies, but also in their characters and capacities. Contexts in which men and women did things interchangeably were rare; contexts in which they did different tasks or the same tasks differently were the norm. In theory, at least, men were strong, rational, and able to engage in public interaction; women were weaker, liable to be swayed by feelings, and principally capable of acting within the household sphere. Hence, in Athens in any case, women may have been formally unable to own property and to represent themselves in law courts; they did not participate in politics, and they probably did not attend the theatre. Prestigious male roles involved defending the city militarily, performing athletically in gymnasia and participating in the governance of the city; prestigious female roles involved domestic productivity, modesty and bearing children. Sexuality was asymmetrical – male sexuality was freely acknowledged as a social force, female sexuality was subject to strictures of seclusion and sanction. The 'public eye' was assumed to be a male eye, and it judged women according to a standard of *aidos* (modesty or shame).[18] Images of women in sculpture and on painted pottery tend to portray female desire in a way that emphasizes passivity and justifies aggressive male desire.[19] This gender ideology led Greeks – or at least the authors amongst them – to prescribe a spatial segregation; with inferiors such as slaves running their errands, respectable women were supposed to remain closeted modestly within the home.

There is no doubt that the Classical world was not gender-neutral, and that there were fundamental differences between men and women. Yet this picture of gender segregation and male domination has raised two related controversies. The first element of this is that picture is derived predominantly from legal texts, philosophical treatises, poetry, and artistic representations. These present the world incompletely and from a male perspective, and have often been analysed almost entirely from a male point of view. Did reality on the ground actually correspond to this idealized, prescriptive formula?

The answer is 'in some ways, but often not'. As ideals, the normative roles for men and women seem to have been widely shared. But we should not take the resulting prescriptions for how to live too rigidly. For example, in the theory of satirical commentators, respectable women remained indoors in a space where they would not encounter unrelated males; modestly out of the public gaze, they worked thriftily and productively for the good of the household. Images of women dressing and weaving indoors are common in myth, poetry and pottery (Plate VIIb), creating a mixture of beauty and labour which created the ideal feminine object of desire, the maiden.[20] On the other hand, incidental mentions in texts and inscriptions make clear that women often held jobs of many sorts including selling cloth, ribbons, food, and vegetables, nursing, washing, weaving, dying, and sewing cloth, inn-keeping, playing music and prostitution.[21] Women's labour in the fields was widespread and economically important.[22] Not all of these working women were slaves. Similarly, in theory, a strict sexual morality of chastity outside of the marriage bed applied to women, but extra-marital liaisons were the stuff of

comedy and presumably not unknown in daily life. The doctrine of female seclusion has similarly been critiqued as an overstated, elite ideal at odds with actual practice as known from both the archaeology of households[23] and literary and legal texts.[24] As Bundrick remarks:

the concept of female seclusion in Classical Athens originated with 19th-century male perceptions of women's ideal roles, fed by Victorian sensibilities with more than a hint of Orientalism; ironically, this view continues to be promoted by many feminist scholars with a different agenda. More moderate in perspective, but no less feminist in outlook, is the proposition that gender roles in the Athenian family were fluid, and that seclusion was a literary construct more than a working reality.[25]

The main thrust of such rigid and unrealistic prescriptions may well have been not so much to confine women as to underline class differences. They provided an idealized standard which many households were inherently unable to meet for economic reasons. Thus, for example, different standards of public exposure and sexual approachability were applied to slaves; similarly, (presumably upwardly-mobile) speakers in Athenian courts apologize for the fact that poverty made their mothers perform publicly visible or menial tasks. Female seclusion thus provided an unattainable 'regulatory fiction' (see following discussion) which used the supposedly innate characteristics of the female body as a way of separating classes.

Secondly, and relatedly, what was the status of Classical women? Were they systematically oppressed by patriarchy or were they autonomous, powerful, and in control? The answer is far from clear. Classical women lived under significant legal, economic and political restrictions.[26] A modern visitor to ancient Athens would probably be shocked by the extent of ingrained, casual misogyny. Occasional female poets, athletes or warriors should not obscure the fact that women were generally culturally devalued as weaker, less politically central, and less able to participate in rational discussion, and they were excluded from important venues such as the political assembly, the theatre, the gymnasium and the symposium. It has often been observed that valued statuses for men stressed their own physical or mental qualities, while valued statuses for women were relational, identifying them as daughters, sisters and spouses.[27] The result is ambiguity or contradiction: gender ideology portrayed women as under men's control, but social life also required women to affirm and participate actively in marriage and community.[28]

Yet women were not mere subordinates or slaves. They could occupy important roles, particularly in ritual, for instance as priestesses and as participants in cults such as that of Dionysos. They participated in their own networks of sociality and commensality.[29] They had their own domain of value and influence; men who spent too much time inside the home rather than in public places were suspect, effectively making spatial exclusion a two-edged sword. Gendered space within houses probably provided complementary, somewhat fluid realms rather than female confinement.[30] Literary mentions portray male-female relations of trust and affection,[31] and the general volume of misogynistic literature itself is testimony to the fact that who women were and what they did was important and struck at points of male vulnerability. Moreover, they could exert significant control over their own affairs. Males and females had different forms of production, leading to economic complementarity within the *oikos*.[32] In theory, the male head of household controlled his wife's wealth, principally held in her dowry, but she could threaten to take it back by divorcing him, thus holding a kind of veto over household affairs. Major economic decisions would have often, perhaps normally involved consensus amongst members of the household.[33] Even places where masculinity was asserted could be used as points of vulnerability; male sexual power was questioned in role-reversal plays such as Aristophanes' 'Women at the Assembly' and in his 'Lysistrata' in which the women of Athens hold a sex-strike to stop a war. Moreover, as lyrics by Sappho suggest, female desire was important in its own right, not merely a reflection of male sexuality, and the power of female sexuality is acknowledged in literature in Euripides' 'Hippolytos'.

At the end of the day, forcing Classical women into simple boxes of prisoners or equals really reveals more about our own political fixations than about ancient society. The situation was probably similar to that in recent, traditional Mediterranean societies: in theory, gender segregation and patriarchy prevail; but in practice, one finds household solidarity and cooperation, and supposedly governed women are often surprisingly influential in decision-making.[34] Probably, the best way to make sense of it is to see Classical society as involving the intersection of two kinds of units, the household (*oikos*) and the city (*polis*). In theory, the household involved a balanced complementarity of male and female roles, while civic relations involved the exclusion of women.[35] Yet such a conceptual division was not hermetic. As noted, women held prominent ritual positions in the *polis* as priestesses, officiating at public rites.[36] Ideological representations of the family emphasize its unity and solidarity rather than divisions within it.[37] For example, new legislation in the mid-fifth century BC which restricted Athenian citizenship to only people both of whose parents were citizens placed a new political emphasis upon mothers and

Figure 48. Woman on funerary stela (© Trustees of the British Museum).

wives; one unintended result was the increasing representation of women and family groups in the only public context in which they could be displayed, funerary stelae (Figure 48).[38]

There was real inequality in that women did not have access to the system of public esteem in which men participated, and hence had to work indirectly to do things which men could do without mediation.[39] But this was accompanied by genuinely complementary forms of value, opportunity and exclusion in other ways and by a social world in which men and women shared a strong common interest in the affairs of the household. Ultimately, the ambiguity about Classical gender inequality does not result from gaps in the ancient evidence available to us, although there are gaps; it was a genuine feature of social relations, and this ambiguity was one of the great strengths of the Classical gender order which made it so durable.

Men and men

As the asymmetry in male-female relations suggests, masculinity was a key social value. In some ways, men were conceptualized as the moral centre of society, women as the 'other'.[40] Most fundamentally, Greek masculinity seems to have been understood much as 'honour' in more recent Mediterranean societies: the capability to act effectively to assert one's will in competitive situations, to fulfil one's civic and domestic responsibilities and to protect one's interests, household and dependents. It is overgeneralizing to suggest that all Mediterranean societies are homogeneous and ancient Athens was the same as modern Spain or Algeria. But there is historical evidence to suggest that competition and dominance were latent in male-male interactions, while women were represented as an object (of desire, of control, of protection). For example, men could be prosecuted legally for crimes resulting from *hubris*, an overly aggressive masculinity resulting in sexual crimes not only against women but against younger males.[41] This gender ideology was developed in several high-profile institutions. Warfare was important in the strife-ridden world of the *poleis*, and military service was expected of every adult male. In the citizen infantry, war was an arena in which personal honour was gauged and reputation forged. Athletics was another. The gymnasium (literally, the 'place of nudity', from the custom of exercising naked) was dedicated to the cultivation of male bodies, which was also thought to be morally important. In its careful grooming of the male body as a sign of elite status, this continued late prehistoric traditions of the 'warrior's beauty' attested both in Homeric literature and in material items such as razors and tweezers.[42] Finally, the symposium was a formalized male drinking party which encompassed anything from serious intellectual and literary discussion to conventionalized homoerotic seduction to bawdy revelry with prostitutes.

At this point one might ask: Why are so many men in Greek art naked? Nudity was a male thing. Nakedness in women was rare both in life and in art; when it occurred, as in prostitutes shown on pottery, it marked the woman as part of an alternative, generally excluded social order. But in real life, men went nude in very few contexts, principally athletics and bathing. So why are men so often sculpted and painted nude, both when no context is shown and in particular contexts such as (rather impractically) when fighting on the battlefield? Both actual male nakedness and nudity in sculpture were a cultural costume rather than the mere absence of clothes, and nudity was used to express a range of meanings from godlike beauty to vulnerability and abjection.[43] In sculptures, however, heroic nudity[44] was principally a vehicle for emphasizing male beauty. The beautiful body was not identified by specific physical features, but by its harmonious proportions and symmetry; even depictions of athletes do not emphasize specific musculature in an anatomical sense as modern body builders do, but instead represent generically beautiful bodies which happen to be engaged in athletics.[45] This harmony of proportions was both a gift from the gods and the result of careful cultivation. Beyond this, the beautiful male body came in two distinct varieties; these are neatly encapsulated in the pair of statues known as the Tyrannicides, supposedly the first individual portraits erected in Athens, which commemorated two men who assassinated one of the last tyrants of Athens in 514 BC (Figure 49). One is the fully mature male, bearded, grave and robust. The other is the beardless, graceful male just reaching adulthood. The distinction does not signal only age differences, but also a deeper conceptual complementarity between mature males whose desire motivates social relations and the object of their desire, Apollo-like males exemplifying male beauty at its peak. This distinction laid the basis for Greek homoeroticism, which was not considered a lifelong, exclusive, sexual orientation but rather a natural erotic attraction towards a highly desirable object. In art and poetry, at least, homoeroticism took the form of a highly conventionalized courtship between an older, bearded man and a younger, beardless protégé. For the younger man, it was considered a transient phase, and it was considered shameful for a fully adult man to take a passive or 'female' part in a sexual relationship. Whether or not one follows Foucault's controversial analysis of Greek male homosexuality as a power discourse, it seems inescapably part of a narcissistic meditation upon male beauty.[46]

In the streets of the city

In the streets of the Classical city, bodies came in many more types than simply male and female. Two other important distinctions were citizen versus foreigner and free versus slave. Foreigners were 5–10 per cent of the Athenian population and comprised both Greeks from other city-states and non-Greeks. What it meant to be a citizen or foreigner seems somewhat ambiguous, as was the status of citizen itself.[47] Foreigners were subject to numerous legal restrictions. They were subject to taxes and civic duties but did not enjoy either political representation or public benefits. They were not allowed to own landed property, they paid special poll taxes and they had less legal protection. Yet literary, historical and artistic evidence suggests that they seem to have lived on equal terms with Athenians at all levels of society, working, living and dressing interchangeably. In sculpture and pottery, for instance, foreign identity is rarely indicated except where it was particularly relevant to some narrative point (for instance, adding Scythian or Phrygian attire to a warrior to indicate some military role other than the Greek infantryman). Physiognomy was rarely used to show 'others'. Even legendary figures thought to come from Africa such as Andromeda were usually depicted like any other figure.[48] The system thus combined sharp legal and institutional exclusions with cultural mobility and assimilation.

Figure 49. The 'Tyrannicides' (Naples, National Archaeological Museum, © Deutsches Archäologisches Institut – Rom).

Slavery was a more important stigma. Male and female slaves accounted for perhaps one-third to one-half of the population; almost all households included slaves and many industries relied upon their labour extensively. Much as in eighteenth-century America, a society attentive to equality amongst its citizens paradoxically took slavery as unquestioned.[49] Political theorists such as Aristotle (in his *Politics* I.2.2) justified slavery as natural by defining masters as capable of reason and slaves as using the body rather than the mind. Slaves were mainly ethnically different people drawn in from places such as Persia, Scythia, Thrace, the Levant and Egypt. Slaves were born into their status, or originated from war captives or a long-distance slave trade spanning the Black Sea, the Eastern Mediterranean and the Central Mediterranean. Slavery was a legal condition; they were not entirely without rights but were excluded from some property ownership, judicial representation and a political voice. How slavery translated into living conditions varied greatly. Skilled craftspeople could be well-off and relatively autonomous under the light control of their owner, and household slaves formed an inferior but omnipresent part of the household, participating in meals, rituals and celebrations as well as work. Agricultural slaves and particularly slaves in mines and quarries were worked hard, often brutally. Slavery was a bodily condition: slaves could be sexually used, beaten and tortured to give evidence in court. Yet it was not made visible on the body with specific costumes, badges or gestures.[50]

The streets of Athens thus present a paradoxical situation. There were important legal and institutional differences between people, between bodies. There were class differences between rich and poor. But there was also social mobility. Social distinctions were stressed in particular places and contexts – courts, assemblies, households. They were not made visible in many public areas; slaves, foreigners and citizens shared the streets and marketplaces, looking similar and often doing the same jobs for similar wages. Streets and marketplaces thus were 'free spaces' where important, fluid discussions between different kinds of people took place.[51] Hence the differences between bodies were invoked flexibly and situationally, not rigidly categorized across contexts.

Lives, deaths and the ritual state of the body

Bodies are stories, or to the extent that people live within a master biographical narrative, stories have bodies. The major points of the Classical Greek lifespan were marked with rituals which made visible the important relations between people. In fact, many votives recovered archaeologically were associated with transitions between sickness and health or between stages in life. Birth was a dangerous moment for both infant and mother: women giving birth were equated with men fighting on a battlefield, both facing socially valued perils. Infants remained socially outside the family until they were nine days old, and although concrete information is debatable, unwanted infants may have been exposed during this period. During growth, children reaching adulthood dedicated their old toys at shrines. Marriage was the next point marked ceremonially. In theory, women married in their late teens, men about ten years later. Marriages were often, perhaps usually, contracted between families, and they were celebrated formally with feasts, processions and group hymns outside the nuptial chamber; ribald songs celebrated the consummation of the marriage. Even reaching old age was marked with rites, as when women gave up their mirrors, no longer useful now that they have passed the age of beauty.

Death was conceived of as the soul's journey to an underground land of the dead (Figure 50). The soul, led by Hermes the Soul-Leader (or *psychopomp*), was conducted to Hades, the land of death. While there were many ways of burying people under different circumstances,[52] normative death rituals involved the washing, dressing and anointing of the body by the women of the household, a period of lying in state accompanied by ritualized mourning, a procession to the cemetery, and then either cremation or burial (Plate VIId).[53] Here two points are important. First, these rites of passage at birth, marriage and death shared a common structure in which the body was washed, clothed and decorated in a way appropriate for its new state, followed by collective public commentary by the group of relatives and friends affirming its new state. In this way, the changing body was channelled through an idealized life narrative. Secondly, the public dimension was important; each one provided an occasion in which not only the new body but also others' relations to it could be witnessed. For instance, marriage not only involved consummation of a sexual relationship but public recognition of this, and carrying out funerary rites was an important duty towards the dead, particularly one's father, and also part of a claim to heirship.

The body was ritually regulated at many other points as well, particularly through prescriptions about purity and purification.[54] Prescriptions about ritual purification abounded; for instance, in many cities one was forbidden to enter a sacred place after having had sexual intercourse or having given birth, and killing often created a ritual impurity which had to be expiated. Such beliefs about ritual purity were not holdovers from an earlier superstitious era. Instead, they coincided, and in some ways complemented, the development of law codes from the seventh century BC onwards. Although ritual regulation of the body may have served as a preventative to discourage antisocial behaviours, it was much less shaped by an explicit, coordinated theology than it was in later eras such as medieval times (cf. Chapter 6). Instead, it seems to have been intended to allow social acknowledgement of important bodily states which were not visible on the body.

Humans, animals, gods

As we have seen in other periods, human bodies are defined in part through contrasts with non-human bodies, and the borders between these categories may be defined differently in each culture. Greeks drew a clear, but mobile, line between humans and animals.[55] This may seem counter-intuitive given the popularity of human-animal hybrids in Greek art and mythology, but it is clear that they combined humans and animals precisely to underline the difference between then. Creatures such as centaurs, minotaurs and sirens, for example, were shown artistically with a clear join between discrete human and animal parts (Figure 51, Plate VIIc). These composites were a commentary on humans. They were used principally to point out the potential of humans to go wrong, to become bestial. A satyr violates the moderation humans should follow, to let pleasure and desire become drunkenness and licentiousness like a goat. Hence, human-animal mixtures do not represent fluid transformations as in perspectivism (see Chapter 3) but instead provide a literary way of displaying an exaggerated inner nature. The same is true for transformations of humans into animals, plants and trees (as in Circe's transformation of Odysseus's sailors into pigs); as a punishment or tragic destiny it reveals an inner nature.

In contrast, the border between human and divine was much more open. Visually, it is an oft-remarked feature of Classical art that there is no clear distinction between how humans and divinities are represented.[56] Without a caption or context, we cannot distinguish whether a *kouros* represents Apollo or a dead youth. Even in fragmented bodies of votives, it is sometimes unclear whether (for example) an ear represents the afflicted ear of a sufferer or the ear of the god it was hoped would hear the prayer. Except for truly large or splendid sculptures (such as the gilded Athena at the Parthenon), the bodies of deities are marked only by their perfection: gods simply have super-bodies and are super-humans. This mirrors the lack of a simple boundary between human and divine. The space between them is filled by a chain of heroes and demigods, and mythology is littered with interaction such as sexual relations, parenthood, and fostering between gods, heroes and ordinary humans. Effectively, humans and gods formed parts of a continuous field of possibilities.

Close encounters of alternative kinds

Bodies were encountered in Athens in circumstances set apart from quotidian reality. The two most important were drama and religious ritual. Dramas were performed only during two religious festivals dedicated to Dionysos, the Lenaia in January and the Dionysia in March. These festivals brought the city together in a program of events in honour of the god of wine and disorder. The Dionysia began with a raucous procession bearing large wooden phalluses and wine. The carnivalesque atmosphere bracketed the festival off as a time of role reversal or antistructure.[57] Even the style of acting marked theatrical performances as taking place in a different kind of space, with no attempt at naturalism of voice or gesture; actors wore oversized, rigid masks and declaimed speeches were interspersed with formal choral commentary. If we accept that one role of the dramatic festival was to bring Athenians, in a moment outside of daily time, together in a sense of their shared self, it is fascinating to consider how different kinds of dramas did this. Tragedies explored such lofty, un-quotidian themes as human relationships with the gods, the obligations of blood and kinship, and destiny. Comedies similarly provided moral prescription for ordering matters such as war, politics, and the relations between men and women, but through exaggeration, parody and laughter; comic actors in exaggerated costumes showed off grotesque anti-bodies which defined the beautiful male body by negation. 'The comic body is all things that the individual Greek, whatever his or her social background, hoped that his body was not' (Figure 52a).[58] In both, the assumed general point of view was that of the adult male citizen. This is clearest in the satyr plays, obscene burlesques written by the same erudite authors responsible for grave and lofty tragedies and viewed by the same audiences. Satyr plays were acted by actors wearing hugely exaggerated phalli and stepping out of the normal bounds of civility (Figure 52b). Satyr plays invoke a world of aggressive, misogynistic male sexuality for the audience to share in transitorily; this may have been an undercurrent in Greek masculinity accessed only during moments of dissolution of structure.

Religious practice was based upon formalized interaction with gods and goddesses. The most ceremonial events were elaborate sacerdotal procedures carried out with large casts of professional ritualists at major sanctuaries; these involved sacrifice and invocations on behalf of the entire community at an altar and often before a statue of the deity. Less elaborate rites involved private prayers at sanctuaries and shrines, and informal prayers in passing a wayside statue or local altar. Two points are striking here. First, such interactions almost always involved an element of reciprocity, a libation, sacrifice or obeisance accompanying a prayer or request for favour. Secondly, in ritual practice, no distinction was made between the image of the deity and the deity himself or herself: the statue receiving the sacrifice or prayer was not a

Figure 50. Charon the ferryman, shown on a lekythos intended for death rituals (© Trustees of the British Museum).

(a)   (b)   (c)

Figure 51. Hybrids. A. Minotaur (Photograph © National Museum, Athens). B. Sphinx (photo Robb; photo courtesy of 3rd Ephorate of Prehistoric and Classical Antiquities, Kerameikos Museum, Athens; © Hellenic Ministry of Education and Religions, Culture and Athletics). C. Satyr (© Trustees of the British Museum).

representation of the god, the statue *was* the god. The vision of the god was an epiphany, a culmination of the ritual process.[59] Ritual settings prepared the viewer to experience a different kind of visuality than that of ordinary life. Ritual practices such as decorating, feeding or supplicating activated or animated the image and 'blurred the distinction between the statue as inanimate matter and the god'. This point is almost impossible to understand with an ontology descended from Christianity and its 'representationalist' paradigm in which physical things are separate from, and hence can only stand for, spiritual things rather than actually be them. What is an exceptional, miraculous occurrence in Christianity (the Incarnation), was a daily phenomenon in Greek religion.

This fact – that the hard-headed, business-like thinkers who observed nature narrowly, invented formal logic and historical writing, and calculated fine profit margins also believed in seemingly absurd myths and the animation of images they had made themselves – led Veyne (in *Did the Greeks believe their myths?*[60]) to propose that classical Greeks could switch contextually between different standards of truth (this concept, multimodality, has already been introduced in Chapter 2). The idea that people can switch between contradictory modes of thought as they move from one context to another is consonant with both the findings of anthropologists studying other cultures and with our own experience, if we are honest about it (for instance, in the oft-noted paradox that the same people may be capable of great humanity and tenderness and great brutality). It seems clear that Greek ritual practice involved multimodality in switching between mental frameworks within which people interacted with the (images of the) gods.

Intellectual theorizations of the body: Philosophers, doctors

Intellectual discourses of the body existed, of course, but were surprisingly fragmented. The nature of the body per se was not a major philosophical focus, and it tended to turn up principally in understated contrast to the soul, and even this latter aspect of humanity was not widely elaborated. Pre-Socratic philosophers, for example, mostly had little to say about the body, although Pythagoras and Empedocles taught that souls transmigrated amongst bodies during reincarnation (a doctrine underlying their vegetarian diets). Socrates seems to have seen the body as a material liability which distracted attention from the soul, and Plato developed this theme explicitly in his famous allegory of the cave: what we sense as material worldly reality is merely a shadowy reflection of an ideal higher truth.

The two most important philosophical discussions of the body are Plato's body map for the republic and Aristotle's biological systematization of living things, both of which remained highly influential through the Middle Ages. In the *Timaeus*, Plato presents an extraordinary synthetic account of how the different parts of the body come into being. Much of it draws upon Hippocratic medicine (e.g. the idea that health results from a proper balance of the elements making up the body), but much is also original and strikingly different from all received theology (e.g. the account of how a single divinity created the different parts of the body). In *The Republic*, Plato makes an analogy between the human body and the city-state.[61] The workers, like the abdomen, are productive and make things; the warriors, like the thorax, are brave and protect the rest; the philosopher-king, like the head, is rational and guides everything else. The just state is the one that preserves the balance amongst these (much as the healthy body preserves harmony amongst its elements) so everybody can play the part they are best suited for. This asserted both the organic unity of the state and a natural hierarchy amongst its parts. Similarly (in the *History of Animals*), Aristotle arranged all living things into the Scale of Nature from most rudimentary to most complex, based upon their complexity, vitality and movement. Humans, naturally, were at the top, having vegetative capacities of reproduction, sensitive capacities of movement and rational capacities of thought. Aristotle also made major steps in using the human body to justify inequality, both in his defence of slavery as natural and in his assertion that males were responsible for the active element in procreation, the female only providing an inert, passive substrate.

Three facts about how the Greek philosophers treated the body are striking to the anthropological (rather than philosophical) eye. First, such basic principles as they held in common were also widely shared with the general public. Most obviously, they generally start with a division between the material body and the soul, which represents contact with divinity or higher reality in some form and which can last on after death. In the general imagination, the soul escaped from the body after death and undertook a journey to Hades; philosophers provided a range of alternate interpretations. Similarly, the idea of a virtuous moderation, proportion or balance amongst body parts was widely shared. Gender provided the other cardinal point of understanding; the Greek adult male body was taken to be the 'unmarked' basic standard from which difference was assessed.[62] Secondly, philosophers varied amazingly. From this point of departure, one gets a feeling of philosophers combining personal observation, logic, and individual inclination to wing it

 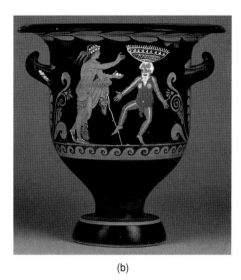

(a) (b)

Figure 52. Grotesque anti-bodies: A. Clay figurine (© Trustees of the British Museum). B. Satirical actor depicted on pottery (© Trustees of the British Museum).

creatively. Unlike the medieval period, there was very little control upon personal interpretation. Thirdly, philosophical views rarely focused on daily life and dealt more commonly with abstract concepts. They often focused upon relatively abstract, detached notions (such as the nature of truth) upon which their opinions remained paradoxical and far from common thought. Their political views were often completely counter to the state (for example, Plato was decidedly anti-democratic) and in spite of Plato's vision of the philosopher-king there is no record of any important public process being changed by philosophical views. Similarly, many philosophers were religious sceptics whose views had little to do with theological orthodoxy and normal ritual practice. As Aristophanes' parody of rhetoric-spouting, fee-grubbing philosophy teachers in 'The Clouds' shows, philosophers were well-known figures, but it remains doubtful that Classical philosophy provided a general spearhead of truth rather than a fashionable cultural pastime amongst a minority of educated, urban, upper-class men.

Surviving medical texts in the Classical period are limited principally to the Hippocratic writings by Hippocrates and his followers, with some work by Aristotle. Hippocratic writers conceptualized the human body as essentially a container for fluids – not a surprising view, given that dissection of the human body was not done until the Hellenistic period (and rarely even then), limiting knowledge about the body's internal anatomy and physiology other than that gleaned from animal bodies or witnessed on the battlefield. The Hippocratics originated the doctrine that the body contained four fluids or 'humours' (blood, phlegm, bile and black bile); health resulted when these remained in their proper balance.

This made the body permeable rather than bounded; a repeated argument in Classical science was that people from different places had different physiognomies because of environmental influences such as heat, cold, moistness or dryness. Equally, the body was thus fluid rather than fixed and stable. Treatment was therefore basically non-invasive and aimed at maintaining or restoring this balance and ameliorating the patient's symptoms. The permeability and fluidity of the body meant that external treatments of diet and exercise could modify it. This view was passed down via the Roman writer Galen to provide the basis for medieval medical thought (see Chapter 6).

In some ways, medical writing was amongst the most gender-neutral ways in which Greeks thought about the body. Votive models of the body in parts show both males and females; there is little sense of an association between women and interiority which arises in later periods (for instance, in eighteenth century discussion of the location of genitalia). Gender comes in principally in discussing how the womb relates specifically to female illnesses. Yet both the Hippocratic and Aristotelian traditions found women to be inferior to men. In the latter, women were cold and unable to produce life. In the former, menstrual blood produced difficulties in achieving a balanced bodily constitution. Both traditions took the male body as the universal baseline. Moreover, it was believed that menstrual blood could build up dangerously in the body, a situation which could be prevented by intercourse, thus tying women's health into sexual and political relations between the sexes.[63] Small dolls pictured on the grave stelae of girls probably served to teach girls these facts about their own bodies. An alternative interpretation is that these are not dolls but votive offerings dedicated for a safe passage through menarche.[64]

As with philosophy, medical thought was influential and well-recognized, yet it remained at odds with many other elements of the Classical world. Doctors treated wealthy clients for a range of conditions, but many, perhaps most people, would have been treated by other kinds of practitioners (midwives, local practitioners of herbal lore, family members). The fact that medical knowledge was developed by the Hippocratics' detailed observation and written and taught as a distinct body of knowledge suggests that it stood in opposition to more diffuse, less formalized healing practices. Moreover, the idea remained common that illness was caused by spiritual factors rather than physical causes. Regardless of whether a particular episode was ascribed to divine judgment, sufferers often supplicated gods for healing.[65]

Votive body parts reveal another side to how illness was conceptualized.[66] These are representations of body parts which were deposited at shrines and cult sites, often in supplication for healing (Figure 53). Arms, legs, hands, feet, eyes, ears and even internal organs such as the womb are common. Because of the Hippocratic view of the body as a container for liquids rather than a deep structure of organs and tissues, votives from Greece typically contain few internal organs (in contrast to votives from the Central Mediterranean and from later periods). Votive body parts become common in the fourth century BC and remain widespread throughout classical antiquity. The parts were used for various purposes (such as in rites of passage of puberty or to represent the worshipper – with heads, hands, or, for pilgrims, feet), but the most common was to ask for divine help in healing; hence they are often found in sanctuaries of the healing god Asklepios.[67] The ill body, as represented in votives, differed from how the body was conceptualized in official medical writings and in other practices. Although the god Asklepios was dreamt to have cut people up to heal them (as recorded in accounts of healing at his sanctuary at Epidauros), the Hippocratic medical writings generally treat the body as an integrated whole; illness results from the relations amongst its components. In contrast, votives divide the body into parts and localize the ailment in a single place. Dividing the human body was in itself a controversial idea. Illness was sometimes conceptualized as fragmentation of the body. Not only did official medical practice eschew both surgery and dissection, but other treatments of the body such as burial practice emphasize the need for whole bodies; although the body was cut open in battle, only barbarians such as the head-hunting Gauls mutilated their enemies; and amongst Greeks, only Bacchanals in the grips of religious ecstasy tore humans to pieces.

For Greeks, the interior was accessed only in transgressive practices. Votives ran counter to this general view that the body should remain whole. Although in many contexts the emphasis was upon the whole body, the ordering of its parts and on social harmony, votives remind us that in other contexts the body could be fragmented and divided.

The Classical Greek body world: Coherence and contradiction

Like other worlds of bodily belief and practice, the 'Classical body' revealed in this review is a mass of coherences and contradictions. There were some principles which would have remained unquestioned by virtually all Greeks and were applied across many different contexts. The most obvious is the idea of male and female gender as a universally applicable set of distinctions and as a fixed point for identity and self-understanding. The habitus of gender was enacted practically, as males and females did different activities in different places, times and groups. It was proclaimed discursively, in texts of all kinds describing the essential gulf between men's and women's natures. Masculine and feminine natures were seen both as complementary and set within a fundamental asymmetry. This was tied into a conceptual spatiality which viewed the world as composed of different institutions which brought people of different kinds together: the household (*oikos*), which brought males and females together into domestic relations, and the tribe (*phyle*) and city (*polis*), which brought unrelated males together in political relationships.

Other related principles for understanding the body included the idea of beauty as a balance or harmony between the parts making up something, whether it was the parts making up the body or the activities within a healthful and virtuous life. This was expressed visually in sculpture and textually in philosophy and literature. It was enacted practically in regulations such as those allowing men participation in a wide range of experiences (including eating, drinking and sexual pleasures) as long as excess was avoided. It was also expressed in anti-bodies, grotesque lampoons of exaggeration in satire, comedy and visual art. An emphasis on wholeness and proportion in turn structured understandings of health and illness. In turn, the body became a metaphor for union in division in political theories such as Plato's, a map for the harmonious but hierarchical relations between the elements making up society.

A third principle for understanding the body was the idea that people's bodies were transient, material things animated by a soul. Epitaphs stress the pathetic contrast

Figure 53. Votives: leg dedicated to Aesclepius (© Trustees of the British Museum).

between the beauty of the living person and the ugly dust enveloping them in death. The soul escaped from the body in death, to be led to an underworld populated by the spirits of the dead. As Odysseus's visit to the underworld suggests, unlike a Christian afterlife, for most people Hades was neither a place of reward nor of punishment, but a rather dreary place thronged with souls longing for news of the living. Having an animating principle without a body to experience the joys of life was a mixed blessing, it seems.

Across contexts, these principles create a sense of recognizability, of coherence or predictability. However, this world was far from flat or unvaried. The body world of Classical Greece was rich and complex. There were medical bodies, philosophical bodies, working bodies, ritual bodies, divine bodies, hybrid bodies. An Athenian could have argued with his or her compatriots about these principles or about how to apply them in a particular case. Do we trust the reality of our bodily senses as ordinary perception suggests or see through them to a higher reality, as some philosophers argued? Is illness sent by the gods or a purely medical phenomenon? Should a sufferer go to a temple, to a village healer or to a doctor? Are women faithful, reliable partners in the household, objects of sexual desire, or thriftless shrews? Under what circumstances can a male be homoerotic and still masculine? Is it glorious to die in battle or is death simply the beginning of a long, sad existence as a shade in Hades? Controversy was not limited to differences of opinion

amongst people, however. As one passed from one context to another, beliefs about the body shifted. During the anti-structure of a festival, people collectively experienced virtue-driven tragic destinies and bestial humour. A sculpture addressed ritually became the body of the god. The whole, undivided body which represented the social harmony and correct ordering of parts was divided in votives, which addressed individual needs.

Perhaps the greatest ambiguity was political. Clear theoretical lines of political division existed between slave and free, between citizen and foreigner, and between man and woman, yet these seem to have been blurred in practice as often as not. Slaves were degraded and stripped of rights, yet often lived intimately with the families they served, participated in household rituals, and dressed and worked similarly to the free. Resident foreigners could not vote or own property but worked, paid taxes and even served in arms alongside citizens. Women theoretically remained confined to the household, but worked, socialized and had affairs outside the home. Inasmuch as it is worth commenting upon general intellectual tendencies, Classical Athens seems notable in the amount of free play about ideas and practices, not only in intellectually creative spheres such as drama, poetry and philosophy but in everyday practices such as whether to bury or cremate. Even the simple dichotomy of human and divine lent itself to elaboration into a complex field of possibilities and interactions. Politically, this meant that, at the same time as proclaiming discrete, universally applicable categories, an inextricable part of the social order was the blurring of these categories in practice.

With such a proliferation of bodies, and such potential for shifting how they were performed and understood contextually, perhaps the most surprising thing about the Greek body world is how little attempt there was to regulate it, simplify it, or control it institutionally. This is in clear contrast to the medieval world we turn to in Chapter 6.

The Classical body as cultural politics

There were many more Classical Greek bodies than the marble ones we find in sculpture, and this fact alone should alert us to the error of reading Classical sculpture as 'the' Classical body. Classical sculpture was a political statement, a loud and influential voice but ultimately one voice amongst many. As art, Classical sculpture's work was to fashion cultural imagination for social or political purposes. How did Classical sculpture work politically?

We can start by disclaiming any strong link between Classical aesthetic styles and democracy *per se*. On a simple empirical level, the Classical style of sculpture was made and appreciated throughout the Greek world, in tyrannies, oligarchies and democracies, as well as in places such as Olympia, Delphi and other sanctuaries where people from all kinds of regimes came together. It evidently filled a void in Greek politics, as it spread rapidly throughout the Greek world to places where *kouroi* had never been common, such as Italy and Sicily. But it reached its most florid peak in Athens, where the state's wealth allowed several phases of major building programs, notably a sweeping reconstruction of the city following the victory over the Persians in 480 BC, followed by the Periclean building program in the 440s and 430s BC and culminating in the completion of the Parthenon. Here there was an explicit sense of association between art and individuals, but nonetheless Athenians were wary of allowing sculpture to glorify individuals such as victorious generals; they restricted the magnificence of funeral ceremonies and monuments, and they fostered very particular forms of sculpture such as herms which had distinct democratic overtones. This illustrates not a fundamental connection between the Classical style and democracy, but that the political possibilities the new style offered, which were based upon a common Greek political process, could be customized for a wide range of concrete situations.

At a superficial level, the politics of art is evident. Classical sculptures were public art. They occurred as objects of veneration in temples, as decoration upon public monuments, and as dedications at sanctuaries; their only privately sponsored use was in grave monuments, which were still located in public spaces. Their political role is made clear from their technological characteristics: with their expensive materials, fine design and visibly flawless craftsmanship, they served as a 'technology of enchantment',[68] impressing the viewer.

Many of the images they presented were central to the state's political agenda; in Athens between the late sixth century and the end of the fifth century BC, we find images of foundational Athenian heroes such as Theseus and episodes such as the wars with the Centaurs and the Amazons, 'portraits' of the eponymous founders of Athens' ten tribes, political figures such as the Tyrannicides, and memorials of the city's war dead that set the stage for patriotic rites of commemoration.[69] *Kouroi* are traditionally viewed as images of the Archaic aristocracy; herms, it has been argued, are a democratic answer to *kouroi*. The armed hoplite in Athenian art is clearly a reference to the citizen infantry; as noted earlier, a change to family scenes and women on grave markers after 450 BC may reflect new citizenship laws which required Athenian descent from both parents.[70]

But much Classical sculpture addresses other themes, particularly the grave stelae which present family scenes and private grief. The deeper political role of Classical sculpture concerns not its overtly political manifestations but its fundamental style: the 'Greek Revolution', the question of why this aesthetic style of body representation itself should have developed.

Art, vision and community

Art works. 'Art' as something created purely for the aesthetic pleasure of the connoisseur is a recent invention.[71] Most ancient and prehistoric 'art' was created to accomplish a particular social purpose (this is still true of the vast majority of images we create today – a cereal box label, a stamp design, a corporate logo). This is equally true – perhaps above all true – for Greek 'art', which must be extracted from the mythology of aesthetic revolution if we are to understand what it is really about. Art may be considered a specialized technology for achieving social effects.[72] Moreover, style is important. *How* something is represented, as opposed to what is represented, may be the central message. Even 'naturalistic' forms of art whose goal is to represent the world closely make use of arbitrary conventions which the viewer must share to 'see' the image properly.[73] Other ancient art traditions used conventions such as comic-book style sequences to show the passage of time and making important characters larger than minor characters; Greek art uses conventions of perspective and foreshortening to create an illusion of seeing 'naturally'.

Greek art is often seen in terms of an intellectual quest to envision the essential within the specific, to bring forth a Platonic ideal of a horse from a picture of a specific horse.[74] But such condensation and interpretation of reality into a more transcendental form is always a political act. What, then, does style accomplish? It makes representations intelligible, of course. But beyond that, it draws the viewer in. As Mitchell asks, 'What do pictures want?'[75] The act of viewing is not an innocent one; it creates, or recreates, the conditions of seeing in the viewer.[76] This is all the more so when we are dealing with representations of bodies; bodies project stories before and behind them, and viewing a body is an act which must take place within a potential or projected, if not real, relationship between viewer and viewed. Berger[77] has pointed out how the female nude paintings cast the spectator in the role of a male sexual protagonist potentially dominating the objectified woman. In parallel, feminist literary and film theorists and psychoanalysts developed the notion of the gaze as a relation of power between subject and object, a line of thought which has had considerable influence upon feminist art historians.[78]

This implies that there is an inescapable relationship between the stylistic conventions of art and the sense of being a subject capable of viewing it. Moreover, when it is explicitly political or community art, we may make the further link that the persona of the viewer is central to the sense members share of what the basis of their community is. As Stewart notes,

> When I enjoy an image constructed to satisfy the public eye, I implicitly align my glance with the gaze that shaped it. When the two merge as the image comes into focus, I immediately take on the role of a representative of the image's originally intended constituency of viewers – in the case of the Greeks, the citizen body or one of its sub-groups.... My spectatorial role of cultural representative strengthens as my enjoyment grows, ensnaring me in a self-reinforcing loop of complicity – a potent nexus in a culture that believed firmly in art's magnetic effect upon the eyes.[79]

As Tanner[80] insightfully notes, the naturalism of Greek art appropriates bodily responses to commit the viewer to social roles. What was the political aesthetics of this style?

As a starting point, the first stage of monumental human sculpture, the Archaic *kouroi* and *korai*, are generally considered aristocratic statements. They were used either to mark upper-class graves or as dedications at venues of wealth and ostentation such as pan-city games. They were costly and are rather infrequent, although occasionally numerous at particular sanctuaries. Archaic elites played on two rhetorics of leadership, an 'aristocratic' rhetoric based upon luxury, Orientalising styles, and birth, and a 'middling' rhetoric based upon local roots, sobriety and moderation, and representation of the community. *Kouroi* and *korai* formed part of the 'aristocratic' sense of leadership. Hence, they stress the basic gender asymmetry between the nude, independently beautiful male and the clothed, relationally praiseworthy female. The only point they really make about the male is the beauty of the male body, nude as in athletic contexts. This is presented in a blank, context-free purity which states, rather aristocratically, that virtue and beauty are autonomous of circumstances and action; they simply exist. If we look at art as creating a relationship between viewer and object, what is striking about the *kouroi* is that, in portraying only the beardless young male, they choose to present the male body at what was considered the momentary peak of its beauty. Whether or not the *kouroi* had homoerotic overtones, it defines the viewer as a mature male who is looking upon another class of body, not potentially himself. This moment of perfect beauty is an object to be enjoyed, mourned over, or dedicated to a god; but it is an object external to the viewer.

Inasmuch as there is a general political shift throughout the Greek world around the end of the sixth century BC, it is the victory of the 'middling' strategy over the 'aristocratic' strategy. Greek cities were never equal; they were built upon deep inequalities of slavery, gender and wealth. But with the growth of population and trade, elites could no longer simply play the aristocratic card; politics increasingly involved the participation of the larger mass of free adult males. The process was most marked in Athens, which extended legal enfranchisement in the assembly to all male citizens, but it happened throughout the hundred-odd *poleis* of the Greek world. In some cities, this meant the increasing importance of citizen assemblies; in others it meant the rise of tyrants, themselves invariably aristocratic, who appealed demogogically to the masses against the aristocracy. It is important to realize that here we are talking not only about the institutions of government, which differed from city to city, but also about the social process, the political classes, reflexes and options, which shared much in common everywhere. Some cities cycled through many institutional options in the turbulent late Archaic and early Classical periods.

Inasmuch as 'art' was produced for specific tasks, mass participation provides a context for key elements of Classical sculpture. Most notably, the customers shifted; whereas sculpture continued to be produced for wealthy patrons to use as grave markers and dedications, the *polis* became a major patron, commissioning religious and memorial sculptures on a large scale. Related to this, art treated a much broader range of subjects and themes – not only the gods, but mythological, historical, individual and family scenes. In terms of bodies and style, there are two fundamental shifts. One is that art now portrays adult men as well as youths. Although this seems simple and obvious, it dramatically changes the relationship between viewer and art. Previously, art had offered the viewer something external to enjoy; now, art allowed the relationship of self-identification for all adult males. This allowed art to be not only about beautiful males but about political males, and it allowed the dynamic of subjectification discussed earlier; art could be used to present ideal types of the viewer himself.

In stripping away the layers of relational significance embodied in classical sculpture, gender is the first, inescapable great division. The classical gender dynamic was implicit in sculpture. Females are shown acting relationally to men, women and children (as wives, mothers, sisters, daughters or mistresses of servants). Although men are often shown in family scenes, they are also often shown actively in a world only of other men (as athletes, soldiers or citizens). For both men and women, personhood involved many relationships; these are foregrounded in representations of women, while men are often shown either acting on their own or in male-only contexts. Moreover, the semantics of nudity underline this asymmetry. Females were rarely nude in sculpture because exposing the female body to a male desire assumed to be ever-present was an act of vulnerability, not only for the woman but also for the social unit of which she formed a part. Women are almost always shown clothed and often making decorous gestures of modesty or reserve as well. Even the supposed first female nude, Praxiteles' Aphrodite of Knidos (Figure 54), simply makes this situation explicit; her nudity is not voluntary, she is ineffectively shielding her body from a male view which can nonetheless penetrate it from several directions. This is perhaps the purest example of a gaze which constructs the viewer in 'potentially different narrative possibilities – as the invited lover, as the stranger blundering at a private moment, as an unseen voyeur'.[81] Male nudity, in contrast, was understood in terms of an assertive, empowering beauty.

The human body was also a sign of social class. This is most obviously referenced in the iconography of male pursuits. For late Archaic grave markers,

> It is very frequently not labor but leisure which identifies the dead man as one who competed in the areas of masculinity. Athletics was an amateur activity which only the wealthy could engage in on any scale.... To put athletic prowess on display was not simply to show that one was a man whose naked body could compete with other men, it was to show that one was a member of an elite.[82]

This is certainly true for the top end of athletes, who needed private wealth to fund long trips to Panhellenic games and high-capital sports such as horsemanship and chariot-racing. Less elite men certainly participated in athletics, as literary sources and finds of athletic paraphernalia such as strigils in unspectacular graves attest, but even so the connotations of upper-class self-cultivation remained: it was a care of the body for those who had the leisure, money, and energy to pursue it. Even after the mid-fifth century BC, when it was more common to present men in grave markers as members of families, reference to their role as athletes is common; the understated reference to Eupheros' athletic prowess in his grave stela (Figure 44) places him firmly in this class. Moreover, these later grave markers typically show men as central figures in the household, as the head of the *oikos* or as its heir; of course, the

peripheral kinsmen and slaves would not have merited a grave marker in any case.

On the political stage, politicians and intellectuals were typically drawn from a small core of historically prominent, wealthy families. Warfare itself was a rich source of class distinctions. Because soldiers supplied their own gear and horses were expensive, cavalry were typically drawn from the wealthy elite. The prominent representation of horsemen in scenes such as the battle with the Amazons upon the Parthenon friezes makes a claim about the role of this class in defending Athens, and showing the dead youth Dexileos as a horseman on his grave marker places him in at the top level of society. Further down the scale, the core of Greek armies was the heavily armed infantryman, the *hoplite*. Both citizens and resident foreigners were obliged to serve as infantrymen. Men who were not citizens or who lacked means to equip themselves with armour, sword, spears and shield served in other ways, as lightly armed auxiliaries or as sailors rowing triremes. Naval service was particularly important for the lower classes who had no arms but their arms, so to speak, and Athens' imperial success owed much to its dominance of the seas. Yet representations of armed and fighting men almost always show them as hoplites, to the exclusion of auxiliaries and sailors (Figure 55). When specific men are represented, this underlines their claim to belong to the citizen class. More importantly, the omnipresent images of fighting infantrymen made the claim that Athens' security and success was due specifically to this citizen class.

Aspirational bodies: Style as a regulatory fiction

The object of aesthetic enjoyment in the Archaic period thus evolved into the basis for an imagined community of political citizenry in the Classical period. So far, so good: but one could depict gendered and class-marked bodies in a great many ways. How should we read the *aesthetics* of Classical sculpture – the peculiar blend of idealism and naturalism, the shift in style from a more rigid, schematic style to a more 'lifelike' one that has made Classical sculpture seem to come alive?

The first step is to debunk, or at least contextualize, the idea of naturalism. As Gombrich pointed out,[83] Greek art is mimetic: unlike Near Eastern or Egyptian art of the time, it claims to imitate nature. However, this does not mean a quasi-photographic realism. The naturalism of Greek art was an illusion created through representational conventions. The bodies represented in sculpture mismatched the crowd of bodies in the streets. Entire classes of bodies were not represented: the infirm, the poor, slaves and foreigners turn up rarely and then only

Figure 54. Praxiteles' Aphrodite of Knidos (© Museum of Classical Archaeology, Cambridge).

universe of the physically and socially perfect; where are the squat, the blemished and the lumpy?

Similarly, although we have got beyond not-quite-of-this-world smile of the Archaic *kouros*, the faces of Classical sculptures remain generic. In contrast to the 'warts and all' style for which Roman portraits are sometimes notorious, Classical Greek faces tend to be symmetrically regular, with conventionalized beauty. Such individuality as they have is often bestowed not by the irregularities and disconformities which mark living faces but by the stereotyped features emblematic of idealized values the individual was reputed to have held (hence sculptures of Socrates, legendary for ugliness, show a highly conventionalized, rhetorical ugliness). They are not the faces people had; they are the faces the person should have had, given their character.

Anatomical 'naturalism' was thus used *not* to depict what the eye saw faithfully, but for another purpose, to engage the viewer, to allow recognition of a continuity between real bodies such as the viewer's own body and the idealized bodies represented. It provides a middle ground between an absolute schematism which reduces variation to a simple matching with generic categories (either one identifies with the symbol on male restroom doors or with the one on female restroom doors) and an absolute descriptivism which provides a one-to-one match between a representation and a specific person (as in portrait photography and DNA fingerprinting). The images simultaneously present bodies realistic enough for viewers to potentially identify themselves with, but which also conform to general, idealized categories of person. Modern examples of such imagery tend to occur in our own forms of exhortational art. Shop mannequins, for instance, present the viewer with idealized bodies in generic postures whose individuality has been intentionally

as accessories or complements to citizens rather than as people in their own right. Those who were represented were shown in a narrow range of social roles and activities; for example, unlike vase paintings which were much cheaper and suited to a wider range of contexts, there is almost no reference in sculpture to work. Finally, the body itself is shown in an idealized way. The philosophical ideal of beauty involved harmony and proportion; in 'naturalistic' sculpture, body proportions are dictated by a formal canon of relationships between the parts (one famous sculptor, Polykleitos, supposedly even wrote a now-lost textbook on body proportions to accompany his visual canon, the Doryphoros [Plate VIIa]). It is a

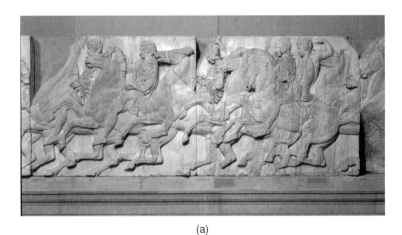

(a)

(b)

Figure 55. Armed men: cavalry and hoplites. A. North Frieze, Block XLII, Parthenon (© Trustees of the British Museum). B. Frieze from the Nereid Monument (© Trustees of the British Museum).

blurred. A middle-class clothing catalogue, similarly, uses photographs to show off a lifestyle which you can buy into; the models and settings are carefully chosen to show a realistic, attractive, but entirely generic target picture.

By offering realism and detail without individuality, the picture allows the viewer to project himself or herself into the world of the image. However, that act of projection is contingent: you can be the body depicted in its essential qualities provided that you embrace the essential values and apply them to yourself. This act of self-identification may be a simple moment of recognition; it often also involves objectifying actions to fit yourself to the ideal through bodily techniques such as exercise, diet, clothing and self-decoration. As working political images, Classical sculpture functioned much more like the bodies in any lifestyle magazine or clothing catalogue than like high art or the detailed, individualising bodies of recent portraiture. It provided aspirational bodies, bodies which engaged the viewer and allowed him to project himself into an ideal order. The males fighting centaurs on the Parthenon frieze could represent the essence of any male citizen, provided that the male citizen agreed that what made an Athenian citizen were the qualities essentialized in them.

This interpretation – that classical sculpture presents a carefully blank, quasi-universal human to serve as an aspirational political object – goes a long way towards addressing some of its most salient qualities. One is its very blankness, its apparent lack of distinctions, its apparent presentation of people simply as humans qua humans. We know that social distinctions in Classical Greece – rich and poor, citizen and foreigner, Greek and non-Greek, slave and free – could certainly be sharp-edged and divisively applied. But such distinctions, beyond gender, are rarely visible in sculpture.[84] Why? In part, because they are assumed; there was no need to signal visually that the infantrymen are free men because virtually by definition they would be so. In part, however, it is asserted that the distinctions are not relevant in a particular ethical context; all men, citizens and foreigners, can aspire to the ideals promoted in sculpture, hence there is no need to distinguish them visually. This may be the importance of nudity as a costume; even as it purports to display the beautiful male body free of encumbering distinctions of dress, it is at the same time both a universal and easily achieved condition and strongly associated with particular elite male contexts. The same logic of aspiration applies to the quality of the male body itself. In classical belief, bodily beauty reflected careful and attentive cultivation to exercise, balance and moderation, activities involving moral virtues. The perfect sculptural body supposedly represents the universal aspect of all male bodies, yet it shows the fruit

of attention and self-care attainable only by a few. The class-marked aspects of athletics and participation in the gymnasium have already been mentioned. It is also worth noting that the body in sculpture is not marked by work; no roughness of skin, no hypertrophied muscles or occupational deformities, no slackness from a sedentary occupation, unscarred by toil, accident or misfortune. It even dies beautifully!

The political strength of Classical sculpture, thus, was precisely that it was apparently apolitical. It was not allied with a narrow sectional order or exclusionary categorical distinctions; but this simply meant that its use of social distinction was not blunt and categorical but subtle and contingent. It drew its power from the universalizing assertion that it simply showed what a body really is; this assertion was accompanied by silences on other kinds of bodies one encountered every day, and upon the differences of degree between bodies which could potentially have been the sculpted one and were not. The body thus created a labile category to which a broad range of people can consider themselves belonging, in various ways, not because they actually have bodies like those sculpted but because they potentially could have them, at least in essence. In this flexible, aspirational quality, it fit the particular nature of inequality within the Classical world, its combination of tenacious class stratification with a lack of formal, rigid exclusionary distinctions. For women it provided a positive ideal to aspire to which both gave them power but kept them within the *oikos*. For men, it identified a sectional ideal as universal, but in a way which allowed all men to potentially aspire to it even if few would achieve it. In the process, it provided an 'objective' democratic standard for legitimating those men who did live up to the ideal.

This has much in common with Butler's concept for modern Western society of the regulatory ideal,[85] which we discussed briefly in Chapter 2. For Butler, gender in Europe and America is produced through people's actions, by the way they try and live up to particular kinds of standards (which are never fully attainable[86]) of maleness and femaleness. For example, how a person sits (legs together or legs apart), what a person wears (skirt or trousers), how they have their hair (long or short) or how they behave (aggressive or passive) all help to produce a form of gender. Today we are surrounded by images of different kinds of bodies, many of which are lauded for being thin or muscular or decried for being fat; these images help to produce our regulatory ideals of what a body should be. Like these media images of 'good' and 'bad' bodies, Classical statuary provided an ideal towards which practices could be aimed, even if they were never achieved. This in turn helped to confirm

(a)   (b)

Figure 56. Herms. A. Marble herm from Siphnos, late Archaic (photo National Archaeological Museum, Athens, © Hellenic Ministry of Education, Religions, Culture and Athletics/Archaeological Receipts Fund). B. Herm on red-figure vase (State Hermitage Museum, St. Petersburg, photograph © State Hermitage Museum. Photo by Vladimir Terebenin, Leonard Kheifets, Yuri Molodkovets).

the notion that statues captured the ideal form of male and female dress, behaviour and comportment. The fact that most statues, other than herms, were encountered within specific contexts added to this. It was particularly in relation to immortality captured in temples, sanctuaries and cemeteries that these bodies that extended beyond the context of human time and activities were suitable for display.

Spatiality: Herms and the phallic panopticon

This discussion may help us understand one of the most curious and least often discussed aspects of Classical sculpture, the herms – the plain pillars made human only by the addition of a head of Hermes and an erect phallus (Figure 56).[87] Herms are unusual in two ways. First, they show men with erect phalli. Ithyphallic males are shown elsewhere only in situations where men are carried away with sexual enthusiasm – typically satyrs in Dionysiac moments (Figure 51c). The erect phallus is portrayed as something comic, exaggerated, grotesque. Herms are different. Their head is serene, with the standard beauty of a mature, bearded male and the gravitas of an important god waiting to receive prayers and supplications. They keep a calming and beneficent eye on things. So why do they need an erection to do so?

Secondly, other statues of gods and goddesses were usually located in their 'official' places – inside temples, sanctuaries, shrines or public monuments. Herms, in contrast, were everywhere. This is attested by literary accounts, by archaeology and by the not infrequent depictions of herms as scenery in vase paintings (Figure 56). They were erected alongside roads between towns, at crossroads and marketplaces, and by the doorways of individual homes, marking the transition between the household and the city. Other gods were fixed in place; you had to seek them out. Herms, in contrast, saw every journey, they were unavoidable. They had blanket coverage.

Hermes was a liminal god, the god of transitions, the conductor of the dead, and something of a trickster; as divine statues, herms received prayers and libations. It is important not to discount the genuine religious role of herms out of an unjustified assumption that sexuality cannot be religious. But herms are also a logical extension, almost to an extreme, of the argument outlined previously. They present a minimalist male body distilled down to its most fundamental essentials, the head and the sexual organs. It is for this reason that they have often been regarded as a specifically democratic form, a reaction against the aristocratic *kouroi*. In terms of the earlier outline, they are closer to the schematic end of the spectrum; although they still exclude women, the infirm or very aged, and the beardless youths, they reduce categorical identification almost to a simple yes/ no checklist. At the same time, 'the herm was seen to re-present the male viewer with himself'.[88] The herm presented sexuality as a fundamental and socially positive fact: 'The herm's phallus represented the citizen's power, not in a violent sense, but with implications of potency, authority, and maturity – and, crucially, the successful reproduction of the democratic citizen body'.[89] It is these meanings which underlie the formula of the erect phallus as apotropaic, as signalling prosperity and warding off ill fortune.

Moreover, placing images is an essential element in creating landscapes of meaning, in making inhabitable spaces. Herms were ubiquitous; Athens and the countryside around it effectively became a network of spaces connected by herms. It is thought-provoking to compare herms to bodily icons which sum up entire belief systems in other times and places. For much of medieval and recent Christianity, the cross or crucifix was omnipresent, making all or most social activity happen under the watchful eye of the crucified Incarnate and presencing the paradox at the core of the body-spirit split. In more recent times, one thinks of the importance of vision as a vector of control and discipline in Foucault's analysis of the surveying panopticon (cf. Chapter 7); the current version of this, closed-circuit television coverage, turns the relationship inside out and makes the body of the observed citizen the omnipresent icon. Herms, too, were images which arrested the passer-by, subjected movement and action to the god's watchful eye, and made evident the divine basis for the collective citizen body. They provided the phallic panopticon.

The later history of the Classical body

Politics and the body: Exporting the Classical body

Greek overseas settlement and trade provides a direct, complementary insight into how politics and the body related. This is particularly the case when we consider how much of the material transactions between Greeks and non-Greeks involved body-related paraphernalia: perfumes and oils in small vases, wine and drinking gear, strigils and mirrors and other items of personal care, and human body representations on pots, mirrors and statues. If these items found their way into non-Greek houses and tombs, did a Greek understanding of the body do too?

Treatments of colonialism have changed dramatically in the last decade. The traditional view both popularly and in academia was relatively simple: in the colonial encounter, things from the centre were better (thus Greek art was better art than native Italic art, European technology and institutions were better than Native American ones, and so on). Hence, in cases in which the civilizing party's custom was adopted, there is no need to explain it; where it was not adopted, it is either because the natives were too remote or because they were recalcitrantly barbarian and refractory to the march of civilization. The huge sea-change in this view is generally known under the rubric of post-colonial theory.[90] A key tenet is that we cannot see the colonial encounter simply in terms of the dichotomized identities of colonizer and colonized, with inevitable dominance of the former over the latter. Instead, colonialism involves a complex process in which many people occupy mediating positions, balancing different obligations and identity claims, working both systems to create a liveable accommodation between them. In the Mediterranean, this line of research has been best used to deconstruct narratives of 'Romanization', which see it simply as the execution of a rational military-administrative design planned in Rome.[91] There is also an emerging body of work for relations between Greeks, Phoenicians and native peoples.[92]

The Etruscan body[93]

The Etruscans were a populous and prosperous people living in western Central Italy who both competed with Greeks for control over the Central Mediterranean and traded extensively with them.[94] For example, because of the Etruscan taste for using Athenian red-figure vases as grave goods, far more of these pots have been found in Etruria than in Athens itself! Etruscans took up Greek wares and ideas avidly; beyond pottery, Etruscan sculpture from the sixth century BC is heavily influenced by Greek art, both in its focus upon the body and in its idealized-naturalistic style. Traditionally, this has simply been explained as the natural spread of civilized products and ideas to barbarians.[95] Yet there is considerable evidence to the contrary. Etruscans were active agents in formulating their own use of Greek bodily practices. They possessed a well-defined body world distinct from the Classical one.[96] To take an example, hand-held bronze mirrors are an extremely common archaeological find in Etruscan burials from the late Archaic and early Classical periods; they not only allowed people, mostly women, to view themselves, but they are also often engraved with mythological or quotidian scenes. Mirrors were originally Greek and many scenes engraved upon them parallel those on their Greek counterparts, but they rapidly took different forms and were deposited in significantly different ways (as burial goods rather than at sanctuaries, for instance).[97] Although Etruscans imported masses of Greek dining and drinking pottery, they fitted

Plate I. Mesolithic burial at Vedbaek, Denmark, ca. 5000 BC (picture: Aaron Watson).

Plate II. A Bronze Age cremation, Pitten, Austria, ca. 1600 BC (picture: Aaron Watson).

Plate III. Kerameikos, Athens, ca. 430 BC. A family conducts a burial rite outside the Dipylon Gate while the life of the city passes around them (picture: Aaron Watson).

Plate IV. Canterbury, England, fourteenth century AD. A group of pilgrims to the shrine of St. Thomas makes their way through the city (picture: Aaron Watson).

Plate V. Hanging a criminal, Tyburn, London, ca. 1750 AD (picture: Aaron Watson).

(a)   (b)   (c)   (d)

(e)   (f)   (g)   (h)

Plate VI. Gallery of historical images, part 1. A. 'Lion man' figurine, Hohlenstein Stadel, Germany, Upper Palaeolithic. Note the seamless merging of animal features and human-like posture and behaviour (Photo Thomas Stephan, © Ulmer Museum). B. 'Venus' of Hohlestein Fels, Germany, Upper Palaeolithic. In some contexts Palaeolithic people identified and represented the human body as clearly bounded and distinct from animals (Photo © Eberhard Karls, University Tübingen). C. Neolithic female figurine, Vinča, Serbia, fifth millennium BC. Typical of Neolithic figurines, it is small, clay and female; but it also shows an unusual local tradition of ritually masking the face (© Trustees of the British Museum). D. Neolithic house-figurine, Macedonia, fifth millennium BC. An unusual, eloquent merging of several Neolithic key symbols: the body and the house (Photo © Irena Nasteva). E. Statue-stela, Lunigiana, Italy, late third – early second millennium BC. The body is reduced to a tabular surface for display, marked only by anatomical divisions and gender icons (Photo: Robb). F. Figurine, Romania, Bronze Age (late second millennium BC). Dress became an elaborate vocabulary for female identity and social distinction (Photo courtesy of Nona Palincas, Sorin Oanță-Marghitu and History National Museum of Romania/Bucharest). G. Rock art, Tanum, Sweden, Bronze Age (later second millennium BC). A typical association between weapons and a graphically depicted masculinity (Photo: Harris). H. Golden death mask, Mycenae, Greece (Bronze Age, mid-second millennium BC). With social hierarchies such as in the Shaft Graves at Mycenae, the Bronze Age metallization of the social body became ever more resplendent (National Archaeological Museum, Athens, © Hellenic Ministry of Culture/Archaeological Receipts Fund).

(a)

(b)

(c)

(d)

(e)

(f)

(g)

(h)

Plate VII. Gallery of historical images, part 2. A. The 'Doryphoros' ('Spear-bearer') sculpture (Classical Greece, fifth century BC) presents a schematised ideal of masculine beauty deriving both from ideas of proportion and balance and from class-based practices (© Museum of Classical Archaeology, Cambridge). B. Red figure pyxis, 440–415 BC. Except rarely, Classical Greek women were portrayed clothed, often in family groups, emphasizing gendered ideals of self-presentation, spatial segregation and centrality to the family (© Trustees of the British Museum). C. Red figure psykter, c. 500–470 BC. Unlike Palaeolithic hybrids, Classical Greek hybrids have clearly distinguishable human and animal elements; their hybridity and antisocial behaviour underlines the rigid distinction between humans and animals (© Trustees of the British Museum). D. Death in Classical Athens: women mourning a dead body in front of a funerary stela, white-ground lekythos, Athens, c. 435–425 BC (© Trustees of the British Museum). E. Medieval theology of the body summed up in an image: a demon and an angel fight for the soul escaping from the dead body (© Koninklijke Bibliotheek, The Hague). F. A 'Zodiac Man' from medieval science showing which astrological signs exercised influences on each part of the body (reproduced by kind permission of the Master and Fellows of Trinity College Cambridge). G. A monstrous composite of body parts: this carved 'gryllus' under a church seat belongs to a world of incongruously comic, obscene, monstrous, or threatening imagery around the margins of medieval orthodoxy (© Victoria and Albert Museum, London). H. The medieval Everyman as pilgrim, experiencing and balancing radically different views of the body: the poet Chaucer, depicted in the Ellesmere manuscript of the *Canterbury Tales* (reproduced by permission of the Huntington Library, San Marino, California [EL 26 C 9]).

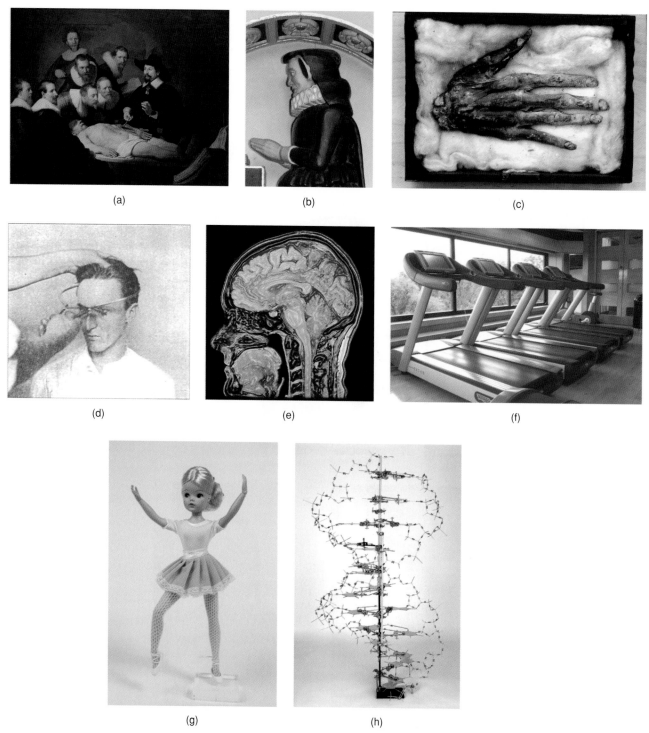

Plate VIII. Gallery of historical images, part 3. A. Rembrandt's 'Anatomy lesson of Dr Nicolaes Tulp' shows a seventeenth century demonstration of the mechanism of the forearm (© Royal Cabinet of Paintings Mauritshuis, The Hague). B. Even as theologians denounced the dead body as worthless carrion, Early Modern memorials often elaborated the body in death more than ever before (photo: Robb). C. In an Early Modern belief of the inherent magical potency of the body, the 'Hand of Glory', the preserved hand of an executed criminal, was used to facilitate further nefarious enterprise. It could, for example, ensure the members of a household remained asleep while they were burgled (by permission of Whitby Museum). D. From the mid-nineteenth century, scientific observation of the body was increasingly used for 'racial' classification. This photo shows a measuring device used by the Czech anthropologist Aleš Hrdlička being employed to quantify the body, in this case the breadth of the head (Hrdlička 1919, fig. 12). E. MRI scan, late twentieth century: scanning technologies bring the areas often associated with the soul or psyche ever more within the medical gaze (image via Wellcome Library London, © Mark Lythgoe & Chloe Hutton). F. Treadmills, twenty-first century. As with the Victorian treadmill, the body is disciplined through repetitive interaction with machines, but the focus has shifted from social correction to medical discourses of health and perfecting the body's appearance as part of consumer culture (photo: Robb). G. 'Sindy' doll, late twentieth century Britain. Like American 'Barbie' dolls, these popular toys fostered gender ideals, not only of appearance but of gendered activities and gestures (© Victoria and Albert Museum, London). H. The DNA model: replica of Crick and Watson's original model. DNA has provided a new master metaphor for the body, that of material information, but it has also been understood within existing ideas about what bodies are (© MRC Laboratory of Molecular Biology).

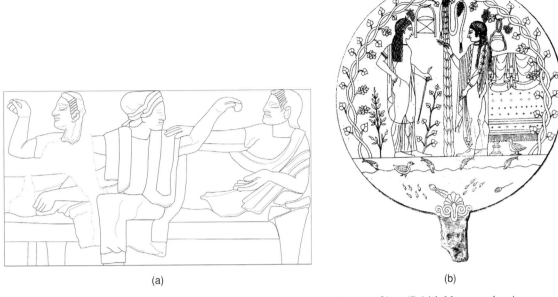

(a)   (b)

Figure 57. Etruscan body imagery. A. Men and women dining, Etruscan frieze (British Museum, drawing by Vicki Herring). B. Etruscan women in a 'dressing scene', engraved bronze mirror (Izzet 2007: fig. 2.7, image courtesy of Vedia Izzet).

these imports into their native tradition of commensality. Unlike Greeks, Etruscans dined in mixed-sex parties, something which would give rise to reports amongst the narrow-minded Greeks and Romans of the permissiveness of Etruscan women (Figure 57). Although there are gymnasium scenes reminiscent of Greek ones, Etruscan art has far less male nudity than Greek art. Although Etruscans seem to have appreciated Athenian vases with robust scenes of sex and violence, Etruscan art has very little of the explicit homoerotic themes of some Greek art, implying differences in sexual practices. Etruscans were more interested in the interior of the body than Greeks were, with an international reputation as soothsayers able to forecast the future based upon the internal organs of animals, and perhaps occasionally humans.[98] As these examples suggest, the Greek body world did not travel as a package; Etruscans chose specific items from the material culture and ideas on offer and fitted them into their own lifeways and views of the body.

The monumental human body in the
Central Mediterranean

One of the most distinctive elements of Classical Greece was the human body in monumental statuary. How did this fare in the overseas encounter?

The answer is: decidedly mixed, as the images in Figure 58 show (all are from the edges of the Greek world). Monumental statuary is fairly common around the Central Mediterranean in the period between 800 BC and 300 BC (Figure 59), but this statuary takes a very wide

range of forms. Greek-style 'naturalistic' sculpture used three-dimensional space to show rounded people with a range of anatomical features. The people who adopted it most enthusiastically were the Campanians in Southern Italy and the Etruscans in Central Italy. The former are no surprise, living in an area densely populated with a multi-ethnic mixture of Greek colonists, Etruscan colonists and native Italic people. Etruscan sculpture shows a rapid mastery of new techniques of modelling, but these were used to create sculptures on Etruscan themes in Etruscan ways. As noted previously, male nudity is much rarer and the choice of subjects is much less focused upon male beauty and includes specifically Etruscan deities and situations.

Elsewhere in Central and Southern Italy, the uptake was limited. In several regions, people held resolutely to the inherited prehistoric tradition of tabular statue-stelae (Figure 33, Chapter 4). This is true of the Ligurian Lunigiana tradition of Copper and Bronze Age stelae found around La Spezia northwest of Etruria.[99] Sculptors here probably had contact with Greek ideas mediated through Etruscans (one Iron Age Lunigiana stela in fact bears an inscription in Etruscan). In the Iron Age, under the influence of new sculptural traditions, Lunigiana stelae become decidedly less schematic, for instance in representing more details of clothing and regions of the body such as the legs (Figure 58a). But they maintain their traditional style of showing the body as a tabular slab rather than going over to sculpture in the round. To the east of the Etruscans, in Adriatic Central

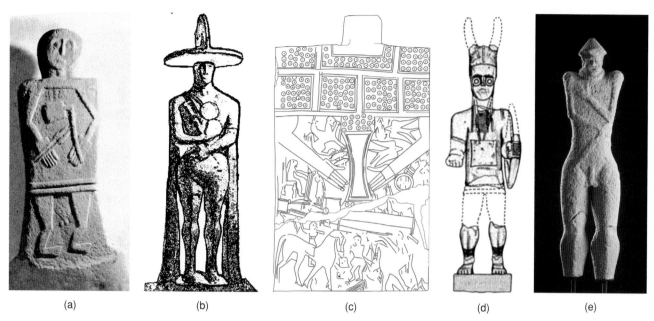

(a)   (b)   (c)   (d)   (e)

Figure 58. Human statuary around the edges of the Greek world. A. Lunigiana stela, Liguria, northern Italy (photo: Graziosi 1974: fig. 138). B. Capestrano 'warrior', east-central Italy (drawing: Robb). C. Daunian stela, Puglia, south-eastern Italy (drawn by Vicki Herring). D. Monte Prama, Sardinia (drawn by Vicki Herring after Tronchetti 2005: fig. 18). E. Hirschlanden, Germany (© P. Frankenstein and H. Zweitasch, Landesmuseum Württemberg, Stuttgart).

Italy among the Picenes, the Capestrano Warrior statue (Figure 58b) is clearly made by people adopting the idea of three-dimensional sculpture, but they have dispensed with heroic nudity, left it in native garb and cowboy-hat-like headgear, and used body proportions completely foreign to the Greek canon. The most interesting case is that of the Daunians, on the Adriatic coast of Puglia. Here there arises a flourishing tradition of sixth and fifth centuries BC anthropomorphic grave markers (Figure 58c) which show male and female figures with elaborate surface ornamentation depicting dress, hair style, weaponry and inset scenes.[100] The Daunians are not far from the Greek colonies at Taranto and Metaponto, Greek traders were sailing the Adriatic, and the Daunians had regular contacts with Greeks and Etruscans from the sixth century BC. Yet they seem to have remained stubbornly independent of any Greek aesthetic influence (for instance in maintaining local styles of geometric pottery). Their human body representations show no acknowledgement at all of the Greek tradition, remaining entirely within the native tradition of showing the body as a slab affording a surface for schematic display.

Further afield, in Sardinia, developments similar to that in Etruria seem to have occurred. Local people adopted the basic concept of sculpture in the round to produce monumental statues at Monte Prama from Phoenicians and Greeks, but the sculptures are basically large stone versions of the body as it was represented in the local tra-

dition of small bronze statuettes (Figure 58d).[101] To the north of the Classical world, the early Iron Age Hallstatt group maintained autonomous traditions of body representation on pottery and in other media, and these are strongly echoed in Iron Age Alpine rock art at Valcamonica. However, Hallstatt people also erected monumental statues or grave markers occasionally, and archaeological finds from sites such as the Heuneberg and Manching show that south-western Hallstatt groups were in contact with Greek traders via the Rhone valley. One result is the Hirschlanden stela (Figure 58e), which resembles nothing so much as a tabular statue, with arms and weaponry in a traditional posture, which has been fleshed three-dimensionally to create a hybrid stela-in-the-round.

Thus, the Greek body did not travel unchanged. Everywhere it travelled, the Greek body was reinterpreted to fit into local body worlds and political relations, ranging from complete adoption through hybrid reworking of various elements to complete rejection. This is not too surprising. Greeks overseas were much more interested in selling than propagandizing; the ideological target of Classical sculpture was the Greek community itself rather than the world outside it.

Votives[102]

We encountered votive body parts earlier in our discussion; these representations of discrete body parts, usually made of clay but also found in stone, were offered at

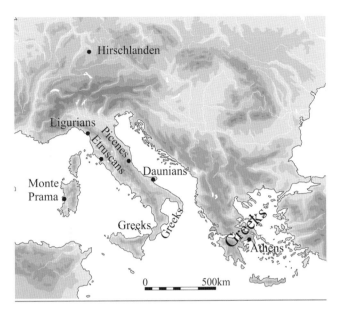

Figure 59. The Central Mediterranean and surrounding areas, showing locations of statuary traditions referred to in the text.

temples and sanctuaries in prayers for healing the ailing part. From the fourth century BC onwards, they became increasingly common throughout the Mediterranean area. Their history is surprisingly complex. As votives spread throughout the Greek world, its neighbours and its heirs, they changed in ways which reflected the concerns and beliefs of the people using them. In Etruria, for example, assemblages of votives include many more internal organs than in Greek areas, because of the long-standing Etruscan interest in divination through the organs of sacrifices which meant that Etruscans were much more familiar with, and interested in, internal organs. In Roman Gaul, the practice of dedicating votives arrived with the Romans, who had taken the practice in turn from the Greeks. Amongst the Gauls, special attention was paid to heads, which was probably related to a long-standing tradition of head-hunting and head cults here. As yet another permutation, in some areas of the Eastern Mediterranean, particularly in the Lydia and Phrygia, images of body parts such as eyes, arms, legs, breasts and phalli, which were clearly derived from votives, were carved upon large stone stelae inscribed with prayers, confessions of sins and accounts of how these sins were expiations. These 'propitiatory stelae' reformulate the body part imagery from votive traditions in new ways deriving from the complex theological debates which were taking place in the Eastern Mediterranean in the last two centuries before Christ – a theological ferment involving the reformulation of many older religions and providing the matrix for the birth of Christianity.

How well did the Greek body travel?

As these three examples show, Greek ideas and practices about the body certainly made their way to people outside the Greek world. Yet, even when these recipients lived around the edges of the Greek colonial world, or directly within the Roman Empire for that matter, the process was not the steamroller of culture and high art rolling inevitably over less desirable ways of living. It was always a political process; but it was local politics that mattered. Gauls in Southern France bought wine and pottery from Greeks at Marseilles, but used them according to their own pattern of political feasting.[103] Etruscan elites had a mass uptake of Greek body-related paraphernalia, including new ways of ornamenting their bodies, competing athletically, and representing the body. There is no doubt that this changed the Etruscan way of life; but it was not an uncritical acceptance and it did not make them become Greeks in many fundamental outlooks. Similarly, Greek sculptural techniques were adopted in some places, rejected in others, and merged with previous traditions of representation in others. How votives were received and used seems to have depended in large part upon prior attitudes towards the body.

It is worth asking what this says about the relationship of the body, style and politics. If specific elements of style and iconography could be adopted piecemeal and fitted into other ways of doing politics, does this undermine our earlier argument for a close fit between political life and the aesthetics of the body? Not necessarily; the fact that culture has functional relations within it does not mean that it is hermetically sealed, and the fact that it can adopt elements from outside does not mean that internal relations do not exist. Transplanting a practice into a new context often redefines it. Hence, a style or practice which fit coherently into an edifice of Greek cultural politics may have meant something much differently when a sculptor in Central Italy, Sardinia, or on the banks of the Danube decided to try it out when he or she sat down to make a traditional statue.

Conclusion: The body and politics

When Eupheros' mourning family gathered around his grave at Kerameikos, outside the main gate of Athens, to pour libations, sing songs of lamentations and mark the place with a stela, they were grieving as private citizens. Surely such moments of private grief and mourning have little to do with the political ideology of the city-state in any direct, heavy-handed way. The epitaphs on Classical grave markers still move us with their pathos.

Yet, in some ways, the body is always political. The body is never generic; it is a particular kind of body, with the capacity to have particular kinds of experiences and enter into specific social relationships. The body world of Classical Greece was richly multiple and multimodal. Bodies were inescapably gendered and aged. Beyond this, they could be politically marked or unmarked as Athenian or foreign, free or slave. They could be shaped by menial toil or by the cultivated training of the gymnasium. Philosophers saw the body in a wide range of ways, including as a transitory container for the soul and a map of the polity. The ritual purity of the body was of deep concern to some; to others, this was superstitious nonsense. Refined discussion of beauty alternated with cruel lampooning of grotesque, deformed bodies. Bodies could be understood and treated medically via a range of theories, therapies, prayers and magic.

Eupheros' body, living, took part in all of these discourses and more. Aside from gender, which fundamentally arranged social relations between men and women, most of these discourses were not overtly political. Yet as Foucault[104] has reminded us, some forms of power are most powerful when they are invisible, when they appear to be doing nothing more than making an abstract statement about beauty or order. And nothing makes politics more invisible than submerging it in the body. We are intuitively familiar with the politics of the body in our own lives. The grossest bodily divisions – the politics of 'race', gender, and sexual orientation – hang on with depressing tenacity. Class divisions are equally embodied in many forms: work and dress, food and sport, even gesture and habitus. If the body is central to modern politics, which are supposedly founded upon the assumption that all bodies are equal, it is no surprise that the body is even more overtly politicized in other settings. For example, we have seen in Chapter 3 that Mesolithic bodies possessed something of the fluidity of hunter-gatherer politics in which boundaries between groups, like boundaries between ontological categories, were permeable and flexible. Chapter 4 underlined the association between ancestral burials, territory and local origins which was fundamental to the politics of Neolithic village life; the politicization of bodies changed in the fourth and third millennia BC with the introduction of a new kind of political personhood which was intimately associated with new conceptions of the body.

In Classical Athens, the politics of the body – at least, of the sculpted body – was to provide a regulatory ideal,[105] which, rarely achieved and probably never fully achievable, nevertheless provided a reference point for the fashioning of lived lives. It provided a carefully generic, idealized, but 'naturalistic' body which served as a medium of aspirational self-understanding for free adult male members of the *polis*. In presenting the people of Athens with themselves, transformed, the mirror of art performed first of all acts of selection, of eradication, making invisible not only whole sectors of the population but also whole aspects of the lives of those who remained – work, for instance. It transformed the body into an idealized body, the body the citizen would have had if able to embody the class-marked ideal of the adult male cityman. The politics of art was implicit not only in its subject matter but in its style too. In transforming the mutable, politically complex body of living Eupheros into a stone proclamation of this regulatory ideal, the political gaze did not provide the 'kiss of the prince' so much as the gaze of the Gorgon.

Superficially, politics regulates bodies; every political order includes prescriptions or proscriptions about what to eat, what to wear, how to have sex, what kinds of people can do certain jobs and so on. But the relationship is reciprocal; in a deeper current, the body regulates politics. The body provides a sense of identity as a specific kind of person, a basis for community, an understanding of difference. These things are experienced through the action of the habitus, and they are political resources.[106] Thus, on one level, the rise of Classical 'naturalism' in sculpture reflects a shift from aristocratic to mass politics, with the new style providing ideological images of civic virtue. But while this is true, it is also reductionist. There was no concerted, intentional ideological campaign behind the style; there was no simple mapping of artistic events on to political events; most importantly, a simple, unidirectional functionalism does not explain why people actually responded to the new style in a politically productive way, something which depended upon sharing its presuppositions. Most of the necessary beliefs and practices (for instance, the definition of male and female identities) pre-existed this style, and were so deeply held that there can be little question of sculptors or patrons manipulating them. Instead, both politics and style responded to habitus. The body thus formed an ideological resource for politicians, but it was more than this. It was also part of the cultural framework which generated political behaviour by teaching citizens about their bodies. To the extent that the flow of politics presumed and was channelled by ideas of personhood, the body created politics.

The later politics of Classical sculpture

We still live with Classical sculpture, and its history between the Greeks and now has always been political. It is an entertaining tale to trace briefly. In the Hellenistic period, sculptors developed the Classical body into new genres such as more realistic portraiture. However, they also made use of the now-venerable Classical style. One result was that, for the first time, Classical sculpture acquired a sense of antiquity; this is the moment when the Classical actually became 'classical', in contrast to more contemporary styles. Hellenistic and Roman collectors procured Classical originals and made copies of them. Moreover, the context of sculpture changed; while it continued to be used for public religious and patriotic monuments, it also moved into private homes as decoration purely for 'aesthetic' enjoyment. 'The female nude as the site and the public display of heterosexual desire', as a unifying political force, may be the reason for the great popularity of the female nude based upon the Aphrodite of Knidos, which really first becomes common at this time.[107]

Socially, the survival and popularity of Classical sculpture in post-Classical times were not simply chance. As other elements of the Greek world (such as dress, and weaponry) were allowed to pass, Hellenistic and Roman elites took over a large dose of Greek high culture – literature, history, medicine, the theatre – as something to be consumed in creating a specific cultured, aristocratic self-image. Sculpture formed part of this package of reworked cultural capital. This really sets the pattern for subsequent uses of Classical sculpture. With its rediscovery by artists in the Renaissance and by art historians in the Enlightenment, Greek art provided an image of idealism in the sense of noble aspirations summed up in the human form – but it also provided a historical genealogy for Western art and civilization. Therefore, there is an irresistible attraction to the shaky belief that Classical sculpture is somehow inherently twinned from birth with democracy. 'Classical' is always an oppositional term; it depends for meaning upon contrast with something that is not 'Classical'. Revolutionary France was heroically neo-Classical, but since then the Classical body has acquired generally conservative overtones. More generally, it has acquired the aura of high culture; it still legitimates a social order, but it does so not by embodying the virtue of the citizens but rather by embodying the history, education and symbolic capital which distinguished classes with taste and education from those without. Again, it is the reductio ad absurdum which makes clearest the distance we have travelled. Male beauty is gone; we have lost almost completely the naked men which dominated Classical sculpture-scapes (and many of those which survive have acquired fig leaves!). Sculptures may be adapted to fit Christian ideas about how humans relate to the divine.[108] When we want to suggest aspirational bodies to emulate, we use other media (above all

photography) and we do so mostly in the service of capitalism ('buy this lifestyle!') rather than political order. Yet the female body remains fair game for the possessive gaze and Classical sculpture remains familiar as an idiom for taste. The cement nude at the garden centre is now completely removed from scandalous divine eroticism of Praxiteles' Aphrodite; it exists to give an innocuous touch of gentility to one's flowerbed.

NOTES

1. The Classical body has been the subject of scholarship in at least four often unrelated lines of research. For gender, sexuality and the body, see: Blundell 1995; Cole 2004; Fantham et al. 1995; Foxhall and Salmon 1998; Kampen 1996; Koloski-Ostrow and Lyons 1997; McClure 2002; Monserrat 1997; Pomeroy 1995; Porter 1995; and Wyke 1998a; 1998b. Within art history, Osborne 2011 presents a recent synthesis of the body in visual arts. See also: Dunbabin 1986; Flynn 1998; Nochlin 1994; Osborne 2006; and Squire 2011. For history of medicine, see Dean-Jones 1996; Grmek and Gourevitch 1998; Horstmanshoff, Van Der Eijk, and Schrijvers 1995; King 1998a; 1998b; King 2005; Kuriyama 1999; Longrigg 1998; and Von Staden 1992. Beyond literature on the body, for the history of Classical art, Boardman 1978; 1985; 1995 presents a magisterial summary of traditional scholarship; more recent synthesis can be found in Beard and Henderson 2001, Osborne 1998a, Pollitt 1972, Spivey 1996, and Stewart 2008. Berard et al. 1989 review the varied imagery of Classical Athens, and Oakley 2004 reviews the visual evidence for Athenian deathways. Good general introductions to the history and politics discussed in this chapter are provided by Cartledge 1993a; Pomeroy et al. 2007, Samons 2007, and Shapiro 2007, and by the Joint Association of Classical Teachers' *World of Athens* 2008 2nd edition revised by R. Osborne.
2. Gell 1992.
3. We are grateful to Lin Foxhall for emphasizing the importance of this point to us.
4. Haynes 1984; Pollitt 1972.
5. Said 1978.
6. Fullerton 2000, 115.
7. We follow general usage in using the term "Classical" both to refer broadly to the Greek and Roman worlds generally and narrowly to refer to the fifth and fourth centuries BC in Greek-speaking areas. It will usually be clear from the context which is meant.
8. Morris 1992.
9. Gombrich 1962, 99.
10. Osborne 1998a, 137.
11. Haynes 1984; cf. Tanner 2006, 36–37.
12. Fullerton 2000, 121–122.
13. Pollitt 1972, 23, 68.
14. Tanner 2006, 12.

15. Dover 1978; Foucault 1978; 1985; 1988; Halperin 1990.
16. Fantham et al. 1995; Pomeroy 1995.
17. Blundell 1995; Lefkowitz and Fant 1982; Wyke 1998a, 1998b.
18. Stewart 1997.
19. Osborne 1996.
20. Lewis 2002; Ferrari 2002.
21. Brock 1994.
22. Scheidel 1995.
23. Antonaccio 2000; Nevett 2011.
24. Cohen 1989.
25. Bundrick 2008, 310.
26. Schaps 1998.
27. Leader 1997.
28. Stehle and Díaz 1996.
29. Burton 1998.
30. Antonaccio 2000.
31. Lefkowitz 1983.
32. Lyons 2003.
33. Foxhall 1989.
34. Cohen 1989; Seremetakis 1991.
35. Leader 1997.
36. Connelly 2007.
37. Closterman 2007.
38. Osborne 1997a.
39. Johnstone 2003.
40. Walters 1998.
41. Cohen 1991.
42. Treherne 1995.
43. Hurwit 2007; Stewart 1997.
44. Osborne 1997b.
45. Osborne 2011.
46. Foucault 1985.
47. Osborne 2011.
48. Osborne 2011.
49. Cartledge 1993b.
50. Osborne 2011.
51. Vlassopoulos 2007a; 2007b.
52. Papadopoulos 2000.
53. Oakley 2004.
54. Osborne 2011.
55. Hughes 2010.
56. Osborne 2011.
57. Turner 1969.
58. Osborne 2011, 229.
59. Bettinetti 2001; Elsner 2007; Gordon 1979; Osborne 2011; Tanner 2006.
60. Veyne 1982.
61. Brock 2006.
62. Sassi 2001.
63. Dean-Jones 1996; King 1998a; 1998b.
64. Reilly 1997.
65. Van Der Eijk 2005.
66. There is a large recent literature on votives, which is summarized in Hughes 2008 and Hughes in press.
67. Glinister 2006.
68. Gell 1992.
69. Stewart 2008, Chapter 7.
70. Osborne 1997a.
71. Tanner 2006.
72. Gell 1998.
73. Gombrich 1962.
74. Pollitt 1972; Stewart 2008.
75. Mitchell 2006.
76. Berger 1972.
77. Berger 1972.
78. Brown 1997; Kampen 1996; Koloski-Ostrow and Lyons 1997.
79. Stewart 2008, 18–19.
80. Tanner 2001.
81. Osborne 2011, 209.
82. Osborne 1998b, 29.
83. Gombrich 1962.
84. Osborne 2011.
85. Butler 1993, 1; cf. Harris 2005, 41–42.
86. Butler 1990, 176.
87. Osborne 1985; Quinn 2007.
88. Osborne 1985, 54.
89. Quinn 2007, 90.
90. Bhabha 1994; Gosden 2004; Moore-Gilbert 1997; van Dommelen 2006; 2011.
91. Millett 1992; Webster 2001; Woolf 1997.
92. van Dommelen 2006.
93. Here we draw extensively on the work done by Simon Stoddart.
94. Izzet 2007.
95. Boardman 1978; 1985.
96. Stoddart 2009.
97. Izzet 2007, 212.
98. Bonfante 1986.
99. Ambrosi 1972.
100. Nava 1988.
101. Tronchetti 2005; Tronchetti and van Dommelen 2005.
102. This draws on the work of Jessica Hughes (e.g. Hughes 2008).
103. Dietler 2010.
104. Foucault 1977; 1978.
105. Butler 1990; 1993.
106. Butler 1990; 1993.
107. Salomon 1997, 212.
108. Hughes 2011.

6

The body and God

Oliver J. T. Harris and John Robb[1]

Life is a pilgrimage[2]

Canterbury, England, sometime in the thirteenth or fourteenth century (Plate IV). A group of pilgrims approaches the cathedral, one of the four great holy destinations of Medieval Europe. They are dusty and tired from several days travel from London; some have come much further before this last stage. Yet as their bodies travel the well-worn path from the main road through the town, via the pilgrim's entrance in the north side of the Cathedral, to the crypt where St. Thomas's body was first buried and, finally, to the Trinity Chapel where the saint now rests, their spirits become elevated. Some go simply to pray in the presence of the holy; others go to thank the saint for helping them or to ask for a cure for an illness which has defied doctors and healers. The pilgrims' piety is genuine, spontaneous, but not unscripted; they are guided by the footsteps of a century of pilgrims before them, by practiced gestures such as kneeling and praying, by the didactic pictures around them of the saint's miracles of healing (Figure 60). There are sensory prompts too – the vault soaring to heaven, the sweet incense of the Mass and the music echoing in the roof which moves their bodies from the ordinary to the presence of God.

Human bodies travel a road of hardship and pain, but, with the help of encounters with holy bodies such as the miracle-working bones of St. Thomas, they can struggle through to a heavenly destination. This sense of a bodily journey is embodied in the common image of *homo viator*, the human voyaging through life as a pilgrimage:

'This world nys but a thurghfare ful of wo,
And we been pilgrymes, passinge to and fro.'
['This world is but a thoroughfare full of woe,

But there are other bodies in this crowded world besides the pious and the saint. There is a world of learned bodies. Amongst the pilgrims themselves, there may be physicians, astrologers and alchemists who read the Bible little, relying instead upon their knowledge of the humours and the stars to heal bodies, to predict their fortunes, and to change the nature of matter. Within each pilgrim, learned or unschooled, there is a bodily vitality sometimes interpretable as fleshly sin but not reducible to it. Gluttony and excess are to be condemned, but not eating and drinking; lust may be sinful, but love is also a bodily emotion to these medieval people. The tavern and good company beckon, stories and brawls unfold, the town with its delights thrusts up against the walls of the cathedral and the travellers will experience both. Even in the church itself, the experienced pilgrim may have an eye out for adventures of love. The vitality of the body comes out irrepressibly not only in the pageantry of dress and action along the way, but in the anti-bodies jeering at solemnity and holiness. In the corners of one's eye, the comic and obscene peep out, the grotesques and gargoyles leering down at the pilgrims from high in the stonework of the cathedral. Our pilgrims can be forgiven for shifting their focus. What is the margin and what is the central text, what is the wayside pleasure and what is the real goal?

This chapter explores medieval bodies, focusing principally upon Christians in Western Europe in the later Middle Ages. It asks two basic questions. First, how did medieval people actually understand their bodies? In the historical panorama we have been telling up to this point, the really unique innovation of the medieval period was religion. For the first time in European history, a monotheistic religion was backed up by a strong theocracy and a sophisticated intellectual tradition. Christianity aspired to a monopoly of belief and, in many spheres of life, it came close to achieving it. Moreover, from the very start, Christianity was a religion of bodily paradox. From the virgin birth through the resurrection, the miracles of Jesus were miracles of physical impossibility – walking on water, multiplying loaves and fishes, healing the sick and raising the dead. These explicitly divided the spiritual from the material and asserted the primacy of the former, which could reorder the physical world at will. Such a development must have been shaped by understandings of the body, and it must have had sweeping consequences for such understandings. So, our second question: what was the relationship between the body and God?

Medievalness familiar and strange

Medieval Europe is locked in traditional grand narratives. Every schoolchild knows how the Roman empire collapsed in the fifth to sixth centuries AD, leaving Europe prey to the barbarian ravages of the so-called Dark Ages; how Christianity and the feudal system emerged painfully from the wreckage as the political basis of Western Europe's ancestral kingdoms; how the centuries of ignorance were relieved only by the tenth and eleventh centuries when revivals of Classical learning filtered through Moorish Spain and the Arab East; how the high and late Middle Ages were dominated by kingly splendour, dynastic wars and devastating plagues; and how humanism, movable type and the discovery of the Americas ushered in a new era by 1500.

Recent scholarship has tended to efface both the teleologies and the punctuational episodes in such narratives. Rome fell, as an empire; but studies of late antiquity have shown continuity throughout the Mediterranean from the Classical world rather than rupture, particularly in on-the-ground daily life. Huns, Goths, Lombards, Vandals, Franks and other cataclysmically invading hordes tended to be absorbed into the peoples they encountered, leaving an inextricably mixed heritage, or, often, surprisingly little trace. Classical learning was not lost but transmitted by figures such as Isidore of Seville (560–636), whose twenty-volume encyclopaedia intended to summarize all knowledge was read throughout Europe throughout the Middle Ages. Moreover, critique of traditional grand narratives of the Middle Ages often rests upon a change of scale and perspective. What is medieval history a history *of*? To recall issues raised in Chapter 2, a political narrative shows punctuated change when an economic or social narrative normally shows continuity or gradual shift. The lens of educated, elite networks may show a decline into intellectual darkness when a portrait of the other 98 per cent of the population reveals little change. Religious theory according to theologians may little resemble popular belief or religious, magical or medical practice. It is perfectly reasonable to ask, as one historian has done,[4] whether women had a 'fall of Rome'.

These issues are central to a history of the body, an entity which existed in discourses across all of human experience from the muddy ploughman plodding behind his horse to the erudite philosopher debating the nature of Eternity. In this chapter, the Middle Ages will look sometimes familiar, sometimes strange, in the light of other visions. Throughout, we try to follow Bynum's[5] call to history, that however we look at the past, we cannot lose sight of the people in it and what is wonderful in their lives and works.

From the Classical to the Christian world

The setting in which Christianity was born provided abundant ingredients for understandings of the body. On one hand, the prevalent view of the body in Judaism was a materialistic one: the body was understood in terms of flesh and blood, ordinary experience, pleasure and pain; it was subjected generally to illness and universally to death. Moreover, a body was identity: a person *was* his or her body. At the same time, some Jewish apocalyptic cults such as the Pharisees believed that the bodies of the faithful would be resurrected at the end of the world to live again. This resurrection was generally understood as a revival of the material body itself; this would rescue the identity of the dead from dissolution and oblivion.

The Classical inheritance (see Chapter 5) provided three key elements. First, the background assumption was that the body and the self were identical; the self was located in the living, sensing, gendered, aged, socially recognized body, the locus of universal and inescapable things like gender, pleasure, pain and death. The second element was the soul or *eidos*, something associated with this body but that was severed from it at death. This concept turns up commonly in images of death; the lamenting souls of the dead populate the dismal realm of Hades. In Plato's influential philosophy the concept of soul was significantly elaborated; the spirit was a distinct plane of existence which lay behind the visible world of immediate experience. It was the plane of eternal, quintessential and ideal forms which were reflected imperfectly in the transient material things of the world. Finally, Classical medicine supplied the Hippocratic/Galenic model of the humoural body. This model saw the body as fluid both literally, in that its constitution was determined by its mixture of the four elemental humours, and conceptually, as the balance of humours in the body was continually in flux and open to environmental influences.

Faced with such an array of heterogeneous elements, Christianity was both conservative and revolutionary. It was conservative in that both late antiquity in the Mediterranean and the early medieval period north of the Alps drew directly and heavily upon earlier periods, not only for technologies, economies and geographies but for concepts as well. Conversion was not a lightning reorientation but a piecemeal process of negotiation and adaptation which incorporated indigenous elements. Medical, scientific and philosophical concepts were basically

Figure 60. Pilgrims. Stained glass window, shrine of St. Thomas, Canterbury Cathedral (photo: Robb).

taken from Classical authorities without rupture and often without much modification. Similarly, practices such as the deposition of votive body parts continued, even when the deity being supplicated changed. In magical practices, Classical charms and curses, by and large, were winnowed and adapted to a new framework of belief rather than invented anew.[6] The same is true for most aspects of bodily practice in daily life – how people dressed, moved about through their houses, used tools and worked, produced food and ate depended much more on local pre-Christian ways than upon any revolutionary new way of life. Whereas traditional accounts of the end of the Roman Empire prioritize the male worlds of public life, economics and politics, fundamental aspects of women's lives remained little changed, particularly 'the constancy of marriage and motherhood as the central facts of almost all women's lives' and 'their place in a gender hierarchy predicated upon male superiority'.[7]

Even ways of dealing with the dead, which one might expect to reflect eschatology closely, show a curious absence of linkage with religion. Christians did not cremate, but cremation was already waning in favour of inhumation in much of the Roman world by the onset of Christianity. The only marked change was bringing burials within the limits of settlements, broaching the Greek and Roman taboo upon polluting death. Outside of the Mediterranean, pre-Christian and early Christian burials are often distinguished by, at most, a reduction in how many objects were placed in the grave with the deceased.[8] Another pervasive element of the early historical body world, gender, also shows little discontinuity. Early Christians generally concurred with their forebears about what made men and women different, drawing both upon Classical medical writers such as Galen and

Aristotle to portray the female body as a weaker or inferior version of the male and upon earlier ideas of honour, violence, and modesty as a basis for gendered codes of space, activity, violence, and sexual behaviour.

Yet Christianity was a complete cultural revolution in one particular sense. Earlier and other ways of looking at the world had cheerfully accepted contextuality as a fact of life. Classical religion, medicine, sexuality and daily practices such as clothing and ornamenting the body tended to form different spheres of life, regulated by different codes and conceptualizations. In contrast, Christianity proclaimed a universal belief system, in the sense that one set of beliefs should encompass all aspects of life. In a process of 'desecularisation', Christianity 'annexed areas of life formerly independent of religious cult and belief'.[9] Moreover, Christianity was a religion of the body in a fundamental sense; or, to some extent, a religion *against* the body. It was doctrinally centred around an idea of spirit which opposed it to matter and which prescribed the regulation of the material order by the spiritual. The body became the object of spiritual regulation. Theologians now had to formulate the official Christian views on the whole gamut of bodily behaviours such as foodways, sexuality, dress, magic and healing. The effect was to reorder the Classical inheritance: while the material remained much the same, it was fitted into an entirely new overarching conceptual structure.

Medicine exemplifies this; early Christian thinkers had to decide to what extent Classical medical approaches could be encompassed within Christianity (for instance, by arguing that God had made therapeutic plants for humans to use) or to what extent health and illness were simply ordained by God and addressed through prayer.[10] It is likewise with the regulation of bodily appetites. To the extent that ancient people thought explicitly about how one should eat, the key ideas were the enjoyment of good food and the Hippocratic/Galenic medical concept of a balance in the diet. As Christianity spread from Jews to Gentiles, basic foodways throughout Europe essentially were the same as non-Jews had practiced everywhere. But the need to develop a specifically Christian way of eating was satisfied by identifying a system of fast days (typically one or two days a week plus holy days and Lent) and foods which were abstained from during them. This was supplemented by additional restrictions for people in holy orders and exemplia of self-prescribed asceticism in the exceptionally holy. Underlying this was a deep suspicion of bodily pleasure, which had to be held in check. The same approach was largely applied to questions of sexuality, only more so. Sexuality was of little importance to Classical religions. In contrast, Christian theologians from Paul onwards were deeply worried by sexuality. By about 400 AD, thinkers such as Augustine had formulated the basic positions which would last through the Middle Ages, annexing it to the realms of life under religion's governance. At the most basic level, carnal desire was spiritually destructive and needed to be controlled. Yet it was recognized that sex was necessary for reproduction, and that sexual desire could not be entirely eliminated. Hence, as Gregory the Great said, sex was not sinful as long as it was procreative and you didn't enjoy it! Thus, in theory, while people unable or unwilling to remain chaste were allowed to marry, both contraception and sexual acts other than intercourse purely for procreation were immoral. Moreover, chastity was enjoined for men and women in religious life.

Where is 'the medieval body'?

Paradoxically, in current academic literature, 'the medieval body' is both everywhere and nowhere. Bodies are ubiquitous: theologians debate and pronounce about them, doctors practice upon them, courtly etiquette and violence enact codes of embodied behaviour and so on. Yet the huge literature on such things has no centre of gravity; no single consensus. There is surprisingly little discussion of the body per se. There are three reasons for this. First, except for some theological and scientific work, in much of the literature on the medieval body, the body is a vehicle for gender, political status and sanctity. It acts as a signifier, enacting coded discourses about these things. It is simultaneously foregrounded and made invisible; the gaze slides off it rapidly on to whatever signification it carries. Secondly, the topic is fragmented academically more than in any other period except perhaps for the Classical world. Political and social historians, historians of gender, religion and medicine, literary critics and archaeologists all discuss the body. But they use materials ranging from chivalric romances, theological disquisitions and medical texts which circulated amongst tiny but influential international literati to scriptural formulae which resonated throughout the Middle Ages, manor court records of small village fracas, and the skeletons of everyday citizens. Which is really 'the' body?

Finally, such cacophony also reflects a genuine multiplicity which few scholars have fairly squared up to. Difference lies in the body itself, not only in our disciplinary treatments of it. While clerics rail against the flesh, medical writers may recommend sex as a healthful therapy and courtly writers idolise adulterous love. Peasants gorge themselves and fornicate gleefully while ascetics mortify their bodies. Doctors prescribe diets and medicines to treat the ailing while priests prescribe penitence.

The body in death was corrupt and repugnant flesh, yet saints' relics were revered as powerful. Women were considered inherently weak and sinful but write some of the most moving spiritual ecstasies of the Middle Ages. Even in the narrow world of theological doctrine, there was no simple unanimity: medieval thinkers gave quite different readings to the notion of 'soul' and how it related to a physical body, and what gave it a specific identity. Even in imagery, we have warlike bodies such as the Lewis chessmen, sacred bodies such as those of Christ and the saints, the working bodies of the ploughmen, and inexplicably obscene bodies such as the Sheela Na Gig of medieval Britain and Ireland, a roughly carved woman with genitals exposed.

This profusion of bodies is well captured by Caroline Walker Bynum in a widely-cited overview.

> It would be no more correct to say that medieval doctors, rabbis, alchemists, prostitutes, wet nurses, preachers and theologians had a 'concept' of 'the body' than it would be to say that Charles Darwin, Beatrix Potter, a poacher, and the village butcher had 'a' 'concept' of 'the rabbit'.[11]

Yet at the same time, there were widely shared ways of thinking about the body. The real sticking point here is not whether the medieval body existed, but whether it existed as a 'concept', with the implication that it was a single, sharply definable thing which was uniform throughout the period. As we discuss later, there clearly was no single 'medieval body'. Yet medieval people's multiple bodies did not form an orderless cacophony; instead, they related to each other within a liveable experience.

The three bodies of the medieval world

The intersection of earlier traditions and Christianity created a complex medieval body world. Although many of its aspects were widely shared throughout Europe from late antiquity through the sixteenth century, some elements were not, and the illustrative sources are more revealing for the later Middle Ages. As noted earlier, we focus here principally upon the high and later Middle Ages (ca. 1000–1500 AD) of Western Europe.

The doctrinal body: The body as theological battleground

The doctrinal body – the body as the Christian Church saw it – is virtually a cliché; indeed, expressions such as 'keeping body and soul together' still loom large in our language. In some ways, this is the most visible medieval body: the voice of the Church is loud in text and visual

Figure 61. The perfect body of theology: Jesus (twelfth century, Italy; © Victoria and Albert Museum, London).

Table 7. *Theological dualisms*

Forms of existence	Spirit: matter
Components of the human person	Soul: body
Temporality	Eternal: transient
Value	Transcendental: worldly
Moral orientation	Pure: sinful
Enactments	Prayer, asceticism: sensual indulgence

art (Figure 61). There is no doubt that this formed a major part of the European framework of thought. Even scholars who have argued that medieval theology was often not strictly and mechanistically dualistic note that the twin, opposed concepts of 'body' and 'soul' provided widely shared terms of discourse throughout the Middle Ages.[12]

Throughout medieval culture, one encounters this opposition (Table 7). In simplest form, this dichotomy structured European thought from late antiquity onwards, not only to the end of the Middle Ages but in many ways up to the present (see Chapters 7 and 8). The body was flesh, mortal and liable to sin and corruption. The soul was spiritual, divine and eternal, whether its eternal existence was delightful in heaven or tormented in hell (Plate VIIe).

These two components of personhood were promulgated in theological discourse; a vast range of texts, images and practices communicated, enacted and reproduced them. Although we must not overestimate the homogeneity of medieval theology, there were common principles. To start with, the body/spirit duality framed the human life story. In most medieval theories, the two were joined at conception and parted at death.

Death was understood as the death of the body, when the connection between the two was severed. The body returned to dust, and the soul went to face its reckoning, the reward of virtue or the wages of sin (Plate VIIe). The medieval 'good death', expressed through a well-articulated *ars moriendi* (the art of dying), was by and large aimed at negotiating this transition, with a generally simple and levelling burial rite accompanied by prayers and masses designed to relieve the soul of the dead of punishments for the sins inevitably committed during bodily life (Figure 62a).[13] Soul and body remained separate until the Last Judgment, when the bodies of the righteous would be resurrected. Although this general framework was believed throughout the Middle Ages, the later Middle Ages saw a particular florescence in theory and imagery about life after death (Figure 62b). The idea of Purgatory became increasingly important throughout the Middle Ages. It was believed that immediately after death, the souls of most people (even the generally virtuous) would go to Purgatory, where they could be purified of their sins before the final judgment. Although Purgatory was painful, its pain purged sin and ultimately led to the soul's reward in Heaven. Thus, pardons and indulgences were developed to lighten the posthumous punishment of the dead, and in both literature and art there was a graphic emphasis on memento mori depictions of the gruesome fate of the corpse in the grave and the torments of the damned. Medieval images of the Day of Judgment show the naked dead raised from their graves and herded off by demons either to the company of saints in Heaven or to torment within the monstrous Jaws of Hell.

Just as the life of Christians was structured in a narrative of body-soul relations, the body of Christians was defined by contrast with other bodies, good and bad. Christianity was founded upon the bodily paradox of an incorporated deity which brought opposites together in a divine union.[14] Christianity was defined by holy, miraculous bodies which defy the very nature of ordinary bodies. The paradigm, of course, was Christ's body, the perfect body and, in cosmic geography, isomorphic with the earth at the centre of creation (Figures 61 and 63).

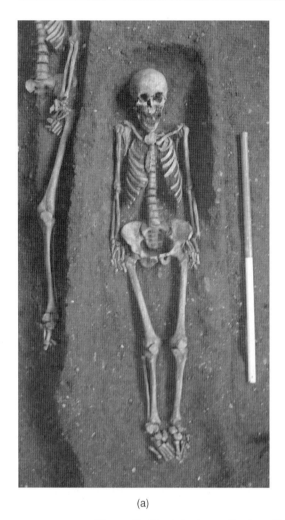

(a)   (b)

Figure 62. Death in the medieval world. A. St. John's College, Cambridge: medieval burials (fourteenth century) (Photo courtesy of Cambridge Archaeological Unit and Craig Cessford). B. The transience of worldly vanity (© The British Library Board, Arundel 83, f. 127).

Saintly bodies bridged the gap between normal people and Christ, and could therefore act as intermediaries with a kind of delegated power to work miracles. The power of God worked through the saint because the saint's soul (and by implication, body) was pure. The historical tradition of venerating saints as particular spiritual guardians and intercessors dates originally to between the third and fourth centuries AD[15] and lasts through the modern period (in modern Catholicism, for instance). Its early focus was principally the graves of saints as places where miracles were possible, particularly healing; saints' graves and monuments provided foci for pilgrimages (Figures 60 and 64). The remains of the saints themselves were a somewhat later focus, perhaps because most Early Christian holy places were in the Eastern Mediterranean. As centres of piety in Northern and Western Europe expanded, relics could be moved more easily than shrines. Relics such as bones, hard, dry and clean, also defied the aesthetic horror of the corruption of the body;[16] rich jew-

elled reliquaries presented the aesthetic doctrine that the exterior form of the body revealed the inner moral state (Figure 65).[17] Fascinatingly, once the power of saintly relics was validated by spiritual hierarchies, it formed the basis for a complex worldly economy circulating relics.[18]

The standard human body was assumed to be a Christian body. Non-Christians (such as Jews, Muslims or other pagans) had different bodily habits of dress and diet and were sometimes pictured as unable to control appetites (such as lust) and as having bodies which defied natural order. Jewish men were sometimes believed to menstruate; Jews were sometimes alleged to kidnap, murder or eat Christian children, and sexual relations between Christian women and Jewish or Muslim men were censured. Similarly, the varied disfiguring diseases termed 'leprosy' were understood, theoretically at least, as manifestations of a spiritual disfigurement, a propensity towards lust.[19]

The ideal body of Christianity was male, and women provided another alternative body. Both Galen and Aristotle provided scientific views on why women's bodies were weaker or inferior to males; early theologians quickly reinforced the view that women were inherently weaker, both physically and morally; their soft, wet bodies were more susceptible to bodily appetites such as lust than men's hard, dry ones. Hence, even as women's souls were just as worth saving as men's and there were outstandingly spiritual women throughout the Middle Ages, there was nevertheless a widespread theoretical misogyny. Spiritual women were sometimes thought of as facing the special challenge of overcoming their nature as women. Although there was no simple dualism equating women with flesh and sin and men with spirit and virtue, one element of such denigration was the body-soul distinction: soul was opposed to body, and if you were to assign a moral ranking to the two terms, souls were morally superior to bodies. Hence if you were reaching for a concept to denigrate women, lepers or Jews, 'body' would do.[20]

What did such framing images have to do with the daily practices of the body? Consider 'sin' as a way of organizing experience. Virtually all of the body's appetites were reclassified within Christianity as potential manifestations of spiritual defect (Figure 66). Lust and gluttony were obviously bodily acts; fighting could be due to anger, wearing finery could reflect pride, laziness could be ascribed to spiritual sloth. For most of these, the pole of virtue was defined by ascetic, appetite-free holy men and women. This was mirrored, in a diluted form, by restrictions and regulations on dress, diet, and sexuality. The pole of sin was defined by exemplary sinners consumed by a single obsession, of the kind described by Dante in *The Inferno*. Humans sat in the middle between the poles of absolute sin and absolute virtue. It was generally acknowledged that ordinary people could not attain saintly standards of bodily purity and self-denial, but they should not stray outside of a permitted range of pleasures and indulgences. And if they erred, they faced

Figure 63. The divine body as the earth: God outside the world looking in, the Divine Spirit as a circle of fire enveloping the world and Christ's perfect body at the earthly centre. Thirteenth century illustration of Hildegard of Bingen's *Liber divinorum operum* (© The Art Archive/Biblioteca Civica Lucca/Gianni Dagli Orti).

strict consequences drawn up in 'penitentials', detailed lists of punishments for infractions. Medieval penitentials were virtually manuals of things not to do, particularly for sex and food. This conceptual set-up made a person's spiritual state always contingent upon his or her bodily actions, always monitored. Even when a particular action was not sinful, the fact that practices such as eating, wearing clothes, sexual acts and so on could potentially be sinful meant that, for the faithful, the body was always subject to monitoring. The framework of sin

Figure 64. Sufferers praying for miracle of healing, shrine of St. Thomas, Canterbury Cathedral. The box depicted on the altar contained the saint's relics (photo: Robb).

created a spiritual panopticon; it made the body a perpetually contested battle ground between the sacred and the sinful.[21]

The result was widespread practices of regulation of the body. People were enjoined to eat within moderation, and the pleasures of eating were further restricted by fasting (as noted earlier), which meant abstaining from particular foods, typically meat. Under some regimes, fast days accounted for almost half the year between two regular fast days a week, saints' days and Lent. Whether or not the average medieval European would actually have eaten meat every day without such rules is moot; these practices established the point that eating fell under the larger jurisdiction of the Church. Similarly, sexual behaviour was always monitored.[22] Theologians throughout the Middle Ages debated sexuality, ranging from a relatively harsh view that all sexuality was sinful to a more liberal Augustinian view that permitted sex between married spouses for purposes of procreation. Underlying these divergent views, however, was the common denominator that sex was a carnal matter, inherently opposed to spirituality, and that it was always necessary for spiritual authority to have a view upon sex – to regulate, condemn, contain, justify or approve it.

Dualism or habitus?

How did distinctions between body and soul actually work? Complexly, in a word. 'Belief' was as complicated in the medieval period as at any other time in history. Although theological pronouncements sound clear and programmatic, most people lived in 'a spectrum of faith, belief, and unbelief'.[23] Thus, 'lived religion' was a creative process. On the one hand, the opposition between body and soul recurs throughout the period. On the other

hand, what people actually meant by these terms and how the terms fit into broader world views varied a lot. Many thinkers saw persons as made up of a combined body and soul, but others favoured a three-way model, with people made up of an intellectual spirit located in the brain, an emotive soul located in the heart, and an animal or fecund being located in the viscera – itself a model which goes back to Plato.

'Body and soul' thus cannot be read off as a fixed script, a structuralist programme rigidly dictating medieval thought in a homogeneous and unchanging way. What 'body' and 'soul' provided was shared terms of discourse. As Bynum notes, 'throughout the Middle Ages, theorists who dealt with eschatology tended to talk of the person not as soul but as soul and body'.[24] People often agreed on the existence, nature and categories of sin even as they disputed what actually constituted a particular sin and what to do about it. Generally, both heretics and inquisitors fervently believed in God, just in different ways. This shared repertory of concepts also extended to the body. Although theorists differed about exactly what the soul was, few people are on record as denying its existence altogether; similarly, excluding perhaps a few extreme heretics, nobody in the Middle Ages thought the soul was bad or (unlike many Native Americans) believed

Figure 65. The reliquary's outward magnificence manifested the spiritual brilliance of its contents. Reliquary of St. Eustace (© Trustees of the British Museum).

Figure 66. The Seven Deadly Sins, Hieronymous Bosch (© The Art Archive/Museo del Prado, Madrid/ Gianni Dagli Orti).

in an afterlife which was morally neutral or which was more or less the same as this life. Similarly, the pleasures of the flesh were understood as carnal enjoyment rather than as (say) sacraments, political acts, or simple fun not subject to moral evaluation; in enjoying pleasures consciously regarded as worldly or carnal, the terms of one discourse of the body were used to define and encapsulate actions within another. In other words, even as controversies raged, there was quite a lot of background consensus about how the world was put together, embodied in shared terms of disagreement.

In terms of a medieval body world, what we are looking at here, in fact, is habitus, a system of generative dispositions or terms of thought that come into play in loose, often contradictory logics (cf. Chapter 2). At the

core of this particular habitus was the idea that the flesh and the senses were inherently suspect, and that the body was a theological battleground between virtue and sin. This was combined with an attitude we might call spiritual individualism. Having defined earthly life as a quest for salvation, Christianity made this quest an individual one. The souls which passed before the heavenly judge were individual ones, and on earth, the unit of moral action was the individual body, bounded and governed by an individual soul, under command of the individual's will and reflecting the state of the individual soul. In this, the doctrinal body provided a completely different model than the changing, permeable and relational body envisioned by scientists and doctors (see discussion later in this chapter).

The problem with women, part I

As with the study of the Classical period, much of the original impetus to examine the medieval body came from questions about the status of women and the desire to write a genuine women's history. The results are distinctly mixed, as discussed below. Within theology, women laboured under pervasive asymmetries. Men represented the standard human spiritual condition; women were different, a special case or anomaly. Moreover, women were different because, generally, they were worse off. Sin entered the world through the temptation of Eve, and there was a tendency to associate the flesh with women, who were often thought to be weaker, less rational, and more liable to sin.[25] This underwrote much of the institutionalized misogyny we have already seen, both in actions (for instance in restricting spiritual authority to male clerics) and in attitudes (such as characterizing women as more sexually voracious). To take just one example, extra-marital sex was stigmatized for both men and women, but discussion of how to deal with sexual desire after one's spouse had died generally focused not upon widowers (who were expected to remarry) but upon widows (who often were not). Similarly, penitential manuals on sexual sins often assumed that, in sex acts, women were the seducers, while the penance was aimed at the man being seduced. Augustine and Aquinas, the two best-known theologians, 'viewed women's differing sexual nature with an acceptance that was muted at best, little more than resigned acceptance of the Creator's mysterious ways. Moreover, few others shared their relative breadth of vision. Misogyny permeates the assumptions of most medieval writers'.[26]

At the same time, in other ways, women were regarded as spiritual equals. At least as far as gender went, Christianity offered equal-opportunity salvation. Women's souls were worth saving, as images of resurrection show. All men and women had human souls and Christ was sent to earth for all humans. There is no sense at all that men's and women's souls differed; the difference lay in their bodies. Although this sounds obvious (it has always been part of the familiar Christian tradition), one could imagine alternative realities, equally plausible in anthropological terms, in which men and women were considered to differ all the way down to the very basis of their spiritual nature. Many, perhaps most sins were defined in relatively gender-balanced ways. Sexuality was often thought in terms of a 'marriage debt' which husband and wife reciprocally owed each other. Moreover, such theoretical misogyny, whilst real, did not exhaust women's experiences; there remained the gap between 'woman' as a category and the actual lives of particular women.

Even within the spiritual world, there were female superstars. The Virgin Mary, whose cult increased in popularity particularly in the later Middle Ages, provided the example par excellence of feminine purity and sanctity, although this could at times provide also a rod with which to censure women unable to live up to such an impossible standard of purity. Mary was a particularly important exemplar for religious communities which needed a solid model of virginity. Female religious orders provided communities within which women could define their own terms of life. As leaders of such communities, women could wield spiritual authority. The most famous, Hildegard of Bingen (Figure 63), who led female monastic communities in the Rhine valley, was a visionary who episodically experienced the presence of God directly, but she was also a theologian, scientist and musician who corresponded with leading intellectuals.[27] Other female saints, visionaries and leaders, however, showed that women everywhere could potentially participate deeply in the spiritual life of Christianity.

Medicine and science: The body as a system of affinities

In many ways, the medical/scientific body is the medieval body that is most straightforward to understand. This is because it was codified in writing, shared more or less homogenously amongst a widely spread educated intelligentsia, and relevant to more or less discrete spheres of life, principally science and medicine. Most medical writers in medieval Europe were Christians and many were clerics, and medical theory was typically couched within an overarching framework of church doctrine. But there are important reasons for considering the medical/scientific body separately from the doctrinal body. Unlike Christian theology, most scientific theory was inherited directly from Classical writers. Moreover, the borders of the Christian world were much less distinct in medical matters than in religious matters; many Classical texts were transmitted to the medieval West via Muslim writers such as Avicinna, and Muslim, Jewish and Christian medical practitioners exchanged information.[28] Most importantly, medical concepts of the body were used for different purposes than doctrinal concepts – understanding and healing the body as opposed to saving the soul – and in many ways, the fundamental underlying principles of the body were different.

Medieval scientific theories of the body descend directly from Classical models, principally the Hippocratic and Galenic writings (cf. Chapter 5). These were transmitted both directly via early medieval writers such as Isidore of Seville and indirectly via the rediscovery and

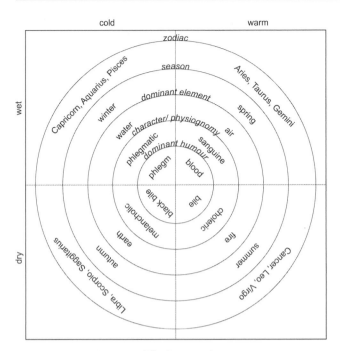

Figure 67. The humoural system.

suspected, particularly in someone of a sanguine complexion and temperament, bleeding was normally prescribed to relieve the excess. Where should the patient be bled? This was governed by a combination of factors including not only the particular symptoms to be relieved but also environmental factors such as the season and position of the stars (Figure 68).

Medieval health care was never a single unified field. Scientifically educated physicians were rare, university-educated people trained in philosophy and science; they cared for the very top of society. Fractures and wounds clearly could not be ascribed to humoural imbalance; if they were dealt with by specialists at all, they were dealt with by surgeons, who were informally educated technicians of lower status. For common complaints and for common people, most healing was in the hands of women, who were widespread village or family healers with herbs and folk remedies.[30] Although physicians wrote about women's medical issues, in practice women also generally dealt with gynaecology and obstetrics. At the popular end, healing practices often shaded off into magic, with efficacious herbs and practical treatments

augmentation of Classical scientific writings by Arabic writers such as Avicenna, from about 900 AD onwards. Aristotle was also a major influence; for instance, in the concept that the heart is the seat of the spirit (a model which lasted until Harvey's physiological explorations in the 1600s, cf. Chapter 7).[29] The core concept was the doctrine of the humours. The body contained four basic fluids or 'humours' (blood, phlegm, yellow bile or choler, and black bile or melancholy) (Figure 67). Each humour was associated with a physiognomy and temperament for individuals in whose particular constitution it predominated, and with environmental qualities, seasons, foods, and therapies. For instance, individuals with an excess of blood relative to other humours in their personal constitution were sanguine, with florid countenances and open, outgoing temperaments.

The key to health lay in moderation and balance rather than excess. When the humours were in balance, the body was healthy. When one of the humours was lacking or over-abundant, the imbalance created ill health. In practical terms, this view treated the internal structure of the body basically as a black box, not surprisingly in a period in which dissection was rare and internal surgery dangerous. The body's state was deduced from external signs such as its temperature, colour, pulse, breathing and emissions (uroscopy, or the examination of urine, was a standard diagnostic technique [Figure 69]). Likewise, physicians addressed illness through non-invasive means such as herbs and drugs, diet and external therapies. For example, in cases where an excess of blood was

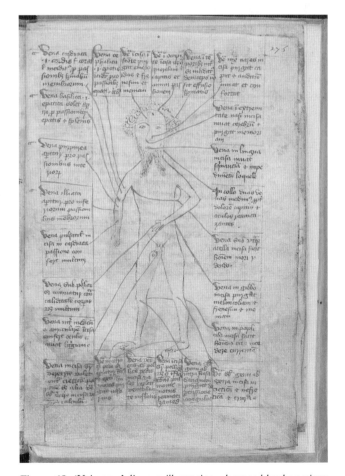

Figure 68. 'Vein man' diagram illustrating where to bleed a patient for specific conditions (© Wellcome Library, London).

combined freely with healing charms and bits of religious doggerel.[31] There was probably a spectrum between theoretical medicine and 'folk' healing rather than a complete division; for instance, written charms could only be used by the literate, who may sometimes have been low-ranking clerics.

The important point here, however, is the intellectual model underwriting scientific and medical understandings of the body. The humoural theory was not merely a medical model. It relied upon a broad set of correlations and affinities extending into the cosmos. Each humour was associated with environmental qualities which aligned it with the elements constituting the world. Earth, like phlegm, is cold and dry; fire, like choler, is warm and dry; air, like blood, is warm and moist; and water, like black bile, is cold and moist. Coincidences between planetary and stellar events – particularly the zodiac – and bodily events (such as birth) affected the individual's constitution and fortune (this is the ancestral origin of modern astrology), and also the appropriate therapy (hence images such as the 'zodiac man', Plate VIIf). The system of affinities extended beyond the human body and the cosmos. The body here was in effect a microcosm of the world around it, a point we return to later and in Chapter 7. Plants could be used for medical purposes based not only upon observed therapeutic effects but also upon how they looked or what environments they were associated with. Albertus Magnus, for example, catalogued the magic properties of stones, which often depended upon aspects such as their colour and place of origin. Magical charms requiring ingredients of particular colours or collected at particular times were an attempt to proactively use such affinities to affect the human body.

Unlike the doctrinal body, the medical body was permeable and porous. In scientific theory, the boundaries of the body were not clearly demarcated and controlled by the individual will; effluvia such as hair, blood and fingernails were potent magical ingredients which helped channel influences between individual and environment (for example, in a love or healing charm). Moreover, people's moral characteristics did not depend only upon their will or virtue; they were shaped by their environment. Thus, in a view descending from Hippocrates, climate shaped both the form and psychological characteristics – an argument used by Aristotle to explain why natives of Greece loved freedom and natives of Asia were servile by nature. The climatic theory was transmitted through writers such as Isidore of Seville and Albertus Magnus and was invoked throughout medieval times to explain cultural difference.[32] Finally, the body was constantly in flux.[33] It absorbed and emitted potent liquids, solids and vapours; its constituent elements changed through dietary and environmental influences. It was liable to be invaded by external agents. As already noted, leprosy, for example, was thought to connote moral deformity (another example of the medieval tendency to find correspondences between outer appearances and inner natures) and to be contagious; hence lepers needed to be segregated.[34] However, the body was changeable not only through diseases, but also through alien intentions (for instance, as transmitted through charms to hurt, heal or effect mood changes such as falling in love) and even demonic or spiritual influences. In fundamental contrast to the self-contained, morally bounded, stable body which doctrine prescribed, it was a relational, contingent body.

The problem with women, part 2

Medical writers were as concerned as theologians about the problem with women, and as certain that women were problematic. Men were bounded, stable, warm, and dry; these qualities were associated with the right hand, the south and east and with air and fire. Women were associated with the weak or problematic side of the equation – permeable, mutable, cold, wet, unbounded, porous, north and west, the earth and water.[35] Women's bodies were more susceptible to demonic possession because their bodies were more open, more porous, and had more penetrable cavities, particularly related to the viscera.[36] As a part of medieval habitus, such distinctions were often left implicit or invoked contextually.

Reproduction was the real crux. The Classical inheritance included two principal views on the subject. The Aristotelian view was that women provide formless matter (a horrifying concept in itself to a medieval mind) to a new infant; form comes from the male's semen. The Galenic view, in contrast, was that conception needed male and female sperm; menstrual blood was matter which nourished the foetus. Both views were influential in medieval times. Underlying the varied discourses (some written by women such as Hildegard of Bingen and 'Trota', a twelfth-century woman doctor in Salerno)[37] were important commonalities. Above all, men were treated as the normative, standard body from which women differed, and medical theory underlined the unstable fluidity of the female body and the danger of menstrual blood.[38] Moreover, woman was viewed as cold and wet; intercourse was needed to warm the female body, otherwise female seed could build up and suffocate her.

Conceptually, medieval women's bodies were considered unstable, resisting boundaries. In this respect they were similar to other 'monstrous bodies' such as the monstrous races on the margins of the earth. Unlike other monstrous bodies, however, women's bodies were

Figure 69. Therapies: Uroscopy. Paris, fifteenth century (© Wellcome Library, London).

close at hand rather than remote, necessary to society rather than imaginative constructions. Hence, male authors tried to encapsulate them discursively in several ways. These medical theories could sometimes have quite repressive consequences. In the Galenic tradition, it was believed that pregnancy could not occur without female orgasm. It was therefore impossible for a woman to become pregnant through rape, since the fact of pregnancy in itself was taken to imply her pleasure and consent.[39]

Critique of the female body was always ambivalent, of course; like sexuality, it was the source of life. By sin, not just death entered the world, but also fertile carnality. Menstruation was both a mark of that sin – the 'curse of Eve' – and a necessary companion of fertility. Moreover, motherhood was recognized as an important source of identity and value for women – the exemplar being, of course, Christ's mother, Mary. Hence debates such as that over whether the Virgin Mary menstruated.

> Logic might tell them that a Virgin with an Immaculate Conception ought not to menstruate, but Christology, observation and common sense told then she must have. So menstruate she did. Similarly, if experience suggested that women lived longer than men whereas Aristotle had held the contrary view, ways were found to vindicate the Philosopher's judgment without in any way denying the validity of their own more immediate data. [40]

The vital body: Medieval con gusto

Finally, we can turn to a third medieval body – one which is pervasive but almost invisible in academic discussion. The body possessed a vitality and identity simply through the process of living. Rather than beginning with abstract propositions, let's talk about food and sin.

Worries about sin are well-documented through penitentials, which were manuals instructing priests what to ask about in hearing confessions and what sort of penitence to hand out for each kind of sin. In one fourteenth-century penitential, under the sin of gluttony, the priest was supposed to ask whether the person confessing

> has over-indulged in a pleasing fashion in food or drink, either by quantity or variety. If he has been accustomed to eat greedily, hastily, or with undue ardor. If he has eaten excessive quantities. If he has sought delicate or overly expensive food. If he has vomited. If he is often drunk. If through gluttony he has vomited the Eucharist. If he has encouraged others to eat or drink too much through malice or vainglory. If he has frequented taverns and taken others there. If he has forced someone to drink to excess. If he has eaten meat at times when he should not.[41]

The list goes on and on . . .

The essential point here is simple, but has, paradoxically, somehow remained virtually invisible in a great deal of discussion of the medieval body. Such detailed and probing catalogues of sin do not grow in a vacuum; they are not purely formal exercises or priestly paranoia. They are convincing evidence of the exuberance and creativity with which people lived their bodies. In an ordinary confession, it was anticipated that the priest might well meet someone who had eaten more than he or she should have done purely for the pleasure of it, who habitually got as drunk as a monkey or a bear (to use common medieval images), who had whiled away hours convivially in the inn, who had succumbed to the temptation of eating meat when it was prohibited. At the risk of stating the obvious, it is only because people eat with energy and gusto outside religion that fasting can have any meaning within religion.

The point is simple. We cannot take the doctrinal body in isolation. Much as the structure of a tree or animal presupposes the invisible but constant earthward pull of gravity, the theological body could only exist in constant tension with another body. Throughout the medieval period, we can observe the action of a tacitly acknowledged 'vital body' which exerted a constant pull of inherent appetites, desires and needs. Concepts such as virtue, spirit and salvation were defined fundamentally through contrast with what the body, on its own, was inherently likely to feel and do in the very process of living. Characteristically, this theory of the body was not articulated in texts; it emerges through practices and habits, through censure, through material culture and through humour and satire. This vital body, lived in specifically medieval rather than universal ways, was part of medieval theories of the body.

The body in practice

The body was omnipresent and irrepressible in daily life. Toil, illness, pain and death were daily, inescapable, universal experiences. Most people, women and children included, worked with their hands and their backs; their routine experience was like that of the labourers picturesquely working their way through their annual rounds in illustrated books or pictures made for aristocrats, although possibly less clean (Figure 70). Physical work defined a labouring class, one of the three estates or traditional social divisions. Most men and women ate food they or their neighbours produced, and inhabited rather than wore their surprisingly limited wardrobes. Medical care was limited and pain was familiar and sharp.

Yet the life of the body was marked by pleasures and emotions. Emotions were explicitly embodied,[42] and often expressed through external signs such as copious tears, changes in colour, temperature or pain.[43] Even the emotion of religious experience was embodied in powerful fashion.[44]

Sexuality and love were powerful forces (Figure 71). The anti-sex party has been heard from previously in this chapter. The opposition is usually spear-headed by Chaucer's Wife of Bath, who famously argued that God provided humans with sexual organs for a purpose. There is abundant evidence for sexual behaviour.[45] In literature, sex is dealt with salaciously and humorously. Old English riddles had obscene double entendres ('What hangs at a man's belt and goes into a small dark hole? A key'.) In later times, the short satirical and comical stories known as fabliaux, which were aimed at literate, usually courtly audiences but which were probably mirrored by oral stories amongst other classes, made jest of sexuality. Common targets of satire were lecherous clerics and impotent old men; the protagonists were lusty young men and women who used cunning wiles to satisfy their desires. At times, it was fashionable in romantic literature to glorify adulterous liaisons. In practice, most cities had tolerated brothels; the London centre of the trade, the bathhouses on the south bank of the Thames, were actually owned by the Bishop of Southwark. In many places through the earlier Middle Ages, it was known and

indeed tolerated for clergy to have long-standing sexual companions. Legal and religious codes specified penalties for a wide range of sexual transgressions, suggesting again that it was not infrequent to encounter sexual infractions. Court records cite fornicators and adulterers engaged in an astonishingly active and creative gamut of sins. The overall impression is that fighting sexual desire theologically was like fighting the ocean's unstoppable tides.

This does not mean that medieval sexuality simply expressed some primordial bodily urge, however. Instead, it reproduced particular kinds of bodies, historical forms of sexuality in Foucault's terms (cf. Chapter 2). As Karras argues,[46] unlike modern sexuality, medieval sexuality was always asymmetrical, with male sexuality defined as inherently transitive (acting upon another) and female sexuality as inherently receptive. Hence sexual acts were inherently gendered and asymmetrical rather than mutually participatory; penalties typically applied to men taking the woman's role and vice versa.

Nor was the bodily pull limited to purely physical desire. Although courtly literature overflows with elegant, if sometimes rather studied and artificial, discussion of love, it is harder to get a sense of everyday desire. Yet occasional glimpses show that it was not just the upper classes who longed for intimacy. Love charms were a staple of medieval magic throughout Europe.[47] Popular lyrics express this plaintively and directly:

> O Western wind, when will thou blow,
> That the small rain down can rain?
> Christ, that my love were in my arms
> And I in my bed again[48]

Similarly, in the private correspondence of the Paston letters, a young woman writes privately to her future husband in February 1474: 'Mine heart me bids evermore to love you truly over all earthly thing'.[49] Four years later, now married, her husband is away in London on business, and she writes a chatty, newsy letter about their relatives and neighbours, but adds a postscript: 'Sir, I pray you if ye tarry long at London that it will please you to send for me, for I think long since I lay in your arms'.[50]

The same energy was put into living the body's life in other ways. Medieval foodways are often cited as a means by which status and opulence were displayed, but eating as much and as well as one could was an act of pleasure for everybody. Whenever economically possible, there was a trade in delicacies such as wine, spices and dried fruits; talented cooks were attached to elite households, and menus included many kinds of sweetmeats and savouries. People of all statuses enjoyed celebratory meals, from peasants concluding a harvest to aristocrats

Figure 70. 'Work in August', stained glass roundel (© Victoria and Albert Museum, London).

Figure 71. Medieval sexuality, Bodleian Library (Douce Mss. 6: 160v-161r, image © Bodleian Library, Oxford).

entertaining one another. Food was a locus of status distinctions, and even humble cuisine was prized for its taste and seasonings, its ability to provide women with an arena of culture under their control, and special meanings such as festivity.[51] One of the funniest illustrations is found in creative evasion of monastic rules. Benedictine monks were forbidden to eat meat within their refectory. Yet many monks came from wealthy families and were accustomed to a rich and tasty diet. By the later Middle Ages, it was common to build a small side room (termed a 'misericord' or 'place of mercy', apparently without irony!)

apart from the main dining hall where monks could happily eat meat without breaking the actual letter of the law.

We could mirror this point with a wide range of bodily practices from dance and music to sport and violence. People of all ranks enjoyed music and dance in contexts from professionals performing before royalty to a village celebration (Figure 72a). Music moved people deeply, and even sacred music sometimes carried emotional subtexts of sexual desire.[52] Because the same melodies were often used for sacred and popular music, people hearing

(a)   (b)

Figure 72. Bodily practices: A. Musicians, fourteenth century England, Luttrell Psalter (© The British Library Board, Add. 42130, f.176). B. Hunting, fourteenth century England, Smithfield Psalter (© The British Library Board, Royal 10 E. IV, f.253v).

music in a sacred setting might well think of the lyrics of love or spring they knew – particularly if they did not understand the Latin of the holy version. To take another example, hunting (Figure 72b) provided food for upper-class tables, but it also was a sport which combined aristocratic display, specialized lore, and the physical thrill of the chase and kill. It ranged from a polite pastime to an obsession.

Like hunting, other sports displayed the capacity for violence. Males competed in various warlike engagements ranging from wrestling and archery for prizes at the village fair to aristocratic jousting and swordplay in tournaments. Violence, both in informal fighting, in warfare and in play, provided a complex expressive idiom.[53] Underlying this language of brutal gesture, in many ways, the capacity for violence defined the most common form of masculinity.[54] Fighting and defending oneself was about male gender. It was also used to mark the body in particular ways, with certain areas of the body often deliberately defaced to mark particular kinds of real or perceived transgressions.[55]

Then there was clothing. From head coverings distinguishing married women from girls to the regalia and liveries of nobles and their followers, dress was part of a visual language marking the lived body with different identities, or allowing the performance of different identities. It was part of the 'performance of self'.[56] This is most obvious with opulent dress: 'the sheer cost of luxury garments ensured that clothes carried immense semiotic weight'.[57] Hence sumptuary laws were often aimed principally at young males in elite contexts, as part of an ordering of male power relations.[58]

Gluttony, lust, wrath, pride, avarice, sloth – the body grounded the catalogue of the sins (Figure 66). Only envy or covetousness is missing, and even so people struck with envy are often portrayed medievally as showing bodily symptoms such as weeping in chagrin! Yet all of these attest an absorption in daily bodilyness far removed from the image of sanctimonious sin-counting we might expect from theological views. We have tried to give a sense so far in this chapter of the sheer omnipresence and business of a body pursuing its own concerns in daily life in spite of attempts to regulate it. In fact, this irrepressibility turns up widely in scatological and sexual humour, in carnivalia and in grotesque, parodic bodies around the margins of serious images that we discuss in a later part of this chapter.

There are really three key points here.

1. First, much, perhaps most, of bodily life was simply not reducible to the theological or medical paradigms. This is most visible in what people *did* rather than what they wrote, drew or sculpted; the textual record over-emphasizes doctrine and science, and over-states the uniformity and systematicity of medieval thought.[59] In situations in which it did not require medical remedy or religious curb – and this was a lot of daily life – the body lived with far more variety, with eager engagement and with commitment than was required by any medical or theological agenda. Theological discourse in particular is principally negative or restrictive; but in its ability to enjoy, embody or experience, the body had an innate, positive, creative vitality.

2. Secondly, the body's characteristics and actions provided an essential basis for identity, for daily social relations such as gender and for the self. This is best exemplified by the problem of resurrection explored later in this chapter.

3. Finally, the scientific and theological paradigms attempted to explain the vital body (through physiological theories of its constitution or theological theories of its innate materialness and sinfulness) and to regulate it. But these theories were attempts – however partial and unsuccessful – to encapsulate discursively something outside themselves, something to which they did not give origin. Medieval people took the body's desires and necessities as matter-of-fact, obvious and natural. In this sense, the medieval understanding of, and participation in, the appetites, pleasures and troubles of the vital body was an implicit theorization of the body in itself.

The vital body as a political resource

The place where the vital body is most obvious, in text and images, is when the body becomes politicized. To the extent that specific qualities of the body were abstracted, enacted and exaggerated to create political power, they were the qualities of the vital body: its ability to fight, to dress, to consume, to enjoy. Hence, for every attribute of the vital body, one end of the scale was defined by the worldly splendour of princes.

In all of these things, bodily experience was expected to be demonstrated publicly and expressively. Worldly magnificence was appreciated; from the sumptuary laws of urban dress to the magnificence expected of imperial feasts and the courage expected of chivalric leaders, the ability to fulfil the body's mandates provided an important basis for social distinction. The higher one climbed in the social scale, the more formalized the ritual etiquette through which bodily respect was created by gestures of distance, subjection and care.[60] Kings, queens, magnates and aristocratic ladies were expected to dress magnificently and expensively (Figure 73a). The same

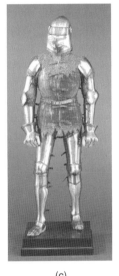

Figure 73. The vital body as a political resource. A. Charles VI receiving English ambassadors, manuscript of Froissart (© The British Library Board, Harley 4380 f. 40). B. Bishop's robe (image © Victoria and Albert Museum, London). C. The metallized body of the knight (image © Metropolitan Museum of Art).

held true for prelates of the Church, whose vestments, paraphernalia such as croziers and thrones, and buildings showed a carefully graded, theatrical magnificence (Figure 73b). Feasts at aristocratic courts featured foods which were not only tasty and expensive but also arranged for maximum visual effect – centrepiece dishes were sometimes gilded – and served with theatrical rituality. The entry ticket for aristocratic fighting was a horse, squire, weapons and armour, an assemblage costing many times more than most people's annual wage, and the result was to transform the body into a shining, ponderous, unstoppable, metalized simulacrum (Figure 73c). The same principle worked in reverse to disintegrate political

bodies. Exemplary executions (stripping, hanging, quartering, emasculating) of traitors such as Hugh Despencer the Younger were aimed at destroying the body as site of aristocratic masculinity with connotations of prowess, health, display, self-control.[61] Executed bodies were not buried in consecrated ground, but – in these exemplary cases – were displayed publicly, often in many places at once. In all of these things, the bodies at the top of society were made into performative superbodies, and the body which was performed superlatively was not the medical or sacred body but the vital body.

Living as (or with) women

It is with the vital body that medieval women come into their own. As we have seen, theologians and medical writers differed about exactly how and in what contexts women were problematic, but they generally agreed that the female body was troublesome in ways in which male bodies never were. Medieval women manoeuvred in a world structured by males;[62] for example, the male gaze was reproduced in art to control women.[63] Except for prostitutes, women's work was rarely sex work per se, but being a servant nevertheless often involved sexual vulnerability.[64]

In spite of this, women often constructed lives with autonomy and value. It is clear that this often involved exploiting the gap between woman as an ideal or category and being an individual woman in a particular situation. To take an example we are unusually well-informed about (thanks to an archive of private correspondence), Margaret Paston was an ordinary woman of the land-owning class in fifteenth-century Norfolk.[65] We do not know if she would have agreed with theoretical ideas about the spiritual and physical weakness of women, or even have been aware of them. Her marriage was arranged for her, and she fought with her own daughters who attempted to resist the marriages arranged for them. But Margaret also led the household during her husband's long absences in London on family business. She raised seven children, kept tabs upon local politics, collected rents and defended her family's interests in turbulent times. Although, as a woman, she did not fight, on several occasions she organized armed defences against assaults by aggressive neighbours. One gets a definite sense that Margaret was too busy with holding her family's own in projects of management and upward mobility to be a weak, inferior, woman!

There is no reason to suppose that Margaret Paston was unusual. Women had diverse life experiences, affording many opportunities for asserting their identity.[66] In general, as this suggests, family relations were a source of power and identity for women. Within the sphere of a family enterprise – and most enterprises involved the joint labour of families – their work was essential. Women did fundamental economic production such as spinning and weaving. Household tasks and family business created spheres of effective action such as providing food and healing. Rather than seeing medieval life-spaces as ungendered or entirely masculine, we must see many spaces as places of female autonomy and control, even within castles, a category of space nominally gendered as masculine.[67]

Deeper sources of female power were rooted in the body itself. Sexuality did not merely involve vulnerability to male power and desire. Women also had the power to enjoy sexuality, and it gave them power over males; the doe-eyed, dependent, often duped male lover or husband is a familiar figure in literature. Maternity itself provided a trump card. However much medical and theological writers decried the female body, it remained unanswerable that women's fertility was responsible for the reproduction of society.[68] Motherhood was an important social relation, and the ability to have children was an important component of social identity. Motherhood was not merely a biological relationship but a social process, an ideal of nurturing towards which women actively worked.[69]

The other route to empowerment was to explore alternative possibilities for feminine identity. The best-studied is female religious devotion, which provided a different kind of experiential autonomy. Women of means could choose a religious vocation within a convent or nunnery, and pilgrimage offered women a source of strength, empowerment,[70] as well as being a way of travelling, a kind of liminal space where daily restrictions were relaxed. But beyond this, both within convents and outside them, women sometimes experienced intense spirituality, sometimes feeling Christ's suffering through their own bodies.[71] The physical symptoms spiritual women displayed in these cases sometimes looked disconcertingly and dangerously like those displayed in cases of demonic possession – trances, immobility, fits, uncontrollable crying – and the issue tended to be decided by whether the spirit entered into the heart (as a holy spirit) or into the lower body (as a corrupting demon).[72] Clerical authorities were often clearly ambivalent about the effusive, uncontrolled spirituality these women displayed, especially as the women often were outside the church's institutional control hierarchies.

Interestingly, masculinity was also subject to lived reinterpretation. Maleness provided a general, somewhat amorphous or polyvalent concept. Although theologians or medical theorists might have a clear idea on maleness

as an abstract ideal, what it actually meant to be masculine was developed to fit a given situation. The result was multiple historically situated masculinities.[73] Masculinity was different for aristocrats, working men and scholars.[74] Moreover, medieval masculinity involved competitive performance between males. If the vital body provided the basis for politicized identities, by definition, higher status males were more enabled to perform masculinity. Hence, subordinate men used a form of 'complicit masculinity' which adhered to the common political ideal of masculinity without the tensions or risks of directly challenging authority.[75] The best-known example is that of clerics. Clerics, enjoined to chastity, were excluded from a central male-defining field of action, sexuality. The same was true to some extent of fighting. Clerical masculinity thus posed a problem to which people created a range of solutions. Some clerics simply participated in ordinary forms of asserting their masculinity such as drinking, fighting and loose behaviour. Others devised specifically monastic forms of masculinity;[76] for instance, clerics sometimes took up the rhetoric of spiritual armour and battle and portrayed saints as warriors in spiritual combat.[77]

Individual and biography, or why bother to resurrect the body?

The most striking example of how important the lived or vital body was is found in the fascinating question of resurrection.[78] From the beginning, it was a central tenet of Christianity that believers would live after death, but even in early Christian times, groups such as the Sadducees denied the resurrection and scripture was quite vague on how this was actually supposed to happen. It was up to theologians to supply the essential details. How exactly did a person's identity continue after death?

As Bynum notes, Christianity developed amongst people for whom bodily change and flux were theoretically inexplicable and to whom corpses were horrifying.[79] Resurrection involved resolving a contradiction. The body had to maintain its continuity, its fundamental identity, in order for a particular believer to be resurrected, but the body was also constantly in change, in flux – becoming ill, dying, becoming fragmented after death and decomposing.

There were basically two possible solutions to this paradox. One could merge the concept of resurrection with the doctrinal dualism between matter and spirit, and argue that the dead were resurrected spiritually, without literal continuity of the body. Resurrected bodies would thus be without matter, sex, age and bodily needs, like angels. This Platonic solution was proposed by Origen

Figure 74. Christ leading the dead out of Purgatory in the Harrowing of Hell. The dead are shown naked as worldly distinctions are levelled in death, but they still retain individuality in bodily features of age, gender and facial appearance. Alabaster carving (© Victoria and Albert Museum).

in the third century AD and it was occasionally revived throughout the medieval period, for example by Duns Scotus in the thirteenth century. It was logically coherent and philosophically elegant. If the body was corrupt, sinful flesh, soon reduced to worms and dust, why bother resurrecting it at all? The soul would suffice.

The problem, however, is that this solution just did not *feel* right.[80] Resurrection without the material body did not feel like a continuation of the self. Hence, the dominant theological tradition, extending from Jerome and Augustine around 400 AD through the length and breadth of the Middle Ages, insisted upon the resurrection of the material body itself, not just its soul (Figure 74). This was a 'doctrine of comfort' in which death was not a loss of self.[81]

The theology of late antiquity rejected what were, philosophically speaking, the best solutions available. Instead of admitting flux, of allowing otherness, of lodging self

in some sort of internally coherent and dynamic pattern (as did Origin), the majority of patristic theologians focused increasingly on material bits. They were willing to sacrifice philosophical coherence for the oxymoron of incorruptible matter.[82]

In terms of a doctrinal dualism, this did not make much sense. If the body was merely an incidental encumbrance or temporary housing for the soul, why not leave it mouldering in the earth? And as practical theology, this opened a real can of worms (so to speak). Would resurrected bodies have sex, age, social rank? Would people dying as small children or as decrepit elderly people have to remain so throughout eternity? What if parts were missing? Theologians provided some answers; for instance, some claimed that children would be resurrected as they would have been at the age of 33, the age at which Jesus died and hence the perfect age. Others, such as Augustine, claimed that everybody would be resurrected at this age. Similarly, it was accepted that God could, omnipotently, reassemble the disturbed bodies of the dead from their scattered parts. (Thus, in congested late medieval churchyards, virtually every burial disturbed an earlier one, but there was little effort to prevent such disturbance; keeping all burials inside consecrated ground was more important than placing them in less crowded extramural spaces). Wounds would be healed and bodies made perfect (though the holy scars of martyrs would remain visible). But most of these dilemmas never reached a widely-accepted, authoritative solution, and some became surprisingly convoluted. Cannibalism provided a surprising extreme test case for reasons that seem completely unexpected to us. Of course cannibalism was bad; but theologically, the real problem was sorting out whose body was whose. What if the parts of one body had been eaten and had become assimilated into the body of somebody else? Whose body would they belong to at resurrection?

The real point is that theologians stuck to a doctrine which contradicted a simple spirit-flesh dualism model and tied them into philosophical knots because they also shared an underlying sense that the body was essential; that a person, to be a person, had to have not only the soul but also the body. The core of Christianity was not just the soul, but the soul's relation to the body, to matter; this was most densely exemplified by the incarnated Christ and the Resurrection as the victory over the body's death.

To put it another way, all the things which made an individual an individual – their age, their gender, their individual life-history, their activities, abilities, appetites, pleasures and pains – were experienced by and registered in the body. In this sense, identity derived from the biography of the individual body. As in all cultures, gender was fundamental. Even when science and theology were deeply ambivalent at best about the female body, visions of the afterlife generally insisted that people remained male and female. Similarly, age was an essential part of the self (Figure 75a). The body's story was one of metamorphosis.[83] Age was an important part of identity. Aries' pioneering argument that medieval people did not recognize childhood[84] has become increasingly difficult to sustain.[85] Categorizations of the stages of life portrayed the young body as appropriate for love; the aged body was understood as a metaphor for worldly vanity, and old age was a time for the expiation of sin and preparation for salvation.[86] Moreover, throughout life, personal identity was written permanently on the body in a way which went beyond physiognomy, in clothing, in gestures, in signs of work, strength and ability (Figure 75b-f). The image of Fortune's Wheel, which suggested that worldly vanities were mutable and could be overturned at any instance, was a common literary trope, but such transformations happened mainly in literature (and even then rarely so; in chivalric legends, for instance, peasants who exhibit prowess almost always turn out to be noblemen in disguise). To the extent that bodies were situated in histories and daily routines, there is little sense that the country people labouring in the fields or signifying their identity as they ride on pilgrimage will realistically change bodily tracks through life with the armour-encased knight riding to war or the splendid lord feasting at table. Such transformations belonged to the world of bodily disorder (see discussion that follows).

Thus living after death without the actual body would not actually be life after death, a survival of a particular individual person. Hence, paradoxically, whereas on the one hand theology proclaimed dualistically that the soul would be much better off free of the body; on the other hand, it was not clear that the soul without the body would not lose everything that made one that person. In fact, it was believed that saints (who of course skipped Purgatory and went straight on to Heaven) would want their bodies back, and hence their happiness would really be complete only after the day of resurrection. The body, in all its sensory experience and history, was essential to the self. This contradiction should come as no surprise in a religion founded upon bodily paradox, nor for that matter to students of anthropological dualisms, which customarily unite irreconcilable opposites. The real point is that, in spite of a sometimes quite sustained doctrinal onslaught on its very nature, the body's colourful, powerful vitality fought back. As in the Classical world, life was situated in what the body actually did and felt.

Living between three bodies: Tensions and accommodations

We have presented the medieval body as three opposed, pure logics:

1. A theological logic in which the fleshly body is coupled to a spirit within a dualistic model, regulated to curb its threatening appetites and influenced only by its moral soul's ability to govern it.
2. A scientific body in tune with affinities of cosmos, qualities and things, permeable to external influences and constantly in flux.
3. A lived body of sensations, positive appetites, change and history, identified as the experiential locus of a person's self and biography.

Body worlds always contain multiple, incommensurate ideas; lived bodily experience involves switching between these, yet this can involve contradictions and tensions (Chapters 1 and 2). Writing on the medieval body has tended to follow two lines. One is normative, stressing one of these bodies (usually the theological). The other is to see bodies as fluid, unstable, subversive or multiple,[87] finding people living interstitially. Both are correct but incomplete. Normative views have to face an important question. 'Which norm applies and what did it mean in a particular context?' Negotiated, unstable views have to have some points of reference to negotiated with or against. Fortunately, the medieval body offered lots of scope for ambiguity, contradiction and manoeuver.[88]

In the medieval period, some people constructed ways of living that were committed to pursuing logics of the vital or doctrinal body almost exclusively. Real or literary ascetics mortified their flesh to live the doctrinal model of the body as purely as possible; but there were doubtless also sometimes committed heretical scientists or atheistic hedonists as well, though they rarely got written up to the same extent. But most people did not live pure logics; they were contextually tolerant, exclusionary, flexible, rigid, pious or sceptical.[89] The three medieval theories of the body meshed or collided in a variety of ways.

Multimodality: Switching logics and tensions between them

The multimodality of belief is far clearer in the medieval period than in earlier times, precisely because of the Church's innovative, theocratic attempts to impose a single modality of belief (even when that doctrine itself was at times self-contradictory). Our cacophony of medieval bodies, thus, really represents different ways of thought which only look contradictory when we

(a)

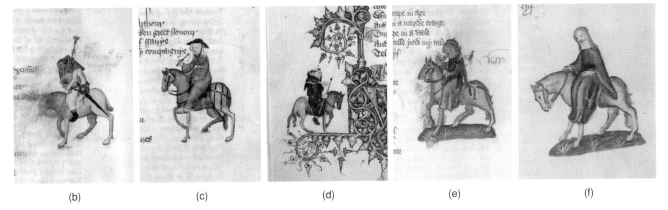

(b)   (c)   (d)   (e)   (f)

Figure 75. A. Individuation in the body: the 'Ten Ages of Man' (© The British Library Board, Arundel 83, f.126v). B through F. Pictures of various Canterbury pilgrims: B: Miller. C. Wife of Bath. D. Friar. E. Nun's Priest. F. Second Nun. Ellesmere manuscript of *Canterbury Tales* (reproduced by permission of the Huntingdon Library, San Marina, California [EL 26 C 9]).

assume – as both medieval theorists and modern theorists tend to – that humans must live according to a single exclusive, universally applied logic.[90]

Switching modes of bodily understanding is clearest when the jurisdiction between approaches was well-demarcated. The 'vital body' model provided the experiential framework for much of ordinary life, as well as being the dominant paradigm in situations of ostentation and splendour such as the political pageantry of worldly pomp. When consulting a physician for medical diagnosis and treatment, one operated under the scientific model of the body, and the same model dominated when philosophers and scientists addressed questions such as what the body was composed of and how its composition related to that of the earth and heavens. The doctrinal model came into play, via the notion of sin, in the ongoing regulation of the body's behaviours. It was relevant in acts of worship in which sensory prompts such as music, incense, gesture and architecture prompted feelings of rising above the body, and rites at major life events such as birth, baptism, marriage and death reaffirmed the body's subordination to divine order. Moreover, as the dualistic model implied that the life of the body inherently risked falling into sinful thoughts and acts, the person maintained a running balance of sin – much of it bodily – which was periodically redressed or cancelled out through confession, penitence, pardon and the intercession of others through prayer. Although zeroing out this spiritual indebtedness was an ongoing lifelong task, death was a particularly important moment, when the last rites guided the soul, freed of its body, towards salvation. In the shadow of death, ordinary activities seemed worldly distractions from the urgent need to turn towards a heavenly life.

Disputed Borderlands: Between doctrine, medicine and the lived body

While people passed through these varied contexts and mentalities constantly and smoothly – or at least with conventionalized bumps and jolts such as ritualized contrition – the underlying bones of the system are clearest in the disputed borderlands (Figure 76). These are situations where it was not clear what standard applied, and it is fascinating how long-standing tensions between alternative ways of understanding the body generated the same discussions over and over.

The most obvious ones concerned the lived body and the doctrinal body. We have already mentioned the conflicting theologies of the resurrection of the body. Another obvious one is the question of at what point permitted pleasure turned into sin. Sexuality generated tensions between conflicting discourses.[91] How do you reconcile the sexual desire of the lived body with the denial demanded of the spiritual body? It is striking that basically the same solutions were proposed from the fifth through the fifteenth centuries – a longevity which reflects not only the direct influence of textual sources such as Paul and Augustine but also the limited tools and options for resolving the problem available within a long-lasting world view.

A second borderline question is the status of women. In both doctrinal and medical theory, women were categorically weaker, socially dependent and morally more subject to sin. Yet in daily experience, women worked hard, had strong voices in family decision-making, defended their rights, followed the path of virtue, and often owned property, wielded political influence, and spoke with their own intellectual or spiritual voices. Recurrent discussions of the nature and status of women make it clear that tensions surrounding the discrepancy between the lived body and various theoretical bodies could not be settled by simple fiat.

Similarly, throughout the Middle Ages, chronic tensions between the spiritual and physical world were often mapped onto social divisions (between churchly and temporal powers) or onto differing interpretations of religion. Worldly power was based upon force, wealth and political legitimacy; spiritual power was based upon access to God and salvation. The conflict of king and pope is a medieval cliché, but its association with the body is clear in things such as imagery contrasting temporal power, however splendid and merited, as transient and decaying with the body, in contrast to the riches of the spirit. Within religion throughout the Middle Ages, the Church was perennially split between moral aesthetics of magnificence and display and ideals of poverty and service. High-end clergy such as those staffing cathedrals were more favourable to worldly ostentation; monastic orders such as the Franciscans agonized more about abstention from wealth. But in some sense, the debate was applicable to the entire religious establishment as the poles of magnificence and abstention formed universal points of reference or tools of thought; both cathedral-style magnificence and satires upon luxury-loving, worldly clergy were reinvented everywhere throughout the Middle Ages, within – as well as between – all branches of the Church.

Borderlands between doctrine and medicine were similarly negotiated. Magic in the Greco-Roman world was morally neutral. With Christianity, however, the spirits who were the operatives in magic were increasingly seen as evil, so that the Church increasingly came to condemn all magic.[92] Yet evidence from burials shows that people continued to use magical charms, whether or not the Church approved.[93] Perennial tensions between

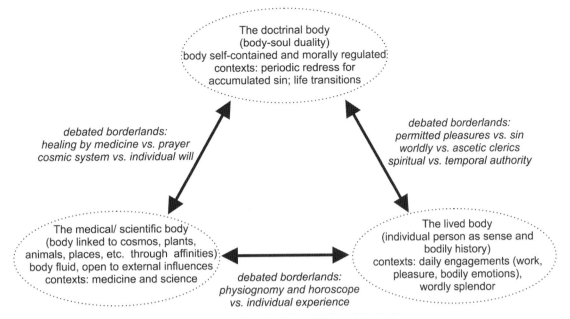

Figure 76. Medieval multimodalities of the body.

magic and the Church culminated in late medieval and Early Modern witch persecutions; although some of these were doubtless politically motivated, underlying tensions between doctrine and magic provided a ready pretext. Similarly, with the Church's focus upon individual moral accountability and the power of God, early Christians were ambivalent about medicine.[94] Hippocratic ideas of balance and moderation conflicted with Christian ideas about asceticism. For example, sexuality was normally regarded theologically as morally dangerous, but physicians following a traditional Galenic doctrine of balance and moderation sometimes prescribed sexual activity, outside marriage if necessary, as a therapy. Christian dogma was suspicious of charms and amulets, and there was particular tension about sexual medicines, abortions and contraceptives.[95] In later medieval times, religious writers treated pain as the soul's experience of sin, whereas medical authorities treated it as a practical diagnostic to a physical problem.[96] Disease, in Christian doctrine, was linked to sin, although this interpretation was invoked mostly when it affected other people![97]

In practice, this meant that sufferers had multiple options, both for interpreting medical conditions and for trying to heal them.[98] Was madness due to humoural imbalance or demonic attack? Was leprosy a matter-of-fact medical condition which could affect anyone, or was it an outward sign of moral deformity?[99] Was plague due to environmental 'miasmas' – which one could therefore escape by moving – or was it a scourge for humanity's sin? On a deep, conceptual level, such discussions resulted

from a contradiction between the porous, fluid, interconnected view of the body in medicine and science and the bounded, individual moral body of Christianity. Pragmatically, many sufferers chose to try both healing and prayer. These could be complementary, with medical treatment sometimes addressing symptoms while prayer addressed the underlying causes. Hence treatment worked, usually fairly seamlessly, by accommodating both theories. The first step was classifying the condition and its probable cause and first route of treatment. Fractures were obviously physical in origin and, for those with formal medical care, sent one to a surgeon. Most diseases fell under a physician's jurisdiction. But ailments which baffle all doctors are a cliché of miraculous saintly healing; if the first recourse failed, it was a sign of the limitations of human endeavour or of some deeper divine intention, and treatment changed gears, shifting to prayer. Different saints had jurisdiction over different ailments, and a major impetus for pilgrimages to shrines such as Canterbury was either to ask for saintly healing or to thank the saint for helping one recover from illness. Theology provided the ultimate explanation when all else failed. For example, the Black Prince of England (Edward, son of Edward III, who lived from 1330 to 1376) was everything one hoped – manly, martial and a born leader. When he died of a mysterious, lingering ailment which led to the effusion of blood from his body, this was hard to understand, as such effusions were thought to be feminine and unholy (cf. the popular belief that Jewish men menstruated) – so it was interpreted as a divine punishment en route to redemption for this hero.[100]

Finally, scientific views of the body always had the potential to clash with lived experience. The question of women's theoretical nature versus reality has already been mentioned. The treatment of lepers affords another fascinating example. Lepers were often imagined in theology and literature as one the great 'others' of the medieval mind: impurity, contagion and corruption made flesh. Yet there was also a developed body of practical medical lore on the disease, and yet more strikingly, people often devoted significant resources to caring for lepers, for example by founding hospitals where they could live in some comfort.[101] This care for lepers as humans enmeshed in social relations is hardly what one would predict from textual images such as the lecherous lepers begging to degrade Isolde in the romance of Tristram.

More generally, the scientific view of the body provided a rather abstract mechanism which always risked running afoul of direct observation. There were cases of failed medical diagnosis and therapy. And what did one do when theories of character and physiognomy failed – when someone who, by horoscope or physiognomy, should have had a sanguine character behaved cholerically or fell into melancholy? It is striking that astrological descriptions of physiognomy and character typically are written as generalities, leaving room for exceptions. Committed believers of physical theory could always point to intervening factors which blurred and complexified its application to a particular case, but it is also clear that simply disbelieving physical theory was also an option. Marginal manuscript images of foxes and apes acting as doctors suggest that physicians were not uncommonly a target of parody (Figure 82b).

The point is that people switched between the three basic understandings of the body continually – as they went from one context to another, and within a particular context as circumstances warranted. Whilst the borderlands in which it was not clear which model of the body applied were sometimes policed or contested, it was equally common for this conceptual switching to work seamlessly. To the extent that one model provided a meta-theory which attempted to encompass the others, it was clearly the doctrinal body; God, as the ultimate cause, trumped causes deriving from within his Creation. But it is clear that in practice the relative jurisdictions of the different models were also determined by negotiation and compromise: the theological view demanded from lived bodies only what they could be persuaded to pay. It theoretically demanded all, but in practice, as long as gross excess was curbed, it took its share mostly at key moments of ritualised contrition and spiritual payback.

The high medieval grand synthesis: The body as cosmic geography

Body worlds provide the elements and reflexes for thinking rather than thought itself. Medieval thinkers trying to creatively understand the world improvised around general themes rather than simply repeating scripted views. In this process, they were helped by some well-understood medieval intellectual reflexes:

- An encyclopaedic, systematizing and ordering impulse to link all the different provinces of knowledge, on the basis of laying clear the hidden order which pervaded God's creation.

- The general belief that the outward form of bodies should reflect their inner spiritual state.[102] Hence a person's physiognomy displayed their moral nature, disfiguring diseases such as leprosy bore a moral stigma, saints' corpses were supposed to remain miraculously incorrupt and sweet-smelling, and an 'aesthetic of preciousness'[103] meant that reliquaries were sometimes made of materials as precious as their contents.

- The idea that order or structure was replicated on several planes of reality. A common exegetical method was to assume that reality could be read on four different levels: literal/historical, allegorical, moral and analogical. Hence, for example, bestiaries were simultaneously natural histories, allegories, and moral orders, with each animal exemplifying a particular moral quality. This idea of repeated patterning on different levels of reality is an important element of the scientific system of affinities amongst personalities, climates, elemental qualities, heavenly bodies, animals and minerals. It also underwrites the common medieval literary technique of allegory in which a story is told through symbolic references (in the most famous example, the *Romance of the Rose*, a courtly lover pursues his beloved in the form of a perfect rose).

- Specific theological-spatial tropes such as a distinction between centres (which represented wholeness and perfection) and peripheries (which represented moral disorder or ambiguity), and between higher and lower as ways of comparatively ordering things.

These reflexes were the essential tools by which the Classical inheritance was transformed into something distinctly medieval and Christian (for instance, by adding systematizing Christian values to a Ptolemaic cosmos of concentric spheres, to a Classical geography, and to natural histories derived from Pliny and Aristotle). They were also essential in elaborating views of the body and reconciling opposed views.

One of the grand synthetic edifices of the Middle Ages was the *scala naturae* or Great Chain of Being. This concept arranged all material things in a ladder-like spiritual hierarchy from inanimate, mutable matter to eternal, rational, divine beings: minerals, then plants, then animals, then humans, then angels and finally God.[104] Humans occupied a critical middle link, sharing in both the flesh of beasts and the rational spirit of angels; this gave them a unique hybrid identity and with it, the necessity to regulate their bodies through moral choices. The Great Chain of Being drew upon the dualistic body/spirit view of the human body but also elaborated it to provide a philosophical way of understanding relations between people and animals, to authorize moral distinctions between humans and to legitimate gender hierarchy and the divine right of kings.

Synthesis applied to one-off improvisations about the body as well. To take one example, the twelfth-century British chronicler, Gerald of Wales, describing his trip to Ireland, tells the following story:

> Roderick, king of Connaught, had a white tame goat, remarkable for its flowing hair and the length of its horns. This goat had intercourse, bestially, with the woman to whose care it had been committed; the wretched creature [the woman] having seduced it to become the instrument of gratifying her unnatural lust, rather than that the animal was the guilty actor. O foul and disgraceful deed! How dreadfully does the lord of brutes, discarding his natural privileges, descend to the level of brutes, when he, rational animal, submits to such intercourse with a beast. For although on both sides it is detestable and abominable, it is by far the least that brutes should be entirely submissive to rational creatures.[105]

Gerald here draws upon common ideas such as the inherent lasciviousness of women. He also invokes the Great Chain of Being: because humans are higher up the scale and possess reason, they have the responsibility of moral choice, and hence this is not merely a sexual offence but an inversion of natural order. Thus the woman was to blame, not the goat! But as part of a Norman rule over conquered Ireland, Gerald is also interested in characterizing Ireland as a place of moral disorder. Hence he combines ideas of natural order and spatiality to characterize peripheries such as Ireland as places where bodily order breaks down and humans and beasts can mix in forbidden ways.[106]

As far as bodies are concerned, the grandest medieval synthesis was the concept of the body as microcosm. The body as microcosm was particularly a fourteenth to fifteenth century trope.[107] As we have seen, scientific views were based upon linkages between the body, the elements and the zodiac. The ordered parts of the body also provided a way of thinking about parts of society. The lower body, like the peasantry, was fertile and productive but grossly material, while the head and heart, seats of the spirit and soul, represented the clergy and nobility.[108] Each part of the universe could be conceptualized as elements of a giant body, and each part of the body in turn related to different elements of the universe.

The body-cosmos linkage is elaborated in other ways as well. This is laid out beautifully in *mappae mundi* maps such as the Hereford, Ebstorf and Psalter maps (Figure 77, Figure 78) that underline the homology between the earth and bodies, especially sacred bodies.[109] As codifications of a high medieval multilevel reality, these both incorporate actual geographical knowledge and treat geography as a representation of an underlying moral order. The human body and the earth could be equated as outstanding examples of God's creation, and the most perfect human body was that of Christ. A revealing thirteenth-century illustration shows an exemplarily beautiful human body at the centre of Creation; the concentric layout, surrounded by the winds and the waves of the encircling ocean, make clear that it is to be read as the earth (Figure 63). Enveloping it is a red Holy Spirit, and outside this, in the place in the cosmos assigned to the eternal, unchanging prime mover, God himself. In terms of geography, Classical writers such as Herodotus and Hippocrates contributed quasi-anthropological discussions of how climate leads people in different continents to have skins of different colours, and they supplied catalogues of 'monstrous races' which inhabited the periphery of the known world. To this, medieval synthesizers added Christian concepts of spiritual centrality and nature reflecting an underlying moral order. Hence the basic 'T-O' form of the map which arranged the three known continents inside the perfect form, a circle; Jerusalem, the sacred city of Jesus' life and death, lay at the centre of the earth, and by extension of Creation.

Bodies are integrated in two ways. In the human world, the centre is a place of moral order where humans have proper normal bodies. At the margins – conventionally represented on *mappae mundi* in Africa – the natural order of bodies breaks down and there are monstrous races: people with dogs' heads or monstrously long ears, Cyclopses, cannibals, headless people with faces in their chests, people who bound along on one huge foot and many others. Monstrous races were not just bizarre superstitions or ignorance. Inherited from Classical writers, they served to provide monsters defining negatively at the margins the reason and order in the centre.[110] Secondly, on the cosmic level, the earth itself could be understood as the body of Christ. Although this remains implicit,

Figure 77. Psalter Map, cosmological geography (© The British Library Board Add. 28681, f.9).

Figure 78. Psalter Map, detail showing 'monstrous races' at margins of the earth (© The British Library Board Add. 28681, f.9).

the Ebstorf Map in fact makes this explicit, with Christ's head, hands and feet protruding from his body, the circular earth.

The literary equivalent was John Mandeville, the fourteenth century writer. In his *Travels*, probably the single most influential travel book ever written,[111] Mandeville claimed to have spent years travelling in the East. Whether he did or merely synthesized and elaborated upon others' accounts, his account simultaneously reveals geographical knowledge and the moral order immanent in the world. Mandeville's *Travels* parallel the geographical vision of the *mappae mundi*. Of interest here is how geographical order, in the medieval grand synthesis, was a bodily order.

Mandeville's *Travels* are written, in part, as a guide to pilgrims going to the Holy Land, and the presumed body of both the author and the readers is a 'normal' human, Christian body. It is the body of somebody who sins but who aspires to salvation (a project of which pilgrimage itself was part), who has needs for food, drink, rest, conveyance, and knowledge of the bodily perils of travel,[112] who enjoys good wine[113] and who is not averse to seeing wonderful sights en route. Against this default vision of presumed Bodies Like Us, the traveller encounters three distinct types of Other Bodies. Interestingly, these are

rooted in the three medieval discourses of the body. The first is holy bodies. The Holy Land itself

> is blessed and hallowed and consecrated by the precious blood of Our Lord Jesus Christ, in which land it pleased Him to take life and blood by Our Lady Saint Mary and to travel round that land with His blessed feet.[114]

As this suggests, what makes the Holy Land holy is bodily connections and events. Some places are marked by bodily miracles such as the preservation from burning of a virgin wrongly accused of fornication,[115] or by the relics of saints which pilgrims may wish to go view. But many others are marked by the events of Jesus' life: where he was born, circumcised, baptized, fed, imprisoned, scourged, crucified, buried and resurrected and where he taught and worked miracles. In some places the landscape itself is marked by the Lord's body:

> Upon that hill [Jehosaphat] Our Lord stood when he mounted into Heaven; men can still see the footprint of his left foot in a stone He stood upon.[116]

Other footprints of Jesus could be seen in a rock at Nazareth.[117] Jesus' incarnation and sacrifice brought together paradoxically the dualistic contradictory elements of body and spirit; it was the descent of spirit in the world to provide humans with salvation. As in maps of the time, Jerusalem is sacred because of its identification with the sacrifice of Jesus' body, and the sacrifice happened here because of its centrality.[118] This is sacred corporeal geography.

The other bodies Mandeville encounters, however, exemplify other theories of the body. As he travels beyond the Holy Land into the Orient, Mandeville describes the strange peoples he meets. He provides a bodily anthropology, for instance describing the Tartars in terms of how their men and women look, eat, dress, fight and treat the dead.[119] These are the categories of the lived body which his readers use to understand their own lives and others. The same terms of thought are used to describe the court of the Great Khan, which is distinguished by bodies which are human but superlative: they are beautiful, splendidly clothed, extravagantly fed, martially powerful, elegantly comported, insuperably numerous, ceremonially arrayed and hierarchical. These are the virtues of the lived body, the worldly qualities of political splendour and bodily enjoyment. Hence, the court of the Great Khan provides the ne plus ultra of worldly embodiedness, much as the Holy Land provides a land of sacred bodies: 'There is beneath the heavens no lord so rich, so mighty, nor so great as the Great Khan, nor above or below the earth'.[120]

Finally, there is the scientific discourse of order. Natural order prevails in most places. Where people vary, it can be for scientific reasons:

> The people of India are not naturally disposed to travelling beyond their own country, for they live under the planet of Saturn . . . because Saturn is so slow-moving, men who live under him have no great desire to move around much, but stay in their own lands and desire no other. It is quite the opposite in our own country. We are in a climate under the rule of the moon, which is a planet that moves quickly – the traveller's planet. So it gives us the desire to travel and visit different countries of the world.[121]

But on the margins of the ordered world, in furthest India and Asia, all bets are off: natural order breaks down, the traveller encounters monstrous bodies: cannibals, bearded women, people dwelling in nakedness and enjoying lust without shame, people like beasts without reason or speech, giants, Cyclopses, dwarfs, blemmies, people with lips like parasols, with no mouths, ears to their knees, dogs' heads or horses' feet, arboreal quadrupeds, and hermaphrodites. The natural ordered relations between parts of the body, amongst humans, and between humans and animals, are all disturbed. Although a Biblical cause is mentioned offhandedly for this catalogue of monstrosities derived from Classical geographers (such beings may descend from a branch of humanity which interbred with demons[122]), there is little real attempt to explain such beings; it is simply what one would expect at the margins of the concentrically ordered world.

A masterpiece of synthesis, Mandeville's *Travels* brings together ideas of the holy body which combines divine spirit and flesh, the worldly qualities, pleasures and capacity for political splendour of the lived body, and the scientific idea of bodies as a locus of natural order and disorder. They are, moreover, all understood by the implicit contrast with the traveller's expectations about bodies. In literally making sense of the bodily world, the traveller and pilgrim had no choice but to switch freely between multiple modes of understanding other bodies and his or her own.

Subversive glimpses: Grotesques, tensions and marginalia

Some of the most disconcerting, surprising or funny images of the Middle Ages are marginal grotesque bodies.[123] In the margin of a manuscript of the *Romance of the Rose*, a nun picks penises from a tree full of phalluses (Figure 80). Though satirical and risqué, perhaps this is not too unexpected in a work about love. But what about

holy books? In books of prayers such as the Macclesfield Psalter, the Rutland Psalter and others from twelfth to fourteenth century England and France, deformed monsters made of random assortments of human and animal parts run amok. They play trumpets through their buttocks, ride on donkeys, ape human acts jeeringly and mock priests and kings. Some images make use of the allegorical turn of mind; when a knight jousts with a giant snail, the snail may allude to female genitalia (Figure 82a).[124] Others just seem to be extravagant, random fragments of bodies at play (Figure 82c).

Besides the margins of manuscripts, the other places in which grotesques turn up are in church architecture and everyday material culture. In material culture, face jugs had comic, sometimes distorted faces below the rim; 'puzzle jugs' spilled the contents on the user when one attempted to pour from them. Small carved items such as knife handles represented themes from popular play such as the 'Green Man' which formed part of spring festivities.[125] Such images seem to represent the lived body at play. Images in church architecture are more inexplicable. At the French Benedictine monastery of Cuxa, in the cloister – a space of silent, pious reflection – monstrous human-demons leer or threaten from the tops of the columns. Some are gobbling up human victims greedily (Figure 83).[126] At many cathedrals, small grotesque faces adorn gargoyle waterspouts high above the churchgoers walking below, glowering or making rude faces (Figure 81). Carvings on the bottom of wooden choir seats (*misercordia*) show not only scenes of everyday life but ape-like humanoids japing and cavorting. Amongst the most debated are the Sheela Na Gigs (Figure 79). These are stone carvings of women and sometimes men lewdly exhibiting their genitals. They are usually placed around the outside of churches, often high up on the walls or tower. Sheela Na Gigs are neither erotic nor doctrinal; they may have been apotropaic, marking liminal zones.[127] Like other stone carvings, these represented a substantial investment of labour by skilled craftspeople, surely monitored by architects and clerics. But if we can assume that they were not simply obscene jests, we are much less certain of what doctrinal or other significance placing them in solemn holy places might have had. Nowhere in medieval theology or medicine is there a suggestion of why images of vulvas should be apotropaic.

How can we make sense of bizarre, satirical or even obscene imagery in supposedly serious contexts? We can dispense immediately with the view that they show rude craftsmen and illustrators at play, perhaps having a satirical fling at their superiors. Woodcarving, stone-carving and manuscript illumination would have been painstaking, skilled and monitored tasks, not the venue

Figure 79. Sheela Na Gig (© Trustees of the British Museum).

Figure 80. Nun picking penises from a tree. Mss. of *Roman de la Rose*, Bibliotheque Nationale, Paris (redrawn by Vicki Herring).

for a quick, anti-authoritarian graffiti, and in many cases (particularly in architecture and manuscript illumination) they are clearly part of a planned or conventional layout. There is no reason to suppose that viewers and readers did not appreciate them. These are not acts of resistance to authority but moments of disorder sanctioned by the commissioning authorities.

A subtler explanation sometimes proposed is theological. Holy things stood at the centre of a world whose margins were populated with monsters; grotesque images around the margins of holy places and texts remind us of the threatening demons and chaos from straying away from true faith. Hence, the disturbing, threatening monsters carved in the cloister at Cuxa (Figure 83) served to give a visual form to the sins and desires of the flesh, as a way of helping the monks understand and master their own bodily nature. The body is a microcosm of the world; their deformed bodies thus make clear their nature; sin is a deformity of the soul. 'These monstrous

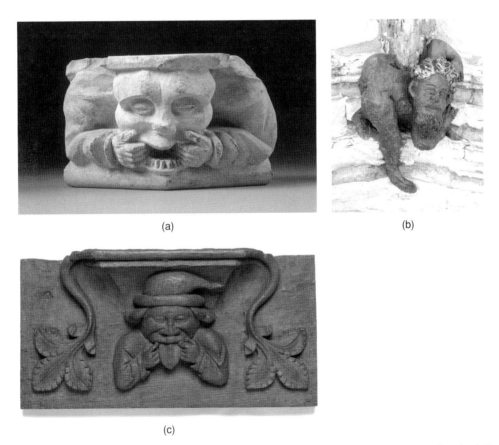

(a)

(b)

(c)

Figure 81. Architectural grotesques. A. Grotesque corbel (© Victoria and Albert Museum, London). B. Ceiling boss, Norwich Cathedral (photo: Robb). C. Misercord (church seat) with carved grotesque pulling face (© Victoria and Albert Museum, London).

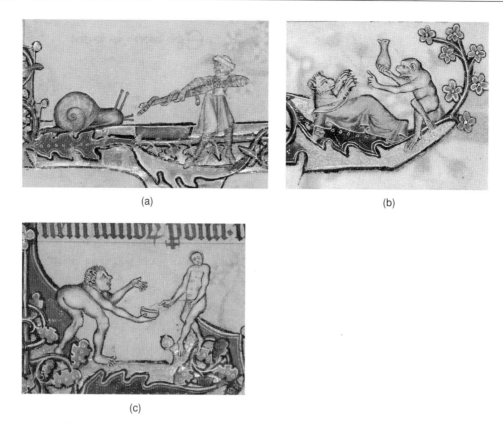

Figure 82. Grotesque marginalia, Macclesfield Psalter. A. Knight jousting with snail. B. Ape mimicking doctor performing uroscopy. C. Man urinating into a bowl held by a grotesque. (All images © The Fitzwilliam Museum, Cambridge.)

and deformed creatures carved in stone made tangible the malevolent spirits that caused the monk to disobey and served as the starting point for the cleansing of memory and for spiritual reform'.[128] Such a theological rationalization is perfectly plausible for grotesques such as at Cuxa, which were certainly part of a monastically planned conceptual design. Grotesques emphasize the earthiness of the body, its appetites, its ability to copulate, defecate, and consume, and to disorder social relations. Such appetites and abilities were threatening, particularly to monks seeking to master their fleshly natures, and they were portrayed in bodily form; the gaping jaws on the Cuxa monsters are mirrored in the huge reptilian mouths ready to swallow damned souls at the entrance to Hell (Figure 74).

But this gives us a narrow monkly take on marginal grotesques as a general category of representation. Having equated grotesques and the fleshly aspects of human existence, it sees the latter as something only to be feared, condemned and resisted. What about humorous or satirical marginalia perched near cathedral roofs and under choir seats? What about the puckish, capering grotesques in manuscripts which must have expressed whimsy, parody or *joie de vivre* as much as any theological warning?

Marginal art created moments of permitted disorder around the edge of serious contexts; it was a form of carnival which could be directed against anything serious, whether kingly power, pretentions to holiness, or simply the order of nature.[129] The medieval world was full of marginalized peoples: the poor, exiles, lepers, Jews, brigands, prostitutes and the disabled.[130] Much marginal art responds to social tensions, targeting the people at the centre – the holy, the learned or the powerful. Another target is order itself. The view of the medieval world from texts and images tends to be dominated by seriousness and order, but this is continually questioned by sexual and scatological humour, social satire, grotesque images such as the Sheela Na Gig and Carnival itself. Amongst these things, marginal images self-consciously juxtapose or comment upon the central messages they lurk around in a way which acknowledges the limits to order without undermining it. It is a necessary recognition of the varied nature of the world, the limits of order and the need to sometimes relax or waive pretensions to control.

Here the important point is how bodies enter into this. In some contexts (as in the cloister carvings discussed earlier), grotesque bodies personify a struggle between appetite and control. Camille[131] expresses it elegantly: 'It

Figure 83. Cuxa monastery cloister, France: carving of grotesque monster consuming a human head-first (Metropolitan Museum of Art, photo: Robb).

was because sex was marginalized in medieval experience that it so often became an image on the edge'. Similarly, the viscera and lower body were the seat (so to speak) of the base animal instincts. This underwrote scatological humour such as in Chaucer's Miller's Tale, in which a parody of courtly love culminates in a traumatic encounter between a tremendous fart and a red-hot iron. A popular form of marginalia thus consists of the gryllus, a capering human reduced to simply a bottom with legs, as in Plate VIIg with its appropriately phallic nose. In other contexts, the struggle is between bodies which conform socially and ones which transgress manners and bodily proprieties, or which (like beggars, lepers and prostitutes) are marginal to the social world. In others, what is transgressed is the natural order: how body parts make up a body, the border between humans and animals. The linkage to the broader argument we have made in this chapter is clear: it is an acknowledgement that there is more than one track to human bodily existence. Moreover, the struggle between modes of having a body is never a cut and dried victory for any one view. Images of women and men obscenely exposing their genitalia lurk high on the walls of many churches. Is this a repulsive warning against lust?[132] Did comical manuscript imagery have a sharp-edged subtext denigrating women?[133] Even in serious theological contexts, liminal moments such as Carnival may be irrepressible; they may even add to the understanding of the context.

The real question this leaves us with, then, is why marginal images are marginal, rather than placed at the centre or left out entirely. The answer may have to do with the inherent balance or tension in medieval bodies. In spite of attempts to proclaim a dominant theological monocorporealism, with fleshly appetites ever present and grot-

esque bodies running riot around the edge and threatening to erupt into the text, this balance was precarious and often ambiguous. What was the true life of the body? Was the goal of pilgrimage penitence for the soul, or was it the pleasure of wayfaring en route? The balance between image and frame is never as clear as it is presented.

Conclusions: Living the medieval body

We can now come back to what the 'medieval body' was and was not. Analytically, the medieval body was *not*:

- A simple empirical generalisation specifying a single dominant idea of 'the body', a homogeneous characterisation without contradictions.
- A rigid structuralist set of dualisms (soul, body/male, female/pure, impure, etc.) playing out without variation over the centuries.
- A clearly bounded and codified phenomenon (e.g. as part of a list of traits characterizing medieval 'culture').

Medieval people held multiple, clashing views of the body; yet these views shared terms of discourse, they were used generatively in thought and action, and they formed part of a way of life which involved shifting gears on a daily and lifetime basis between them. More than anything else, the 'medieval body' provided a heterogeneous set of recurrent terms of discourse with which people could live their lives: a set of assumptions about the nature of reality which provide the basic tools of thought for large regions and long periods. Although these were often defined in tension – asceticism as denial of the world, worldly pleasures as denial of the sinfulness of the flesh – at some level they shared a vocabulary or were defined within an overarching tension. In this chapter, we have emphasized the underlying structural contrasts between different views of the body. Yet the texture of daily experience may have been much less fragmented; the same people participated in all three modes of understanding (for instance, most writers on the medical body were trained within religious orders), and all three ways of looking at the body offered a lot of ground for compromise and synthesis. Thus, living the body in medieval social life involved weaving together multiple ways of being embodied, living tensions within an overall ontology. It shares some characteristics of habitus[134] such as the generative 'loose logic' with which underlying concepts were embodied in physical and emotional reflexes and used to negotiate unforeseen situations. However, the concept of habitus really applies to individual lives; 'the body' here really refers to an intellectual construction extending over several centuries.

We began this chapter by asking how Christianity changed understandings of the human body. What was the effect of monotheism? There are really two answers to this. The first is the one we may arrive at by taking texts and images at face value, the answer the Church would have liked to have been true. The second is more complex.

As a system of thought, medieval Christianity was distinguished above all by its 'capacity to produce system'.[135] Amongst earlier and contemporary Western religions, only Judaism was comparable in its aspirations to bring all aspects of thought and action under a single moral purview. Through concepts such as sin, Christianity laid claim to authority over many areas of life not considered relevant to earlier religions. Many of these involved the body: dress, eating, marriage, sexuality, medicine, burial, magic and so on. In many of these areas, the specific concepts of the Classical intellectual inheritance changed little. But the overall effect was more or less like passing a powerful magnetic field through a scrapyard of scattered metal remains. The constituent elements remained much the same, but their arrangement changed entirely, drawing them into new, systematic alignments.

The result was monocorporeality, which, as a doctrinally centralized monotheism, produced an insistence on a single theoretical and enacted understanding of the body. In theory, at least, theology had the right to pronounce authoritatively on any aspect of bodily life. These formed a very strong 'our body' in contrast to the 'other' bodies of Jews, Muslims and heretics. The result was an ontological edifice which lasted for at least a millennium with considerable homogeneity and continuity.

Yet the paradigm of the body as the earthly container for the spirit, while providing real terms of thought, was too simple. It was encased in a more complex theology which had its own contradictions: notably, the alternate view of the body as an essential component to personal identity was implicit in the doctrine of resurrection. This betrayed a deeper multiplicity; there were two other principal ways of understanding the body. One was a powerful intellectual view applied in science and medicine, which saw the body as enmeshed in a set of relations and affinities with heavenly bodies, elemental substances and qualities, and environments. In contrast to the spiritual view which saw the body as isolated from its surroundings in its rigid individualistic accounting of sin, this view saw the body as fundamentally changing in flux with its surroundings; knowledge of these affinities and connections was the key to healing the body. The other view was of the body as a locus of emotions, capacities, appetites and histories, through whose expression the person experienced life. This was rarely if ever explicitly stated, but it is evident in the vitality of the body as it experienced pleas-

ures, work and expressive activities. Characteristic medieval positions (such as discussions of sin) cannot be understood as simple statements of a free-standing theological view, but make sense only in terms of a constant tension against the implicit counterweight of this lived body.

Living such a situation was both normal and complex. The general accommodation was a negotiated compromise between modes of embodiment, with the theological view providing a framing narrative whose key components were a biography beginning with baptism and continuing through death to salvation, and a regulatory notion of sin which specified the limits of the permissible. Intellectually, there were various ways of formulating a synthesis more or less seamlessly, for instance by integrating the medical/scientific view within an appreciation of the body as a beautiful and complex creation of God. In the analogical and synthetic reasoning typical of medieval intellectual reflexes, this sometimes resulted in mapping the body onto the earth and the cosmos – the body as a microcosm of Creation.

On the experiential level, it was recognized that each view really applied to different situations, and people shifted between modes of understanding the body as they went from context to context, through the rhythms of weeks, years, journeys or lives. With such tensions between the scientific body, the theological body and the lived body, a purely doctrinal view dominated at key biographical moments. In much of the rest of life, there was a negotiated compromise, an institutionalized admission that one mode could not handle it all. Such an admission was also evident in marginalia, in satirical or grotesque images complementing an official view and reminding us of the body's ever-present potential for chaos and disorder, a potential allowed to escape as monsters or absurdities on condition that they remained in the margins.

Having multiple views of bodies was a resource in some ways, a complex way of dealing with a complex world. It allowed alternative, complementary ways of addressing phenomena such as illness. It allowed multiple, contradictory views of women, reconciling theoretical misogyny and practical equality in various settings. Ambiguity created room for creative manoeuver. At the same time, ambiguity generated tensions. Was illness a response to environment or sent by God? Why did spiritual salvation actually require the body, and how exactly did the body maintain its continuity and stability when resurrected? What were the permissible limits of appetite? Should clerics be ascetic or magnificent? In some ways, medieval history involved the long, slow working out of contrasts between these views, a process evident in the cyclical discussions of borderline issues, often in quite similar terms.

Coda: Life's pilgrimage and the disconcerting episode of Chaucer's retractions

The medieval body was not simple or constant. Life was a complex mosaic produced by intersecting rhythms: ordinary days and holy days, the turning months of the year (a favourite theme of illustrators), the stages of a human's life, health and illness, the turning of Fortune's wheel. Our pilgrims changed as they made their way through the long path to twin destinations, the grave and the world of pain and punishment beyond it. The body itself changed too. Sometimes it was understood as a locus of sensual pleasure, pain, work, joy and illness. Sometimes it was part of cosmic clockwork, its humours subject to the influence of heavenly bodies like the sea whose tides shifted with the moon. Sometimes it was the theological battleground where sin and virtue fought out the battle of life, with the soul at stake.

Chaucer's *Canterbury Tales* is the greatest unfinished work in the English language, but some time before the poet (Plate VIIh) died in 1400, he closed it with a Retraction. In this final couple of paragraphs, he begs the reader to pray for his soul and repudiates all of his works – naming them one by one, from his early courtly poems to his last, most worldly masterpiece. He excepts only his translations of Boethius' philosophy and some saints' lives and moralities. All his other works – three decades of writing, thousands of lines of verse – were renounced as mere worldly vanity. In effect, the greatest medieval English poet disavowed his entire career.

Why did he do this? Literary scholars have always found it inexplicable. The *Canterbury Tales* shines amongst medieval literature for its balanced humanism and vitality, its gently satirical nature but also its affectionate interest in people as people. Chaucer's retraction cannot be read as ironic (for instance, as a sly way of listing the author's 'greatest hits') without shallowly discounting the evident sincerity of its religiosity. The retraction clearly goes beyond a gesture of conventional piety; it was common to ask the reader to pray for the author's soul, but why disavow a whole shelf full of works which were perfectly conventional according to ordinary morality? Nor was it a reaction to the parts of his work later critics have found low or lewd, the sexual and scatological; the blanket renunciation of worldly vanities encompasses a dozen works of impeccably refined courtliness as well. In short, there is no explanation which we can square with Chaucer's keen interest in people and the world, his erudition and *joie de vivre*. We are left with explanations such as that proposed by Robinson:[136] 'Such a repudiation may be deplored as weakness of mind or explained as a sign of broken health in old age'. It is a let-down we forgive out of affection or respect, a feeble and ill old man foreswearing his muse.

But this conclusion tells more about us and our expectations than about Chaucer as a medieval person. As Arnold drily notes, 'people did not live their lives awaiting death at every moment'.[137] One's point of view did not remain the same throughout the pilgrimage, whether swapping vulgar stories in a hostelry, reading someone's humoural constitution in their face, bowing to the worldly pomp of knights and prioresses, or approaching the holy destination in piety and repentance. If we assume that people had one static medieval mindset, changing one's point of view situationally thus becomes an aberration, an inexplicable straying. But as we have seen, this is not how medieval people thought about their bodies and their place in the world. Instead, they alternated between several quite distinct logics of the body which could, with effort, be reduced to a single coherent scheme but which always threatened to burst from facile reconciliations and spill out into open conflicts, censure and absurdity. Life as a journey was much like the emblematic pilgrimage Chaucer narrates: for most people, it was neither a spiritual journey to salvation nor a pleasure junket affording opportunities for amusement and dalliance, but both at the same time. And it was understood that times for play alternated with times for learning, ceremony, and spiritual reverence or fear; as you neared your destination, your frame of mind necessarily changed.

The author of the 'Retraction' was an old man, feeling illness changing his own body and sensing the approach of death. This was perhaps the archetypal medieval moment to shift frames. Hence, a plea for forgiveness of sins and worldly vanities – including even innocent literary ones – is neither a pious formality lacking in feeling, nor a betrayal of vitality. They belong to another world, another context, another bodily frame of understanding. Putting one world of bodies away and readying oneself for another was simply what one did, seriously, in the face of mortality. It is a completely normal, deeply felt moment, the medieval multimodality of the body enacted as biographical narrative. We can hope that it brought him peace.

NOTES

1. We are particularly grateful to Dr Helen Foxhall-Forbes and Dr Craig Cessford for detailed comments upon this chapter. All errors and omissions remain the authors'.
2. Writings on the medieval body are extensive but patchy. Work by Caroline Walker Bynum, the doyenne of the subject, spans gender studies, popular culture and the history of religions (Bynum 1992a; 1992b; 1995a; 2007).

In many ways, work began with French social historians; the classic works include Ariès 1962; 1981; Le Roy Ladurie 1978. Elias' work is also crucial: Elias 1978; 1982. In early Christian theology, Brown's (1981; 1990) work has been significant. Reynolds 1991 and Arnold 2005 are key for lived religion. For general histories of magic, see Flint 1991; Kieckhafer 1989. Medieval death is discussed by Gilchrist and Sloane 2005 and Binski 1996. For medieval sexuality, one of the better-studied topics, see Brożyna 2005; Bullough and Brundage 2000; Harper and Proctor 2011; Karras 2005; and McCarthy 2004. There is a substantial but uneven literature on gender and women (e.g. Bennett 1993), medieval masculinities (e.g. Hadley 1998; Karras 2001; Lees 1994), and particularly women's spirituality (Bynum 2007; 1992a; 1992b). Conrad et al. (1995) provide a good overview of medieval medicine. Holsinger (2002) reviews the effect of post-colonial theory, particularly building upon the Annales tradition of attention to daily life and peasant politics. Perhaps because the topic is fragmented amongst history, the history of medicine, literature, theology and gender studies, there is relatively little work directly upon the concept of the body per se, although see Kay and Rubin 1994 and Cohen 2003. One very recent account that develops a related set of arguments to those proposed here comes from Roberta Gilchrist (2012). This was published after we had submitted our manuscript to press, otherwise it would have figured much more heavily in our analysis.

3. Chaucer 1933; modern translation by Neville Coghill: Chaucer 1951, 95.
4. Smith 2000.
5. Bynum 1995b.
6. Flint 1991.
7. Smith 2000, 565; cf. Richlin 2010.
8. The Church did not ban grave goods, as has been sometimes suggested; indeed, St Cuthbert was buried with a massive pectoral cross.
9. Conrad et al. 1995, 72–73.
10. Conrad et al. 1995.
11. Bynum 1995b, 8.
12. Bynum 1995b, 19. Writers (such as Paul) sometimes discuss a three-part human made of body, soul and spirit. However, interestingly, they tend to worry about how the soul and the spirit differed from each other; the contrast of both with the body was clear.
13. Gilchrist and Sloane 2005; Binski 1996.
14. Zimmerman 2008.
15. Brown 1981.
16. Bynum 1995a.
17. Simons 1994.
18. Geary 1986.
19. Zimmerman 2008.
20. Abulafia 1994.
21. Angels were simultaneously genderless and gendered, in a somewhat paradoxical way; as pure spiritual beings they were free from the liabilities of the flesh, but as mediators between God and humans, presumably they shared human characteristics such as gender to help people relate to them.
22. Bullough and Brundage 2000; Harper and Proctor 2011; Karras 2005.
23. Arnold 2005, 168.
24. Bynum 1995b, 19.
25. Pain in childbirth was thought to have been punishment for Eve's sin (and more generically, the inherent sinfulness of the flesh); Mary was believed not to have suffered pain in childbirth.
26. Wood 1981, 711–712; cf. Nelson 1997.
27. Flanagan 1998.
28. García-Ballester 2001.
29. Webb 2010.
30. Cabre 2008.
31. Kieckhafer 1989.
32. Bartlett 2001.
33. Cohen 2003.
34. Rawcliffe 2006; Zimmerman 2008.
35. Coon 2008.
36. Caciola 2000.
37. Flanagan 1998; Green 2001.
38. Cadden 1993; Jose 2008.
39. S. Miller 2010.
40. Wood 1981, 724–725.
41. Woolgar 2010, 14.
42. Of course emotions are always embodied (Harris and Sørensen 2010): the point is that medieval people explicitly recognized this in a way which some modern accounts of emotions as cognitive events tend to deny.
43. Le Roy Ladurie 1978, 140.
44. Stevenson 2006.
45. Bullough and Brundage 2000; Harper and Proctor 2011; Karras 2005.
46. Karras 2005.
47. Kieckhafer 1989.
48. O Western Wind, anonymous, a popular sixteenth century English verse.
49. Davis 1983, 234.
50. Davis 1983, 253.
51. Woolgar 2010.
52. Holsinger 2001.
53. Meyerson and Thiery 2003.
54. Smith 2008; M. Johnson, personal communication.
55. Groebner 2009.
56. Crane 2002; Jaritz 2000; Phillips 2004.
57. Phillips 2007, 23.
58. Phillips 2007.
59. Arnold 2005.
60. Phillips 2005.
61. Rollo-Koster 2003; Westerhof 2007.
62. Nelson 1997.
63. Caviness 2001b.
64. Karras 2004.
65. Davis 1983.

66. Lester 2011.
67. Gilchrist 1994; 1999.
68. Wood 1981.
69. Parsons and Wheeler 1996.
70. Craig 2003.
71. Bynum 2007.
72. Caciola 2000.
73. Hadley 1998; Lees 1994.
74. Karras 2001.
75. Phillips 2007.
76. Coon 2010; Nelson 1998; Thibodeaux 2010.
77. Smith 2008.
78. Bynum 1995a.
79. Bynum 1995a, 56.
80. Bynum 1995a.
81. Bynum 1995a.
82. Bynum 1995a, 112.
83. Bynum 2005.
84. Ariès 1962.
85. Hanawalt 2002.
86. Shahar 1994.
87. Caviness 2001a; 2010; Cohen 2003; Rubin 1994.
88. Rubin 1994.
89. Arnold 2005; Reynolds 1991.
90. Reynolds 1991.
91. Karras 2005.
92. Bailey 2001.
93. Gilchrist 2008.
94. Conrad et al. 1995, 74.
95. Conrad et al. 1995, 168.
96. Cohen 2000.
97. Conrad et al. 1995, 75–76.
98. Archambeau 2011. The Anglo-Saxon writer St Bede gives five principal reasons for illness, including simply to allow a saint to demonstrate his or her powers through miraculous intervention.
99. Rawcliffe 2006.
100. Green 2009.
101. Rawcliffe 2006.
102. Simons 1994.
103. Sekules 2001, 94.
104. Lovejoy 1936.
105. Gerald of Wales, *The Topography of Ireland*, cited in Brożyna 2005, 92.
106. Cain 2002.
107. Camille 1994; Sekules 2001, 120–125.
108. Camille 1994.
109. Birkholz 2006.
110. Mittman 2006; Münkler 2002.
111. Mandeville 1983; cf. Higgins 1997.
112. Mandeville 1983, 100–101.
113. Mandeville 1983, 100.
114. Mandeville 1983, 43.
115. Mandeville 1983, 75.
116. Mandeville 1983, 87.
117. Mandeville 1983, 95.
118. Mandeville 1983, 43.
119. Mandeville 1983, 156ff.
120. Mandeville 1983, 156.
121. Mandeville 1983, 120.
122. Mandeville 1983, 145.
123. Bovey 2002; Camille 1992.
124. Camille 1992, 35.
125. Hall 2001.
126. Dale 2001.
127. Borland 2011; Karkov 2001.
128. Dale 2001, 430.
129. Camille 1992.
130. Geremek 1990.
131. Camille 1992, 40.
132. Weir and Jerman 1986.
133. Caviness 2001a.
134. Bourdieu 1977.
135. Binski 1996.
136. Editor's Introduction to Chaucer 1933, 15.
137. Arnold 2005, 168.

7

The body in the age of knowledge

Oliver J. T. Harris, John Robb and Sarah Tarlow

A matter of life and death[1]

One cold crisp morning in 1753, a crowd gathers at Tyburn, in London, around a gallows standing at a crossroads (Plate V). The crowd contains adults and children, men and women, rich and poor. Mothers nurse children, men chat to each other whilst smoking clay pipes. Hawkers sell food and drink to refresh the spectators. For a better view of the hanging, people with a little cash pay for a seat in the stands the enterprising locals have erected.

A cart approaches, bringing the condemned man, a murderer who has been sentenced not just to be hanged but to be dissected afterwards at the college of surgeons. In fact, the men working for the anatomists – 'blackguards', from their black coats – wait with their own cart to take the body away. They are attracting a few comments and glances from other members of the crowd, but their presence has been legalized by the Murder Act, passed by Parliament the previous year. The guilty man stands erect, listening to the priest accompanying him in the cart, nodding to the words, and joining in with the prayers where appropriate. The crowd offers cheers and catcalls as they approach the scaffold. The criminal, now positioned underneath the gallows on a second cart – this one designed specifically for the purpose – continues to listen to the priest. He is then given the opportunity to speak his last words. He urges them to avoid making the mistakes which have led him to a life of iniquity and to live as good Christians. His greatest regret is not his death, which will arrive momentarily, but the cut of the surgeon's knife as his body is dissected.

Following his words, the condemned man is masked and hanged. But this is not the end of events. A young woman is led up to the dangling corpse and the executioner raises the body's hand to touch her neck. It is a frightening moment, but the touch of a hanged man's hand is a traditional cure for neck complaints, which she has suffered from for years; her family has arranged this moment with the executioner. All of this is watched by the priest, the crowd and the surgeons' men, the latter scuffling with relatives of the hanged man who hope to seize his body for a less disgraceful burial.

This single moment – a convicted felon is hanged – reveals the cacophony of beliefs about the body which typifies the Early Modern period,[2] and the diversity of the body world in this period. Religious views espoused by the priest (and echoed by the condemned man in his ritualized final speech) tended to see the body simply as an unpleasant, earthy and fleshy thing afflicted with temptation. It was natural for the body to expiate the sins the individual committed. Yet the body was also a site of social display. Prominent and important bodies were richly dressed, bewigged, and ornamented; stigmatized bodies were degraded. Hanging criminals was nothing new, but dissecting them was. Many crimes were punished capitally; thus hanging alone was not sufficient punishment for a crime as serious as murder, and the Murder Act of 1752 exacted dissection as a further punishment. Post-mortem dissection was something to be feared and avoided, a punishment worse than 'mere' death. The law too was caught up in these beliefs. But dissection also made the body a site of scientific exploration by anatomists, who were increasingly interpreting it a machine, whose parts needed to be identified, located and recorded. Alongside these social, religious and scientific beliefs, a fourth strand can be detected in our scene. These are what we might term folk beliefs about the body, such as the popular faith in the magical potency of the hanged man's hand. These different beliefs were all present in the Early Modern body world, and despite their apparent contradictions, many were held to be true by the same people.

The Early Modern period is a foundational moment in the history of our world. The medieval period seems distinctly 'other'; by the nineteenth century we move amongst familiar ideas, techniques and practices. Capitalism, science, medicine, art, and music all look back to this period as the moment when modern life as we know it began to coalesce. So too with the body; most accounts of the 'modern' body trace its distinctive characteristics to this period (cf. Chapter 2). This period is sometimes depicted as the march of knowledge and increasing scientific understanding of the body. In the simplest version, the period could be seen as a transition from the medieval idea of the body as microcosm to a modern idea of body as machine.[3]

Table 8. *Key dates in the Early Modern period*

c. 1439	Invention of the printing press in Germany. By 1500, more than 200 cities in Europe had presses that had produced between 8 and 20 million books.
1453	End of the Hundred Years War.
1492	Discovery of the New World.
1517	Martin Luther writes his *95 Theses* and nails them to the door of the castle church in Wittenburg, sparking the reformation.
1532–1534	A series of acts of Parliament initiated by Henry VIII break England away from Rome, opening the door to Protestantism.
1536	The dissolution of the monasteries begins in England.
1543	Vesalius publishes *De Humani Corporis Fabrica*.
1545–1563	The council of Trent begins the Counter-Reformation.
1616	Harvey announces his discovery of the circulation of blood.
1618–1648	The Thirty Years War, involving most of Europe.
1620	Bacon publishes *Novum Organum*.
1633	Galileo put under house arrest by the Catholic church.
1637	Descartes publishes *Discourse on Method*.
1642–1649	The English Civil War, ending with the decapitation of Charles I and the appointment of Oliver Cromwell as Lord Protector.
1660s	Period narrated by Samuel Pepys' *Diary*.
1687	Newton publishes the *Principia*.
1688	The 'Glorious Revolution': the installation of William and Mary as King and Queen of England at the invitation of Parliament.
1761	Giovanni Battista Morgani publishes his three volume treatise on *The seats and causes of diseases investigated by anatomy*. This is the start of modern pathology.
1789	The storming of the Bastille and start of the French Revolution.

In this chapter, we tackle two questions. First, is this image of the transition – a shift from belief to science, driven by increasingly accurate knowledge of the 'natural' world – accurate? Or is the story more complicated, as the different currents of understanding the body tangling in our vignette suggest? Secondly, how did the transition happen? Much of the literature on the Early Modern body is written in terms of 'high discourse': it is about what happened in the literate, educated world of anatomists, scientists, theologians and poets. But what did this have to do with changes in how people lived their daily lives, in the way they went to work, or moved through space?

The historical background

The Early Modern period covers a host of upheavals both in Britain and across Europe and has produced a vast scholarship in many disciplines. This chapter uses changes in Britain during this period as a lens to examine wider transformations in Europe and beyond.

Historians have noted strong continuities between the medieval period and the Early Modern period, and periodizations of history also reflect particular theoretical agendas. As in Kelly's provocative question, 'Did women have a Renaissance?'[4] Europeans' lives were dramatically

different in 1750 compared to 1450, but the change was incremental and gradual, and there were strong continuities in many aspects of life.

Society, 1450–1789

The Early Modern period is traditionally defined as beginning with the European invention of the printing press (in what would become Germany around 1440) and the European discovery of the New World (by Columbus in 1492), and as ending with the French Revolution and the first stirrings of the industrial revolution (Table 8). These are, of course, arbitrary landmarks. What is clear is that this was a time of enormous upheaval in Europe. There was profound religious change. With the Reformation and Counter-Reformation, different forms of Christianity vied for supremacy. Religious developments had profound implications for the social order. Before and during the French Wars of Religion (1562–1598), accusations of heresy, sexual deviance and infanticide were used to demean minority sects.[5] In Britain:

If anything were certain in 16th century England, it would be that everything changes, even the immutable; that everything is relative, even the absolute. In the space of a single generation from 1530 to 1560 there were no fewer than five state religions, five different and competing monotheisms, incompatible versions of the one God.[6]

Conflict between Catholics and Protestants in Britain was settled decisively only in 1688 by the 'glorious bloodless revolution' and the installation of William and Mary, at the invitation of Parliament, as King and Queen of England and Scotland. On the continent, religious conflict continued through the seventeenth century, particularly during the Thirty Years War (1618 to 1648), fought across what was then the Holy Roman Empire. It is estimated that perhaps a third of the population of the Empire lost their lives during that war.[7]

Politically, two developments stand out. The first is the gradual formation of nation states. Some European states (such as Spain, England and France) emerged from the Middle Ages, but throughout the post-medieval period there was increasing unification and centralization as the fragmented map of medieval principalities evolved into the familiar states of today. The last major countries to emerge were Germany and Italy, unified during the mid to late nineteenth century. Secondly, absolutist monarchies increasingly evolved into forms of government which incorporated parliaments or other forms of representation, reflecting the increasing power of urban, educated, industrial classes at the expense of traditional rural aristocracies. This is most marked in England, where the struggle between Parliament and monarchy began with the English Civil War which concluded in 1649 with the beheading of Charles I. The monarchy was restored in 1660, but the balance of power continued to shift towards Parliament over the next century. Elsewhere in Europe, a real sense of rebellion can be detected, culminating with the revolution in France in 1789.

The Early Modern period was a time of scientific transformation, as the scepticism instilled by the Renaissance began to translate itself into new ways of looking at the world. In sixteenth-century Italy, the Flemish anatomist Vesalius led the new craze for dissection, an enterprise which would come to change the subject of its enquiry, the human body, even as it became perhaps the metaphor of choice for the period. Francis Bacon began to develop his scientific principles in the early seventeenth century and these influenced Newton, who outlined a new physics and mathematics in his masterpiece, the *Principia* in 1687. Philosophically, the major figure of the seventeenth century was René Descartes, whose ideas about the relationship between body and soul and body and mind were to have a great impact on how people thought about the body over the next 300 years. These scientific theories were accompanied by new social theories. One example is John Locke's notion of natural rights, which in turn

had a profound influence on Thomas Jefferson. Jefferson drafted the Declaration of Independence of the United States in 1776, which declared that all men were created equal (though Jefferson did not apply this to the slaves he owned).

Social and material changes between 1450 and 1789 included a swelling European population, literacy becoming more widespread, and an increasing growth of major cities. To support increasing urban populations, trade expanded as well. Although most industrial work was still carried out in workshops rather than factories, some industrial enterprises were sizeable indeed. Social change affected the countryside too. Although the enclosure of the British landscape is often portrayed as happening later, much took place before 1750, changing rural people's engagement with their landscape, but also wider attitudes to space, place and the body.[8]

This is also the period in which Europe became imperial and colonial. Russia reached out across vast swaths of the east, swallowing up diverse Muslim and indigenous populations. Spain, Portugal, France, England and the Netherlands appropriated the forests and prairies of North America, the great Aztec cities of Mexico, rich Caribbean islands, and the rain forests, pampas and cordilleras of South America. From South Africa to India, Australia to Pacific tropical islands, colonists, traders and military adventurers encountered new worlds. As well as generating vast wealth for Europe, the colonial encounter challenged ideas about bodies. Medieval Europeans had imagined bodies on the margins of the known world; Early Modern Europeans actually met them.

Society 1789–1900

Although most of this chapter focuses on the period before 1789, it is important to mention some later changes, particularly the industrial revolution. Aspects of the industrial revolution were already in place by 1789. Machines had already begun to emerge that made it sensible, for the first time, to move the process of production together under one roof, in what were termed manufactories, rather than relying on a series of cottage industries, each producing different aspects of the finished product. In the 1760s and 1770s, these machines included Arkwright's Spinning Frame, Crompton's Spinning Mule and Hargreaves' Spinning Jenny, all designed to increase the speed at which spinning took place. In the 1760s, James Watt developed usable steam engines. Increased industrialization raised demand for raw materials such as cotton, coal, and iron, from both domestic sources and overseas colonies.

With the advent of factory labour, population began to shift away from the countryside and towards the cities. In 1750, two-thirds to three-quarters of the British population lived in the countryside; by 1850, the majority of the population lived in cities. In turn, this was coupled with a huge increase in population. In Britain, for example, the population increased from around 6 million in 1740 to around 12 million in 1801, and more than doubled again to 27.5 million by 1851.[9] As rural populations remained stable, these huge increases took place in the great industrial and commercial cities. Surging towns brought with them new kinds of social relations, principally through new kinds of work in factories, mines and urban services. These new ways of living and working were tied up with routines linked to mass production and factory labour that can be directly linked to the rise of capitalism throughout both the Early Modern and Modern periods. These new routines were also linked to new ways of understanding and experiencing the body.

Progress and improvement began to be dominant tropes in the explicit discourse that surrounded life from the end of the eighteenth and throughout the nineteenth centuries.[10] Indeed, they are still with us today. The central idea was that progress and improvement are natural and proper, and should be strived for in all walks of life. Thus we see emphasis on the improvement of the countryside, of urban conditions, and of the lives and minds of the urban population. It can also be seen as directly related to the idea of improving the self through posture, manners and deportment, as well as the new forms of bodily discipline in contexts such as the school, the hospital and the prison.[11] These were written through the laws of the land as well as in people's daily routines. Ideas of development, progress and change are central to two theories developed in the mid-nineteenth century that have been at the heart of almost everything written about the body since that time: Marx and Engel's theories about capitalism and Darwin's theory of evolution. As Marxist and Darwinian ideas spread over the next century, for the first time, ideas about the body created through scientific research became an almost universal aspect of how ordinary people understood their worlds. Darwin's theories in particular created new understandings of nature, and his thought played a crucial, if unintended, part in the emergence of new conceptions of race, biology and hierarchy amongst human beings.

From medieval to modern body worlds: Narratives and counter-narratives

Such sweeping changes could not happen without equally dramatic transformations in body worlds. At the beginning of this period, the idea of the body as a microcosm of the world was strong. This drew on the Galenic tradition of the humoural theory of the body we introduced

Figure 84. Summer: the body as microcosm in the seventeenth century (Property of Duke University Medical Center Library, Trent Collection, History of Medicine Collections, Durham, NC. Image provided by Wellcome Library, London).

in Chapter 6. In a broader sense, the body was part of a system of affinities and qualities which incorporated the world within it. Figure 84 captures one element of this. It is one of four 'anatomical fugitive' sheets that relate particular seasons to the human body alongside other scientific and moral matters. In this case, the season is summer, and it is tied to particular natural events, bodily qualities and even to particular places. This microcosmic structure related not just to nature but also to politics, a concept which originated in Plato and Aristotle and was developed by medieval thinkers (cf. Chapter 6). Using the hierarchy and integration of parts of the body to express social organization was a familiar and important Early Modern image. The house, the state and the universe were the body writ-large.[12] Yet it was also adapted to changing times. Thomas Hobbes' *Leviathan*, published in 1651, shows society as homologous to the body, with the king as its head and the subjects as its torso (Figure 85). For Hobbes, a royalist, the body of the English state had done the unthinkable two years before: it had chopped its own head off. However, *Leviathan* also reflects new political debates, seeing the monarch not as simply inevitable and divinely ordained but as a defence against civil disorder made up by the consent of its members, a concept shown graphically by the way in which the body of the state is made up of the mass of its constituent subjects.

By the end of the period, a very different view of the body dominated. Epistemological developments by Descartes and others shifted the idea of the person from

Figure 85. Part of the title page of Hobbes' *Leviathan* (1651) (© The British Library Board, c05160–02 Egerton 1910, f.1).

a unity of body and soul to a material shell housing the mind. Science and medicine increasingly represented the body as a machine, one whose breakdown and death, far from being natural, represented a failure that required investigation. The person, from one perspective, became ever more separated from the body and subjected to a materialist philosophy, eventually became the subject of psychological theories. How did this change come about?

There is one way of telling this story that would be familiar to most of us. It is one of progress and increasing rationality: scepticism towards superstition and a new empiricist methodology that peeled back the mysteries of the world, leaving behind only the cold, hard, facts of science. So whereas the body at the beginning of the period was *mis*understood as being made up by the four humours and governed by the soul, by the end of the period it was properly revealed to be a biological machine, driven by organs such as the heart-pump, until disease or age led to mechanical breakdown. This is a story of the *men* who drove this change, and the technologies they invented along the way to help them. Thus it was Vesalius who began dissecting the body, Harvey who identified the circulation of the blood, and Morgagni who began the study of pathology. Jenner discovered that small doses of cowpox could prevent the onset of the far more deadly smallpox in 1796, and Lister's experiments with antisepsis in the 1860s greatly increased the chances of surviving surgery. Within this story, each discovery drives the next, the human thirst for knowledge rolling inexorably forward. As time progressed, the vitalism that saw human bodies as driven by God's spirit was replaced with ideas of mechanism. This was not just a new way of seeing the body;

it was a better way, a more rational way, that separated thoughts from emotions, minds from bodies and subjects from objects, so that the world could be studied in splendid objective contemplation. This progress in knowledge about the body continues to the present day.

But the modern body has many alternative histories. In fact, most social historians of the body would consider a simple narrative of scientific progress part of our own world view rather than a real historical account of what happened. It accepts a particular story that people, especially from 1750 onwards, constructed for themselves.[13] It accepts as absolute the distinctions and differences between people and things, politics and science, mind and body, and knowledge and belief that were instituted in this period.[14] Instead, we need to consider alternative stories, ones that recognize how the progress of medicine wasn't just a better way of seeing the body; it was a new way of looking altogether.[15] The body was always a way in which power, identity and politics were understood and reproduced, and these were as important as medical advances in shaping the modern body.

Alternative histories place the body within social relations. Thus, for example, the German sociologist Norbert Elias used manuals on social comportment as sources to argue that body boundaries were increasingly policed in the Early Modern period.[16] People were instructed about how to blow one's nose, how to consume one's food or where and when to urinate and defecate; particular bodily functions were increasingly censured and tabooed, and material cultures from handkerchiefs to plumbing were produced to help manage bodily behaviours. Rather than emphasizing martial prowess, which had been the case in the medieval period, bodily and emotional control became more important.[17] A second example is the great French historian and philosopher Michel Foucault (see Chapter 2). Foucault analysed how clinics, prisons, schools, factories and asylums emerged in the Early Modern period as new technologies for disciplining the body. Foucault pulled together changes in all aspects of life to demonstrate how they produced new understandings of the body. Crucially, he employed the notion of discourse to examine how different kinds of architecture, social structure and debate brought certain possibilities for the body into existence. Thus the architecture of prisons, as we will see, created certain kinds of possibilities for bodily action and thus for understanding bodies at all.[18] Moreover, in tracing the history of sexuality, Foucault showed how it formed a discourse by which power could be exercised upon people.[19] Foucault did not seek origins for these practices but instead looked at how they come together through particular genealogies to have historical impact.

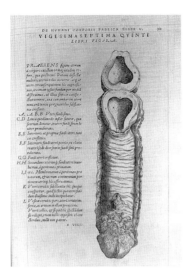

Figure 86. Vesalian image showing female genitalia as an inversion of male genitalia (© Wellcome Library, London).

As a third example of counter-narrative, Thomas Laqueur[20] argues that since classical times the body was understood as being either one of two genders (either male or female) but could only be of a single sex: males and females were understood as having the same sexual organs, although the female version was the inversion of the male. Thus the vagina was an inverted penis, the ovaries internal testicles and so on. This argument is supported by images taken from Vesalius' work (Figures 86 and 89), by details such as how nosebleeds, which occur in both men and women, were understood as similar to menstruation, and by anecdotal stories which reveal the fear that women could turn into men if vigorous exercise caused their penis to fall out from inside them. In the eighteenth century, Laqueur argues, this 'one-sex' model was replaced by a 'two-sex' model which saw males and females as fundamentally different and incommensurate. Laqueur emphasizes that the move to the two-sex model *preceded* the discovery of scientific evidence for anatomical difference by almost two hundred years. Instead, he suggests that as the Enlightenment, the French Revolution and other notable events in the eighteenth century drove forward the argument that all people were created equal, so discrimination against women began to be more difficult to justify. The 'discovery' of the two-sex model produced an authoritative-sounding 'scientific' account of why women were inferior which served to defend traditional institutional discrimination and misogyny.[21]

All three of these master visions of where 'the modern body' came from have been widely critiqued. Laqueur's model has been challenged as simplistic, over-generalized or restricted to narrow intellectual contexts; for instance, eighteenth-century erotic writings show a different understanding of male-female differences,

and seventeenth-century midwives clearly appreciated the uterus, an organ with no male parallel.[22] Similarly, Elias can (rightly) be accused of only a partial reading of the sources, and forms of bodily discipline in some contexts clearly predate the transition identified by Foucault. But, significantly, critique has not reverted to simply asserting accounts of medical and scientific progress. Instead, critics have accepted the fact that the modern body requires a *social* history, whether it is the one provided by Elias, Foucault, or Laqueur or another, more complex one. It would be ingenuous to dispute that modern science and medicine – reaching back to the seventeenth century – involve some very sophisticated understandings of the body and effective ways of exploring and treating it. The point is that these are not the only understandings possible, they are never free from their cultural and social matrix, and their history is also a history of power, metaphor and the practices of daily life. To explore this in more detail, we now turn to a closer examination of religion, philosophy, science and medicine and their relationship to the Early Modern body world.

Post-medieval religion: The increasingly worldly body and the body in death

As we saw in Chapter 6, medieval theology opposed the worldly, appetite-ridden flesh and the soul, yet paradoxically regarded the person as the union of these. From the sixteenth century onwards, theologians increasingly severed the links between these two components of the person.

The Protestant Reformation was a major factor in rethinking the relations of body and soul throughout Northern Europe. One target of Protestant reformers was the doctrine of purgatory.[23] Purgatory was a central doctrine in late medieval and Early Modern Catholicism. It referred to the period after death but prior to the resurrection and the Day of Judgment, where a person's ultimate fate would be decided. Purgatory was thus a temporary limbo for souls awaiting judgment, a place in which they suffered pains to expiate their sins in life; this pain focused not on the earthly body (which lay in the ground awaiting resurrection) but on the soul itself. Crucially, these pains could be eased by the prayers of the living, whether by the dead person's loved ones or by priests paid to say masses on their behalf. Furthermore, Purgatory provided a place for popularly-imagined monsters, ghouls and goblins which the church was reluctant to recognize as belonging to the kingdoms of either God or Satan.[24] For Protestant reformers, however, the whole concept was deeply problematic. For them, people would be saved or damned by their own faith alone, not by the actions of others after their death. But abolishing Purgatory radically affected the relationship between the living and the dead, and thus also attitudes towards the dead body. Previously, the funeral had begun the process of praying for the soul of the dead person; now, such prayers offered no benefit. Theologians thus began to bemoan elaborate funerals accompanied by candles, incense and other regalia as an entirely unnecessary worldly vanity. According to Zacharie Boyd, a seventeenth century Glaswegian Protestant theologian, memorials were a waste of money that could better be spent on charity.[25]

During the seventeenth century, to Protestant and particularly Puritan theologians, the body was increasingly thought of as standing for all worldly interests. Worse than this, its appetites made it particularly sinful. Decrying the body had been a long-standing strand of Christian theology; but, increasingly, the body was seen as a base and worthless device whose only purpose was to serve as a temporary vehicle for the soul. Given this, bodies needed to be disciplined by the soul, so that the temptations to sin could be reduced or at least managed during life. For one Protestant theologian, William Sherlock, writing towards the end of the seventeenth century, the body was not just the container of the soul but its enemy who had to be fought at all times.[26] The only purpose for treating the dead with dignity was to comfort the bereaved or to improve the moral standing of the living. Even burial on consecrated ground was of no interest to some theologians; if your body was burnt and scattered on the four winds, God could still resurrect you. Because God in Heaven would not care about where people were buried, why should people themselves care about it? For Boyd, the possibility of being released from the body was something to desire greatly, and what happened to it after that was of little importance.[27]

Of course, this extreme point of view was not held by everyone. Some theologians, notably Thomas Becon, one of the foremost critics of Purgatory in the sixteenth century, argued that the body ought to be cared for after death because it had at one stage held the soul. He also cited a second reason: a continuing belief in the genuine resurrection of the physical body. Other theologians continued the long-standing medieval debates about the importance of the body, and what condition it would be in in the afterlife.[28] This is a point about which there seems to have been little coherence in the Early Modern and Modern periods. Sherlock, writing a century later than Becon, felt the resurrected body was quite different from the one people had in life; it was light and ethereal rather than worldly.[29] Even those who seemed to be more committed to a literal resurrection were still loathe to argue that a complete body in death was necessary for a complete body in the afterlife. Thus despite their disagreements, theologians of all stripes followed St Augustine and concurred that the treatment of the body after death had no bearing on the likelihood or possibility of a successful transition into heaven.

In any case, it seems clear that within theological discourse, the body was becoming increasingly separated from the soul. It is interesting in this context to contrast Becon, writing in 1568, and Sherlock, writing in 1689. As we will see, between these two dates, the Cartesian 'moment' had come and gone, and many authors were employing the new philosophical tools of the Enlightenment to proclaim their distance from the earthly ties of the body, whether to conduct 'pure' research or just to be 'pure' theologically. In either case, the emotional, porous, sexual body was something of which to be free, or at least to discipline, whilst the mind or the soul (depending on your point of view) was the thing to be celebrated. Thus Sherlock declares:

> methinks when we see the senseless and putrefying Remains of a brave Man before us, it is hard to conceive that this is all of him! Or was there a more Divine inhabitant, which animated this Earthly Machine, which gave life, and Beauty, and Motion to it, but is now removed?[30]

Hence, there was an increase in the popularity of memento mori depictions, which had been known throughout the medieval period but which now experienced a resurgence (Figure 87a).

In actual religious practice, funerary practices remained remarkably similar after the Reformation. Catholic grave goods such as rosaries, bulls and pardons, disappeared, although these were probably rare in any case. Aside from this, most of the features of Early Modern and Modern burial had been established well before the period began, including the use of coffins, east-west burial and, in some cases, commemoration by permanent memorial. Although some theologians argued that burial was a useless disposal of the soul's worthless material shell, for most people, the body remained at the heart of the funerary ritual which continued to ensure that bodies were interred in consecrated ground, facing the right way, and ideally as close to the church as possible.

Paradoxically, in some ways this separation also made funerals more elaborate. With the Protestant abolition of Purgatory, funerals became the last point of mediation between the living and the dead. This increased the role of the funeral as a key ritual marking the end of life. Hence, in Britain, the funeral service changed over the late

(a)

(b)

Figure 87. Seventeenth century death, theological and social: A. Memento mori inscription, Norwich Cathedral. B. Memorial to a Jacobean noblewoman with long biographical inscription, Salisbury Cathedral (photographs: Robb).

sixteenth and early seventeenth centuries. The salvation-oriented aspect of the funerals notably decreased, while the sermon was extended, which both offered moral lessons for the living as well as a memorial for the deceased.[31] Later in the seventeenth century, the popularity of commemorative memorials began to increase as well. Medieval royalty had effigy tombs, of course, but they rarely included inscriptions; the pinnacle of society needed no identification beyond their heraldic armour. As commemorative memorials descended the social scale to minor nobles and bourgeois, inscriptions mushroomed virtually into curricula vitae, reciting the dead person's career, social connections and virtues at considerable length (Figure 87b, Plate VIIIa).[32]

Philosophy: From soul and body to mind and nature

Philosophy and theology were closely linked at the beginning of the Early Modern period. Philosophy, like anatomy at this point, was in a very real sense a branch of theology in that it primarily focused on the workings of God. As time moved on, however, they became increasingly separated from one another. Philosophy, often taking its lead from the radical scepticism of Descartes, sought to understand the natural world as it existed. God was outside of the natural realm, and thus had to be studied through different means.

Descartes is a good place to begin, although he was only one of a number of philosophers to play a key role in redirecting the field. Descartes developed a radical

scepticism based on the idea that the only thing a thinker could logically be sure of was that they were thinking; this argument was captured in that most famous of philosophical maxims *cogito ergo sum* ('I think, therefore I am'). It follows logically from this that thought – that is, the mind – must be the seat of reason. Anatomists began to demonstrate compellingly that the body could be understood as a material mechanism; in a famous image captured brilliantly by Rembrandt, one could make the hand of a dead person move by pulling on a tendon in the forearm (Plate VIIIa). Such demonstrations led Descartes to argue that the force that stimulates the body to move, the soul/mind, must be separate from it.[33] That this did not capture the phenomenological reality of experience was something Descartes himself realized,[34] but it was nonetheless evident to him that mind and body were two separate entities, linked, he suggested, by the pineal gland in the brain. The mind was now the ghost in the machine, the mysterious essence of life which drove it. The explicit relationship Descartes invokes between body and machine is clear when he compares a sick person to a badly made clock.[35] It is an open question whether Descartes was the first to suggest that the body was best thought of as a machine, but the publication of his *Discourse on Method* in 1637 represents the moment when this began to become the dominant metaphor for understanding the human body within philosophy. Rather than a body linked to an eternal soul, the body became increasingly contrasted to the reasoning mind that dwelt within it. Later in the seventeenth century, these distinctions were elaborated by Locke, who suggested in 1694 that the self lay purely in the mind and was therefore entirely independent of the body.[36] The poet Alexander Pope's (1688–1744) famous passage places humans between base matter and divine beings in the traditional medieval *scala naturae* (cf. Chapter 6), but the Enlightenment emphasis is upon reason and the oxymoron which results when it is found in an animal's body:

> He hangs between; in doubt to act or rest,
> In doubt to deem himself a God or Beast,
> In doubt his mind or body to prefer;
> Born but to die, and reasoning but to err....
> Created half to rise and half to fall;
> Great lord of all things, yet a prey to all;
> Sole judge of truth, in endless error hurled;
> The glory, jest and riddle of the world!

Thus this changing philosophical discourse on the body, far from being contradicted by the theology we saw earlier, in fact seems to parallel it. In both cases, people increasingly began to relate *to* their body, whether as a sinful thing in need of discipline or as an object of study, rather than acknowledging that they *were* their bodies.

The Enlightenment reformulation of the body/soul dualism happened subtly, by degrees; the medieval inheritance was transformed without a dramatic rupture. But it had colossal consequences for the newly separated terms that emerged: the material body, the mind, and the separated, bounded, thinker examining them both. Descartes' radical scepticism, combined with the notion of the neutral and disembodied mind provided a whole new way of looking at the world, a new kind of gaze. As this gaze consumed and recorded all that it fell upon, so too the body would be further transformed through a process that would eventually come to be called science.

The empirical gaze: The emergence of knowledge specialists

A brief history of nature

At the heart of this new way of thinking was the idea of nature. 'Nature', as Raymond Williams notes,[37] is probably the most complicated word in the English language, capable of multiple and disparate interpretations.[38] For the ancient Greeks, the whole of nature was a living breathing organism, whilst in medieval times nature was understood in terms of the 'Great Chain of Being' (cf. Chapter 6).[39] The medieval understanding of nature was ambivalent; nature was part of God's majesty and, along with the Bible, a source for understanding divinity, but nature could also be a powerful and malevolent force capable of anything from benign indifference to wanton destruction. Early Modern thinkers inherited the theological concept of human uniqueness: humans alone had mastery over nature, which God had created to serve their needs. For Bacon and others, the purpose of the study of nature was to restore humanity's mastery over nature, lost since the Fall. Indeed, the mastery over nature demonstrated by farming and cultivation was central to the justification of English occupation of both Ireland and parts of the New World: land belonged to those who could dominate and exploit it rather than to 'children of Nature' merely inhabiting it.[40]

So began the study of natural history, the scientific naming of plants and animals, their recording and empirical study. Although a slow-moving and always partial development, such studies (alongside other scientific

developments) were to have unintended consequences. Following the work of Copernicus and Galileo in the sixteenth and seventeenth centuries, thinkers began to classify nature itself as a machine. For Galileo, only God and Man were outside of nature; the rest followed machine-like rules that could be calculated.[41] This was very much the line of reasoning taken by Isaac Newton. Newton, a devout and even mystical Christian, saw nature as an intricate, divinely constructed mechanism. God, a divine clockmaker, set it in motion and then stood outside it, letting it run according to its inbuilt rules without direct intervention. The 'natural philosopher' had the task of deducing these rules from empirical observation.

This echoed Descartes' arguments: the human mind was outside of nature, even if the body remained part of it. Thus we see that the idea of a natural body (cf. Chapter 2) and the concept of the body as machine were closely intertwined. Moreover, the stable and permanent condition of nature gave a baseline against which human change – history – could be measured. This fed into the ideas of seventeenth and eighteenth century political thinkers, particularly Thomas Hobbes, who argued that people had emerged from a basal 'state of nature' and were progressing, through the application of reason, towards a state of perfection. For Hobbes, the 'state of nature' was degraded and human life in it was 'solitary, poor, nasty, brutish and short'. In contrast, for Locke and Rousseau, humans in the 'state of nature' led the prosperous, peaceful and egalitarian lives of noble savages. By 1700, the difference between humans and beasts was increasingly seen in terms of 'culture',[42] a stage of civilization, a process of separating people from nature.[43] This separation was instantiated through the enclosure of the landscape, its mapping, and in the way it came to be represented in painting and continued in the eighteenth and nineteenth centuries (see following discussion). Moreover, the process of industrialization and urbanization pushed 'nature' as a pre-cultural baseline to the margins;[44] 'nature' was now a place away from the city, something you had to travel to visit. Temporally it lay in the past rather than the future.

A further twist in the meaning of 'nature' occurred with the Romantic movement via poets such as Wordsworth. Here 'nature', in the form of the rustic countryside, was lauded over the degraded and polluted city. Across the spectrum of thinkers, nature now was opposed to culture, as body was to mind, even as different sides declared each the superior of the other. It was also now associated not merely with the countryside but particularly with the wild and undomesticated, as opposed to culture even in the form of cultivated fields.[45] From this emerged the love of 'nature', getting 'back to nature', and modern environmental discourses. In tandem with this came a new emphasis on 'technology', represented by the factories and machines that were ever more prevalent. Technology too became a force external to nature, and eventually external to society as well, a subject we return to in detail in Chapter 8.

The final act of change, however, came via Darwin's *On the Origin of the Species* in 1859 and Spencer's concept of the 'survival of the fittest' in 1864. These harkened back to the Newtonian vision of a rule-bound nature, while also claiming that nature, far from being unchanging, was subject to its own process and development. This restored a sense of teleology and direction to nature.[46] Moreover, biological studies challenged human exceptionalism. Classificatory studies such as Linnaeus' *Systema Naturae* in 1735 portrayed humans as one animal amongst others.[47] How did thinkers balance this with the doctrine of human exceptionalism? For many scientists, they did so by invoking the Cartesian compromise: the human body was a material mechanism, it fell within 'nature' and could be studied scientifically, while the human 'soul' or 'mind' was unique and outside nature. The novelty of Darwin and Spencer's evolutionary views – Darwin was low-key about this in *The Origin of Species* but hinted at it in *The Expression of Emotions in Animals and Man* – was to treat humans entirely within a philosophy of materialism, without feeling the need of special clauses to explain the parallel derivation of the human mind or soul from divine sources. You could now understand all aspects of humanity – including reason and psyche – purely from a material, 'natural' basis.

Empiricism, knowledge and knowledge specialists

What were the consequences of this new philosophical approach for how scholars went about their work? If 'nature' was no longer a material veil for divine intention but a machine whose principles of operation could be deduced by human observers, this dictated new modes of study. Knowledge did not have to be mediated through authorities such as Aristotle and Galen, nor through texts such as the Bible. It could be accessed directly through observation.

The preferred sense of the new empiricism was sight. A key moment was the invention of the compound microscope at the very end of the sixteenth century and its use in the seventeenth century, although it was not until the nineteenth century that this device would be used in medical diagnosis. The microscope seemingly reveals truths to the inquisitive eye,[48] but this attitude tells as much about the period it was used in as the machine itself. At the heart of this lay a new relationship with vision,[49] which began to

be privileged above and beyond the other senses as never before. To see increasingly meant also to know, and this radical empiricism, in which everyone needs to see-it-for-themselves, opened the world to be studied through the extended application of the gaze.

Yet a focus upon verification by vision transformed both the observer and the observed. It separated the world into these two distinct categories. The ability to look, to see and, therefore, to understand was the property of an active subject rather than an inactive object.[50] As the mind became increasingly hidden behind the eyes, so it became increasingly separated from the world. It was now possible to look out onto a world, to observe it from a neutral position that was objective, even as it acted to objectify the things it could see. It is 'the harnessing of vision to a project of objectification that has reduced it to an instrument of disinterested observation'.[51] Matter now became ever more firmly separated from reason, as reason became the province of the observing subject, whilst matter was the object of this reasoned enquiry. Although echoing older separations between idea and material, these distinctions became increasingly hard and fast as the new epistemology of empiricism became dominant from the seventeenth century onwards.

Thus, at the start of the period, no clear distinctions existed between art and science. Artists such as Da Vinci straddled the divisions that would later emerge between disciplines and conducted experiments as well as painting pictures. Poets such as the Frenchman Du Bartas wrote works that combined the emergent sciences with art in a way that was hugely popular in the late sixteenth century and early seventeenth century.[52] These connections worked both ways; Vesalius explicitly drew on religious, classical and artistic imagery to both communicate and legitimate his anatomical studies (Figure 89). During the seventeenth century, such links became harder to sustain. Science became an increasingly prestigious and exclusively masculine field, distancing itself from art, poetry and literature. It began to rely less and less on allegories for justification and became increasingly understood as driving knowledge forward for its own sake, despite the best efforts of a few poets and thinkers, including women like Margaret Cavendish.[53] Science became increasingly valorized as the celebration of a clinical, detached and objective view of the world. Latour captures this distinction in the way in which two seventeenth-century thinkers divided the world between them: Robert Boyle and Thomas Hobbes. The former dealt with science and nature, the latter with politics and history. Despite the fact that both were making arguments that inevitably impacted the other, they nevertheless kept their worlds apart, leaving science (an empirical enterprise) on one side of an unbridgeable divide from society (a moral enterprise).[54] We return to this particular event, and its consequences, in Chapter 8.

The creation of the concept of material nature distanced from a knowing mind created 'knowledge' in the modern sense, and with it knowledge specialists. In so doing it also helped create the idea of a 'natural body' suitable for scientific study. Classical and medieval societies had previously contained specialists whose social role included authoritative command of beliefs about the world and the body, but these beliefs were usually justified through some mixture of appeal to received authorities, local logical reasoning (as in the medieval system of reasoning by allegory and affinity) and affirmation of first principles, often religious. 'Natural philosophers' (they were not known as 'scientists' until the nineteenth century) practiced direct and, in theory, objective observation. That this form of reasoning was viewed as part of a collective project of improvement-through-reason is shown by the seventeenth- and eighteenth-century foundation of learned societies in Britain, France and other countries, many of which continue today.

Religion, magic, superstition . . .

One cannot invent 'knowledge' without inventing its opposites. To put it less pithily, once one class of proposition is defined by a particular kind of logical support – appeal to empirical experience – others become implicitly or explicitly defined by a lack of such support. Hence, one defining characteristic of the Early Modern period is an increasing hardening of borders between 'knowledge' and 'belief', and between the fields of action defined in terms of them – science, religion and magic. Although the term 'magic' has a long medieval pedigree, 'knowledge' in the narrow sense of awareness based upon direct experience dates to the seventeenth century, and 'superstition' was first used in the modern sense in the mid-seventeenth century.

There is a huge literature on witchcraft and magic in the Early Modern period,[55] and here we mention only two key points. First, witchcraft, magic and religion all continued strongly in the 'Age of Reason'. These other modes of knowing the world did not go out of existence; indeed, many of them were thrown into sharper relief than ever before by critique and border policing from the new natural philosophy. It will be the mid-nineteenth century before the first major battles between religion and science (for instance), but the seeds were sown in the seventeenth century. Secondly, in many contexts, magic and religion were not defective alternatives to empirical reasoning; they addressed other kinds of concerns through other modes of knowing.

Thus witchcraft persisted, and even became more prominent than ever before. Witchcraft was about more than the practice of magic, which undoubtedly took place in this period;[56] instead, it was about pledging one's soul to the devil. It was this 'crime' that people believed to be widespread throughout Europe, particularly in the Holy Roman Empire. Women were especially vulnerable to witchcraft accusations, both because of the marginal position of older widows in society and (in the medieval tradition; see Chapter 6) because women were seen as more vulnerable to demonic temptations and invasion. Although men were also tried and executed for witchcraft (and were in the majority in Russia[57]), in Western Europe, women made up 75 to 85 per cent of those executed as witches.[58] The extent to which people believed witchcraft to be a widespread phenomenon and a real danger can be gathered from some of the claims about the numbers of witches. Demonologist Henri Boguet claimed there were 1,800,000 witches in Europe! Even without such hysterical claims, witch hunts were a feature across Europe in the sixteenth to eighteenth centuries, particularly in those countries that relied both on inquisitorial investigation practices and torture.[59]

Witchcraft was always entwined with conceptions of the body, and it changed as they changed. It was not until the late seventeenth century that witch hunts began to decline. By this stage, some 60,000 people had been executed, most burnt at the stake. In one Early Modern continuation of the medieval scientific view, the porous, permeable body, particularly women's, was constantly at risk from external forces.[60] When that environment included the Devil and his minions, it is hardly surprising that the body was viewed as a site at risk! By contrast, the Cartesian concept of the body as machine undermined the possibilities for witchcraft.[61] The body as machine was not as vulnerable to outside spiritual forces. Simultaneously, empiricism was related to renewed scepticism of invisible agents of evil, undermining the case for witch trials. The decline in witch trials by the end of the seventeenth century (the last major ones were the Salem, Massachusetts trials of 1692) resulted from wider changes in social life, but changing conceptions of the human body played a part.

Although witchcraft passed, other forms of magic or folk belief about bodies continued. One set of beliefs focused upon the innate potency of the human body. Through the mid-nineteenth century, 'mummy' (the flesh of dead bodies, dried and pounded into a paste-like consistency) was widely used as a medicinal ingredient by both physicians and folk healers (indeed, this use of the word long predates its application to Egyptian mummies). The flesh needed could be obtained from buried bodies or from hanged men. At the core of this was a belief that the dead body, as a substance, possessed an inherent potency.[62] Such beliefs often focused upon the questionable boundaries between life and death. Scientific journals into the eighteenth century were happy to publish articles telling tales of homunculi springing from the powder of a crushed skull. Similarly, it was often believed that a murdered corpse could identify its killer by signs or noises. One example of this kind of belief was the 'Hand of Glory' (Plate VIIIc). This was the idea that the hand of a hanged criminal could bring specific magical powers to the bearer – for example that it would keep people asleep in a house as it was being burgled.[63] More generally, the hand of an executed criminal brought fortune; the hands of hanged men were cut off and preserved as charms or talismans. As in our earlier vignette, the touch of the hanged man's hand was commonly thought to bring healing to particular ailments. These beliefs were by no means only held by uneducated members of the populous. For example, William Harvey – a fixture in narratives about scientific progress for his investigations of the heart's action – firmly believed in the agency of the dead body. These folk understandings provided an important alternative modality with which to engage the body.

Such beliefs changed with the times, as the body took centre stage in the fears and hopes of people right into the nineteenth century. Often these were directly connected to bodily themes like sexuality. This is particularly noticeable in the Gothic romances that flourished in Britain after the publication of Horace Walpole's *The Castle of Otranto* in 1764. Famous novels such as Bram Stoker's *Dracula* (1897) played on bodily desires, sexuality and the boundaries between the living and the dead. More striking still is Mary Shelley's *Frankenstein*, published in 1818. In this novel, a young scientist, Dr Victor Frankenstein, builds a new form of life by reanimating a corpse. Narratives about monsters threatening humans were not new, of course. At different points throughout the medieval and Early Modern period, witches, Jews, Catholics, Protestants, werewolves, vampires and others had provided examples of threatening bodies running amok. Often such stories used bodily anomalies or transformations into animals to underline the body's capacity for destabilizing social relations. With colonial expansion, people with exotic appearances and incomprehensible habits formed another ingredient for bodily utopias and dystopias; as we will see later, the concept of 'race' developed in this period as a particular kind of colonial fantasy. But *Frankenstein* marks a true watershed. It is

no coincidence it appears in the days of Dickens' traumatic childhood, as the urban and industrial explosion of nineteenth century Britain was reaching its crescendo; like the Romantic poets, *Frankenstein* sees the threat to humans not from wilderness but from scientific progress, the cities and their 'dark Satanic mills'. As in Stevenson's *Dr Jekyll and Mr Hyde* (1886), the natural body is not transformed into a monster by magic but by science; and the unnatural monster is also partially a victim. From here on, the dystopic fantasy is about technology's ability to transform monstrously. It is a fantasy which still grips us today – we return to this in Chapter 8.

The medical gaze and the body as machine

Part of the new empiricism was the development of what Foucault called 'the medical gaze'. The Cartesian view was predisposed to this because, as the observing subject was progressively located in the mind, the body became an external object suitable for study through vision. Much as the scientific gaze was a new way of looking at the world, so the medical gaze was a new way of looking at the body. It defined closely and normatively what was normal or healthy and what was not. Moreover, it mapped body space in an increasingly controlled manner; for example, where diseases were located and how they related to particular organs was increasingly specified, to the point that Foucault describes it as 'a new distribution of the discrete elements of corporeal space'.[64] In other words, the emergence of medicine was not a simple process of discovering pre-existing truths about the body, but rather a new way of defining what that body was. This was accomplished by dividing the body into structures, objects and parts that could successfully be identified as mattering. This parsing of the body into internal structures played a key role in how the body came to be understood as a machine. Like machines, bodies could be seen as having parts whose form was repeated, even standardized, which performed specific functions and which might break in predictable ways. Previously, bodies were similar to one another because each was a microcosm of the world around it; now, particularly through studies of comparative anatomy, bodies were regarded as similar based upon machine-like criteria of form, internal organization and function. Just as nature was a machine suitable for study, so was the new natural body.

How did this generalized change work in specific practices? It is worth examining how these areas play out in three key areas: anatomy, autopsy and prosthesis. These emerge, broadly, through time during the sixteenth and seventeenth centuries, at the end of the eighteenth century and during the nineteenth century. They thus reveal the manner in which medicine helped to remake the body world through the Early Modern and Modern periods.

Anatomy

Anatomy was one of the principal ways in which the body was transformed, at least in medical contexts, from a microcosm of the universe to a kind of machine. Anatomy expanded extensively in the sixteenth century. Prior to Vesalius, anatomy and medicine were understood as substantiating Classical sources and the Bible. Through the sixteenth and seventeenth centuries, however, this evolved. The work of Vesalius and others began to challenge Galen's texts.

Initially, anatomical dissection was conceived explicitly as the exploration of the human body.[65] This drew upon the medieval idea of the body as a microcosm of the world. Just as sixteenth-century explorers were charting and colonizing unknown territories in the New World, so anatomists took on the challenge of exploring and colonizing the human body. The body was a mysterious place, full of unknown corners, dark liquids and terrible possibilities. By shining a light on these, by seeing them, anatomists began the process of domesticating the human body philosophically. In doing so, they formed a crucial part of the emergence of the new scientific world view. The knowledge generated by Vesalius and others challenged medieval scholasticism, setting the scene for Bacon and others to propose the first truly empiricist methodologies early in the seventeenth century.

Just as the New World had to be seen to be believed, so did the secrets of the human body. Opening the body was now vital to obtaining knowledge.[66] Nowhere is this geographical exploration of the body more explicitly evoked than in the seventeenth century poet John Donne's quasi-geographical exploration of his lover's body in Elegie XIX:[67]

> Licence my roaving hands, and let them go,
> Before, behind, between, above, below.
> Oh my America! My new-found-land
> My kingdom, safeliest when with one man man'd.

Vesalius' work was based in the paradigm of the body as microcosm, but it laid the ground for what would follow. As Sawday puts it 'the period between (roughly) 1540 and 1640, is, therefore, the period of the discovery of the Vesalian body as opposed to the later invention of the Harveian or Cartesian body'.[68] One goal of dissection, expressed in both anatomy and poetry, was

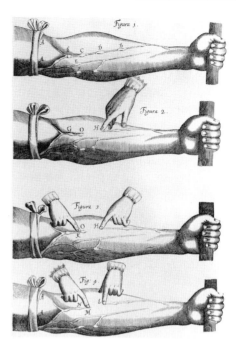

Figure 88. Harvey demonstrated the circulation of blood through ligatures at specific points, much as one would measure a hydraulic system. Illustration from his *Exercitatio anatomica de motu cordis et sanguinis in animalibus*, 1628 (© Wellcome Library, London).

to explore the mysterious natures of different organs. Stomachs, tongues, livers, hearts and other organs were increasingly understood as having 'eerily individuated agencies'[69] which made them behave in contradictory ways. During the sixteenth and early seventeenth century the opening of the body was central to obtaining knowledge precisely because of the manner in which different organs might reveal different qualities. 'Virtue and sin, for example, were often imagined as literally inhabiting bodily innards'.[70]

From beginnings rooted in Classical and medieval medical theory, the explorations of the body also, in one sense, led to the emergence of the idea of the body as machine. The complexity of the body dumbfounded many anatomists, and this was one of the many reasons why a machine began to emerge as a better metaphor than an undiscovered land. Vesalius and other sixteenth-century anatomists thus paved the way for later thinkers such as William Harvey, whose discovery of the circulation of the blood, announced in 1616, marked the beginning of the end for the idea that the body was dominated by four humours. Harvey's investigation of the heart revealed the engine of this machine, the pump which drove it (Figure 88).

Anatomy reached out into daily life, both inspiring and terrifying people.[71] The metaphor spread into literature with Burton's *The Anatomy of Melancholy* (1621), and throughout the sixteenth and seventeenth

Figure 90. Nineteenth century graves in the foreground; fences protect the graves from potential robbing by 'resurrectionists' (photo courtesy of Dr Martyn L. Gorman).

Figure 89. Vesalian image drawing explicitly on classical statuary (© Wellcome Library, London).

centuries, poets explicitly linked dissection to sex. Anatomical dissection was also a public spectacle. Before the late seventeenth century, crowds would attend Vesalius and others working in anatomical theatres across Europe. These were really the Early Modern equivalent of the 'Body Worlds' exhibition (Chapter 1), and were equally sensationalist. Thus in the organisation of these theatres, which really were set up for public viewing, in the performance of dissection, and in the display of the dissected corpse in anatomical books, it is clear that anatomists took great care to legitimate their actions. Sixteenth- and seventeenth-century anatomists took care to show themselves as men acting on God's injunction to 'know thyself'; they sought to reveal His wonder and majesty to the world. As we noted earlier, the display of bodies in books like *De Humani Corporis Fabrica* explicitly drew on Christian and classical imagery to associate itself with scholastic legitimacy (Figure 89). Images of the body demonstrating itself to the person watching drew 'on a dense network of sacred imagery surrounding the figure of Christ in various stages of the passion'.[72]

Thus in its initial centuries, anatomy was not yet legitimated principally by what we would recognize as a scientific drive to know more. Instead, it was proposed as a continuation of older regimes of knowledge. Here, unlike in eighteenth- and nineteenth-century medical school practice, dissected cadavers were not anonymized and denied identity or history; instead that identity became an important part of the process.[73] Only later, once the body was a generic machine, could the investig-

ation of its internal workings be conducted in laboratory-like solitude, cut off from its history and identity: the body as faceless scientific object. Before this the anatomy theatre was an arena for the worship of God, through the spectacular dissection of a known person.

Yet at the same time, for most people, anatomy was not something to be desired but rather something to be feared. Fear of the anatomist's touch continued up through the eighteenth and nineteenth centuries. After the Murder Act of 1752, people who committed murder were turned over to the anatomists after execution, though this could cause outrage and even violence amongst the crowds watching the hanging. Between 1752 and the Anatomy Act of 1832, the demand for bodies rose as the number of executions fell. The 'Resurrectionists' were grave robbers who would dig up freshly buried bodies to supply cadavers for research. Fear of being resurrected for dissection led some people to take steps to prevent this from happening (Figure 90). In one famous case, the so-called Irish Giant, Charles Byrne, is reputed to have asked to be buried at sea, as otherwise anatomists would snatch his extraordinarily tall body for dissection (in the event, however, the anatomist John Hunter succeeded in doing so, and his skeleton is now in the Hunterian Museum in Glasgow). Dissection denied the body a sense of personhood and identity, particularly as dissection concentrated ever more on the generalized objectified body in the cold and distanced world of scientific research. The assumption, which ran counter to theological arguments, was that 'dissected bodies would not resurrect'.[74] In this context, it is interesting indeed to note that some bodies were reconstituted for burial after they had been dissected. For example, following

Figure 91. Autopsied and reassembled body from Humber (c. 1800). The skull, which shows clear sign of undergoing a craniotomy, had been glued back together, and much of the torso, including the ribs and pelvis, had been removed. A wooden stake was inserted where the spine would have been to allow the body to hold together when it was stitched back together for burial. (Photo courtesy of Warwick Rodwell.)

anatomical dissection, the burial in Figure 91 from Barton on Humber had the skull glued back together and a wooden stake inserted where the spine would have been in order to give the body rigidity. For most people, the fear of body snatching (and of being dissected alive in cases of mistaken burial) far outweighed its actual occurrence.

Autopsy

Within this world of research, and as knowledge of the body increased, anatomists began to examine bodies also for their individual characteristics. Rather than merely exploring the bodies of executed criminals, anatomists began increasingly to explore the bodies of people who had died of natural causes. This was not entirely new – the bodies of kings had long been examined to ensure they had suffered a natural death – but its expansion to a much larger proportion of the population, and the understanding of the body it rested on, was novel. In 1761 Giovanni Battista Morgagni published *The Seats and Causes of Diseases Investigated by Anatomy* based on his own personal experience of more than 700 autopsies.[75] Morgagni's work represented the first systematic attempt to catalogue the effects of disease on the human body, though it was not until the early nineteenth century that this could be linked to the diagnosis of live patients. Autopsy was a predictable step in the development of the concept that the body was a machine; once its basic functioning and normal condition were understood, broken down examples could be diagnosed. As the French doctor Marie Francois Xavier Bichat put it 'open a few corpses, and the airy wisdom of the ancients will disappear'.[76] Bichat belonged to the Paris School in post-revolutionary France.[77] Using the hospitals surrounding Paris (there were more hospital beds there than in the whole of Britain at the time) they had access to thousands of diseased corpses which they set about dissecting and understanding. Not only did the

Paris School advance the understanding of disease and medicine, they also completed the transformation of anatomy. As the 'Bills of Death' written out for each death in eighteenth-century London attest, it was now normal practice to investigate and assign a cause of death. That cause of death had to be accountable in medical terms, even if it was only 'old age'; 'God's will' is conspicuous in Bills of Mortality by its absence.[78] People needed to understand how and why a particular machine had come to break down.

Anatomy and autopsy were essential in producing the medical gaze. Through both, the body became a space through which new kinds of understanding could be articulated. The new language of medicine, and the places and spaces it describes, were not neutral arbiters, but rather particular ways of looking at the world and speaking about it. As physicians began to link the results from autopsies to diagnosis, the relationship between symptom and disease increasingly became one between sign and signified. Symptoms in living patients could now be understood as signifying a deeper problem, usually located within the organs. Foucault traces this change in the simple physician's question of 'what's the matter with you?' becoming 'where does it hurt?' revealing the ways in which medicine now located disease and pain in space.[79]

Prosthesis

Prosthesis was the next logical step in the mechanization of the body. By the nineteenth century, the increased use and technical sophistication of prosthetics meant they played an important role in producing new understandings of the body. Prosthetics of various kinds had been in use for centuries at this point. But particularly after the 1850s, discourses about prostheses reveal the ongoing changes in how the body was understood.[80] Moreover, while some amputees disregarded the severed limb, others wished to be buried with it in order to ensure bodily wholeness after Christian resurrection.[81] For the living, as the materialist bent of the nineteenth century continued, integrity of the body came to be explicitly linked to the integrity of the mind. Loss of part of the body threatened the wholeness and well-being of the mind. Although a majority of patients with serious amputations died, warfare and accidents resulting from increasingly industrialized workplaces meant that a significant number of people were living without a limb. Furthermore, with improved surgical techniques and anaesthesia, by the end of the century not only were more amputations being performed, more people were surviving them.

Prosthetics assumed a natural body; they were designed to look and function increasingly realistically

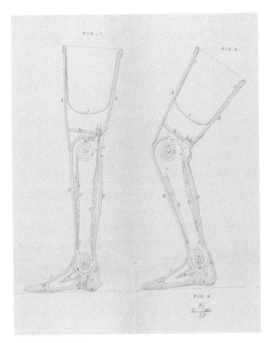

Figure 92. Patent for the design of a prosthetic leg by William Edward Newton, 1857 (© Wellcome Library, London).

and to match the capabilities of the original limb. This idea of prosthesis also added to the notion of the body as machine, where parts could be manufactured to replace the old ones; these parts would be equivalent to (and sometimes even superior to) their original (Figure 92). Engineered prosthetic limbs were explicitly marketed to be ever more life-like, ever more capable of replacing that which had been lost.[82] Prosthetics addressed the psychological effects of amputation. The stump in particular was seen almost as a separate agent, one given to hysteria, not least in the commonly held feeling of the 'phantom' limb (this is the notion, familiar today, that amputees continue to sense the absent limb). Prosthetics restore the image of bodily integrity. Although they may not have answered theological questions about the fate of dismembered bodies in the next world, they at least restored its wholeness in this one. For injured male soldiers, for example, this also restored a sense of masculinity often based on bodily wholeness and prowess; they literally re*membered* the patient.[83]

Anatomy from the sixteenth century, autopsy from the eighteenth and the increasing development of prosthetics in the nineteenth century are three broadly chronological developments in the history of medicine that were intimately bound up with the production of new ways of understanding the body. Other aspects of 'science' also contributed to this new way of thinking, for instance Bacon's seventeenth century development of a scientific methodology itself, and research into sexual difference, which also began to transform the body from a

hierarchically ordered microcosm of the universe to a biologically defined and sexed machine. Each played a role in redefining the body as a natural machine, with diagnostic procedures and replacement parts in case of failure. The development of anatomy in particular underlines a fundamental irony: a technique which originated to bring together God and Galen ultimately drove them apart.

Social presentation and interiority: The body as person

As we have seen, medieval people located a sense of personhood in the lived body, and in the union – inviolable even after death, via the doctrine of resurrection – of body and soul. As these areas – theology, philosophy, the study of nature and medicine – emerged together to create a new body world and with it an understanding of the body as a machine rather than as a microcosm of the world around it, the mind was split off from the physical body. As the physical body became increasingly distanced from the locus of reason and spirit, what became of the person and the sense of individual identity?

By and large, Renaissance thinkers continued the medieval tradition of treating the body's external features as an outward manifestation of internal character, for instance with Shakespeare's Richard III whose deformity manifests his inner villainy.[84] This was both an aesthetic concept of the material world reflecting an essential spiritual design and a consequence of medical theory in which emotions, thought, imagination and appearance affected and were affected by the humours.[85] Similarly, it is clear that at the start of the Early Modern period, bodies, especially those of women, were considered to be extremely porous to influences of environment, diet and external events. In fact, even souls could be transformed by both diet and digestion.[86] Words, for example, were understood to affect the body directly, and particular events such as changes in the weather could alter the balance of humours, transforming people's moods, health and well-being. This is revealed in all sorts of practice from eating and attitudes towards the dead, to the way magical spells using particular words could be used to 'expose the fragility' of the boundaries between self and the world.[87] As in the medieval period, this openness to external influences was an opportunity for magical as well as medical practices upon the body.

The rise of the Enlightenment view, and the emergence of the body as machine, had two interesting consequences. First, as anatomy, and later the medical gaze more generally, came to define the location of the body in space, so the boundaries of the body came to be increasingly policed. It may seem counter-intuitive to suggest that a practice such as anatomy that so clearly fragments the body had a role in keeping it enclosed, yet this is precisely what slowly occurred through the Early Modern and Modern periods. Fragmenting the body allowed each piece to be named, domesticated and controlled. The body became a form of property, and like all property it needed to be bounded and defined. Thus, simultaneously, the practice of anatomy both pulled apart different parts of the body and constituted what it was that made up a body in the first place. Divisibility and indivisibility emerge together at the expense of permeability.[88] This coincided with social changes involving the increased boundedness and spatial control of the body (see discussion later in this chapter).

Secondly, where was the person? How was the experiencing subject understood? The 'body as machine' view never supplanted other views of how the body related to the person; rather, it supplemented them. It is here we gain additional signs of multimodality in this body world. Whereas in science, theology and philosophy the body was ever more machine-like and separated from the person, in other areas the body became increasingly associated with the unique individual – the body as person. Here, it is worth noting two senses in which Early Modern people felt that the body remained the locus of subjective experience.

The first is through the life of the body – dress, food, drink, music, dance, sex, fighting and so on. There is no evidence that seventeenth- through nineteenth-century people were any less interested in the pleasures of the body than in previous or later centuries. Outside relatively narrow Puritan circles, dress (sometimes remarkably elaborate) continued to be a medium of self-presentation. With rising literacy and middle-class prosperity, this is the period in which we see the rise of the cookbook, with abundant evidence that cooks were interested not only in sustenance and economy but the pleasures of the table as well. Glimpses of private life through diaries such as Samuel Pepys' and satirical works of Swift and Hogarth show the enduring attraction of the licit and illicit pleasures of the flesh.

Even in death, the body was not only a site of mourning as the bereaved said farewell to a loved individual; it remained a last moment of social display as funerals were conducted with ostentation befitting the social position of the dead person and sometimes remarkably ornate monuments were erected. As noted earlier, distancing the soul from the body both in life and in the afterlife paradoxically focused attention on burial as a final commemoration of the person. Thus, men like Sherlock, Boyd and Becon decried the body, declaring it to be filthy and

disgusting, mere carrion as soon as the soul had departed. Indeed Boyd argued that 'the losse of burial is no great losse',[89] and for him, as we have already noted, all memorial services and inscriptions were a waste of money and a demonstration of sinful pride. Despite this, many of these same churchmen were buried with pomp and circumstance in places of note. Sherlock was entombed at St Paul's, while Becon was probably buried at Canterbury Cathedral. More generally, large and ostentatious monuments proclaiming the deceased's religious piety are widespread, despite the fact that doctrinal thought explicitly declared such memorials to be height of vanity. In fact, as we move into the Modern period, so the prominence, permanence and frequency of tombstones increased; in the eighteenth and nineteenth centuries, tombstones moved from being the preserve of the well off to being standard for most of the population.[90]

Discourse and practice here do not tally with one another. The increased emphasis on the dignity of the corpse also helps explain why it was that many people regarded the possibility of being dissected with great abhorrence, even going to extensive lengths to protect their graves. Similarly, throughout this period there is growing evidence for embalming, which became more widespread and more technologically sophisticated. The body was permanently discarded at death, but people remained emotionally attached to it; hence attempts to hang onto it for a bit longer, to retard the decaying effects of death, at least cosmetically.[91]

The body was thus still a place where personhood was enacted; if anything the added emphasis on comportment, culture, boundaries, dress and so on increased the association between body and person. It is interesting how little scientific theorists had to say about such lived experiences. Having located subjectivity in the reasoning mind and dedicated themselves to understanding the body's physical structure, there was very little attempt to develop any 'scientific' psychological theory until the mid- to late-nineteenth century. Phrenology may have been the first such effort. Developed by the Swiss physician Gall in the later eighteenth century, phrenology held that a person's character could be read in cranial bulges which revealed the development of different areas of the brain where characteristics such as intelligence, confidence and sensitivity were located (Figure 93). Although phrenology was generally, and justifiably, abandoned by 1900, one can understand how it filled a vacant niche defined by intellectual developments of its time. It neatly tied together developing ideas about the brain which were important in racial classification (see discussion later in this chapter) with an attempt to get at inner character through 'scientific' means. It effectively attempted

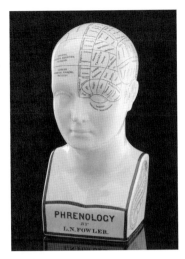

Figure 93. Phrenological model showing where in the skull various mental faculties were supposedly located (© Science Museum London, Wellcome Images).

to make inner subjectivity visible externally as part of the 'medical gaze'. But until, and besides, this abortive effort, scientists were generally content to leave experience and comportment to poets, romantic philosophers such as Rousseau, and moralizing theologians. This of course, would change dramatically in the twentieth century with the development of psychology, psychiatry and pharmacology.

Secondly, in the Enlightenment view, the mind increasingly was internal, hidden from the scientist's view; it was the examiner, not the examined.[92] This rendered the surface of the body increasingly superficial, a mechanical product with little connection to mind or individuality. The internal character of the person was understood as lying inside, not immediately visible. This transition is clear within the increasingly popular genre of portrait painting. By and large medieval depictions of people have little concern with individuality; people are given the stock features to denote their 'type' or qualities such as beauty or manliness. Renaissance humanists such as Leonardo and Ghirlandaio sought increasingly to portray individuality via the face and features, although in general the story line of the personality portrayed was straightforward: eminence, thoughtfulness, beauty, prosperity. It is in the seventeenth and eighteenth centuries that the balance shifts and portrait painters increasingly sought to capture the interior character. The painter's eye sought out details of expression and gesture which revealed an 'inner' nature, sometimes at odds with the official story line of wealth or social position. Moreover, it is in this period that we see the first true self-portraits, with the implication that painting was not so much an act of depicting a surface body but one of seeking to reveal an inner self (Figure 94). It is not coincidental that the first documented usage of the term 'introspection' to mean 'looking inwards to seek knowledge of oneself' dates to 1676, when one M. Hale defined 'introspection' as

The actings of the Mind or Imagination itself, by way of reflection or introspection of themselves.[93]

Thus portraiture became almost a branch of divination, and people like Oliver Cromwell could confidently demand that their artists painted them 'warts and all'. At the same time this also helped to affirm the importance of the individual and their association with their body. This ran counter to the opposition between body and mind as we have seen, and this represents clear evidence for multimodality within this body world. This association between body as person, just like body as machine, would continue in importance in future periods as we will see in Chapter 8.

(a)

(b)

(c)

Figure 94. Representations of known people. A. Medieval: bust of Princess Marie de France, fourteenth century. B. Early Renaissance: Domenico Ghirlandaio, 'Portrait of a Woman' (ca. 1487). C. Early Modern: self-portrait, Rembrandt, 1660. (All three images © The Metropolitan Museum of Art.)

Disciplining the body

Our discussion thus far has kept fairly closely to the 'wigs in salons' style of writing intellectual history through the actions of scientists, philosophers and artists, though with occasional forays into the more popular world of magic and burial. Yet most people in this period probably never heard of Descartes, Vesalius or Harvey; they lived outside the intellectual spheres which bulk large in the history of religion, philosophy and medicine. We now turn to other aspects of the body world, the important changes in how bodies were enacted on the ground in daily life. Sometimes these changes contradicted or reacted against what was happening in intellectual circles; sometimes they overlapped with them. One of the most striking and powerful features of the post-medieval body is the way in which, by the mid-nineteenth century, mechanistic and materialistic trends in medicine and science converged dramatically with the daily experience of bodily discipline in homes and industrial workplaces.

Civilizing bodies: Distance and boundedness

From later medieval times onwards, there has been an increasing emphasis upon controlling the body. This particularly involves fixing and policing the boundaries of the body: concealing its exhalations and leakages, restraining and synchronizing its gestures. Although not as widespread as sometimes claimed, later medieval and modern manuals of comportment increasingly dictate how to blow the nose, how to move at a dinner table, how to approach others in public, and so on.[94] Posture in particular was important, and the demands on people's bodies became increasingly specific and strict, in part because of Renaissance theories of microcosmic body geometries. Dancing and fencing were taught which placed specific controls on bodily deportment.[95] Clothes began to be produced that would forcibly shape the body; it is in the sixteenth century that the whalebone corset makes its first appearance. The central concept behind many of these developments was self-control; as the body became more of a machine and less of a map, good breeding was revealed in restraint, in the reasoning mind's control. These things were also affected by an increase in laws surrounding hygiene (amongst others), showing the importance of the state in exerting social pressures.

Domestic space: The body at home

As anyone who has visited a museum of 'period rooms' will know, the Early Modern period saw a sweeping reorganization of domestic space. Just as the structures of the body became defined and individuated through the processes of anatomy, so domestic spaces were increasingly defined and individuated in the Early Modern period. Even prosperous medieval houses tended to have few rooms and little furniture by modern standards. This does not reflect primitive simplicity or material poverty; instead, people lived together with little concern for privacy and rooms tended to be used for multiple functions, with movable, general purpose furniture. From the sixteenth century onwards, rooms began increasingly to be defined and furnished for particular purposes, and for particular people. In the medieval period, servants and masters ate together in a single hall, seated in a manner that expressed their relative status; servants now became increasingly separated from the main body of the house, eating away from the family and spending more time outdoors. Bedrooms began to be separated off and put into more 'private' areas of the house, those furthest away from public access. During the seventeenth century, the list of particular rooms becomes ever longer. Other activities such as entertainment that had previously taken place outside the house (for instance, in inns) began to take place within it, and these too required further specialized rooms. This process reached new levels in the eighteenth century with the widespread adoption of Georgian architecture and ground plans, where servants could be relegated to the back of the house and special rooms were used for functions such as receiving guests and dining formally.[96] The same differentiation increasingly occurred in public spaces as well, for instance, as inns began to provide separate chambers and beds for travellers. Many people could not afford such spatial niceties, of course; both urban and rural poor continued to live in small, undifferentiated houses with many people crammed together in each room. Unburdened by middle-class sensibilities, when the poor were charitably provided with extra rooms to allow boys and girls to sleep separately, they often rented them out to gain extra income instead.[97] But the idea of separating and dividing spaces to segregate people and functions – modern 'privacy' – steadily became more widespread amongst society as a whole.

Below the level of architecture we can trace some of the dividing technologies of this period in more intimate bodily practices. Cooking and eating became increasingly separated spatially, socially and materially. Sixteenth century foods were cooked and served in similar pots; by 1750 a whole range of distinctive material containers had emerged to cook, serve and preserve food in.[98] Plates and dishes differentiated, and cutlery was provided rather than each eater using his or her own knife. It was in this period that forks became widely popular, starting in Italy and eventually moving across Europe.[99] Long benches were increasingly replaced by individual stools or seats, with each person now sitting in a separate and defined place.[100] Like formal dances, the formal dinner service, as a social technology, fitted household members, guests and servants into an intricate social ritual of precedence and rank, differentiation and coordinated action.[101]

The new technologies of food consumption and new kinds of architecture further bounded bodies off from one another. Each body could be seen, like the collections of crockery or cutlery as one part of a broader set. Each individual piece was like the others, could be replaced by another, but each piece at the same time played its role in the overall construction. The body was both a part of a machine, but also a machine in its own right. It was in the rhythmic practices of daily life and with and through the changes in material culture that this aspect of the body world became prominent.

The body in the landscape: Boundedness, order and vision

The routine experience of living, moving and dwelling in particular kinds of architecture or landscapes impacts directly on how people come to understand their own bodies (cf. Chapter 3). As with dissection and the medical gaze, and in domestic spaces, the body's relationship to space was becoming increasingly tightly defined in the scale of landscapes as well.

Throughout the Early Modern period and the nineteenth century, the landscape was increasingly enclosed. In the process of enclosure, communal farmland was appropriated by private landowners intent upon maximizing profit from grazing or arable farming. Enclosure was part of a general shift from a modest mercantile economy to an aggressively capitalist one. What enclosure also brought with it, however, were new bodily practices and new ways of experiencing landscape. People had to find new routes through the landscape as old paths were blocked, new forms of access to land they had worked all their lives. Particularly where the change was swift and dramatic, people's experience of landscape could change very rapidly, creating, as Johnson suggests, 'new forms of social and cultural boundedness'.[102] Moreover, instead of farming in ways that involved collective responsibility for fields, people worked in fields through relations of employment, often exploitative, whose units were individuals and whose boundaries were boundaries of power. The daily routines that made up people's lives, the unthinking practices that formed the habitus of living in the landscape, must also have changed.[103]

At an even greater scale, as the house, body and local landscape became increasingly bounded, so did the nation state, with firmer borders, policed by new kinds of armies fighting new kinds of war. Just as bodies came under threat both from within and without in the new discourse of medicine, so the nation state was under threat from foreign enemies and domestic rebels, the latter anxiety only increasing in Europe after 1789. These boundaries were marked and defined precisely through the new forms of maps that began to develop, adding another aspect to the manner in which cartography changed people's relationships with space.[104]

The Enlightenment vision also reordered the aesthetics of landscape via projects of cartography, landscape design and painting. Medieval maps were mostly cosmological imaginings (Chapter 6); cartography in a modern sense originated from the seventeenth century onwards, and was associated with economic and political control, both in local land surveying and in overseas colonial expansion. Cartography was based upon a vision of Cartesian intelligence, and was invented as a way of showing the world that is not from the spatial standpoint of any viewer at all. This physically impossible representation derives from assuming a disembodied, purely rational viewer who does not stand at any single point but is omnipresent and objective. Space here is uniform and absolute rather than understood from the embodied experience of the viewer (as in perspective drawings or medieval route-maps). Once invented, cartographic understandings changed how people understood and moved in the landscape.[105] In contrast, landscape gardening by architects such as Lancelot 'Capability' Brown placed the embodied viewer firmly in the landscape, but manipulated it to project a socially contextualized vision. One element was the idea of 'nature', which here meant a carefully designed stage-set from which signs of human presence had been artfully erased, in contrast with the civilizing presence of human rationality. As landscape was increasingly understood as a passive backdrop, so it was increasingly feminized, associated with women and suitable for men to take control of and dominate through rationality.[106] Landscape designs based upon rational geometric principles instilled a habitus based upon the principle that 'man's' domination of Nature, and the upper class's domination of society, was based upon their command of Reason.[107] This echoed in the landscape the opposition of mind and body, reinforcing these distinctions.

Landscape painting similarly projected a new 'way of seeing'.[108] The genre originated in the sixteenth century in Italy and the Netherlands and was associated with forms of perspective that located the viewer at a single central point and allowed them to survey and control space visually.[109] As a genre, landscapes became increasingly popular particularly in the nineteenth century, precisely as more people became distanced from 'nature'. Landscapes allowed the spectator to appropriate views through this gaze. Just as the countryside itself was being divided and enclosed, so new forms of representation emerged that allowed people to objectify, appreciate, and alienate it. Pictures, and access to them by the wealthy, thus reified the consequences of enclosure.[110] As a form of discourse, landscape pictures simultaneously place the viewer at the centre and render them absent, outside the frame, gazing at the workers who, like cattle, so often feature in them. They enact a separation between the seeing-eye and the world around them and a class-based connoisseurship which identified the possessing eye with the seeing-eye.

Discipline, not punish: The body as part of a social machine

One of the most striking changes in the Early Modern body world is summed up under Foucault's term 'discipline'. As we saw at the beginning of this chapter, this refers to a sweeping shift in how the body was treated across a range of contexts, including in the workhouses of the poor, the asylums of the insane and schools for children. The shift happened above all in the eighteenth century. As we saw in Chapter 2, Foucault contrasts the punishment of criminals in the early eighteenth century with how criminals were dealt with by 1800. In the former, prison tended to be for short stays to hold prisoners before punishment, not as a punishment in itself. When an assassin who had killed the French king was put to death in 1757, the execution was spectacular and exemplary. As in high-profile medieval executions, the criminal was paraded through the streets, mocked and reviled, and tortured in ways designed to cause the most pain and humiliation possible. The violent ritual demonstrated the horror of his crime. Just eighty years later, prison had become institutionalized in a way which still looks familiar today. More people were held in prison as a punishment in itself, with sentences, not physical pain, calculated to match the severity of crimes. Detailed guidelines specified the spaces prisoners occupied, the arrangements to survey them, the timetables of seclusion, exercise and activity they followed, and the surveillance arrangements to control them. In effect, prisoners were micromanaged, with the position and habits of their bodies planned rationally to create calculated effects upon them. Rather than a spectacle aimed at demonstrating the power of the state over the body of the criminal, punishment was

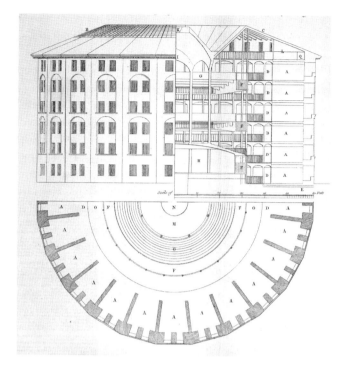

Figure 95. Surveillance and bodily routine: Bentham's 'panopticon' design for model prisons (© Cambridge University Library).

now a process of measured discipline.[111] This is not to say that the spectacular display of the punished corpse came to an end suddenly. In Britain, the public gibbeting of corpses continued until the 1830s. Nevertheless this process was in decline as the disciplining of bodies increased.

This disciplining of bodies became increasingly widespread throughout Europe in the nineteenth century. The number of criminals executed began to drop, and as new crimes were added to the statute books – particularly ones designed to protect private property – the numbers incarcerated began to rise. Initially, more people died in prison from disease than had previously been executed, but the nineteenth century saw extensive prison reforms. Diets, sleep, clothing, exercise and punishment regimes were carefully planned. Prisoners were sometimes integrated into economically productive work. Prison spaces were designed to allow prisoners calculated amounts of knowledge, movement, and vision. Prison reformers separated kinds of prisoners to prevent moral contagion.[112] Monitoring regimes were created to ensure that regimes were followed. Some did so through purpose-built architecture; in the most celebrated of these, Bentham's ideal 'panopticon' which anticipated modern video surveillance, all areas of a prison could be seen from a single central control point (Figure 95). Such changes were controversial in ways surprisingly familiar today; some reformers aimed at rehabilitating and re-educating

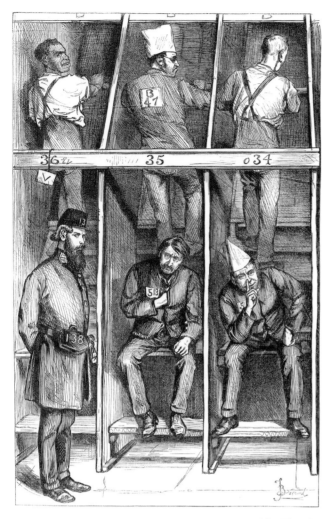

Figure 96. The treadmill in a Victorian prison (© Victorian picturelibrary.com).

prisoners, while others wanted prison to be a proper punishment and deterrent. Yet, even those advocating harsh punishment called for a typically nineteenth century form of it, private and routinized through starvation diets and physical labour, rather than by inflicting pain on the body publicly. For both sides of the debate, prisoners' bodies were now disciplined.

Such regimes created a new 'microphysics of power' (in Foucault's phrase) through which the state disciplined and habituated prisoners' bodies, producing new kinds of bodily experience. As in domestic practices and landscapes, technology acted to separate and divide bodies from one another, to increase the sense of bounded and separated individuals. The prison itself became machine-like, and the individual prisoners were forced to take their place as one part of the machine – in some cases, literally so, on devices such as the treadmill which conveniently merged industrialized work and punishment (Figure 96). In turn, the metaphor of body-as-machine would

have begun to take shape for prisoners, as well as those more familiar with the philosophical concept. The body as machine was thus forcibly demonstrated.

The most essential point of Foucault's argument is that these changes were not restricted to prisons; they happened in clinics, schools, armies and workplaces – in fact, in any environment in which large numbers of bodies were assembled and coordinated. In armies, for example, the eighteenth century saw the advent of formal military drill, in which groups of soldiers learned to march in formation, to shoulder arms, reload, fire, advance and withdraw, not only acting as a group but coordinating specific bodily gestures. These collective gestures were instilled through repetitive practice and they redefined the individual soldier's body as a small part whose effective functioning depended upon precise coordination with a large machine made of other bodies, technologies and spaces. Similarly, much as in prisons, reformers in clinics and schools phrased their goals and methods in terms of educating the body, and nineteenth century educational and health institutions used much the same tactics: carefully constructed spaces divided into areas of specific function, timetables specifying movements, gestures and activities, repetition and routine to instil bodily habits.[113] In all these areas, we see the efforts of the state, which was becoming more powerful in the Early Modern period, acting on the bodies of its citizens. Laws were passed on hygiene, sexuality, work hours, disposal of the dead, manners of dying and being born (including on suicide, abortion, violent crime and warfare). The state thereby became tightly bound up with the disciplining of the human body. Classic examples of this were the acts of Parliament passed in 1666, 1678 and 1680 that insisted that all bodies prepared for the grave should be buried in wool. These both regulated the bodies of the dead and the practices of the living and acted to support dominant commercial interests.[114]

The body at work

Nowhere were these changes more directly brought home to people than where they worked. For millions of people, particularly in the nineteenth century, the factory became the workplace. Factories harnessed the mechanical energy of water mills and steam to manufacture things on unprecedented scales. Together with their supply and distribution chains in mining, industrialized agriculture, shipping and international trade, canals and railroads, they generated huge wealth for middle and upper classes and huge, if impoverishing, employment for the poor. Some of the largest cities in Britain, such as Birmingham and Manchester, sprang up very rapidly as factory towns, and the conflicts of factory life engendered entire social theories such as Marxism. Factories were part of an agenda linking rationality to efficiency, modernity and progress. For example, in *The Wealth of Nations*,[115] the influential Scottish economist Adam Smith pointed out that one person alone making pins could make 20 pins in a day, but if ten people gathered together and divided up the work into different tasks, they could make thousands, with an increase of between 240 and 4,800 times more. Whatever these ten hypothetical pin-makers felt about it, the rationalized productivity of factories underwrote Europe's explosive nineteenth century economic growth.

What is important here is the factory's effect upon bodies, both materially and conceptually. As in the prison, school and hospital, factories divided activity into discrete tasks and allocated them to finely differentiated groups of people. An Early Modern potter saw a vessel through most stages of production alone or in a small working group. A century later, at a typical factory in Stoke-on-Trent, a blue and white china plate, one of the most ubiquitous Victorian consumer goods, passed through the work stations of more than twenty separate workers who did narrowly-defined, repetitive tasks such as dipping moulded plates into a basin of clay slip as quickly as possible thousands of times a day (Figure 97). Unsurprisingly, this period saw the first studies of occupational health as an extension of the medical gaze, as such repetitive, intense gestures took their toll on the bodies of workers. Timing, integration and workflow were imposed and fixed rather than set flexibly by workers, as delays in one stage could halt the entire process. The organisational machine of the factory thus came to encompass both physical mechanisms and the people who served and operated them. The increasing interaction people had with machines helped to popularize understandings of technology as a new factor in people's lives, something external to both society and nature and potentially transforming both (cf. Chapter 8).

Underwriting the whole were the twin concepts of rational design and surveillance. Rational design supported the analysis of tasks and workflow. Significantly, in rational design, workers' bodies were treated as a means for producing; like any tools, they had their needs and limitations, and the goal of rational design was to work around these to integrate them into a larger machine which would maximize productivity. Surveillance was a way of making sure operations ran according to plan. Workers' bodies were overseen both bureaucratically through records such as time-keeping, and literally, through overseers and managers; like prisons, factories were often designed in ways which allowed visual surveillance of workers. As Foucault noted, regimes of surveillance become internalized, conditioning the body. Factory life had a temporal regime entirely different from the farm or workshop, with time measured, divided, remunerated and regulated through fixed working hours and break times, instilling a different sense of time in workers and managers.[116]

In many ways, the best contemporary ethnographers of this change were Marx and Engels, whose theories specifically discussed how the conditions of work became internalized in the workers' consciousness, abilities and sense of self. It was through the imposition of discipline, particularly through factories, that many people came to understand their bodies as machines. By taking part in the routinized, timed, planned machine-like operations which integrated the worker's body as a part in a larger machine, the countless thousands who were excluded from intellectual circles of philosophical and medical discourse helped to develop the widening conception of the mechanistic body.

The body overseas: The emergence of 'race'

Thinking about rationality, social change and bodies brings us to one final development of the Early Modern period which remains important today: the concept of 'race'. The body is always implicated in colonialism; we saw in Chapter 5 how the Classical Greeks exported some of their understandings of the body along with the sculptures, wines, perfumes, and other items of trade. The period between 1500 and 1800 was the great period of European worldwide colonialism, when empires spanning the globe were created. Colonialism involved bodies in many ways. Whether supplying clothing such as furs and silks and stimulants such as tea and coffee to Europe, colonial outlets for products made in the mills of Sheffield or Manchester, or bodily encounters such as violence or sexuality, it was an embodied process. We have already encountered one example of this, the ontological misunderstanding about bodies and souls which grew out of the encounter between French Jesuits and Native American Hurons in sixteenth century Canada (Chapter 2). However, one of the most enduring legacies was the conceptual way in which bodily difference came to be classified.

From a modern perspective, it may be surprising that 'race' was not a fundamental *biological* category until relatively recently. For example, although the term was used since the seventeenth century, it was only in the eighteenth century that the term 'Negro' acquired its pejorative qualities, having previously been merely descriptive. Race acquired its full biological definition only in the

(a)   (b)

Figure 97. Machines and bodies. A and B. Images of nineteenth century factory workers in the workplace (© English Heritage NMR).

later nineteenth century.[117] The concept has a complex history.

The microcosmic view of the body saw differences in physique and appearance as the outcome of geography and climate. Slavery in the sixteenth and seventeenth century was typically justified not through racial hierarchy but through the language of economics, and the idea that certain groups would be more suited to some climes than others.[118] For example, it was argued that tropical Africans could work on Caribbean plantations in conditions which would kill Europeans. Yet alongside the work of Blumenbach, Montesquieu and others who saw race in these terms, other kinds of thinking began to emerge. As we have seen from 1700, the term 'culture' increasingly came to be used to describe human accomplishments. Through the eighteenth century, as ideas of classification and boundary came to be applied to differences between people, the term began increasingly to be associated with ideas of *cultures*, of particular groups whose nature made them behave in different ways. Within Europe, such differences were discussed by German authors in terms of *völker* or 'peoples'. By 1800, Johann Gottfried von Herder could argue that the world was populated by different cultures whose character created their history. Hence the apparent backwardness of African cultures, Herder argued, was because of their innate mental state.[119] These were essentialist arguments: culture was increasingly understood as being carried biologically and transmitted hereditarily within each kind of people. Colonial experience gave seeming evidence for this. Encounters in the New World had shown human beings living in an apparent 'state of nature'. Beyond this,

the appalling mortality rates of Native Americans exposed to European diseases was taken as evidence of their bodily weakness and the natural superiority of the Europeans.[120]

During the early nineteenth century, these debates developed further. Three concepts were key. First, as we have seen earlier, in the 1700s, Linnaeus and others first undermined the doctrine of human uniqueness and suggested that humans were part of the animal kingdom. As such, humans were fair game for the eighteenth-century drive for empirical, material study and classification. At the same time, human distinctiveness for at least some humans could be rescued if it was argued that some groups of humans were unique, or more perfect, while others were closer to animals. Hence, the particularly 19th century classification of humans into 'higher' and 'lower' races, to the extent that James Hunt in 1863 could argue that there was less difference between a gorilla and a chimp than between a white man and a black man; it was common amongst nineteenth-century anthropologists to see 'black' races as midway between 'white' races and apes.[121] Secondly, as history was increasingly understood as a story of progress, difference between peoples was forced into a temporal or evolutionary framework; difference had to be gauged in terms of being 'advanced' or 'backwards'. The final key concept was the idea that mental capabilities were related to physical characteristics, and the obsessional measurement of different parts of the anatomy could reveal these underlying social and racial types. Thus nineteenth century anthropologists such as Paul Broca in Paris and Samuel Morton in Philadelphia invented a range of 'scientific' techniques such as craniometry to measure skulls, faces, hair, and body proportions (Figure 98, Plate VIIId). The overriding goal was to enable empirical scientists to objectively classify the people of the world into discrete, hierarchically ranked 'races'.[122]

All the ingredients of 'race' as a tool for classifying bodily variation were now present, allowing scientific observation to provide physical causes and evidence for why different 'races' had incommensurate abilities and historical destinies. The master narrative characterized the history of the world in terms of more or less evolved races. Mapped onto world political economy, this provided an explanation for why some people were 'civilized' and others remained 'savages'. Thus, although Spencer's and Darwin's ideas about evolution were not in themselves racist, they fitted precisely into the agenda of those who wanted to argue that European domination simply reflected the victory of the most advanced 'race'. Authors such as Gobineau, writing at the end of the nineteenth century, saw race as everything, a biological structure at the heart of history. Race was now a fundamental biological category. The political context and consequences of this are only too familiar. Nineteenth-century imperialism drew on this form of biologically driven racism to justify European domination of Africa, Australia, Asia and the Americas. Just as the study of gender had been used to 'scientifically' justify the subjugation of women despite Enlightenment appeals for universal equality,[123] so the 'science' of race was used to provide 'objective' support for European domination, even as its vaunted scientific method turned to ever increasing nuances of difference in an attempt to hold up a concept with little actual validity.[124] Although anthropologists such as Franz Boas, Aleš Hrdlička and (in Nazi Germany) Karl Saller dissented, the doctrine that biologically discrete races were inherently different physically, psychologically and intellectually continued to be promulgated by prominent anthropologists such as Earnest Hooton through the mid-twentieth century. The same toxic ingredients underwrote Gustaf Kossinna's racial anthropology in Germany which provided the ideological basis for Nazi beliefs in a superior 'Aryan' race. Although anthropologists widely abandoned the concept of 'race' after World War II, the concept still forms part of many people's popular understanding of the body.

Historical process in the modern period

Our vignette of a Tyburn hanging in the 1750s falls about midway through an extraordinarily rich and interesting period in the history of the body. There can be no doubt that how people understood the body changed dramatically between 1450 and 1900. An Elizabethan such as Shakespeare would probably have understood the body much more as his or her medieval ancestors did than as his or her Victorian descendants would. In the crowd that flocks around the gallows at Tyburn, we can see some of the changes in progress. The theology preached to the condemned man is post-Reformation, yet not too much different from traditional Christian doctrine. The crowd contains believers in the magical potency of the dead man's hand. Yet the anatomists' assistants waiting to take the executed criminal away reminds us of dissection, a practice that has been growing in social importance for more than two centuries now and whose meaning has been steadily shifting to converge with developments in philosophy. At this point, however, most of the changes in how the body was understood are still mostly in the intellectual realms of science, philosophy and art. In dealing with criminals, the emphasis is still firmly upon 'punish' rather than 'discipline', and the practical effects of the industrial revolution have yet to be felt.

There are two main story lines in this segment of history. One is a real change in how the body was understood. Between 1450 and 1900, an entire body world has changed. The other, equally instructive, is how this change happened and what this tells us about the nature of historical body worlds.

From medieval to modern bodies

The change in how the body was understood can be summarized briefly, at the cost of some schematism. At the end of the Middle Ages, there were several competing ways of understanding the body (Chapter 6): doctrinally as a battleground between the soul and the flesh, scientifically in terms of a system of cosmological affinities, and in lived experience. To the extent to which these coalesced into a single metaphor, the body was understood as a microcosm of the world around it. Internally it was dominated by the four humours and was seen as permeable to the outside world, capable of both leaking out and of being influenced by foods, words and actions in a very direct and immediate way. Theologically, the 'body as microcosm' view made the body an example of God's creation.

Over three centuries or so, the body came to be understood very differently. Philosophers began to separate mind from body, associating the former with the newly constructed concept of culture, and the latter with nature, a world now seen as obeying fixed mechanical rules. These new epistemologies also built on a radical scepticism which entrenched the separation of body and mind. The former was susceptible to the ravages of nature, and

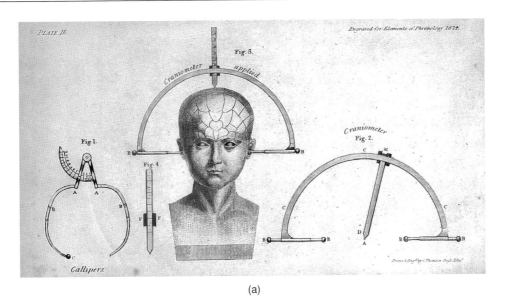

(a)

(b)

Figure 98. Nineteenth century 'scientific' techniques and racial classification. A. Craniometer and skull measurement techniques (© Wellcome Library, London). B. The unilinear scale of human races and lower relatives according to Nott and Gliddon (1868) (image: Gould 1981, 32, fig. 2.1). As Gould notes, the chimpanzee cranium is falsely inflated here and the 'Negro' jaw has been extended to suggest that the former should possibly rank higher than the latter.

to weaknesses of emotion and desire; the latter, through its ability to reason, could separate itself from the world and take up an objective position. As such the body itself was also seen as mechanical, external to the person. Anatomists had been practicing since the sixteenth century, initially to explore the inner geography of the microcosmic body. Yet by the seventeenth century, anatomy increasingly shifted its semantic direction and became directed at identifying the mechanical structures of the body and deducing how they related to their function. Increasingly this created the possibility for an objectifying, medical gaze to be applied to the bodies of both the living and the dead, further creating them as objects suitable for study. From anatomy, which helped to develop a detailed understanding of the body's internal spatial relations, via autopsy which developed the medical gaze that further objectified the body, to the role of prosthetics specifically designed to 'complete' an otherwise partial body, medical discourses helped to produce the idea of the body as a natural machine. The newly powerful nation states aided in this by helping procure specimens for dissection through changing laws.

So far, so good: a coherent Cartesian intellectual agenda harnessed anatomical dissection in the interests of empiricism and transformed the duality-and-unity of soul and body to a much more pronounced disjuncture of mind and matter. Yet there are a number of surprising counter-developments as well. Protestant theologians bemoaned the body as a sin-filled earthly prison for the soul, one that was worthless and should be abandoned. Yet in spite of this, the body remained identified enough with the person to an important site of affection and commemoration in burial, social display and stigma. As much as the new laws imposed by the state provided machine-like bodies for dissection, they also punished bodies as persons in a public way. Furthermore, having converted the soul to a pure reasoning mind, sixteenth and seventeenth century thinkers were at something of a loss about where to locate the individual personality. Emergent instead was a model of personhood that understood surface to be superficial, and depth to equal truth. Without the medieval assurance of a spiritual unity between surface and depth, they had to develop a rather vague and free-floating concept of an inner person, a self *within* the body but not fundamentally related to it. This inner person was revealed through acts such as introspection. Yet at the same time this existed in tension with another modality that increasingly associated the body and the bounded individual. Portraiture acted to reveal this close coincidence in the manner it sought to capture the 'real' person.

At the same time as these issues were fermenting in intellectual circles, parallel changes were taking place in the practices of everyday life. From the seventeenth century onwards, the body's relationship to space was increasingly defined not only in portraiture, landscape painting, anatomy and medicine, but in more concrete ways as well: in homes as space became internally divided and dedicated to particular social functions; in the landscape as rural areas became enclosed, bounded and appropriated, rearranging rights and work rhythms. The increasingly tightly defined relations between human bodies and space helped to insist on the policing of the boundaries of the human body, and its decreasing permeability to the outside world.

These changes gained in tempo throughout the 1700s, but the biggest change in daily life came in the late eighteenth and early nineteenth century. As the bodily regimes of work shifted to industrial production, workers performed repetitive, standardized gestures to service a real and organizational machine which had to be kept running. Nothing could make clearer a functional redefinition of the human body as a machine within a machine, a specialized part performing specific roles in an overall process. Similar changes occurred in the organization of other settings: houses, machines, factories, schools and hospitals and in the laws that governed them. Bodies and technologies co-constitute each other.[125] As factories that produced individual material things through particular stages with singular functions in specialized spaces came into existence, so houses, schools, prisons and hospitals developed equivalent bounded locales with unique tasks and objectives, producing individual citizen bodies. People on the margins of society, too, were forced to experience the new logic of body as machine. In clinics, asylums and prisons the controlled rhythms of daily practice, the controlled times of eating, and the watchful eye of surveillance technology acted to force bodies into routines that separated people out, controlled them, identified their particular maladies and sought to fix them through discipline. New kinds of bodies could be identified through these processes, the body of the prisoner, or the lunatic or the patient, each requiring correction. Whereas philosophers, theologians and doctors formulated new doctrines about bodies, new forms of landscape, architecture and work instilled equally sweeping changes in how the body was practically understood. The notion of technology as an external force acting on society that these changes helped to instantiate was captured in moments of rebellion, such as when the 'Luddites' a group of nineteenth-century textile weavers destroyed mechanized looms.

Beyond narratives of scientific progress: Social context and multimodality

At this point, an official disclaimer for the reader is called for. The narrative of scientific progress exerts an almost irresistible suction upon us. But it would misleading to see the history of the body between the seventeenth and nineteenth centuries simply as a story of scientific progress, of rational enquiry gradually overcoming inherited superstition. It would be naïve to deny that the body-as-machine metaphor and empirical observation have proven extraordinarily successful over the last several centuries at understanding the physiology and function of the body. But that is not what is at stake. Any metaphor for understanding the human body is useful in bringing to the fore, or creating, some aspects of it at the expense of others, and every metaphor arises from a particular social context. Thus, we can list briefly a number of ways in which history belies such a simple narrative.

1. The trajectory of 'body as microcosm' to 'body as geography' to 'body as machine' implies a uniformity and shared view. As Stevens notes, there were 'a myriad of published opinions on the human mind and body circulating in the 17th century'.[126] Moreover, Early Modern thinkers held all sorts of beliefs we now consider peculiar. Bacon, for example, believed that human movement was a series of explosions that took place within the body,[127] whilst Robert Fludd was happy to accept Harvey's understanding of the blood while nevertheless pursuing microcosmic understandings of humanity.[128] Narratives of progress usually pick out the ideas we continue to share teleologically as ancestors and dismiss the rest as passing errors, but this distorts how the thinkers we study really thought.

2. Intellectual developments happened within a social context, a context in which intellectual models were also power models. The most obvious example is gender. Whether or not one accepts Laqueur's controversial theory of the invention of biological sex in the eighteenth century, it is clear that philosophical dichotomies of intellect and matter, reason and emotion were used to impose social hierarchies between males and females. Even further: to the extent that Enlightenment thinkers inherited gendered models of the body and personhood, it is not a case of perverting correct logic to impose social inequality so much as reasoning in a tradition in which such dichotomies were always already gendered. The same hierarchical dichotomy was later used to legitimate 'racial' inequalities. The concept of 'race' itself, historically, is a scientific superstition which results from an encounter between the prestigious habits of scientific observation, an evolutionary narrative of progress and reason, and the need to convert difference into an unquestionable symbol of naturalised inequality in colonial situations.

3. A top-down, intellectual-driven narrative overlooks the fact that explicitly theoretical contexts were only some amongst many. Alternative narratives are always present.[129] For example, studies of the different conceptions of the body present in eighteenth century erotic texts reveal that 'knowledge about bodies was...not created in the fields of science and medicine and rearticulated in other domains'.[130] Moreover, as we have seen, for many people, some of the most compelling evidence that the body was like a machine was experiential, through daily routines of work, education and home. In fact, to the extent that philosophers and scientists drew upon their own experience for metaphors and self-evident facts, it is as likely that the daily experience of social life conditioned intellectual theorizing as the reverse. For example, to thinkers working in the eighteenth and nineteenth century when fields such as agriculture and industry were being overhauled through a social doctrine in 'improvement',[131] the concept of inevitable progress through rationality may have appeared self-evident.

4. As we have already seen, ideas of the body in any society are multimodal, with different understandings invoked in different contexts. This period, a well-documented chaos of ideas, affords one of the clearest examples of this. Understanding and acting upon the dead body, for example, could involve concepts of social display and performance, such as ostentatious burial for the prominent and dissection for the stigmatized; unauthorized 'folk' belief, such as belief in the magical potency of the hanged man's hand; scientific concepts of anatomical dissection; and theological discourses arguing that the corpse was little more than empty carrion which could be discarded. These different beliefs did not provide a menu of truth and errors a thinker could choose from; they provided different approaches for different contexts and problems. They were thus often combined in ways which seem contradictory to us. Thus, as we saw earlier, William Harvey not only formulated a mechanistic theory of how the heart pumped blood around the body; he was also a firm believer in the curative powers of a dead person's hand.[132]

To give a sense of how completely normal it was to alternate between multiple ways of experiencing the body, we cannot do better than listen to Samuel Pepys, a civil servant who recorded his daily life in London in the 1660s in his private diary in candid, shrewd detail. In Pepys' diary, the body world of his time really comes to life.

Pepys loved the pleasures of the body – good food and wine, good company, music, dance and the theatre – and he notoriously rarely missed an opportunity to dally with a pretty woman. Moreover, he understood thoroughly the importance of self-presentation and the social body; something of a careerist, he liked costly clothes and understood dressing for success, and when his brother died, he paid extra to have him buried in the central aisle of the church, a place of status. Yet he was also unquestioningly, if conventionally, religious. Wanting to rule his body and habits in accordance, he repeatedly swore off his pleasures in bouts of moralising, only to relapse again quickly into a satisfied complacency. In keeping with the Protestant theology of his time, he clearly considered funerals and monuments a way of honouring the dead rather than any form of spiritual intercession. Nevertheless, he finds the grave-digger's too-casual treatment of recently dead bodies disconcertingly callous:

> so to my brother's and to church, and with the grave-maker chose a place for my brother to lie in, just under my mother's pew. But to see how a man's tombes are at the mercy of such a fellow, that for sixpence he would, (as his owne words were) "I will justle them together but I will make room for him;" speaking of the fulness of the middle isle, where he was to lie; and that he would, for my father's sake, do my brother that is dead all the civility he can; which was to disturb other corps that are not quite rotten, to make room for him. (March 18, 1663)

Like many other Londoners, Pepys attended hangings as public entertainments, on one particularly crowded occasion paying extra to stand upon a wagon for a better view:

> And there I got for a shilling to stand upon the wheel of a cart, in great pain, above an houre before the execution was done; he delaying the time by long discourses and prayers one after another, in hopes of a reprieve; but none came, and at last was flung off the ladder in his cloake. A comely-looked man he was, and kept his countenance to the end: I was sorry to see him. It was believed there were at least 12 or 14,000 people in the street. (21 January 1664)

A man of scientific interests at a time when natural philosophers such as Boyle and Harvey were actively rewriting theories of the body, Pepys attended lectures by surgeons, and on one occasion spent most of the day at the dissection of an executed criminal, intrigued by seeing the anatomical structures laid bare.

> After dinner Dr. Scarborough took some of his friends, and I went along with them, to see the body alone, which we did, which was a lusty fellow, a seaman, that was hanged for a robbery. I did touch the dead body with my bare hand: it felt cold, but methought it was a very unpleasant sight....Thence we went into a private room, where I perceive they prepare the bodies, and there were the kidneys, ureters [&c.], upon which he read to-day, and Dr. Scarborough upon my desire and the company's did show very clearly the manner of the disease of the stone and the cutting and all other questions that I could think of. (February 27, 1662)

Pepys read critically a book written by a fellow member of the Royal Society presenting a rigorous scientific criterion for proving the existence of witches. He noted with interest his first encounter with "mummy", the preserved human flesh used in medical preparations.

> And so parted, I having there seen a mummy in a merchant's warehouse there, all the middle of the man or woman's body, black and hard. I never saw any before, and, therefore, it pleased me much, though an ill sight; and he did give me a little bit, and a bone of an arme. (May 12, 1668)

If Pepys himself is somewhat non-committal about the magical aspects of the human body, he provides reliable witness that they were taken seriously by many of the educated and prosperous circle in which he moved.

All of the views of the body we have discussed above turn up in this Restoration Everyman: the cutting-edge scientific body, the theology of burial and the revulsion towards the dead body, the body as a site of social pleasure, display and stigma, and even the magic body. What is most remarkable is how Pepys weaves these different views together as he lives without any apparent ontological strain other than an occasional bit of self-censure, repugnance or skepticism.[133]

The process of change: Transformation by continuity

The transition from medieval to modern body worlds really follows a model we might call 'transformation by continuity'. Over several centuries, something remarkably different emerged, yet this happened without any moment of rupture or erasure.[134] Each strand of medieval multimodality continued to develop by degrees until it reached something quite different from its point of departure. Theology saw the medieval self break apart through the slow distancing of body and soul. Philosophy saw soul transform into mind. Medicine started out rooted in Galenic humoural theory and microcosmic models and, passing through geography, wound up with the body as a machine. Perhaps the only really new element was the concept of discipline; yet this was not entirely unrelated to other strands of belief, and earlier examples can be detected.

The body was made of multiple, contextual historical strands; yet these did not form an orderless accumulation. In some cases they clearly echoed and reinforced each other. Preachers decrying the dead body as mere carrion to discard would have understood doctors analysing its structures as a spiritually empty machine, although the latter might have seen the body as beautiful rather than repulsive. Is this *zeitgeist*, a set of general intellectual reflexes at work? At other times, however, the interactions between modes of thought, and the different needs underlying them, generated completely counter-intuitive historical patterns. For example, Protestant theologians denouncing the body as useless carrion seems only to have increased the attention paid to the dead body, not only by the general public but even by the theologians who made these pronouncements. Similarly, the more the body was seen as purely material, the more there developed a sense of an elusive 'inner' self hiding somewhere within it, heightening the tension between the body as machine versus the body as person.

Recently, the cultural historian Dror Wahrman has asked, 'is the expectation for logical consistency itself culturally or historically specific?'[135] The answer has to be yes. In the medieval period, there was a widely agreed-upon meta-theory of the body, the Christian doctrinal view. It was not necessarily the view most people followed in most contexts, but it was the one which purported to supply a universal theoretical framework enveloping and conditioning other understandings, and it had considerable institutional and spiritual power to apply sanctions to people violating it too obviously or in the wrong contexts. The Early Modern period is fascinatingly complex in part because it is much more questionable whether there was any such meta-theory. Instead, for two centuries between about 1650 and 1850, there seems to have been a widely accepted sort of negotiated compromise. It ran along Newtonian lines: God created the world and the spiritual realm was His jurisdiction; the material world ran upon its own built-in rules without direct divine intervention. This gave a free warrant for understanding the body, like the Copernican universe, as a mechanism, while ruling that questions about the psyche and the subjective experience of living were somebody else's problem. Like all such arrangements, it was not necessarily logically ten-

able, but that was not the point; it was eminently liveable. As long as one did not ask the wrong question, that is; carefully constructed blind spots ensured that (aside from a few agonized intellectuals) most people rarely asked inconvenient things such as 'where in the material body is the soul actually located?', 'what makes "I" feel like "me"?', 'why are people reluctant to throw a deceased relative on the rubbish heap?' or 'why should hanged men's bodies have different magical powers?' It was, in effect, a warrant for a quite practical multimodality.

This balance of metaphorical logics lasted for several centuries. It was not without tensions, variations or arguments; indeed, these dissensions were not a defect in it but a fundamental part of it. Ultimately, however, what seems to have destabilized it was the balance of practical experience. As industrial capitalism grew, it created bodies whose overwhelming experience of practical activity was that of performing a mechanical function, standardized, repetitive and in concert with other parts. This converged with similar logics in other domains of experience: the increasing depth of knowledge and success in treatment available in medicine which was predicated upon a body-as-machine model, the bounded, divided and ordered spaces within houses and landscapes, the regulated, bounded and controlled bodies within institutional regimes such as the school, hospital, prison and army. Such experiences reinforced each other hegemonically, either intuitively through habituation or explicitly under theories about improvement, rationality and progress.

Such accumulated experience tipped the balance, and from the mid-nineteenth century onwards, the meta-theory of the body was increasingly that of a machine. The body as microcosm was reduced to residual medical practices such as bleeding patients to rebalance their humours and to an occasional political metaphor about 'heads of state'. Religious views continued to be held strongly, though their relation to materialist doctrine remained vague and labile. A sign of the tipping point, if not the tipping point itself, was in the middle of the nineteenth century, when two of the great metanarratives were put down on paper: Darwin's *On the Origin of the Species*,[136] published in 1859, and Marx and Engel's *Das Kapital*,[137] published in 1867. Neither felt any need to appeal to religion for support. In fact, Darwinian arguments implicitly suggested a purely materialistic model for the origins of human uniqueness, including the intellectual and emotional, and Marx and Engels specifically created a materialist theory for the origins of human consciousness. In doing so, they were making territorial claims to the special preserve which the Newtonian compromise had long kept sacred from the encroaching of empirical science.

It was little wonder that Nietzsche was able to declare in 1882 that God was dead, and the moral compass of Christianity had been lost. Freud and psychology would follow, reclaiming the inner self in non-religious, scientific terms. This was not the path that Descartes, Newton and others had started on, but it was the consequence nonetheless.

A mechanistic understanding of the body never eradicated other views of course; asserting this would do a disservice to legions of truly spiritual Victorians, and for that matter, a great many spiritual people today. We continue to believe contradictory things about the body in different situations (cf. Chapters 1, 2, 8 and 9). But the mid-nineteenth-century shift did accomplish one thing: after centuries of overt multi-vocality, once again there was a meta-theory of the body, a totalizing frame which (in spite of evidence to the contrary) claimed to encompass and explain the other voices clamouring to speak for the body. And that meta-theory was a materialistic, mechanistic body.

NOTES

1. This chapter draws heavily upon Tarlow 2011, which provides a detailed study of the body in death and much relevant background. A good general introduction to the period is Wiesner-Hanks 2006. We also use some of Tarlow's earlier work, notably Tarlow 2007. Once again, the literature for this period on the body is immense. The key texts that provide an overall, if highly contested, picture come from the synthetic works of Laqueur (e.g. 1991) and Elias (e.g. 1978; 1982) and most of all Foucault (e.g. 1973; 1977; 1978). On the history of anatomy, the outstanding text remains Sawday 1995 and for later periods Richardson 1989. A broader introduction to the history of medicine is Porter 2001. It is also worth examining texts on medicine in the particular periods in question e.g. Gentilcore 1995 and Tapper 1995. For work on changing households, landscape and material culture, a good starting point is Johnson 1996. Historical studies of attitudes towards the body and reproduction include Fissell 2005, and the relationship between parts and wholes is covered by Hillman and Mazzio (1997a; 1997b). Broader studies of gender are Gowing 2003 and Harvey 2004. The history of the concept of nature was studied brilliantly by Collingwood (1945) and Thomas (1983); and the relationship between body and environment is discussed in a highly informative edited volume (Floyd-Wilson and Sullivan Jr 2007). The emergent role of scientists and the consequence for dichotomous thinking is also discussed by Latour 1993. A good introduction to the origins of concept of race is Hannaford 1996. Finally, our main source on theology is Tarlow 2011 (who provides further references) and Gittings' (1999) study of the relationship at death between the secular and the sacred. A good study

of one particular religious set of responses to the body is Strasser 2004.
2. Tarlow 2011.
3. Foucault 1978
4. Reeves and Adams 1993; Shepard and Walker 2008; Wiesner-Hanks 2008.
5. Racaut 2002.
6. Mullaney 2007, 71.
7. Wiesner-Hanks 2006, 292.
8. Johnson 1996; Tarlow 2007, 46.
9. Tarlow 2007, 30.
10. Tarlow 2007.
11. Elias 1982; Foucault 1977; Vigarello 1989.
12. Sawday 1995, 23.
13. Tarlow 2007.
14. Latour 1993.
15. Foucault 1973.
16. Although, it should be acknowledged that Elias' readings are selective.
17. Elias 1978; 1982; 1983.
18. Foucault 1973; 1977.
19. Foucault 1978.
20. Laqueur 1991.
21. Laqueur 1987; 1991.
22. Fissell 2005; Gowing 2003; Wahrman 2008. On erotic writings, see Harvey 2004. On midwives and the uterus, see Hillman and Mazzio 1997b.
23. Tarlow 2011, 23.
24. Tarlow 2011, 77.
25. Tarlow 2011, 29.
26. Tarlow 2011, 27.
27. Tarlow 2011, 27–29.
28. Dacome 2006.
29. Tarlow 2011, 26–27.
30. Sherlock 1690, 36.
31. Gittings 1999.
32. We return to this and its relationship with the theologians we discuss here later in this chapter.
33. Sawday 1995, 158.
34. Stevens 1997, 269.
35. Descartes 2008 [1641].
36. Dacome 2006, 89, 74.
37. Williams 1976, 219.
38. Berger 1972, 219.
39. Collingwood 1945; Macnaghten and Urry 1998, 3.
40. Thomas 1983, 27, 14.
41. Collingwood 1945, 103; Thomas 2004.
42. Olwig 1993, 315; Thomas 2004, 82.
43. Olwig 1993, 315.
44. Thomas 1983, 301.
45. Olwig 1993, 313.
46. Collingwood 1945, 14.
47. Thomas 1983, 52.
48. But see Latour 1993; 1999 on the history of laboratory vision.
49. Ingold 2000.

50. Latour 1993.
51. Ingold 2000, 273.
52. Sawday 1995.
53. Sawday 1995, 88–91, 249.
54. Latour 1993, 15–32.
55. The classic starting point remains Thomas 1973, but see also Davies 2007; Hutton 1995; 1996 amongst others.
56. Levack 1987.
57. Kivelson 2003.
58. Wiesner-Hanks 2006, 386.
59. Levack 1987.
60. Floyd-Wilson and Sullivan Jr 2007.
61. Levack 1987, 218–220.
62. Tarlow 2011, 164–167.
63. Tarlow 2011, 168.
64. Foucault 1973, xviii.
65. Sawday 1995, 24.
66. Hillman 1997, 83.
67. Sawday 1995, 24.
68. Sawday 1995, 23.
69. Hillman and Mazzio 1997a, xii.
70. Hillman 1997, 82.
71. Sawday 1995; Tarlow 2011.
72. Sawday 1995, 118.
73. Tarlow 2011.
74. Dacome 2006, 103.
75. Porter 2001, 410.
76. Foucault 1973.
77. Porter 2001.
78. Reeves and Adams 1993.
79. Foucault 1973.
80. O'Connor 1997.
81. Richardson 1989.
82. O'Connor 1997, 761–762.
83. O'Connor 1997.
84. As always, things are more complex with the Bard. It is a matter of debate whether Shakespeare depicted Richard as a hunchback *because* the character is evil or whether it was *because* of his hunchback – and thus his inability to be a lover – that he was 'determined to prove a villain'. This latter view hints towards the later attitudes that declared that it was the internal character that could be transformed, and external appearance did not reflect this.
85. Floyd-Wilson and Sullivan Jr 2007; Paster 2007; Pollard 2007; Schoenfeldt 1997, 253.
86. Sutton 2007, 15.
87. Pollard 2007, 183.
88. Sawday 1995, 25–26; cf. Hillman and Mazzio 1997a, xv.
89. Boyd 1629, 1046.
90. Mytum 2006; Owen 2006.
91. Tarlow 2011, 89.
92. Royer 2004, 74.
93. Oxford English Dictionary online; the work cited is M. Hale, *Primitive Originat. Mankind* (1677), i. ii. 55.
94. Elias 1978; 1982; 1983.
95. Vigarello 1989.
96. Johnson 1996, 169–170.
97. Tarlow 2007, 129–132.
98. Johnson 1996.
99. Rebora 2001.
100. Johnson 1996, 170–172.
101. Leone and Potter 1999.
102. Johnson 1996, 72.
103. Johnson 1996, 70–75.
104. Anderson 2006, 170–178; Thomas 2004, 99.
105. Ingold 2000, Chapter 13.
106. Olwig 1993, 324.
107. Leone 1984.
108. Berger 1972.
109. Cosgrove 1984.
110. Olwig 1993, 318, 331.
111. Foucault 1977.
112. Tarlow 2007, 151–155.
113. Foucault 1977.
114. Tarlow 2011, 136.
115. Smith 1995 [1776].
116. Lucas 2005.
117. Arendt 1973; Hannaford 1996, 210; Malik 1996.
118. Chaplin 2001, 21; Hannaford 1996; Malik 1996, 21.
119. Hannaford 1996, 229–232; Malik 1996, 79.
120. Chaplin 2001, 9.
121. Malik 1996, 87; Thomas 1983, 4, 42; Thomas 2004.
122. Gould 1981.
123. Laqueur 1991.
124. Gould 1981; Malik 1996, 120.
125. Latour 1999; cf. Chapter 8, this volume.
126. Stevens 1997, 270.
127. Paster 2007, 110.
128. Stevens 1997, 278.
129. Wahrman 2008.
130. Harvey 2002, 219; cf. Harvey 2004.
131. Tarlow 2007.
132. Tarlow 2011.
133. Pepys, Samuel (1893). *The Diary of Samuel Pepys*. Edited by H. B. Wheatley. London: George Bell. Entries for 18 March 1663, 26 January 1664, 27 February 1662, 12 May 1668, 24 November 1666, and passim.
134. Cf. Strathern 1992a, 7.
135. Wahrman 2008, 588.
136. Darwin 2008 [1859].
137. Marx 1990 [1867].

8

The body in the age of technology

Oliver J. T. Harris, Maryon McDonald
and John Robb

Introduction: Home is where the heart is[1]

We have introduced the preceding chapters with vignettes which show people making or transforming bodies. Even when the pictures we have drawn might seem to be exceptional rather than everyday (as with a Tyburn hanging), they still reveal something important about bodies at that time. When we pass into the twentieth and twenty-first centuries, we have moved into a world of the hospital or clinic, with all the attendant changes in understandings of bodies so ably outlined by Foucault.[2] We are in a world now where bodies have, in an important sense, been standardized through medicine. We can imagine a 'human body' that might seem, in significant respects, to be interchangeable across the globe. We can imagine a human body in the interiority of which disease can be detected through a range of external tests, screenings and imaging. For that disease there may, happily, be treatment and perhaps a cure.

So let's have two brief vignettes to illustrate what this might mean. We move for a moment to 2013 in England. A thirty-five year old man who has been diagnosed with 'heart failure' is carrying a rucksack on his back as he walks home from the shops with his wife. It is his wife who carries the shopping. The rucksack, to which the man appears connected by tubes and wires, emits a steady background noise. Inside it is a mechanical heart. This device has temporarily taken on the function of the man's own heart that has failed. It is keeping him alive, for the moment. He is waiting for a heart transplant.

This mechanical heart makes use of the body as machine. It is a fine piece of 'bio-engineering' in which new digital technologies as well as the mathematical and structural skills of engineers and the medical understandings of the cardiovascular 'system' and its 'pump', and more, seem to have been brought into happy union. In a

second situation, a messier version of the body as machine can be found in the meantime in a nearby hospital, in its operating theatre – where a heart transplant is taking place. The heart to be implanted has been procured from a deceased donor; it is checked, its structures cleaned and, as a working model, it is implanted in a recipient.

The body as machine takes a different form when we then go to Spain, where donated hearts are more plentiful, and watch an American scientific researcher experiment with a donated heart that was too 'marginal' in its capacities to be used for transplant. The researcher 'dissolves' the heart's existing cells with a form of detergent. Gradually, all that is left is a partially translucent structure which she calls the heart's 'architecture'. Then we enter definitively a cellular world. Stem cells are added to the structure. Through a combination of, we are told, 'cells plus architecture plus physiology' the stem cells gradually morph into something resembling a heart, re-covering the structure. Heart cells in a petri dish will beat; stem cells added to this structure will, it is hoped, become a heart. This is still experimentation. No such heart has yet been transplanted into a human being. We can see, however, that this is the world born of modern experimental physiology more than anatomy, and the heart-to-be is not simply a product of the technology that made visible the cell – but of the cell turned into technology.

In these vignettes, we have taken a lot for granted: information technology, sophisticated bio-engineering, systems thinking, cells, immunology and other molecular universes and more. All of these bodies have developed since the time frame of our last chapter. This is a world now of scientific modernity in which modernity itself has been both defined by scientific objectivity – and castigated and rejected in part because of it. The world of 'science' that has produced apparent advances, such as those we have already seen, has also been condemned and required to pay attention to social concerns. From the lurid headlines of tabloid newspapers, it might seem as if the human body is in crisis here, under threat from a host of new technologies that question the boundaries of human and machine, human and animal, and culture and nature (cf. Chapter 1). In the more sober realms of Parliament, the law courts and the pronouncements of medical ethics, there is a clear concern with these technologies: witness the reams of regulation accompanying medical experimentation and research. Although for those at the cutting edge of these fields, talk of the 'body in crisis' might feel like hyperbole, their concern with regulating and managing change reveals that there is a problem. For those who might gain from the transplants and pacemakers that we touched on in our vignettes, the benefits may be very clear, but such gains seem for others to be hedged by a threatening potential. From many perspectives it certainly seems like the previously secure boundaries of the body are being put in question by ever more powerful and invasive technology. Things we have taken to be separate seem to be coming ever closer together.

Technology and society

In entering this chapter, we have bypassed the construction of new national, imperial and post-national boundaries in Europe and the construction of disciplines within the universities. Instead, we have stepped into a world familiar with nature and culture, with society and the economy, and with both historiographical pasts and modern futures, all with their myriad specialists. In the twentieth century there were also two World Wars and then the Cold War. 'Scientists', familiar figures by now, gained a high public profile in physics and military science particularly. This public profile was not unproblematic. The 1960s have become an important historical pivot. Amidst demographic changes, increased studentification, and the re-invention of the category of 'youth', a new 'generation' was self-consciously establishing itself in contra-distinction from its parents. Old certainties such as progress, reason, positivism and the whole project of modernity were put in question. This was a time when a world of cultural diversity was rethought, a time of civil rights marches in the United States, a time of decolonization and counter-cultures, a time when the alternative worlds of regionalism, particularism and relativism appealed, and when new nationalisms and new identities, ethnic and national, began to crowd the map in Europe and beyond.[3]

In the 1960s some of this dissent turned to rage against a science and technology that was apparently external to and threatened 'society' – as it had done already in two world wars. Until the 1990s, the focus of concern was largely developments in physics; nuclear weapons seemed poised to destroy society at any moment. With new developments in genetics particularly, however, this focus shifted to the biological sciences. This became the age of biotechnology, an age of new bodies – and new rage has ensued.[4] Where the weapons of mass destruction had threatened the destruction of human society, now the new biotechnology seemed to promise something far more shocking: the remaking of what it means to have a human body and to be a human being at all.

These fears rest on the way technology seems to threaten to tear up the rule book. The bodies that make us human seem now to be about to be pierced, pulled apart, fragmented, scanned and objectified as never before. Biol-

ogy is supposed to be the realm of the natural, which for many has also meant the fixed and innate. Understandings of who your relatives are, who you should live with, from whom you inherit property and with whom it is acceptable to breed, are supposed to be based firmly in natural 'laws'. Darwinian evolution, originally itself modelled on human kin relationships, had come to provide the model on which understandings of nature were based.[5] Ideas of genetic variation supported cultural taboos on incest, for example. The basic presuppositions here now seem contested. To take just one example we touched on in Chapter 1: IVF[6] has introduced the concept of surrogacy, giving a child both a genetic mother and the birth mother. Which is legally or morally the *real* mother? Yet this question reveals much older concerns: reproductive technologies such as the eugenic breeding or mechanical creation of humans had formed part of both utopian and dystopian visions long before such technologies became practicable. Even in the 1950s,[7] artificial insemination had raised issues of parenthood, adultery and inheritance.

There are clearly some concerns quite specific to medical and *bio*-technology, and we will return to them later. However, some of the worries are underlined and exaggerated by more general concerns about technology. These have a significant history going back into the period covered by the last chapter – one example being the famous destruction of mechanized looms by the Luddites in the early nineteenth century. Around the same time, as we saw in Chapter 7, fears about technology began to be expressed by writers such as Mary Shelley in *Frankenstein*. Increasingly romantic perspectives contrasted the 'dark satanic mills' of industrial England with its green countryside, and the control and domination of nature became an increasing matter of concern. As we mentioned during the last chapter, technology became increasingly reified as an external force in this period acting upon 'society', an important point to which we shall return.

Technology and the body: Boundaries (feel like they are) dissolving

More recently, some of the technologies that have seemed to threaten 'society' have done so in part by also threatening 'the body'. In the last chapter, we saw how one dominant mode of conceptualizing the body – as a microcosm – was supplanted, although never fully replaced, by another: the body as machine.[8] We also saw the growth of associations between the individual and the body, the body as person. The increasing emphasis on the individual in the twentieth century, however, has seen this latter modality increase in importance significantly. This concept draws on a secular reading of much older ideas of the unique soul to cast the body as the seat of indivisible, incomparable personhood. It is from the tensions between the body as a comparable, equivalent machine, and the body as unique and special, between the body as 'nature' and the body as 'culture', that much of the worry around technology stems.

Until recent decades, the relationship between bodies and things seemed clear-cut, the boundaries between the two neatly defined by the skin. Although glasses improved vision inside the head, they sat on one's nose, occasionally falling off at inconvenient moments. Although prosthetics such as wooden legs bore weight and helped people move, the body itself appeared to remain unchanged, it was clear where the natural body ended and the machine began. But solutions to such problems become both ever more effective and ever more integrated within the body. When kidneys fail, dialysis machines that maintain the correct balance of water and minerals in the blood have, for some, become portable and integrated. Artificial, implanted pacemakers can already keep the heartbeat regular. Hearing aids replaced earlier ear trumpets, and in turn may be replaced by cochlear implants, already becoming common. Contact lenses bring the corrective to the very surface of the eye, and laser eye surgery and corneal transplants can permanently improve eyesight; vision is being partially restored to some blind people through the transmission of video footage wirelessly to the retina. Continuing the trend, experimental new prostheses are connected to nerve endings to allow the brain to control them directly in much the same way as it controls limbs of flesh and blood (Figure 99). Such devices, at present, are designed to make up for the failings of the organic body, but it is a short step to imagining a world in which mechanical transplants allow people to surpass the body's original capacities. It is no surprise that popular media such as the January 2010 edition of *National Geographic* headline the 'merging of man and machine', and the incoming 'bionic age'.[9]

In other contexts, these machines create new zones in which bodies can exist. The late twentieth and early twenty-first centuries have seen new reflection on the medical diagnoses of death.[10] Life support machines are very much a part of this story. These machines allow the body to enter into a very difficult and troubling zone between life and death, between person and object, and have raised the issue of 'brain death'.[11] This captures the troubling distinction between body and mind perfectly, a moment in which the body (in conjunction with machines) can live when the mind has gone. Brain deaths have been one important source of organ transplants and such transplants are now an established part of modern medicine. The range of possible transplants continu-

ally increases from kidneys, to hearts, to faces. Although largely accepted in one sense – few discussions take place in Europe or North America over whether transplants should be banned or tightly controlled in the manner of cloning or genetic engineering – debates remain.[12] In death, organ transplants offer the potential for fragmentation, and thus the violation of the bounded individual body, something to which some people object.[13] For others, however, this potential transformation is one to be embraced, the chance to 'live on' in another's body. Recipients have reported that transfers of organic material can also transfer aspects of personhood with them, with the donor felt to be continuing to live on in the new host.[14]

More dramatic transformations appear to be promised by genetic engineering, the source of many hopes and fears about the future of 'the human body'.[15] Genetic engineering works directly on an organism's DNA, removing parts that are seen as threatening and replacing them with other sequences of code designed to produce alternative proteins and thus alternative effects. Scientists have been able to combine different DNA strands since 1973.[16] To date, genetic engineering has largely focused on non-humans, particularly crop plants. Potentially, however, it holds the key to preventing the onset of a number of genetically influenced diseases such as cystic fibrosis. Understandings of genetic therapy are tied up with by how we 'read' DNA, often imagined to be the inner essence of a human identity. Anthropologist Rayna Rapp[17] has argued that, with our increasing understanding of how diseases are coded for in DNA, our fate seems to be increasingly biologically programmed.[18] Working with parents and children with a rare genetic condition called familial dysautonomia, which almost exclusively affects Ashkenazi Jews, Rapp has traced the way in which parents put ever more emphasis on the potential for a genetic solution to the problem.[19] Yet as she points out, to date 'genomic knowledge has produced little that is life extending, whereas the old-fashioned clinical gaze has produced quite a lot'.[20] The point here is that, in contrast with the actual reality of genetic engineering, our popular understanding of DNA means that genetic research may create fears of parentless babies, super humans, and animal-human hybrids, but also hopes for miraculous victories over disease. All this might seem to stem from a molecular universe oblivious to the later concerns of epigenetics, but both raise 'ethical' dilemmas often seen as social and external to science. How would such changes be socially determined? Who might have access to these advantages? What kinds of inequality are being created? Furthermore, if the relations between parents and children are defined by passing on DNA,

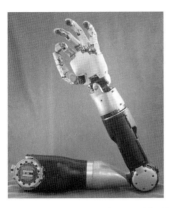

Figure 99. A next-generation prosthesis (© Johns Hopkins University Applied Physics Laboratory. Image courtesy of vandorendesigns.com).

what happens when parts of that DNA come from other human beings, from animals, or from a laboratory, or when more ovaries are transplanted, or when the body parts are grown through tissue engineering?[21]

Further concerns are linked to the potential for cloning. Reproductive cloning involves the production of genetically identical organisms, and is the basis of asexual reproduction. Reproductive cloning of mammals, such as the famous sheep Dolly, involves inserting an adult cell nucleus into an egg cell with no nucleus.[22] This can then, as Dolly showed, grow into another, separate organism. Cloning of a human being remains an area of taboo within both the public and scientific community. Some ethical concerns arise from the fact that cloning a whole animal often leads to biological failure and premature death. Yet even if a simple and guaranteed procedure could be invented, cloning would still raise many ethical issues not only for religious groups, but also for more secular ideas of identity. The Catholic Church has challenged the process because of the way it involves, in their view, the destruction of life. More broadly Pope Benedict XVI has spoken out against the use of embryos in any form of research because of the way it treats them as some*thing* rather than as some*one*. This distinction has been important and we will return to it.

Mass-producing people in cloning vats to fit pre-destined social roles forms the leitmotif of Huxley's famous dystopia *Brave New World*; as this suggests, long before cloning was potentially practical, it threatened the idea of individual identity. Moreover, cloning raises the question of the role of 'nature' once again. What is the status of the parts of a person grown in a laboratory? What of the embryos stored in vast numbers through IVF treatment and available as a source of stem cells?[23] Are they human in any real sense? Do they in themselves, as bearers of human DNA, have rights? Furthermore, if

parts of a person are grown from their own cells, if people are cloned rather than born, what does this mean for human relationships? Should we be looking, as one of the researchers interviewed by Hogle suggests, to 'free humans from the limitations of the body'?[24] Nature, as Strathern[25] points out, is increasingly becoming an issue for design – something some people may find potentially threatening.

Fears and concerns about the ways in which technologies are disturbing the world we take for granted are exemplified by the efforts people put into regulating and shaping these technologies (and their effects). The field of bioethics is one that has emerged to try to ensure that only suitable new forms of technology emerge, that the boundaries of the human are properly policed. Ethics committees and panels, committees of politicians and the broader media all monitor and engage with these issues. Scandals such as that of the Alder Hey hospital in the UK, in which the body parts of deceased children were taken as laboratory specimens without parental knowledge or consent, have underlined the importance of regulation to draw clearly the individual, and the distinction between person and object.[26] Concerns about biotechnology tend to involve worries about positive harm or about tinkering with nature, or to be generated by the way in which both the idea of the 'person' and relationships are disturbed, or by a potential confusion of persons and objects. We have to work hard in Europe to keep person and things, bodies and commodities, and gift and market distinct on these matters.[27] You can donate your body part but you cannot sell it.

This regulation of the relationship between body and technology goes well beyond the medical sphere. Professional athletes for example follow strict regimes which police what they can do to their bodies. They can use specialized training equipment, but not take performance enhancing drugs. Caffeine is acceptable but not diet pills. High energy foods are acceptable but not anabolic steroids. Beyond this, there is other daily regulation on how things and bodies interact, the most obvious examples being that concerning mobile phone use – fine in certain contexts (at home, in public) but not in others (exams, quiet carriages on trains, lecture theatres[28]). It is not just at the extremes of cutting-edge technology that body-technology relationships are regulated.

In many ways, the technologization of the body makes people feel as if they are presented with a Faustian bargain. Each individual innovation is an offer we cannot refuse; it makes sense in terms of its own logic. Vaccinations, corrective eye surgery, hip replacements, transplants for failing organs, medications for mental illness, reproductive technologies for the socially or biologically infertile – there is a growing list. If we can make our daily life healthier, more comfortable, more productive, why should we not do so? Should we willingly refuse to heal a disease, condemning people to suffering and death, allowing people such as the heart patient in our vignette to die? Yet this same logic drives a frenzied development of new technologies, many of which extend changes in the body, or in how we understand it, beyond our comfort zone, fragmenting it, effacing its individuality, erasing boundaries between humans, animals and machines, and making bodies and parts the objects of commodified transactions.[29]

Hence a sense of a slippery slope, a runaway train. In accepting concrete and present hopes and comforts, each of which may be fully justifiable on its own merits, we piecemeal give up something much bigger, the idea of the 'natural' body. Within established dichotomies, the body sits firmly on the side of 'nature', against 'culture' as we saw in Chapter 2. Once built on the foundation of our genes, it is this that makes us human, it is what we feel we have evolved, or been created, to be. But new organic transformations offer to remake nature, or at least assist it in its proper goals; is the body still 'natural' if we have to intervene to make it happen?[30] As we have seen, some of the fears about technology are not so much about technology *per se* but about what technology does to the 'natural' body. Beyond the examples reviewed already, this is shown clearly by comparing cars and cloning.[31] Cloning is a largely theoretical technology without immediate dangers (nobody has ever yet been killed by cloning) which may bring great medical benefits, yet it inspires fears and protests. In terms of real danger, cars are by far the more threatening. They kill many people annually in accidents, they harm many others through pollution, they have severe environmental consequences, and the need for oil to fuel them entangles us in complex, often politically dangerous, relationships. But the car does not threaten to remake our 'natural' body invasively, and we accept cars happily as enhancements to our bodily ability to get from place to place.

Technology, society and the body re-thought

Throughout this volume, we have been critical of the kinds of assumptions that posit the opposition of (for example) nature and culture. If the hopes and fears we feel about modern technology stem from our acceptance of these divisions, how might we understand our relationship to technology differently? The basic assumption at the heart of these fears is that technology and society are separate from one another.[32] A further corollary is that

this technology 'brings itself into being' and is the driving force behind its own adoption.[33] Technology is seen as being 'out there'; it is something that does things to us. It fragments our bodies or forces us to remake them in new ways. Change is not something we can choose to live with or without, but is rather something constantly foisted onto us.

The assumption that technology is an external force driving change is part of what Pfaffenberger has criticized as the 'Standard View of Technology'.[34] In this view, technology is primarily a functional way to control and exploit the world around us. Nature poses challenges to humans which we have overcome through increasingly elaborate material strategies. In recent years, however, this increased elaboration has brought about significant alterations as we shift from using tools to using machines.

> Now we live in a material world. The result of the explosion of technological knowledge has been a massive expansion of Man's reach, but with lamentable and unavoidable social, environmental and cultural consequences: We live in a fabricated environment, mediated by machines. Technology was more authentic when we used tools, because we could control them. *Machines, in contrast, control us.*[35]

This view, which Pfaffenberger caricatures in this quotation, underlies many people's normative perspective of technology in virtually all contexts. At its extremes, it drives not only a concern about where these dominating machines, demanding ever more fuel, space and time, might take us, but an explicit *technophobia*, a fear of technology, its properties and potentials.[36] This can be seen in the writings of Ellul, Mumford and others who 'interpret the history of technology as the progressive obscuring or warping of human nature'.[37] More recently, Postman has declared that the 'uncontrolled growth of technology destroys the vital sources of our humanity'.[38] For Postman,[39] the world in which we currently live is a 'technopoly' in which technology rather than human beings determine our lives. Authors like Postman capture a view more widely held of the dangers of technological determinism, and the absence of 'truly human' virtues – whatever they might be.

Both the standard view of technology and the technophobia that can derive from it have been part of European thought only since the Renaissance,[40] and they have developed alongside the dualities we detailed in Chapter 7. In fact, the term *technology* itself only developed its modern usage in 1706.[41] Drawing on the scholarly work of Shapin and Schaffer,[42] Latour[43] has traced the emergence of the division between science and technology on one side, and society on the other, through the seventeenth-century clash between Robert Boyle, who was investigating what would later become understood as science, and Thomas Hobbes, whose work is now primarily associated with politics. As we saw briefly in the section on knowledge specialists in Chapter 7, whilst Boyle was attempting to develop an empirical science from which politics could be kept separate, Hobbes was developing a political rationale that would not need to bend itself to science.[44] Each emerged out of the fractions and discord of seventeenth-century England; each depended upon both belief and observation; each depended on politics and science. But by separating the two, by denying their common point of origin, each could become master of his own domain.[45] Hobbes' work and that of his intellectual descendants focused on people; Boyle and his descendants focused on things. In this historiography, things (the world of technology and science) became separate from humans (the world of politics and culture), undoing what had previously been a unified enterprise.

These changes also played out elsewhere. Just as we saw mind and body becoming opposed in Chapter 7, so at the same time designing something intellectually and actually doing it physically began to become increasingly separate activities: scientist and technician, architect and builder emerged as separate professions.[46] After this, as technology became increasingly associated with following an externally derived plan, so it became perceived as a force exterior to society itself. Human beings, their abilities, techniques and skills in turn were understood as being detached from the process by which technology – that is things, machines and objects – were brought into being.[47] Technology's role has been to play its part in transforming what has been seen as 'natural' (resources, crops, animals) into what might be perceived to be 'cultural' (petrol, cars, food). The industrial revolution further created a sense of technology as a separate transformative force.[48] People increasingly became marginalized in the process of making things as machines played a greater role in production. In the previous chapter, we argued that people became one part of a larger machine, repeatedly performing simple manual tasks within the larger production processes of factories. By externalizing the term technology, by making it a thing which we could write and talk about, people both distanced themselves from it, and declared its role in driving change.[49]

Latour[50] describes this way of looking at the world as part of the 'Modern Constitution', which rests in part on repeated acts of division, or 'purification' (to use Latour's word), of the world into two opposed camps, whether these be nature and culture, nature and science, or culture and technology. Such distinctions are historically dependent, and some would now find these divisions deeply unsatisfactory. Indeed, in the humanities or in the sciences now, many feel that the perspective Latour describes is not a view that really gets to grips with how people and things interact. Analytically, there is now the possibility instead of thinking of technology as itself social. This does not mean simply thinking of technology as having been socially designed or as having social consequences, all of which of course it does. There is not a social context in which *technology* is designed, emerging from it only to pop back into the social again when it has consequences. Technology and society would, in such models, still be distinct. The point here is that we can rethink technology as inherently social. Instead of treating technology and society as separate things, we are better off thinking of the two as always inseparable, always bringing each other into being and helping to sustain each other.

This has been one of the arguments developed in anthropology for some time now and also in 'science and technology studies', with Latour's work cited in both.[51] In this view, material things and technologies are neither as dominant as the technophobes would have us believe, nor totally pliant as social theories often make them seem. Instead, things and people emerge together in a network, and agency (or the ability to act) is not seen to be dependent on a particular kind of identity. Both things and people can be agents[52] in other words. Take one of Latour's examples: that of the person and the gun.[53] Do guns kill people, or do people kill people? This debate is clearly enmeshed in political baggage, which has served to obscure the rather obvious answer: neither. People with guns kill people. Neither a person without a gun, nor a gun without a person is capable of acting in the same way as when the two are brought together.[54] Thus technology does not produce society (the gun requires the person to aim and fire it) nor does society purely produce technology (creating guns brings in many unforeseen consequences, including the shooting of accidental bystanders and so on). This may all seem rather obscure, but the central point is rather straightforward: technology and society bring each other into being. At the same time, technology has its own relationalities, its own sociality. To put it all another way, 'technology is society made durable'.[55]

When we get to this point, it is clear that both 'technology' and 'society' have changed meaning analytically. 'Society', for followers of Latour, can cover the relationships of the inorganic – and 'technology' can cover pretty much anything from the conceptual to the material. We are not pretending therefore that this point of view is a common one nor is it one constructed for populist appeal. It is one way, however, in which technology, society and the body can be re-thought – and with none of these reified anymore. 'Technology', from within such a view, is no longer a black box posing as an external focus of popular fear.

Incarnation: Technology and the body

> To get used to a hat, a car, a stick is to be transplanted into them, or conversely to incorporate them into the bulk of our own body.[56]

How then does technology relate to bodies rather than to the social world more generally? Rather than getting into theoretical complexities here, let's get into our cars. Although all technologies are equal, some are more equal than others, and cars are undoubtedly one of the defining technologies of our times. Many of us spend an enormous amount of time in cars, commuting to work, shopping or pursuing leisure activities. Cars are the largest purchase most of us make after our houses (themselves another master technology), and the car industry structures the economy as much as the needs of cars structure the landscape we inhabit.

For the driver, the car provides a paradigmatic example of an extended body. Cars transport bodies; yet the process is not neutral and non-sensory. Instead, the car has transformed our experience of movement.[57] The car feeds clues about motion to the body of the driver through multiple senses, not only through the eyes, but through hearing (the sound of the engine, the constant monitoring for anything unusual) and through vibrations.[58] The whole body monitors this latter aspect as the car travels over differing kinds of road surface, gripping with the tyres to different extents. An experienced driver in normal circumstances feels these changes unconsciously rather than monitoring them explicitly. The same is true for monitoring movements in different directions at high speed, for judging distances between your car and others, and so on. Normally, such reflexes are internalized and form part of a closed cycle encompassing the habituated gestures needed to drive. How often does one consciously think about changing gear? It bypasses thought; the car and body become blurred as the brain receives signals from the ears and through the skin and in turn sends a signal to the hands and feet which cooperate together to change the car's gears. The same is true for steering, signalling, and other ways of changing what the car does simultaneously as it changes what your body does. The innocent body does not simply get into a car and drive off; learning to drive is not merely about understanding how a car works, but about learning to grasp, without conscious reflection, a host of complex signals, principles and

embodied actions.[59] We become particularly conscious of this body-car entanglement when something sudden and unexpected happens – for instance when another car swerves unexpectedly into our lane and we have to slow down sharply to avoid an accident. Our response includes not only the appropriate mechanical response – hitting the brakes – but bodily changes too: a shot of adrenalin pumping through the body, often anger or aggression. The car, quite literally, is experienced as an extension of the body, and extends that body in a unique way.[60]

How is this functional embodiment created technologically? Like a carefully fitted prosthetic, cars focus specifically upon the body of the driver. Here cars focus on what Thrift calls the 'phenomenological space of habitability' to produce 'new bodily horizons and orientations'.[61] Ergonomically, seats can be positioned for the particular driver; the cabin provides a heated, padded, sealed-off, musically enhanced, space. Light entering is polarized by glass, road noise is minimized, door locks secure the cabin space from outside threats; all of these reinforce the separation between inside and outside. The body itself is enveloped in a cocoon of gadgets: controls are at hand and at eye, mirrors extend the driver's visibility, car seats accommodate small bodies, seat belts restrain the body, cup holders keep refreshment within reach, and hands-free headsets allow drivers to legally carry on telephone conversations. Many vehicles have 'cruise control' mechanisms to maintain speed automatically and some have speed-limiting devices. Interestingly, a major thrust of recent technological development is to intermingle car and driver ever more.[62] Computer software now often controls windscreen wipers, lights, traction control and ABS brakes.[63] The latest cars already have bumper video-links to aid parking in tight spaces and automatic warnings about too-close encounters with other traffic. Navigation is increasingly controlled by computer systems such as GPS-based satellite navigation, sometimes fitted with robotic voices. Where the driver used to tell the car where to go, now it can be the other way around.

On the road, car space is social in much the same ways that bodily 'personal space' is. Communicating with other drivers largely depends upon basic signals: indicators, flashing of headlights, the raised hand to say thanks, the raised finger to say something else. Yet in spite of the simplicity of such signals, the road forms a social universe in which people experience themselves as surrounded by others. Drivers infer the personality of other drivers (Careful? Dangerous? Polite? Rude?) based upon how they move their cars in relation to yours; a car persistently driving too closely behind one often evokes the same feeling of intrusive presence and annoyance that somebody standing too close to one does. 'Road rage' is an extreme example of such interactions. People who habitually drive in several countries often note distinct national styles of driving in which the positioning and movement of cars on the road has much in common with that of bodies in ordinary interaction. Make and model of car, and what can be seen of the driver, flesh out the social persona ('that's just what I would expect of somebody driving a bright red Mercedes four-by-four[64] with personalised number plates...'). Drivers interact with other users of the road and with the landscape. The sense of speed engendered by driving may make other forms of movement, such as being stuck behind a bicycle or tractor, annoyingly slow. Traffic can be an emotional hell. Other emotions can be engendered through speed or the sense of success elicited by avoiding jams, taking short-cuts and getting home quickly.[65] These are embodied sensations, a central part of the sensuous bodily experience of moving through the city and landscape of the present day.[66]

Cars, in turn, are designed with our bodies, and therefore ideas about our bodies, in mind. Seats are shaped to fit particular kinds of bodies, and those with specific needs often have cars that are specifically designed for them (e.g. wheelchair access). The size of cars indicates the needs of the particular body towards which it is aimed: the people carrier for the extended family, the sports car for the rampant and rich bachelor, the standard saloon for the nuclear family. Above all, cars are related to the sense of *individual* freedom which many see as being paramount. With a car, you don't need to wait for the vagaries of public transport, you can set off as and when you choose. This means you do not need to live close to where you work, you can pursue leisure activities across different contexts. The car is designed to facilitate a single individual in this freedom, but also to allow the families with which these individuals live to come along as well. It is little wonder then that the car has even greater importance in the United States than in Europe, given the increased emphasis on a sense of individual freedom within the former.

Cars are not, however, just things we drive about in. They are the scene for all sorts of other practices both licit and illicit. For drivers on major highway corridors, cars can be the scene of office work – reading reports, replying to emails and so on.[67] Despite the difficulty of performing office work whilst driving, in an environment that is not designed for it, workers 'artfully combine'[68] the dashboard, passenger seat and steering wheel to accomplish the tasks they need to finish on the road. People eat and sleep in cars (technologically enabled through fully reclining seats, tray tables and specific venues such as drive-through restaurants). Passengers can be entertained by built-in video screens. They conduct their social lives in cars via mobile telephones and laptop computers with wireless connections and prepare their social faces by applying cosmetics using mirrors built into standard windshield shades. One in fourteen Americans resides in a mobile home of some form.[69] People have sex in their cars, deal and take drugs in their cars; cars are the sites for a wide range of embodied activities which are in turn shaped by the space the car offers to perform them in.

We have now reached the destination of this ethnographic mini-journey. In some ways, it is easy to draw a border between car and body: the car is what remains when you climb out of it. But in other ways, the car remains with you and helps constitute your body. You carry away with you the capacity to be somewhere else at high speed, the sensation of moving quickly, the habituated reflexes of the driver or passenger, the knowledge of places and distances moved through in fast, detached, road-bound ways. Reciprocally, the car remains as it has to be to accommodate your body, not only as baggage to be transported but as something to be connected to its world via some senses (predominantly vision) but not via others (temperature, rushing air), informed, coddled, entertained and kept safe. To the traveller, car and body are incomplete without each other; together, the combination of car and body makes travel possible, but it is travel of a specific kind with different senses, restrictions and possibilities. As Haraway[70] notes, 'the machine is not an *it* to be animated, worshiped, and dominated. The machine is us, our processes, an aspect of our embodiment'.

Going beyond this detailed example of the car, bodies are constantly caught up in a host of technologies that not only provide us with various 'affordances'[71] but condition how we can act in the world; they train our bodies to move in certain ways.[72] Tools of different kinds allow us to think differently, because of the way in which they provide the fuel for metaphors, because of the connections they create between people, because of the way they can embody biographies, connections and relationships. Physically, using tools or machines repetitively creates detectable changes to both muscular and skeletal structure, for example. Similarly, repeated use of different kinds of tools alters the way the brain works, creating and reinforcing alternative neural pathways.[73] Hence, tools literally produce our bodies as we engage with them.[74] Experientially, technology, the things, objects, architecture, tools and devices that surround us are what makes the world understandable and, more than this, inhabitable. The world is revealed to us through our engagement with material things, through the way they show up to us.[75]

Bodies today emerge from a mosaic of technologies as we touched on in Chapter 2: people interact through portable media devices that extend the boundaries of bodies and the ways bodies can communicate;[76] cosmetic surgery transforms bodies in line with both a racialized and sexualized notion of beauty;[77] more commonplace 'reflexive body techniques'[78] including exercise (Plate VIIIf), brushing one's teeth and shaving[79] all help to shape bodies through interactions with technologies. Each of these form a reciprocal relationship with bodies, generally constituting the way these situated, habituated and contextualised forms (including gendered forms) of being human become possible. These technologies range from the invasive – plastic and cosmetic surgery – to the extended – mobile phones, smart phones, wireless internet and so on. Our daily interactions with things from toothpaste to tarmac are 'materializing practices' and it is through these practices that bodies are produced.[80] Thus bodies and things do not pre-exist as givens in the world but are instead, constantly changing as they bring each other into being recursively, rather than one simply imposing any 'will' on the other.[81] As Thrift[82] has suggested, it is precisely because of the human body's ability to 'co-evolve' with things that human beings have become what they are.

Where then does the boundary between the body and technology lie? Try an unexpectedly disconcerting thought experiment. Take anybody you know and progressively strip away their material things – sensory and social prosthetics such as headphones and mobile phones; external shells such as coats and hats; increasingly intimate layers of clothing; signifiers of memory and relationships such as rings and heirlooms; prosthetics which almost form part of the body such as dentures and contact lenses; the body and things inside it – the carefully styled hair, tattoos, pinned bones and pacemakers. The naked being is a different social being; as concentration camp guards from Auschwitz to Guantanamo Bay know, stripping away material personhood limits one's ability to act. And yet the traces of technology remain within the body itself, formed by exercise, by nutritional regimes, by vaccinations, and by habits latent in the back which knows how to carry and the fingers which know where the keys on the keyboard are.

We also need to take on board the reverse aspect of this equation. Just as technologies constitute bodies, so bodies help to constitute technology. As Shilling has noted 'basic bodily needs remain a *source* of technological innovation'.[83] Need emerges in particular social, historical and material contexts. Plastic surgery did not emerge *ex nihilo* to shape our understanding of bodies, but rather in a world in which physical 'perfection' was becoming ever more salient and saleable.

To take a simple example, consider the problem of failing eyesight, something which is very common after the age of about forty. There is a long and rapidly accelerating sequence of technologies for dealing with this beginning towards the end of the thirteenth century: reading stones, rivet spectacles, old-fashioned pince-nez spectacles, modern-style eyeglasses with earpieces offering simple magnification, eyeglasses with lenses custom-fitted to a particular patient's vision, bifocals, varifocals, scratch-proof surfaces, glare reduction lenses, contact lenses of many varieties, laser vision correction surgery.[84] From our perspective, it seems obvious that if poor vision can be corrected, it should be. Hence, technology seems an autonomous, external force whose history simply reflects progressive technical perfection to a functional need. Yet eyeglasses were technically feasible, and known in Europe since the thirteenth century, long before the widespread market for them came in during the sixteenth century.[85] Initially, they addressed problems of farsightedness, only turning to myopia in the fifteenth century (although the technical requirements were not excessively different).[86] In an era in which it was assumed that bodily imperfection and change was simply a fact of life, in which it was assumed that old age meant sitting by the fire 'sans teeth, sans eyes, sans taste, sans everything' (as Shakespeare says[87]), there was no active search for remedies to inevitable degeneration. Forms such as the pince-nez glasses without earpieces allowed the nearsighted to read, but not necessarily to see while being physically active.

The widespread use of spectacles increases through the Early Modern and Modern periods, just as the beginnings of ideas of a medical, healthy body come to prominence.[88] At this time they were largely sold by street peddlers. Prescription spectacles and opticians really date to the twentieth century. This was the era in which the idea of medical technology as a way of maintaining the mechanical body to a uniform standard came to the fore on a mass scale, along with the adoption of a young and economically productive body as the standard for people of all ages. The recent acceleration in varieties such as improved bifocals,[89] varifocals and contact lenses is driven principally by the development of eyeglasses as a commercial product, parallel to the proliferation of consumer choice in other fields. Similarly, new medical procedures are developed through economic and social choices, not by technological progress as a disembedded force. Laser corrective surgery may not have been the most urgent life-saving innovation to develop, but it is obviously a welcome development in a prosperous society that does not want to age.

Thus, our 'social' expectations of the body also help to determine technology. To return to an example from

Chapter 2, there are many technologies that exist principally to structure how bodies are spaced together or apart; these range from plastic bars separating groceries at the supermarket checkout line to seating, partitions, cubicles, dividers and screens, bed designs suited for particular kinds of relationships, signage, table service, and many others. The sense of personal intimacy and bodily boundaries underlying these is a product of relatively recent ideas about the body.[90] In the last chapter we saw how ideas of the 'individual' emerged in context with individualised tasks at work, individualised seating, cutlery and crockery and so on. These conceptions of the body now in turn demand particular kinds of individualised technologies designed for singular, separate and bounded bodies.

The conclusion is straightforward. Bodies and technology are co-constitutive. People and things are both central to the notion of practice, and it is through practice that bodies are continually remade.[91] This is something we have encountered throughout this book. To give just two examples, in the Neolithic we saw how pottery created new links between houses, bodies and vessels, and in the Bronze Age we described how metals and the body together forged new possibilities for social display and thus personhood. What is most interesting about this is what it does to the common metanarrative of technology driving bodily change. Rather than technology as an external force, driving change in how we understand the human body, there is no prime mover here. Trying to tease out where technology stops and the body begins in the present or in the past demands that we try and separate out things that, in many ways, were never divisible in the first place. Whereas the body has been thought of as something apparently stable but under threat from a separated and externalized technology, we can see that technologies and bodies might be conceptualized alternatively as utterly imbricated with one another, and interacting in innumerable ways.

Multiple bodies: Body and technology in biotechnology

Technologies of everyday life, from mobile phones to cars, are caught up in emergent and co-constitutive relationships with bodies. So, too, are the new biotechnologies. Just as cars are constructed to meet the perceived needs of individual commuters and nuclear families, and in doing so alter the capacities of those bodies, so the work surrounding DNA (whether in genetic modifications or fingerprinting) builds on, transforms and is transformed by pre-existing understandings. Thus we use DNA signatures to trace ancestry in a manner that would be familiar

to people in the nineteenth century, or to identify individuals as criminals just as fingerprinting or phrenology allowed us to before. In the aftermath of terrorist atrocities like 9/11, we rely on the promiscuity and unbounded nature of DNA (we leave it behind wherever we go) to restore a sense of individuality to otherwise unidentifiable remains in a manner which people in the 1950s, say, would also have recognized as important.[92] Similarly the new reproductive technologies we have already described do not create afresh concepts of parenthood but rather emerge from our categories of what it means to be a mother and a father. Fertility treatments now often reflect the concept that any healthy body should be able to have children that are its direct biological offspring regardless of its age, fertility or social relations. The different hearts described in our vignettes that opened the chapter all act to sustain the body in the same way a 'natural' organ would do – they do not seek to exceed its capabilities.

It is worth reminding ourselves for a moment that body-changing technologies already permeate our ordinary lives. Pharmaceutical products give just one of many examples. Immunizations permanently change the way our immune system deals with certain diseases, allowing different and presumably better futures to exist for the altered body.[93] The vast majority of children and adults in the western world are now immunized against a wide range of diseases, and these permanent biological alterations to our children's bodies are often viewed as a moral imperative rather than with fear. Other products also alter our physical and embodied states. Increasing numbers of children are prescribed Ritalin, and many adults alter their mood through drugs like Prozac.[94] Painkillers and prescription drugs are taken for allergies, asthma and other complaints. Other bodily transformations can be achieved using drugs which allow particular kinds of activities. Steroids, for example, can swell athletes' muscles and transform their physical capacities, whilst Viagra can bring its own forms of gender performativity and pleasure. All of these vaccines, drugs and painkillers are produced through the interaction of people and things, and allow bodies to emerge that are capable of doing different things, living in different ways and responding differently to various situations.

Scanning technologies

Imaging machines provide a particularly well-studied example of the consequences new technologies can have for how we conceptualize bodies.[95] They inevitably draw on our existing understandings but also create new bodies. These screening technologies include a wide range of commonly used techniques of which mammograms, foetal scans and brain imaging are just three examples. We cite these here to remind ourselves of how, in an important sense, we live through different bodies. We do this contextually in our developmental and daily lives anyway but medical technologies can seem to add to the bodies available.[96]

Mammograms work by using low-level x-rays to examine women's breasts for cancerous tissue. They are now widely used to screen women routinely for breast cancer. Lives are saved through this process, although the numbers are not large, and emphasis upon them hides repeated cases of misdiagnosis, particularly of false positives.[97] While we commonly perceive mammograms as simply revealing what is already there, they also produce new bodies, and new embodiments of the bodies depicted. Screening can produce either healthy or ill bodies based on new criteria; a body can be 'ill' even if it is entirely asymptomatic. And once a body has been classified mechanically as 'healthy' or 'ill', it affects ideas of identity and self with it, as well as the range of options open for future embodied practice. The body is clearly constituted through technology here, but at the same time ideas of a comparable internal set of structures that can be revealed through particular practices (whether anatomy of the dead or scanning of the living) also clearly draw on existing ideas of the body: so 'the body' constitutes technology as well.

Another screening example with similar consequences is foetal scans. These use ultrasound images to inspect a foetus in a pregnant woman's uterus. The ultrasound image brings the foetus, which might previously have been detected inferentially, to the surface.[98] This foetus is of course a cyborg – visible only in its conjunction with machines.[99] Whilst we might wish to view the foetal scan as merely revealing what we already know to be the case, there is never anything 'mere' about the act of revealing, because to reveal is always simultaneously to create. Ultrasound images, in combination with the physical changes going on in a woman's body, thus produce new bodies – foetal bodies, pregnant bodies and the new relationships between them. It is this complexity of conjoined individuality that constantly raises the pregnant woman as a subject for both ethical and legal debate.[100] The ultrasound image can produce the sense of the foetus as an individual person separate from the mother: 'culturally speaking, we can see the person when the person appears as an individual, and we see an individual when we see a body'.[101] Expectant parents now show ultrasound images to friends and relatives, keep them in photo albums and display them on social networking sites, much like baby pictures. This production of an individual is of course central to anti-abortion groups' usage of these images;

they are by no means politically neutral.[102] Just as our sense of the foetal body and the pregnant body are produced by these technologies, so this scanning technology both draws on and is encouraged by our understanding and construction of bounded, individualized bodies.

Brain scans, a third example, have increasingly been used to diagnose disorders such as chronic fatigue syndrome, attention deficit disorder, Gulf War Syndrome and others.[103] These diseases are contested, with their physical bases and symptoms questioned. Sufferers face a battle to have their condition recognized, both legally and medically, to obtain treatment, compensation or changed working conditions.[104] Brain scans are central here because they are often used to support diagnosis, to show that the condition is not just 'in the patient's mind' but rather in the brain, and therefore 'real'. It is worth noting the tenacity of the historical mind:body dichotomy here. The former is 'cultural', constructed and not the purview of medicine, the latter is 'natural'. If the disorder can be found (literally) within the body, then it must be a 'real', medical, physical condition – giving the sufferer a stronger claim for treatment or compensation.

But brain scans such as those produced by functional magnetic resonance imaging machines (fMRI) play a contested role. In Dumit's[105] account, scientists and machine operators were reluctant to use scans as definitive evidence. Yet because the images offered tantalisingly physical proof, they were accepted far more readily in courtrooms than they were in the laboratory as 'hard proof' of the physical reality of the condition. Such 'proof' can appease not only courts and companies but the sufferers themselves, providing validation of their condition. Once again, then, technology does not simply reveal the existence of the disease but shapes it as a socio-medical reality. Moreover, the reality of these disorders is verified as much in disability hearings, courtrooms, insurance companies and doctors' surgeries as at the conjunction of brain and imaging machine. This also allows the truth of these conditions to be contested in differing locales: 'for sufferers and their families, this landscape of differential diagnosis can provide an opportunity for them to help control the answers by *changing the venue* where the questions are asked'.[106] Diagnosis here relies on far more than the technology merely revealing what was already there. Each form of scanning or imaging technologies not only creates new 'representations' of human bodies, they also create new truths and new bodies.[107] The images shown in Figure 100 circulate between different contexts: medical labs, textbooks, image libraries, homes, police stations and so on.[108] This allows bodies to act in new ways and in new surroundings. These images give bodies new powers and new potentials – in many ways,

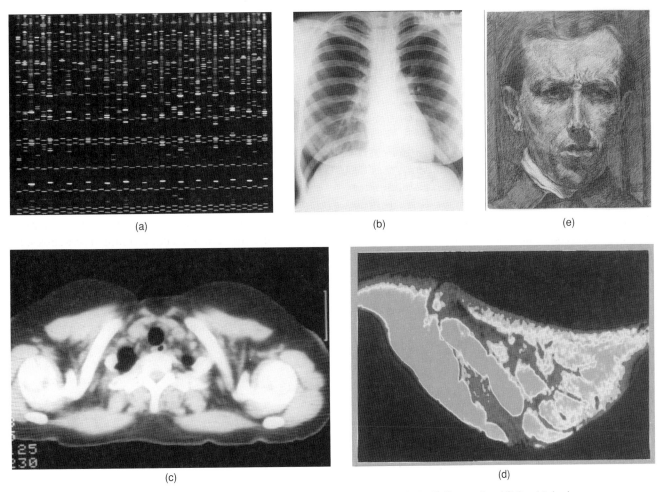

Figure 100. Some of the multiple bodies of scanning technologies. A. DNA fingerprints (© Sue Moberly, via Wellcome Images). B. X-ray. C. Computerized tomography (CT) scan. D. Mammogram (all © Wellcome Images). E. Self-portrait of Umberto Boccioni, 1910 (© Metropolitan Museum of Art). See also the enhanced MRI in Plate VIIIe.

new bodies. Alongside these new potentials, the images draw on older ideas and concepts.

Scanning technologies create, therefore, as much as they reveal and draw on our existing understandings of the body and our social needs in doing so. Biotechnology is also constitutive of bodies and vice versa, in the way we have already suggested; the stark novelty now is that bodies themselves have become technologies. The creation of cell-lines is one obvious example, with the HeLa line perhaps the most famous, as the first 'immortal cell line' created from human materials.[109] A more established example has long been offered by the donation of whole bodies for medical education[110] but the use of human tissue in medicine and research has gathered new controversy – and new regulation and ethical formulation around it.[111] We have touched on just a few other examples in this chapter: stem cells, organ transplants, cloning, DNA and new reproductive technologies. We have moved from bodies as machines to molecular

and sub-molecular bodies, with technology constructing these bodies – and with the bodily material now rendered technology. In the way we have presented this, we have tried to make clear that, analytically, technology and the body and society are not a priori separate entities although they may be seen as such; instead, each inheres in the other. If we take this viewpoint back to earlier chapters, it becomes clear that bodies and technologies have always been imbricated the one in the other.

Many of the medical technologies discussed here – from eyeglasses to scanning technologies – both depend on and help to create the idea of a standard healthy universal body whose functioning can be monitored mechanically, specified bureaucratically and which can be repaired mechanically when it falls short (as we mentioned briefly in Chapter 2). It is this (largely mythical) figure against which the real thing – the leaky, smelly, ill and diseased body – is compared. The body, whether ill or well, is a material reality, but our understandings of this material never prefigure its engagement with environing circumstances, people, the world or with history. Just as with the technologies more commonplace in daily life that we just listed (from cars to mobile phones to tooth brushes), new technologies do not arise inevitably and independently; they are developed specifically to fit perceived social needs.[112] These 'needs' are themselves already embodied.

Thus, no coherent 'brave new world' is emerging from the wreckage of ideas. Instead, when we examine the different vectors of new technologies in detail, they deal with different issues in each case, and the same technology can be used in radically different ways. Scanning technologies offer us different and multiple bodies, depending on the specific corporealities depicted,[113] and may then be embodied in turn. They can also advance a sense that the individual's health is bureaucratically defined and managed, something which meshes well with a perceived growth of governmental biopower[114] in the form of biometric databases. But like DNA fingerprinting and its uses, this depends upon a traditional idea of the 'individual' and the individual, disciplined body as the basal unit of 'society'. New reproductive technologies blur biological relations at the same time as DNA-supported family genealogies perpetuate an entirely traditional model of descent. Transplants, cloning and DNA sequencing create the ability to fragment the body into ever-smaller pieces, but the uses of such techniques (healing a person, tracing somebody's identity) depend upon images of original unity,[115] emphasizing the uniqueness perceived at the heart of European and American personhood.

Conclusion: Dominant modalities

The previous sections have dealt with two issues. First, we have glimpsed some of the hopes and fears people have about the body and modern technology. It became clear that the basis for many fears involved a premise, now contested, that the body and technology were separate things, and that the latter was bearing down on the former, transforming it out of all recognition. We then turned to the second issue: how can we think differently about the relationship between the body and technology? By examining both the technologies we encounter in everyday life (e.g. the car) and a few modern medical and 'bio'-technologies, we have suggested that just as technology changes the body (as it inescapably does) so it in turn is shaped by our own prior assumptions about what the body is and what the body needs, and is shaped by the bodies that embody such realities.

Hacking has summarized a point well-known now to social scientists – that 'the effects of new technologies

are not determined by the technologies themselves but by how they mesh with a view of a person living in the world, a way of life. New conceptions and practices fit into existing moral codes and attitudes'.[116] A novel technology per se does not instigate controversy. New reproductive technologies such as surrogate motherhood may lead to social confusion only if understanding and discussion starts from a baseline belief that children should receive their biological substance from only two individuals and that these biological parents must also be the child's social and legal parents. A key point of any worries about technology is the conviction that our own bodies are 'natural' and hence any departure from them 'unnatural'. Yet, examples from other technologically advanced parts of the world and the historical difference traced in this book show how this view is a particular one of its time. What is going on at present is not the replacement of a 'natural' body by a culturally defined one but a conflict between different bodies. The idea of nature versus culture, as Strathern puts it, 'belonged to a world structured by divisions and dichotomies, where, in struggling to be free of machines, people perceived themselves to be dominated by them'.[117]

Building from the material in the last chapter, and as noted in the introduction, we can see that within the bodily ontologies available, two tend to dominate. Perhaps the most widely held conception of the body in the Euro-American world is that it is equivalent to the person, to the unique and bounded individual. We see this in many instances. For example, a cultivated sense of personal space and privacy only make sense if you take for granted the idea that distance and visibility between two physical bodies reflects, or creates, a social relationship between two people. Bodies are only bodies because they are social in their materiality[118] and they are clearly both social and multiple: most people might feel differently about undressing in front of a stranger or a crowd from how they would feel about undressing in front of their spouse, their cat or their wardrobe. This modality of the body as person links the sense of bounded self we discussed in Chapter 1 to the idea of an inner self, accessible through introspection, we touched on in Chapter 7.

Yet there are also arenas in which not the body as person but the body as machine emerges, our second dominant modality. This became prominent, as we saw in Chapter 7, from the coming together of many different elements including discourses in science, medicine, philosophy, the disciplining devices of schools, hospitals, prisons and asylums and the daily experiences of home, work and landscape. There are many contexts in which people's bodies might be, or might have been, objectified in some way – if only because many modern workplaces have been organised in ways that have treated workers as 'a cog in the machine'. But for most of us, the contrast is most obvious in medicine. In medical practice, the body is occasionally treated as thing-like, its properties dictated by material processes. For example, medical treatment to help a broken ankle heal might normally require stabilizing and aligning the bones and assuring the flow of blood and nutrients to the area, not spiritual repentance, psychotherapy, blood vengeance or a witchcraft trial to ascertain the cause of the injury; it is basically the same whether the ankle belongs to a saintly person or a sinner, a Scorpio or a Sagittarius, a stranger, friend, lover or enemy. This opposition between the natural, material body and social relationships has emerged out of the practices and dichotomies popularized through the Early Modern and Modern periods as we saw in Chapter 7.

In medical education and in everyday medical encounters, tension between treating the patient as a person and treating his or her body as a material thing is latent, and situations in which it can loom large are hedged with protocols of various kinds.[119] Privacy, uniforms, situational expectations and professional manners create a routinized space in which it is understood that doctors can see and touch patients in ways that would be inappropriate for them as private individuals. This is often established subtly through small boundary-setting mannerisms; for example, dentists and doctors inspecting one's face at very close quarters avoid looking directly into one's eyes in a way which would suggest the physical intimacy of friends or lovers. The work of von Hagens, which we saw in Chapter 1, creates such controversy precisely by flouting these boundaries. Real people are objectified and transformed into things; they are not presented merely as medical subjects, but rather playing chess or basketball. The horror for some, and fascination for others, emerges not only from the objectification of bodies, therefore, but the way this objectification is subverted outside the suitably reverential ground of scientific practice.

Where then, do these attitudes come from? As we saw in the previous chapter, and then discussed in this chapter in relation to technology, the work of anatomists, scientists and philosophers alongside changing regimes of discipline at home and at work, led to the hardening and codification of a particular, dualistic way of thinking about the world. Although many of the specific oppositions (mind/soul versus body, nature versus culture and so on) appear to have long histories that can take them back at least as far as Classical Greece (see Chapter 5), they nonetheless became increasingly firmly set in the Early Modern period. It was through redefining matter as an inert substance, as Descartes did, that people became able to clearly differentiate themselves from it,

to privilege mind over body, to separate and oppose culture and nature.[120] Our concepts of the body as machine and the body as person can be read directly on to the dominant concerns with the body as natural versus the person as cultural, and on to dichotomies of technology and society. These are the multimodalities of our time, and whilst we might school ourselves, as do medical students, to accept that the body is a machine in certain contexts, the subjective, the personal and the individual constantly return to haunt this. Whilst we may analytically reject these dichotomies (as we clearly have earlier in our discussion), and recognize their historical contingency, they nevertheless form important components in commonplace understandings of not only the technologies of daily life but also those of the twenty-first-century biosciences.

This tension between body as machine and body as person is often encapsulated in the kinds of fears and concerns with which we opened this chapter. Fear of technology through the nineteenth and twentieth centuries came to be felt and expressed, in the mode of Frankenstein, through visions of a progressively technologized body. Modernity seems constantly to produce new things which cannot be defined as either culture *or* nature. As we saw in Chapter 7, in *Frankenstein*, Mary Shelley uses the figure of the monster to stand as one of these hybrids, as a creature that is neither nature nor culture, and as such is the wellspring of our fears. If the body is just a machine, surely it should be improved in all the usual ways: new parts, repairs, new kinds of engineering, the installation of a computer and so on? But on the other hand, if it is a person, then its 'natural' integrity should be respected. Until recently, the understanding of the body as machine was a metaphor or an analogy: it was not *literally* true. Modern medical technologies, however, threaten to cross the divide between analogy and reality, and to make the metaphors material.[121] Where the machines and the factories of the industrial revolution increasingly made people understand their body as *if* it were like a machine, we now seem to have the potential to make it truly machine-like.[122] As we saw in our vignettes: where before the heart was like a pump, now it may literally *be* a pump. Biotechnology furthers the tension in the boundaries between nature and culture as well as between person and object; its products defy easy classification.

Even while changing, bodies at every scale always carry their histories with them. Rather than a 'modern body' replacing a 'pre-modern body', what we have seen is a gradual shift. Alongside continued elements of a microcosmic view of the world (in horoscopes and phrases like the 'head of state'), it is two bodies – the body as machine and the body as person – that have come to dominate, emerging from Medieval and Early Modern perspectives that contrasted the soul/person with the material form (see Chapters 6 and 7). What has changed, however, is both the emergence of a new master discourse (science) in replace of another (religion) and the ability of that discourse to undermine the very separations that led to its emergence in the first place. If we wish, we can punctuate this with historical 'turning points' – the 'birth of the prison',[123] or the discovery of DNA and so on – but such moments are always the long-term product of historical process rather than being any instantaneous externally generated cause. Moreover, the idea that we live in unique, perpetually changing time is itself part of modernist self-definition. The idea that technology is now causing revolutionary change rests partly on the perception that, before the present, the body was static, an unchanging a-historical constant. New technologies and practices constitute new kinds of bodies, but we should emphasize the *familiarity* of change in contrast to the assumptions of stability. New genetic technologies may change the corporeal realities of ageing, but so did medicine in the twentieth century. Human-machine cyborgs may extend human capacities to act on the world as never before, but so did the invention of pottery. Organ transplants may allow parts of one person's body to move to another's but so, in an important sense, did the exchange of polished stone axes. Such considerations of both scale and experiential reality suggest that change is not always quite as dramatic as it might otherwise appear.[124]

As the medieval gave way to the early modern and thence to the twentieth century, long-standing concepts and practices rarely vanished; what happened instead was a shift in relations amongst bodily modalities. Between 1600 and 2000, for example, there was no single moment in which people in Europe and the United States stopped believing in the body as animated by a spirit and started to believe in it as a purely material thing. Instead, both of these perspectives were present before and after that period. The concepts of body as person and body as machine, and related attitudes to technology, are part of these long-term historical trends. Are bodies changing? Undoubtedly yes. But are they changing in a manner that is unprecedented? No. Instead, it is ideas of the 'natural' body, which bodies are commonly imagined to be, that are under sustained pressure in the current world. In the final chapter we turn to our conclusions from this wide-ranging study of the body in history, and we will examine the extended history of these different modalities there.

NOTES

1. Although this chapter covers the most limited time frame of any of our case studies, the literature is no smaller, and once more reaches across diverse modes of thought. For a general account of literature referring to what we have earlier called the modern body world, the reader is directed to Chapter 2 (which discusses several examples). This chapter focuses more closely on the relationship between bodies and technologies and thus concentrates on a slightly different literature. As well as Foucault's (1973) understanding of emerging medical practice, the key texts from anthropology include Strathern's essential analysis of English kinship and modern medical technologies (1992a; 1992b), the work of Franklin (e.g. 2003; 2006), Lock (2000; 2003) and Mol (2002). Excellent edited volumes include Franklin and Lock (2003) and Lock, Young and Cambrosio (2000). More broadly, the world of modern material culture has recently formed an important area of study for anthropologists (e.g. Buchli 2002). One oft-cited introduction to this is Miller (2010) and an edited volume with a more explicitly theoretical slant, Miller (2005b). Technology (Pfaffenberger 1992) and science and technology studies, strongly influenced by actor-network theory (e.g. Law 2002), are important; the work of Latour is pivotal (for one summary, see McDonald 2012). The best introduction to Latour's ideas is perhaps Latour (2005), although we more heavily cite other works by him (e.g. Latour 1993; 1999). Shilling (2005) also provides an informative account of bodies' relations with technology in modernity.
2. Foucault 1973.
3. McDonald 2012; 1989.
4. Brodwin 2000; McDonald 2012.
5. Strathern 1992a.
6. In vitro fertilization, which is involved with up to 5 per cent of births in some countries (Franklin 2006, 177).
7. Strathern 1992a, 40–41.
8. Foucault 1978
9. cf. Knappett 2005, 18.
10. Lock 2002; Lock 2003; McDonald 2011.
11. Lock 2000; 2003.
12. Diagnoses of death and their acceptance can vary, however. Brain death was only legally recognized in Japan in 1997, and has been problematic for families and physicians alike. As a consequence, far fewer cadaveric organs have been recovered for transplantation (Lock 2000, 235).
13. Sharp 2000.
14. Rabinow 1996, 149; Sharp 2000, 305.
15. Strathern 2005, 15.
16. Strathern 2005, 25.
17. Rapp 2003, 130.
18. Of course, new studies have made this picture more complex. DNA is not simply a fixed code but something that is changeable; it is a two-way messaging system (Franklin

2003, 75; 2006, 160). Geneticists have long been surprised by the way their work is absorbed by the public (Strathern 2005, 167), but it is increasingly clear that it is a very particular aspect of DNA and genetic engineering (one that fits with accepted ideas of natural selection and architecture and within commonplace dichotomies such as nature and culture) that is widely focused on. The role of mitochondrial DNA, for example, equally essential to reproduction, has played a less active role in the public imagination (Parisi 2007, 38).

19. Rapp 2003, 136–144.
20. Rapp 2003, 142–143.
21. Brown 1999; Hogle 2003; Strathern 1992b; 2005.
22. Known as somatic cell nuclear transfer (Franklin 2006, 169).
23. Franklin 2006, 174.
24. Hogle 2003, 81.
25. Strathern 1992a, 47.
26. Parry 2005.
27. McDonald 2012; Pottage and Mundy 2004.
28. In the last two cases, this is an ideal at least.
29. Strathern 1996.
30. Strathern 1992b, 58.
31. cf. Strathern 2005, 18.
32. Ingold 2000, 313.
33. Strathern 2005, 92.
34. Pfaffenberger 1992, 493.
35. Pfaffenberger 1992, 494 (our emphasis).
36. cf. Spacapan and Oskamp 1990, 14.
37. Mitcham 1979, 164; cf. Ferkiss 1993.
38. Postman 1993, xii.
39. Postman 1993, 48.
40. Strathern 2005, 93.
41. Mitcham 1979, 184.
42. Shapin and Schaffer 1985.
43. Latour 1993.
44. Latour 1993, 27.
45. Latour 1993.
46. Ingold 2000, 295.
47. Ingold 2000, 315.
48. Pfaffenberger 1992.
49. Strathern 2005, 94–95.
50. Latour 1993.
51. Latour 1987; 1991; 1993; 1999; 2005.
52. Or more properly actants in Latour's terms.
53. Latour 1999; cf. Fowles 2010; Knappett 2005; Robb 2004.
54. See Fowles 2010 for a sophisticated discussion of how the political aspects of this debate are more complex than Latour supposes, particularly around the importance for the U.S. right of the absent as well as the present gun.
55. Latour 1991.
56. Merleau-Ponty 1962, 143.
57. Thrift 2008, 75.
58. Dant 2004, 73.

59. Crossley 2004, 38.
60. Dant 2004, 74; Thrift 2008, 81.
61. Thrift 2008, 83.
62. Thrift 2008, 85.
63. Thrift 2008, 83.
64. With apologies to any readers who drive such vehicles impeccably.
65. Sheller 2004.
66. Thrift 2008.
67. Laurier 2004.
68. Laurier 2004, 26.
69. Hart, Rhodes, and Morgan 2002; cited by Thrift 2008, 80.
70. Haraway 1991, 180.
71. Gibson 1979.
72. Mauss 1990; Merleau-Ponty 1962.
73. Bloch 1998; Malafouris 2004.
74. Sofaer 2006; Taylor 2005, 745; Chapter 2.
75. As we saw in Chapter 2, most of the time we do not pay direct attention to the things themselves, they are humble, staying in the background, remaining ready-to-hand (cf. Heidegger 1962; Miller 1987; 2005a; 2010a; Olsen 2010). Yet, in thinking about our most routinized encounters with matter – stumbling around the kitchen making coffee first thing in the morning, for example – they form the basis of our sensory experiences, our habituated routines, our orientations for action.
76. cf. Strathern 2005, 26.
77. Crossley 2006, 31; Gill, Henwood, and McLean 2005, 49; Sharp 2000, 307–308; Taylor 2005, 748.
78. Crossley 2004; 2005; 2006.
79. Bickle 2007.
80. Taylor 2005, 744.
81. Haraway 1991; 1993; Ingold 2000; Knappett 2005; Latour 1993; 2005; Thrift 2008; Thomas 1996.
82. Thrift 2008, 10.
83. Shilling 2005, 175, original emphasis.
84. Veyrat, Blanco, and Trompette 2008.
85. Veyrat, Blanco, and Trompette 2008.
86. Maldonado 2001, 39.
87. *As You Like It*, Act II. Scene VII.
88. Foucault 1977; Veyrat, Blanco, and Trompette 2008.
89. Invented by Benjamin Franklin in the eighteenth century.
90. cf. Foucault 1978.
91. Taylor 2005, 744; Thrift 2008, 8.
92. ap Stifin 2008.
93. Hables Gray, Figueroa-Sarriera, and Mentor 1995, 2; Thrift 2005, 247.
94. Thrift 2005, 247.
95. Edwards, Harvey, and Wade 2010.
96. cf. Mol 2002.
97. Kaufert 2000, 173–177.
98. Taylor 2005.
99. Sharp 2000, 317.
100. cf. Strathern 2005, 29.

101. Strathern 1992a, 50.
102. Sharp 2000, 301.
103. Dumit 2000.
104. Dumit 2000, 210.
105. Dumit 2000.
106. Dumit 2000, 217, original emphasis.
107. cf. examples in Edwards, Harvey, and Wade 2010; Oudshoorn and Pinch 2005.
108. See Latour (1999, chapter 2) for a full discussion of the importance of the circulating referent.
109. Landecker 2003; 2007; Rabinow 1996.
110. McDonald forthcoming.
111. Nuffield Council on Bioethics 2011; Price 2009.
112. The point has been made many times that medical technologies are not outside of 'culture' and acting upon it, but are part of it. For the cases outlined here, it is worth stressing, however, that people rarely interact with technology in an unmediated way. Institutions, including governments, health authorities, businesses, law enforcement, charities and associations, play their role in the way people and things come together. Institutions play an important role not least because of their size, their ability to spread across both time and space. Scale, time and history are central to this relationship as well as to the broader narratives of change to which we turn in Chapter 9.
113. Mol 2002.
114. Foucault 1978, 140.
115. Strathern 1992b, 157.
116. Hacking 2007, 81.
117. Strathern 2004, 37.
118. Lambert and McDonald 2009.
119. See Good 1994; McDonald 2011; 2012; forthcoming; and Sinclair 1997 for references and examples.
120. Mitcham 1979, 185–187.
121. Strathern 1992b, 2–3.
122. Hacking 2007.
123. Foucault 1977.
124. contra Thrift 2006, 192.

9

The body in history: A concluding essay

Oliver J. T. Harris and John Robb

Far from the body having to be effaced, what is needed is to make it visible through an analysis in which the biological and the historical are . . . bound together in an increasingly complex fashion. . . . Hence I do not envision a 'history of mentalities' that would take account of bodies only in the manner in which they have been perceived and given meaning and value; but a 'history of bodies' and the manner in which what is most material and most vital in them has been invested.

Michel Foucault[1]

History can be read as a series of forms of embodiment which come into being and then act as historical forces.

Chris Shilling[2]

The paradoxical body

Reality exists, but it is complex. More than complex – it is contradictory, patterned and unpatterned, ambiguous, multiple. It is a forest to walk through which you can understand as a riotous Van Gogh landscape, a sepia photograph of memory, an expressionist moodscape, a technical blueprint, a sensory Calvary of pleasures and pain, or a blindfolded world of bird calls, leaves rustling in the wind, and the footfalls of unseen beasts. In such a world, there is no representation without misrepresentation; there is no remembering some things without forgetting others. Much as we would like it to be otherwise, twenty-first-century Western academics have not managed to escape the human condition and achieve a way of understanding the body (and the world) which does not rely upon metaphors as much as other people do. The question is not which metaphors are true and which are false, but which ones help us understand particular things about the body.

Thus: what is 'the human body'? One answer – the one with which many readers probably embarked upon this book – is the practical, common-sense, no-nonsense view: the body is a natural, physical object which carries out biological processes such as breathing, nourishing itself, excreting, growing, reproducing and dying. All the rest is dressing it up in 'culture'. Yet this view is itself a historical product; it emerged with the 'body as machine' metaphor in the sixteenth century (Chapter 7). It isn't a complete view of the body; people of that time (and indeed today) invoked several other understandings of the body to fill in its blind spots and to deal with many other situations in which it was not very useful to see the body only as a physical object. Moreover, the conceptual basis of this view is questionable. It presumes that 'nature' is distinct from 'culture'; thus a universal 'natural' body pre-exists the 'social' body. Yet humans can never not be social. The very structures and processes of the physical body itself always develop within social relations.[3] Social mating patterns bring together a particular sperm and a particular egg with their cargo of DNA to create a new body already endowed with a social position. Social relations feed the body abundantly or inadequately, let it grow or stunt it; they prescribe it a regime of activity which shapes its bones and muscles, which wears it out at forty or which delivers it in good condition to a golden old age. Social relations categorize the body and mark it inside and outside with its identities, teaching it the dance of meaningful gestures that make up unthinking, effective social action and practical efficacy. In doing so, they consign it to a particular social destiny. It is our social setting which helps to ward off illness and patch the body up, or to leave it vulnerable to insult and injury. Society prolongs or kills the body. In all of this, social relations interact with physical processes to bring forth something which is only partially captured by imposed categories such as 'nature' and 'culture'. If reproduction, growth, nutrition, activity, illness and death – biological processes – always happen in and through social contexts, where is the presocial, 'natural' body?

At the other end of the spectrum, some theorists have argued that the body is first and foremost a product of cultural discourse. This is often tacit; social constructionists such as Bourdieu, Foucault, and most feminist theorists acknowledge the biological body but regard it as of little relevance to the body's real social existence. Hence, this view implies that, if Paleolithic people did not recognize the human body as a distinct kind of object, it is inapplicable to apply the concept of 'body' to the Paleolithic; if Neolithic people equated an axe with a body, an axe was in all respects a human body at that time. Although most useful theorizations of the body have originated in this social constructivist perspective, it leaves little ground for comparative analysis, as each society can ultimately be understood only within its own terms. By denying any non-trivial biological side to the body, it quietly reproduces the nature:culture distinction even while loudly denouncing it. It also leaves little scope for understanding the body as a material object. However the material processes involved in birth, growth, nutrition, reproduction, illness and death are defined, they exist and are not trivial. Just as there is no material body pre-existing the social body, so there is no social body pre-existing its material counterpart.

Thus, both approaches miss the point, in our view. It seems more useful to take the position that the biological processes involved in things like birth, growth, illness and death pose existential challenges which all societies must interpret and react to physically in some way. Thus, 'the body' is in part the understanding given to the biological structures, processes and capacities of the human organism; these create a conceptual space which all societies fill somehow, even if they do so in ways almost unrecognizably different from ours. But, critically, when people interpret 'the body', they do so in practical, physical ways such as feeding it, injuring it, healing it, forming its appearance, and making it work, which create the physical object. The 'body' is not an absolutely existing precondition for this interpretation and action; it emerges as a lifelong, contingent result of it.

This in turn throws the spotlight upon the existential possibilities of the body. Here is where the body becomes entirely paradoxical. In some ways, it is obvious to understand bodies as integral wholes. They travel around as a unity; you don't send your left leg out to work while your right leg stays home and does the housework. Yet it is equally obvious that bodies can and sometimes must be understood as partible. However you divide the body into parts and understand what each part does, hands are formed differently and do different things than eyes, tongues, genitals or stomachs. Moreover, the body as a whole-in-parts possesses inherent spatial affordances which most cultures acknowledge, such as up-down orientation and right-left bilateral symmetry. To take another contradiction, in some ways the body is inescapably individual. People are recognizably different and not interchangeable, and physical sensations directly affect the nerves of a particular body, not all bodies. The physical structures which are associated experientially with a sense of being a given, named 'I' tend to show continuity from one day to the next. Yet the body is also inescapably relational. Bodies show visible resemblances to other bodies; they share identities of family, kinship and social group which are manifest physically in habits and appearances; they are formed by the actions of other bodies, through

sex, care, nourishment, exchange, violence, and so on. As we experience every day in relationships, families and groups, even feelings such as pain or happiness move contagiously from one person to another. The body is thus also simultaneously relational all the way down. And so on for many other antinomies. Is the body stable and fixed, or constantly in flux? Is the body bounded or permeable? Is it distinctly human or can it also be animal, machine or place? The answer to such antinomies is: 'Yes, both'.

The body thus contains inherently antithetical possibilities, and the situations in which the body is involved often require us to acknowledge these. To take one trivial illustration, European and American systems of justice identify and punish bodies as bounded individuals morally responsible for their own actions. In legal contexts, we don't lock up criminals' families, just the criminals themselves. At the same time, in other contexts, our system of identities may recognize the relational effects people have on each other via kinship, ethnic identity, shared substances such as DNA or blood, psychological therapy, and legal responsibility for family members.

Much in the same way, seeing the body as a machine has proven an extraordinarily productive metaphor for exploring the body's functional relations in the physical world. But it also requires suppressing or forgetting all the ways in which the body is *not* like a machine, or refuses to be *only* a machine. Thus for every new technological breakthrough based upon the body's similarity to a machine, there springs up a new bioethical dilemma, a set of regulatory rules, or even just some unforeseeable baroque twist such as people making new kinship links with complete strangers based upon internet-based DNA assays, multiple parenthood based upon new permutations of biological material, or computer-synthesized voices which cannot be listened to until they have been given a gender. Such cases serve to show us the limits of a mechanistic view of the body, which cannot work socially until it has been adjusted to, bolted on to, or encapsulated within other ways of understanding the body. The same is true for all the understandings of the body we have explored in this book, and many others which were never thought of in Europe. No single metaphor exhausts its possibilities.

This may perhaps explain the long-term evolutionary success of confusion, or at least of the peculiarly human way of being confused – switching between systematic but partial and contradictory visions. It is impossible to imagine other things that think – a computer or a cat – being confused in this way. But we are beings living in a complex, often indeterminate world, living contingent lives in which sharing some make-it-up-as-you-go-along social context with others is often more fundamental to getting by than any measurable bottom-line 'real world' success or failure. In this knowledgescape, for making sense of inherently ambiguous objects such as the body, multimodality of belief is a resilient, durable and endurable strategy; a universalizing clarity is rigid, brittle, partial and often brutal, a luxury reserved for philosophers, saints, tyrants and robots.

Body worlds: Living in bodies

In Chapters 1 and 2 we introduced the idea of 'body worlds' as a heuristic tool for thinking about the omnipresence of bodies in human lives. Our case studies have set out a series of historically contingent body worlds. In each case, the body was experienced and understood complexly, and in a way which blurs any distinction between the social and the material. The body is society made flesh, and it is always as intricate as society.

What we have learned gives substance to body worlds as historical phenomena. We have seen how the body mediates between high level logics, abstract beliefs, and concrete on-the-ground practices. Generalized, abstract, often implicit propositions underwrite a multitude of more concrete, context-specific beliefs and practices, and the body is the medium for their interaction. Take gender: recent feminist critiques have made clear how gender in the West today is produced through a series of enacted performances incorporating dress, behaviour, ways of walking, eating, sitting and standing. These are daily, real life, practices. In acting out these ideals, however, people both draw on and sustain a broader opposition between male and female, an underlying dichotomy that structures the more obvious gender signs people notice and discuss. In this analysis, it is useful to distinguish between generalized, cross-context beliefs and situated practices. People live in a historically inherited world of abstract beliefs and tendencies, more or less in line with Bourdieu's concepts of habitus and doxa. These in turn provide the materials called in to formulate specific fields of action – rule-bound and meaningful ways of doing particular things.

Body worlds capture these relationships between broad contextual beliefs and daily practices. Produced through practices, beliefs, material things, architecture, landscapes, language, ideas, beliefs and institutions, they structure the possibilities of the kinds of people a person can be, not only for gender but also in terms of age, ethnicity, relational or individualized modes of personhood and so on. These structuring principles are best thought of as regulatory ideals.[4] Whilst never fully attainable, these ideals, which exist in as well as guide people's practices, provide the blueprint against which identities can be measured. By acting in a gender-appropriate way (however that might have been defined in a particular time and place) people both sustain and reproduce that gendered ideal. As such regulatory ideals form a crucial bridge in body worlds between muddling through the choices of daily life and the broader, deep time beliefs which structure it.

Body worlds are neither systematic nor chaotic; they usually contain multiple partial systems of logic. This is multimodality. Within any body world, there are always multiple ways of understanding the body, of having bodies, of being bodies. These can exist in explicit contrast with one another – is the body a replicable machine which needs to be disciplined through universal health care, or the location of my unique personhood, the home of an inviolable individual? Or they can exist in a subtler coexistence, with people moving contextually from one mode to another depending on the context in which one finds oneself. The existence of multimodality, however, does not simply mean there are multiple beliefs about a single 'real' (biological) body.[5] Bodies can act differently and have different capacities within these different modes, meaning there are real material consequences to multimodality, and the histories we trace would be very different if we did not recognize its essential role. Multimodality gives a body world the ways of achieving a liveable balance in recognizing and acting upon the body's paradoxical, self-contradictory existential possibilities.

The long history of the human body

In the largest view, that of macro-history, the body's history can be outlined through changes in basic conceptualizations. These are answers to questions like: What defines the human body? What qualities does it have? What is it like?

Summarizing this history briefly is challenging. There can be no doubt that fundamental understandings of the body evolved over the millennia. Yet the core ideas tended to be multiple, span multiple periods and evolve gradually rather than abruptly (see following discussion); this alone should discourage us from trying to characterize each period in terms of a single master metaphor or kind of body. Moreover, in this book, we discuss some moments of the history of the human body in Europe. For both practical and theoretical reasons, ours is a partial history and it certainly does not exclude other versions. But such a history has never been attempted.

In some ways, pictures tell the story better than we can with words. Our reconstruction drawings are designed to bring a human vividness to key moments in the history we relate. This is particularly so given that our chapters range through so many kinds of disparate evidence. We do not want readers to compare a world of dry and alien-looking stone tools with a world of vivid and intimate medieval lyrics or Renaissance portraits; we hope readers will see people facing the human challenge of dealing with death amidst the confusions of life, whether in Mesolithic Denmark or Classical Greece (Plates I–V). In the following gallery of images (Plates VI–VIII), as in the images throughout Chapters 3 through 7, ancient people have their own voice. Each image tells us something about how ancient or recent people understood and engaged with human bodies. Epochal changes are visible in the sequence; at various points the body is separated from animals, decorated with jewellery, gold and weapons, standardized and idealized, connected to the universe and separated from it as it becomes ever more machine like. Yet we also see long-term continuities crossing such thresholds, and contradiction and discord within any period, as the body is variously valourized and demonized, idealized and materialized, individualized and generalized.

The limits of the body: The upper Paleolithic through the Neolithic

In the Upper Paleolithic (ca. 40,000–10,000 BC) and Mesolithic (ca. 10,000–6000 BC), there are few anthropomorphic images, which may suggest a symbolic investment in landscape and animals instead of the human body. Although some forms of art, such as the famous 'Venus' figurines (Plate VIb), suggest that in some contexts the body was understood as distinctly human, this is the period in which there seems to be least symbolic attention paid to defining the limits of the body, both physically and in terms of bounding humanity from animality and other categories of being conceptually. Human-animal mixtures in art and burials suggest relatively fluid transformation between states of being, possibly animistically (Plate VIa). Multimodality is elusive for the Palaeolithic, in part because of the nature of the evidence and in part perhaps because, in societies with loosely defined authority structures, contextual differences in understanding bodies would probably have been softly modulated rather than sharply contrasted. However, foragers were likely to have moved between understandings of the human body as continuous with animals and environments and as distinct from them, as fluidly similar across groups and as sharply localized.

The situation changes with the Neolithic (ca. 6000–3000 BC), in which hunter-gatherer societies transformed into farming communities, with social innovations including sedentary village life, monumental landscapes and burial in formal cemeteries. Two changes dominate. First, the body becomes an obvious focus of structured distinctions. For the first time, distinctly human representations in art are common, mostly in figurines in Balkan and Mediterranean Europe (Plate VIc). Burials suggest that the body in death became a new focus of social action. In both art and burials, the human body is clearly distinguished from animals, which suggests that redrawing human-animal distinctions accompanied domestication; domestic animals were probably regarded as property, as important social valuables, rather than as prey, as peers, or as potential transformations of people (all of which had been true of wild animals in the preceding periods). The increasingly clear definition of the human body is echoed by the increasingly defined social spaces in which the body moved, on scales from the routinized encounters of domestic architecture to the village and its territory, marked by the remains of the dead. In some places, the body and the house are explicitly connected (Plate VId). A typical Neolithic response to social geography was to draw sharp group boundaries and then define relations across them through exchange, warfare and ritual participation – all things which were present earlier but which became more important here, along with their underlying premise of fundamental social difference. As with the sense of place and the body's routinized inhabitation, this suggests a shift to a more highly structured, human-centric body world.

Secondly, this did not result in a simple, homogeneous definition of the body. Imagery and material culture stresses gendered forms of social value, but in a context-dependent way making use of the body's potential for difference rather than its potential for similarity. For example, participation in warfare, in labour, or in the gendered activities associated with figurines remained socially valued but separate – a heterarchical form of organizing social identities.

What caused this shift in how the body was understood? The biggest reorganization of human life at this point was the transition to a sedentary agricultural lifestyle. But we cannot simply regard changes in the body as the cultural reflex of an economic/ecological transformation. The transformation was not a simple, externally forced event; it varied locally and cultural values and propensities guided it as well as being its outcome. For example, the shift to sedentism or to domesticated foods was probably carried out regionally for a wide range of motives, including the attractions of sociality, the political uses of food and the formation of group identities, rather than simply being a response to food source security. Moreover, although there remained varied ways of understanding human bodies in the Neolithic – for instance, in the continued importance of hunting in some contexts, in funerary treatments which broke down the boundaries of the individual body, and in masks suggesting ritual transformations – the cumulative effects of convergent developments in many fields of action involving the body would have shifted the overall ontological sense of the body from a fluid, permeable and partible understanding to one which was much more structured in terms of identities, movements and definition. This sense of the body, its needs and relations to others, would then have made it correspondingly unimaginable to return to a different kind of body world.

The body and social relations: From the Neolithic through the Bronze Age

Much of Europe witnesses the emergence of a new form of political personhood in middle prehistory (between about 3500–1400 BC, between the later Neolithic and the Middle Bronze Age[6]). This was organized symbolically around a cross-contextual, interchangeable form of value represented in a handful of gendered symbols, principally weaponry and some ornaments, which recur across contexts such as burial, exchange, material culture, and iconography. It is clear that these objects had become central symbols tied into a widely shared habitus. Most fundamentally, the body went from being a site of difference, an accumulation of heterogeneous qualities and citations relevant in different contexts, to being a site of similarity, of values relevant *across* contexts. This is summed up in monumental human representations found across Europe in which the constituent elements are subordinated to a schematic, standardized template (Plate VIe). The body effectively becomes reduced to a surface for display of a small group of key symbols and practices that unite varied institutions around the persona of male and female political leaders. Politically, following this transition, the body's potential for similarity grounded a situation in which more or less equal people competed for parity in bodily social distinctions; rarely but sometimes spectacularly, hierarchies developed. Metals begin as a key symbol enhancing the body by clothing it in visual manifestations of social value and extending it prosthetically. This is increasingly expressed in the metallization of the body with the explosion of metalwork from the Middle Bronze Age onwards. In the Late Bronze Age to the Iron Age (ca. 1400–700 BC), the value systems defined in the previous period intersect, patchily, with the development of economies focused around accumulation rather than display and redistribution, resulting in the use of the body to represent hierarchical difference, particularly in the Medi-

terranean but increasingly in the Iron Age of Central, Northern and Western Europe (Plate VIh).

What is remarkable is how a new social constitution came into being without massive technological or economic change (metals typically accompanied or followed rather than preceded the change), and without 'evolutionary' steps such as increased inequality. The change emerged through the internal reorganization of prestige systems. Many elements of the Copper/Bronze Age world were widespread practices within the Neolithic: the use of animals as social valuables, gendered associations such as males and weaponry (Plate VIg), the use of ornaments to make social distinctions (Plate VIf), and an association between ancestral bodies and places where the living lived. Metals were caught up in this transformation and played an important part in expressing it; until well into the Bronze Age, rather than providing the principal cutting edges, they were mostly a form of bodily display. Likewise, the monumentalization of bodies within the landscape began earliest in the mid-fifth millennium BC Atlantic fringe with menhirs and monuments representing generalized ancestors. Over time, the bodies represented by these stones became increasingly gendered and marked with status objects, and this converged with the rise of gendered stelae elsewhere in Europe. Neolithic exchange networks circulated ornaments, obsidian, flint and axes; as metalwork came in, exchange networks were gradually reorganized around them both geographically and conceptually. Patterns of warfare changed, becoming more gendered. The point is that most fields of action show continuity but also shifted gradually in how they were assigned to overarching interpretive concepts such as prestige, gender and personhood. The result was a gradual convergence around a stable core of a handful of symbols recurring across contexts – the emergence of a generalized rather than situation-specific idea of social value and prestige. This was a cumulative shift in how social value was imputed to the body. It underlines the body's role as an organizer of social relations.

As before, the transition was never complete in effacing alternative ways of looking at the body. For example, while exchange and monumental ritual were related in some ways (in focusing attention around central social figures past or present) they were also used to create different forms of meaning – often idiosyncratically expressed local identities vs. standard expressions of trans-local networking. Similarly, some evidence (such as bog bodies) suggests the vitality of magical and other practices outside the definition of the gendered prestige system throughout the Bronze and Iron Ages. Detailed study of the rise of cremation in Central Europe between 1700 BC and 1300 BC shows both how different ways of dealing with the body coexisted and how changes in bodily practice resulted from micro-scale local shifts in practice rather than large-scale causes. During this period, cremation went from a rare practice to being the normal practice for disposing of the dead. Fine-grained study shows that this happened locally over the course of a few generations.[7] Rather than a single, flip-the-switch change from inhumation to cremation, the change happened through ongoing tinkering with variations possible within the inherited repertoire of practices. Yet cremation, which destroyed the body dramatically, was heterodoxical in terms of one basic Bronze Age principle, that values and identity should be displayed on the body. The resulting accommodation was to develop new ways of burying cremated bodies accompanied by status- and gender-marked ornaments and grave goods.

The body and politics: Representations of the body in the Classical world

The Classical Greek body has always been viewed in terms of art: for the first time the body is portrayed 'naturalistically', with attention to real anatomical structures, lifelike poses, and individual details (Plate VIIa). Before about 500 BC, Archaic period sculptures such as kouroi were rigid, formalized within a narrow range of postures and facial expressions. A generation later, Classical sculptures presented the body in more fluid detail and in all sorts of dynamic postures and activities. To many art historians, sculpture really seems to 'come to life' at this point, establishing a tradition of naturalistic, individual, action-oriented representation which endures down to the present day. This has been traditionally linked to aspects of our own society we trace to the Classical period, particularly Classical Greece (fifth to fourth centuries BC): humanism, individualism, democracy. Yet, ascribing the Classical body to specific political regimes (such as democracy) is illusory; this form of representation was attractive throughout the Greek world in city-states with all forms of government. Ascribing it to a zeitgeist of humanism and individualism simply restates the problem in descriptive terms, as well as prioritizing representations over actual social practices.

Probably the best place to start here is the relationship of Classical sculpture to 'the Classical body'. There were demonstrably multiple Classical bodies: its purity is ritually regulated in some contexts but not others, common bodily practices run the gamut from delicately refined to exuberantly obscene, there are varying, freely developed, medical theories of the body, and there is great variation in burial practice (Plate VIId). Politically, important distinctions (such as those between free people and slaves and between Greeks and non-Greeks) were surprisingly invisible in bodily terms. Cross-cutting all of this is a strong gender differentiation which prescribes different natures, behaviours, forms of prestige and spheres of life to men and women (Plate VIIb). Although men and women were theoretically separated, with men having greater social power, this too was variably practiced and cannot be taken at face value. Such proliferation of bodies no doubt owes much to Classical Greece's status as an urban, literate society with widely shared elements of habitus (such as gender), a complex division of labour and diverse range of social contexts, but without any attempt at overriding intellectual or theological control.

Within such a proliferation of bodies, the 'naturalistic' body of Classical sculpture must be seen as an innovation in one particular form of action rather than a sweeping change in how bodies were understood and experienced in all contexts – the rise of a particular form of representation which has proven historically very influential. In Classical sculpture, public imagery of the body takes on a new burden of class relations. This is expressed in norms of beauty promulgated particularly through male nudes. Far from being individualistic or naturalistic, Classical sculptures present the human body in an idealized, schematized and generic way. They are much like shop mannequins and models in catalogues nowadays: they present carefully generic individuals whose role is to provide a focus for the viewer to project himself or herself into the picture. This new style for representing the body, particularly in political and ritual contexts, provides stylized aspirational bodies whose virtues are ostensibly universal but in fact strongly class-marked. The new body was tied to elite fields of action such as athletics, cavalry and hoplite warfare (restricted to the independent citizenry of means), affluent burials and public ritual dedications. In essence, it promoted an ideal of the socially enabled male citizen body formed to perfection through participation in a range of restricted activities. Alternative bodies were depicted with gender-specific idioms (e.g. females, normally depicted clothed [Plate VIIb] and in gestures of modesty), as iconographically marked foreigners, or as monsters or grotesques (Plate VIIc). Yet we cannot reduce the naturalistic body in art to simply a consequence of an external political inequality; instead, it formed an act of self-identification by a political class which was understood to be constituted by at least the aspiration to such bodies. It grew out of the inherited idea – already existing in the Archaic and indeed in the late prehistoric period – of the gendered body as the locus of social value and increasingly social capital. It then adapted these ideas in new ways, fitting them to a more broadly based political world. In so doing, it defined the qualities of an idealized participant in political (not simply democratic) society. This in turn worked to enlist citizens to act appropriately for their class. Once the concept of the citizen body was established, it formed a powerful ideological resource throughout antiquity.

The body and God: The medieval body

What happens when a new element enters the situation, an overriding belief, backed up by spiritual and temporal hierarchies, in a monotheistic religion? This is the situation of Medieval Christian Europe (ca. 400 AD to 1500 AD). Although this change occurred throughout Europe from late antiquity onwards, we discuss it here principally in later medieval Western Europe.

Monotheism created aspirations to monocorporeality: an attempt to refocus discourses of the body around a single, spiritual focus. The idea that humans consisted of an earthly, material body combined with a spirit which endured after death was found both in Classical culture and in ancient Judaism, although it was not a particularly prominent element of either. From the start, Christianity built this distinction into miraculous paradoxes of the body, notably the Resurrection, which pitted the earthly body and sacred spirit against each other and subordinated the former to the latter. In medieval times, the pervasive body-soul dualism structured theological understanding of the nature of humanity (Plate VIIe). It supplied diffuse, omnipresent terms of thought and reaction and was promulgated through institutions of the church and through daily practices of bodily regulation via ideas of piety and sin. But there were at least two other defining medieval models for the body. In science, the Galenic doctrine of the humours portrayed the body as fluid and permeable to external influences, and as enmeshed within a complex system of affinities between bodily humours and qualities, temperaments, seasons, climates, stellar constellations and other objects (Plate VIIf). This underwrote practical theories of medicine, in which such affinities were manipulated to maintain the body in health. There is also an exuberantly lived body, expressed not only in bodily appetites and practices such as eating, sexuality, fighting, dance and song, but also in political idioms such as the worldly splendour of princes.

All three modes of understanding the medieval body grew out of ancient traditions – the earlier Judaic and Greek idea of the spirit, Classical medical and scientific writers, and the lived body of daily life. To return to a metaphor we used in Chapter 6, the overall effect of Christianity was more or less like passing a powerful magnetic field through a junkyard: the components often remained much the same, but they were repositioned according to a new master alignment. Christianity was bound by practices of fidelity to texts and promulgated by people focused upon liturgical standardization. The-

oretically, it had aspirations to regulate any and all aspects of life, and it was often backed by state and institutional power.

But the Church's attempt at monocorporeality was never successful; throughout the medieval period, the situation was really one of multimodality in which these three models of the body existed simultaneously in tension. These three modes had quite different underlying logics; for instance, the bounded, stable, individually morally accountable body of religion contrasts with the fluid permeable bodies of medicine, in which health, character and morality are open to the ever-changing influences of heavenly bodies, environments and magical affinities. Intellectually, systematic thinkers attempted to reconcile or unify them, for instance by defining the limits of permissible worldliness or by merging the Galenic and spiritual models into a grand synthesis which placed the body at the heart of an encyclopaedic, systematizing exploration of Creation expressed in geographical terms – the 'body as microcosm' idea. Theologically, the entangled, rather self-contradictory doctrine of the resurrection of the body attempted to merge a spiritual concept of divinity with a strongly felt commitment to the lived physical body as the locus of individual identity. But most people alternated between these views in the course of daily life and over their lifetime. Ultimately, in most forms of textual and visual discourse, the spiritual version of the body provided at least a meta-theory which attempted to encapsulate and circumscribe the others. At the same time, tensions between ontologies of the body generated recurrent debates such as arguments over clerical poverty versus worldliness, female sexuality and similar borderland issues, and because of the repressive role of hierarchies, negotiations particularly between earthly and spiritual views of the body often resulted in tacit expressions of a balance such as marginalia. Alternative voices are pervasive (for instance in licentious literature such as fabliaux, and in the grotesque, often obscene, marginalia guarding the frames of the most sacred buildings and manuscripts [Plate VIIg]) and everyday life probably consisted of an undeclared, continually negotiated truce between different ways of experiencing bodily life: the human as pilgrim along a varied route between the theological bookends of baptism and death (Plate VIIh).

The body and knowledge: The modern period

Between about 1500 AD and 1900 AD, the traditional medieval understandings of the body as a material container for the soul and as a microcosm of Creation were increasingly replaced by a new image, the body as machine. The human body was increasingly seen as a functional mechanism with a purely physical being; its needs governed its structures and processes. This development is traditionally ascribed to the growth of anatomical dissection and natural science (Plate VIIIa), with discoveries such as William Harvey's characterization of the heart as a pump for circulating blood the key moments in its formulation, and with nineteenth century materialist theories such as Darwin's and Marx's its logical extension. Yet there is at least one other, convergent strand of historical development, the idea of the disciplined body as outlined by Foucault.[8] Discipline conceptually involved seeing the individual human body as an interchangeable part of a larger social 'machine' and subjecting it to therapy or training to render it fit for its purpose. Particularly from the eighteenth century onwards, the body was increasingly disciplined in workplaces, schools, prisons, clinics and similar settings. The effect was to train it to act as a part within a purpose-oriented, rationalised social whole.

While the modern period provides a legitimating narrative in which scientific knowledge drives changes in how the body is conceptualized, the historical reality was far more complex. For one thing, it is not simply a case of one paradigm replacing another. As in the medieval period, there were multiple ways of understanding the body throughout the modern period, including scientific, spiritual, social, and magical. Often the same individuals (including prominent scientists and theologians) participated freely in all of them. The same theologian who decried the body might demand to see it celebrated in death (Plate VIIIb). Although there was a gradual, and debated, change in the meta-theory framing these multiple discourses of the body, people continued to move fluidly between different understandings in different contexts. Moreover, 'science' itself as a defined kind of endeavour was emerging at the same time and under varied historical forces. For the first time, 'knowledge' was opposed to 'belief' and 'nature' was defined as a separate realm from the human world. The complex history of the term 'nature' and its move from God's Creation through base matter to romanticized ideal forms a key component of our understandings of the human body to this day.

Key practices and ideas about the body also evolved. For example, anatomical dissection began prior to this period as a quasi-geographical, microcosmic exploration of God's creations; only gradually did it acquire the purpose of individuating the function of each structure identified as in a machine. Conceptually, the body was first described as machine-like in the seventeenth century, part of a process that firmed up the separation of body and soul and placed God outside the universe (as in the Newtonian image of God as the divine watchmaker). Yet this was only one of several competing theories of how God, the universe and the body related, and it spread little beyond philosophical and medical discourse. It was only from the later eighteenth century, once daily life was transformed through discipline at home and work, through changes in landscape, architecture and material culture, and as medicine began to have a significant practical impact, that the concept of the body as machine really took off outside philosophical circles.

Relations between different modes of understanding the body evolved gradually but distinctly. At the beginning of the period science, daily life and social practices were couched in a Christian meta-theory of body/soul duality, but once God was successfully placed outside the immediate world of nature through the Newtonian arrangement, this dominance became increasingly distant. Multimodality is at its clearest in this period from circa 1600–1750. Social, folk/magical, religious and scientific doctrines surrounded the body and individual people moved between them.[9] In many of these, the human body, particularly exceptional dead bodies, was believed to have an inherent magical potency (Plate VIIIc). By the end of the period, growing industrialization and the concurrent dominance of the mechanistic model meant science began to assert itself as the dominant modality for the first time. The great materialist edifices of the nineteenth century (Darwin and Marx) could leave God out entirely in explaining human origins and conditions. Effectively, from about the mid-nineteenth century onwards, the emphasis on empirical methods, scientific research and knowledge over 'belief' raised a new form of meta-discourse. Rather than religion, where a unicorporeality based on liturgical adherence was preached, what mattered now was science, which defined itself through a shared method, rather than a shared doctrine. The classification of people, racially, socially and sexually took place at an unprecedented rate (Plate VIIId). This image of progress wrote itself through nineteenth century attitudes to landscape, society, poverty, discipline and the body and is pervasive today.

The body and technology: The twentieth and twenty-first centuries

At the end of the twenty-first century, new technological capabilities seem to repeatedly drive us ever further from a 'natural' body into a brave new world populated by beings which blur the line between human bodies and technology. Innovation after innovation threatens 'natural' boundaries such as the differences between humans, animals and machines; developments in neuroscience threaten to reduce the last hiding place of the individual psyche to anatomy and biochemistry (Plate VIIIe); technologically assisted reproduction happens through new mechanical processes and evolves previously unforeseeable patterns of parentage. Such developments drive the understanding of the body as a purely material entity still further, increasingly threatening the inherited sense of bounded individuality and personhood based upon the Cartesian mind-body duality. These concerns are evident not only in the media hype around issues such as cloning, face transplants and stem cell technology, but, more substantially, also in the huge regulatory apparatuses spawned all around the 'ethical' edges of new biotechnologies. To some it may seem, therefore, that technology is threatening the body and indeed wider society.[10]

Yet the situation is far more complex. For one thing, technology is not an external force which acts upon the body; the body and technology mutually define each other. In daily life, bodies are understood through their interaction with objects such as clothing, computers, and cars, and these technologies conversely are designed to respond to the body's needs and character (e.g. Plate VIIIf). Similarly, medical technologies such as the wide range of scanning technologies (ranging from x-rays and ultrasounds to CT and MRI scans [Plate VIIIe]) are developed in response to the body's social as well as medical needs, and they define the multiple bodies of medical practice, rather than simply revealing aspects of a single body which is already there. Moreover, narratives of technophobia originate in the inherited terms we have traced from the medieval and Early Modern periods; within this way of thinking people already separate the material world of technology and the 'natural' body it acts upon from other ways of understanding the body (as a person, as a housing for a soul or personality). To the extent that fears about medical technology reflect tensions, they are not tensions between the body and technology; they are tensions between inherited, different ways of understanding the body. Technologies and bodies have been caught up in producing each other for millennia – biotechnologies are just the latest example of this.

How does this particular set of circumstances relate to the broader body world we touched on through our vignettes in Chapter 2? The discipline of the machine-like body with authority coordinating the parts, segregated, specialised spaces for different purposes and discourses of interiority and privacy for the lurking refuge of the non-mechanical runs through the ordered world of classical music, and the strictly gendered spaces of bathrooms. The medical intrudes not only in the doctor's surgery but in daily concerns about nutrition, exercise and alcohol; in fact, health, rather than punishment or industrialised work, is an increasingly prominent discourse for regulating and disciplining the body (Plate VIIIf). In each case, it is the standardized, replicable, universal, body as machine that is the matter of concern. Yet at the same time there is more to our current body world than this. The body as person, as a unique and bounded individual, is a central concern, developed from the medieval ideas of the soul and now reformulated through the commercial potentials of capitalism. Although we have focused here principally upon medicine and technology, there remain huge spheres of habitual action and consumer culture that are based upon the idea that one's body is one's self, in social presentation, in psychology, and in relations with others. Practices of authority and distancing (Chapter 1) and the varied perfect bodies of exercise, dress, and gender (Chapter 1, Plate VIIIf, Plate VIIIg) belong to this world. The idea of personal space, of a unique individuality expressible through taste, cultivated or not, of a property-owning irreducible identity is the alternative modality manifest in the world outside the clinic. DNA is thought of as bridging these divides, both that which makes us truly human in a material, mechanistic sense, and that which makes us uniquely individualized (Plate VIIIh).

Lessons from macro-history: How change happens

Yet the aim of this book has not been just to present these narratives in isolation. A deep-time history of the body gives us an opportunity for general or comparative analysis. What does this history tell us about why and how the human body changed?

Beyond prime movers: The body in historical process

One value of drawing together a grand narrative is to tackle the usual suspects – the prime movers we might intuitively look to for big causes of historical change. On the simplest level of comparative analysis, it is clear that we cannot say that (for example) new religious ideas or scientific discoveries are the main forces generally responsible for changes in how bodies are perceived or understood, if only because beliefs about, and experience of, the body demonstrably changed in societies lacking either formal institutionalized religion or scientific knowledge. As we argued at the end of Chapter 2, the most basic step we have to make is from seeing the world in terms of linear causation ('x causes y in circumstances z') to one of contingent causation ('x causes y given all the other processes creating the context in which x *can* cause y').

Understandings about the body specifically exemplify this problem. A simple model of causation assumes that the causal forces are autonomous and external to the situation being explained. Although this is probably never strictly true in an absolute sense, it may be a workable assumption in understanding some historical problems. But in most cases, isolating separable causes and effects is somewhat artificial; any element interesting enough to provide an important cause will itself be embedded in many of the same processes as its supposed effect, as well as reciprocally influenced by it. This is eminently true with the body. Because the body is integral to social relations, it is difficult to argue logically that social, political, economic, technological, or intellectual changes provide an external, independent cause of changes in body worlds, because these same changes are effected, and affected, through actions shaped *by* body worlds.

We see this in all periods. In the Neolithic, for example, changes in conceptualizing the body coincided with sedentism and agriculture, but it is not obvious that sedentism and agriculture were prior facts which drove change in how people thought about their own bodies. If we un-black-box 'sedentism' and 'farming', we see that the motivations for becoming sedentary farmers – or doing so in a particular way, or resisting the transition – may have included social relations based upon sharing food, gendered forms of labour, ideas of territory and group belonging, and meaningful relations and distinctions between humans and animals. Similarly, as the process of Neolithicization progressed and tentative experiments in farming became consolidated as an accepted, widespread and normal way of life, it was accompanied by a sedimentation in habitus of concepts about the differences between human and animal bodies, how bodies were spatially positioned and routinized, and how bodies were valued through activity. This habitus became a conditioning factor in subsequent social economic and political change.

Likewise, it has been traditional to ascribe social changes in the third and second millennia BC to the introduction of metals, but metals really became widespread as a body technology important within the context of social changes already in progress. People were already beginning to elaborate particular distinctions in bodies through display and weaponry when metals offered a new technology for exploring this further. Problems with the 'prime mover' paradigm for causation are similarly evident when we consider the role of politics in Classical Greece. Although there were important political innovations in the Classical period which were directly related to new ways of representing the body ideologically in art, these innovations came about in a setting deeply conditioned by pre-existing ideas of the body such as the tradition of personifying male political value in the activity and appearance of elite male bodies. With both religion in Medieval Europe and science in Early Modern Europe, it is clear that while we can 'black-box' these factors as causal agents changing how ideas of the body developed, in both cases religion and science evolved out of prior ways of understanding the body and evolved to accommodate alternative, contradictory ways of understanding it. So it is only by an act of artificial analytical excision that we can see them as external causal factors in any way.

Multi-scalar historical patterning: Swirls and scales

Working at any scale involves theoretical choices (cf. Figures 5a and 5b, Chapter 2). For example, at one scale, it would be entirely valid to say that 'medieval Europeans considered the human body to be a microcosm of divine Creation'. However, if we zoom in the microscope of historical analysis, we are forced to add 'except in other contexts when they thought something completely different, and except for a lot of illiterate peasants who never really heard of this idea, and for some theologians who disagreed for various reasons, and maybe women didn't believe it as much as men, and we're not too sure about the Muslims, Jews, and heretics either . . . ' This situation characterizes every historical setting: a clear picture at one scale decomposes into a ragged, heterogeneous mass of pixels when seen from closer up, which then calls the larger picture into question.

Scholars have traditionally dealt with this problem simply by seeing generalization as a trade-off between factual accuracy and significance, and choosing the preferred scale of generalization at which they are comfortable working (or, more accurately, their disciplinary history usually chooses it tacitly for them). In this approach, stories told in terms of smaller units may contribute evidence to support larger narratives – the individuals who provide thumbnail stories to prop up social history. Conversely, narratives of larger units may provide the convenient, excusably distorted glosses which form Lecture 1 of the course or the 'background' chapter of the book.

But this smuggles in two prejudicial, or at least unexamined, assumptions. The first is that there is only one true historical story to tell and we are trying to capture it as accurately as possible; in other words, that truth resides at one scale of analysis (the situation 'on the ground') and not others. In all of the fields we traverse here – prehistory, history of various kinds, Classics, anthropology – there has been a tendency to focus upon small-scale analysis, to look at individual lives and patterns of historical change happening within a century or two at most. This has often been accompanied by an implicit or explicit suspicion of large-scale narrative as (at best) over-generalizing to the point of triviality and (at worst) marshalling spurious, totalizing meta-narratives which mask conflict and legitimate modern inequalities. The second assumption is that we know what the true, bottom-line units of history actually are. In other words, we narrate the story in terms of people, or groups, or societies, empires, or classes, because we understand these units as having a real existence which guarantees that the story about them will be the true one.

The large-scale history of the body really makes three points about the 'scale debate'. First, while close-up analysis of history is important and worthwhile, as an increasing number of researchers have pointed out, it leaves important, larger-scale stories untold.[11] It does not seem helpful to simply declare truth to reside exclusively at one scale, whether this is on-the-ground micro-histories of a handful of people or continent-wide, centuries-long generalizations. As DeLanda has pointed out, it is no less reductionist to assume 'society' is simply a sum of its aggregate parts, than it is to presume that individual people are merely dupes carrying out the social roles dictated for them by high level systems. Similarly, it makes no sense merely to locate the 'true' level of causality at the middle ground, in the moment where structure and agency meet, for example. Privileging any single scale will always be reductionist, whether it is micro-reductionist, macro-reductionist or meso-reductionist.[12]

The question really is: "what is history a history of?"[13] When we write histories at different scales, we are not merely creating more or less accurate versions of a single, empirical story. Instead, we are creating different *kinds* of narratives about different kinds of things. It is like describing a starling. The genetic or biochemical account we write at a molecular level is no more or less accurate than the functional anatomy account describing the bird's bones, organs and feathers, the behavioural account describing the bird's nesting and feeding, or the ecological account describing how the starling relates to plants, trees, insects, hawks and humans. In this sense, when we juxtapose bodies, we inherently pose research questions. Juxtapositions at different scales do not raise the same question at different scales of accuracy; they pose qualitatively different kinds of question (Figure 101).

Exactly the same point could be made about the various black-boxed narratives we use to understand the body in history, for example, the famous Aphrodite of Knidos by the Greek sculptor Praxiteles (Chapter 5)

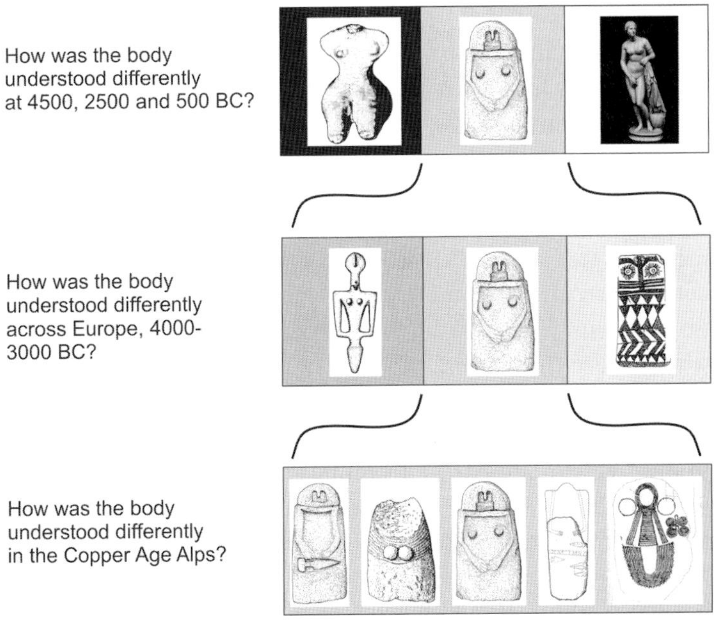

How was the body understood differently at 4500, 2500 and 500 BC?

How was the body understood differently across Europe, 4000-3000 BC?

How was the body understood differently in the Copper Age Alps?

Figure 101. Multi-scalar analysis of the body in history.

(Figure 102). As Strathern remarks, patterns are always fractal; equally complicated pictures emerge at all scales of analysis.[14] In other words all parts of an assemblage are in themselves assemblages.

Because the body is the medium of how society acts through individuals, but also of how people act back to create social understandings, the body creates history at multiple scales. Methodologically, the implication is that we cannot reduce the history of the body to a single scale. To continue with our example, we can read Praxiteles' Aphrodite of Knidos (Figure 103) as a single moment in terms of human agents: a particular sculptor created a striking new statement about beauty and divinity. However, such a story implicitly presumes other, intersecting stories. Praxiteles worked conventionally within the social medium of sculpture as an activity: he reproduced rather than redefined networks of patrons, religious authorities, marble suppliers, slaves, places, materials and tools.[15] The sculpture thus fitted into, and presumed, an institutional history spanning the entire Classical period. Within

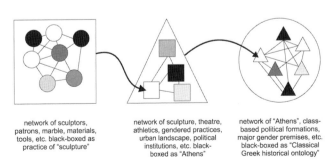

network of sculptors, patrons, marble, materials, tools, etc. black-boxed as practice of "sculpture"

network of sculpture, theatre, athletics, gendered practices, urban landscape, political institutions, etc. black-boxed as "Athens"

network of "Athens", class-based political formations, major gender premises, etc. black-boxed as "Classical Greek historical ontology"

Figure 102. Black-boxing and scales of analysis: Praxiteles' Aphrodite of Knidos.

sculpture as a historical genre, to create even such a striking new statement, Praxiteles worked within a tradition or corpus which furnished him with precedents, ideas and limits. Some of the agency of creation must certainly be seen as the long playing out of a much longer process of distributed cognition involving humans, non-humans and traditions of practice.[16] The Knidian Venus itself, indeed, played a part in this process in a way entirely extraneous to the sculptor's and patrons' intentions. From Hellenistic times, at least a century after the deaths of everyone involved in creating the sculpture, it began to be adopted as a pattern for the female nude in secular contexts. Furthermore, the whole process must be seen in the context of a much longer-term history of habitus and gender. Since late prehistory, there had been an unbroken tradition of women's focusing attention on self-presentation via clothing and jewellery (Chapter 4). In Greece, since Archaic times at least, this had resulted in a double standard in which the female body, seen as beautiful but socially vulnerable, was hedged with restrictions of modesty and shame and always strictly portrayed clothed (Plate VIIb). Praxiteles' Aphrodite thus, scandalously, unveiled a respectable, even divine female body to the public gaze. Yet the public gaze was a male gaze, and even while asserting the power of the goddess's beauty, the sculpture did so in gestures of intimacy and vulnerability. Effectively, this creative, potentially subversive gesture was captured by the longer-term weight of gender relations; throughout its subsequent history, the female nude was always ambiguous, potentially asserting the power of the female body while simultaneously furnishing an object for male consumption.

Secondly, narratives at different scales will reveal different processes of change. Stereotypically, practices change readily and flexibly in historical circumstances. A charismatic preacher leads a new sect whose logic echoes current social developments; oppressed peasants exploit a legal loophole to develop alternative pathways to political autonomy; a network of intellectuals working on new problems develops a local discourse which questions things previously taken as authoritative. Such small-scale, local changes in belief and practice are well-theorized in practice theory, in the sociology of science and in other ways (such as Barth's anthropology of knowledge).[17] In contrast, underlying abstract propositions are usually 'embedded', 'sedimented' and resistant to change. Empirically, one can trace continuities in the basic propositions defining the world of a medieval Christian, a Roman peasant, or a Neolithic British farmer over centuries or more. These are the kind of long-lasting, regionally shared configurations which Annales historians termed *mentalités* – although they were always as

much material as they were mental. Theoretically, such conservatism results from the commitment with which basic values are held (as Bourdieu implies). It may also be because (as Rappaport notes) such abstract values must be enacted and reproduced through practical action, and fields of practical action usually include ways of rationalizing moments when one's abstract logic does not work (for instance, when worldly evil appears to triumph, contradicting a faith in divine plan).[18] They are thus often buffered from the slings and arrows of change. The multimodality of belief also fosters conservatism by allowing a historical constellation of beliefs to accommodate completely contradictory experiences of the world without radical change.

The second point concerns the emergent effects of scale. In this book, we have focused mostly on larger scales of analysis because, in spite of pioneering efforts such as Foucault's and Laqueur's, the grand scale has been the neglected dimension of body history. One of the most interesting conclusions, indeed, has been simply that one *can* write a large-scale history of body worlds which is more than merely a summary of masses of smaller-scale detail. The acid test of this is whether patterns emerge at the large-scale which are not visible at smaller scales. To return to the starling example, anyone who has watched a flock of birds wheeling through the sky will understand how the 'flock' only possesses a temporary and amorphous unity, but, as each bird cues its flight off its neighbours, the aggregate flock, and each bird within it, moves and swirls along a different flight path than any individual bird would do on its own.

Thus, in this history, body worlds possess emergent effects not visible from their component elements.[19] They do not enforce rigid uniformity upon how people understand the body; they supply the tools of thought, the terms of argument and the limits to the thinkable. One emergent effect is the long-term coherence of tradition. As the Neolithic and Bronze Age examples show, people do not continue to use the same bodily practices over centuries or even millennia because they lack creativity, but because their creativity is situated. Continually addressing problems which are perceived within similar terms, and with similar tools of thought at hand, they reinvent broadly similar solutions. A second emergent effect concerns the ecology of modes of understanding. Sometimes quite distinct fields of practice converge in a way which gives greater weight of authority to concepts that capture a theme central to both of them – something which may escape a less global analysis. The most obvious example from this work is the eighteenth-nineteenth-century convergence between mechanistic models of the body in scientific discourse and in daily experience of workplaces and

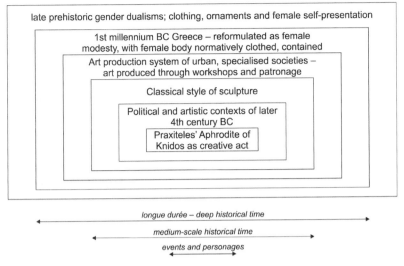

late prehistoric gender dualisms; clothing, ornaments and female self-presentation

1st millennium BC Greece – reformulated as female
modesty, with female body normatively clothed, contained

Art production system of urban, specialised societies –
art produced through workshops and patronage

Classical style of sculpture

Political and artistic contexts of later
4th century BC

Praxiteles' Aphrodite of
Knidos as creative act

longue durée – deep historical time

medium-scale historical time

events and personages

Figure 103. The multi-scalar history of the Aphrodite of Knidos.

body worlds. This is when inherited, competing terms of thought generate recurrent tensions and debates about the body – effectively arguments in a *longue durée* system of collective thinking or distributed cognition playing themselves out over the time scale of concrete political and social dramas. Medieval debates over issues such as sexuality, women, and clerical worldliness or asceticism demonstrate this well, but we may perhaps see it in repeated vacillations in Copper and Bronze Age Europe in the meaning of burial: was it about displaying the prominence of selected individuals or about demonstrating the equality and solidarity of the group?

institutional life (Chapter 7). The ability of the body-as-machine concept to make sense of both industrial experience and the emergent intellectual view of the body propelled it forward in a way that could not have happened if only one of these had been present. Often an existing mode of discourse provides a gravitational pull, assimilating new experiences and making them comprehensible. Neolithic burial was a way of reconstituting the mythological history of the group; politically central people in the Copper and Bronze Ages were memorialized in these inherited terms as prominent ancestors. How non-scientists understood DNA when it was discovered makes much the same point (see following discussion).

Another common high-level interaction seems to have been long-standing accommodations in which existential needs were divided between modes of understanding the body. Medieval and modern examples of such conceptual divisions of labour have already been well-discussed. In Greek history, a gender-neutral model of the soul, afterlife and mourning seems to have been invoked in contexts of death at the same time as a deeply gender-divided approach was taken to most contexts of life. In prehistory, too, we might see such accommodation in the persistence of hunting as symbolic activity in agricultural worlds; and, in the Paleolithic, we see divisions between contexts in which the human body was represented as amorphous and transformable and ones in which the female body is individuated quite clearly and distinctly. As we stated when we opened this chapter, body worlds or historical ontologies thus always include long-standing ways of coping with situations both in which it is useful to think 'the body is x' and 'the body is not x'.

Yet such divisions of labour also generate one of the most striking examples of emergent dynamics within

It's not about invention! continuity and bundles of modes

One important, somewhat counter-intuitive implication of the long history of the body is that 'new' attitudes and understandings are almost never actually new. In virtually all of our cases, there is never a clean transition of the kind where 'first people thought A, then X happened and afterwards, they thought B'. Instead, the pattern tends to be one of redefinition through continuity.[20] Both A and B are almost always present both before and afterwards, but the relations between them have changed.

Theoretically, this makes sense. An entirely new body world can arise only if people are blank slates waiting to be written. In the history of humanity, this has yet to occur. Instead, revolutionary new theories solve problems defined within old terms of thought; startling new evidence is fitted into existing possible ways of thinking. For example, key Classical means of embodying gender and status originated in the Iron or even Bronze Ages; early Christianity harnessed Classical and Judaic beliefs about body, soul and resurrection to new evangelical propagation and theological elaboration. The discovery of DNA provides a recent example. If anything would be a dramatic sudden event reorienting ideas about the body, surely this would. Yet, as Strathern remarks, researchers were surprised not only by how popular the concept of DNA immediately became, but also by how the public seized on particular elements of it.[21] The point is not that DNA has had no effect upon how we think about the body (see following discussion); the point is that the discovery of DNA was fitted into strong prior structures of how we already understood the body, and this conditioned how both research and public understanding of it unfolded. As a molecule, DNA provides a set of instructions for producing proteins which in turn help to form specific biological structures. How these instructions result in a particular body depends upon variable factors, notably developmental interaction between the organism and its environment. DNA does *not* produce a complete, lowest common denominator organism which is then customized by environment; in some cases, DNA provides alternate developmental pathways which growth switches between according to circumstances. But when DNA was unveiled to the world, it immediately became fitted into the long-standing 'nature' versus 'culture' dichotomy described in Chapter 7. DNA became the ultimate trump card for 'nature' – the unchangeable, fixed material source; the secret of being. In the manner in which scientific research is presented to the public, therefore, this underlies an assumption that the cause of something biological can and should be ascribed either to 'nature' or 'nurture' rather than 'both indivisibly' or 'the interaction between DNA and developmental factors'. This in turn means that support is thrown behind research aimed at determining mathematically the 'heritability' of everything from specific diseases to intelligence and personality, as well as programs of genetic screening which make us see unborn bodies in new terms (Chapter 8). Taking DNA as an oracle of the organism's true, fixed, material nature has harnessed it to identity discourses from the personal (as in DNA-based genealogies) to the national (as in books using genetic studies to reconstruct the 'origins of the British' or other groups). It has also facilitated such things as adopted children or children born from donated sperm or eggs seeking their 'real' parents. This of course is based on a much older idea of traceable biological descent – through substances such as 'blood'. Nowhere does scientific knowledge tell us that kinship based on molecular amounts of DNA, most of which is widely shared, has no phenotypical manifestation, and has no correlation with any social, historical or psychological variation, is more 'real' than kinship based upon years of living together as a family. This is a frame our social history has taught us to put around DNA.

Realizing that change and continuity are inseparable and that beliefs almost never arise abruptly changes how we have to understand the history of body worlds. A few cardinal points about the texture of change emerge:

- As historical units, body worlds tend to consist of bundles of alternative modes of understanding the body; they are given unity not by single master metaphors but by the accommodations and tensions between these modes.
- Over time, these strands evolve internally, for instance with the transformation of Neolithic hunting and weapon technologies into a much wider ranging

and non-context specific idea of the male Bronze Age 'warrior', or with the evolution of the medieval body/soul distinction into the modern material machine/inner psyche distinction.

- Within the overall ensemble of ways of understanding the body, change often comes about as emphasis shifts from one strand to another; a contextual variation becomes a widely shared, generalizable truth or vice versa. So the opposition between body and soul in the Classical period, which was merely one minor element in the body world at that time, emerged and became the dominant central element in understanding the body in medieval times; its influence continues today.
- Modes of understanding the body are often closely tied to particular fields of practice: while one understanding of the body underwrites medicine or death rites, another may be reproduced through sexuality, dress or kinship. But this reciprocal relationship, through which a practice cites and reiterates generalized principles and generalizes those principles that are used to interpret a practice, is historically dynamic and always subject to remapping. As discussed in Chapter 2, practices can be mapped on to quite different high level interpretations, while generalized beliefs, as they evolve, can spawn or lose the practice which reproduce them. The changing interpretation of anatomical dissection between the sixteenth and twentieth centuries provides an example (Figure 104). We can trace an unbroken historical thread from Classical medical theory through medieval medicine, Early Modern medicine and recent medicine. For much of this thread, medical theorists only cut up a tiny number of bodies (such as those of medieval kings, to verify causes of death for political reasons), and medical views were often subordinated to them as an investigation of the body as a microcosm of God's creation. As we saw in Chapter 7, as anatomy took off, it moved from metaphors of quasi-geographic exploration to machines as the internal complexity of the body became increasingly difficult to explain. A single field of practice – anatomy – had been remapped through religious and Classical medical understandings to the new world of science. It had begun as a way of bringing Galen and God together but ultimately finished by aspiring to demolish both.

Causal explanation and partial patterns of history: How does change happen?

The points set out in the preceding section cover a basic reading of historical process. However, here we must address frankly one frustrating aspect of this view of

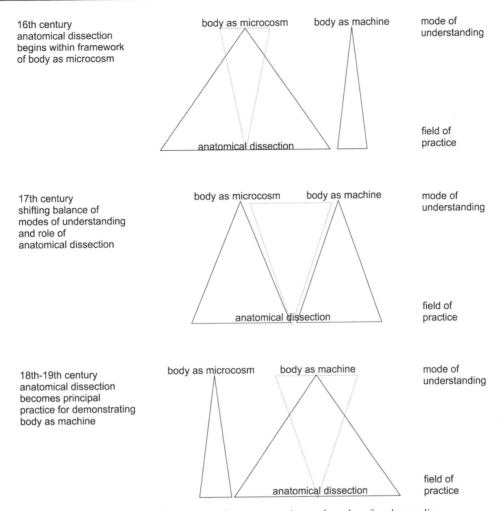

16th century
anatomical dissection
begins within framework
of body as microcosm

17th century
shifting balance of
modes of understanding
and role of
anatomical dissection

18th-19th century
anatomical dissection
becomes principal
practice for demonstrating
body as machine

Figure 104. Historical remapping between practices and modes of understanding.

history which some readers will find frustrating: causal explanation. What makes change actually happen?

We sympathize with the desire to find a genie ped-alling frantically away inside the machine, to unmask the hero or villain of history ('aha! it was technological progress [or class conflict, or reproductive strategies, or the will to power] all along!'). But (as noted), history does not afford explanation according to any simple causal model in which a specifiable input results in changes in the body. Instead, history represents the intersection of multiple historical factors, a negotiation between histor-ical contingency and structure, balancing explanation and interpretation. With enough thick description at enough different levels of scale, description segues seamlessly into interpretation; you arrive at a specification of why history could not be otherwise. 'Explanation' consists of high-lighting heuristically particularly influential relationships within a local network. (If there is a hero or a villain in history, it is the protean body itself!) In fact, the most con-vincing and satisfactory histories have always been written in this manner.

Yet neither is history merely a series of unique occur-rences without recognizable patterning. What gives it legibility is partial patterning, tendencies that can be parsed in the medium level vocabulary of process. Such partial patterns derive their repeatability and structure from the characteristics of the processes of bodily action generating them.

Here we simply give an example of the process. Con-sider the recurrent problem of how changes in practices relate to changes in deeper, embedded conceptual struc-tures – how variant understandings of the body come to spread across multiple fields of practice and become 'black-boxed' or institutionalized as orthodoxy – and in how complex historical ontologies have their own internal dynamics. In the cases discussed in this book, three mech-anisms or partial patterns seem to recur. These can be seen heuristically as three formal models for the kinds of causal patterns that bring about the changes identi-fied previously, or (perhaps more accurately) as a vocab-ulary for recognizing fragments of pattern in the swirl of history.

- *Practice-led historical unbalancing.* In this model, alternative modes of understanding the body are associated with particular, important fields of practical action. These fields of action have their own historical trajectories, and they provide conceptual examples or ways of thinking which people can generalize to other fields of action. There are two clear examples of this in our work. The most obvious one, already discussed extensively, is how medical science expanded its scope immensely between the seventeenth and twentieth centuries, and in the process became the paradigm conceptual example of the 'body as machine' mode of thinking. To take another example, Classical sculpture in ancient Greece took an inherited class-based habitus of an aristocratic male and innovated a new visual idiom which embodied important values of new, more broadly based, politics. Sculpture then became an important ideological vector for new political processes and senses of identity. Sculpture did not drive political process, but neither was it simply a reflex of politics. Instead, there was reciprocal development of the field of action and the overall concept of a politicized citizen body. Monumental representation provided only one of many disparate ways of understanding the human body in the Classical world. But the shift in the use of monumental sculpture from privately to publicly sponsored contexts was associated with a nuanced shift in the aspirational male habitus from a more socially restricted to a more open view. Because this was a public, highly visible context associated with key political developments, the new sculptural style provided an ideological idiom for making new forms of political identity and participation accessible to the relevant citizenry.

- *Convergence through redefining.* As we have seen, the relationship between fields of action and underlying abstract understandings of the body is fluid; a traditionally mandated gift can emphasize relations of superiority, subordination or equality, a ritual can hammer home several competing theologies. Hence, as each generation reproduces traditional practices, they can redefine what these mean and how they relate to each other. When such reinterpretation is systematic, it can result in assembling a new abstract structure of belief out of existing practices and ideas. Again, there are several clear examples of this from our work. An obvious case is early Christianity, which took a range of existing practices and bodies of thought – medical and scientific knowledge, philosophical concepts and most aspects of daily life – and attempted to subordinate them to a theological framework. The result – at least in theory – was a convergence of previously unrelated elements within a new struc-

ture of belief. An equally interesting example occurs at the beginning of the metal ages in prehistory. As noted earlier, throughout Europe, the archaeology of the end of the Neolithic shows continuity, with most practices of daily life and settlement developing directly from local forebears. At the same time, there are differences of emphasis. For instance, the practice of ornamenting the body continues uninterrupted in a series of gradual developments, as do exchange, warfare and burial. Yet the result was convergence among previously unrelated practices to create a new, widely shared abstract ideological concept. The same process is visible to some extent in reverse in other cases. We can see this with the disintegration of previously strongly unified ways of understanding the world as practices carry on but the underlying conceptual connections between them are de-emphasized, allowing different fields of practice to go their own way. The breakup of a strongly expressed theological view of the body in the modern period provides a key example; the core views remain strong but many forms of action, including anatomy and sexual reproduction, formerly under its jurisdiction, no longer are.

- *Emergent reorganization.* Finally, at times, a new way of conceptualizing the body emerges from the unintended, self-reinforcing effects of major life choices. Unlike the previous model, this may have little to do with the human reinterpretation of existing practices and much to do with the emergent logic of systems. There are two clear examples of this process here. One (already mentioned) is how industrial discipline in the later eighteenth and earlier nineteenth centuries really instilled a mechanistic, materialistic view of the body through practical experience in clinics, prisons, schools, factories and the army. In this sense, the change in belief results from recognizing the self-imposing, immanent logic of a new system of organization encompassing humans, things and institutions. The other example is the emergence of an increasingly bounded and structured concept of the body during the transition to the Neolithic. In this model, people began to experiment with Neolithic lifeways and sedentism for a range of reasons, but these lifeways had broad-ranging unintended consequences which tended to increasingly impose the new way of life through economic commitments, spatial regimes and conceptual structures. The Neolithic body was created partially through representations which suggest a bounded human body predicated upon new distinctions from animals and new associations with landscapes, and through new social regimes of habituated daily space and encounter. It thus made flesh the immanent logic of a new, self-reinforcing way of life.

It is no accident that the two paradigm examples of this last process are the Neolithic Revolution and the Industrial Revolution. To the extent that new ideas about the body emerge in tandem with sweeping social, political and economic changes – new bodies for new epochs of history – this third mechanism is probably the central process involved. However, we should not overstate the case for a Big Mechanism Of Change. Both transitions, when unpacked from their overstated black boxes, happened through small incremental steps and continuities. In both cases, changing conceptions of the body (place bound, different from animals for the Neolithic; disciplined and docile for the nineteenth century) were as much the cause as they were the result of the changes that took place. Overall, much, perhaps most, of the accumulated change in our story happened quietly rather than in big 'revolutions'.

Power, monocorporeality and the changing nature of change

Finally, consider a conundrum. Change can be described through recurrent, partial patterns of the kind exemplified earlier. These derive from the body and how people understand it and act through it. Yet the body is *itself* historically contextualized, never generic, and it changes through time. If change flows through and from the body, then what are the consequences of changing bodies for the nature of change itself? The rather obvious logical consequence of this is, therefore, that the processes by which the body changes are themselves subject to change. *The nature of the change itself changes.*

With the coming of sedentism and the Neolithic, for instance, body worlds were increasingly manifested through practices surrounding people with a growing range of material things,[22] a quantum step forward in objectification of belief and identity; the game of chess played out between people and things became increasingly positional rather than mobile. But Neolithic body worlds developed other bodily affordances, exploiting the body's potential for difference to create identity and value in diverse contexts. This was a world of heterarchy – with different fields of practice developing different and incomparable schemes of value and prowess. This tended to create a social world which muted the extent to which innovation in any one context such as ritual, trade or warfare could spread widely across contexts. Change was dissipated along myriad small fracture lines rather than spreading across society, adding a distinct stability to long-term history. The innovation of later prehistory was to allow equivalences between different objects and activities around a form of value that was

more and more compatible with multiple different contexts, something which allowed increasingly the potential accumulation of value in the body and with it the potential for hierarchy. Structurally, innovations in one aspect of life could be harnessed to others, effectively making things like crafting, growing food and fighting more politically dynamic than before. When the body was harnessed to politics on a larger scale in Classical Greece, difference continued to flourish, but increasingly alternative modes of understanding the body were aligned with different forms of participation in an increasingly varied spectrum – for example the invention of medicine as distinct from philosophy, political ideology or religion – a feature of the broader landscapes of understanding which conditioned all future developments. In this sense, literacy and intellectual specialization changed the conditions for the reproduction and transmission of knowledge.[23]

This development of intellectual specialization opened new possibilities, particularly for attempts to politicize one mode of understanding the body and enforce it across all the different elements of a body world. As we described it in Chapter 6, perhaps the defining characteristic of knowledge systems in the medieval period was this first determined attempt to restrict multimodality, to create a single, unified, politicized canon of truth based upon the theological doctrinal body that theoretically applied to all contexts of life. Monocorporeality was never successful as more than a negotiated truce between competing understandings of the body, but it provided a paradigm within which other modes of understanding the body had to develop – even when they eventually outgrew it. Counter-intuitively, one effect of claims to monocorporeality was to render the multimodality of belief more visible than ever before, as discrepancies were recast as heterodoxy.[24]

After the flowering of multiple discourses in the sixteenth and seventeenth centuries, the nineteenth and twentieth centuries saw a second attempt to claim monocorporeality but of a different form. The medieval world had attempted to define a single concept of the body by laying out what a body should be *substantively*. In contrast, the mechanistic idea at the heart of materialist/scientific views defined the body *methodologically*, in terms of how one went about establishing knowledge about it. This was, and indeed is, a much more ambitious and open-ended project. Rather than attempting to conserve a finite truth about the body, the project of understanding the body is harnessed to twin open-ended projects which are inherently restless rather than stable: science and capitalism, which drive forward their own logic of change seeking new potentials for profit. The nature of change, just like the nature of bodies themselves, therefore, has never been stable. Change too has a history – a history caught up in the history of bodies and played out in the different practices, institutions and discourses that have been brought to bear upon it.

This modern attempt at unimodality has not been successful. No single mode of understanding the body can ever truly efface all others in human life; recent attempts by public scientists to dismiss religion entirely are thus paradoxically modelled upon Christianity's attempt to carry out an equivalent manoeuver, and similarly show a misunderstanding of human existence.

In the mirror of history

Back to the 'modern' body

We began this book by looking at our own body world, and returning to the present is a fitting way to end it. In Chapter 2, the point of the rather low-key and impressionistic walk through our own body world was simply to provoke the reader who had never thought about the social life of bodies to realize how peculiar and arbitrary our bodies are, and how deeply they structure our social lives. Now, however, we can think about our body world a bit more critically in the light of history.

One lesson of history is that the 'modern' body is historically layered, and much of it is not particularly 'modern'. Although not all of the models reviewed in Table 1 (Chapter 2) are supported by evidence, many are. But they are all partial; 'the modern body' has never been a single thing. We can trace ideas of the body as containing an inner person back to medieval ideas of the soul, and of the body as machine to Descartes, Harvey and the growth of industrial discipline. The 'civilizing' process of bounding and hiding its physicality began in late medieval times and continued through the modern period. The body's position as earth rather than spirit goes back at least to Classical Greece, before it was extended theologically by Christianity and codified as 'nature' in the seventeenth century. Some of our basic gender symbolism and body divisions date to later prehistoric times, as does a dominant sense of human boundedness from the animal world.

Yet despite its disparate origins, the modern body is not simply a random aggregation of inherited attitudes, perspectives and practices. Like other body worlds it has a historical integrity which is expressed not only in the way one modality, scientific materialism, has attempted to become a dominant category that transcends and links other perspectives, but above all in tensions between concepts of the body. Thus, the twentieth century tension between the body as a person – a unique, bounded individual – and the body as a machine – a replicable,

comparable, standardized form – may descend from early modern tensions between mechanistic and spiritual bodies, but each of these strands has evolved considerably. Moreover, some views, such as the magically potent body, have almost entirely dropped out of the picture. Others, such as the body as a site of social distinction and pleasure, have undergone strong historical vicissitudes. In any case, the point is that each understanding of the body is defined in part by what it is *not*, by opposing views and contextual divisions of the territory.

But we must resist modern exceptionalism; this situation is not peculiar to modernity. One of the most important conclusions which long-term history affords is that, however unique we feel our moment in history to be, body worlds in every other period behave this way too. Any body world we might choose to examine, similarly has elements that can be traced back over thousands of years, the ebb and flow of different modalities, modes of practice that have shifted from one way of thinking about the body to another – perhaps without changing much in themselves. There are deep historical trends leading up to the present; but the Neolithic, Bronze Age, Classical and Medieval periods were just as much the result of powerful deep-time changes. Thus, we would refute one basic, often tacit, presupposition of the 'modern' body literature, which is that modernity is a unique historical moment which requires a different kind of explanation than any other part of the human story. History does not provide a dichotomous picture where a monothetically defined 'pre-modern' suddenly gives way to 'modern'; indeed, characterizing anything as 'pre-' automatically imposes a two-part teleological logic.[25] Body history is not a sudden shift from black to white; it is a spectrum which shades through many equally unique colours.

The body as a matter for concern

If modernity is not a unique moment – or at least, it is not unique in a different way than any other moment in history is unique – what about the worries that the way the body is acted upon by technology is increasingly out of control? We started Chapter 1 with a glimpse of our hopes and fears about the body. We have problematized this point of view extensively since then, but the underlying narrative it reveals is still potent. To put this another way: in Chapter 7 we traced medical intervention through stages of anatomy, autopsy, and prosthesis. What comes next? Presumably, not merely replacing parts of bodies technologically, but actually making bodies. Stem cells, cloning, tissue engineering and gene therapy all appear to offer a moment of dramatic transformation: the natural body vanishes, replaced by the body *as* technology.

This story is based upon two popular master narratives. The first is that history displays inevitable, teleological progress towards objective scientific knowledge. The second is that, as we learn to do things to the body – split it apart, copy it, transform it – that before *seemed* like they were only ever metaphorical, technology is driving our concept of the body to a breaking point where the concept of a 'natural body' vanishes.

But the history of the body belies narratives of either 'crisis' or simple linear progression. This is for the three reasons we rehearsed in Chapter 8. First, in spite of our Frankenstein-like fantasies, technology is not a new, external, force acting upon the body. The development of technology is shaped by the development of the body to which it is addressed. Crisis? We are not on a runaway roller-coaster driven by technology; technology is in the seat with us and our bodies are steering. Secondly, the 'crisis of technology' narrative comes from the Early Modern and modern identification, separation and valourization of 'nature' as fixed, transcendental and prior to society. This is where our sense of the body as a pristine spontaneously growing refuge from the machine originates. Hence, to the extent that new technological developments trigger a sense of crisis, it is created not by the violation of universal axioms but by our inherited historical categories for understanding the world. Thus 'technology' in itself is not inherently a threat to 'nature', it is our historical construction of both terms that makes us see them in this way. Biotechnology feels threatening only because we have inherited a framework of concepts which make it so.

Third, and perhaps most importantly, however much we learn scientifically and can do technologically, humans retain their elastic capability to believe multiple, contradictory things about the body. In many ways, we are still working with the situation as it stood around the end of the nineteenth century: the metaphor of the body as a material machine purports to provide a dominant meta-theory, and this is evident in its extension to increasingly broad fields of discourse (for instance, eating, sexuality and illness are increasingly phrased in terms of health rather than moral terms). Yet we resolutely continue to understand the body in other ways as well. For example, the Early Modern strand of the body as a site of social display or stigma persists in a twentieth-century transformation as consumer culture in which identity is tied to fashioning the body through diet, exercise and clothing. Similarly, the concept of the body as housing the soul seems to have evolved (with a weakening of the social importance of religion) into the idea of the body as an external shell housing an inner psyche to be discovered through self-realization and explored through psychology. Relating to bodies as persons rather than as material things provides perhaps the strongest observable alternative to the materialist functional perspective on the body. The sense of 'crisis' provoked by technology, therefore, really seems to betray tensions between modes of understanding the body which have been around for at least a century.

Two provocative observations can round out this discussion. First, there is no peculiarly modern 'crisis of the body', but many people sometimes feel that there is one, or at least there should be one. Whence comes this feeling? It results from our historically inherited categories; it is not an accurate description of the modern body, it is part of what we believe about the body itself. More globally, a sense of crisis really seems to result from the feeling that the everyday choices and new developments of social life have big implications for what the body is, that they have to be evaluated accordingly and that there is a real danger of making the wrong choice. But if this is so, it seems to be a relatively straightforward implication of having multiple modes of understanding the body; there will always be alternative visions and values, choices to be made, jurisdictional disputes between modes. This is therefore a permanent condition; the idea that there was a simple, unproblematic time before our current confusion is part of the myth of the natural body. If the body is in crisis now, it has always been in crisis.

Secondly, can anything be done? Somewhat puckishly, we would recommend giving up all aspirations to unimodality – to the search for a single, ultimate logical consistency for the body. If our analysis is correct, the sense of crisis arises *not* from the existence of multiple truths about the body – because multimodality works perfectly well to get us through many different situations of life, and has done so for thousands of years. Instead, the sense of crisis springs from our worrying about this fact, and from the heightened tensions caused by trying to extend one truth of the body to all situations. Whether it is medieval theology, Victorian materialism or modern science, would-be meta-theories take something – the body – that is inherently dynamic and multiple and attempt to fix it to a single frame of reference, a single mode of being. In fact, the attempt to impose a unimodality seems to us potentially an actual source of stress. Like medieval attempts to regulate the body's potential for sin, we live with increasingly continual monitoring of the body as more and more aspects of our lives come under scientific-social surveillance, and as regulatory bioethics has to assess how scientific developments meet or violate other expectations about the body. If there is any sense of crisis, it will appear as these fragile, brittle edifices creak under the strain of reality, rather than the more elastic, resilient body worlds of prehistoric Europe, Classical Greece or the Early Modern period.

The future of the body and the bodies of the future

The body has always been a focus for hopes and fears about the future. From Paleolithic shamans through Classical Amazons, medieval shape-changers and monstrous races, and early modern witches, there have always been visions of alternative embodiment. The Enlightenment was marked by an amazing proliferation of philosophical fictional worlds, both utopian places where the reason-governed life was crafted and dystopian places where appetite or reason ran out of control.[26] Virtually every one describes an imaginative body regime, often in entertainingly earnest detail. But the modern trend for fantastic body worlds was really set in the early nineteenth century, with the shift to technophobia which linked *Frankenstein* with twentieth century successors such as *Brave New World*. A rough-and-ready typology of visions of future bodies might include:

- The body's humanity breaks down, releasing beasts within, such as werewolves, vampires and the Mr Hyde submerged within every Dr Jekyll.
- The body's boundaries are violated, as space aliens (*Alien*) or demonic spirits invade it, sap its volition and take it over.
- The boundary of life and death, person and thing becomes blurred, peopling the world with zombies, ghosts or monstrous, despairing immortals.
- Technology takes over the body, as in *Frankenstein*, *Brave New World* and countless science-fiction space epics with robots, cybermen and Daleks.

Such stock fantasies don't tell us much about what future bodies will be like, but they do tell us what we worry about. The first three draw upon old fears about the strain of moral regulation, violation of bodily integrity and loss of personhood with death; the last includes our new fears of technology. It is a bit worrying how rare dreams of future Golden Ages populated with happy superbodies are; perhaps we distrust science too much, or we feel that religion should have a monopoly on such visions. Only a few exceptionally thoughtful works use future visions explicitly to explore embodiment. Ones which stand out include B. F. Skinner's manifesto for behavioural psychology *Walden II*, Stanislaw Lem's and Isaac Asimov's stories exploring the consciousness and humanity of robots, and Ursula Le Guin's anthropological fantasies imagining things such as a world without gender.

There is an almost irresistible urge, at this point, to speculate on what *we* think the future holds for human bodies. Predictions are risky, though; yesterday's apocalypse or paradise turns embarrassingly outdated faster than fresh fish. Nevertheless, perhaps the shape of the past gives a few guarded hints about the shape of things to come.

Throughout the past, ancient, continuous traditions of understanding the body were constantly reinterpreted in the light of new experience, and this process will never stand still. Take the 'body as machine' metaphor, for instance. When machines were assemblages of pumps, valves and levers, the body was too. With electrical technology, the nerves became wires. When high-tech meant a single, stand-alone computer, the brain had 'hard-wired' neurological architecture and 'soft-wired' learned behaviour, the new incarnation of a nature/culture distinction and one which, with ongoing research into neurological plasticity and how the brain changes with experience, seems increasingly inaccurate. With networked computers and decentred clouds of data storage, the metaphor has shifted and the machines our bodies and brains are may become decentred and fuzzily bounded.

Multiple practices create multiple bodies (Chapter 8), and as the semantic field of the body shifts enough, new master metaphors will undoubtedly arise. As we learn more, medicine itself reveals ways in which the body is *not* like a machine. DNA, for example, contains information describing an entire organism in each component of the whole – very unlike the economical partition of functions in a machine. New practices such as genetic profiling, forensic biometrics and tissue culturing suggest that the body may increasingly be defined not in terms of its material components but in terms of the information needed to specify how this material is configured and made individual. Lawsuits over who owns genetic information – the people whose genome it is, or the governmental or commercial groups collecting it – reveal the anxiety about relations between genetic information and persons (Chapter 8).[27] This point has been made graphically by the portrait of Sir John Sulston (who led the team first documenting an entire human genome) – which shows the subject both as he appears 'in person' and as he appears genetically (Figure 105).

Interestingly, this may converge with developments in daily sociality. In spite of fears about virtual identity, the Internet, Facebook and other social media often build upon existing conceptions of identity rather than wiping them clean – for instance, building on ideas of personal and national identity rather than undermining them.[28] Even in radical spaces like Second Life, people usually adopt avatars that resemble themselves in non-virtual

(a)   (b)

Figure 105. Marc Quinn's portraits of Sir John Sulston: A. Sample of his DNA in agar jelly. B. Photograph. (Both images © National Portrait Gallery, London.)

life,[29] and virtual relationships are just as emplaced as the friendships we might expect in more traditional venues.[30] Nevertheless, such developments change the parameters of sociality. Unlike face-to-face encounters, social relationships are dislocated in the material world at least; a virtual relationship can take place anywhere and everywhere – a process which began long ago with letters, telegrams and telephones, of course, but recent technology has extended it enormously. Mobile phones, email and mobile internet browsing make one continuously connected, often with multiple simultaneous relationships. Virtual relating becomes embedded in people to such an extent that being cut off from it prevents one from maintaining significant relationships. Problems of verification arise; are people on the internet who they appear to be? Facebook accounts, Second Life avatars and twitter feeds are all potentially run by multiple people, and a person can have multiple versions of each – the potentials for very different kinds of personhood here are legion. The different worlds of the virtual, the different kinds of place they generate, open up new possibilities for embodiment too.[31] A generation gap is apparent between those who believe that virtual sociality is a proxy for carrying on relations originating in traditional face-to-face encounters and those who regard it as a genuine social life in its own right.

Genetics and virtual sociality may do to the body what medicine and industrial discipline did in the eighteenth and nineteenth centuries or new spatial regimes of boundedness did in the Neolithic. As they converge, the body is redivided into disembodied information and substance. This is, of course, a revival of a Classical division of form and matter, but now potentially as a basic parameter of practical experience. One component of personhood has no location, and can be shared, subdivided,

reproduced and reformulated at will; the other is tied traditionally to a place, to a unique configuration of material substance with some fixity. The two components are held together – at present – by technologies of verifications such as passwords which restrict the permeability, multiplicity and replicability of the virtual person. Note that we are *not* saying that traditional bodies will imminently be replaced by virtual bodies. Visions of travellers who do not transport a physical body but simply use their cloud-based specification to grow a new, disposable body at will wherever they need one remain the stuff of science fiction. Instead, if you approach the body as a bundle of often-contradictory existential possibilities, as we did at the beginning of this chapter, it is clear that we will always need both ways of understanding the body: as unbounded, permeable, fluid, multiple or unlocated, and as integral, fixed, located or grounded in a particular material organism. New developments do not replace our modes of embodiment so much as add to them and change what aspects of life they encompass. And as such, there is clearly space for an emerging view of the body as information.

We would like to close on a note of optimism, in contrast to the gloom that seems to prevail in discussions of today's body. However 'human' is defined, people are irrepressibly human. There is no reason to suppose that the future body will ever become unimodal; this is probably the greatest respect in which it will differ from the relentlessly programmatic future bodies of fantasy. And this is a source of both unpredictability and of comfort. In human history as in engineering, composites are more resilient. To take an example, the Internet is technological, but it is above all social. When computer scientists and defence engineers began putting it together as a nuclear bomb-proof communication system during the late stages of the Cold War, the last thing they could have envisioned would have been Facebook, strangers exchanging dialect poetry and ethnic heritage recipes, the huge virtual garage sale that is Ebay, and the vast burgeoning of free political and social communication the Internet has created – and which, effectively, has created the Internet as it exists today. Similarly, people have always rooted concepts of relatedness in ideas about shared bodily substance. Although organ transplants may challenge our traditional sense of bodily boundedness, people have reacted not by abandoning traditional beliefs but by coming up with creative ways of formulating new idioms of relatedness to cope with situations in which body parts move between individuals (Chapter 8).[32] Even though DNA is not a particularly useful way of conceptualizing many elements of social relatedness, it has been incorporated in the rise of sociality based around shared genetic conditions and information (as in DNA-based genealo-gical groups – most of which operate in virtual space on the Internet!). When one considers the vast gamut of kinship relations people past and present have created to live within, our resources for coping with the multi-tudinous configurations of parenthood possible with new reproductive technologies are surely more than sufficient. The ways in which different modes of embodied sociality envelop and transform technology may be endearingly silly, or they may be painfully-worked out compromises. But the one thing they are *not*, is irrational. They are merely human.

Over the long run, where will such ideas lead? One benefit of taking the really long view – as in taking the wide view, in looking at different ways of living around the world today – is to put change into perspective. The body worlds we have seen in this book are alien, dramatically different, not only from our own but also from each other. Yet they were all liveable human worlds, most of which endured for much longer than ours has so far. We are deeply habituated to our social micro-environment, and being able to transplant faces, grow organs on demand, or be virtually in many places at once may feel like a shock. But when we look at the extraordinary range of body worlds humans have inhabited, such developments require minor tweaks to our ways of understanding the world; the end is not yet nigh. And, while different from ours, other body worlds past and present all have points of contact with our world, ways which they can be made comprehensible by overlap with things we also do and believe. Thus – to take just one possible example – living with a relational rather than absolute body that can be in many places, change between many forms and cross boundaries of humans and animals is not new territory for us. Our ancestors did things like this many times, above all in the Palaeolithic. History is no more linear than it is apocalyptic. Have we been to the future before?

NOTES

1. Foucault 1978, 152.
2. Shilling 2007.
3. Cf. Chapter 2; Sofaer 2006.
4. Butler 1993.
5. Harris and Robb 2012.

6. Depending where you were in Europe: see tables 4.1 and 4.2.
7. Sørensen and Rebay-Salisbury 2008c; 2008d.
8. Foucault 1977.
9. Tarlow 2011.
10. e.g. Postman 1993.
11. In archaeology, see Prentiss, Kuijt, and Chatters 2009; Robb and Pauketat 2012a; in history, see Shryock and Smail 2011 and *Journal of World History*.
12. DeLanda 2006, 4–5.
13. Robb and Pauketat 2012a; for questions of bridging on-the-ground social history to large-scale history, especially from a feminist perspective, see Pomeranz 2007; Wiesner-Hanks 2007.
14. Strathern 2004.
15. For analysis of the Classical art production system, see Gordon 1979; Tanner 2006.
16. Gell 1998.
17. Barth 2002.
18. Rappaport 1979.
19. Finding a vocabulary to express this is challenging as most available terms have considerable theoretical baggage. We resist the term 'belief systems' because it focuses attention too narrowly upon ideas rather than practices and mater-ial things, and it implies things are more systematic than they are. Similarly, 'structures of belief' implied a relatively rigid top-down determinism in which what happens at local scales is merely the playing out of pre-set structures. In one publication (Robb 2012), the term 'historical ontology' has been used for a collection of modes of understanding the body prevalent in a given historical period, but, as termin-ology, this is somewhat opaque. Hence our strategy here is to lead the reader to see what we mean by pointing out how extant terms do not express it!
20. Strathern 1992a, 7.
21. Strathern 2005, 167.
22. Hodder 2012.
23. Barth 2002.
24. Cf. Harris and Robb 2012.
25. Latour 1993; Shryock and Smail forthcoming.
26. See Guadalupe and Manguel 1987 for some wonderful examples.
27. Rabinow 1996.
28. Miller and Slater 2000; Shilling 2005.
29. Boellstorff 2011, 506.
30. Boellstorff 2011, 510.
31. Boellstorff 2011, 517.
32. Sharp 2000.

Epilogue

Marilyn Strathern

A scene from Aachen in northwest Germany, half way through the first decade of the twenty-first century. Several men, gathered intently together, form a rough circle. They are members of an art collectors' society[1] and have chalk in their hands, ready to mark their individual claims on a replica of three aluminium fuel tanks – the originals were the underbellies of aircraft – around which they are crowded. Half a century earlier, just such detritus from World War II had served as flotation for a raft fashioned in Darwin, Australia, by a destitute Scottish artist intending to get to England. Following his landfall in Indonesia, at least one of the original tanks was taken by his rescuers as recompense for their trouble, broken up and turned into things of use. The imagined replica of the whole raft was designed and fabricated by an artist, whom the collectors were hosting, as an explicit commentary on economic relations in the art world, on getting by without money, on reciprocity. The raft was shortly to be broken up, the tanks cut by the collectors themselves, and each bit gifted to them as marked, one idea being that they would get back something proportionate to their collective sponsorship, another that the aluminium would be returned to them refashioned by the artist with Indonesian themes.[2]

For me, what comes from John Robb and Oliver Harris's remarkable book is a sense of the artistry to be found in bodily relations. This book, for a start. The dismemberment of the vessel – it is their vignettes that make me re-image it as having something of the disposal of a body about it – derived from a collective fashioning (through the collectors' subscriptions) and anticipated its redistribution (each collector would keep a part of what they had seen as a whole). This book too would never have come together without the collaboration of the several colleagues on the Leverhulme-funded research project whose names are chalked up on the different chapters, and who receive back their work in a partitioning of sorts. In fact it puts partitioning in a slightly different light: what these colleagues contributed as a portion of their own (whole) work they receive back as a portion of a whole fashioned by the two principal authors. Robb and Harris have carried off an enterprise as every bit as engaging as the artist working with the Aachen collectors.

Any embodiment would have done, but I have needed the concrete analogy for collaboration and partition that the raft provides in order to convey just what a subtle work has emerged from a project so theoretically awkward ('the body'! 'in history'!). Concreteness summons all the limitations of a particular event at a particular social moment while at the same time connecting with a seemingly limitless imagination. Imagination is equally bound of course but that is not how we imagine it (to act out one version of 'the person' who appears in the narrative at the eleventh hour – silly to quarrel anthropologically with the use of the term when I recognize what it depicts). Rather than dwelling on the incommensurability, I can only report on that connection as a visceral sensation. As to the book, because it is an artefact that is composed largely of words, discourses, illustrations and arguments, it conveys the concrete in word-specific ways. Drawing analogies is one such. I refer not to ethnographic analogies, once so popular though now thoroughly domesticated in archaeology, if less so in history, but to the craft to be found in this book and the relations it encapsulates. There is a (bodily) liveliness and vigour to the writing, an analogy perhaps for the fact that body worlds are also lifeworlds.

They are also, inevitably, the end result of what otherwise can be separated into different times and epochs. Indeed multimodality, including the multiplicity of partially coexistent scales through time, is invoked at several junctures, adding a dimension at once challenging and self-evident to what is already descriptively complex in terms of time and space. But in the way it is written, *The Body in History* does not drive to greater and greater abstraction; instead, what comes out of the concrete returns to the concrete. Particularly for archaeologists, this is most easily done with found artefacts – fuel tanks, useful or artistic – to which are returned all the historical and conceptual work that fashions them afresh, whether or not they seem changed thereby. Yet while such items illuminate the present record, they are not the story here. The body never came together in the first place, it was never 'found', to act as a surrogate artefact of this kind. Although the modern anatomically inspired human frame recurs as a reference point, Robb and Harris's focus is on something else, namely that one cannot talk of bodies without acknowledging their life in and as 'body worlds'. The idea of body worlds enables

235

constant return to the concrete. With no apology for the variability to be found in any one moment – on the contrary, the authors revel in it – it is bodies expanded socially, materially and conceptually that are captured in their sequence of particular, located, descriptions. Bodies are in turn known (identifiable) through the form the expansion takes.

Body worlds are both less than and more than the historical epochs or time horizons or cultural arenas by which writers usually attempt to stride across vast domains. The authors repeatedly insist that anything identified with apprehensions of body is inevitably co-constructed with what some anthropologists might call 'other bodies', but which is commonly (as in arguments of naturalist bent) called context or environment. The point is that they put together a series of composites or assemblages that from any one specific perspective has unique and identifiable features. Very simply, the perspectives are created by the evidence that is assembled. Like an analogy, it is through the contingent and arbitrary concreteness of what is selected *as* evidence that identifiable, recognizable particulars are bodied forth.

This is important because the authors and their colleagues' central project is how to demonstrate, even (if possible) account for, long-term processes of change. Assemblages or composites require their particularities in order to raise questions of change through time. So the concreteness to which I have alluded is not just an effect of encountering over and again people realizing body worlds as they live them in their own specific ways,

or a matter of effective literary style in bringing things to life: it is theoretically needed to accomplish the work of comparison.

In one sense, the raft around which the collectors were gathered, intent on apportioning it, was not of course a replica: it was an artwork they were about to take apart. Their intervention was designed by the artist not only to show the contrivance of a whole, individual creation, but (he had conceived the project with ethnographic reference to reciprocity and exchange) also to enable continuing interactions between him and the collectors through the physical dispersal of the object. Readers are at the same time contributors, we know, and will no doubt apportion parts of this book to the worlds with which they too connect. The question that follows, I guess, is what it will do to body worlds that people become conscious of them.

Marilyn Strathern
27 June 2012

NOTES

1. The collection group Twodo, at the Neuer Aachener Kunstverein, who are interested in the distributed ownership to which conjoint artwork gives rise. My thanks for their hospitality and for Michael Stevenson's stimulating invitation.

2. Part of a series of artistic commentaries on cultural economics by artist Michael Stevenson. In this case, at the point of partition, there were still several possible outcomes in terms of gifting and reciprocity.

Bibliography

Abulafia, A. 1994. Bodies in the Jewish-Christian Debate. In *Framing Medieval Bodies*, edited by S. Kay and M. Rubin. Manchester: Manchester University Press, 123–138.

Ahmed, S. 2008. Open Forum: Imaginary Prohibitions: Some Preliminary Remarks on the Founding Gestures of the 'New Materialism'. *European Journal of Women's Studies* 15 (1):23–39.

Albarella, U., and D. Serjeantson. 2002. A Passion for Pork: Meat Consumption at the British Late Neolithic Site of Durrington Walls. In *Consuming Passions and Patterns of Consumption*, edited by N. Milner and P. Miracle. Cambridge: McDonald Institute, 33–49.

Albrethsen, S. V., and E. Brinch Petersen. 1976. Excavation of a Mesolithic Cemetery at Vedbæk, Denmark. *Acta Archaeologica* 47:1–28.

Aldhouse-Green, S., and P. Pettitt. 1998. Paviland Cave: Contextualizing the 'Red Lady'. *Antiquity* 72:756–772.

Ambrosi, A. 1972. *Corpus Delle Statue-Stele Lunigianesi, Collana Storica Dell Liguria Orientale*. Bordighera: Istituto Internazionale di Studi Liguri.

Anati, E. 1994. *Valcamonica Rock Art, Camunian Studies 13*. Capo di Ponte: Edizioni del Centro.

Anderson, B. 2006. *Imagined Communities*. 3rd ed. London: Verso.

Angel, J. L. 1984. Health as a Crucial Factor in the Changes from Hunting to Developed Farming in the Eastern Mediterranean. In *Paleopathology at the Origins of Agriculture*, edited by M. Cohen and G. Armelagos. New York: Academic, 51–74.

Antonaccio, C. M. 2000. Architecture and Behavior: Building Gender into Greek Houses. *Classical World* 93 (5):517–533.

ap Stifin, P. 2008. Excavating and Ordering: The Archaeology of the World Trade Centre. Unpublished M.A. Thesis, Department of Anthropology, University College London.

Aranguren, B. 2006. Primi Dati Di Cronologia Assoluta Dal Livello Funerario Eneolitico Di Grotta Della Spinosa. In *Preistoria E Protostoria in Etruria: VII Incontro Di Studi*, edited by N. Negroni Catacchio. Milano: Centro Studi di Preistoria, 481–489.

Archambeau, N. 2011. Healing Options During the Plague: Survivor Stories from a Fourteenth-Century Canonization Inquest. *Bulletin of the History of Medicine* 85 (4):531–559.

Arendt, H. 1973. *The Origins of Totalitarianism*. London: Harcourt.

Ariès, P. 1962. *Centuries of Childhood: A Social History of Family Life*. London: Jonathan Cape.

Ariès, P. 1981. *The Hour of Our Death*. New York: Knopf.

Arnold, J. 2005. *Belief and Unbelief in Medieval Europe*. London: Hodder Arnold.

Bailey, D. 2005. *Prehistoric Figurines: Representation and Corporeality in the Neolithic*. London: Routledge.

Bailey, D., A. Whittle, and V. Cummings, eds. 2005. *(Un)Settling the Neolithic*. Oxford: Oxbow.

Bailey, G. 2007. Time Perspectives, Palimpsests and the Archaeology of Time. *Journal of Anthropological Archaeology* 26:198–223.

Bailey, G. 2008. Mesolithic Europe: Overview and New Problems. In *Mesolithic Europe*, edited by G. Bailey and P. Spikins. Cambridge: Cambridge University Press, 357–371.

Bailey, G., and P. Spikins, eds. 2008. *Mesolithic Europe: Overview and New Problems*. Cambridge: Cambridge University Press.

Bailey, M. D. 2001. From Sorcery to Witchcraft: Clerical Conceptions of Magic in the Later Middle-Ages. *Speculum-a Journal of Medieval Studies* 76 (4):960–990.

Bar-Yosef, O. 1998. The Natufian Culture in the Levant, Threshold to the Origins of Agriculture. *Evolutionary Anthropology* 6 (5):159–177.

Barfield, L. 1994. The Iceman Reviewed. *Antiquity* 68:10–26.

Barrett, J., R. Bradley, and M. Green. 1991. *Landscape, Monuments and Society: The Prehistory of Cranborne Chase*. Cambridge: Cambridge University Press.

Barrett, J. C. 1994. *Fragments from Antiquity: An Archaeology of Social Life in Britain, 2900–1200 BC*. Oxford: Blackwell.

Barth, F. 1987. *Cosmologies in the Making: A Generative Approach to Cultural Variation in Inner New Guinea*. Cambridge: Cambridge University Press.

Barth, F. 2002. An Anthropology of Knowledge. *Current Anthropology* 43:1–18.

Bartlett, R. 2001. Medieval and Modern Concepts of Race and Ethnicity. *Journal of Medieval and Early Modern Studies* 31 (1):39–56.

Battaglia, D. 1990. *On the Bones of the Serpent: Person, Memory and Mortality in Sabarl Society*. Chicago: Chicago University Press.

Beard, M., and J. Henderson. 2001. *Classical Art from Greece to Rome*. Oxford: Oxford University Press.

Beihl, P. 2006. Figurines in Action: Methods and Theories in Figurine Research. In *A Future for Archaeology – the Past as the Present*, edited by R. Layton, S. Shennan and P. Stone. London: UCL Press, 199–215.

Beltrán Martínez, A. 1982. *Rock Art of the Spanish Levant*. Cambridge: Cambridge University Press.

Bennett, J. M. 1993. Medievalism and Feminism. *Speculum-a Journal of Medieval Studies* 68 (2):309–331.

Bennike, P. 1985. *Palaeopathology of Danish Skeletons: A Comparative Study of Demography, Disease, and Injury.* Copenhagen: Akademisk Forlag.

Benson, D., and A. Whittle, eds. 2007. *Building Memories: The Cotswold Neolithic Long Barrow at Ascott-under-Wychwood, Oxfordshire.* Oxford: Oxbow.

Berard, C., C. Bron, J. Durand, Frontisi-Ducroux, F. Lissarrague, A. Schnapp, and J. Vernant. 1989. *City of Images: Iconography and Society in Ancient Greece.* Princeton: Princeton University Press.

Berger, J. 1972. *Ways of Seeing.* Harmondsworth: Penguin.

Bettinetti, S. 2001. *La Statua Di Culto Nella Pratica Rituale Greca.* Bari: Levante.

Bhabha, H. K. 1994. *The Location of Culture.* London: Routledge.

Bickle, P. 2007. I'm Your Venus: Making Surfaces on the Body. *Journal of Iberian Archaeology* 9/10:257–270.

Bickle, P. 2009. Scene by the Brook: Early Neolithic Landscape Perspectives in the Paris Basin. In *Creating Communities: New Advances in Central European Research*, edited by D. Hofmann and P. Bickle. Oxford: Oxbow, 132–141.

Binski, P. 1996. *Medieval Death: Ritual and Representation.* London: British Museum Press.

Birkholz, D. 2006. Mapping Medieval Utopia: Exercises in Restraint. *Journal of Medieval and Early Modern Studies* 36 (3):585–618.

Bloch, M. 1998. *What We Think They Think: Anthropological Approaches to Cognition, Memory and Literacy.* Oxford: Westview Press.

Blundell, S. 1995. *Women in Ancient Greece.* Cambridge, Mass.: Harvard University Press.

Boardman, J. 1978. *Greek Sculpture, the Archaic Period: A Handbook.* London: Thames and Hudson.

Boardman, J. 1985. *Greek Sculpture, the Classical Period: A Handbook.* London: Thames and Hudson.

Boardman, J. 1995. *Greek Sculpture: The Late Classical Period and Sculpture in Colonies and Overseas.* London and New York: Thames and Hudson.

Boast, R. 1995. Fine Pots, Pure Pots, Beaker Pots. In *Unbaked Urns of Rudely Shape: Essays on British and Irish Pottery for Ian Longworth*, edited by I. Kinnes and J. Varndell. Oxford: Oxbow, 69–80.

Bocquet-Appel, J. P. 2002. Paleoanthropological Traces of a Neolithic Demographic Transition. *Current Anthropology* 43 (4):637–650.

Bocquet-Appel, J. P. 2009. The Demographic Impact of the Agricultural System in Human History. *Current Anthropology* 50 (5):657–660.

Bocquet-Appel, J.-P., and O. Bar-Yosef, eds. 2008. *The Neolithic Demographic Transition and Its Consequences.* New York: Springer.

Bocquet-Appel, J.-P., and J. Dubouloz. 2004. Expected Palaeoanthropological and Archaeological Signal from a Neolithic Demographic Transition on a Worldwide Scale. *Documenta Praehistorica* 31:25–33.

Boellstorff, T. 2011. Virtuality: Placing the Virtual Body: Avatar, Chora, Cypherg. In *A Companion to the Anthropology of the Body and Embodiment*, edited by F. E. Mascia-Lees. Oxford: Wiley-Blackwell, 504–520.

Bonfante, L. 1986. *Etruscan Life and Afterlife.* Detroit: Wayne State University Press.

Bonsall, C. 2008. The Mesolithic of the Iron Gates. In *Mesolithic Europe*, edited by G. Bailey and P. Spikins. Cambridge: Cambridge University Press, 238–279.

Bordo, S. 1993. *Unbearable Weight: Feminism, Western Culture and the Body.* Berkeley and London: University of California Press.

Borić, D. 2002. The Lepenski Vir Conundrum: Reinterpretation of the Mesolithic and Neolithic Sequences in the Danube Gorges. *Antiquity* 76:1026–1039.

Borić, D. 2005a. Body Metamorphosis and Animality: Volatile Bodies and Boulder Artworks from Lepenski Vir. *Cambridge Archaeological Journal* 15:35–69.

Borić, D. 2005b. Deconstructing Essentialisms: Unsettling Frontiers of the Mesolithic-Neolithic Balkans. In *(Un)Settling the Neolithic*, edited by D. Bailey, A. Whittle and V. Cummings. Oxford: Oxbow, 16–31.

Borić, D. 2007. Images of Animality: Hybrid Bodies and Mimesis in Early Prehistoric Art. In *Image and Imagination: A Global Prehistory of Figurative Representation*, edited by C. Renfrew and I. Morley. Cambridge: McDonald Institute, 83–100.

Borić, D. 2008. First Households and 'House Societies' in European Prehistory. In *Prehistoric Europe: Theory and Practice*, edited by A. Jones. Oxford: Wiley-Blackwell, 109–142.

Borić, D. 2009. Absolute Dating of Metallurgical Innovations in the Vinča Culture of the Balkans. In *Metals and Societies. Studies in Honour of Barbara S. Ottaway*, edited by T. K. Kienlin and B. W. Roberts. Bonn: Habelt, 191–245.

Borić, D. 2010. Happy Forgetting? Remembering and Dismembering Dead Bodies at Vlasac. In *Archaeology and Memory*, edited by D. Borić. Oxford: Oxbow, 48–67.

Borić, D. 2011. Adaptations and Transformations of the Danube Gorges Foragers (C. 13,000–5500 Cal. BC): An Overview. In *Beginnings – New Research in the Appearance of the Neolithic between Northwest Anatolia and the Carpathian Basin*, edited by R. Krauß. Rahden: Verlag Marie Leidorf, 157–203.

Borić, D. in press. Mortuary Practices, Bodies and Persons in the Neolithic and Early-Middle Copper Age of Southeast Europe. In *The Oxford Handbook of Neolithic Europe*, edited by C. Fowler, J. Harding and D. Hofmann. Oxford: Oxford University Press.

Borić, D., J. Raičević, and S. Stefanović. 2009. Mesolithic Cremations as Elements of Secondary Mortuary Rites at Vlasac (Serbia). *Documenta Praehistorica* 36:247–82.

Borić, D., and J. E. Robb, eds. 2008. *Past Bodies: Body-Centred Research in Archaeology.* Oxford: Oxbow.

Borić, D., and S. Stefanović. 2004. Birth and Death: Infant Burials from Vlasac and Lepenski Vir. *Antiquity* 78: 526–544.

Borland, J. 2011. Audience and Spatial Experience in the Nuns' Church at Clonmacnoise. *Different Visions: A Journal of New Perspectives on Medieval Art* 1 (3):1–45.

Boulestin, B., A. Zeeb-Lanz, C. Jeunesse, F. Haack, R.-M. Arbogast, and A. Denaire. 2009. Mass Cannibalism in the Linear Pottery Culture at Herxheim (Palatinate, Germany) *Antiquity* 83:968–982.

Bourdieu, P. 1977. *Outline of a Theory of Practice*. Cambridge: Cambridge University Press.

Bourdieu, P. 1990. *The Logic of Practice*. Stanford: Stanford University Press.

Bovey, A. 2002. *Monsters and Grotesques in Medieval Manuscripts*. London: British Library.

Boyd, B. 2002. Ways of Eating/Ways of Being in the Later Epipalaeolithic (Natufian) Levant. In *Thinking through the Body: Archaeologies of Corporeality*, edited by Y. Hamilakis, M. Pluciennik and S. Tarlow. New York; London: Kluwer Academic/Plenum, 137–152.

Boyd, B. 2005. Transforming Food Practices in the Epipaeolithic and Pre-Pottery Neolithic Levant. In *Archaeological Perspectives on the Transmission and Tranformation of Culture in the Eastern Mediterranean*, edited by J. Clarke. Oxford: Oxbow, 106–112.

Boyd, B. 2006. On 'Sedentism' in the Later Epipalaeolithic (Natufian) Levant. *World Archaeology* 38 (2):164–178.

Boyd, Z. 1629. *The Last Battell of the Soule in Death*. Edinburgh: Heires of Andro Hart.

Boyle, K. 2006. Neolithic Wild Game Animals in Western Europe: The Question of Hunting. In *Animals in the Neolithic of Britain and Europe*, edited by D. Serjeantson and D. Field. Oxford: Oxbow, 10–23.

Bradley, R. 1984. *The Social Foundations of Prehistoric Britain*. London: Longmans.

Bradley, R. 2000. *The Good Stones: A New Investigation of the Clava Cairns*. Edinburgh: Society for the Antiquaries of Scotland.

Bradley, R. 2002. *The Past in Prehistoric Societies*. London: Routledge.

Bradley, R. 2006. Danish Razors and Swedish Rocks: Cosmology and the Bronze Age Landscape. *Antiquity* 80:372–389.

Bradley, R. 2007. *The Prehistory of Britain and Ireland*. Cambridge: Cambridge University Press.

Braithwaite, M. 1984. Ritual and Prestige in the Prehistory of Wessex, C. 2200–1400 BC: A New Dimension to the Archaeological Evidence. In *Ideology, Power and Prehistory*, edited by D. Miller and C. Tilley. Cambridge: Cambridge University Press, 93–110.

Brennand, M., and Taylor, M. 2003. The Survey and Excavation of a Bronze Age Timber Circle at Holme-next-the-Sea, Norfolk, 1998–1999. *Proceedings of the Prehistoric Society* 69:1–84.

Brinch Petersen, E., and C. Meikeljohn. 2003. Three Cremations and a Funeral: Aspects of Burial Practice at Mesolithic Vedbaek. In *Mesolithic on the Move*, edited by L. Larsson, H. Kindgren, K. Knutsson, D. Loeffler and A. Åkerlund. Oxford: Oxbow, 485–493.

Brittain, M., and O.J.T. Harris. 2010. Enchaining Arguments and Fragmenting Assumptions: Reconsidering the Fragmentation Debate in Archaeology. *World Archaeology* 42 (4):581–594.

Brock, R. 1994. The Labor of Women in Classical Athens. *Classical Quarterly* 44 (2):336–346.

Brock, R. 2006. The Body as a Political Organism in Greek Thought. In *Penser Et Représenter Le Corps Dans L'antiquité*, edited by F. Prost and J. Wilgaux. Rennes: Presses Universitaires de Rennes, 351–359.

Brodwin, P., ed. 2000. *Biotechnology and Culture: Bodies, Anxieties, Ethics*. Bloomington, Ind.: University of Indiana Press.

Brody, H. 1997. *Maps and Dreams: Indians and the British Columbia Frontier*. Long Grove, Ill.: Waveland Press.

Brøndsted, J. 1940. *Danmarks Oldtid 2. Bronzealderen*. Kopenhagen: Gyldendal.

Brown, N. 1999. Xenotransplantation: Normalizing Disgust. *Science as Culture* 8 (3):327–355.

Brown, P. 1981. *The Cult of the Saints: Its Rise and Function in Latin Christianity*. Chicago: University of Chicago Press.

Brown, P. 1990. *The Body and Society: Men, Women and Sexual Renunciation in Early Christianity*. London: Faber and Faber.

Brown, S. 1997. 'Ways of Seeing' Women in Antiquity: An Introduction to Feminism in Classical Archaeology and Art History. In *Naked Truths: Women, Sexuality and Gender in Classical Art and Archaeology*, edited by A. O. Koloski-Ostrow and C. L. Lyons. London: Routledge, 12–42.

Brożyna, M. 2005. *Gender and Sexuality in the Middle Ages: A Medieval Source Documents Reader*. Jefferson (NC) and London: MacFarland and Co.

Brück, J. 2004. Material Metaphors. The Relational Construction of Identity in Early Bronze Age Burials in Ireland and Britain. *Journal of Social Archaeology* 4:307–333.

Brück, J. 2006a. Death, Exchange and Reproduction in the British Bronze Age. *European Journal of Archaeology* 9 (1):73–101.

Brück, J. 2006b. Fragmentation, Personhood and the Social Construction of Technology in Middle and Late Bronze Age Britain. *Cambridge Archaeological Journal* 16 (3):297–315.

Brück, J. 2009. Women, Death and Social Change in the British Bronze Age. *Norwegian Archaeological Review* 42 (1):1–23.

Buchli, V., ed. 2002. *The Material Culture Reader*. London: Berg.

Bullough, V., and J. Brundage. 2000. *Handbook of Medieval Sexuality*. London: Routledge.

Bundrick, S. D. 2008. The Fabric of the City: Imaging Textile Production in Classical Athens. *Hesperia* 77 (2):283–334.

Burns, L. 2007. Gunther Von Hagens' Body Worlds: Selling Beautiful Education. *American Journal of Bioethics* 4:12–23.

Burton, J. 1998. Women's Commensality in the Ancient World. *Greece & Rome* 45 (2):143–165.

Busby, C. 1997. Permeable and Partible Persons: A Comparative Analysis of Gender and Body in South India and Melanesia. *Journal of the Royal Anthropological Institute* 3:261–278.

Butler, J. 1990. *Gender Trouble: Feminism and the Subversion of Identity*. London Routledge.

Butler, J. 1993. *Bodies That Matter: On the Discursive Limits of 'Sex'*. London: Routledge.

Butler, J. 2004. *Undoing Gender*. London: Routledge.

Bynum, C. 1992a. *Fragmentation and Redemption: Essays on Gender and the Human Body in Mediaeval Religion*. London: Zone.

Bynum, C. 1992b. *Holy Feast and Holy Fast: The Religious Significance of Food to Medieval Women*. Berkeley: University of California Press.

Bynum, C. 1995a. *The Resurrection of the Body in Western Christianity, 200–1336*. New York: Columbia University Press.

Bynum, C. 1995b. Why All the Fuss About the Body? *Critical Inquiry* 22:1–33.

Bynum, C. 2007. *Wonderful Blood: Theology and Practice in Late Medieval Northern Germany and Beyond*. Philadelphia: University of Pennsylvania Press.

Bynum, C. W. 2005. *Metamorphosis and Identity*. New York: Zone.

Bynum, W., and L. Kalof, eds. 2010. *A Cultural History of the Human Body*. Oxford: Blackwell.

Byrd, B. F., and C. M. Monahan. 1995. Death, Mortuary Ritual, and Natufian Social Structure. *Journal of Anthropological Archaeology* 14:251–287.

Cabre, M. 2008. Women or Healers? Household Practices and the Categories of Health Care in Late Medieval Iberia. *Bulletin of the History of Medicine* 82 (1):18–51.

Caciola, N. 2000. Mystics, Demoniacs, and the Physiology of Spirit Possession in Medieval Europe. *Comparative Studies In Society And History* 42 (2):268–306.

Cadden, J. 1993. *The Meanings of Sex Difference in the Middle Ages: Medicine, Science, and Culture*. Cambridge: Cambridge University Press.

Cain, J. 2002. Unnatural History: Gender and Genealogy in Gerald of Wales's Topographia Hibernica. *Essays in Medieval Studies* 19:29–43.

Camille, M. 1992. *Image on the Edge: The Margins of Medieval Art*. London: Reaktion.

Camille, M. 1994. The Image and the Self: Unwriting Late Medieval Bodies. In *Framing Medieval Bodies*, edited by S. Kay and M. Rubin. Manchester: Manchester University Press, 62–99.

Canci, A., S. Minozzi, and S. M. B. Tarli. 1996. New Evidence of Tuberculous Spondylitis from Neolithic Liguria (Italy). *International Journal of Osteoarchaeology* 6 (5):497–501.

Cartledge, P. 1993a. *The Greeks: A Portrait of Self and Others*. Oxford and New York: Oxford University Press.

Cartledge, P. 1993b. Like a Worm I' the Bud? A Heterology of Classical Greek Slavery. *Greece & Rome* 40 (2):163–180.

Casini, S., R. De Marinis, and A. Pedrotti. 1995. *Statue-Stele E Massi Incisi Nell'europa Dell'età Del Rame*. Vol. 3, *Notizie Archeologiche Bergomensi*. Bergamo: Civico Museo Archeologico.

Casini, S., and A. Fossati. 2004. *Le Pietre Degli Dei: Statue-Stele Dell'età Del Rame in Europa – Lo Stato Della Ricerca*. Vol. 12, *Notizie Archeologiche Bergomensi*. Bergamo: Civico Museo Archeologico.

Cauvin, J. 2000. *The Birth of the Gods and the Origins of Agriculture*. Cambridge: Cambridge University Press.

Caviness, M. H. 2001a. Reframing Medieval Art: Difference, Margins, Boundaries. http://dca.lib.tufts.edu/Caviness/ (accessed 13 March 2012).

Caviness, M. H. 2001b. *Visualizing Women in the Middle Ages: Sight, Spectacle and the Scopic Economy*. Philadelphia: University of Pennsylvania Press.

Caviness, M. H. 2010. Feminism, Gender Studies, and Medieval Studies. *Diogenes* 57 (1):30–45.

Cessford, C. 2005. Estimating the Neolithic Population of Çatalhöyük. In *Inhabiting Çatalhöyük: Reports from the 1995–1999 Seasons*, edited by I. Hodder. Cambridge: McDonald Institute 323–326.

Chaplin, J. E. 2001. *Subject Matter: Technology, the Body, and Science on the Anglo-American Frontier, 1500–1676*. Cambridge, Mass.: Harvard University Press.

Chapman, J. 2000. *Fragmentation in Archaeology: People, Places and Broken Objects in the Prehistory of South-Eastern Europe*. London: Routledge.

Chapman, J., and B. Gaydarska. 2006. *Parts and Wholes: Fragmentation in a Prehistoric Context*. Oxford: Oxbow.

Chaucer, G. 1933. *The Complete Works of Geoffrey Chaucer*. Edited by F. N. Robinson. Cambridge, Mass.: Riverside Press.

Chaucer, G. 1951. *The Canterbury Tales*. Translated by N. Coghill. Harmondsworth: Penguin.

Chauvet, J.-M., E. Brunel Deschamps, and C. Hillaire. 1996. *Chauvet Cave: The Discovery of the World's Oldest Paintings*. London: Thames and Hudson.

Childe, V. G. 1942. *What Happened in History*. London: Penguin.

Childe, V. G. 1950. *Prehistoric Migrations in Europe*. Oslo: Aschehoug.

Chippindale, C., and P. S. Taçon. 1998. *The Archaeology of Rock-Art*. Cambridge: Cambridge University Press.

Clark, A. 1997. *Being There: Putting Brain, Body and World Back Together Again*. Cambridge, Mass.: MIT Press.

Clarke, D. V., T. G. Cowie, and A. Foxon. 1985. *Symbols of Power at the Time of Stonehenge*. Edinburgh: National Museum of Antiquities of Scotland.

Clendinnen, I. 1999. *Reading the Holocaust*. Cambridge: Cambridge University Press.

Closterman, W. E. 2007. Family Ideology and Family History: The Function of Funerary Markers in Classical Attic Peribolos Tombs. *American Journal of Archaeology* 111 (4):633–652.

Clottes, J. 2000. Art between 30,000 and 20,000 BP. In *Hunters of the Golden Age: The Mid Upper Palaeolithic of*

Eurasia, 30,000 – 20,000 BP, edited by W. Roebroeks, M. Mussi, J. Svoboda and K. Fennema. Leiden: Leiden University Press, 87–103.

Cochrane, A., and I. Russell. 2007. Visualizing Archaeologies: A Manifesto. *Cambridge Archaeological Journal* 17 (1):3–19.

Cohen, D. 1989. Seclusion, Separation and the Status of Women in Classical Athens. *Greece and Rome* 36:3–15.

Cohen, D. J. 1991. Sexuality, Violence, and the Athenian Law of 'Hubris'. *Greece & Rome* 38:171–188.

Cohen, E. 2000. The Animated Pain of the Body. *American Historical Review* 105:36–68.

Cohen, J. J. 2003. *Medieval Identity Machines*. Minneapolis: University of Minnesota Press.

Cohen, M., and G. Armelagos. 1984. *Paleopathology at the Origins of Agriculture*. New York: Academic.

Cole, S. G. 2004. *Landscapes, Gender and Ritual Space: The Ancient Greek Experience*. Berkeley: University of California Press.

Coles, J. 1962. European Bronze Age Shields. *Proceedings of the Prehistoric Society* 28:156–190.

Coles, J. 1968. Neolithic God-Dolly from Somerset, England. *Antiquity* 42:275–278.

Coles, J. 2005. *Shadows of a Northern Past. Rock Carvings of Bohuslän and Østfold*. Oxford: Oxbow.

Coles, J., and A. Harding. 1979. *The Bronze Age in Europe*. London: Methuen.

Collard, M., K. Edinborough, S. Shennan, and M. G. Thomas. 2010. Radiocarbon Evidence Indicates That Migrants Introduced Farming to Britain. *Journal of Archaeological Science* 37:866–870.

Collingwood, R. G. 1945. *The Idea of Nature*. Oxford: Clarendon Press.

Conneller, C. 2004. Becoming Deer: Corporeal Transformations at Star Carr. *Archaeological Dialogues* 11:37–56.

Conneller, C. 2005. Death. In *Mesolithic Britain and Ireland: New Approaches*, edited by C. Conneller and G. Warren. Stroud: The History Press, 139–164.

Conneller, C. 2011. *An Archaeology of Materials: Substantial Transformations in Early Prehistoric Europe*. London: Routledge.

Connelly, J. B. 2007. *Portrait of a Priestess: Women and Ritual in Ancient Greece*. Princeton: Princeton University Press.

Conrad, L., M. Neve, V. Nutton, R. Porter, and A. Wear. 1995. *The Western Medical Tradition: 800 BC to AD 1800*. Cambridge: Cambridge University Press.

Coon, L. 2008. Somatic Styles of the Early Middle Ages. *Gender & History* 20:463–486.

Coon, L. 2010. *Dark Age Bodies: Gender and Monastic Practices in the Early Medieval West*. Philadelphia: University of Pennsylvania Press.

Cosgrove, D. 1984. *Social Formation and Symbolic Landscape*. London: Croom Helm.

Craig, L. A. 2003. 'Stronger Than Men and Braver Than Knights': Women and the Pilgrimages to Jerusalem and Rome in the Later Middle Ages. *Journal of Medieval History* 29 (3):153–175.

Crane, S. 2002. *The Performance of Self: Ritual, Clothing, and Identity During the Hundred Years' War*. Philadelphia: University of Pennsylvania Press.

Cristiani, E., and D. Borić. 2012. 9500-Year-Old Late Mesolithic Garment Embroidery from Vlasac (Serbia): Technological, Use-Wear and Residue Analyses. *Journal of Archaeological Science* 39 (11):3450–3469.

Crossley, N. 2004. The Circuit Trainer's Habitus: Reflexive Body Techniques and the Sociality of the Workout. *Body and Society* 10 (1):37–69.

Crossley, N. 2005. Mapping Reflexive Body Techniques. *Body and Society* 11 (1):1–35.

Crossley, N. 2006. In the Gym: Motives, Meaning and Moral Careers. *Body & Society* 12 (3):23–50.

Croucher, K. 2010. Bodies in Pieces in the Neolithic Near East. In *Body Parts and Body Wholes*, edited by K. Rebay-Salisbury, M. L. S. Sørensen and J. Hughes. Oxford: Oxbow, 6–19.

Croucher, K. 2011. Anatolia. In *The Oxford Handbook of the Archaeology of Ritual and Religion*, edited by T. Insoll. Oxford: Oxford University Press, 826–845.

Croucher, K. 2012. *Death and Dying in the Neolithic Near East*. Oxford: Oxford University Press.

Crumley, C., R. Ehrenreich, and J. Levy. 1995. *Heterarchy and the Analysis of Complex Societies*. Washington, D.C.: American Anthropological Association.

Csordas, T., ed. 1994. *Embodiment and Experience: The Existential Ground of Culture and Strength*. Cambridge: Cambridge University Press.

Cummings, V., and O. J. T. Harris. 2011. Animals, People and Places: The Continuity of Hunting and Gathering Practices across the Mesolithic Neolithic Transition in Britain. *European Journal of Archaeology* 14 (3):361–382.

Cummings, V., and A. Whittle. 2004. *Landscapes of Special Virtue: Megaliths in the Neolithic Landscapes of Wales*. Oxford: Oxbow.

Dacome, L. 2006. Resurrecting by Numbers in Eighteenth-Century England. *Past and Present* 193:73–110.

Dale, T. E. A. 2001. Monsters, Corporeal Deformities, and Phantasms in the Cloister of St-Michel-De-Cuxa. *Art Bulletin* 83 (3):402–436.

Dant, T. 2004. The Driver-Car. *Theory, Culture and Society* 21 (4/5):61–79.

Darwin, C. 2008 [1859]. *On the Origin of Species*. Oxford: Oxford University Press.

Davies, O. 2007. *Popular Magic: Cunning-Folk in English History*. London: Hambledon Continuum.

Davis, N. 2009. New Materialism and Feminism's Anti-Biologism: A Response to Sara Ahmed. *European Journal of Women's Studies* 16 (1):67–80.

Davis, N., ed. 1983. *The Paston Letters: A Selection in Modern Spelling*. Oxford: Oxford University Press.

de Lumley, H., M. Fonvielle, and J. Abelanet. 1976. *Vallée Des Merveilles*. Nice: Union International des Sciences Pre- et Proto-historiques.

De Marinis, R. C., and G. Brillante. 1998. *La Mummia Del Similaun: Ötzi, L'uomo Venuto Del Ghiaccio*. Venice: Marsilio.

Dean-Jones, L. 1996. *Women's Bodies in Classical Greek Science.* Oxford: Oxford University Press.

DeLanda, M. 2006. *A New Philosophy of Society: Assemblage Theory and Social Complexity.* London: Continuum.

Deleuze, G., and F. Guattari. 2004. *A Thousand Plateaus: Capitalism and Schizophrenia.* London: Continuum.

Delson, E., I. Tattersall, J. A. Van Couvering, and A. S. Brooks. 2000. *Encyclopedia of Human Evolution and Prehistory.* 2nd ed. New York: Garland Publishing.

Descartes, R. 2008 [1641]. *Meditations on First Philosophy: With Selections from the Objections and Replies.* Oxford: Oxford University Press.

Descola, P. 1992. *In the Society of Nature: A Native Ecology in Amazonia.* Cambridge: Cambridge University Press.

Dietler, M. 2010. *Archaeologies of Colonialism: Consumption, Entanglement, and Violence in Ancient Mediterranean France.* Berkeley: University of California Press.

Dixon, P. 1988. The Neolithic Settlements on Crickley Hill. In *Enclosures and Defences in the Neolithic of Western Europe,* edited by C. Burgess, P. Topping, C. Mordant and M. Maddison. Oxford: British Archaeological Reports, 75–87.

Dobres, M.-A. 2000. *Technology and Social Agency.* Oxford: Blackwell.

Dolfini, A. 2011. The Function of Chalcolithic Metalwork in Italy: An Assessment Based on Use-Wear Analysis. *Journal of Archaeological Science* 38 (5):1037–1049.

Dorfer, L., K. Spindler, F. Bahr, E. Egarter-Vigi, and G. Dohr. 1998. 5200-Year-Old Acupuncture in Central Europe? *Science* 282:242–243.

Douglas, M. 1973. *Natural Symbols.* London: Pelican Books.

Dover, K. J. 1978. *Greek Homosexuality.* New York: Vintage.

Dumit, J. 2000. When Explanations Rest: 'Good-Enough' Brain Science and the New Socio-Medical Disorders. In *Living and Working with the New Medical Technologies: Intersections of Inquiry,* edited by M. Lock, A. Young and A. Cambrosio. Cambridge: Cambridge University Press, 209–232.

Dunbabin, K. M. D. 1986. Sic Erimus Cuncti. . . . The Skeleton in Graeco-Roman Art. *Jahrbuch des Deutschen Archäologischen Instituts* 101:185–255.

Edwards, J., P. Harvey, and P. Wade, eds. 2010. *Technologized Images, Technologized Bodies.* Oxford: Berghahn.

Elias, N. 1978. *The Civilising Process: The History of Manners.* Oxford: Basil Blackwell.

Elias, N. 1982. *The Civilising Process: State Formation and Civilisations.* Oxford: Basil Blackwell.

Elias, N. 1983. *The Court Society.* Oxford: Basil Blackwell.

Elsner, J. 2007. *Roman Eyes: Visuality and Subjectivity in Art and Text.* Princeton: Princeton University Press.

Evans, J. 1971. *Prehistoric Antiquities of the Maltese Islands.* London: Athlone.

Fairén-Jiménez, S. in press. Rock Art in the Neolithic of Iberia. In *The Oxford Handbook of Neolithic Europe,* edited by C. Fowler, J. Harding and D. Hofmann. Oxford: Oxford University Press.

Fantham, E., H. P. Foley, N. B. Kampen, S. Pomeroy, and H. Shapiro. 1995. *Women in the Classical World: Image and Text.* New York: Oxford University Press.

Fedele, F. 2007. Monoliths and Human Skeletal Remains: Ritual Manipulation at the Anvòia Ceremonial Site, Ossimo (Valcamonica, Italy). *Notizie Archeologiche Bergomensi* 12:49–66.

Fedele, F. 2008. Statue-Menhirs, Human Remains and Mana at the Ossimo 'Anvòia' Ceremonial Site, Val Camonica. *Journal of Mediterranean Archaeology* 21:57–79.

Ferkiss, V. C. 1993. *Nature, Technology and Society: Cultural Roots of the Current Environmental Crisis.* London: Adamantine Press.

Ferrari, G. 2002. *Figures of Speech: Men and Maidens in Ancient Greece.* Chicago: University of Chicago Press.

Fiedorczuk, J., B. Bratlund, E. Kolstrup, and R. Schild. 2007. Late Magdalenian Feminine Flint Plaquettes from Poland. *Antiquity* 81:97–105.

Finlayson, B., and G. Warren, eds. 2010. *Landscapes in Transition.* Oxford: Oxbow.

Fissell, M. E. 2005. *Vernacular Bodies: The Politics of Reproduction in Early Modern England.* Oxford: Oxford University Press.

Fitzpatrick, A. P. 2011. *The Amesbury Archer and the Boscombe Bowmen. Bell Beaker Burials at Boscombe Down, Amesbury, Wiltshire, Wessex Archaeology Report 27.* Salisbury: Wessex Archaeology.

Flanagan, S. 1998. *Hildegard of Bingen: A Visionary Life.* London: Routledge.

Flint, V. I. J. 1991. *The Rise of Magic in Early Medieval Europe.* Princeton: Princeton University Press.

Floyd-Wilson, M., and G. A. Sullivan Jr, eds. 2007. *Environment and Embodiment in Early Modern England.* New York: Palgrave McMillan.

Flynn, T. 1998. *The Body in Sculpture.* London: Weidenfield and Nicolson.

Fontijn, D. 2002. *Sacrificial Landscapes. Cultural Biographies of Persons, Objects and 'Natural Places' in the Bronze Age of the Southern Netherlands, C. 2300–600 BC.* Vol. 33/34. Leiden: Praehistorica Leidensia.

Formicola, V., and A. P. Buzhilova. 2004. Double Child Burial from Sunghir (Russia): Pathology and Inferences for Upper Paleolithic Funerary Practices. *American Journal of Physical Anthropology* 124 (3):189–198.

Forty, A., and S. Küchler, eds. 1999. *The Art of Forgetting.* Oxford: Berg.

Foucault, M. 1973. *The Birth of the Clinic: An Archaeology of Medical Perception.* London: Tavistock.

Foucault, M. 1977. *Discipline and Punish: The Birth of the Prison.* London: Allen Lane.

Foucault, M. 1978. *A History of Sexuality, Volume 1: The Will to Knowledge.* Harmondsworth: Penguin.

Foucault, M. 1985. *The History of Sexuality, Volume 2: The Use of Pleasure.* New York: Pantheon Books.

Foucault, M. 1988. *The History of Sexuality, Volume 3: The Care of the Self.* New York: Vintage Books.

Fowler, C. 2000. The Individual, the Subject, and Archaeological Interpretation. Reading Luce Irigaray and Judith Butler. In *Philosophy and Archaeological Practice: Perspectives for the 21st Century*, edited by C. Holtorf and H. Karlsson. Göteborg: Bricoleur Press, 107–133.

Fowler, C. 2001. Personhood and Social Relations in the British Neolithic with a Case Study from the Isle of Man. *Journal of Material Culture* 6:137–163.

Fowler, C. 2004a. *The Archaeology of Personhood: An Anthropological Approach*. London: Routledge.

Fowler, C. 2004b. Identity Politics: Personhood, Kinship, Gender and Power in Neolithic and Early Bronze Age Britain. In *The Archaeology of Plural and Changing Identities: Beyond Identification*, edited by E. C. Casella and C. Fowler. New York: Springer, 109–134.

Fowler, C. 2004c. In Touch with the Past? Monuments, Bodies and the Sacred in the Manx Neolithic and Beyond. In *The Neolithic of the Irish Sea: Materiality and Traditions of Practice*, edited by C. Fowler and V. Cummings. Oxford: Oxbow, 91–102.

Fowler, C. 2010. Pattern and Diversity in the Early Neolithic Mortuary Practice of Britain and Ireland: Contextualising the Treatment of the Dead. *Documenta Praehistorica* 37: 1–22.

Fowles, S. 2010. People without Things. In *An Anthropology of Absence: Materializations of Transcendence and Loss*, edited by M. Bille, F. Hastrup, and T. F. Sørensen. New York: Springer, 23–41.

Foxhall, L. 1989. Household, Gender and Property in Classical Athens. *Classical Quarterly* 39 (1):22–44.

Foxhall, L., and J. Salmon, eds. 1998. *Thinking Men: Masculinity and Its Self-Representation in the Classical Tradition*. London and New York: Routledge.

Franklin, S. 2003. Re-Thinking Nature-Culture. *Anthropological Theory* 3 (1):65–85.

Franklin, S. 2006. The Cyborg Embryo: Our Path to Transbiology. *Theory, Culture and Society* 23 (7–8):167–187.

Franklin, S., and M. Lock, eds. 2003. *Remaking Life and Death: Toward an Anthropology of the Biosciences*. Sante Fe: School of American Research Press.

Frieman, C. 2010a. Imitation, Identity and Communication: The Presence and Problems of Skeuomorphs in the Metal Ages. In *Lithic Technology in Metal Using Societies*, edited by B. V. Eriksen. Højbjerg: Jutland Archaeology Society, 33–44.

Frieman, C. 2010b. Skeuomorphs and Stone-Working: Elaborate Lithics from the Early Metal-Using Era in Coastal, Northwest Europe. Unpublished Ph.D. Thesis, Institute of Archaeology, Oxford University.

Fugazzola Delpino, M. A., and V. Tinè. 2003. Le Statuine Fittili Femminili Del Neolitico Italiano: Iconografia E Contesto Culturale. *Bullettino di Paletnologia Italiana* 93–95:19–51.

Fullerton, M. 2000. *Greek Art*. Cambridge: Cambridge University Press.

Gallay, A. 1995. Les Stèles Anthropomorphes Du Site Mégalithique Du Petit-Chasseur À Sion (Valais, Suisse). In *Statue-Stele E Massi Incisi Nell'europa Dell'età Del Rame*, edited by S. Casini, R. De Marinis and A. Pedrotti. Bergamo: Civico Museo Archeologico, 167–194.

Gamble, C. 1999. *The Palaeolithic Societies of Europe*. Cambridge: Cambridge University Press.

Gamble, C. 2007. *Origins and Revolutions: Human Identity in Earliest Prehistory*. Cambridge: Cambridge University Press.

García-Ballester, L. 2001. *Medicine in a Multi-Cultural Society: Christian, Jewish and Muslim Practitioners in the Spanish Kingdoms, 1222–1610*. Aldershot: Ashgate Variorum.

García Sanjuán, L., D. W. Wheatley, P. Fábrega Álvarez, M. J. Hernández Arnedo, and A. Polvorinos del Río. 2006. Las Estelas De Guerrero De Almadén De La Plata (Sevilla): Morfología, Tecnología Y Contexto. *Trabajos De Prehistoria* 63:135–152.

Geary, P. 1986. Sacred Commodities: The Circulation of Medieval Relics. In *The Social Life of Things*, edited by A. Appadurai. Cambridge: Cambridge University Press, 141–168.

Geertz, C. 1973. *The Interpretation of Cultures*. New York: Basic Books.

Gell, A. 1992. The Technology of Enchantment and the Enchantment of Technology. In *Anthropology, Art and Aesthetics*, edited by J. Coote and A. Shelton. Oxford: Blackwell, 40–67.

Gell, A. 1993. *Wrapping in Images: Tattooing in Polynesia*. Oxford: Clarendon.

Gell, A. 1998. *Art and Agency: An Anthropological Theory*. Oxford: Clarendon Press.

Gentilcore, D. 1995. Contesting Illness in Early Modern Naples: *Mircaolati*, Physicians and the Congregation of Rites. *Past and Present* 148:117–148.

Geremek, B. 1990. The Marginal Man. In *Medieval Callings*, edited by J. Le Goff. Chicago: University of Chicago Press, 347–373.

Gerritsen, F. 2003. *Local Identities. Landscape and Community in the Late Prehistoric Meuse-Demer-Scheldt Region, Amsterdam Archaelogical Studies 9*. Amsterdam: Amsterdam University Press.

Giannitrapani, M. 2002. *Coroplastica Neolitica Antropomorfa D'Italia: Simboli Ed Iconografie Dell'arte Mobiliare Quaternaria Post-Glaciale*. Vol. 1020, International Series. Oxford: British Archaeological Reports.

Gibson, A. 2004. Burials and Beakers: Seeing beneath the Veneer in Late Neolithic Britain. In *Similar but Different: Bell Beakers in Europe*, edited by J. Czebreszuk. Poznan: Adam Mickiewicz University, 173–192.

Gibson, J. 1979. *The Ecological Approach to Visual Perception*. Boston: Houghton Mifflin.

Giddens, A. 1984. *The Constitution of Society: Outline of the Theory of Structuration*. Cambridge: Polity.

Gilchrist, R. 1994. Medieval Bodies in the Material World: Gender, Stigma and the Body. In *Framing Medieval Bodies*, edited by S. Kay and M. Rubin. Manchester: Manchester University Press, 43–61.

Gilchrist, R. 1999. *Gender and Archaeology: Contesting the Past*. London: Routledge.

Gilchrist, R. 2008. Magic for the Dead? The Archaeology of Magic in Later Medieval Burials. *Medieval Archaeology* 52:119–159.

Gilchrist, R. 2012. *Medieval Life: Archaeology and the Life Course*. Woodbridge: Boydell and Brewer.

Gilchrist, R., and B. Sloane. 2005. *Requiem: The Medieval Monastic Cemetery in Britain*. London: Museum of London Archaeological Services.

Gill, R., K. Henwood, and C. McLean. 2005. Body Projects and the Regulation of Normative Masculinity. *Body & Society* 11 (1):37–62.

Gilman, A., R. M. Adams, A. M. B. Sestieri, A. Cazzella, H. J. M. Claessen, G. L. Cowgill, C. L. Crumley, T. Earle, A. Gallay, A. F. Harding, R. J. Harrison, R. Hicks, P. L. Kohl, J. Lewthwaite, C. A. Schwartz, S. J. Shennan, A. Sherratt, M. Tosi, and P. S. Wells. 1981. The Development of Social Stratification in Bronze Age Europe [and Comments and Reply]. *Current Anthropology* 22 (1):1–23.

Gimbutas, M. 1965. *Bronze Age Cultures in Central and Eastern Europe*. The Hague: Mouton.

Gimbutas, M. 1974. *The Gods and Goddesses of Old Europe, 7000–3500 BC*. London: Thames & Hudson.

Gimbutas, M. 1991. *The Civilization of the Goddess: The World of Old Europe*. San Francisco: Harper and Row.

Gittings, C. 1999. Sacred and Secular: 1558–1660. In *Death in England: An Illustrated History*, edited by C. Gittings and P. C. Jupp. Manchester: Manchester University Press, 147–173.

Glinister, F. 2006. Reconsidering 'Religious Romanization'. In *Religion in Republican Italy*, edited by C. E. Schultz and P. B. Harvey. Cambridge: Cambridge University Press, 10–33.

Godelier, M. 1986. *The Making of Great Men: Male Domination and Power among the New Guinea Baruya*. Cambridge: Cambridge University Press.

Godelier, M., and M. Strathern. 1991. *Big Men and Great Men: Personifications of Power in Melanesia*. Cambridge: Cambridge University Press.

Goffman, E. 1974. *Frame Analysis: An Essay on the Organization of Experience*. Cambridge, Mass.: Harvard University Press.

Gombrich, E. 1962. *Art and Illusion*. London: Phaidon.

Good, B. 1994. *Medicine, Rationality and Experience*. Cambridge: Cambridge University Press.

Gordon, R. L. 1979. The Real and the Imaginary: Production and Religion in the Graeco-Roman World. *Art History* 2 (1):5–34.

Goring-Morris, N., and L. K. Horwitz. 2007. Funerals and Feasts During the Pre-Pottery Neolithic B of the Near East. *Antiquity* 81:902–919.

Gosden, C. 2004. *Archaeology and Colonialism: Cultural Contact from 5000 BC to the Present*. Cambridge: Cambridge University Press.

Gould, S. J. 1981. *The Mismeasure of Man*. 2nd ed. New York: W. W. Norton.

Gowing, L. 2003. *Common Bodies: Women, Touch and Power in Seventeenth-Century England*. New Haven: Yale University Press.

Graham, S., and N. Thrift. 2007. Out of Order. *Theory, Culture & Society* 24 (3):1–25.

Gräslund, B. 1994. Prehistoric Soul Beliefs in Northern Europe. *Proceedings of the Prehistoric Society* 60:15–26.

Graziosi, P. 1974. *L'arte Preistorica in Italia*. Firenze: Sansoni.

Graziosi, P. 1980. *Le Pitture Preistoriche Di Porto Badisco*. Firenze: Martelli.

Green, D. 2009. Masculinity and Medicine: Thomas Walsingham and the Death of the Black Prince. *Journal of Medieval History* 35 (1):34–51.

Green, M. 2000. *A Landscape Revealed: 10,000 Years on a Chalkland Farm*. Stroud: Tempus.

Green, M. 2001. *The Trotula: A Medieval Compendium of Women's Medicine*. Philadelphia: University of Pennsylvania Press.

Grimm, L. 2000. Apprentice Flintknapping: Relating Material Culture and Social Practice in the Upper Palaeolithic. In *Children and Material Culture*, edited by J. S. Derevenski. London: Routledge, 53–71.

Grmek, M. D., and D. Gourevitch. 1998. *Les Maladies Dans L'art Antique*. Paris: Fayard.

Groebner, V. 2009. *Defaced: The Visual Culture of Violence in the Late Middle Ages*. Cambridge, Mass.: MIT Press.

Grosman, L., N. D. Munro, and A. Belfer-Cohen. 2008. A 12,000-Year-Old Shaman Burial from the Southern Levant (Israel). *Proceedings of the National Academy of Sciences of the United States of America* 105 (46):17665–17669.

Guadalupe, G., and A. Manguel. 1987. *The Dictionary of Imaginary Places*. New York: Harcourt Brace Jovanovich.

Guilaine, J., and J. Zammit. 2005. *The Origins of War: Violence in Prehistory*. Oxford: Blackwell.

Hables Gray, C., H. J. Figueroa-Sarriera, and S. Mentor. 1995. Cyborgology: Constructing the Knowledge of Cybernetic Organisms. In *The Cyborg Handbook*, edited by C. Hables Gray, H. J. Figueroa-Sarriera and S. Mentor. London: Routledge, 1–14.

Hacking, I. 2007. Our Neo-Cartesian Bodies in Parts. *Critical Inquiry* 34:78–105.

Hadley, D., ed. 1998. *Masculinity in Medieval Europe*. London: Longman.

Hall, M. A. 2001. An Ivory Knife Handle from the High Street, Perth, Scotland: Consuming Ritual in a Medieval Burgh. *Medieval Archaeology* 45:169–188.

Hallowell, A. I. 1955. *Culture and Experience*. Philadelphia: University of Pennsylvania Press.

Hallowell, A. I. 1960. Ojibwa Ontology, Behaviour and World View. In *Culture in History: Essays in Honor of Paul Radin*, edited by S. Diamond. New York: Columbia University Press, 19–52.

Halperin, D. 1990. *One Hundred Years of Homosexuality, and Other Essays on Greek Love*. New York: Routledge.

Halstead, P., ed. 1999. *Neolithic Society in Greece*. Sheffield: Sheffield Academic Press.

Hamilakis, Y., M. Pluciennik, and S. Tarlow, eds. 2002. *Thinking through the Body: Archaeologies of Corporeality*. London: Kluwer Academic/Plenum Publishers.

Hampel, F., H. Kerchler, and Z. Benkovsky-Pivovarová. 1981. *Das Mittelbronzezeitliche Gräberfeld Von Pitten in Niederösterreich. Ergebnisse Der Ausgrabungen Des Niederösterreichischen Landesmuseums in Den Jahren 1967 Bis 1973 Mit Beiträgen Über Funde Aus Anderen Perioden, Band 1: Fundbericht Und Tafeln, Mitt. Prähist. Komm. Österr. Akad. 19/20.*

Hanawalt, B. A. 2002. Medievalists and the Study of Childhood (Observations on the Image of the Child in the Medieval and Renaissance Periods). *Speculum-a Journal of Medieval Studies* 77 (2):440–460.

Hanks, B. 2008. The Past in Later Prehistory. In *Prehistoric Europe: New Methods and Theories*, edited by A. Jones. Oxford: Blackwell, 255–284.

Hannaford, I. 1996. *Race: The History of an Idea in the West.* Washington, DC: Woodrow Wilson Center Press.

Haraway, D. 1991. *Symians, Cyborgs and Women: The Re-Invention of Nature.* London: Free Association Press.

Haraway, D. 1993. The Biopolitics of Postmodern Bodies: Determinations of Self in Immune System Discourse. In *Knowledge, Power and Practice: The Anthropology of Medicine and Everyday Life*, edited by S. Lindenbaum and M. Lock. London: University of California Press, 364–410.

Harding, A. 1994. Reformation in Barbarian Europe, 1300–600 BC. In *The Oxford Illustrated History of Prehistoric Europe*, edited by B. Cunliffe. Oxford: Oxford University Press, 304–335.

Harding, A. 1999a. Swords, Shields and Scholars: Bronze Age Warfare, Past and Present. In *Experiment and Design: Archaeological Studies in Honour of John Coles*, edited by A. Harding. Oxford: Oxbow, 87–93.

Harding, A. 1999b. Warfare: A Defining Characteristic of Bronze Age Europe? In *Ancient Warfare: Archaeological Perspectives*, edited by J. Carman and A. Harding. Stroud: Sutton, 157–173.

Harding, A. F. 2000. *European Societies in the Bronze Age.* Cambridge: Cambridge University Press.

Harding, A. F. 2007. *Warriors and Weapons in Bronze Age Europe, Archaeolingua Series Minor 25.* Budapest: Archaeolingua.

Harding, A. F., R. Sumberova, A. K. Outram, and C. Knüsel. 2008. *Velim: Violence and Death in Bronze Age Bohemia.* Praha: Archeologicky Ustav.

Harper, A., and C. Proctor. 2011. *Medieval Sexuality: A Casebook.* London: Routledge.

Harris, O. J. T. 2005. Agents of Identity: Performative Practice at the Etton Causewayed Enclosure. In *Elements of Being: Identities, Mentalities and Movements*, edited by D. Hofmann, J. Mills and A. Cochrane. Oxford: British Archaeological Reports, 40–49.

Harris, O. J. T. 2009. Making Places Matter in Neolithic Dorset. *Oxford Journal of Archaeology* 28 (2):111–123.

Harris, O. J. T. 2010. Emotional and Mnemonic Geographies at Hambledon Hill: Texturing Neolithic Places with Bodies and Bones. *Cambridge Archaeological Journal* 20 (3):357–371.

Harris, O. J. T. 2011. Constituting Childhood: Identity, Conviviality and Community at Windmill Hill. In *(Re)Thinking the Little Ancestor: New Perspectives on the Archaeology of Infancy and Childhood*, edited by M. Lally and A. Moore. Oxford: British Archaeological Reports, 122–132.

Harris, O. J. T. in press. 'Blessed Are the Forgetful': Social Tensions between Remembering and Forgetting at Two Neolithic Monuments in Southern England. In *Living Landscapes: Exploring Neolithic Ireland in Its Wider Context*, edited by R. Schulting, N. Whitehouse and M. McClatchie. Oxford: British Archaeological Reports.

Harris, O. J. T., and J. E. Robb. 2012. Multiple Ontologies and the Problem of the Body in History. *American Anthropologist* 114 (4):668–679.

Harris, O. J. T., and T. F. Sørensen. 2010. Rethinking Emotion and Material Culture. *Archaeological Dialogues* 17 (2):145–163.

Harrison, R., and V. Heyd. 2007. The Transformation of Europe in the Third Millennium BC: The Example of Le Petit-Chasseur I + III (Sion, Valais, Switzerland). *Praehistorische Zeitschrift* 82 (2):129–214.

Hart, J. F., M. J. Rhodes, and J. T. Morgan. 2002. *The Unknown World of the Mobile Home.* Baltimore: Johns Hopkins University Press.

Harvey, K. 2002. The Substance of Sexual Difference: Change and Persistence in Reproductions of the Body in Eighteenth-Century England. *Gender & History* 14 (2):202–223.

Harvey, K. 2004. *Reading Sex in the Eighteenth-Century: Bodies and Gender in English Erotic Subculture.* Cambridge: Cambridge University Press.

Haynes, D. 1984. *Greek Art and the Idea of Freedom.* London: Thames and Hudson.

Hedges, R., A. Saville, and T. O'Connell. 2008. Characterizing the Diet of Individuals at the Neolithic Chambered Tomb of Hazleton North, Gloucestershire, England, Using Stable Isotopic Analysis. *Archaeometry* 50:114–128.

Heidegger, M. 1962. *Being and Time.* Oxford: Blackwell.

Henshall, A. 1972. *The Chambered Tombs of Scotland. Vol. 2.* Edinburgh: Edinburgh University Press.

Herdt, G. 1996. Mistaken Sex: Culture, Biology and Third Sex in New Guinea. In *Beyond Sexual Dimorphism in Culture and History*, edited by G. Herdt. New York: Zone Books, 419–445.

Hershkovitz, I., H. D. Donoghue, D. E. Minnikin, G. S. Besra, O. Y. C. Lee, A. M. Gernaey, E. Galili, V. Eshed, C. L. Greenblatt, E. Lemma, G. K. Bar-Gal, and M. Spigelman. 2008. Detection and Molecular Characterization of 9000-Year-Old Mycobacterium Tuberculosis from a Neolithic Settlement in the Eastern Mediterranean. *PLOS One* 3 (10).

Higgins, I. M. 1997. *Writing East: The 'Travels' of Sir John Mandeville.* Philadelphia: University of Pennsylvania Press.

Hillman, D. 1997. Visceral Knowledge: Shakespeare, Skepticism, and the Interior of the Early Modern Body. In *The Body in Parts: Fantasies of Corporeality in Early Modern Europe*, edited by D. Hillman and C. Mazzio. London: Routledge, 81–105.

Hillman, D., and C. Mazzio. 1997a. *Introduction*. In *The Body in Parts: Fantasies of Corporeality in Early Modern Europe*, edited by D. Hillman and C. Mazzio. London: Routledge, xi–xxix.

Hillman, D., and C. Mazzio, eds. 1997b. *The Body in Parts: Fantasies of Corporeality in Early Modern Europe*. London Routledge.

Hodder, I. 1990. *The Domestication of Europe: Structure and Contingency in Neolithic Societies*. Oxford: Blackwell.

Hodder, I. 2006. *The Leopard's Tale: Revealing the Mysteries of Çatalhöyük*. London: Thames and Hudson.

Hodder, I. 2007. Çatalhöyük in the Context of the Middle Eastern Neolithic. *Annual Review of Anthropology* 36 (1):105–120.

Hodder, I. 2012. *Entangled: An Archaeology of the Relationships between Humans and Things*. Oxford: Wiley-Blackwell.

Hodder, I., and C. Cessford. 2004. Daily Practice and Social Memory at Çatalhöyük. *American Antiquity* 69 (1): 17–40.

Hodder, I., and L. Meskell. 2011. A 'Curious and Sometimes a Trifle Macabre Artistry'. *Current Anthropology* 52:235–263.

Hofmann, D., and A. Whittle. 2008. Neolithic Bodies. In *Prehistoric Europe: Theory and Practice*, edited by A. Jones. Oxford: Wiley-Blackwell, 287–311.

Hogle, L. F. 2003. Life/Time Warranty: Rechargeable Cells and Extendable Lives. In *Remaking Life and Death: Toward an Anthropology of the Biosciences*, edited by S. Franklin and M. Lock. Sante Fe: School of American Research Press, 61–96.

Holbraad, M. 2007. The Power of Powder: Multiplicity and Motion in the Divinatory Cosmology of Cuban Ifá (or *Mana*, Again). In *Thinking through Things: Theorising Artefacts Ethnographically*, edited by A. Henare, M. Holbraad and S. Wastell. London: Routledge, 189–225.

Holmes, K., and R. Whitehouse. 1998. Anthropomorphic Figurines and the Construction of Gender in Neolithic Italy. In *Gender and Italian Archaeology: Challenging the Stereotypes*, edited by R. Whitehouse. London: Accordia Research Centre, 95–126.

Holsinger, B. W. 2001. *Music, Body and Desire in Medieval Culture: Hildegard of Bingen to Chaucer*. Palo Alto: Stanford University Press.

Holsinger, B. W. 2002. Medieval Studies, Postcolonial Studies, and the Genealogies of Critique. *Speculum* 77 (4):1195–1227.

Höpfel, F., W. Platzer, and K. Spindler. 1992. *Der Mann in Eis: Bericht Über Das Internationale Symposium 1992 in Innsbruck*. Vol. 1. Innsbruck: Eigenverlag der Universität Innsbruck.

Horstmanshoff, H. F. J., P. Van Der Eijk, and P. H. Schrijvers, eds. 1995. *Ancient Medicine in Its Socio-Cultural Context*. Amsterdam: Editions Rodopi.

Houston, S., D. Stuart, and K. Taube. 2006. *The Memory of Bones: Body, Being, and Experience Amongst the Classic Maya*. Austin: Texas University Press.

Hrdlička. 1919. Anthropometry C. Anthropometry on the Living. *American Journal of Physical Anthropology* 2 (3):283–319.

Hughes, J. 2008. Fragmentation as Metaphor in the Classical Healing Sanctuary. *Social History of Medicine* 21 (2):217–236.

Hughes, J. 2010. Dissecting the Classical Hybrid. In *Body Parts and Body Wholes*, edited by K. Rebay-Salisbury, M. L. S. Sørensen and J. Hughes. Oxford: Oxbow Books, 101–110.

Hughes, J. 2011. The Myth of Return: Restoration as Reception in Eighteenth-Century Rome. *Classical Receptions Journal* 3:1–28.

Hughes, J. in press. The Biography of a Votive Offering from Roman Italy. In *Ex Voto: Votive Images across Cultures*, edited by I. Weinryb. Ann Arbor: University of Michigan Press.

Hurwit, J. A. 2007. The Problem with Dexileos: Heroic and Other Nudities in Greek Art. *American Journal of Archaeology* 111:35–60.

Hutton, R. 1995. The English Reformation and the Evidence of Folklore. *Past and Present* 148 (1):89–116.

Hutton, R. 1996. *The Station of the Sun: A History of the Ritual Year in Britain*. Oxford: Oxford University Press.

Ingold, T. 1999. On the Social Relations of Hunter-Gatherer Bands. In *The Cambridge Encyclopedia of Hunters and Gatherers*, edited by R. B. Lee and R. Daly. Cambridge: Cambridge University Press, 399–410.

Ingold, T. 2000. *The Perception of the Environment: Essays in Livelihood, Dwelling and Skill*. London: Routledge.

Ingold, T. 2007. Materials against Materiality. *Archaeological Dialogues* 14 (1):1–16.

Izzet, V. 2007. *The Archaeology of Etruscan Society*. Cambridge: Cambridge University Press.

Jackes, M., D. Lubell, and C. Meiklejohn. 1997. Healthy but Mortal: Human Biology and the First Farmers of Western Europe. *Antiquity* 71:639–658.

Jacobs, S.-E., and J. Cromwell. 1992. Visions and Revisions of Reality: Reflections on Sex, Sexuality, Gender, and Gender Variance. *Journal of Homosexuality* 23:43–69.

Jaritz, G. 2000. Social Grouping and the Languages of Dress in the Late Middle Ages. *Medieval History Journal* 3:235–259.

Johnson, M. 1996. *An Archaeology of Capitalism*. Oxford: Blackwell.

Johnstone, S. 2003. Women, Property, and Surveillance in Classical Athens. *Classical Antiquity* 22 (2):247–274.

Joint Association of Classical Teachers. 2008. *The World of Athens*. 2nd ed. Cambridge: Cambridge University Press.

Jones, A. 2006. Animated Images: Images, Agency and Landscape in Kilmartin, Argyll, Scotland. *Journal of Material Culture* 11 (1/2):211–225.

Jones, A. 2007. *Memory and Material Culture*. Cambridge: Cambridge University Press.

Jose, L. 2008. Monstrous Conceptions: Sex, Madness and Gender in Medieval Medical Texts. *Comparative Critical Studies* 5 (2–3):153–163.

Joyce, R. 2005. Archaeology of the Body. *Annual Review of Anthropology* 34:139–158.

Kampen, N. B., ed. 1996. *Sexuality in Ancient Art.* Cambridge: Cambridge University Press.

Karkov, C. 2001. Sheela-Na-Gigs and Other Unruly Women: Images of Land and Gender in Medieval Ireland. In *From Ireland Coming....* edited by C. Hourihane. Princeton: Princeton University Press, 313–331.

Karras, R. M. 2001. *From Boys to Men: Formations of Masculinity in Late Medieval Europe.* Philadelphia: University of Pennsylvania Press.

Karras, R. M. 2004. Women's Labors: Reproduction and Sex Work in Medieval Europe. *Journal of Women's History* 15 (4):153–158.

Karras, R. M. 2005. *Sexuality in Medieval Europe: Doing Unto Others.* London: Routledge.

Kaufert, P. A. 2000. Screening the Body: The Pap Smear and the Mammogram. In *Living and Working with the New Medical Technologies: Intersections of Inquiry,* edited by M. Lock, A. Young and A. Cambrosio. Cambridge: Cambridge University Press, 165–83.

Kaul, F. 1998. *Ships on Bronzes: A Study in Bronze Age Religion and Iconography.* Copenhagen: The National Museum of Denmark.

Kay, S., and M. Rubin. 1994. *Framing Medieval Bodies.* Manchester: Manchester University Press.

Kelly, R. 1993. *Constructing Inequality: The Fabrication of a Hierarchy of Virtue among the Etoro.* Ann Arbor: University of Michigan Press.

Kieckhafer, R. 1989. *Magic in the Middle Ages.* Cambridge: Cambridge University Press.

Kienlin, T. L. 2008. Der 'Fürst' Von Leubingen: Herausragende Bestattungen Der Frühbronzezeit Als Bezugspunkt Gesellschaftlicher Kohärenz Und Kultureller Identität. In *Körperinszenierung – Objektsammlung – Monumentalisierung: Totenritual Und Grabkult in Frühen Gesellschaften,* edited by C. Kümmel, B. Schweizer and U. Veit. Münster: Waxmann, 181–206.

Kimmig, W. 1964. Seevölkerbewegung Und Urnenfelderkultur. In *Studien Aus Alteuropa,* edited by R. V. Uslar and K. J. Narr, 220–283.

King, H. 1998a. *Hippocrates' Woman: Reading the Female Body in Ancient Greece.* London: Routledge.

King, H. 1998b. Reading the Female Body. In *Gender and the Body in the Ancient Mediterranean,* edited by M. Wyke. Oxford: Blackwell, 199–203.

King, H., ed. 2005. *Health in Antiquity.* Oxford: Routledge.

Kirby, V. 1997. *Telling Flesh: The Substance of the Corporeal.* London: Routledge.

Kivelson, V. A. 2003. Male Witches and Gendered Categories in Seventeenth-Century Russia. *Comparative Studies In Society And History* 45 (3):606–631.

Klíma, B. 1988. A Triple Burial from the Upper Palaeolithic of Dolní Věstonice. *Journal of Human Evolution* 16:831–835.

Knappett, C. 2005. *Thinking through Material Culture: An Interdisciplinary Perspective.* Philadelphia: University of Pennsylvania Press.

Knauft, B. 1989. Body Images in Melanesia: Cultural Substances and Natural Metaphors. In *Fragments for a History of the Human Body, Part III,* edited by M. Feher. New York: Zone, 192–278.

Knauft, B. 1993. *South Coast New Guinea Cultures: History, Comparison, Dialectic.* New York: Cambridge University Press.

Kohring, S. 2011. Social Complexity as a Multi-Scalar Concept: Pottery Technologies, 'Communities of Practice' and the Bell Beaker Phenomenon. *Norwegian Archaeological Review* 44 (2):145–163.

Koloski-Ostrow, A., and C. Lyons, eds. 1997. *Naked Truths: Women, Sexuality and Gender in Classical Art and Archaeology.* London: Routledge.

Kristiansen, K. 1998. *Europe before History.* Cambridge: Cambridge University Press.

Kristiansen, K. 1999. The Emergence of Warrior Aristocracies in Later European Prehistory and Their Long-Term History. In *Ancient Warfare. Archaeological Perspectives,* edited by J. Carman and A. F. Harding. Stroud: Sutton, 175–189.

Kristiansen, K. 2002. The Tale of the Sword – Swords and Swordfighters in Bronze Age Europe. *Oxford Journal of Archaeology* 21 (4):319–332.

Kristiansen, K., and T. B. Larsson. 2005. *The Rise of Bronze Age Society: Travels, Transmissions and Transformations.* Cambridge: Cambridge University Press.

Kuijt, I. 1996. Negotiating Equality through Ritual: A Consideration of Late Natufian and Prepottery Neolithic A Period Mortuary Practices. *Journal of Anthropological Archaeology* 15:313–336.

Kuijt, I. 2008. The Regeneration of Life: Neolithic Structures of Symbolic Remembering and Forgetting. *Current Anthropology* 49 (2):171–197.

Kuriyama, S. 1999. *The Expressiveness of the Body and the Divergence of Greek and Chinese Medicine.* New York: Zone.

La Guardia, R., ed. 2001. *Archeologia E Arte Rupestre. L'Europa, Le Alpi, La Valcamonica. Convegno Internazionale Di Archeologia Rupestre 2, 1997.* Milano: Comune di Milano, Settore Cultura Musei e Mostre.

Lambek, M., and A. Strathern, eds. 1998. *Bodies and Persons: Comparative Perspectives from Africa and Melanesia.* Cambridge: Cambridge University Press.

Lambert, H., and M. McDonald, eds. 2009. *Social Bodies.* Oxford: Berghahn.

Landecker, H. 2003. On Beginning and Ending with Apoptosis. In *Remaking Life and Death: Toward an Anthropology of the Biosciences,* edited by S. Franklin and M. Lock. Sante Fe: School of American Research Press, 23–59.

Landecker, H. 2007. *Culturing Life: How Cells Became Technologies.* Cambridge, Mass.: Harvard University Press.

Lanting, J. N., and J. D. Van der Waals, eds. 1976. *Glockenbecher Symposium Oberried 1974.* Haarlem: Bussum.

Laqueur, T. 1987. Orgasm, Generation, and the Politics of Reproductive Biology. In *The Making of the Modern Body: Sexuality and Society in the Nineteenth Century,* edited by C. Gallagher and T. Laqueur. London: University of California Press, 1–41.

Laqueur, T. 1991. *Making Sex: Body and Gender from the Greeks to Freud.* Cambridge, Mass.: Harvard University Press.

Larsson, L. 1989. Late Mesolithic Settlements and Cemeteries at Skateholm, Southern Sweden. In *The Mesolithic in Europe: Papers Presented at the Third International Symposium, Edinburgh 1985*, edited by C. Bonsall. Edinburgh: John Donald, 367–378.

Larsson, L. 1993. The Skateholm Project: Late Mesolithic Coastal Settlement in Southern Sweden. In *Case Studies in European Prehistory*, edited by P. Bogucki. London: CRC Press, 31–62.

Larsson, L., H. Kindgren, D. Loeffler, and A. Åkerlund, eds. 2003. *Mesolithic on the Move.* Oxford: Oxbow.

Latour, B. 1987. *Science in Action: How to Follow Scientists and Engineers through Society.* Cambridge, Mass.: Harvard University Press.

Latour, B. 1991. Technology Is Society Made Durable. In *A Sociology of Monsters: Essays on Power, Technology and Domination*, edited by J. Law. London: Routledge, 103–131.

Latour, B. 1993. *We Have Never Been Modern.* Cambridge, Mass.: Harvard University Press.

Latour, B. 1999. *Pandora's Hope: Essays on the Reality of Science Studies.* Cambridge, Mass.: Harvard University Press.

Latour, B. 2005. *Reassembling the Social: An Introduction to Actor Network Theory.* Oxford: Oxford University Press.

Laurier, E. 2004. Doing Office Work on the Motorway. *Theory, Culture and Society* 21 (4–5):261–277.

Law, J. 2002. *Aircraft Stories: Decentering the Object in Technoscience.* London: Duke University Press.

Le Roy Ladurie, E. 1978. *Montaillou: Cathars and Catholics in a French Village, 1294–1324.* London: Scholar Press.

Leader, R. 1997. In Death Not Divided: Gender, Family, and State Classical Athenian Grave Stelae. *American Journal of Archaeology* 101:683–699.

Lees, C., ed. 1994. *Medieval Masculinities: Regarding Men in the Middle Ages.* Minneapolis: University of Minnesota Press.

Lefkowitz, M., and M. Fant. 1982. *Women's Life in Greece and Rome.* Baltimore: Johns Hopkins University Press.

Lefkowitz, M. R. 1983. Wives and Husbands. *Greece & Rome* 30 (1):31–47.

Leone, M. 1984. Interpreting Ideology in Historical Archaeology: Using the Rules of Perspective in the William Paca Garden in Annapolis, Maryland. In *Ideology, Power, and Prehistory*, edited by D. Miller and C. Tilley. Cambridge: Cambridge University Press, 25–35.

Leone, M. P., and P. B. Potter, eds. 1999. *Historical Archaeologies of Capitalism.* New York: Kluwer Academic/Plenum.

Leroi-Gourhan, A. 1968. *Art of Prehistoric Man in Western Europe.* London: Thames and Hudson.

Leroi-Gourhan, A. 1993. *Gesture and Speech.* Cambridge, Mass.: MIT Press.

Lester, A. E. 2011. In the Singular and Plural Cases: The Lives of Medieval European Women. *Journal of Womens History* 23 (1):187–200.

Levack, B. P. 1987. *The Witch-Hunt in Early Modern Europe.* London: Longman.

Lewis-Williams, J. D. 2002. *The Mind in the Cave: Consciousness and the Origins of Art.* London: Thames and Hudson.

Lewis-Williams, J. D., and J. Clottes. 1998. *The Shamans of Prehistory: Trance Magic and the Painted Caves.* New York: Abrams.

Lewis, S. 2002. *The Athenian Woman: An Iconographic Handbook.* London: Routledge.

Lightfoot, E., B. Boneva, P. Miracle, M. Šlaus, and T. C. O'Connell. 2011. Exploring the Mesolithic and Neolithic Transition in Croatia through Isotopic Investigations. *Antiquity* 85:73–86.

Lock, M. 2000. On Dying Twice: Culture, Technology and the Determination of Death. In *Living and Working with the New Medical Technologies: Intersections of Inquiry*, edited by M. Lock, A. Young and A. Cambrosio. Cambridge: Cambridge University Press, 233–262.

Lock, M. 2002. *Twice Dead. Organ Transplants and the Reinvention of Death.* Berkeley: University of California Press.

Lock, M. 2003. On Making up the Good-as-Dead in a Utilitarian World. In *Remaking Life and Death: Toward an Anthropology of the Biosciences*, edited by S. Franklin and M. Lock. Sante Fe: School of American Research Press, 165–192.

Lock, M., and P. Kaufert. 2001. Menopause, Local Biologies, and Cultures of Aging. *American Journal of Human Biology* 13 (4):494–504.

Lock, M., and V.-K. Nguyen. 2010. *An Anthropology of Biomedicine.* New York: Wiley-Blackwell.

Lock, M., A. Young, and A. Cambrosio, eds. 2000. *Living and Working with the New Medical Technologies: Intersections of Inquiry.* Cambridge: Cambridge University Press.

Lomborg, E. 1973. *Die Flintdolche Dänemarks. Studien Über Chronologie Und Kulturbeziehungen Des Südskandinavischen Spätneolitikums, Nordiske Fortidsminder, Serie B, Bind 1.* København.

Longrigg, J. 1998. *Greek Medicine: From the Heroic to the Hellenistic Age. A Source Book.* London: Duckworth.

Lovejoy, A. O. 1936. *The Great Chain of Being.* Cambridge, Mass.: Harvard University Press.

Lucas, G. 1996. Of Death and Debt: A History of the Body in Neolithic and Early Bronze Age Yorkshire. *European Journal of Archaeology* 4:99–118.

Lucas, G. 2005. *The Archaeology of Time.* London: Routledge.

Lyons, D. 2003. Dangerous Gifts: Ideologies of Marriage and Exchange in Ancient Greece. *Classical Antiquity* 22 (1):93–134.

Macnaghten, P., and J. Urry. 1998. *Contested Natures.* London: Sage.

Malafouris, L. 2004. The Cognitive Basis of Material Engagement: Where Brain, Body, and Culture Conflate. In *Rethinking Materiality: The Engagement of Mind with the Material World*, edited by E. DeMarrais, C. Gosden and C. Renfrew. Cambridge: McDonald Institute for Archaeological Research, 53–62.

Maldonado, T. 2001. Taking Eyeglasses Seriously. *Design Issues* 17 (4):32–43.

Malik, K. 1996. *The Meaning of Race: Race, History and Culture in Western Society*. London: Macmillan Press.

Mallegni, F., and G. Fornaciari. 1980. I Resti Scheletrici Umani Del Villaggio Neolitico Del Centro Di Foggia. *Archivio per l'Antropologia e la Etnologia* 110:461–496.

Mallory, J. 1989. *In Search of the Indo-Europeans*. London: Thames and Hudson.

Mallory, J. P., and D. I. A. Telehin. 1995. Statue-Menhirs of the North Pontic Region. In *Statue-Stele E Massi Incisi Nell'europa Dell'età Del Rame*, edited by S. Casini, R. De Marinis and A. Pedrotti. Bergamo: Civico Museo Archeologico, 319–332.

Malone, C., S. Stoddart, D. Trump, A. Bonanno, and A. Pace, eds. 2009. *Mortuary Ritual in Prehistoric Malta: The Brochtorff Circle at Xaghra Excavations (1987–1994)*. Cambridge: McDonald Institute for Archaeological Research.

Mandelbrot, B. B. 1967. How Long Is the Coast of Britain? Statistical Self-Similarity and Fractional Dimension. *Science* 156:636–638.

Mandelstam Balzer, M. 1996. Sacred Genders in Siberia: Shamans, Bear Festivals and Androgyny. In *Gender Reversals and Gender Cultures*, edited by S. P. Ramet. London: Routledge, 164–182.

Mandeville, J. 1983. *The Travels of Sir John Mandeville*. Harmondsworth: Penguin.

Maraszek, R. 2009. *The Nebra Sky-Disc*. Halle/Saale: Landesmuseum für Vorgeschichte.

Marciniak, A. 2005. *Placing Animals in the Neolithic: Social Zooarchaeology of Prehistoric Farming Communities*. London: UCL Press.

Marriott, M. 1976. Hindu Transactions: Diversity without Dualism. In *Transaction and Meaning: Directions in the Anthropology of Exchange and Symbolic Behaviour*, edited by B. Kapferer. Philadelphia: Institute for the Study of Human Issues, 109–137.

Marx, K. 1990 [1867]. *Capital: A Critique of Political Economy*. London: Penguin.

Mauss, M. 1990. *The Gift: The Form and Reason for Exchange in Archaic Societies*. London: Routledge.

McBrearty, S. 2007. Down with the Revolution. In *Rethinking the Human Revolution*, edited by P. Mellars, K. Boyle, O. Bar-Yosef and C. Stringer. Cambridge: McDonald Institute, 133–151.

McCartan, S. B., R. Schulting, G. Warren, and P. Woodman, eds. 2009. *Mesolithic Horizons*. Oxford: Oxbow.

McCarthy, C. 2004. *Love, Sex, and Marraige in the Middle Ages: A Sourcebook*. London: Routledge.

McClure, L., ed. 2002. *Sexuality and Gender in the Classical World: Readings and Sources*. Oxford: Blackwell.

McDermott, L. 1996. Self-Representation in Upper Paleolithic Female Figurines. *Current Anthropology* 37 (2):227–275.

McDonald, M. 1989. '*We Are Not French!' Language, Culture and Identity in Brittany*. London: Routledge.

McDonald, M. 2011. Deceased Organ Donation, Culture and the Objectivity of Death. In *Organ Transplantation: Ethical, Legal and Psycho-Social Aspects: Expanding the European Platform*, edited by W. Weimer, M. A. Bos and J. J. Busschbach. Eichengrund: Pabst Science Publishers, 267–273.

McDonald, M. 2012. Medical Anthropology and Anthropological Studies of Science. In *Companion to the Anthropology of Europe*, edited by U. Kockel, M. Nic Craith and J. Frykman. Oxford: Wiley-Blackwell, 459–479.

McDonald, M. forthcoming. Bodies and Cadavers. In *Objects and Materials: A Routledge Companion*, edited by P. Harvey, E. Casella, G. Evans, H. Knox, C. McLean, E. Silva, N. Thoburn and K. Woodward. London: Routledge.

McFadyen, L. 2007. Making Architecture. In *Building Memories: The Neolithic Cotswold Long Barrow at Ascott-under-Wychwood, Oxfordshire*, edited by D. Benson and A. Whittle. Oxford: Oxbow, 348–354.

Meiklejohn, C., C. Schentag, A. Venema, and P. Key. 1984. Socioeconomic Change and Patterns of Pathology and Variation in the Mesolithic and Neolithic of Western Europe. In *Paleopathology at the Origins of Agriculture*, edited by M. Cohen and G. Armelagos. New York: Academic, 75–100.

Mellars, P., K. Boyle, O. Bar-Yosef, and C. Stringer, eds. 2007. *Rethinking the Human Revolution*. Cambridge: McDonald Institute.

Mellars, P., and C. Stringer, eds. 1989. *The Human Revolution: Behavioural and Biological Perspectives on the Origins of Modern Humans*. Edinburgh: Edinburgh University Press.

Meller, H. 2002. Die Himmelsscheibe Von Nebra – Ein Frühbronzezeitlicher Fund Von Außergewöhnlicher Bedeutung. *Archäologie in Sachsen-Anhalt* 1:7–20.

Merleau-Ponty, M. 1962. *Phenomenology of Perception*. London: Routledge.

Merritt, J. T. 1997. Dreaming of the Savior's Blood: Moravians and the Indian Great Awakening in Pennsylvania. *The William and Mary Quarterly* 54 (4):723–746.

Meskell, L. 1995. Goddesses, Gimbutas, and 'New Age' Archaeology. *Antiquity* 69:74–86.

Meskell, L., and R. Joyce. 2003. *Embodied Lives: Figuring Ancient Maya and Egyptian Experience*. London: Routledge.

Meyerson, M. D., and D. Thiery. 2003. '*A Great Effusion of Blood'? Interpreting Medieval Violence*. Toronto: University of Toronto Press.

Miari, M. 1995. Il Rituale Funerario Della Necropoli Eneolitica Di Ponte S. Pietro (Ischia Di Castro, Viterbo). *Origini* XLIV:351–390.

Michelaki, K. 2008. Making Pots and Potters in the Bronze Age Maros Villages of Kiszombor-Új-Élet and Kláraflava-Hajdova. *Cambridge Archaeological Journal* 18 (3):355–380.

Midgley, M. 2008. *The Megaliths of Northern Europe*. London: Routledge.

Miller, D. 1987. *Material Culture and Mass Consumption*. Blackwell: Oxford.

Miller, D. 1994. *Modernity, an Ethnographic Approach: Dualism and Mass Consumption in Trinidad*. London: Berg.

Miller, D. 2005a. Materiality: An Introduction. In *Materiality*, edited by D. Miller. Durham: Duke University Press, 1–50.

Miller, D., ed. 2005b. *Materiality*. London: Duke University Press.

Miller, D. 2010. *Stuff.* London: Polity.

Miller, D., and D. Slater. 2000. *The Internet: An Ethnographic Approach.* Oxford: Berg.

Miller, S. A. 2010. *Medieval Monstrosity and the Female Body.* London: Routledge.

Miracle, P., and D. Borić. 2008. Bodily Beliefs and Agricultural Beginnings in Western Asia: Animal-Human Hybridity Re-Examined. In *Past Bodies: Body-Centred Research in Archaeology,* edited by D. Borić and J. Robb. Oxford: Oxbow, 101–113.

Mitcham, C. 1979. Philosophy and the History of Technology. In *The History and Philosophy of Technology,* edited by G. Bugliarello and D. B. Doner. Urbana, Ill.: University of Illinois Press, 163–201.

Mitchell, W. J. T. 2006. *What Do Pictures Want?: The Lives and Loves of Images.* Chicago: University of Chicago Press.

Mithen, S. 1996. *The Prehistory of the Mind: A Search for the Origins of Art, Religion, and Science.* London: Thames and Hudson.

Mithen, S. J. 1990. *Thoughtful Foragers: A Study of Prehistoric Decision Making.* Cambridge: Cambridge University Press.

Mol, A. 2002. *The Body Multiple: Ontology in Medical Practice.* London: Duke University Press.

Monserrat, D. 1997. *Changing Bodies, Changing Meanings: Studies on the Human Body in Antiquity.* London: Routledge.

Moore-Gilbert, B. 1997. *Postcolonial Theory: Contexts, Practices, Politics.* London: Verso.

Morley, I. 2007. New Questions of Old Hands: Outlines of Human Representation in the Palaeolithic. In *Image and Imagination: A Global Prehistory of Figurative Representation,* edited by C. Renfrew and I. Morley. Cambridge: McDonald Institute, 69–81.

Morris, I. 1992. *Death-Ritual and Social Structure in Classical Antiquity.* Cambridge: Cambridge University Press.

Mullaney, S. 2007. Affective Technologies: Towards an Emotional Logic of the Elizabethan Stage. In *Environment and Embodiment in Early Modern England,* edited by M. Floyd-Wilson and G. A. Sullivan Jr. New York: Palgrave McMillan, 71–89.

Mummert, A., E. Esche, J. Robinson, and G. J. Armelagos. 2011. Stature and Robusticity During the Agricultural Transition: Evidence from the Bioarchaeological Record. *Economics & Human Biology* 9 (3):284–301.

Murphy, W. A., D. zur Nedden, P. Gostner, R. Knapp, W. Recheis, and H. Seidler. 2003. The Iceman: Discovery and Imaging. *Radiology* 226 (3):614–629.

Mussi, M. 2000. Heading South: The Gravettian Colonisation of Italy. In *Hunters of the Golden Age: The Mid Upper Palaeolithic of Eurasia, 30,000 – 20,000 BP,* edited by W. Roebroeks, M. Mussi, J. Svoboda and K. Fennema. Leiden: Leiden University, 355–374.

Mussi, M., J. Cinq-Mars, and P. Bolduc. 2000. Echoes from the Mammoth Steppe: The Case of the Balzi Rossi. In *Hunters of the Golden Age: The Mid Upper Palaeolithic of Eurasia, 30,000 – 20,000 BP,* edited by W. Roebroeks, M. Mussi, J. Svoboda and K. Fennema. Leiden: Leiden University, 105–124.

Myers, F. 1986. *Pintupi Country, Pintupi Self: Sentiment, Place, and Politics among Western Desert Aborigines.* Washington DC.: Smithsonian Institution Press.

Mytum, H. 2006. Popular Attitudes to Memory, the Body, and Social Identity: The Rise of External Commemoration in Britain, Ireland and New England. *Post-Medieval Archaeology* 40 (1):96–110.

Nanda, S. 1999. *Neither Man nor Woman: The Hijras of India.* 2nd ed. Belmont, Calif.: Wadsworth.

Nanoglou, S. 2005. Subjectivity and Material Culture in Thessaly, Greece: The Case of Neolithic Anthropomorphic Imagery. *Cambridge Archaeological Journal* 15 (2):141–156.

Nava, M. L. 1988. *Le Stele Della Daunia: Sculture Antropomorfe Della Puglia Protostorica Dalle Scoperte Di Silvio Ferro Agli Studi Più Recenti.* Milano: Electa.

Needham, S. 2005. Transforming Beaker Culture in North-West Europe: Processes of Fusion and Fission. *Proceedings of the Prehistoric Society* 71:171–217.

Nelson, J. 1997. Family, Gender and Sexuality in the Middle Ages. In *The Routledge Companion to Historiography,* edited by M. Bentley. London: Routledge, 143–165.

Nelson, J. 1998. Monks, Secular Men and Masculinity. In *Masculinity in Medieval Europe,* edited by D. Hadley. London: Longman, 121–142.

Nevett, L. C. 2011. Towards a Female Topography of the Ancient Greek City: Case Studies from Late Archaic and Early Classical Athens (C.520–400 BCE). *Gender & History* 23 (3):576–596.

Nieszery, N. 1995. *Linearbandkeramische Gräberfelder in Bayern.* Rahden/Westfalen: Marie Leidorf.

Nilsson Stutz, L. 2003. *Embodied Ritual & Ritualized Bodies: Tracing Ritual Practices in Late Mesolithic Burials.* Lund: Acta Archaeologica Lundensia.

Nochlin, L. 1994. *The Body in Pieces: The Fragment as a Metaphor of Modernity.* London: Thames and Hudson.

Nordbladh, J., and T. Yates. 1990. This Perfect Body, This Virgin Text: Between Sex and Gender in Archaeology. In *Archaeology after Structuralism: Post-Structuralism and the Practice of Archaeology,* edited by I. Bapty and T. Yates. London: Routledge, 222–237.

Nott, J. C., and G. R. Gliddon. 1868. *Indigenous Races of the Earth.* Philadelphia, PA: J. B. Lippincott.

Nuffield Council on Bioethics. 2011. *Human Bodies: Donation for Medicine and Research.* London: Nuffield Council on Bioethics Report.

O'Connor, E. 1997. 'Fractions of Men': Engendering Amputation in Victorian Culture. *Comparative Studies In Society And History* 39 (4):742–777.

O'Shea, J. M. 1996. *Villagers of the Maros: A Portrait of an Early Bronze Age Society.* New York-London: Plenum Press.

Oakley, J. H. 2004. *Picturing Death in Classical Athens.* Cambridge: Cambridge University Press.

Oestigaard, T. 2004. Death and Ambivalent Materiality – Human Flesh as Culture and Cosmology. In *Combining the Past and the Present: Archaeological Perspectives on Society,* edited by T. Oestigaard, N. Anfinset and T. Saetersdal. Oxford: Archaeopress, 23–30.

Oliva, M. 2000. The Brno II Upper Palaeolithic Burial. In *Hunters of the Golden Age: The Mid Upper Palaeolithic of Eurasia, 30,000 – 20,000 BP*, edited by W. Roebroeks, M. Mussi, J. Svoboda and K. Fennema. Leiden: Leiden University, 143–153.

Olsen, B. 2010. *In Defense of Things: Archaeology and the Ontology of Objects*. Plymouth: Altamira Press.

Olwig, K. R. 1993. Sexual Cosmology: Nature and Landscape at the Conceptual Interstices of Nature and Culture: Or What Does Landscape Really Mean? In *Landscape: Politics and Perspectives*, edited by B. Bender. Oxford: Berg, 307–343.

Orbach, S. 1978. *Fat Is a Feminist Issue*. London: Paddington Press.

Orschiedt, J., and M. N. Haidle. 2006. The LBK Enclosure of Herxheim. Theatre of War or Ritual Centre? References from Osteoarchaeological Investigations. *Journal of Conflict Archaeology* 2:153–167.

Ortner, S. 1972. On key symbols. *American Anthropologist* 75:1338–1346.

Orton, D. C. 2008. Beyond Hunting and Herding: Humans, Animals and the Political Economy of the Vinča Period. PhD thesis, Department of Archaeology, University of Cambridge.

Osborne, R. 1985. The Erection and Mutilation of the Hermai. *Proceedings Of The Cambridge Philological Society* (211):47–73.

Osborne, R. 1996. Desiring Women on Athenian Pottery. In *Sexuality in Ancient Art*, edited by N. B. Kampen. Cambridge: Cambridge University Press, 65–78.

Osborne, R. 1997a. Law the Democratic Citizen and the Representation of Women in Classical Athens. *Past & Present* (155):3–33.

Osborne, R. 1997b. Men without Clothes: Heroic Nakedness and Greek Art. *Gender & History* 9:504–528.

Osborne, R. 1998a. *Archaic and Classical Greek Art*. Oxford: Oxford University Press.

Osborne, R. 1998b. Sculpted Men of Athens: Masculinity and Power in the Field of Vision. In *Thinking Men. Masculinity and Its Self Representation in the Classical Tradition*, edited by L. Foxhall and J. Salmon. London: Routledge, 23–42.

Osborne, R. 2006. 'Reflections on the Greek Revolution' in Art: From Changes in Viewing to the Transformation of Subjectivity. In *Rethinking Revolutions through Ancient Greece*, edited by S. Goldhill and R. Osborne. Cambridge: Cambridge University Press, 68–95.

Osborne, R. 2011. *The Histories Written on the Classical Greek Body*. Cambridge: Cambridge University Press.

Oudshoorn, N., and T. Pinch. 2005. *How Users Matter: The Co-Construction of Users and Technology*. Cambridge, Mass.: MIT Press.

Owen, K. 2006. The Reformed Elect: Wealth, Death and Sanctity in Gloucestershire: 1550–1640. *International Journal of Historical Archaeology* 10 (1):1–34.

Palincaş, N. 2010. Reconfiguring Anatomy: Ceramics, Cremation and Cosmology in the Late Bronze Age in the Lower Danube. In *Body Parts and Bodies Whole: Changing Relations and Meanings*, edited by K. Rebay-Salisbury, M. L. S. Sørensen and J. Hughes. Oxford: Oxbow, 72–88.

Papadopoulos, J. K. 2000. Skeletons in Wells: Towards an Archaeology of Social Exclusion in the Ancient Greek World. In *Madness, Disability and Social Exclusion: The Archaeology and Anthropology of 'Difference'*, edited by J. Hubert. London: Routledge, 7–118.

Parisi, L. 2007. Biotech: Life by Contagion. *Theory, Culture and Society* 24 (6):29–52.

Parker Pearson, M., and Ramilisonina. 1998. Stonehenge for the Ancestors: The Stones Pass on the Message. *Antiquity* 72:308–326.

Parry, B. 2005. The New Human Tissue Bill: Categorization and Definitional Issues and Their Implications. *Genomics, Society and Policy* 1 (1):74–85.

Parsons, J. C., and B. Wheeler, eds. 1996. *Medieval Mothering*. New York: Garland.

Paster, G. K. 2007. Becoming the Landscape: The Ecology of the Passions in the Legend of Temperance. In *Environment and Embodiment in Early Modern England*, edited by M. Floyd-Wilson and G. A. Sullivan Jr. New York: Palgrave McMillan, 137–152.

Pavuk, J. 1972. Neolithisches Graberfeld in Nitra. *Slovenska Archeologia* 20:5–105.

Pepys, S. 1893. *The Diary of Samuel Pepys*, edited by H. B. Wheatley. London: George Bell.

Peresani, M., I. Fiore, M. Gala, M. Romandini, and A. Tagliacozzo. 2011. Late Neandertals and the Intentional Removal of Feathers as Evidenced from Bird Bone Taphonomy at Fumane Cave 44 Ky B.P., Italy. *Proceedings of the National Academy of Sciences* 108 (10):3888–3893.

Perry, E. M., and R. Joyce. 2001. Providing a Past for 'Bodies That Matter': Judith Butler's Impact on the Archaeology of Gender. *International Journal of Sexuality and Gender* 6:63–76.

Pettitt, P. 2011. *The Palaeolithic Origins of Human Burial*. London: Routledge.

Pettitt, P., and P. Bahn. 2003. Current Problems in Dating Palaeolithic Cave Art: Candamo and Chauvet *Antiquity* 77:134–141.

Pettitt, P., M. Richards, R. Maggi, and V. Formicola. 2003. The Gravettian Burial Known as the Prince ('Il Principe'): New Evidence for His Age and Diet. *Antiquity* 77:15–19.

Pfaffenberger, B. 1992. Social Anthropology of Technology. *Annual Review of Anthropology* 21:491–519.

Phillips, K. M. 2004. Courtly Love Undressed: Reading through Clothes in Medieval French Culture. *Paragon* 21 (1):166–167.

Phillips, K. M. 2005. The Invisible Man: Body and Ritual in a Fifteenth-Century Noble Household. *Journal of Medieval History* 31 (2):143–162.

Phillips, K. M. 2007. Masculinities and the Medieval English Sumptuary Laws. *Gender & History* 19:22–42.

Pollard, T. 2007. Spelling the Body. In *Environment and Embodiment in Early Modern England*, edited by M. Floyd-Wilson and G. A. Sullivan Jr. New York: Palgrave McMillan, 171–186.

Pollitt, J. J. 1972. *Art and Experience in Classical Greece*. Cambridge: Cambridge University Press.

Pomedli, M. M. 1991. *Ethnophilosophical and Ethnolinguistic Perspectives on the Huron Indian Soul*. Lewiston/ Queenston/ Lampeter: Edwin Mellen.

Pomeranz, K. 2007. Social History and World History: From Daily Life to Patterns of Change. *Journal of World History* 18 (1):69–98.

Pomeroy, S. 1995. *Goddesses, Whores, Wives, and Slaves: Women in Classical Antiquity*. New York: Schocken.

Pomeroy, S., S. Burstein, W. Donlan, and J. T. Roberts. 2007. *Ancient Greece: A Political, Social and Cultural History*. 2 ed. Oxford: Oxford University Press.

Porr, M., and K. W. Alt. 2006. The Burial of Bad Durrenberg, Central Germany: Osteopathology and Osteoarchaeology of a Late Mesolithic Shaman's Grave. *International Journal of Osteoarchaeology* 16 (5):395–406.

Porter, J. I., ed. 1995. *Constructions of the Classical Body*. Ann Arbor: University of Michigan Press.

Porter, R. 2001. *The Cambridge Illustrated History of Medicine*. Cambridge: Cambridge University Press.

Postman, N. 1993. *Technopoly: The Surrender of Culture to Technology*. New York: Vintage Books.

Pottage, A., and M. Mundy, eds. 2004. *Law, Anthropology and the Constitution of the Social: Making Persons and Things*. Cambridge: Cambridge University Press.

Prentiss, A. M., I. Kuijt, and J. C. Chatters, eds. 2009. *Macroevolution in Human Prehistory: Evolutionary Theory and Processual Archaeology*. New York: Springer.

Price, D. 2009. *Human Tissue in Transplantation and Research*. Cambridge: Cambridge University Press.

Price, T. D., ed. 2000. *Europe's First Farmers*. Cambridge: Cambridge University Press.

Pryor, F. 2001. *Seahenge: New Discoveries in Prehistoric Britain*. London: Harper Collins.

Quinn, J. C. 2007. Herms, Kouroi and the Political Anatomy of Athens. *Greece & Rome* 54 (1):82–105.

Rabinow, P. 1996. *Essays on the Anthropology of Reason*. Princeton: Princeton University Press.

Racaut, L. 2002. Accusations of Infanticide on the Eve of the French Wars of Religion. In *Infanticide: Historical Perspectives on Child Murder and Concealment 1500–2000*, edited by M. Jackson. Aldershot: Ashgate, 18–34.

Radovanović, I. 1997. The Lepenski Vir Culture: A Contribution to Interpretation of Its Ideological Aspects. In *Antidoran Dragoslavo Srejović Completis Lxv Annis Ab Amicis, Collegis, Disciplulis Oblatum*. Beograd: Centar za arheološka istraživanja, Filozofski fakultet, 85–93.

Rapp, R. 2003. Cell Life and Death, Child Life and Death: Genomic Horizons, Genetic Diseases, Family Stories. In *Remaking Life and Death: Toward an Anthropology of the Biosciences*, edited by S. Franklin and M. Lock. Sante Fe: School of American Research Press, 129–164.

Rappaport, R. 1979. *Ecology, Meaning and Religion*. Berkeley: North Atlantic Press.

Rawcliffe, C. 2006. *Leprosy in Medieval England*. Woodbridge: Boydell Press.

Ray, K., and J. Thomas. 2003. In the Kinship of Cows: The Social Centrality of Cattle in the Earlier Neolithic of Southern Britain. In *Food, Culture and Identity in the Neolithic and Early Bronze Age*, edited by M. Parker Pearson. Oxford: British Archaeological Reports, 37–44.

Rebora, G. 2001. *Culture of the Fork: A Brief History of Food in Europe*. New York: Columbia University Press.

Reeves, J., and M. Adams. 1993. *The Spitalfields Project. Vol. 1, the Archaeology: Across the Styx*. York: Council for British Archaeology.

Reilly, J. 1997. Naked and Limbless: Learning About the Feminine Body in Ancient Athens. In *Naked Truths: Women, Sexuality and Gender in Classical Art and Archaeology*, edited by A. O. Koloski-Ostrow and C. L. Lyons. London: Routledge, 154–173.

Renfrew, C. 1973. Wessex as a Social Question. *Antiquity* 47:221–225.

Renfrew, C. 1974. Beyond a Subsistence Economy: The Evolution of Social Organization in Prehistoric Europe. *Bulletin of the American School of Oriental Research* 20:69–95.

Renfrew, C. 2007. *Prehistory: The Making of the Human Mind*. London: Weidenfeld and Nicolson.

Reynolds, S. 1991. Social Mentalities and the Case of Medieval Scepticism. *Transactions of the Royal Historical Society (Sixth Series)* 1:21–41.

Rice, P. C. 1981. Prehistoric Venuses: Symbols of Motherhood or Womanhood? *Journal of Anthropological Research* 37:402–414.

Richards, M. 2000. Human Consumption of Plant Foods in the British Neolithic: Direct Evidence from Bone Stable Isotopes. In *Plants in Neolithic Britain and Beyond*, edited by A. Fairbairn. Oxford: Oxbow, 123–135.

Richardson, R. 1989. *Death, Dissection and the Destitute*. London: Penguin.

Riches, D. 1986. *The Anthropology of Violence*. Oxford: Blackwell.

Richlin, A. 2010. Gender in the Early Medieval World East and West, 300–900. *Journal of Womens History* 22 (4): 268–281.

Robb, J. E. 1994. The Neolithic of Peninsular Italy: Anthropological Synthesis and Critique. *Bullettino di Paletnologia Italiana* 85, 1994:189–214.

Robb, J. E. 1997. Intentional Tooth Removal in Neolithic Italian Women. *Antiquity* 71:659–669.

Robb, J. E. 2001. Island Identities: Ritual, Travel, and the Creation of Difference in Neolithic Malta. *European Journal of Archaeology* 4:175–202.

Robb, J. E. 2004. The Extended Artifact and the Monumental Economy: A Methodology for Material Agency. In *Rethinking Materiality: The Engagement of Mind with the Material World*, edited by E. DeMarrais, C. Gosden and C. Renfrew. Cambridge: McDonald Institute for Archaeological Research, 131–139.

Robb, J. E. 2007. *The Early Mediterranean Village: Agency, Material Culture and Social Change in Neolithic Italy*. Cambridge: Cambridge University Press.

Robb, J. E. 2008a. Meaningless Violence and the Lived Body: The Huron–Jesuit Collision of World Orders. In *Past Bodies: Body-Centred Research in Archaeology*, edited by D. Borić and J. E. Robb. Oxford: Oxbow, 89–99.

Robb, J. E. 2008b. Tradition and Agency: Human Body Representations in Later Prehistoric Europe. *World Archaeology* 40:332–353.

Robb, J. E. 2009a. People of Stone: Stelae, Personhood, and Society in Prehistoric Europe. *Journal of Archaeological Method and Theory*, 16:162–183.

Robb, J. E. 2009b. Towards a Critical Ötziography: Writing Prehistoric Bodies. In *Social Bodies*, edited by H. Lambert and M. McDonald. Oxford: Berghahn Books, 100–128.

Robb, J. E. 2010. Beyond Agency. *World Archaeology* 42 (4):493–520.

Robb, J. E. 2012. History in the Body: The Scale of Belief. In *Big Histories, Human Lives: Tackling Problems of Scale in Archaeology*, edited by J. E. Robb and T. R. Pauketat. Santa Fe: SAR Press, 77–100.

Robb, J. E. in press a. Burial and Human Body Representations in the Mediterranean Neolithic. In *The Oxford Handbook of Neolithic Europe*, edited by C. Fowler, J. Harding and D. Hofmann. Oxford: Oxford University Press.

Robb, J. E. in press b. Material Culture and Structural Causation: A New Model for the Origins of the European Neolithic. *Current Anthropology*.

Robb, J. E., and P. Miracle. 2007. Beyond 'Migration' Versus 'Acculturation': New Models for the Spread of Agriculture. In *Going Over: The Mesolithic/Neolithic Transition in Western Europe*, edited by A. Whittle and V. Cummings. London: British Academy, 97–113.

Robb, J. E., and T. Pauketat. 2012a. From Moments to Millennia: Theorizing Scale and Change in Human History. In *Big Histories, Human Lives: Tackling Problems of Scale in Archaeology*. Santa Fe: SAR Press, 3–33.

Robb, J. E., and T. R. Pauketat, eds. 2012b. *Big Histories, Human Lives: Tackling Problems of Scale in Archaeology*. Santa Fe: SAR Press.

Roebroeks, W., M. Mussi, J. Svoboda, and K. Fennema, eds. 2000. *Hunters of the Golden Age: The Mid Upper Palaeolithic of Eurasia, 30,000 – 20,000 BP*. Leiden: University of Leiden.

Rogers, J., and A. Waldron. 1995. *A Field Guide to Joint Disease in Archaeology*. New York: Wiley.

Rollefson, G. O. 1983. Ritual and Ceremony at Neolithic, 'Ain Ghazal (Jordan). *Paleorient* 9 (2):29–38.

Rollefson, G. O. 1986. Neolithic 'Ain Ghazal (Jordan): Ritual and Ceremony, II. *Paleorient* 21 (1):45–52.

Rollefson, G. O. 1998. 'Ain Ghazal (Jordan): Ritual and Ceremony III. *Paleorient* 24 (1):43–58.

Rollo-Koster, J. l. 2003. The Politics of Body Parts: Contested Topographies in Late-Medieval Avignon. *Speculum* 78 (1):66–98.

Roux, V., B. Bril, and G. Dietrich. 1995. Skills and Learning Difficulties Involved in Stone Knapping: The Case of Stone-Bead Knapping in Khambat, India. *World Archaeology* 27:63–87.

Rowlands, M. 1984. Conceptualizing the European Bronze and Early Iron Age. In *European Social Evolution: Archaeological Perspectives*, edited by J. Bintliff. Bradford: Bradford University Press, 147–156.

Rowlands, M. 1999. Remembering to Forget: Sublimation and Sacrifice in War Memorials. In *The Art of Forgetting*, edited by A. Forty and S. Küchler. Oxford: Berg, 129–145.

Rowley-Conwy, P. 2001. Time, Change and the Archaeology of Hunter-Gatherers: How Original Is the 'Original Affluent Society'? In *Hunter-Gatherers: An Interdisciplinary Perspective*, edited by C. Panter-Brick, R. Layton and P. Rowley-Conwy. Cambridge: Cambridge University Press, 39–72.

Rowley-Conwy, P. 2004. How the West Was Lost. *Current Anthropology* 45 (Supplement, August-October):S83-S113.

Rowley-Conwy, P. 2011. Westward Ho! The Spread of Agriculture from Central Europe to the Atlantic. *Current Anthropology* 52 (S4):S431–S451.

Royer, K. 2004. Dead Men Talking: Truth, Texts and the Scaffold in Early Modern England. In *Penal Practice and Culture, 1500–1900: Punishing the English*, edited by S. Devereaux and P. Griffiths. London: Macmillan, 63–84.

Rubin, M. 1994. The Person in the Form: Medieval Challenges to Bodily 'Order'. In *Framing Medieval Bodies*, edited by S. Kay and M. Rubin. Manchester: Manchester University Press, 100–122.

Russell, N. 1998. Cattle as Wealth in Neolithic Europe: Where's the Beef? In *The Archaeology of Value*, edited by D. W. Bailey. Oxford: British Archaeological Reports, 42–54.

Sahlins, M. 1985. *Islands of History*. Chicago: Chicago University Press.

Said, E. W. 1978. *Orientalism: Western Conceptions of the Orient*. London: Routledge.

Salomon, N. 1997. Making a World of Difference: Gender, Asymmetry and the Greek Nude. In *Naked Truths: Women, Sexuality and Gender in Classical Art and Archaeology*, edited by A. O. Koloski-Ostrow and C. L. Lyons. London: Routledge, 197–219.

Samons, L. J., ed. 2007. *The Cambridge Companion to the Age of Pericles*. Cambridge: Cambridge University Press.

Sanchidrián, J. L. 2005. *Manual De Arte Prehistórico*. Barcelona: Ariel.

Sandars, N. K. 1985. *Prehistoric Art in Europe*. 2nd ed. Harmondsworth: Pelican.

Sassi, M. M. 2001. *The Science of Man in Ancient Greece*. Chicago: University of Chicago Press.

Saville, A., E. Hall, and J. Hoyle. 1990. *Hazleton North: The Excavation of a Neolithic Long Cairn of the Cotswold-Severn Group*. London: English Heritage.

Sawday, J. 1995. *The Body Emblazoned: Dissection and the Human Body in Renaissance Culture*. Abingdon: Routledge.

Scarre, C. 2007. Monuments and Miniatures: Representing Humans in Neolithic Europe 5000–2000 BC. In *Material Beginnings: A Global Prehistory of Figurative Representation*, edited by C. Renfrew and I. Morley. Cambridge: McDonald Institute for Archaeological Research, 25–37.

Scarre, C. 2008. Beings Like Themselves? Anthropomorphic Representations in the Megalithic Tombs of France. In *Arte Rupestre Do Vale Do Tejo E Outros Estudos De Arte Pré-Histórica*, edited by L. Oosterbeck and C. Buco. Braga: CEIPHAR, 73–96.

Scarre, C. 2011. *Landscapes of Neolithic Brittany*. Oxford: Oxford University Press.

Schaps, D. M. 1998. What Was Free About a Free Athenian Woman? *Transactions of the American Philological Association* 128:161–188.

Scheidel, W. 1995. The Most Silent Women of Greece and Rome: Rural Labour and Women's Life in the Ancient World (I) *Greece & Rome* 42 (2):202–217.

Schmidt, K. 2003. Göbekli Tepe – Southeastern Turkey. The Seventh Campaign, 2001. *Neo-Lithics* 1 (2):23–25.

Schmidt, K. 2004. 2003 Campaign at Göbekli Tepe (Southeastern Turkey). *Neo-Lithics* 2 (3):3–8.

Schmidt, K. 2006. Göbekli Tepe Excavations 2005. *Kazi Sonuçlari Toplantisi* 28 (2):97–110.

Schoenfeldt, M. 1997. Fables of the Belly in Early Modern England. In *The Body in Parts: Fantasies of Corporeality in Early Modern Europe*, edited by D. Hillman and C. Mazzio. London: Routledge, 243–261.

Schulting, R., and L. Fibiger, eds. 2011. *Neolithic Violence in a European Perspective*. Oxford: Oxford University Press.

Schulting, R., and M. Wysocki. 2005. 'In This Chambered Tumulus Were Found Cleft Skulls...': An Assessment of the Evidence for Cranial Trauma in the British Neolithic. *Proceedings of the Prehistoric Society* 71:107–138.

Sekules, V. 2001. *Medieval Art*. Oxford: Oxford University Press.

Seremetakis, C. N. 1991. *The Last Word: Women, Death and Divination in Inner Mani*. Chicago: Chicago University Press.

Shahar, S. 1994. The Old Body in Medieval Culture. In *Framing Medieval Bodies*, edited by S. Kay and M. Rubin. Manchester: Manchester University Press, 160–186.

Shapin, S., and S. Schaffer. 1985. *Leviathan and the Air-Pump: Hobbes, Boyle and the Experimental Life*. Princeton, NJ: Princeton University Press.

Shapiro, H., ed. 2007. *The Cambridge Companion to Archaic Greece*. Cambridge: Cambridge University Press.

Sharp, L. A. 2000. The Commodification of the Body and Its Parts. *Annual Review of Anthropology* 29:287–328.

Shee Twohig, E. 1981. *The Megalithic Art of Western Europe*. Oxford: Clarendon.

Sheller, M. 2004. Automotive Emotions: Feeling the Car. *Theory, Culture and Society* 21 (4–5):221–42.

Shennan, S. 1982. Ideology, Change and the European Bronze Age. In *Symbolic and Structural Archaeology*, edited by I. Hodder. Cambridge: Cambridge University Press, 155–161.

Shennan, S. 1993. Settlement and Social Change in Central Europe, 3500–1500 BC. *Journal of World Prehistory* 7:121–161.

Shepard, A., and G. Walker. 2008. Gender, Change and Periodisation. *Gender and History* 20:453–462.

Sherlock, W. 1690. *A Practical Discourse Concerning Death*. London: W. Rogers.

Sherratt, A. 1981. Plough and Pastoralism: Aspects of the Secondary Products Revolution. In *Pattern of the Past: Studies in Honor of David Clarke*, edited by I. Hodder, G. Isaac and N. Hammond. Cambridge: Cambridge University Press, 261–305.

Sherratt, A. 1984. Social Evolution: Europe in the Later Neolithic and Copper Ages. In *European Social Evolution: Archaeological Perspectives*, edited by J. Bintliff. Bradford: Bradford University Press, 123–134.

Sherratt, A. 1994. The Emergence of Élites: Earlier Bronze Age, 2500–1300 BC. In *The Oxford Illustrated History of Prehistoric Europe*, edited by B. Cunliffe. Oxford: Oxford University Press, 244–276.

Shilling, C. 2003. *The Body and Social Theory*. 2 ed. London: Sage Publications.

Shilling, C. 2005. *The Body in Culture, Technology and Society*. London: Sage.

Shilling, C. 2007. The Challenge of Embodying Archaeology. Paper read at Research Seminar 'Past Bodies', at The McDonald Institute for Archaeological Research, University of Cambridge.

Shryock, A., and D. L. Smail. 2011. *Deep History: The Architecture of Past and Present*. Berkeley: University of California Press.

Shryock, A., and D. L. Smail. forthcoming. History and the 'Pre-'. *American Historical Review*.

Sieveking, A. 1979. *The Cave Artists*. London: Thames and Hudson.

Simmons, A. H. 2007. *The Neolithic Revolution in the Near East: Transforming the Human Landscape*. Tucson: University of Arizona Press.

Simons, W. 1994. Reading a Saint's Body: Rapture and Bodily Movement in the Vitae of Thirteenth-Century Beguines. In *Framing Medieval Bodies*, edited by S. Kay and M. Rubin. Manchester: Manchester University Press, 10–23.

Sinclair, A. 1995. The Technique as Symbol in Late Glacial Europe. *World Archaeology* 27:50–62.

Sinclair, S. 1997. *Making Doctors: An Institutional Apprenticeship*. London: Berg.

Sjøvold, T., W. Bernhard, O. Gaber, K. H. Künzel, W. Platzer, and H. Unterdorfer. 1995. Verteilung Und Größe Der Tätowierungen Am Eismann Von Hauslabjoch. In *Der Mann Im Eis: Neue Funde Un Ergebnisse, 2*, edited by K. Spindler. Vienna: Springer, 279–286.

Skeates, R. 2011. *An Archaeology of the Senses: Prehistoric Malta*. Oxford: Oxford University Press.

Smith, A. 1995 [1776]. *An Inquiry into the Nature and Causes of the Wealth of Nations*. London: Pickering & Chatto Ltd.

Smith, A. T. 2001. The Limitations of Doxa: Agency and Subjectivity from an Archaeological Point of View. *Journal of Social Archaeology* 1 (2):155–71.

Smith, J. M. H. 2000. Did Women Have a Transformation of the Roman World? *Gender & History* 12:552–571.

Smith, K. A. 2008. Saints in Shining Armor: Martial Asceticism and Masculine Models of Sanctity, Ca. 1050–1250. *Speculum-a Journal of Medieval Studies* 83 (3):572–602.

Smith, M., and M. Brickley. 2009. *People of the Long Barrows: Life, Death and Burial in the Earlier Neolithic.* Stroud: The History Press.

Sofaer, J. 2006. *The Body as Material Culture: A Theoretical Osteoarchaeology.* Cambridge: Cambridge University Press.

Sofaer Derevenski, J. 2000. Rings of Life: The Role of Early Metalwork in Mediating the Gendered Life Course. *World Archaeology* 31 (3):389–406.

Soffer, O., J. A. Adovasio, N. L. Kornietz, A. A. Velichko, Y. N. Gribchenko, B. R. Lenz, and V. Y. Suntsov. 1997. Cultural Stratigraphy at Mezhirich, an Upper Palaeolithic Site in Ukraine with Multiple Occupations. *Antiquity* 71:48–62.

Soffer, O., P. Vandiver, B. Klíma, and J. Svoboda. 1993. The Pyrotechnology of Performance Art: Moravian Venuses and Wolverines. In *Before Lascaux: The Complex Record of the Early Upper Palaeolithic,* edited by H. Knecht, A. Pike-Tay and R. White. Boca Raton: CRC Press, 259–275.

Sommer, U. 2001. 'Hear the Instruction of Thy Father, and Forsake Not the Law of Thy Mother': Change and Persistence in the European Early Neolithic. *Journal of Social Archaeology* 1:244–270.

Sørensen, M. L. S. 1987. Material Order and Cultural Classification: The Bronzes from Late Bronze Age Scandinavia. In *The Archaeology of Contextual Meaning,* edited by I. Hodder. Cambridge: Cambridge University Press, 90–101.

Sørensen, M. L. S. 1991. Gender Construction through Appearance. In *The Archaeology of Gender,* edited by D. Walde and N. D. Willows. Calgary: University of Calgary, 121–129.

Sørensen, M. L. S. 1997. Reading Dress: The Construction of Social Categories and Identities in Bronze Age Europe. *Journal of European Archaeology* 5 (1):93–114.

Sørensen, M. L. S. 2000. *Gender Archaeology.* Cambridge: Polity Press.

Sørensen, M. L. S. 2006. Gender, Things, and Material Culture. In *Handbook of Gender in Archaeology,* edited by S. M. Nelson. Berkeley: Altamira Press, 105–135.

Sørensen, M. L. S. 2010. Bronze Age Bodiness – Maps and Coordinates. In *Body Parts and Bodies Whole: Changing Relations and Meanings,* edited by K. Rebay-Salisbury, M. L. S. Sørensen and J. Hughes. Oxford: Oxbow, 54–63.

Sørensen, M. L. S., and K. Rebay-Salisbury. 2008a. From Substantial Bodies to the Substance of Bodies: Analysis of the Transition from Inhumation to Cremation During the Middle Bronze Age in Central Europe. In *Past Bodies: Body-Centered Research in Archaeology,* edited by D. Borić and J. Robb. Oxford: Oxbow, 59–68.

Sørensen, M. L. S., and K. Rebay-Salisbury. 2008b. The Impact of 19th Century Ideas on the Construction of 'Urnfield' as a Chronological and Cultural Concept: Tales from Northern and Central Europe. In *Construire Le Temps: Histoire Et Méthodes Des Chronologies Et Calendriers Des Derniers Millénaires Avant Notre Ère in Europe Occidentale,* edited by A. Lehoërff. Lille: CNRS, 57–67.

Sørensen, M. L. S., and K. Rebay-Salisbury. 2008c. Interpreting the Body: Burial Practices at the Middle Bronze Age Cemetery at Pitten. *Archaeologia Austriaca* 89 (2005):153–175.

Sørensen, M. L. S., and K. Rebay-Salisbury. 2008d. Landscapes of the Body: Burials of the Middle Bronze Age in Hungary. *European Journal of Archaeology* 11 (1):49–74.

Souvatzi, S. 2008. *A Social Archaeology of Households in Neolithic Greece.* Cambridge: Cambridge University Press.

Spacapan, S., and S. Oskamp. 1990. People's Reactions to Technology. In *People's Reactions to Technology: In Factories, Offices and Aerospace,* edited by S. Oskamp and S. Spacapan. London: Sage, 9–20.

Spikins, P. 2008. The Bashful and the Boastful: Prestigious Leaders and Social Change in Mesolithic Societies. *Journal of World Prehistory* 21:173–193.

Spindler, K. 1994. *The Man in the Ice.* London: Weidenfeld and Nicolson.

Spindler, K., ed. 1995. *Der Mann Im Eis: Neue Funde Un Ergebnisse, 2.* Vienna: Springer.

Spivey, N. 1996. *Understanding Greek Sculpture: Ancient Meanings, Modern Readings.* London: Thames and Hudson.

Squire, M. 2011. *The Art of the Body: Antiquity and Its Legacy.* London: I. B. Tauris.

Srejović, D. 1972. *Europe's First Monumental Sculpture: New Discoveries at Lepenski Vir.* London: Thames and Hudson.

Stehle, E., and A. Díaz. 1996. Women Looking at Women: Women's Ritual and Temple Sculpture. In *Sexuality in Ancient Art,* edited by N. B. Kampen. Cambridge: Cambridge University Press, 105–116.

Stevanovic, M. 1997. The Age of Clay: The Social Dynamics of House Destruction. *Journal of Anthropological Archaeology* 16:334–395.

Stevens, F. 2008. Elemental Interplay: The Production, Circulation and Deposition of Bronze Age Metalwork in Britain and Ireland. *World Archaeology* 40 (2):238–252.

Stevens, S. M. 1997. Sacred Heart and the Secular Brain. In *The Body in Parts: Fantasies of Corporeality in Early Modern Europe,* edited by D. Hillman and C. Mazzio. London: Routledge, 263–282.

Stevenson, J. 2006. The Material Bodies of Medieval Religious Performance in England. *Material Religion* 2 (2):204–232.

Stevick, R. 1964. *One Hundred Middle English Lyrics.* New York: Bobbs-Merrill.

Stewart, A. 1997. *Art, Desire and the Body in Ancient Greece.* Cambridge: Cambridge University Press.

Stewart, A. 2008. *Classical Greece and the Birth of Western Art.* Cambridge: Cambridge University Press.

Stoddart, S. 2009. The Etruscan Body. *Accordia Research Papers* 11:137–152.

Strasser, U. 2004. Early Modern Nuns and the Feminist Politics of Religion. *Journal of Religion* 84:529–554.

Strathern, A., and M. Strathern. 1971. *Self-Decoration in Mount Hagen.* London: Duckworth.

Strathern, M. 1988. *The Gender of the Gift: Problems with Women and Problems with Society in Melanesia.* Cambridge: Cambridge University Press.

Strathern, M. 1992a. *After Nature: English Kinship in the Late 20th Century.* Cambridge: Cambridge University Press.

Strathern, M. 1992b. *Reproducing the Future: Anthropology, Kinship and the New Reproductive Technologies.* Manchester: Manchester University Press.

Strathern, M. 1996. Cutting the Network. *Journal of the Royal Anthropological Institute* 2:517–535.

Strathern, M. 2004. *Partial Connections.* Oxford: Altamira Press.

Strathern, M. 2005. *Kinship, Law and the Unexpected: Relatives Are Always a Surprise.* Cambridge: Cambridge University Press.

Sutton, J. 2007. Spongy Brains and Material Memories. In *Environment and Embodiment in Early Modern England,* edited by M. Floyd-Wilson and G. A. Sullivan Jr. New York: Palgrave McMillan, 14–34.

Svoboda, J., B. Klíma, L. Jarosová, and P. Skrdla. 2000. The Gravettian in Moravia: Climate, Behaviour and Technological Complexity. In *Hunters of the Golden Age: The Mid Upper Palaeolithic of Eurasia, 30,000 – 20,000 BP,* edited by W. Roebroeks, M. Mussi, J. Svoboda and K. Fennema. Leiden: Leiden University Press, 198–217.

Svoboda, J., V. Lozek, and E. Vleck. 1996. *Hunters between East and West: The Palaeolithic of Moravia.* New York: Plenum Press.

Talalay, L. 1993. *Deities, Dolls and Devices: Neolithic Figurines from Franchthi Cave, Greece.* Bloomington: Indiana University Press.

Tanner, J. 2001. Nature, Culture and the Body in Classical Greek Religious Art. *World Archaeology* 33 (2):257–276.

Tanner, J. 2006. *The Invention of Art History in Ancient Greece: Religion, Society and Artistic Rationalisation.* Cambridge: Cambridge University Press.

Tapper, M. 1995. Interrogating Bodies: Medico-Racial Knowledge, Politics and a Study of Disease. *Comparative Studies In Society And History* 37:76–93.

Tarlow, S. 2007. *The Archaeology of Improvement in Britain, 1750–1850.* Cambridge: Cambridge University Press.

Tarlow, S. 2011. *Ritual, Belief and the Dead Body in Early Modern Britain and Ireland.* Cambridge: Cambridge University Press.

Taylor, J. S. 2005. Surfacing the Body Interior. *Annual Review of Anthropology* 34:741–756.

Thibodeaux, J., ed. 2010. *Negotiating Clerical Identities: Priests, Monks and Masculinity in the Middle Ages.* Basingstoke: Palgrave MacMillan.

Thomas, J. 1996. *Time, Culture and Identity: An Interpretive Archaeology.* London: Routledge.

Thomas, J. 1999. *Understanding the Neolithic.* London: Routledge.

Thomas, J. 2002. Archaeology's Humanism and the Materiality of the Body. In *Thinking through the Body: Archaeologies of Corporeality,* edited by Y. Hamilakis, M. Pluciennik and

S. Tarlow. London: Kluwer Academic/Plenum Publishers, 29–45.

Thomas, J. 2004. *Archaeology and Modernity.* London: Routledge.

Thomas, J. 2005. Ambiguous Symbols: Why There Were No Figurines in Neolithic Britain. *Documenta Praehistorica* XXXII:167–175.

Thomas, J. 2007. Mesolithic-Neolithic Transitions in Britain: From Essence to Inhabitation. In *Going Over: The Mesolithic-Neolithic Transition in Western Europe,* edited by A. Whittle and V. Cummings. London: British Academy, 423–440.

Thomas, K. 1973. *Religion and the Decline of Magic.* London: Penguin.

Thomas, K. 1983. *Man and the Natural World: Changing Attitudes in England 1500–1800.* London: Allen Lane.

Thorpe, I., and C. Richards. 1984. The Decline of Ritual Authority and the Introduction of Beakers into Britain. In *Neolithic Studies,* edited by R. Bradley and J. Gardiner. Oxford: British Archaeological Reports (B.A.R), 67–78.

Thrift, N. 2005. Beyond Mediation: Three New Material Registers and Their Consequences. In *Materiality,* edited by D. Miller. London: Duke University Press, 231–255.

Thrift, N. 2006. Donna Haraway's Dreams. *Theory, Culture and Society* 23 (7–8):189–195.

Thrift, N. 2008. *Non-Representational Theory: Space, Politics, Affect.* London: Routledge.

Thwaites, R. G. 1898. *The Jesuit Relations and Allied Documents: Travels and Explorations of the Jesuit Missionaries in New France 1610–1791. Volume XIII: Hurons: 1637.* Vol. 13. Cleveland: Burrows.

Tilley, C. 1994. *A Phenomenology of Landscape: Places, Paths and Monuments.* Oxford: Berg.

Tilley, C. 1996. *An Ethnography of the Neolithic: Early Neolithic Societies in Southern Scandinavia.* Cambridge: Cambridge University Press.

Tilley, C. 1999. *Metaphor and Material Culture.* Oxford: Blackwell.

Tilley, C. 2004. *The Materiality of Stone, Explorations in Landscape Phenomenology 1.* Oxford: Berg.

Tilley, C. 2008. *Body and Image: Explorations in Landscape Phenomenology 2.* Walnut Creek: Left Coast Press.

Tilley, C. 2009. *Interpreting Landscapes: Geologies, Topographies, Identities, Explorations in Landscape Phenomenology 3.* Walnut Creek: Left Coast Press.

Tooker, E. 1964. *An Ethnography of the Huron Indians, 1615–1649.* Vol. 190, Bureau of American Ethnology Bulletins. Washington: Smithsonian.

Treherne, P. 1995. The Warrior's Beauty: The Masculine Body and Self-Identity in Bronze Age Europe. *Journal of European Archaeology* 3:105–144.

Trigger, B. G. 1976. *The Children of Aataentsic: A History of the Huron People to 1660.* Montreal: McGill-Queen's University Press.

Trigger, B. G. 1978. Early Iroquoian Contacts with Europeans. In *Handbook of North American Indians, Volume 15:*

Northeast, edited by B. G. Trigger. Washington: Smithsonian Institution, 344–356.

Tringham, R. 2000. Southeastern Europe in the Transition to Agriculture in Europe: Bridge, Buffer or Mosaic. In *Europe's First Farmers*, edited by T. D. Price. Cambridge: Cambridge University Press, 19–56.

Tringham, R., and M. Conkey. 1998. Rethinking Figurines: A Critical View from Archaeology of Gimbutas, the 'Goddess' and Popular Culture. In *Ancient Goddesses: The Myths and the Evidence*, edited by L. Goodison and C. Morris. London: British Museum Press, 22–45.

Tronchetti, C. 2005. Le Tombe E Gli Eroi: Considerazioni Sulla Statuaria Nuragica Di Monte Prama In *Il Mediterraneo Di Herakles*, edited by P. B. Raimondo Zucca. Rome: Carocci, 145–167.

Tronchetti, C., and P. van Dommelen. 2005. Entangled Objects and Hybrid Practices: Colonial Contacts and Elite Connections at Monte Prama, Sardinia. *Journal of Mediterranean Archaeology* 18:183–208.

Turner, B. S. 1996. *The Body and Society: Explorations in Social Theory*. London: Sage.

Turner, V. 1969. *The Ritual Process: Structure and Anti-Structure*. Chicago: Aldine.

Ucko, P. and Rosenfeld, A. 1967. *Palaeolithic Cave Art*. London: Weidenfeld and Nicolson.

Van Der Eijk, P. 2005. *Medicine and Philosophy in Classical Antiquity: Doctors and Philosophers on Nature, Soul, Health and Disease*. Cambridge: Cambridge University Press.

van Dommelen, P. 2006. Colonial Matters:. Material Culture and Postcolonial Theory in Colonial Situations. In *Handbook of Material Culture*, edited by C. Tilley, W. Keane, S. Küchler, M. Rowlands and P. Spyer. London: Sage, 267–308.

van Dommelen, P. 2011. Postcolonial Archaeologies between Discourse and Practice. *World Archaeology* 43 (1):1–6.

Vander Linden, M. 2006. For Whom the Bell Tolls: Social Hierarchy vs Social Integration in the Bell Beaker Culture of Southern France (Third Millennium BC). *Cambridge Archaeological Journal* 16 (3):317–332.

Vander Linden, M. 2007a. For Equalities Are Plural: Reassessing the Social in Europe During the Third Millennium BC. *World Archaeology* 39 (2):177–193.

Vander Linden, M. 2007b. What Linked the Bell Beakers in Third Millennium BC Europe? *Antiquity* 81:343–352.

Vandiver, P., O. Soffer, B. Klíma, and J. Svoboda. 1989. The Origins of Ceramic Technology at Dolní Věstonice. *Science* 246:1002–1008.

Vanhaeren, M., and F. d'Errico. 2005. Grave Goods from the Saint-Germain-La-Rivière Burial: Evidence for Social Inequality in the Upper Palaeolithic. *Journal of Anthropological Archaeology* 24:117–134.

Vella Gregory, I. 2007. Thinking through the Body: The Use of Images as a Medium of Social Expression in Sardinia from the Neolithic to the Iron Age. *Journal of Mediterranean Studies* 17:23–46.

Verhoeven, M. 2002. Ritual and Ideology in the Pre-Pottery Neolithic B of the Levant and Southeast Anatolia. *Cambridge Archaeological Journal* 12 (2):233–258.

Veyne, P. 1982. *Did the Greeks Believe in Their Myths?: Essay on the Constitutive Imagination*. Chicago: University of Chicago Press.

Veyrat, N., E. Blanco, and P. Trompette. 2008. Social Embodiment of Technical Devices: Eyeglasses over the Centuries and According to Their Uses. *Mind, Culture and Activity* 15 (3):185–207.

Vigarello, G. 1989. The Upward Training of the Body from the Age of Chivalry to Courtly Civility. In *Fragments for a History of the Human Body, Part 1*, edited by M. Feher, R. Nadoff and N. Tazi. New York: Zone Books, 149–199.

Vilaça, A. 2005. Chronically Unstable Bodies: Reflections on Amazonian Corporealities. *Journal of the Royal Anthropological Institute* 11:445–464.

Viveiros de Castro, E. 1998. Cosmological Deixis and Amerindian Perspectivism. *Journal of the Royal Anthropological Institute* 4:469–488.

Viveiros de Castro, E. 2004. Exchanging Perspectives: The Transformation of Objects into Subjects in Amerindian Ontologies. *Common Knowledge* 10 (3):463–484.

Vlassopoulos, K. 2007a. Free Spaces: Identity, Experience and Democracy in Classical Athens. *Classical Quarterly* 57 (1):33–52.

Vlassopoulos, K. 2007b. *Unthinking the Greek Polis: Ancient Greek History Beyond Eurocentrism*. Cambridge: Cambridge University Press.

Von Staden, H. 1992. The Discovery of the Body: Human Dissection and Its Cultural Contexts in Ancient Greece. *Yale Journal of Biology and Medicine* 65:223–241.

Wahrman, D. 2008. Change and the Corporeal in Seventeenth- and Eighteenth-Century Gender History: Or, Can Cultural History Be Rigorous? *Gender & History* 20 (3):584–602.

Walters, J. 1998. Manhood in the Graeco-Roman World. In *Gender and the Body in the Ancient Mediterranean*, edited by M. Wyke. Oxford: Blackwell, 191–193.

Webb, H. 2010. *The Medieval Heart*. New Haven: Yale University Press.

Webmoor, T., and C. L. Witmore. 2008. Things Are Us! A Commentary on Human/Things Relations under the Banner of a 'Social Archaeology'. *Norwegian Archaeological Review* 41 (1):1–18.

Weiner, A. 1992. *Inalienable Possessions: The Paradox of Keeping-While-Giving*. Berkeley: University of California Press.

Weir, A., and J. Jerman. 1986. *Images of Lust: Sexual Carvings on Medieval Churches*. London: Batsford.

Wels-Weyrauch, U. 1988. Mittelbronzezeitliche Frauentrachten in Süddeutschland, Beziehungen Zur Hagenauer Gruppierung. In *Dynamique Du Bronze Moyen En Europe Occidentale. Actes Du 113éme Congrès National Des Sociétés Savantes, Strasbourg 1988*. Paris: Commission de Prè- et Protohistoire, 117–134.

Wels-Weyrauch, U. 1991. *Die Anhänger in Südbayern, Prähistorische Bronzefunde 11 (5)*. Stuttgart: Franz Steiner.

Wels-Weyrauch, U. 2008. Stachelscheibencolliers: Nur Zur Zierde? In *Durch Die Zeiten. Festschrift Für Albrecht Jockenhövel Zum 65. Geburtstag*, edited by F. Verse, B. Knoche, J. Graefe, M. Hohlbein, K. Schierhold, C. Siemann, M. Uckelmann and G. Woltermann. Rahden/Westfahlen: Marie Leidorf, 275–290.

Wenger, E. 1998. *Communities of Practice: Learning, Meaning and Identity*. Cambridge: Cambridge University Press.

Westerhof, D. 2007. Deconstructing Identities on the Scaffold: The Execution of Hugh Despenser the Younger, 1326. *Journal of Medieval History* 33 (1):87–106.

White, R. 1993. Technological and Social Dimensions of 'Aurignacian-Age' Body Ornaments across Europe. In *Before Lascaux: The Complex Record of the Early Upper Paleolithic*, edited by H. Knecht, A. Pike-Tay and R. White. Boca Raton: CRC Press, 277–300.

White, R. 1997. Substantial Acts: From Materials to Meaning in Upper Palaeolithic Representation. In *Beyond Art: Upper Palaeolithic Symbolism*, edited by D. Strattman, M. Conkey and O. Soffer. San Francisco, CA: California Academy of Sciences, 93–121.

Whitehouse, R. 2006. Gender Archaeology in Europe. In *Handbook of Gender in Archaeology*, edited by S. M. Nelson. Walnut Creek, CA: AltaMira Press, 733–783.

Whittle, A. 1996. *Europe in the Neolithic. The Creation of New Worlds*. Cambridge: Cambridge University Press.

Whittle, A. 2003. *The Archaeology of People: Dimensions of Neolithic Life*. London: Routledge.

Whittle, A., and V. Cummings, eds. 2007. *Going Over: The Mesolithic-Neolithic Transition in Western Europe*. London: British Academy.

Whittle, A., F. Healy, and A. Bayliss. 2011. *Gathering Time: Dating the Early Neolithic Enclosures of Southern Britain and Ireland*. Oxford: Oxbow.

Wiesner-Hanks, M. 2007. World History and the History of Women, Gender, and Sexuality. *Journal of World History* 18 (1):53–67.

Wiesner-Hanks, M. E. 2006. *Early Modern Europe, 1450–1789*. Cambridge: Cambridge University Press.

Wiesner-Hanks, M. E. 2008. Do Women Need the Renaissance? *Gender and History* 20:539–557.

Williams, R. 1976. *Keywords: A Vocabulary of Culture and Society*. London: Fontana Press.

Wood, C. T. 1981. The Doctor's Dilemma: Sin, Salvation, and the Menstrual-Cycle in Medieval Thought. *Speculum-a Journal of Medieval Studies* 56 (4):710–727.

Woolgar, C. M. 2010. Food and the Middle Ages. *Journal of Medieval History* 36 (1):1–19.

Wyke, M. 1998a. *Parchments of Gender: Deciphering the Bodies of Antiquity*. Oxford: Clarendon.

Wyke, M., ed. 1998b. *Gender and the Body in the Ancient Mediterranean*. Oxford: Blackwell.

Wysocki, M., A. Bayliss, and A. Whittle. 2007. Serious Mortality: The Date of the Fussell's Lodge Long Barrow. *Cambridge Archaeological Journal* 17 (1 (supplement)):65–84.

Zilhão, J. 2007. The Emergence of Ornaments and Art: An Archaeological Perspective on the Origins of 'Behavioral Modernity'. *Journal of Archaeological Research* 15 (1): 1–54.

Zilhão, J., D. E. Angelucci, E. Badal-Garcia, F. d'Errico, F. Daniel, L. Dayet, K. Douka, T. F. G. Higham, M. J. Martinez-Sanchez, R. Montes-Bernardez, S. Murcia-Mascaros, C. Perez-Sirvent, C. Roldan-Garcia, M. Vanhaeren, V. Villaverde, R. Wood, and J. Zapata. 2010. Symbolic Use of Marine Shells and Mineral Pigments by Iberian Neandertals. *Proceedings of the National Academy of Sciences of the United States of America* 107 (3):1023–1028.

Zimmerman, S. 2008. Leprosy in the Medieval Imaginary (Europe). *Journal of Medieval and Early Modern Studies* 38 (3):559–587.

zur Nedden, D., and K. Wicke. 1992. Der Eismann Aus Der Sicht Der Radiologischen Und Computretomographischen Daten. In *Der Mann Im Eis: Bericht Über Das Internationale Symposium 1992 in Innsbruck*, edited by F. Höpfel, W. Platzer and K. Spindler. Innsbruck: Eigenverlag der Universität Innsbruck, 131–148.

Zvelebil, M. 2009. The Mesolithic and the 21st Century. In *Mesolithic Horizons*, edited by S. B. McCartan, R. Schulting, G. Warren and P. Woodman. Oxford: Oxbow, xlvii–lviii.

Index